MAN'S DISORDER
AND GOD'S DESIGN

MAN'S DISORDER AND GOD'S DESIGN

The Amsterdam Assembly Series

A one-volume edition of four books including

I. The Universal Church in God's Design
II. The Church's Witness to God's Design
III. The Church and the Disorder of Society
IV. The Church and the International Disorder

HARPER & BROTHERS, PUBLISHERS
NEW YORK

AUTHORIZED VERSION
of the Amsterdam Assembly Series
including the Message and the Section Reports
of the Assembly
published for the World Council of Churches
by Harper & Brothers

MAN'S DISORDER AND GOD'S DESIGN
Printed in the United States of America

FOREWORD

TO THE METHODIST EDITION

DURING the next four years, the Methodists of the world will move forward unitedly in the Advance for Christ and His Church. This quadrennial movement has two objectives: (1) A teaching and preaching endeavor in which Methodists may achieve a deeper understanding of and commitment to *Our Faith, Our Church, Our Ministry,* and *Our Mission;* and (2) A World-wide Advance in which Methodists may share in a ministry of relief and in carrying the Gospel of Christ to the peoples of the world.

The preamble to the Advance for Christ and His Church, adopted by the General Conference, reads:

The peoples of the world rise from the ruins of war, hungry and hopeless, confused and disillusioned; but deeper than the hatred alive in many hearts is the desire for love and fellowship, for peace and understanding. The Church must hear its Master speak, "Inasmuch as ye did it unto one of the least of these my brethren, ye did it unto me. . . . If thine enemy hunger, feed him."

The yearning of the common man for life abundant is bound to the conviction that only ignorance and selfishness stand between him and the realization of his dream. Man is ready scientifically to solve the problems of producing enough of food, clothing, and housing to meet his physical needs; but man is not ready spiritually to solve the problems of living together, of establishing justice and brotherhood, and thereby to meet the needs of his soul. We must hear our Lord, "Seek ye first the Kingdom of God and his righteousness and all these things shall be added unto you. I came that ye might have life and that ye might have it more abundantly. Ye cannot serve God and Mammon."

Whether we take up arms and nation march against nation in war, or take up tools and the workers of the world labor in peace; whether we acquiesce in inequality, deepen class consciousness and drift into class war, or use intelligence to create equal opportunity and discover the larger unity that lies in brotherhood; whether we continue to discriminate against our fellow man, or build a society in which a man's opportunity to earn his living is based upon his character and his capacity and not upon his color, will be determined at last by the faith to which we give our minds and hearts. "And He taught His disciples to pray, Our Father who art in heaven, hallowed be Thy name; Thy kingdom come; Thy will be done on earth as it is in heaven."

"Follow Me," He said. In an hour when materialistic ideologies struggle for the soul of man, the church must win his heart and save his soul. We have heard His command, "Go ye." We march forward for Christ and His Church, in the knowledge that life is found by losing it. Thus, in the full gift of self, both we and the church shall come alive to serve and to save.

The Crusade for Christ was the response of the people called Methodists to the leading of the Holy Spirit in an hour of unprecedented crisis and unparalleled need. From the beginning, the Crusade was blessed of God because it came from God. This we devoutly believe. We have sought again to discover God's will for us.

We bring to you a Quadrennial Plan to be known as The Advance for Christ and His Church.

This volume entitled *Man's Disorder and God's Design* which contains the preliminary studies prepared for the First Assembly of the World Council of Churches, together with the Reports of the Sections and the Message from the Assembly to the Churches of the World, is sent to each Methodist minister in the United States. It is to be used as the basic text in the Period of Preparation, from January 1, 1949, to June 30, 1949, during which we shall give ourselves to the study and devotion essential to the Advance. We ministers will preach and teach with power only in so far as we are intellectually and spiritually prepared. It is believed that if the ministry of the church gives itself to serious study of "The Universal Church in God's Design," "The Church's Witness to God's Design," "The Church and the Disorder of Society," and "The Church and the International Disorder," we will be the better prepared for the succeeding phases of the first objective of The Advance for Christ and His Church. In addition to this volume, a *Study Guide and Annotated Bibliography* will be sent to each minister. It is hoped that, in addition to individual study, discussion groups will be organized in each one of the Districts, and that the great themes herein presented may be considered critically and creatively by all the ministers of the church.

Following the Period of Preparation, a Preaching Mission will be conducted in major cities throughout the world. These Mass Meetings will be addressed by Bishops, ministers, pro-

FOREWORD TO THE METHODIST EDITION

fessors, and laymen; and are designed not only to focus attention on *Our Faith, Our Church, Our Ministry,* and *Our Mission* but also to result in a spiritual experience in which our people may be recommitted to *Our Faith, Our Church, Our Ministry,* and *Our Mission.*

During the preaching and teaching endeavor, the emphases will be scheduled, as follows:

November, 1949, through June, 1950—*Our Faith*
October, 1950, through January, 1951—*Our Church*
February, 1951, through June, 1951—*Our Ministry*
October, 1951, through January, 1952—*Our Mission*

In the first period, in which the church centers attention upon *Our Faith,* eight booklets will be prepared. These booklets are to be used by clergy and laity alike. During the month of November, 1949, the entire church will study the booklet entitled *Our Faith in God.* The fact of an entire church simultaneously preaching, thinking, and studying *Our Faith in God* is an event of spiritual significance. The subjects of the following months are: December, *Our Faith in Christ;* January, *Our Faith in the Bible;* February, *Our Faith in Love;* March, *Our Faith in Prayer;* April, *Our Faith in Immortality;* May, *Our Faith in the Holy Spirit;* June, *Our Faith in the Kingdom of God.*

Methodists have chosen this volume which comes from the World Council of Churches, not only because of its intrinsic worth but as a symbol of co-operation in the ecumenical movement. As Methodists advance spiritually in the knowledge that other communions are also advancing, there will come upon us a realization of the fact that we are one, and that the Kingdom of God is being established upon the earth.

WILLIAM C. MARTIN
General Chairman,
The Advance for Christ
and His Church

G. BROMLEY OXNAM
One of the Presidents of
The World Council of Churches

lesson, and layout and are designed not only to focus atten
tion on Our Faith, Our Church, Our Ministry, and Our Mission
but also to result in a spiritual experience in which our people
may be recommitted to Our Faith, Our Church, Our Ministry,
and Our Mission.

During the preaching and teaching endeavor, the emphases
will be scheduled, as follows:

November, 1949, through June, 1950—Our Faith
October, 1950, through January, 1951—Our Church
February, 1951, through June, 1951—Our Ministry
October, 1951, through January, 1952—Our Mission

In the first period, in which the church centers attention upon
Our Faith, eight booklets will be prepared. These booklets are
to be used by clergy and laity alike. During the month of November, 1949, the entire church will study the booklet entitled
Our Faith in God. The fact of an entire church simultaneously
preaching, thinking, and studying Our Faith in God is an event
of spiritual significance. The subjects of the following months
are December, Our Faith in Christ; January, Our Faith in the
Bible; February, Our Faith in Prayer; March, Our Faith in
Prayer; April, Our Faith in Immortality; May, Our Faith in the
Holy Spirit; June, Our Faith in the Kingdom of God.

Methodists have chosen this volume which comes from the
World Council of Churches not only because of its intrinsic
worth but as a symbol of co-operation in the ecumenical movement. As Methodists advance spiritually in the knowledge that
other communions are also advancing, there will come upon us
a realization of the fact that we are one, and that the Kingdom
of God is being established upon the earth.

WILLIAM C. MARTIN,   G. BROMLEY OXNAM,
General Chairman,   One of the Presidents of
The Advance for Christ,   The World Council of Churches
and His Church

CONTENTS

GENERAL PREFACE

GENERAL INTRODUCTION

VOL. I.   THE UNIVERSAL CHURCH IN GOD'S DESIGN

VOL. II.   THE CHURCH'S WITNESS TO GOD'S DESIGN

VOL. III.   THE CHURCH AND THE DISORDER OF SOCIETY

VOL. IV.   THE CHURCH AND THE INTERNATIONAL DISORDER

FIRST ASSEMBLY OF THE WORLD COUNCIL OF CHURCHES MESSAGE

GENERAL PREFACE

THIS book, with its companion volumes, was written in preparation for the First Assembly of the World Council of Churches in Amsterdam, Holland, August 22nd-September 4th, 1948.

Two years and a half in advance of the Assembly, the Provisional Committee of the Council determined that the main theme for the Assembly should be :

MAN'S DISORDER AND GOD'S DESIGN

and that this theme should be considered under four aspects :

1. The Universal Church in God's Design.
2. The Church's Witness to God's Design.
3. The Church and the Disorder of Society.
4. The Church and the International Disorder.

These topics were not chosen at random. They represent burning concerns of all the churches in this crisis of civilisation. The first reveals the growing determination of the various churches to rediscover the divine intention for the Church, and the right relationship of the various churches to one another. Of that determination, the World Council itself is both an evidence and a concrete result. The second testifies to the obligation recognised by all churches alike to claim for Christ the whole world and all aspects of life. From the outset it has been recognised that the World Council would be still-born unless evangelism were its life-blood. The third and fourth subjects bring Christian faith directly to bear upon two critical areas of disorder in contemporary civilisation, the social and the international. They deal with the familiar query : What has the Church to contribute to society in its present extremity ?

Preparation of the delegates for the consideration of these issues at Amsterdam was entrusted to the Study Department Commission of the World Council of Churches. Commissions consisting of leading Christians, both clerical and lay, from various parts of the world, were formed to deal with the four topics. Each Commission held two meetings and came together again on the eve of the Assembly for the final stages of preparation. A volume was outlined on each topic, and writers of chapters were carefully selected. In almost every instance, their contributions have been subjected to searching criticism by the Commission concerned, both individually and corporately, and by a considerably wider circle of experts. In most cases, chapters have been rewritten in the light of this truly ecumenical scrutiny at least once, in some instances two or more times. Thus, the volumes which are here presented represent the outcome of a comprehensive interchange of thought and conviction among leaders of virtually all Christian Communions (except the Roman Catholic). It will be understood that in these circumstances the World Council of Churches itself is not committed to the opinions expressed in the volumes.

But quite apart from its literary results, the process of ecumenical thinking possesses in itself an educational and inspirational value which should not be underestimated. Especially for people in isolated areas of the world, this interchange of documents and comments means an opportunity, eagerly grasped, to share in a vital conversation with brethren from other churches and countries. The wide interest taken in the theme of the Assembly is also evidenced by the fact that several collaborating groups are now preparing similar volumes, dealing with the same set of subjects from a national or confessional perspective.

All these studies are founded on earlier work—the sequence of ecumenical conferences of the past two decades, especially the Oxford Conference on " Church, Community and State " in 1937, the patient enquiries of the Faith and Order movement, the labour of ecumenical study groups in many lands, and the programme of the Study Department of the World Council which continued, hampered but unabated, through all the years of the war.

Serious effort has been made to assure that this discussion be truly ecumenical, representative equally of Christian churches in every part of the world. But difficulties of effective communication have to a considerable degree frustrated that aim. It has not been possible to secure as many contributions as was hoped from the Eastern Orthodox world and from the Churches of Asia, Africa and Latin America. This limitation, while real and regrettable, is less grave than might at first be supposed. For no fact stands out more clearly than that, in the basic problems confronted both by the Churches and by the societies in which they are set, ours is in truth one world.

Although the volumes of the present series were prepared to serve the particular occasion of the Amsterdam Assembly, they deal with issues of continuing and urgent importance for the whole of Christendom. It is hoped, therefore, that they may have a wide usefulness beyond and after the Assembly, and they are here presented to all thoughtful people, within and outside the churches, for that purpose.

GENERAL INTRODUCTION

THE World Council of Churches has come into being at a moment of peril for all mankind which is without precedent in the whole of human history. Frustration and fear grip the minds of men and women. This is true not only of the masses who feel themselves caught in a fate over which they have no power, but hardly less of their leaders who hold in their hands the guidance of events which they are unable to control.

At this fateful moment, the theme of the first Assembly of the Council—MAN'S DISORDER AND GOD'S DESIGN—is singularly relevant and needs little interpretation.

MAN'S DISORDER is inescapably manifest in every aspect of the world's life to-day. It is not merely a result of the recent war. Before the war, the sickness of civilisation was far advanced. The disappearance of common standards, the denial of a law of God above the wills of men and states, the disintegration of family life, the dissolution of community, loss of faith save the false faith in human wisdom and goodness, emptiness and meaninglessness in the souls of men—these symptoms of sickness were clear enough. At almost every point, war and its aftermath have aggravated MAN'S DISORDER. And now has been added the greatest dread of all, that man's mastery of atomic energy foreshadows the annihilation of man and all his works.

The Church carries a large share of responsibility for MAN'S DISORDER ; and it is for that responsibility that the churches must give account. This is true : if the churches had been faithful to their commission from Christ, if they had spoken the word of truth committed to them, if they had rightly interpreted to the world the causes of its sickness, if they had ministered to the world grace and power, above all if they had manifested in their own life the only true medicine for the healing of the nations— if they had done all this, humanity might not have come to its present extremity. On the contrary, MAN'S DISORDER finds its most pointed expression in the disorder of the Church itself.

We live in an age when the Christian Church in many parts is rediscovering its divine mission. But precisely at that moment it discovers also its own weaknesses. To men whose deepest need is spiritual rebirth, it has not exhibited the power of the Spirit. To a world whose deepest need is community, the Church which claims to be the Body of Christ, professing one Lord, one faith, one baptism, one God and Father of all, has presented division and disunity. These are sins for which the Church is responsible to God and to man. Its first act must therefore be, not condemnation of the world, but confession and contrition.

In this plight, our only hope lies in GOD'S DESIGN, His design for the world and for the Church.

GOD'S DESIGN is the divine purpose for men and nations, manifest in the acts of God in Christ. In His life, death and resurrection, in the coming of the Church and the outpouring of the Holy Spirit, a new beginning has been made in human history. In Him, God has begun a work of new creation and redemption. In Him, a reign of love and forgiveness has been inaugurated, moulding the hearts and lives of men, calling them to find their common centre and desire in Him, and so to discover that real community for which mankind is longing. In Him, the Church is continuously reborn from death to life. In Him, there is also revealed GOD'S DESIGN for the ordering of human society, a design that is an act both of judgment and of redemption.

Adopting MAN'S DISORDER AND GOD'S DESIGN as the theme for its first Assembly and as the title of the present series of volumes, the World Council of Churches has committed itself to a double task. It must seek to comprehend MAN'S DISORDER in the light of GOD'S DESIGN, in order that the churches may mediate to the world both a true understanding of its distress and the grace and power to find the way out. And it must bring the churches to face, with relentless realism, their involvement in the world's folly as well as their own distinctive disorders, in order that they may be ready to receive from God the rebirth and true unity which He purposes for them.

HENRY P. VAN DUSEN,
President of Union Theological Seminary
Chairman of the Study Department Commission

MAN'S DISORDER AND GOD'S DESIGN

Volume I

THE
UNIVERSAL CHURCH
IN
GOD'S DESIGN

THE
UNIVERSAL CHURCH
IN
GOD'S DESIGN

AN

ECUMENICAL STUDY

PREPARED UNDER THE AUSPICES OF THE

WORLD COUNCIL OF CHURCHES

VOLUME ONE

CONTENTS

List of Contributors

Introductory Chapter   13

I THE DOCTRINE OF THE CHURCH:
SOME INTERPRETATIONS   17

1 The Church in the Light of the New Testament   18
GUSTAF AULÉN

2 The Church of the New Testament   31
CLARENCE T. CRAIG

3 The Church—her Nature and Task   43
GEORGE FLOROVSKY

4 One, Holy, Catholic, Apostolic Church   59
J. A. F. GREGG

5 The Living Congregation of the Living Lord Jesus Christ   67
KARL BARTH

II THE SHAME AND THE GLORY OF THE CHURCH   77

1 The Disorder of Man in the Church of God   78
H. RICHARD NIEBUHR

2 The Church of God amid the Disorder of Man
(a) Her Witness in Occupied Europe   89
ARNE FJELLBU
(b) The Witness of the German Church Struggle   97
EDMUND SCHLINK

III SIGNS OF HIS APPEARING   109
Evidences of New Life in the Church Universal   110
OLIVE WYON

IV THE ECUMENICAL MOVEMENT   134

1 Regional and Confessional Loyalties in the Universal Church   135
OLIVER S. TOMKINS

2 The Ecumenical Movement and the Younger Churches   147
PAUL DAVID DEVANANDAN

3 The Roman Catholic Church and the Ecumenical Movement
(a) KRISTEN E. SKYDSGAARD   155
(b) Comments by a Roman Catholic Writer   169

4 The Significance of the World Council of Churches   177
W. A. VISSER 'T HOOFT

Membership of the Commission   201
Index   202
Report of Section I

CONTRIBUTORS

AULÉN, Gustaf, D.D., Bishop of Strängnäs, Sweden; formerly Professor of Systematic Theology at University of Lund. Author of *Christus Victor*, etc.

BARTH, Karl, D.THEOL.., Professor of Theology at the University of Basel. Author of *Kirchliche Dogmatik*, etc.

CRAIG, Clarence, D.D., Professor of New Testament, Yale University. Author of *The Study of the New Testament*, etc.

DEVANANDAN, Paul D., PH.D., Professor of History of Religions at the United Theological College, Bangalore. Author of *The Concept of Maya*, etc.

FJELLBU, Arne, D.D., Bishop of Nidaros, Trondheim, Norway; formerly secretary of Norwegian Student Christian Movement. Author of *Sielesorg, Den kristne Moral*, etc.

FLOROVSKY, George, D.D., Professor of Dogmatics, Orthodox Theological Institute, Paris. Author of *Eastern Fathers of the Fourth Century* (Russian), and *The Ways of Russian Theology* (French), etc.

GREGG, J. A. F., D.D., Archbishop of Armagh and Primate of all Ireland; formerly Professor of Divinity at Trinity College, Dublin. Author of *Decian Persecution, The Wisdom of Solomon*, etc.

NIEBUHR, H. Richard, PH.D., Professor of Christian Ethics, Yale University. Author of *The Social Sources of Denominationalism, The Meaning of Revelation*, etc.

SCHLINK, Edmund, D.THEOL., Professor of Systematic Theology and Director of Ecumenical Institute at the University of Heidelberg. Author of *Bekennende Kirche und Welt*, etc.

SKYDSGAARD, Kristen E., D.D., Professor at University of Copenhagen. Author of *Metafysik og Tro; en dogmatisk Studie i nyere Thomisme*.

TOMKINS, Oliver S., Assistant General Secretary of World Council of Churches; formerly Editor of *Student Movement* Magazine.

VILLAIN, Maurice, DR. EN THÉOL.

VISSER 'T HOOFT, W. A., D.D., General Secretary of World Council of Churches. Author of *The Kingship of Christ*, etc.

WYON, Olive, D.D., Secretary of Study Department of World Council of Churches. Author of *The School of Prayer*, etc.

INTRODUCTION

THE CHURCH IN THE WORLD TO-DAY

IN the hopeless world of our time, the one hope lies in the Church of Christ. This appears to be a fantastic claim. Nevertheless, we make it. It is for this reason that an Assembly of Churches, meeting on a world-wide scale in the year 1948, puts the question of the Church itself in the forefront of its consideration. For us, who meet, this is inevitable. We meet because we believe that the Church of Jesus Christ is the greatest reality on earth, and we belong to it.

It is the ground and justification of our coming together. From many countries and cultures, in spite of deep differences and even disagreements, the language we possess is the language of the Church; it is the language of the Bible, of prayer, of our fathers in the faith. For us the Church is certainly no mere idea. It is a strong reality of history and of geography. From whatever tradition we come, our roots lie deep in the past; recent years have seen the Church in many countries emerge from suffering and persecution with a deepened awareness of its own essential nature; recent centuries have seen the spread and growth of the Christian churches in lands where, a few generations ago, they were unknown; more recently, churches which often seemed strange, foreign growths have become a true part of the native life of the cultures which they invaded. Above all, and in all this, the Church is first and last the point in our experience at which eternity penetrates time, and where history gains meaning, for it is the point at which the Living God has condescended to continue meeting us; it is the point at which the Word Who once became Flesh is still to be encountered.

We know well that to many minds among our contemporaries, this preoccupation of Christians with the Church must appear to be not only unwarrantably self-centred, but even completely irrelevant. Such minds, assessing the great forces that are stirring in the world of 1948, do not consider the Christian Church as a relevant factor. To some, in so far as it is relevant, it is mischievous, because it represents the last stronghold of many ideas that are rightly doomed. A few pay it the compliment of considering it dangerous. Far more feel they can safely ignore it in any estimate of the resources of men to face mankind's own problem in our time.

Such men can call much witness to their support. The Christian churches have emerged with an ambiguous record in the development of science in recent centuries; now opposing it blindly; now capitulating without reserve to its findings; at all times speaking with an uncertain voice. In the great political and economic conflict of our time, Christian witness is again divided. Confronted with Communism, Christian bodies speak with contradictory voices or maintain a discreet silence. In the tidal-wave of nascent nationalism in the rising powers of Africa and the East, the Church appears again either to be inextricably confused with the western, alien domination which is being repudiated, or else to be a negligible force in the nationalisms which engulf it. In every major crisis of our time, the Church may thus appear as irrelevant and impotent. Can a World Assembly of Christians justify putting *the Church* in the fore-front of the picture? Indeed, is an Assembly of Churches of any importance to the world of 1948? These are questions which many minds will expect to have answered, and Christians cannot deny that they are questions which have a right to be asked.

It is true to say that the Christian Church makes high claims for itself. It is truer to say that the Gospel makes high claims for the Church; and the Church cannot ignore any claim made by the Gospel, even when it is a claim relating to itself. The Gospel claims that God, Who has made and still rules the world, has won a victory in history itself against the forces which oppose Him. This took place when God raised from death a certain Jesus of Nazareth, vindicating Him as His "anointed one" and gave Him universal Lordship. Although men may deny it, Jesus Christ *is* Lord and human history is the scene of His Lord-ship. Human history is also the story of Christ's waiting. His sovereignty is yet to be shown in unmistakable power. Mean-while He has given to a community, which lives in history, the duty to proclaim His rule and the power to exhibit it to all who can grasp the real meaning of what God has done through Him. God acts in history and the Church holds the thread run-ning through it which gives a clue to its meaning.

In various times and at various places, the hidden meaning

becomes clearer. There are times when human society becomes so corrupt and so lawless, when institutions of justice and humanity so break down, that the Church's clue which leads to the Author of order and love is more readily seen. There are times when man's inability to transcend his own limitations makes clearer the dependence of Christians upon a power and a capacity for renewal which come from beyond themselves. There are times when the bitter conflicts which divide men are more nearly transcended and more quickly healed within the Christian community than outside it.

We claim that our own time has been one of such times. Although we admit, with as much honesty and insight as have been given us, the extent to which the disorders of the world have infected the Christian community, we are still able to claim that God has shown amongst us powers of resistance, healing and unification for which we claim no credit for ourselves but give glory to Him.

The story of the "Christian resistance" in many countries during recent years can be read in two versions. To some it will appear only that organized Christianity showed unexpected resilience and boldness, not only in resisting Nazi invaders of other countries, but even in resisting the rise and spread of Marxism in Germany itself. Professor Einstein, from outside the Christian ranks, paid an ungrudging tribute to the way in which the churches stood and fought when political parties, trades unions and universities had capitulated. He spoke in terms which many have been ready to endorse. But we also claim that the "Christian resistance" has a deeper meaning. It is the meaning of Christian *renewal*. For those who accept the Lordship of Jesus Christ over all human life, the struggle is of wider significance than the war itself; it is the dramatic sharpening of a struggle that is always going on between the Kingdom of Christ and all man-centred systems. For this reason, the struggle is not over. The temptations to relax, to subside into controversy over lesser issues, to lose the unity of the days of conflict, to look back to easier times instead of moving forward into uncertain ones, these are to be expected, but they are to be resisted and overcome if the struggle is seen in its full Christian dimensions. Christian renewal is not a past event to look back on: it is a quality of life in which always to live.

War proved powerless to break the unity in which Christians

are bound together. Although there were some who completely subordinated their universal loyalty to Christ to the claim of nationalism, there remained strong expressions of the transcending unity. Churches supported the missionary work of enemy nationals; prisoners of war received, in the name of Christ, spiritual ministrations from their enemies; even before the war had ended, ecumenical plans were made for reconstruction and inter-church aid; within a few months of the cessation of fighting, both in Europe and Asia, the work of reconciliation had begun; Christians were meeting again, face to face, to resume interrupted conversation on their uninterrupted common tasks. We believe that these facts, and many more, point to a deep unity to which we must give ever clearer expression.

And so, above all, we believe that the Spirit which has been at work amongst Christians for some decades, leading them into continually closer co-operation and understanding, has found clearest symbolic expression in the World Council of Churches. We believe that this council is but one aspect of a wider and deeper activity of the same Spirit of God in our time, working far beyond the limits of our formally organized fellowship and in ways which we have yet to recognize.

We claim that God is working amongst His chosen community for their *renewal* and their *unity* in ways some of which we can already discern. Because He is the Lord of Creation, as well as Lord of the Church, we claim that what is happening to us is also of unpredictable significance for the whole of mankind.

We belong to the Church: the Church does not belong to us. We claim that the hope of the world lies in the Church because the only hope of man lies in the love of God and the Church is that area of human life where man responds to God's love. In spite of all its failure, cowardice, and even betrayal, the Church remains the place in human life where man admits that he does not belong to himself. The fear and pain of the world, in 1948 or in any other year, meet their answer only in that community which truly understands that we belong to Christ and Christ belongs to God, Whose love is our hope.

I

THE DOCTRINE OF THE CHURCH:
SOME INTERPRETATIONS

The fundamental problem of the Church is the existence of the churches. This is not an abstract, theological proposition; it is our admission of a fact of life.

The first fact to face is that there is no agreed Christian interpretation of the doctrine of the Church. Even the Church which has the strongest appearance of unity and the most exclusive claims in the face of other Christians, the Church of Rome, has no dogmatic definition of its theology of the Church.

In this section we lay bare the dilemma from which we start. Five scholars have here interpreted, briefly, the biblical evidence for the nature of the Church. None of them writes as an official spokesman of his tradition; none claims any other authority than his personal authority as a theologian, standing in a particular tradition. They differ in important respects in their conclusions. But they illustrate the situation in Christendom to-day.

But, as it would be untrue to conceal their differences, it would be equally untrue to minimize their agreements. The whole history of the ecumenical movement testifies to the wide area of Christian agreement and to its continual enlargement and definition.

These essays must be read in the context of the whole work of the Faith and Order movement, especially the Declaration of Unity of the Edinburgh Conference 1937. *It is only the unity which exists that makes possible the exploration of our differences. It is only the unity which we believe that God has already given which affords hope that the honest search for biblical truth will, not create unity, but more and more reveal it.*

1

THE CHURCH IN THE LIGHT OF THE
NEW TESTAMENT

by Gustaf Aulén

I JESUS AND THE CHURCH

IN the New Testament, Christianity appears in the form of the Church. To be a Christian is to be a member of the Church, to have a share in the new *koinonia*, the new communion. However, the question has been raised about the relationship between this Church and Jesus Himself. Sometimes exegesis has denied the existence of such a relationship. It has been said that Jesus had no intention of creating a Church, and that the idea of a Church was quite unfamiliar to His teaching and to His aims. An interpretation of the Gospels that does not recognize any connection between Jesus and the Church cannot be maintained. Such an interpretation misunderstands the central message of the Gospel.

Jesus appears as the Messiah of Israel. His task was to fulfil God's promises to His people. He did not come to teach a new religious doctrine, but to proclaim a *message* and deliver an invitation: " The time is fulfilled, and the Kingdom of God is at hand: repent ye and believe the Gospel " (Mark i, 15). He addressed His invitation to His people, to Israel. When He called individuals, He called them to be disciples, to enter the messianic people that He gathered around Himself, to enter the new *koinonia*, the chosen people, the true Israel, that would share in the fulfilment of the promises.

As regards Jesus and the Church, we must not confine our investigations to the statements which speak directly about the *ecclesia*. It is much more important to observe how the idea of a new fellowship continually appears in the Gospels, and how it represents there a constitutive element. Some few examples may be mentioned: Jesus speaks of Himself as the bridegroom among the wedding guests, He speaks of the wedding feast, of the temple to be built (Mark xiv, 58), of the corner-stone that has been laid. Other examples are actions such as the calling of the

Twelve, the sending out of the apostles as authorized agents, the feeding of the five thousand, the Last Supper and so on. The idea of the Church, the *koinonia*, gathered around the Messiah, is indissolubly united with the idea of the Messiah. In the Gospels we find everywhere the consciousness of a new, super-individual order, a new continuity, created by and based upon Christ. This continuity cannot be considered as only an idea, as an invisible continuity. On the contrary, it was something very concrete and realistic: Jesus Himself with His apostles and disciples. In and through this *koinonia* the individual was made a participant in the new age (*aeon*), the Kingdom of God, the new life and the glory to come. The Church that appeared through the events of Pentecost had not only relation to certain statements and actions of Jesus, but was inseparably connected with His appearance as Messiah, as Christ. The continuity between Jesus and the apostolic Church is unbroken. This statement can be denied, but only if we deny that Jesus appeared as Messiah. No Messiah can exist without an *ecclesia* belonging to him. Therefore, faith in Christ and the *koinonia* of the Church belong necessarily together. The realm belongs to the King.

II THE CHURCH AS THE BODY OF CHRIST

The biblical view of the Church is most comprehensively expressed in the formula: the Body of Christ, *soma Christou*. When the Church is called the Body of Christ, that means first of all that Christ and the Church belong together as an inseparable unity. The Church has its existence in and through Christ, and just as we cannot imagine the Church without Christ, so we cannot imagine Christ-Kyrios without His domination, without the communion that belongs to Him. Where Christ is, there is also His Church: and where the Church is, there Christ is found also. Communion with Christ is a communion in and through the Church. Christ is incarnate in His Church. The Church, while subject to the conditions of this earth and this time, is the revelation of the living and active Christ. Here He meets us and works with us.

Therefore, when the Church is called the Body of Christ, this expression is not to be understood merely as figurative. This word visualizes in a very concrete way that Christ and the Church are a unity. It tells us that Christ is living in the Church and at the same time gives life to the Church. When Christ in the Epistles to the Ephesians and Colossians is described as "the Head "—" He is the head of the body, His church " (Col. i, 18) —the intention is not to describe how Christ is separated from the Church, to separate the head and the body as two different parts. On the contrary, the intention is to emphasize their inseparable continuity and unity. Christ is not the isolated head, but the head of His body. And the Church is not the body as isolated from the head, but the Body of Christ. The Body of Christ is Christ Himself, the Risen Christ, alive and active on earth. As the Head of the Body He is the authority that every member has to serve and to obey. He is the life-giving power and the living hope of the Church.

We find the same view of the relation between Christ and the Church in many other biblical expressions, for instance in the words of St. John about the vine and the branches, and in the words in the Epistle to the Ephesians about the Church as a holy temple in the Lord: "Christ himself being the chief corner stone: in whom all the building fitly framed together groweth into a holy temple in the Lord" (Eph. ii, 20-21).

All these three statements about the Church emphasize not only the unity of the Church and Christ, but also the communion of Christians within the Church. The body has many different members with different tasks, but they are all part of the same body. All the branches belong to the same vine, and thus have communion with each other. The stones do not lie isolated. As "living stones" they are joined together in a holy temple, each fitted into its place. Therefore these symbols also represent the communion of the members in the Church. But this communion depends wholly and entirely upon communion with Christ.

III THE CHURCH AND THE NEW AGE

The *koinonia* of the Church means that a new age has appeared in this world of sin and death. God has given mankind a new beginning when He gave us Christ as Lord and made Him the Head of a new humanity. To be a member of the Church means to have been made a participant, in this new age, of the *regnum Christi* that at the same time is a *regnum gratiae*. It means to have received the gift of the justification that Christ has acquired through His sacrifice and His victory over the devil and all the evil forces in the world. Opposing the dominion of sin and death and the old Age, stands the dominion of grace and life, ruling by " the righteousness of God " (Rom. i, 17).

However, the old Age has not disappeared. It is still existing here on earth. But in the midst of this old Age the Church as *regnum Christi* represents the new Age. The Church is not *of* the world, but she lives *in* the world. Because " grace and truth came through Jesus Christ " (John i, 17), she lives in the age of fulfilment. Because she still lives in the old Age of sin and death, she lives in a permanent fight against the evil forces of destruction, and the fulfilment that has come is at the same time a promise of a glory to come when the Kingdom of God will be wholly and entirely realized. Therefore the view of the Church, living and fighting in this world, is an eschatological view. The Church exists on the border between two worlds, having part in the misery of this world, and at the same time having a quality that transcends every present age of history.

As members of the Church, Christians live in two worlds. Living in the " old Age ", in " Adam ", the Christian is a sinner, mixed up in the sinfulness of the world. Living in the new Age, *in regnum gratiae,* he is redeemed and justified, transferred from the kingdom of darkness to the Kingdom of the Son of God's love. As long as the Christian lives here in this world he must, therefore, wage a permanent struggle against sin and the whole nature of the world, the power of which, however, is broken through Christ.

This duality will last until the new Age is fulfilled in glory. The Christian is, according to the view of the New Testament, *simul justus et peccator,* at the same time justified and a sinner. This formula from the Reformation is quite in harmony with the realistic view of the New Testament. The New Testament speaks very openly about the sins, divisions and infirmities to be found in the Church. At the same time it speaks of the Church as one in Christ, as holy and as a communion of saints. The Church is a " Communion of Saints ", not in the sense that her members are holy or " saintly " from a moralistic point of view, not in the sense that they are " perfect "; but the Church is called the Communion of Saints because Christ as the head of the Church is her holiness, and because His Holy Spirit is active in the Church for the sanctification of her members.

IV THE CONSTITUTIVE ELEMENTS OF THE CHURCH

The New Testament gives us a very clear view of the constitutive elements of the Church. The Church that was revealed as a living reality on the first Whit-Sunday was a creation of the Holy Spirit, working through the divine message concerning the victorious Christ as Saviour and Lord. This message appeared in double shape, as Word and as Sacrament, holy action. The gift of the Spirit was the sign that the new Age had come, and that the promises to the Fathers had been fulfilled. The Church was constituted as a community of the baptized, gathered around the Holy Communion as the centre of their worship.

The Church was born into life as a spiritual continuity where the forces of the divine forgiveness and the world to come were at work. In the same way the message about Christ was spread around the world by the apostles and their assistants and successors. And everywhere the Sacraments appeared as an essential part of the life of the Church. Therefore, according to the New Testament, the constitutive factors of the Church are the Word of God and the Sacraments of Baptism and the Eucharist. The Word and the Sacraments are bearers of the divine action. The Spirit, working through Word and Sacraments, uses the apostles and their assistants and successors as instruments and servants. The Word and the Sacraments claim the ministry as their servant.

V THE WORD OF GOD

Primarily the Word of God is Christ Himself. He is, as the only-begotten, the Word in a unique sense, from the beginning being with the Father. When Christ appeared on earth, the Word of God was incarnate. "The Word became flesh and dwelt among us, full of grace and truth" (John i, 14). This incarnate Word is the foundation of the Church—"For other foundation can no man lay than that is laid, which is Jesus Christ" (1 Cor. iii, 11).

However, this same Word speaks to us and acts with us in the message given to us in the Bible, in the *Gospel*. Therefore, also this message appears as the Word of God and as the basis and life-giving power of the Church for all ages and generations.

Everything in the message proclaimed by the apostles has its centre in Christ. That is true also when the message of the apostles refers to the Old Testament scriptures. The Old Testament then appears as a witness to Christ as "the One who is to come". It is interpreted in the light of God's act fulfilled in Christ, to which the apostolic message bears testimony.

The meaning of the Word of God as Gospel would be completely misunderstood if considered only as a doctrine. The Gospel appears as the witness of the apostles and as the message about Christ delivered by them as "ambassadors on behalf of Christ". In the New Testament we find this message in all its purity and firmness. But at the same time it is not only a human message. Christ Himself is in the Gospel. He is Himself the Gospel and through the Gospel He follows up His work among and with us. Therefore the words of the message are "living words", "the words of eternal life" (John vi, 68). When Christ is at work in and through the Gospel, God releases man from the bonds of darkness and leads him through the faith that He kindles into the *Regnum gratiae* whose Lord and Head is Christ, where peace and joy and hope reign.

According to this biblical view, the Christian conception of the Word must reject theories that mechanize the Word, and fail to see that the Word appears in the form of a human witness, as well as theories according to which the character of the divine message appears in a spiritualized way. The Spirit speaks in and through the Word. Only in this way is the Spirit given. The Spirit speaks and acts in and through the Word. A Spirit outside the Word and independent of the Word of God is not God's holy Spirit.

The Word of God does not appear only as Gospel. It appears also as Law. They both pertain to the Church, but in different ways. The Law of God is the Law of creation, *of the Creator*. It would lead to misunderstandings if we were to describe this Law as a "natural" Law. But certainly it is a universal Law. It expresses the claim of God on mankind: the claim of Love, that at the same time is the foundation of justice. It is manifested not only in "commandments", but also in the wrath of God, "that is revealed from heaven against all ungodliness and wickedness of men who by their wickedness suppress the truth" (Rom. i, 18).

The Law has been in force since "the beginning". The Gospel on the other hand has its foundation in the promises of God. Because of these promises the Church existed in a preparatory way even under the Old Covenant. But until the fulness of the Gospel appeared in Christ, the Church did not appear as a living reality. The Gospel is building the Church on earth. The Gospel gives the Church her life. Through the Gospel the Church is what she is. However, that does not mean that the Law should have no place in the Church, or that it should be only a matter of secondary importance.

Certainly, from one point of view the Law has been abolished. When St. Paul says that Christ is the end of the Law, that means that the Law is no way to salvation, and that the Law has no right to condemn the man who has been justified by faith in Christ. The Law is abolished *in loco justificationis*, but only there. Otherwise the Law remains in all its power and in all its universal importance. Through the Law, God has declared His will as regards our human relationships. It may here especially be emphasized that the Law of God functions also outside the Church as a *dynamis* for promoting justice and crushing injustice. However, it is the responsibility of the Church as regards all human relationships to keep watch over the sanctity of the Law of God. It is also the duty of the Church, in the ever-changing situations, to interpret the divine Law according to the revelation of God given to the Church.

VI BAPTISM

In the Sacraments, the divine Love gives itself to us through an action.

Through the Sacraments Christ incorporates us with Himself as members of His Body, the Church.

Fundamental and elemental incorporation in the Body of Christ takes place through baptism. By nature we are members of sinful humanity and subject to its conditions. Through baptism we are brought into a wholly new relation. We become members of the Body of Christ according to the words of St. Paul: "for by one Spirit we were all baptized into one Body" (1 Cor. xii, 13). Thus we are born into a new existence given to us through Christ.

However, baptism is not only an act of initiation. It embraces the Christian life in its entirety. It means that the Christian life must be a continually repeated dying with Christ and rising with Him. The baptized can remain a living member in Christ only in this way, as a living branch of the true vine (Rom. vi, 5-11). As long as the baptized lives on earth, he has to live his life infected by sin and unbelief. The Covenant of Baptism is still in force as far as God is concerned, and it is continually calling man through repentance to return to the grace of God as manifested already in baptism.

As the act of incorporation, baptism is an action of the divine *gratia preveniens*: the call of God is the foundation of our membership. It is from this point of view that we must consider the baptism of infants. For the baptism of infants shows us how our membership in the Church has its basis not in our own endeavours and efforts, but solely in the divine Love and grace, and therefore also how this membership is quite independent of human judgments and decisions. At the same time this kind of baptism acts, and must act, as a living conscience in the Church, impressing upon her her duty to take care of the baptized and to give them a Christian education.

As regards the question of the baptism of infants in the Early Church, it seems very probable that such was sometimes the practice already in the time of the New Testament. It is said more than once that someone was baptized with all his family, that is, with wife and children. When the Gospel tells us that Jesus rebuked His disciples because they would hinder the children from coming to Him, it does not seem unlikely that this statement has been preserved because the Early Church here found a justification of the baptism of infants. However, for the justification of infant baptism it is not necessary to refer to isolated statements in the New Testament. The justification has its foundation in the Gospel itself as the Gospel of the free and undeserved grace of God. This Gospel and the baptism of infants belong together.[1]

VII THE EUCHARIST

As an introduction it ought to be emphasized that the institution of the Eucharist on the night when the Lord was betrayed must not be considered as an isolated action. It must be seen

---

[1] It must be remarked, at this point, that critics of this paper who belong to the Baptist tradition, consider these interpretations of the New Testament evidence or of the doctrine of grace to be untenable. For the Baptist interpretation see *The Ministry and Sacraments*, pp. 219-229 (Student Christian Movement Press, 1937).

in connection with earlier holy table communion between Jesus, His disciples and others.

In the Gospel of St. Mark we find that Jesus in the Last Supper would assure His disciples of the continued personal communion between Himself and His disciples. As regards the future He linked His presence to the breaking of the bread: "This is my body." That means: this is I Myself. At the same time He proclaimed that a new covenant would be established in and through His sacrificial death. Drinking the cup would mean to be admitted into this covenant and there to be regenerated.

There is a central concordance between this view and the view of St. Paul. Also here the communion with Christ is the main idea of the Eucharist. When St. Paul speaks of the remembrance—"do this in remembrance of me"—remembrance does not mean only a solemn reminder of Christ's sacrifice and death; it means also His presence in the cultus. This point of view is most strongly emphasized where the breaking of the bread is characterized as "communion of the body of Christ". "The bread which we break, is it not the communion of the Body of Christ? For we being many are one bread and one body; for we are all partakers of that one bread" (1 Cor. x, 16-17). The communion with the living Christ is the soul of the Eucharist. However, it must be added that the view of His presence at the same time has an eschatological character. The eschatological perspective we find as well in the words of Jesus Himself as of St. Paul. "Truly I say to you, I shall not drink again of the fruit of the vine until that day when I drink it new in the Kingdom of God" (Mark xiv, 25). "For as often as ye eat this bread and drink this cup, ye do show the Lord's death till He come" (1 Cor. xi, 26).

The Holy Communion is, in the light of the New Testament, the Sacrament not only of the suffering Love, but also of the victorious Love of Christ. Through this Sacrament He realizes His victorious work of the resurrection in His Body, the Church. This view of the New Testament may be characterized as a very realistic one, because all here depends upon the action of Christ Himself. The view is neither magical nor only spiritualistic-symbolic, but sacramental. Certainly the Holy Communion is a mystery. But this mystery is nothing other than the mystery of the Gospel as a whole: that into this kingdom of death God has sent Him who is the Prince of Life, and that He has called us to be *one* with Him and to share in His Life.

VIII THE MINISTRY OF RECONCILIATION

According to the New Testament, the Ministry of the Church also belongs to the constitutive elements of the Church. The Ministry has its foundation in the mandate of Christ and is a necessary instrument for the edification of the Church through the Gospel and the Sacraments. Thus it appears as a Ministry of reconciliation. The biblical view of the Ministry will be obscured if the Ministry is interpreted either in a mechanical or in a subjective way.

In the New Testament the Ministry is inseparably connected with the Church. Having its origin in the mandate of Christ, it is a divine mission. The task of the Ministry is to serve Christ by serving the Church in her endeavours to penetrate the human world as deeply and as widely as possible. In this work the Ministry possesses authority, given by Christ, but this authority is not a personal authority, only an authority of service.

Everywhere in the New Testament it is emphasized that the Ministry has a divine mandate. The Lord says of His messengers: "As thou hast sent me into the world, even so have I also sent them into the world " (John xvii, 18). The messengers receive power to forgive sins in the name of the Lord (Matt. xviii, 18, cf. Matt. xvi, 19 and John xx, 22-3), but their authority is not their own. They are completely dependent on Christ, they are His instruments and servants (Matt. xx, 26-8; Matt. x, 40). Listening to St. Paul we find that he most strongly emphasizes the divine mandate that he has received, but also that he does not consider his authority as a personal authority; he himself is nothing but a servant (1 Cor. iii, 5 and iv, 1). His confidence comes from God (2 Cor. iii, 5, cf. 2 Cor. iv, 1). The Ministry can serve the Church only by wholly and entirely serving Christ (Gal. i, 10). The centre of the Ministry is reconciliation. Reconciliation claims the Ministry inasmuch as the victory of the reconciliation must be realized in fighting against the evil forces of destruction. The messengers know that in this fight no human power can accomplish anything; they know that Christ is the Victor, and that His messengers are allowed to go out in His name and with His authority.

As we have seen, the New Testament most strongly emphasizes the Ministry as a divine mandate. As Jesus sent out the apostles, so new messengers must be sent to succeed them. Then, from the biblical point of view, the most important thing as regards the legitimacy of the Ministry is undoubtedly that the message is really the apostolic message, that the Gospel is preached just as it is and not in false reinterpretations, and further that the Sacraments are administered according to Christ's will, and as instituted by Him.

Finally, service in the Church is obviously not confined to the Ministry. In fact, all the members of the Church are called to be servants in different ways. It is not possible to be a Christian without being a servant. However, that service which in the New Testament is connected with the word *diakonia* must specially be mentioned. When the Word and the Sacraments are active, action must follow. Service in love is and must be characteristic of the Church. One of the most important tasks of the Church at all times is therefore to give this service a position that adequately corresponds to its importance.

IX   THE NEW TESTAMENT AND THE UNITY OF THE CHURCH

For the New Testament the oneness of the Church is self-evident. Because the Church is the Body of Christ there can be but *one* Church. The unity is described as a unity in Christ or in the Spirit. St. Paul speaks about "one Body and one Spirit . . . one Lord, one faith, one baptism, one God and Father of all" (Eph. iv, 4-5).

This unity is a reality. But at the same time the New Testament very openly speaks of divisions and antagonisms which are a menace to unity. Repeatedly we find in the New Testament exhortations to maintain and realize unity. Christ's prayer is "that they all may be one" (John xvii, 21). St. Paul appeals to the Corinthians that "there be no dissensions among you", "Is Christ divided?" (1 Cor. i, 10 and 13), and he exhorts the Ephesians to be eager to maintain "the unity of the Spirit in the bond of peace" (Eph. iv, 3).

Considering the conditions and manifestations of unity according to the New Testament, we must emphasize that unity is not uniformity—neither uniformity of doctrine, nor uniformity of organization and orders, nor uniformity of life and religious experience.

Undoubtedly the basis of unity is to be found in the message of Christ as it appears in the Divine Word and in the Sacraments. There is no doubt that the New Testament considers this message as the foundation of the Church, without which the Church cannot exist, and therefore also as the basis of unity. But that does not mean uniformity of doctrine or theology. Obviously there are varieties of doctrine in the New Testament. The theology of St. John is not quite the same as the theology of St. Paul, nor the theology of the Epistle to the Hebrews. Nevertheless, in spite of the variety, the message is one and the same, a unity in variety.

Approaching the question of order and organization, here also we find unity in variety. The backbone of the organization is the apostolic Ministry as a divine institution on behalf of the Word and the Sacraments. Inasmuch as the Ministry is a true servant of the divine message, it represents the unity of the Church. However, we do not find any uniformity of order and organization. Obviously there are considerable differences in different parts of the Early Church. It would be wrong to consider the statements of the New Testament concerning questions of organization as fixed laws of the Church, valid for all ages and generations. The biblical view is characterized by firmness as well as by elasticity. Both are indispensable in the life of the Church. Also as regards elasticity, the principle of organization must be: the best means of serving the divine message which is the creative factor in the Church.

Finally, the unity of the Church is not uniformity of life. It is not based upon subjective experiences. The Church is not a union of individual Christians having the same religious experiences. Certainly the gift given to Christians in and through the Church is one and the same: salvation, the " new life ". But the New Testament shows us that this does not lead to uniformity of religious life. On the contrary, just as the light shining through a prism appears in different colours, so the gift of salvation appears in different human experiences and forms. A unity based on subjective experiences and qualifications must break. It cannot but lead to repeated divisions. The true basis of unity is not a subjective but an objective one: Christ acting through the Word and the Sacraments. The Church is not a closed society of specially qualified and " pure " members. The Church reaches as far as the power of Christ and His life-giving

Spirit is active in human souls. It is always a Church in the making, and its boundaries are always being re-defined.

. . . .

We have here considered some features of the biblical view of the Church. In all endeavours to attain deeper unity it must be a help to return to the Bible. Not because we shall find there fixed rules concerning unity: the Bible is not a law for the Church. But there are other important reasons. First, the aim of the ecumenical movement is primarily a renewal of the Church, and no renewal has at any time taken place in the Church without help from the Bible. Secondly, the constitution of the Church is once and for all given and elucidated in the Bible. Thirdly, the Bible is the common ground of all Christians, and theology—as far as it is truly biblical—will undoubtedly promote Christian unity. We turn to the Bible, because the basis of Christian unity can only be the truth.

2

THE CHURCH OF THE NEW TESTAMENT

by Clarence T. Craig

WHEN the man of to-day hears the word "church", it awakens in his mind a wide variety of images. Some think at once of a *building*, ornate or simple, where the worship of God is celebrated. But the early Christians were groups without legal rights to possess institutional property. Amid the ruins of war-torn cities many modern Christians are discovering anew that the Church is not made of stone or brick. The living stones of the true Temple of God are those who worship Him in Spirit and in truth.

Others think of a denominational or territorial body. There are Methodists and Lutherans; Eastern Orthodox and Baptists; the Church of England and of Sweden. All of these names would have been equally strange to the first Christians. More than that, since the Church was by definition the people of God, there could not possibly be more than one. There could not be a Jewish church and a Gentile church, or a Macedonian church and a Judean. Christ had broken down the dividing wall of hostility and made of the different peoples one new man (Eph. ii, 14). In Christ all human distinctions were abolished (Col. iii, 11-12). As there was one God and one Lord and one faith and one baptism, there could only be one Church (Eph. iv, 4-5; i, 23; ii, 16).

Others think of a congregation of like-minded men and women who band themselves together to worship God in the way they choose. Of course the New Testament can use the word for the Christians living in one place (1 Cor. iv, 17), and even for small house communities (Rom. xvi, 5). But these were not groups which had been formed according to the pattern of other social clubs and religious societies. Believers had been called out by God, called into a society which He had created. They were the Elect, the Chosen. This was not their own doing, but it rested in the purpose of God Who sought a People for Himself.

I

If we are to understand the nature of the Church we must begin with the Old Testament. According to Acts vii, 38 there was already a church in the wilderness when God redeemed His people out of Egypt. Terms like new Israel and "Israel of God" would be pointless except against the background of a nation which had been so conceived as the people of God (Gal. vi, 16). If Christians were the "true circumcision" (Phil. iii, 3) and the "real sons of Abraham" (Rom. iv, 16; Gal. vi, 16) this Old Testament background is presupposed. A people of a New Covenant presupposed an Old Covenant. The Greek word *ekklesia* had no special religious connotation, as its use within the New Testament for a political assembly shows (Acts xix, 32, 39-40). It had acquired such significance because of its use in the Septuagint to translate the Hebrew *Qahal*. This was the term for the people of Israel, called out in solemn assembly, or ideally considered as such.

Throughout the Old Testament there is the conception of a People that God has chosen. The Hebrews looked back to Abraham as the one with whom God had made a covenant which would extend to his descendants (Gen. xv, 18; xvii, 7-8). He was the God Who had brought them up out of slavery in Egypt (Amos iii, 1; Hosea xi, 1; xiii, 4; 1 Kings viii, 51 *et passim*) and they were the People whom He had formed for Himself (Isaiah xliii, 21). His law had been revealed to Moses on the Mount (Ex. xxiv, 7-8), and this called for righteousness and the exclusive worship of the one God (Deut. vi, 13-15). They were to be a holy nation, a cult community (Ex. xix, 6; Ps. xcv, 6-7). Election involved responsibility for Israel rather than special privilege (Amos iii, 2). Over and over again the prophets censured Israel for her faithlessness (Isaiah i, 3-4; Hosea v, 3-5). The disasters which befell her were not historical misfortunes but the judgment of God (Micah i, 6; Amos iii, 6). Yet they looked forward to a coming act of redemption when His People would enjoy the full salvation of God (Isaiah ii, 2-4; ix, 2-7). The noblest spirits did not restrict this to Jews alone, but insisted that God wanted Israel to be a light to the nations of the world (Isaiah xlv, 22; xlix, 6; Zech. viii, 20ff.) Yet even here, God's relation was not with isolated individuals, but with a People whom He had chosen.

When the word *ekklesia* is used in the New Testament it is with conscious reference to this Old Testament conception. One can hardly say, therefore, that Jesus founded the Church. The truth rather is that He redeemed the Church. For centuries there had been a people who looked upon themselves as set apart for God. When Christians applied the term *ekklesia* to themselves they re-defined the People of God in terms of the new acts of God for their redemption. It was not to be identified with Israel after the flesh, but with individuals from every tribe, nation, people, and tongue (Rev. vii, 9, etc.). Its adherents were not those who were strictly loyal to Torah, for Christ was the end of the law (Rom. x, 4). Its centre was not in a Temple where sacrifices were continually offered, but in Christ Who had died for their sins and been raised by God from the dead (1 Cor. xv, 3ff.). Though membership in the People of God was determined by different criteria, the basic conception of a Church goes back to the Old Testament. The true Remnant about which the prophets had spoken, had found fulfilment in the Christian community.

II

The gospels clearly indicate that the central message of Jesus did not deal with the Church. It was concerned with *the kingdom of God* and the repentance which was necessary if men should enter it by the gracious mercy of God (Mark i, 14-15). Jesus announced the nearness of the kingdom of God, a message which gave tremendous urgency to His ethical demands. A crisis was at hand; men must stand ready to pay any price to enter God's kingdom (Luke xiv, 25-33). Its approaching consummation meant the resurrection and the judgment, in other words, God's salvation.

But the message of Jesus did not deal exclusively with future events. The rule of God was already *present in His own ministry*. His healings and especially the demon exorcisms were evidence of the dawning powers of the new age (Matt. xii, 28). For those who had eyes to see, the mysterious presence of the kingdom of God was already manifest. The salvation of God had already appeared in the gracious work of Jesus (Matt. xi, 2-6). To reject Him was to refuse that salvation, for Jesus embodied the kingdom in His own person (Mark viii, 38).

Most startling was His announcement concerning *those who would enter* the kingdom when it should come in its fulness. It would not be for the rich but for the poor (Luke vi, 20ff.). It would not be for the wise scribes but for the little children and the childlike (Mark x, 14-15). It would not be for the righteous Pharisees but for the tax-collectors and sinners who were more ready to repent (Matt. xxi, 31). These were the groups which responded to the message of Jesus,· and to them He gave assurance, "Fear not, little flock, for it is your Father's good pleasure to give you the kingdom" (Luke xii, 32).

Did the message of Jesus deal specifically with the Church? Biblical students are still far from agreement on the question. It is not to be solved simply by a discussion of the authenticity of the two passages in which Matthew employs *ekklesia* (Matt. xvi, 18; xviii, 17). It is the idea, not the term which is crucial. Neither 1 Peter nor the Gospel of John uses the word *ekklesia*, yet they are both documents which accord high importance to the Church. Certainly Jesus promised entrance to the kingdom of God to those who sincerely responded to His call. He gathered a group of disciples about Him. He did not form them into separate synagogues, but His disciples attended the appointed Jewish services. They had no separate cult acts during His life-time. Yet, since they were destined to enter the kingdom of God, were they not already the Church, whether gospel passages use that term or not?

Certainly in those who responded to the call of Jesus we find another part of the *background* for the Church. But many interpreters believe that it is inadmissible to apply the term with reference to that time. They believe that the passages which speak of the presence of the kingdom of God all refer to the activity of Jesus and that none relate this presence to the disciples. Other interpreters believe that this is quite accidental in the preservation of the tradition. They hold that since the Church is the anticipation in the present of the kingdom of God, those who were prepared to enter belonged to the Church even during the life-time of Jesus.

III

No one can doubt, however, that *the resurrection of Jesus* was central for the Church of the New Testament. Those who believed that God had raised Christ from the dead comprised the Church. God had vindicated His Messiah and the time of redemption had begun. With His resurrection the New Age was suddenly manifesting its power. Without that resurrection there was no full salvation because it was the ground for the resurrection of believers from the dead. We may say that the Christian Church was the community which had been constituted by God through the resurrection of Jesus.

A further indispensable mark of this community was its possession by the Holy Spirit. The gift of the Spirit had been promised for the end time. When the early Christians interpreted their ecstasy and joy and peace as caused by the Spirit, they meant that this had already come (Acts ii, 16ff.). The risen Christ had sent them the Spirit, the guarantee of His coming in glory. Though Christian tradition has followed Luke in dating the first experience of the Spirit fifty days after the crucifixion, John's Gospel puts this on the day of the resurrection (John xx, 22). That symbolizes the fact that belief in the resurrection and possession by the Spirit are twin signs for the identification of the Church.

The sharing by believers in the blessings of God was expressed through the word *koinonia*. Recent research has made it clear that when this word is followed by the genitive it should be translated not as " fellowship " but as " participation " or " sharing ".[1] The Church was a *koinonia* because its members participated in the same gifts. Sometimes the gift is Christ (1 Cor. i, 9); sometimes the Spirit (2 Cor. xiii, 14); sometimes God Himself (1 John i, 3). Since these were experiences which they shared in common there was a *koinonia* with one another (1 John 1, 7). This led to financial sharing within the brotherhood (Acts ii, 44-5; 2 Cor. viii, 9). Those who participated in the same spiritual blessings also shared their material resources. But there is no evidence that the word was ever used as a name for the group.

Yet many different terms were used. The author of 1 Peter addressed his readers as " a chosen race, a royal priesthood, a holy nation, God's own people " (1 Peter ii, 9-10). A whole series of Old Testament descriptions of Israel are thus applied

---

[1] J. Y. Campbell, " *koinonia* and its cognates in the New Testament ". *Journal of Biblical Literature*, LI, 352-80; H. Seeseman, *Der Begriff koinonia im N.T.* (1933); F. Hauck in *Theologisches Woerterbuch zum N.T.*, III, 804ff.

to the Church. In the Gospel of John we read of the one flock
in which Christ's sheep are united. Yet there are different
folds. The farewell prayer of Christ is for the unity of all those
who believe through the word preached by the disciples (John
xvii, 21). Believers are the branches of the one true vine (John
xv, 1-4). They find their unity in Him, for apart from Him they
can do nothing. To be in Christ, the crucified and risen Lord,
is to be in the Church.

IV

Entrance to the Church was by *faith and baptism*. Faith was
more than accepting the truth of the Christian message. It
involved repentance and a committal of life to the God Who had
raised Christ from the dead; it called for a dedication to Christ
as the Lord of their lives; it was possible through the gift which
God bestowed through His Spirit; it was the experience in which
the redeeming grace of God laid hold on the individual and
incorporated him into the body of Christ. Jesus had called for
a similar faith, but during His ministry He had not baptized.
Very early, His Church practised baptism into the name of Jesus
as the seal of this experience. It is not strange, therefore, that
water and the Spirit are associated over and over again with
entrance into the Christian life.

The life of this brotherhood in Christ was nourished by the
celebration of *the Lord's Supper*. A common meal was the high
point of their worship. It served to commemorate the Last
Supper which Jesus had celebrated with His disciples, when by
parabolic action and significant words He had pointed to His
redemptive death (1 Cor. xi, 23-5); the meal looked forward to
their reunion with Him in the banquet of the kingdom of God
(Mark xiv, 25). But it likewise served to realize His presence as
the unseen host. "The cup of blessing which we bless, is it not
a participation in the body of Christ?" (1 Cor. x, 16). Or, as
another New Testament writer put it, Christ gave them in Himself nothing less than the bread of life (John vi, 48-51).

The New Testament Church was pre-eminently *a witnessing
community*, for its members were under obligation to proclaim
the Word of God and live in obedience to Him. They were
stewards of the mysteries of God, ambassadors of His reconciliation (1 Cor. iv, 1; 2 Cor. v, 18f.). The good news of His salva-

tion was not to be enjoyed in quiet satisfaction. The risen Christ had called them to be His witnesses to the end of the earth (Acts i, 8). Not only did an apostle like Paul respond to that summons. He rejoiced that his converts had sounded forth the Word of the Lord wherever they had gone (1 Thess. i, 8). The urgency of their missionary zeal was intensified because they were convinced that time was very short.

The New Testament Church looked forward eagerly to the speedy consummation of the kingdom of God. They had already experienced a real salvation in Christ. The man who was in Christ was a new creation and already walked in newness of life through the Spirit. The Fourth Gospel goes so far as to say that the believer already possessed eternal life through knowledge of the one true God in His Son. But the powers of evil had not yet been finally overcome. Believers lived in anticipation of the completion of God's reign. There was continuity between the Church on earth and the new age of God, but these are not the same. The city of the living God, the heavenly Jerusalem, lay beyond the coming resurrection (Heb. xii, 22). The Christ Who now ruled in His Church would ultimately reign as King of kings and Lord of lords (Rev. xix, 16).

v

Words are preserved in the gospels which indicate that there was contention over leadership within the Church (Mark ix, 34; x, 35-45). Jesus made it clear that there was no place for lordship among His disciples. Pre-eminence comes only through humble service. As He Himself had been the supreme Servant, those whom He sends forth as heralds of God's saving grace are to be servants of others. The touchstone of a truly *apostolic* ministry is to be found here. Minister and servant are alternative translations of the Greek.

The various ministries which developed in the early Church were due to differing endowments by the Spirit. All were gifts to His Church. Foremost among these was that of the *apostles* (1 Cor. xii, 28f.). An apostle was one who had seen the risen Lord (1 Cor. ix, 1); that distinction was not communicable to anyone else. The Twelve were included among these, for the risen Christ had appeared to that group (1 Cor. xv, 5). That number had been chosen by Jesus from His disciples with reference to the eschatological kingdom (Matt. xix, 28). Only twelve could sit on thrones judging the twelve tribes of Israel. But there were other apostles whom the risen Christ sent forth as missionaries and these were accorded the same authority (Acts xiv, 14; Rom. xvi, 7).

Working with the apostles were *prophets and teachers,* the other ministers of the Word. The preaching of the Gospel was the supreme function. In addition, there were those who possessed *gifts of healing* and who performed other services to the community. Since all believers shared in the priesthood and Christ was the great high priest in Heaven (1 Pet. ii, 5; Heb. iv, 14) there was no place in the New Testament for ministers who should bear the title of priest. There was need for men in various administrative capacities. In many places in the New Testament these bear no specific title (Heb. xiii, 7; 1 Thess. v, 12; 1 Cor. xvi, 15). Only once does Paul refer to bishops and deacons (Phil. i, 1). In the Acts of the Apostles, elders are mentioned in connection with some of the communities (Acts xiv, 23; xv, 6; xx, 17), and this term is used in other New Testament writings (1 Tim. v, 17; 1 Pet. v, 1; 2 John, 1). Ultimately the Church was to develop an administrative hierarchy of bishop, elders, and deacons, but this is not found within the New Testament, which prescribes no one particular pattern of administration.

Was there a single central authority within the primitive Church? How was their unity to find expression amid scattered communities? There is some evidence that Jerusalem tried to exercise a supervisory relationship over the rest of the churches (Acts viii, 14). It is clear that James, the brother of Jesus, held a unique position of leadership there (Acts xv, 13; Gal. ii, 12). As independent an apostle as Paul showed a surprising deference to James, and he raised an offering for the saints at Jerusalem even from poverty-stricken Macedonian churches (Rom. xv, 26). Among the Twelve, Peter was clearly the leader. Since he was the first to whom the risen Christ appeared there was real support for those who ascribed the primacy to him (1 Cor. xv, 5; Matt. xvi, 18). But the New Testament clearly indicates that he did not exercise ultimate authority (Gal. ii, 11f.). That rested only in the living Christ, Who is present where two or three are gathered together in His name (Matt. xviii, 20). The leadership of the Church depended then as now upon those whom He calls.

The nature of the Church is not determined by any form of organization. It is determined by the relation of a community to Christ. He alone is the Head of the Church and He alone has the right to rule. This is set forth in the New Testament in three figures which express what the Church ought to be if it is the true Church.

First, it is a *building* built on the one foundation, Jesus Christ. Other foundation can no man lay than that which is laid in Jesus Christ (1 Cor. iii, 11). The various stones are fitted into that one building (1 Pet. ii, 5). This is not an outward structure but the *Temple* in which God dwells (1 Cor. iii, 16; 2 Cor. vi, 16; Eph. ii, 21) and of which He is the builder. The Temple at Jerusalem might be destroyed, but the new Temple which replaced it was the Church (John ii, 19). God did not dwell in a place but in a people, a people who rested on Christ as their foundation.

The second figure is that of the Church as *the Bride of Christ* (2 Cor. xi, 2; Rev. xix, 7). That symbolized two things, its obedience and its purity. The author of Ephesians did not think in terms of a democratic marriage or of a patriarchal home. Though we may not agree with the figure that is used we can agree upon the importance of the Church's obedience to Christ. Christ had cleansed the Church that she might be " holy and without blemish ". " The saints " is one of the most frequent names for Christians in the New Testament; the conception is epitomized in the phrase of the creed, " I believe in the Holy Catholic Church ". But this holiness did not mean that all the members of the Church were perfect individually. Many weeds were to be found among the wheat (Matt. xiii, 24-30), and our records of the apostolic Church bear eloquent testimony to the weakness and failure of the first followers of Jesus. But the Church in which we believe is the pure bride of Christ, the holy community of the People of God.

The most important of the figures is that of the *Body of Christ*. When in the Fourth Gospel it is said that the body of Christ will replace the temple which the Jews will destroy, this may refer to the Church as well as to the risen presence of Jesus

(John ii, 19). But it is Paul who develops the figure most fully, and it is with his application that one must be concerned in trying to understand its meaning. It is easy to repeat the phrase without taking the metaphor seriously. Though we may not think so realistically as a man of the first century, we may still find important teaching in this figure. If the Church is the Body of Christ it tells us three definite things about its nature.

(a) First, a body provides a vivid expression of *unity amid diversity* (1 Cor. xii, 12, 27; Rom. xii, 5). Paul elaborated this insight in the twelfth chapter of his first letter to Corinth. A body has many members and these have different functions. Yet it needs them all if it is to be truly a body. Modern ingenuity has gone far in supplying substitutes for hands and feet which have been lost in battle or by accident, but this only emphasizes how much we need them all. A body is a whole which needs all of its differing parts.

The bearing of this on the separativeness of our denominations and national churches should be obvious. Since the members are not alike, they dare not remain apart, or the wholeness of the body will not find expression. Only blind bigotry can make the intolerant claim that because the hand is not the eye therefore it is no part of the body. In the Creed we express our belief in the *Catholic* Church. Since that means *wholeness*, the true Church will find its unity not by uniformity but in the midst of diversity. This was certainly the case in the apostolic Church. It had place for a Paul, to whom Christ was the end of the law, and for Matthew, to whom Christ was a new law-giver. It included James with his moralism and John with his mysticism. If there could be place for such divergences in the first century, there should likewise be room within the Church of to-day for similar variety in expression. That inheres in the very nature of a body.

(b) A second function of every body is to be *the agency* for the visible expression of the soul or spirit. We should not be diverted by details of psychological terminology. All that is meant is that though the person is not identifiable with the body, he cannot be identified without it. This truth may become more vivid to us if we distinguish a body from a corpse and a ghost. A corpse weighs as much as the body, but it no longer expresses "the spirit of the departed". A ghost is a spirit which by definition has no effective embodiment in the world of time and space.

If the Church is the body of Christ, this recognizes the fact that He cannot be fully operative in our world as a disembodied spirit. His spirit must act through some bodily expression if its existence is to be manifest. The Church is the indispensable organ through which Christ makes His life effective in the world. Naturally God is not limited in the way that men are limited by their bodily organism. Certainly the risen Christ can never be completely contained within any ecclesiastical institution. But if the Church is the Body of Christ, it is where His Spirit is effective.

This figure should help us to identify the Church. If it is the Body of Christ no outward forms can guarantee the Church's presence. An institution may become a corpse from which the true spirit of Christ has departed. That possibility should not lead to charges against members of the Body whose polity and forms of worship differ from our own. It should awaken the deepest heart-searching within every branch of His Church. The real Body of Christ is the agency which incarnates His Spirit and incorporates His life.

(c) A third analogy is to be found in that a body is an *organism which develops by transformation from within*. A building may increase in size as separate bricks are laid on one another. But a body does not grow by adding fixed and separate parts. It grows as new material is taken up into the organism and made part of an interacting whole. When Paul called Christ "the head of the body", he may have thought of that part as directing growth (Col. i, 18; Eph. iv, 15). Though our conceptions of biology are quite different, we may still appreciate what the New Testament was endeavouring to express. If the Church is the Body of Christ, He is the inner principle of growth. Growth does not come through the external addition of parts which remain unchanged, but through the inner transformation of these as believers are made new creatures in Him.

If the members thus become parts of one body, the result must follow that all are affected by what happens to any part. An injury to a man's arm has an effect on the whole organism. If the Church *is* the Body of Christ, it should be impossible for members in one part of the world to be afflicted without intense pain to the rest. Members that belong to the same body will

suffer together and rejoice together (1 Cor. xii, 26). If this is
not the case, would one not conclude that this member is either
paralysed or is already cut off from the rest of the body?

The Church of the New Testament considered itself to be
the heir of the promises of God in the Old Testament and the
foretaste of a new humanity. It was the community of those
who looked to Christ as their risen Lord and Saviour. He was
the Rock upon which they were built and the Head into which
they grew. It was a community marked by the gifts and the
power of the Holy Spirit. Those who participated in these
blessings shared with each other for they were part of the same
body, the body of Christ. This community had been entrusted
with the gospel of God's salvation, the word of His wisdom and
power. Men and women entered this society on the call of God
by faith and baptism. Their lives were strengthened as they par-
took of the Lord's Supper. Against that fellowship the powers
of death have been without avail, for the struggling Church
militant looks forward to the Church Triumphant which is the
Kingdom of God.

3

THE CHURCH: HER NATURE AND TASK

by George Florovsky

I

IT is impossible to start with a formal definition of the Church. For, strictly speaking, there is none which could claim any doctrinal authority. None can be found in the Fathers nor in the Schoolmen, nor even in St. Thomas Aquinas. No definition has been given by the Ecumenical Councils, nor by the later Great Councils in the West, including those of Trent and the Vatican. In the doctrinal summaries, drafted on various occasions in the Eastern (Orthodox) church in the seventeenth century and taken often (but wrongly) for the "symbolic books", again no definition of the Church was given, except a reference to the relevant clause of the Creed, followed by some comments. This lack of formal definitions does not mean, however, a confusion of ideas or any obscurity of view. The Fathers did not care so much for the *doctrine* of the Church precisely because the glorious *reality* of the Church was open to their spiritual vision. One does not define what is self-evident. This accounts for the absence of a special chapter on the Church in all early presentations of Christian doctrine: in Origen, in St. Gregory of Nyssa, even in St. John of Damascus. Only some passing and scattered remarks can be found even in the *Summa Theologica* of Aquinas. The first systematic treatise on the Church was composed in the West only in the late fifteenth century by the Cardinal de Turrecremata (Rome 1489). "The Church existed for about fifteen hundred years without reflecting upon its nature and without attempting its clarification by a logical conception."[1]

The current definitions we find in our modern catechisms and in the theological text-books are obviously of a late date. Most of them were coined in the age of the Reformation, in the spirit of confessional controversy, and for polemical purposes. They were meant more to meet the needs of a particular age

[1] Bartmann, *Dogmatik*, Bk. II, para. 137.

than to articulate the free self-consciousness of the Church. No
wonder they prove to be inadequate and insufficient under the
changed conditions. They are, all of them, in an eminent sense
"situation-conditioned". And again they are theological, not
doctrinal, statements; they are merely tentative and provisional,
as it were only private opinions of theologians, however widely
(or even "commonly") they may have been accepted. They
belong more to the school than to the Church. There is no
proper teaching authority standing behind them, and therefore
these definitions cannot be regarded as binding, final or complete. Many modern scholars, both Roman and Orthodox, have
plainly stated that the Church itself has not yet defined its own
essence and nature. "Die Kirche selbst hat sich bis heute noch
nicht definiert," says Robert Grosche.[2] Some theologians go
even further and suggest that no definition of the Church is
possible.[3] In any case the true theology of the Church is still
im Werden, in the process of formation. The doctrine of the
Church has hardly passed its *pre*-theological phase.[4]

In our time, it seems, one has to get beyond the modern
theological disputes, to regain a wider historical perspective, to
recover the true "catholic mind", which would embrace the
whole of the historical experience of the Church in its pilgrimage
through the ages. One has to return from the school-room to
the worshipping Church and perhaps to change the school-dialect
of theology for the pictorial and metaphorical language of Scripture. The very nature of the Church can be rather depicted
and described than properly defined. And surely this can be
done only from within the Church. Probably even this description will be convincing only for those of the Church. The
Mystery is apprehended only by faith.

II

The Greek name *ekklesia* adopted by the primitive Christians
to denote the New Reality, in which they were aware they shared,
presumed and suggested a very definite conception of what the
Church really was. Adopted under an obvious influence of the
Septuagint use, this word stressed first of all the organic con-

---

[2] Robert Grosche, *Pilgernde Kirche*, Freiburg im Breisgau, 1938, p. 27.
[3] Sergius Bulgakov, *The Orthodox Church* (1935) p. 12; Stefan Zankow, *Das
Orthodoxe Christentum des Ostens*, Berlin 1928, p. 65; English translation by
Dr. Lowrie, 1929, p. 69f.
[4] See M. D. Koster, *Ecclesiologie im Werden*, Paderborn 1940.

tinuity of the two Covenants. The Christian existence was conceived in the sacred perspective of the Messianic preparation and fulfilment (Heb. i, 1-2).⁷ A very definite theology of history was thereby implied. The Church was the true Israel, the new Chosen People of God, "a chosen generation, a holy nation, a peculiar people" (1 Pet. ii, 9). Or rather, it was the faithful Remnant, selected out of the unresponsive People of old.⁵ And all nations of the earth, Greeks and Barbarians, were to be co-opted and grafted into this new People of God by the call of God (this was the main theme of St. Paul in Romans and Galatians— cf. Ephesians ch. ii).

Already in the Old Testament the word *ekklesia* (a rendering in Greek of the Hebrew *Qahal*) did imply a special emphasis on the ultimate unity of the Chosen People, conceived as a sacred whole, and this unity was rooted more in the mystery of the divine election than in any "natural" features. This emphasis could only be confirmed by the supplementary influence of the Hellenistic use of the word *ekklesia* meaning usually an assembly of the sovereign people in a city, a general congregation of all regular citizens. Applied to the new Christian existence, the word kept its traditional connotation. The Church was both the People and the City. A special stress has been put on the organic unity of Christians.

Christianity from the very beginning existed as a corporate reality, as a community. To be Christian meant just to belong to the community. Nobody could be Christian by himself, as an isolated individual, but only together with "the brethren", in a "togetherness" with them. *Unus Christianus—nullus Christianus*. Personal conviction or even a rule of life still do not make one a Christian. Christian existence presumes and implies an incorporation, a membership in the community. This must be qualified at once: in the *Apostolic* community, i.e. in communion with the Twelve and their message. The Christian "community" was gathered and constituted by Jesus Himself "in the days of His flesh", and it was given by Him at least a provisional constitution by the election and the appointment of the Twelve, to whom He gave the name (or rather the title) of His "messengers" or "ambassadors".⁶ For a "sending forth"

---

⁵ Luke xii, 32: "*little flock*" seems to mean precisely the "remnant", reconstituted and redeemed, and reconsecrated.

⁶ See Luke vi, 13: "whom also *he named apostles*."

of the Twelve was not only a mission, but precisely a commission, for which they were invested with a "power" (Mark iii, 15; Matt. x, 1; Luke ix, 1). In any case as the appointed "witnesses" of the Lord (Luke xxiv, 48; Acts i, 8) the Twelve alone were entitled to secure the continuity both of the Christian message and of the community life. Therefore communion with the Apostles was a basic note of the primitive "Church of God" in Jerusalem (Acts ii, 42: *koinonia*).

Christianity means a "common life", a life in common. Christians have to regard themselves as "brethren" (in fact this was one of their first names), as members of one corporation, closely linked together. And therefore charity had to be the first mark and the first proof as well as the token of this fellowship. We are entitled to say: Christianity *is* a community, a corporation, a fellowship, a brotherhood, a "society", *coetus fidelium*. And surely, as a first approximation, such a description could be of help. But obviously it requires a further qualification, and something crucial is missing here. One has to ask: in what exactly this unity and togetherness of the many is based and rooted? what is the power that brings many together and joins them one with another? Is this merely a social instinct, some power of social cohesion, an impetus of mutual affection, or any other natural attraction? Is this unity based simply on unanimity, on identity of views or convictions? Briefly, is the Christian Community, the Church, merely a human society, a society of men? Surely, the clear evidence of the New Testament takes us far beyond this purely human level. Christians are united not only among themselves, but first of all they *are one—in Christ*, and only this communion *with* Christ makes the communion of men first possible—*in* Him. The centre of unity *is the Lord* and the power that effects and enacts the unity *is the Spirit*. Christians are constituted into this unity by divine design; by the Will and Power of God. Their unity comes from above. They are one only in Christ, as those who had been born anew in Him, "rooted and built up in Him" (Col. ii, 7), who by One Spirit have been "baptized into One Body" (1 Cor. xii, 13). The Church of God has been established and constituted by God through Jesus Christ, Our Lord: "she is His own creation by water and the word". Thus there is no human society, but rather a "Divine Society", not a secular community, which would have been still "of this world", still commensurable with other human groups, but a sacred community, which is intrinsically " not of this world ", not even of " this aeon ", but of the " aeon to come ".

Moreover, Christ Himself belongs to this community, as its Head, not only as its Lord or Master. Christ is not above or outside of the Church. The Church *is in Him*. The Church is not merely a community of those who believe in Christ and walk in His steps or in His commandments. She is a community of those who abide and dwell in Him, and in whom He Himself is abiding and dwelling by the Spirit. Christians are set apart, " born anew " and re-created, they are given not only a new pattern of life, but rather a new principle: the new Life in the Lord by the Spirit. They are a " peculiar People ", " the People of God's own possession ". The point is that the Christian Community, the *ekklesia*, is a *sacramental community*: *communio in sacris*, a " fellowship in holy things ", i.e. in the Holy Spirit, or even *communio sanctorum* (*sanctorum* being taken as neuter rather than masculine—perhaps that was the original meaning of the phrase). The unity of the Church is effected through the sacraments: Baptism and the Eucharist are the two " social sacraments " of the Church, and in them the true meaning of Christian " togetherness " is continually revealed and sealed. Or even more emphatically, the sacraments constitute the Church. Only in the sacraments does the Christian Community pass beyond the purely human measure and become the Church. Therefore " the right administration of the sacraments " belongs to the essence of the Church (to her *esse*). Sacraments must be " worthily " received indeed, therefore they cannot be separated or divorced from the inner effort and spiritual attitude of believers. Baptism is to be preceded by repentance and faith. A personal relation between an aspirant and his Lord must be first established by the hearing and the receiving of the Word, of the message of salvation. And again an oath of allegiance to God and His Christ is a pre-requisite and indispensable condition of the administration of the sacrament (the first meaning of the word *sacramentum* was precisely " the (military) oath "). A catechumen is already " enrolled " among the brethren on the basis of his faith. Again, the baptismal gift is appropriated, received and kept, by faith and faithfulness, by the steadfast standing in the faith and the promises. And yet sacraments are not merely signs of a professed faith, but rather effective signs of the saving Grace—not only symbols of human aspiration and loyalty, but the outward symbols of the divine action. In them our human existence is linked to, or rather raised up to, the Divine Life, by the Spirit, the giver of life.

The Church as a whole is a *sacred* (or consecrated) community, distinguished thereby from " the (profane) world ". She is the *Holy Church*. St. Paul obviously uses the terms " Church " and " saints " as co-extensive and synonymous. It is remarkable that in the New Testament the name " saint " is almost exclusively used in the plural, saintliness being social in its intrinsic meaning. For the name refers not to any human achievement, but to a gift, to sanctification or consecration. Holiness comes from the Holy One, i.e. only from God. To be holy for a man means to share the Divine Life. Holiness is available to individuals only in the community, or rather in the " fellowship of the Holy Ghost ". The " communion of saints " is a pleonasm. One can be a " saint " only in the communion.

Strictly speaking, the Messianic Community, gathered by Jesus the Christ, was not yet the Church, before His Passion and Resurrection, before " the promise of the Father " was sent upon it and it was " endued with the power from on high ", " baptized with the Holy Ghost " (cf. Luke xxiv, 49 and Acts i, 4-5), in the mystery of Pentecost. Before the victory of the Cross disclosed in the glorious Resurrection, it was still *sub umbraculo legis*. It was still the eve of the fulfilment. And Pentecost was there to witness to and to seal the victory of Christ. " The power from on high " has entered into history. The " new aeon " has been truly disclosed and started. And the sacramental life of the Church is the continuation of Pentecost.

The descent of the Spirit was a supreme revelation. Once and for ever, in the " dreadful and inscrutable mystery " of Pentecost, the Spirit-Comforter enters the world in which He was not yet present in such manner as now He begins to dwell and to abide. An abundant spring of living water is disclosed on that day, here on earth, in the world which had been already redeemed and reconciled with God by the Crucified and Risen Lord. The Kingdom comes, for the Holy Spirit is the Kingdom.[7] But the

---

[7] Cf. St. Gregory of Nyssa, *De oratione Dominica*, 3, MG, XLIV, c. 115f.-1160. (Note: In these footnotes, MG and ML refer to *Migne*, series *Greek* and *Latin* respectively.)

"coming" of the Spirit depends upon the "going" of the Son (John xvi, 7). "Another Comforter" comes down to testify of the Son, to reveal His glory and to seal His victory (xv, 26; xvi, 7 and 14). Indeed in the Holy Spirit the Glorified Lord Himself comes back or returns to His flock to abide with them always (xiv, 18 and 28). . . . Pentecost was the mystical consecration, the baptism of the whole Church (Acts i, 5). This fiery baptism was administered by the Lord: for He baptizes "with the Holy Spirit and with fire" (Matt. iii, 11 and Luke iii, 16). He has sent the Spirit from the Father, as a pledge in our hearts. The Holy Ghost is the spirit of adoption, in Christ Jesus, "the power of Christ" (2 Cor. xii, 9). By the Spirit we recognize and we acknowledge that Jesus is the Lord (1 Cor. xii, 3). The work of the Spirit in believers is precisely their incorporation into Christ, their baptism into one body (xii, 13), even the body of Christ. As St. Athanasius puts it: "being given drink of the Spirit, we drink Christ". For the Rock was Christ.[8]

By the Spirit Christians are united with Christ, are united in Him, are constituted into His Body. *One body*, that of Christ: this excellent analogy used by St. Paul in various contexts, when depicting the mystery of Christian existence, is at the same time the best witness to the intimate experience of the Apostolic Church. By no means was it an accidental metaphorical image: it was rather a summary of faith and experience. With St. Paul the main emphasis was always on the intimate union of the faithful with the Lord, on their sharing in His fulness. As St. John Chrysostom has pointed out, commenting on Col. iii, 4, in all his writings St. Paul was endeavouring to prove that the believers "are in communion with Him in all things" and "precisely to show this union does he speak of the Head and the body".[9] It is highly probable that the term was suggested by the Eucharistic experience (cf. 1 Cor. x, 17), and was deliberately used to suggest its sacramental connotation. The Church of Christ is one in the Eucharist, for the Eucharist is Christ Himself, and He *sacramentally* abides in the Church, which is His Body. The Church is a body indeed, *an organism*, much more than a society or a corporation. And perhaps an "organism" is the best modern rendering of the term *to soma*, as used by St. Paul.

[8] S. Athan. Alex., *Epist, 1 ad Serapionem*, MG, XXVI, 576.
[9] St. John Chrysostom, in *Coloss. hom. VII*, MG, LXII, col. 375.

Still more, the Church is the body *of Christ* and His "fulness" *Body* and *fulness* (*to soma* and *to pleroma*)—these two terms are correlative and closely linked together in St. Paul's mind, one explaining the other: "which is His body, the fulness of Him Who all in all is being fulfilled" (Eph. i, 23). The Church is the Body of Christ because it is His *complement*. St. John Chrysostom commends the Pauline idea just in this sense. "The Church is the complement of Christ in the same manner in which the head completes the body and the body is completed by the head." Christ is not alone. "He has prepared the whole race in common to follow Him, to cling to Him, to accompany His train." Chrysostom insists, "Observe how he (i.e. St. Paul) introduces Him as having need of all the members. This means that only then will the Head be filled up, when the Body is rendered perfect, when we are all together, co-united and knit together."[10] In other words, the Church is the extension and the "fulness" of the Holy Incarnation, or rather of the Incarnate life of the Son, "with all that for our sakes was brought to pass, the Cross and tomb, the Resurrection the third day, the Ascension into Heaven, the sitting on the right hand" (Liturgy of St. John Chrysostom, Prayer of Consecration).

The Incarnation is being completed in the Church. And, in a certain sense, the Church is Christ Himself, in His all-embracing plenitude (cf. 1 Cor. xii, 12). This identification has been suggested and vindicated by St. Augustine: "*Non solum nos Christianos factos esse, sed Christum.*" For if He is the Head, we are the members: the whole man is He and we—"*totus homo, ille et nos—Christus et Ecclesia*". And again: "For Christ is not simply in the head and not in the body (only), but Christ is entire in the head and body"—"*non enim Christus in capite et non in corpore, sed Christus totus in capite et in corpore.*"[11] This term *totus Christus*[12] occurs in St. Augustine again and again, this is his basic and favourite idea, suggested obviously by St. Paul. "When I speak of Christians in the plural, I understand one in the One Christ. Ye are therefore many, and ye are yet one: we are many and we are one"—"*cum plures Christianos appello, in uno Christo unum intelligo.*"[13]

---

[10] St. John Chrysostom in *Ephes. hom. III*, MG, LXII, col. 29.
[11] St. Augustine in *Evangelium Joannis tract, XXI, 8*, ML, XXXV, col. 1568; cf. St. John Chrysostom in *1 Cor. hom. XXX*, MG, LXI, col. 279-283.
[12] St. Augustine in *Ev. Joannis tr. XXVIII*, c. 1622.
[13] St. Augustine in *Ps. CXXVII, 3*, ML, XXXVII, col. 1679.

" For our Lord Jesus is not only in Himself, but in us also "—
" *Dominus enim Jesus non solum in se, sed et in nobis.*"[14] " One
Man up to the end of the ages "—" *Unus homo usque ad finem
saeculi extenditur.*"[15]

The main contention of all these utterances is obvious. Christians are incorporated into Christ and Christ abides in them—
this intimate union constitutes the mystery of the Church. The
Church is, as it were, the place and the mode of the redeeming
presence of the Risen Lord in the redeemed world. " The Body
of Christ is Christ Himself. The Church is Christ, as after His
Resurrection He is present with us and encounters us here
on earth."[16] And in this sense one can say: Christ is the
Church. "*Ipse enim est Ecclesia, per sacramentum corporis
sui in se universam eam continens.*"[17] Or in the words of
Karl Adam: " Christ, the Lord, is the proper Ego of the
Church."[18]

The Church is the unity of charismatic life. The source of
this unity is hidden in the sacrament of the Lord's Supper and
in the mystery of Pentecost. And Pentecost is continued and
made permanent in the Church by means of the Apostolic Succession. It is not merely, as it were, the canonic skeleton of
the Church. Ministry (or " hierarchy ") itself is primarily a
charismatic principle, a " ministry of the sacraments ", or " a
divine oeconomia ". Ministry is not only a *canonical* commission, it belongs not only to the *institutional* fabric of the Church
—it is rather an indispensable constitutional or *structural*
feature, just in so far as the Church is a body, an organism.
Ministers are not, as it were, " commissioned officers " of the community, not only leaders or delegates of the " multitudes ", of the
" people " or " congregation "—they are acting not only *in
persona ecclesiae*. They are acting primarily *in persona Christi*.
They are " representatives " of Christ Himself, not of believers,
and in them and through them, the Head of the Body, the only
High Priest of the New Covenant, is performing, continuing and
accomplishing His eternal pastoral and priestly office. He is
Himself the only true Minister of the Church. All others are

---

[14] St. Augustine in *Ps. XC enarr. 1*, 9, ML, XXXVII, col. 1157.
[15] St. Augustine in *Ps. LXXXV*, 5, ML, XXXVII, col. 1083.
[16] A. Nygren, *Corpus Christi*, in *En Bok om Kyrkan, av Svenska teologer*,
Lund, 1943, p. 20.
[17] St. Hilary in *Ps. CXXV*, 6, ML, IX, c. 688.
[18] Karl Adam, *Das Wesen des Katholizismus*, 4 Ausgabe, 1927, p. 24.

but stewards of His mysteries. They are standing *for* Him, *before* the community—and just because the Body is one only in its Head, is brought together and into unity by Him and in Him, the Ministry in the Church is primarily the Ministry of unity. In the Ministry the organic unity of the Body is not only represented or exhibited, but rather rooted, without any prejudice to the "equality" of the believers, just as the "equality" of the cells of an organism is not destroyed by their structural differentiation: all cells are equal as such, and yet differentiated by their functions, and again this differentiation serves the unity, enables this organic unity to become more comprehensive and more intimate. The unity of every local congregation springs from the unity in the Eucharistic meal. And it is as the celebrant of the Eucharist that the priest is the minister and the builder of Church unity. But there is another and higher office: to secure the universal and catholic unity of the whole Church in space and time. This is the episcopal office and function. On the one hand, the Bishop has an authority to ordain, and again this is not only a jurisdictional privilege, but precisely a power of sacramental action beyond that possessed by the priest. Thus the Bishop as "ordainer" is the builder of Church unity on a wider scale. The Last Supper and Pentecost are inseparably linked to one another. The Spirit Comforter descends when the Son has been glorified in His death and resurrection. But still they are two sacraments (or mysteries) which cannot be merged into one another. In the same way the priesthood and the episcopate differ from one another. In the episcopacy Pentecost becomes universal and continuous, in the undivided episcopate of the Church (*episcopatus unus* of St. Cyprian) the unity in space is secured. On the other hand, through its bishop, or rather in its bishop, every particular or local Church is included in the catholic fulness of the Church, is linked with the past and with all ages. In its bishop every single Church outgrows and transcends its own limits and is organically united with the others. The Apostolic Succession is not so much the canonical as the mystical foundation of Church unity. It is something other than a safeguard of historical continuity or of administrative cohesion. It is an ultimate means to keep the mystical identity of the Body through the ages. But, of course, Ministry is never detached from the Body. It is in the Body, belongs to its structure. And ministerial gifts are given inside the Church (cf. 1 Cor. xii).

The Pauline conception of the Body of Christ was taken up and variously commented on by the Fathers, both in the East and in the West, and then was rather forgotten.[19] It is high time now to return to this experience of the early Church which may provide us with a solid ground for a modern theological synthesis. Some other similes and metaphors were used by St. Paul and elsewhere in the New Testament, but much to the same purpose and effect: to stress the intimate and organic unity between Christ and those who are His. But, among all these various images, that of the Body is the most inclusive and impressive, is the most emphatic expression of the basic vision.[20] Of course, no analogy is to be pressed too far or over-emphasized. The idea of an organism, when used of the Church, has its own limitations. On the one hand, the Church is composed of human personalities, which never can be regarded merely as elements or cells of the whole, because each is in direct and immediate union with Christ and His Father—the personal is not to be sacrificed or dissolved in the corporate, Christian "togetherness" must not degenerate into impersonalism. The idea of the organism must be supplemented by the idea of a symphony of personalities, in which the mystery of the Holy Trinity is reflected (cf. John xvii, 21 and 23), and this is the core of the conception of "catholicity" ("sobornost").[21] This is the chief reason why we should prefer a christological orientation in the theology of the Church rather than a pneumatological.[22] For, on the other hand, the Church, as a whole, has her *personal centre* only in Christ, she is not an incarnation of the Holy Ghost, nor is she merely a Spirit-bearing community, but

[19] See E. Mersch, S.J., *Le Corps Mystique du Christ, Études de Theologie Historique*, 2 vols., 2nd edition, Louvain 1936; cf. also the recent Encyclical *Mystici Corporis Christi*.

[20] The image of the Bride and her mystical marriage with Christ (Eph. v, 23f.) expresses the intimate union. Even the image of the House built of many stones, the corner stone being Christ (Eph. ii, 20f.; cf. 1 Pet. ii, 6), tends to the same purpose: many are becoming one, and the tower appears as it were built or one stone (cf. Hermas, *Shepherd*, Vis. III, ii, 6, 8). And again "the People of God" is to be regarded as an organic whole. There is no reason whatever to be troubled by the variety of vocabularies used. The main idea and contention 1. obviously the same in all cases.

[21] Cf. George Florovsky, "Sobornost, The Catholicity of the Church", in *The Church of God, an Anglo-Russian Symposium*, ed. by E. L. Mascall, Londor. 1935.

[22] Such as in Khomiakov or in Moehler's *Die Einheit in der Kirche*.

precisely the Body of Christ, the Incarnate Lord. This saves us from impersonalism without committing us to any humanistic personification. Christ the Lord is the only Head and the only Master of the Church. "In Him the whole structure is closely fitted together and grows into a temple holy in the Lord; in Him you too are being built together into a dwelling-place for God in the Spirit" (Eph. ii, 21-22, Bp. Challoner's version).

The Christology of the Church does not lead us into the misty clouds of vain speculations or dreamy mysticism. On the contrary, it secures the only solid and positive ground for proper theological research. The doctrine of the Church finds thereby its proper and organic place in the general scheme of the Divine Oeconomia of salvation. For we have indeed still to search for a comprehensive vision of the mystery of our salvation, of the salvation of the world.

One last distinction is to be made. The Church is still *in statu viae* and yet it is already *in statu patriae*. It has, as it were, a double life, both in heaven and on earth.[23] The Church is a visible historical society, and the same is the Body of Christ. It is both the Church of the redeemed, and the Church of the miserable sinners—both at once. On the historical level no *final* goal has yet been attained. But the *ultimate* reality has been disclosed and revealed. This ultimate reality is still at hand, is truly available, in spite of the historical imperfection, though but in provisional forms. For the Church is a sacramental society. *Sacramental* means no less than "*eschatological*". *To eschaton* does not mean primarily *final*, in the temporal series of events; it means rather *ultimate* (decisive); and the ultimate is being realized within the stress of historical happenings and events. What is "not of this world" is here "in this world", not abolishing this world, but giving to it a new meaning and a new value, "transvaluating" the world, as it were. Surely this is still only an anticipation, a "token" of the final consummation. Yet the Spirit abides in the Church. This constitutes the mystery of the Church: a visible "society" of frail men *is* an organism of the Divine Grace.[24]

---

[23] Cf. St. Augustine in *Evang. Joannis tract*, CXXIV, 5, ML, XXXV, c. 19f., 7.
[24] See Khomiakov's essay *On the Church*; English translation by W. J. Birkbeck, *Russia and the English Church* (first published 1895), ch. XXIII, pp. 193-222.

III

The primary task of the historical Church is the proclamation of the Gospel. To proclaim the Gospel means inevitably to pass a judgment upon the world. The Gospel itself is a judgment and a condemnation. It lays bare the sin of the world (cf. John iii, 19). There is an ultimate tension, a contrast and an opposition. The Gospel itself is " not of this world ". It is a proclamation of another world " to come ". The Church bears witness to the New Life, disclosed and revealed in Christ Jesus, the Lord and Saviour. This it does both by word and deed. The true proclamation of the Gospel would be precisely the practice of this New Life: to show faith by deeds (cf. Matt. v, 16).

The Church is more than a company of preachers, or a teaching society, or a missionary board. It has not only to invite people, but also to introduce them into this New Life, to which it bears witness. It is a missionary body indeed, and its mission-field is the whole world. But the aim of its missionary activity is not merely to convey to people certain convictions or ideas, not even to impose on them a definite discipline or a rule of life, but first of all to introduce them into the New Reality, to *convert* them, to bring them through their faith and repentance to Christ Himself, that they should be born anew in Him and into Him by water and the Spirit. Thus the ministry of the Word is completed in the ministry of the Sacraments.

"Conversion" is a fresh start, but it is only a start, to be followed by a long process of growth. The Church has to organize the new life of the converted. The Church has, as it were, to exhibit the new pattern of existence, the new mode of life, that of the " world to come ". The Church is here, in this world, for its salvation. But just for this reason it has to oppose and to renounce " this " world. God claims the whole man, and the Church bears witness to this " totalitarian " claim of God revealed in Christ. The Christian has to be a " new creation ". Therefore he cannot find a settled place for himself within the limits of the " old world ". In this sense the Christian attitude is, as it were, always revolutionary with regard to the " old order " of " this world ". Being " not of this world " the Church of Christ " in this world " can only be in permanent opposition, even if it claims only a reformation of the existing order. In any case, the change is to be radical and total.

Historical failures of the Church do not obscure the absolute and ultimate character of its challenge, to which it is committed by its very eschatological nature, and it constantly challenges itself.

Historical life and the task of the Church are an antinomy, and this antinomy can never be solved or overcome on a historical level. It is rather a permanent hint to what is "to come" hereafter. The antinomy is rooted in the practical alternative which the Church had to face from the very beginning of its historical pilgrimage. *Either* the Church was to be constituted as an exclusive and "totalitarian" society, endeavouring to satisfy all requirements of the believers, both "temporal" and "spiritual", paying no attention to the existing order and leaving nothing to the external world—it would have been an entire separation from the world, an ultimate flight out of it, and a radical denial of any external authority. *Or* the Church could attempt an inclusive Christianization of the world, subduing the whole of life to Christian rule and authority, to reform and to reorganize secular life on Christian principles, to build the Christian City. In the history of the Church we can trace both solutions: a flight to the desert and a construction of the Christian Empire. The first was practised not only in monasticism of various trends, but in many other Christian groups and denominations. The second was the main line taken by Christians, both in the West and in the East, up to the rise of militant secularism, but even in our days this solution has not lost its hold on many people. But on the whole, both proved unsuccessful. One has, however, to acknowledge the reality of their common problem and the truth of their common purpose. Christianity is not an individualistic religion and it is not only concerned for the "salvation of the soul". Christianity is the Church, i.e. a Community, the New People of God, leading its corporate life according to its peculiar principles. And this life cannot be split into departments, some of which might have been ruled by any other and heterogeneous principles. Spiritual leadership of the Church can hardly be reduced to an occasional guidance given to individuals or to groups living under conditions utterly uncongenial to the Church. The legitimacy of these conditions must be questioned first of all. The task of a complete re-creation or re-shaping of the whole fabric of human life cannot or must not be avoided or declined. One cannot serve two Masters and a double allegiance is a poor solution. Here the above-mentioned alternative inevitably comes in— everything else would merely be an open compromise or a reduction of the ultimate and therefore *total* claims. *Either* Christians ought to go out of the world, in which there is another Master besides Christ (whatever name this other Master may bear: Caesar or Mammon or any other) and in which the rule and the goal of life are other than those set out in the Gospel—to go out and to start a separate society. *Or* again Christians have to transform the outer world, to make it the Kingdom of God as well, and introduce the principles of the Gospel into secular legislation.

There is an inner consistency in both programmes. And therefore the separation of the two ways is inevitable. Christians seem compelled to take different ways. The unity of the Christian task is broken. An inner schism arises within the Church: an abnormal separation between the monks (or the *élite* of the initiated) and the lay-people (including clergy), which is far more dangerous than the alleged "clericalization" of the Church. In the last resort, however, it is only a symptom of the ultimate antinomy. The problem simply has no historical solution. A true solution would transcend history, it belongs to the "age to come". In this age, on the historic plane, no constitutional principle can be given, but only a regulative one: a principle of discrimination, not a principle of construction.

For again each of the two programmes is self-contradictory. There is an inherent *sectarian* temptation in the first: the "catholic" and universal character of the Christian message and purpose is here at least obscured and often deliberately denied, the world is simply left out of sight. And all attempts at the direct Christianization of the world, in the guise of a Christian State or Empire, have only led to the more or less acute *secularization* of Christianity itself.[25]

In our time nobody would consider it possible for everyone to be converted to a universal monasticism or a realization of a truly Christian, and universal, State. The Church remains

[25] For a more detailed treatment, see George Florovsky, *The Antinomies of Christian History*, in the volume of Orthodox papers, published by the Study Department of the World Council of Churches.

"in the world", as a heterogeneous body, and the tension is stronger than it has ever been; the ambiguity of the situation is painfully felt by everyone in the Church. A practical programme for the present age can be deduced only from a restored understanding of the nature and essence of the Church. And the failure of all Utopian expectations cannot obscure the Christian hope: the King has come, the Lord Jesus, and His Kingdom is to come.

4

ONE, HOLY, CATHOLIC, APOSTOLIC CHURCH

by John A. F. Gregg

I

THE Church is the extension in time and space of the Incarnate Word of God, crucified, ascended, glorified, operating among men through the indwelling in them of His Holy Spirit, Who mediates to it His Victorious Life. Thus, although the Church is visible and tangible, it is a supernatural corporation. Its life is on earth, but its citizenship is in heaven. Its habitat is this globe and the affairs of men are its concern, but the dwelling-place of its spirit is the eternal world. It has here no continuing city; it seeks a city which lies beyond.

The reason for this is found in the constitution of its being. As the Church of the Ascended Christ Whose Body it is, it is no self-constituted Society of like-minded seekers after ideal truth or of admirers of the prophet Jesus; it is a Society founded and constituted by an invisible Head in Whom resides all its vitality and apart from Whom it can do nothing. The distinguishing and confessed characteristic of its being lies in given-ness. "When He ascended up on high, He gave gifts unto men." Christ is its life, its hope, the secret of that revival and restoration of which, because of the fallibility of its human element, it stands in permanent need. This relationship is no mere subjective loyalty, resting on its members' faith and trust (although both are needed). The glorified Christ is the objective, constitutive Reality, without Whom its entire corporate existence would fall to the ground.

The relationship existing between the Head and the members of the Body is on the one hand of a personal and individual kind (though space does not permit us to dwell on it here), and on the other hand of a corporate and comprehensive kind. Various metaphors are employed which seek to suggest the closeness and the permanence of the latter.

(1) **The Church is the Bride of Christ**, bought with His

Blood, liberated from sin by the power of His Cross and quickened by His Life.

(2) The Church is His Body, its many members constituting the fulness of Him, its Head, Who all in all is being fulfilled.

(3) The Church is to Christ as the vine-branches are to the vine-stem. They can bear fruit only as they abide in Him.

(4) The Church is the flock of the Good Shepherd. This gracious and mystical relationship with the heavenly Bishop of our souls is postulated through the whole teaching of the Apostolic writings and underlies the witness of the Constantinopolitan Creed to the One Holy Catholic and Apostolic Church.

Piety is very ready to think of the relationship to Christ in individualistic terms, drawn from or even justified by, such scriptural passages as Psalm xxiii. But such pictures as those specified above, and such a picture as that of the spiritual Temple, a fabric compacted out of countless living stones, force us to recognize that personal devotion to Christ must find its place side by side with the broader and more exacting love of the brethren. There is thus a deep truth underlying the apparently repellent *Extra ecclesiam nulla salus.*

For although when we study the Church in history, we see much that is unworthy and that seems to contradict the idealizing claims made for it, we recognize that, if it is an earthen vessel, it contains and exists for and by a Treasure, and that the actual, which is yet incomplete and growing, must be viewed in the light of this ideal which is at once its inspiration and the goal of its journey through time.

II

The well-known notes of the Church tell how she is One, Holy, Catholic, Apostolic.

(a) She is *One*, and in spite of divisions knows herself as one because her Head is one and the Spirit indwelling her is one. And as there is but one Christ and one Spirit, she can never rest in the thought of herself as anything else than one. She is one in tendency, in sin, in endeavour, in expectation. Are we to feel surprise if a mere nineteen hundred years have not brought into harmony the unruly wills and affections which in secular affairs we see contending together between the nations and between the individuals who compose the nations?

We are only beginning to-day to appreciate the size and complexity and the deep-lying divisions of the human material out of which mankind is built, and it is only as we feel the confusion of that human chaos that we become aware of the vastness and splendour and withal the difficulty of the task that lies before the Church of making Christian believers, let alone the human race, one in Christ. The One Christ has made His Church one. In spite of the obscuring of that unity in the empirical "churches", the common belief in the Person of the one Christ is forcing believers in Him to seek to actualize the unity which belongs to the Church by virtue of its one Head, in Whom it is God's purpose to gather all things together in one.

(b) The Church is *Holy*. She is holy because Christ is holy; holy, not because she can claim to have arrived at any perfection of holiness, but because the head of the Church has consecrated her to holiness. The Church is the redeemed society, the fellowship of those who are being schooled in holiness. Called to be holy, with the means of grace freely offered to them, they respond and are led on in the way of holiness. That there should be some, or many, who fail to respond through ignorance or wilfulness, is neither a condemnation of the Society which seeks their good nor a justification for departing from it on the part of those who shrink from contact with others who seem to be living below the strictest standard.

Whatever the defilement of human sin, even in the regenerate, it is beyond doubt that holiness is the aim, to the pursuit of which the Church is dedicated, and that in Christ the Church is indefectibly committed to holiness as it is to the belief in the forgiveness of sins.

At the worst of times, there has always been a faithful remnant. Whatever may be said by way of detraction, the Church forms a standing conscience to the world, which knows well enough that the sins of Christians do not truly represent the moral standard of the Church but are grossly inconsistent with it. For even when the leaders of the Church have failed signally, the *sensus communis* of the rank and file has carried on the sacred tradition.

Secular society is little conscious of its obligation, but such sense of truth and justice and respect for the individual as it possesses is drawn from, or at least is firmly supported by, the Christian Church, that treasury of the mind and principles of Christ.

.(c) The Church is *Catholic*, or *Universal*. Unlike the Jewish
Ecclesia, which was exclusive as being confined to the covenant-
people, the Christian Ecclesia is universal in its range, and is for
all God's children whatever their race or colour or tongue. As
the visible symbol of the largeness of God's purposes for mankind
and the instrument for effecting them, it is its duty to go into all
the world, to preach the whole Gospel to every creature.

The subject of its teaching is the revealed truth to which the
New Testament, as heir of the Old Testament, the ancient
fathers, the great Councils and the consent of the Church from
age to age bear witness. Its business is not to declare new truths,
but faithfully to hand on the deposit which had been accepted
always, everywhere and by all.

At the same time, the Church is Catholic, because all truth
everywhere is of God, and nothing that is a revelation of the ways
and mind of God can be outside its scope.

Christian thinkers and students and teachers can ill afford to
neglect the assured results of scientific investigation, of intellectual enquiry or critical research. Truth is of God, and the
Church of Christ Who is the Truth must not be unduly slow in
coming face to face with the questionings or the affirmations
which proceed from the minds of honest seekers after truth.

The Church is placed in the world to speak with authority
concerning the revealed Truth which it possesses by age-long
inheritance; but its authority will commend itself the better to
an enquiring age if it is known that it honestly takes account
of, and checks its position and utterances by the light that comes
pouring in from every quarter of God's world.

(d) The Church is *Apostolic*. Our Lord said to the assembled
company on the night of His Resurrection, "As my Father hath
sent me, even so send I you." He gives a mission to His Church
even as He had received His mission from God.

The Church exists by divine authority, and authority in the
Church was committed to the Apostles who were divinely designated as its organs to exercise in it a permanent stewardship of
grace and truth. Thus, not only was a Society established but it
received the beginnings of a structure. The Church grew up
round its Apostolic Ministry. There is a "given-ness" both in
its faith and in its form. In the Church, whether in regard to
the given-ness of its faith or of its ministry, we see an illustration
not of evolution upwards but of devolution downwards. Its

organization was of necessity loose and flexible to begin with, its general ministry passing into the local ministry, but involved in it there lay certain governing elements of authority and continuity necessary for the preservation of its identity. And thus the Church was no self-appointed or self-governing democracy. It acknowledged an abiding and directing constraint upon its freedom exercised by the Apostolic stewards whom Christ in the beginning had set over His earthly household. This authoritative constraint manifests itself down the ages most noticeably in two connections, viz., in the Faith delivered through the Apostles, and in the historic ministry set within it from Apostolic days, "the very nerve and sinew of ecclesiastical unity and communion" (John Bramhall), as the organ for the performance of the corporate actions of the society.

III

The most important duties laid upon this visible Church are three in number—(a) that of witnessing to the revealed Truth of God in Christ, (b) that of the worship of God, and (c) that of teaching men to live as children of the Heavenly Father.

Witness to the Truth. God who in many parts and in many fashions spoke in past days to the Fathers through the prophets, spoke in these last days in a Son. Christianity is Christ, or rather the Godhead as revealed in and through the Person of Christ. The progressive revelation of God through the prophets of the Old Testament is followed and completed by the self-revelation of the Father through the Incarnate Word. And it is to declare God in Christ, and to lead mankind to see the world of men and things in the light of that disclosure that the Church was sent on its way.

The knowledge of the Truth is intended to lead on to *Worship.* Man's highest duty and privilege is, with reverence and godly fear, to acknowledge and bow before and give glory to his Creator, his Father, all holy, all sovereign and all pitying.

The Church has to live in the world as leader and teacher of God's creatures in their adoring wonder at the majesty and perfection and saving grace of God, and in their voluntary submission to, and execution of His will.

Christ, the High Priest of mankind in the heavenly Temple, presents before God His unceasing Self-oblation and intercession, and with Him the Church which is His Body is to be taught to join, as it yields itself to God with the heart-homage of instructed praise and devout thanksgiving.

The Church's duty in the world is also to teach men *how to live*. It is the home and channel of grace through the indwelling Spirit of Christ. It is the supreme witness to love, the love of Christ which binds Him to His spouse the Church and the Church to Him; to the love of its members for one another whereby in the fellowship and peace of the Holy Ghost they live the corporate life of mutual service and loyalty; and to the Christian ethic based on the teaching given by Christ and His Apostles and on the personal example bequeathed by Christ Himself. The visible Church as it discharges these duties exercises an influence on a civilization, often hostile and commonly indifferent, whether for judgment or inspiration, both salutary and vivifying.

Nevertheless the Great Church is not a temporal power. It must not stand in any formal way over against the State. It has no country, no Courts of Justice, no General Headquarters, no Diplomatic Corps, nor does it commit itself to treaties or concordats. The meeting of a General Council is the rarest of events. As a Corporation as much spiritual as temporal it is by nature too elusive for the conduct of secular negotiations, but it must operate on the world indirectly through its members.

Just as the pressure of the atmosphere is silent and imperceptible and yet real and universal, so the visible Church exercises its pressure and its moral authority through its members who are bound to it by bonds invisible as well as visible, who, if they use the Grace given to them, can diffuse the influence of their Society at all points of their contact with the citizens of the secular State. It is in this way that, though the Church must always be more or less at cross-purposes with the world, the standard of public opinion and morals can be upheld and raised, by the determined upward thrust of that *sensus communis* which the Church, in the exercise of its prophetic office, quickens and shapes and builds in the consciousness of its children.

.   .   .   .

The Great Church, for all its supramundane relations, is an institution in this world and discernible as such. The tragedy of our divisions is precisely that we are not agreed about the necessary " marks " by which " the Church " is discerned. Those who belong to the Anglican communion believe themselves to have inherited, by God's mercy and not of their own deserving, the marks of an essential catholicity. However much their expression may to-day have been obscured and need reform, these essentials must be part of any fully Catholic Church.

Essential Catholicism, in its view, involves a background of four fundamental and indispensable elements, viz.: (1) Holy Scripture as the final criterion by which all beliefs claimed as necessarily to be confessed for salvation are to be tested; (2) the full faith of the Apostles' Creed and the Nicene Creed; (3) the unfailing use of the two great Sacraments of the Gospel as ordained by Christ, and (4) the Apostolic Ministry of Bishops, Priests and Deacons, transmitted by those having authority to transmit.

The Book of Common Prayer presents the body of practice accompanying and interpreting for the Church of England these four traditional elements in the Catholic position. But just as in the Anglican system many variations of that book have taken shape in the sister and daughter churches of the Anglican Communion, so in the branches of the Great Church an infinite variety of rite is compatible with loyalty to the Catholic norm, which from early days has admitted without uneasiness the practical necessity in a world-wide fellowship of " *Salvo jure communionis diversa sentire* ", or again of " in things essential, unity; in things doubtful, liberty; in all things, charity ".

In conclusion, a Church claiming to be Catholic must not be content with a self-regarding enjoyment of its Faith. Not merely does it possess the Faith, but the Faith possesses it. And the Faith, by its Apostolic nature, drives it to look outwards and to seek fellowship with other bodies of Christians. The establishment or restoration of communion with separated bodies of Christians must be one of its most serious concerns. For there should be no schism in the Body of Christ. And yet schism is one of the most palpable and painful facts of Christian history. The Great Church's witness to the world, to say nothing of its own growth in holiness, is hampered to an incalculable extent by the divisions prevailing among the baptized members of Christ's Church.

Yet no yearnings after a closer fellowship can justify the

entering into communion with a society which has lost, and shows no desire to recover, its hold upon any one of those few but vital institutions specified above which are the visible pledges of continuity with the undivided Church.

Thus the Great Church to-day is conscious of a tragic tension between necessities seemingly irreconcilable. But the Church is not a voluntary association which can make its own terms. It is a trustee with an unbroken succession of the deposit once for all delivered, and its trust determines coercively for its member-churches how each, as a pillar and buttress of the truth, is to shape its invitations and its responses. Thus, paradoxically enough, many Anglicans who in principle are ardently desirous for fellowship between their own and other communions, are compelled to resist any proposals for union which either deny the sufficiency or threaten the integrity of the Church's inherited faith or order.

Divisions between separated bodies of Christians which recognize in one another the workings of the one Spirit, need not forbid mutual respect, or endeavours after a better understanding or co-operation in social reform, nor need they any longer attract the world's attention and contempt by manifestations of controversial acerbity. On the other hand, comprehension at the cost of unlawful compromise would be no better than a bridge which broke in the middle.

5

THE CHURCH—THE LIVING CONGREGATION[1]
OF THE LIVING LORD JESUS CHRIST

by Karl Barth

THE title of this paper constitutes a *definition* of the idea, "Church". It is a positive description of what the Church *is*. Negatively, however, it goes further, for it tacitly eliminates all that may bear the name of "Church" but is not so in reality: a merely nominal church, an ecclesiastical shell from which the life has fled.

The definition describes the Church as a *congregation,* a subject, which is confronted by, and controlled by another primary subject: *Jesus Christ* as absolute Lord (Creator, Preserver, Owner, Governor); the Church (as "congregation") is only a *living* Church in so far as it is filled with the life of this primary subject, and only if its life is based on this foundation is it a *real* Church.

What the Church is: the congregation *is,* or *exists,* where, and in so far as it dares to live by the act of its living Lord.

The danger menacing the Church: the congregation fails to *exist* when, and in so far as the foundations of its life are shaken by its own sins and errors.

The renewal of the Church: the congregation is preserved and is saved by the ever-new acts of its Lord. The meaning of its life and its calling consists in being continually open to Him, ready to perceive these "signs of His appearing"

I WHAT THE CHURCH IS

The period in which the congregation is living is that of *the End,* that is, the period containing the particular, final History between God and man, which began with the Resurrection of Jesus Christ from the dead, and will reach its close and its con-

---

[1] German: *Gemeinde.* In this paper Barth uses the word "Gemeinde" to denote the *worshipping community*, meeting regularly in a given place, entirely dependent on the continually new activity of the Lord Jesus Christ. (Translator.)

summation in the open manifestation of the reconciliation between God and the whole of creation, already effected in Him.

In this final period the congregation is the *event*[2] which consists in gathering together (congregatio) those men and women (fidelium) whom the living Lord Jesus Christ chooses and calls to be witnesses to the victory He has already won, and heralds of its future universal manifestation.

The congregation is the result of a process by which certain people are differentiated from others, and are drawn into fellowship with one another by Jesus Christ, through a common experience of the Divine Mercy, which is also Judgment, and of the Divine Judgment which is also Mercy, a common experience of gratitude towards God, and a common desire to serve their neighbours, which leads them to the discovery that *together*, they have a mission to the world outside.

The congregation is that event in which the absolute sovereignty of Jesus Christ—its Lord, and also the Lord of the world—finds its proper answer and response in the perfect freedom of obedience of those who have been called, called out, and called together by Him, and summoned to gratitude and to service.

The congregation is that event in which these men—for whom the work of Jesus Christ as the Reconciler of the world with God has become a revealed Word, the Word of Truth, which lays its obligation upon them—unite together over against the world; yet only in order that they may identify themselves with the need and the hope of the world.

The congregation is the event in which the witness of apostles and prophets to Jesus Christ, deposited in Scripture, as such, becomes present, effective and fruitful; and its authority visible and intelligible in a continual process of research, exposition and preaching.

The congregation is the event in which the communion of the Holy Ghost also establishes, with divine power, a human fellowship, derived from the acceptance of the Word of Jesus Christ in and through the witness of the Bible, heard and perceived in common; this produces a concord of faith and creed, of love and its works, of hope and its confidence, made available for all mankind.

---

[2] German: *Ereignis*. The writer means that the Church is not constituted once for all, but that it is continually being re-created by renewed divine activity. No single English word can express this idea, which lies behind the word "event" as used in this paper. (Translator.)

The congregation is the event in which the Sacraments are powerful as the one reality by which men live: Baptism, which incorporates human beings into this special relation to Jesus Christ, and the Lord's Supper, which keeps them in this state of grace, that is, of "belonging to Him", and enables them to fulfil their mission to others.

The congregation is the event in which the divine mission of Jesus Christ is represented and attested: through the preaching of His Word, through the invitation to believe on Him, and also through the manifestation of the temporal, political and social significance of the salvation that has appeared in Him in the midst of the "non-Christian" world (for which nevertheless He died and rose again).

The explanation of the idea of the "Church" by means of the idea of the "congregation" is significant and useful only if "congregation" is explicitly understood as a "living congregation"; that is, as a congregation as described in the preceding paragraphs, which consists in the *event* by which it is *gathered* together: that is, the congregation as the decisive element in this final phase in the story of God's relations with man. It is precisely this history which, as such, constitutes the Church; that is "what the Church *is*".

II THE DANGER MENACING THE CHURCH

The life of the Church is both secured and endangered: its security comes from above; its danger from below.

Its life is secured (*perpetuo mansura est*) by the indissoluble life of its Head, the Lord Jesus Christ, risen from the dead: through the final validity of His work accomplished once for all; through the power of His Word and His Spirit; through the inexhaustible nature of the witness of apostles and prophets to Him; through the validity of the signs instituted by Him in Baptism and the Lord's Supper; and through the unceasing fidelity with which He watches over His congregation.

The life of the Church is *endangered* (the Church can and does fall into temptation), for the following reasons: because the life of Christ's congregation is "creaturely" in character; because it cannot be absolutely protected against the possibility of falling into unbelief or error, into lovelessness and doubt, that is, against the possibility of dissolution and of death; but it can be given a *de facto* protection only, which consists in the occurrence of that "event" in which the activity of Jesus Christ is stronger than all human sin.

One form of this danger which threatens the Church, through human error, can be seen when the Bible, dogma, the catechism, church order, the liturgy, preaching, and sacrament, instead of being documents and instruments within the congregation become mere museum pieces; when the Kingdom of God that has "come upon" men in Jesus Christ becomes a vague realm of venerable truths and exalted moral principles; when the free grace of God's Word and Spirit becomes the routine of a religious and moral code. If in such conditions the congregation affirms what it believes, it does so without joy, because it has no sense of urgent need, no impulse to ask, and seek, and knock, no sense of dissatisfaction; and therefore also no impulse to share with others. Such a congregation—in spite of all its assertions to the contrary—is at heart unsure of itself, uncertain in its faith; hence it can only "keep up appearances" before the world; its reality and its impressiveness are hollow.

Another form of this danger which threatens the Church through human error, appears when the attention and loyalty of the congregation is divided between what it ought to do for the world, in the service of its Lord, and according to His teaching, and what it feels bound to do from all sorts of other considerations—for "the need of the moment", for society at large, for political and economic realities, for the tendencies of the dominant culture with its own philosophy of life and its own ethical tradition, or even for the specific traditions of its own church life and order. When this situation arises, the congregation lives and preaches a so-called "Christianity", which is actually a mixture of elements in which that which is alien to real Christianity always tries to get the upper hand.

Another form of this danger to the Church through human error appears when the congregation absolutely forgets its peculiar endowment and its mission, and devotes itself to the concerns and wishes, the convictions and endeavours of the "Christian" people who constitute its membership, concerns which are foreign, and perhaps even directly opposed to, its relation to Jesus Christ. Then faith in the Gospel degenerates into religiosity, love becomes devotion to certain "ideals", hope becomes confidence in all kinds of social and individual progress.

The Bible is interpreted by alien criteria, and quietly ceases to be read or used. It is then only a question of time before the Creed loses all meaning, public worship ceases, evangelism disappears, and the "Church" of this kind has no vital message for the world; it is dumb and silent. The Church has now itself become the world, a "religious" world, with a prophetic ministry so weak and feeble that the world can well afford to ignore it altogether.

The common element in all forms of this danger to the Church consists in the fact that the history, the movement, the action begun by the first subject, by Jesus Christ, is not continued in the other subject, in His congregation, but suffers from arrested development. The vital current passing and repassing between the Lord and His congregation is blocked by man's sin. The life of the congregation ceases to be "event"; the congregation ceases to be a *living* congregation. But this means that the Church has ceased to exist.

In itself, and as such, the Church could long since, and everywhere, have succumbed to this danger. She could long since have passed away and perished as the result of her own sin. The fact that her disease only affects certain spheres of her life, and does not infect everything, is due to the sovereignty, the faithfulness, and the patience of her Lord. Even then, the Church must be on her guard against this disease, which might be fatal. She must always bear in mind that spiritual carelessness may lead to the final tragedy when, as a congregation, her Lord may say unto her: "Thou hast a name that thou livest, and art dead."

The place of the church that is no longer a church is not replaced by a vacuum. Instead we have the phenomenon of the nominal church, or the church which is merely an ecclesiastical shell: the ecclesiastical *quid pro quo*, endowed with all the qualities (but deprived of all their content) of the really living congregation. In this situation two things may happen: the congregation that has long been dead may be on good terms with society and the State, because it constitutes no threat to the world around it; or—the fact that it is so feeble and has so little influence on the world may bring external judgment upon it. So the phenomenon of the congregation which is dead, and yet still maintains its external existence, must always be regarded from a twofold point of view: on the one hand, as a sign of the extreme gravity of the danger hanging over it, and, on the other hand, as a sign of the patience of God, Who can raise men to new life, even from the grave.

The visible sign of the danger which menaces the Church is the loss of her unity. Her unity stands and falls with that "event" which is the "gathering" of the congregation by the Word and the Spirit of her living Lord, Jesus Christ. If this divine activity is even partially checked, the congregation itself disintegrates, and congregations fall apart. For a living and a dead congregation cannot be a single congregation; there can be neither friendship nor peace between living and dead congregations. Even the necessary service of the living congregation to one that is dead must retain the form of open contradiction until unity in Jesus Christ has once more become an "event", until the dead congregation has once more been quickened into life. Even then the living congregation finds itself plunged into all kinds of difficult and painful questions about the severity and the clemency the situation requires (e.g. the problem of the relation between the Law and the Gospel in the "Church Struggle" and in theological controversy!).

III THE RENEWAL OF THE CHURCH

The life of the Church is preserved, and saved in one way alone: by the renewal of her life as an "event", and thus by the renewal of her "gathering" as a congregation. A church that is not thus engaged in a reformation corresponding to the way in which she was originally "formed", has already fallen into the abyss of non-existence, or, in other words, she has fallen into the hopeless condition of a nominal church, or an empty ecclesiastical shell.

The renewal of the living congregation, which also constitutes her unification, is the work of her living Lord: the new light and the new power of His Word, according to the testimony of the Bible, the new outpouring of His Spirit, and His new Presence in preaching and in worship, in Baptism and the Lord's Supper. No danger can touch Him. He alone, in the power of His endless life, is so triumphantly adequate to deal with the sins and errors of the life of the Christian Church that He can both preserve and save it. He alone is the hope of the Church.

But the congregation must see to it that her church-order

makes room for that "event" which constitutes her renewal by the new acts of her Lord. The task and the significance of church-order consists in so uniting the congregation on the human level that it is rendered as free as possible for all that the Lord Himself can, and will do in her.

The Church is neither the invisible fellowship, nor the visible community, of all those who believe in Christ; nor is it a monarchical, aristocratic, or democratic form of the latter. The Church is the "event" in which two or three are gathered together in the name of Jesus Christ, i.e. in the power of His calling and commission. Church order is concerned exclusively with this event, with the living congregation itself.

The primary, normal, and visible form of this event is the *local congregation*, meeting in a "parish" or "district" with clearly defined boundaries. Such a local congregation is constituted by the possibility and the actuality of regular public worship, i.e. common worship at which the Atonement made by Jesus is proclaimed, as the ground of our hope. The Church lives (she *is*) in this visible, concrete, transaction (prayer, confession of faith, Baptism, Lord's Supper, the proclamation and reception of the Gospel), and in its presuppositions (theology, training of the young), and its consequences (brotherly discipline, pastoral care and other oversight). The Church lives (she actually *is*) in the form of a local congregation, which is the basis of all other forms of her life.

The government that guarantees the unity of the living congregation is the concern of her living Lord alone, and of His Word attested by the Scriptures. Apart from Him there is no ecclesiastical office (*officium*). There can only be the *service* (*Diakonia, ministerium*) of the whole congregation, divided and organized in relation to all that worship requires, both in that which it presupposes, and that to which it leads. For the fulfilment of this service all the members of the congregation are responsible together, as a whole, in which all share; in this service, for practical reasons some may have to take precedence of others, but in principle there are no "higher" or "lower" forms of service. Such service can be shared among the members only on the basis of a recognition of the different gifts bestowed by the one Holy Spirit, Who is promised to all.

The question about church order arises again when we turn to the relation of different local congregations to each other.

Since each of them, in its immediate relation to the one Lord, is in the fullest sense of the word a Church, i.e. a congregation, they can only mutually acknowledge each other, stand by each other in their life as congregations, advise, help, and to this extent, guide one another. But such "guidance", or "direction", is not domination or authority, but service. Neither individual dignitaries nor a clerical body can be considered the organ for this special service; the only organ for such "guidance" is that constituted by a special congregation, viz. a *synodical congregation* (whether regional, national—or ecumenical?) which is made up *ad hoc* of certain members from other congregations, sharing in the same life, and celebrating public worship in the same way.

The task of the synod or "synodal congregation" consists in securing, as far as is humanly possible, the co-ordination and solidarity, the catholic and "ecumenical" character of the life of those individual congregations associated with it. To do this it will set up and exercise a spiritual law in spiritual authority. It will be quite as much concerned about a forward policy as about the need to preserve a good tradition. In all this it will be simply one free congregation among others, standing alongside of, and yet representing them all. But in the fulfilment of its special task, and indeed of the very purpose of its existence, as a true mother-congregation it will see to it that in the special matters with which it is concerned the churches associated with it will receive counsel and challenge to action, advice and rebuke, but above all, evangelical encouragement. "Church government" as such, however, will not be its concern, but must remain in the hands of Him Who is Lord of all His many congregations.

There are, however, some cross-relations between individual local congregations, and other forms and organs of their unity. These are the *free associations for service* in the cause of charity, education, missions at home and abroad; further, within the bounds set by the one gift and calling that makes the Church the Church, there may also be associations for the guidance of Christian thought and policy. Such bodies should regard themselves quite seriously—and not only *de facto* but also *de iure*—as worshipping congregations, and should behave accordingly. In common with the local congregations and their associated synods, they also live by the grace given to the one Church, and in fulfilling their service to the one Church, they too are churches in the full sense of the word.

Church order, like the Church itself, is not an end in itself. It is man's attempt so to serve God's Word in obedience to it, that, in face of the danger menacing the Church, the wisest, boldest and most effective steps are taken to ensure that the immediate meeting and communion of the living Lord Jesus Christ with His congregation shall take place anew. No human effort can ensure this divine encounter. But man *can* clear the obstacles out of the way; and *this* is the purpose of church order.

The objection to the *papal* church order, and, in lesser degree, also to the *episcopal, consistorial,* and *presbyterian-synodal* church order, is that these systems obstruct the free access of God's Word to the actual congregation, and that they come between the congregation and the Word. All these systems of church order are due, more or less, to a quite unnecessary fear of arbitrary human action on the part of those who are chosen and called to be members of the living congregation of Jesus Christ, coupled with a scandalous lack of concern about the arbitrary behaviour of certain officials, chosen and appointed by men, to wield authority within, and over, the Church. Where the renewal of the Church is concerned, fear of the liberty of the Lord Jesus Christ, or fear of the liberty of His congregation is no help at all. Further, an indirect criticism of these systems of church order arises out of the contemporary situation: churches built on these principles are quite unable to show, as they ought, any example in their own Church life to the peoples of the world, who are everywhere in such need of political renewal.

Not even the *Congregationalist* church order is above criticism. Its representatives have not yet been able to offer a satisfactory answer to the problem of the unity of the Church and of the churches. This paper is not a plea for the uncritical adoption of this particular system. But the principle of Congregationalism—the free congregation of the free Word of God —is sound enough. At any rate, certain elements of Congregationalism are absolutely indispensable for other proposals for church order if these are not to lead to disorder, but to create real order. From this standpoint too the ecumenical unity of the Church can be seen more freely than anywhere else. It is obvious that the last remnants of sovereign authority in the idea of a *corpus christianum* are disappearing; this suggests that we should now look in this other (Congregationalist) direction.   Indirectly, this argument receives further confirmation in the reflection that a Church formed on the basis of these principles would be an event of exemplary importance in the political world of the present day.

II

THE SHAME AND GLORY OF THE CHURCH

However diverse our interpretations of the nature of the Church, the whole body of Christians knows certain things quite clearly in experience. We all know the shame of finding the life of our churches permeated by the disorder of the world. The first of the essays in this section deals with the nature and the depth of that disorder.

We all know, too, with gratitude, how the glory of God can be made manifest in the witness of the Church. The second and third essays speak out of the heart of recent experience of that God-given victory. Whilst Bishop Fjellbu writes, for the sake of concreteness, only from the background of Norway, he testifies to an experience equally known to the Church in many other European countries and in parts of Asia. Dr. Schlink and Dr. von Thadden speak for the Church upon whom fell the first and the hardest part of the struggle to manifest God's glory amidst man's disorder.

1

THE DISORDER OF MAN IN THE
CHURCH OF GOD

by H. Richard Niebuhr

I

At the outset of our effort to measure and understand the
disorder of man in the Church of God we shall do well to
remind ourselves of some general guiding principles.

First: we can rightly think and speak of this disorder only in
the way of Christian repentance. There are many false and
essentially disorderly ways of diagnosing what is wrong with the
Church. Outsiders, for instance, may criticize it for failing to
measure up to one of the various standards they employ. As
nationalists or communists, as political liberals or political conservatives, as humanists, naturalists or idealists, they bring their
particular notions of good and evil to bear on the Church and
call on it to change its ways. Within the Church also there are
ways of diagnosing and criticizing disorder which are not
characterized by the spirit of repentance. Fault-finding directed
towards other individuals or groups in the Church is one of
these, for such fault-finding is as distinct from repentance as it
is from brotherly admonition. Again, emotional shame, remorse
and self-accusation in the Church do not always manifest "godly
sorrow" working repentance, but may exhibit the "sorrow of
the world" working death (2 Cor. vii, 9-11). Repentance distinguishes itself from such an attitude in two ways. On the one
hand it is an active turning away from sin rather than a morbid
feeling. On the other hand it is hopeful, looking towards the
healing of diseases, while remorse and shame, in so far as they
remain worldly, are hopeless. Finally, there is a sort of self-
criticism in the Church, which is not repentance in the Christian
sense, because it is the counterpart of faith in the self rather
than of faith in God. When we practise it we do so as those
who believe that by means of one more effort to correct ourselves
we shall overcome our disorder. In such repentance our chief
disorder—our self-will, our determination to direct ourselves,

our faith in ourselves—remains hidden from us. Christian repentance is the counterpart of Christian faith. As faith is the turning towards God in trust and reliance on Him, so repentance is the turning away from the self and its idols as the beings in which we have confidence and from which we expect our salvation. It is only in the spirit of such repentance and such faith that we can be bold enough in the Church to attempt to understand our sin.

Secondly: the disorder to which our attention is called in repentance is not so much the disorder *of* the Church as disorder *in* the Church. In certain ecumenical meetings held in the past representatives of some sections of the Church have objected to statements that the Church needs to repent, or that it is sinful. This objection has a true basis, recognizable by all of us who confess our belief in the Church as an integral part of our statement of faith in the Triune God. The Church as the community and Body of Christ, as the holy and whole people of God, as the City of God in heaven and on earth, is the mediator of grace and not of sin, of order and not of disorder. Disorder resides in ourselves and not in it. Yet disorder is in ourselves not as individuals only but also as organized parts of the Church, as vocational, national, ethnic and historical organs of its body. We are never merely individual church members but always also members of one of the special groups which constitute the whole community. It is in these groups as well as in our privacy that we hear the call to repentance. To-day we learn of our disorder not only as national or denominational parts of the Church, but also as the part of the Church located in the twentieth century.

Thirdly: we do well to remember that our disorder is not so much a state of affairs as an action of disordering, just as, on the other hand, order in the Church is not a static arrangement of its parts but the constant action of ordering by its Head. Individuals called to repentance by the Gospel sometimes seek to evade that call by reflecting that their sin is a state of miserable existence to which they have been reduced by earlier actions of their own or by the actions of their fathers. They ignore the fact that each repetition on their part of a disorderly action of the past involves a new consent of their wills, and that each repetition introduces fresh disorder into their lives. They also forget that they may be acting sinfully when they repeat in a present moment what was at one time right action but is no longer fitting, as when the mature man behaves in a way that was required of the child. In similar fashion organized members of the Church are tempted to place responsibility for present disorder on some action of their fathers. So sectarians tend to blame present church-disorganization on the Constantinian settlement, calling that the fall of Christianity, while Protestants may make the rise of the Papacy, and Roman Catholics the Reformation, the source of the Church's disorder. The call to repentance meets us in the Church not as those who are disordered by past actions, but as those who are disordering by present actions, whether these be repetitions of actions which were sinful in the past and are now sinful, or repetitions of actions which were done sincerely and in obedience to God by our fathers, but which we can only repeat in disobedience to Him.

Our fourth and final preliminary reflection is that man's disorder in the Church of God is a relative thing. As it is certain that we cannot in repentance know our sin without at the same time knowing in faith God's grace, so also it is certain that our disordering action in the Church is nothing absolute or independent, but is dependent on the presence of God's fundamental action of ordering. In the same vision in which we see the abundance of our sin we see the abundance of God's grace. If all were disorder there would be no Church at all. Where there is disease in the physical body, that is, disorder, there must also be health, that is, some right order; otherwise there would be no body at all which could live, even in diseased condition, and as fighting against its disease. This is the condition which we discern in the Church. Hence our repentance does not turn to despair, for it is the counterpart of that faith which knows the present action of divine grace. On the other hand our faith does not lead us into the temptation to become complacent and to accept our sin as inevitable or as not requiring repentance, for it is faith in the Saviour who rouses us out of our despair and our complacency with the question, "Wilt thou be made whole?"

II

When in such repentant faith and believing repentance we examine ourselves in the Church of God we become aware that there is no area of our existence in which sin does not seem to prevail. We are almost baffled by its pervasive, complex and radical nature. Yet we must seek to understand it. In this effort we may be assisted if we use the Scriptural analogy and regard the Church as the Body of Christ, made up of many members or organs. We note, then, that the disorder of man manifests itself in God's Church in at least four spheres: within the organs themselves, in the relations of the organs to each other, in the relations of the organs to the world, and, finally, in their relations to the Head. What in this complex confusion of disorder is symptom, what source or cause, we do not now inquire as we seek to know something of the extent of our distress.

We may regard the groups called denominations, national churches, vocational orders such as the clergy, local congregations and other associations of Christians, as organs of the body. What sorts of disorder are present in them? What sins abound in the intricate inter-relations of individual Christians to one another and to the organic unit? A factionalism like that described in 1 Corinthians doubtless appears in some, perhaps all, the organs. A loveless discipline which simply casts out offenders against the common rule marks the conduct of others. But perhaps the disorder of which we are most aware in many parts of the Church is the sin which is the opposite of both these former ones: loveless lack of discipline. We tend to purchase our unity at the price of principle and our peace with one another at the cost of genuine mutual service. This situation is connected with the character of the membership of our groups.

As in the days of Augustine "there are many reprobate mingled with the good and both are gathered together by the gospel as in a drag-net". Yet we are forced to admit that the drag-net in our case has often been some other agency than the Gospel. Whether we have sought to expand our organizations in the Church through the direct political measures which created state churches, or have as free churches entered into competition for popular support with other Christian organizations and also with secular institutions, in any case, we have managed to bring into our churches many who have made no personal commitment to the Lord and His cause. When we contemplate what happened to the churches of Germany in their hour of sifting and winnowing, there are not many of us in other countries or in other Christian groups who can sincerely say that their membership contains a smaller proportion of the half-hearted, the luke-warm, of potential or actual deniers and traitors. It would doubtless be disorderly on our part to seek to anticipate the ordering action of the Lord of the Church Who sifts the wheat from the chaff on the threshing-floors of history, yet this does not excuse our more present disobedience both in continuing to gather into the Church those whom we do not call by the Gospel, and in withholding from those who have been so gathered adequate instruction and training in the exercise of genuine Christian vocation.

The first of these disordering actions brings into our churches many folk for whom "religion" is a part of a respectable life, or who pick and choose among the many "values" which the Church offers those which appeal to them. When, for the sake of meeting the wishes of such members, we withhold the challenge of the Gospel and turn it into an easy doctrine which demands no hard decisions, no continued self-denial in political and economic as in private matters, no surrender of the whole self to Christ, then we are guilty of the second part of this disorder. What in this realm is sincere adaptation to the needs of people, what self-deception, what is nominal and what is genuine Christianity, none of us can decide for others. Yet that there is much disorder here is patent, and that corporate as well as individual decisions about the conditions and requirements of church membership must be made seems also clear.

III

We have been made most acutely aware in our time of a second group of disorganizing actions in the Church, namely those which set the parts of the Church, the organic members of the body of Christ, at variance with each other and so disturb, distract and inhibit the functioning of the whole body. These disorganizing actions of ours appear in various forms. Sometimes they are actions of self-isolation in which as local congregations, or as national and ethnic churches or as confessional groups we say in effect to other members of the Body of Christ, "We have no need of you." Again they are actions of conflict in which we contend against other parts of the body as though they were alien and inimical to the body itself. While this disorder seems particularly characteristic of the relations of the Protestant and

Roman communities in the Church of Christ, it also appears in inter-Protestant and in Protestant-Orthodox relations. Again there are the disorganizing actions of those who seek special honour or prestige, as when a community of the clergy claim, or permit themselves to receive, a position in the Church which separates them from the lay orders. These various disorganizing actions may have a touch of imperialism in them, as when some one part of the Church undertakes to extend its rule over other parts, as though its own relations to the Head were more direct than that of the rest.

If the manifestations of disorder in these relations are manifold its roots seem to be manifold also. One apparent source is the social interplay in which action calls forth response in kind. As in the political sphere nationalism in one country calls forth nationalism in its neighbours, so, in the Church, self-sufficient denominationalism in one part tempts others to take the same attitude. Attack invites counter-attack so that anti-Romanism and anti-Protestantism, anti-liberalism and anti-orthodoxy flourish together. A second and more prevalent source of disorder lies in the confusion of a part with the whole. Thus a part of the Church regards itself as the whole or as representative of the whole, or it confuses the statement of what is most evidently true for it with the whole truth of the Gospel, or, again, it believes that the rule which it must follow in the performance of its function is the rule which the whole Church and all its other parts ought to follow. It may even believe that its particular function is the one function which the whole Church ought to carry out. Christendom is full of these confusions and so multiplicity of order is converted into disorder by the absolutizing of every relative, ordered pattern of action. The graciousness which marks some of the relations of distinct geographical, historical and vocational organs or groups in the Church is accompanied by much ingratitude to and for each other. We accept the correction, limitation and complementation of one by the other unwillingly and, rather than remain in the community of forgiveness and truly common faith, we separate from each other by withdrawal or excommunication.

These disorders among the organs of the Church appear most evidently in their external organization and even more in their lack of ecumenical order. They are, however, equally present and perhaps more destructive in the spiritual relations, as when in their prayers, their proclamation of the Gospel and their theological deliberation parts of the Church are either unmindful of one another or mind only those things in each other which invite correction. In this situation we impoverish ourselves as well as others, and as a result of our poverty have less and less to give to a world in need.

A multiplicity of special groups in the Church, serving men for God's sake in many diverse places and situations and cultures and performing many special functions, may be a sign of obedience to one Master and hence of order rather than of disorder. The presence in these congregations, denominations, and associations of many different special types of organization may also be indicative of such obedience. What is disorderly is isolation, contempt for each other, the pretension to special honour, the claim of the part to be the whole, the refusal to live in active inter-dependence, the effort to reign over others.

IV

The third sphere in which repentance discovers our human sin in the Church of God is in our relation as organized parts of the Church to the world outside the Church. Faith knows what action in this sphere is commanded by the Lord of the Church. Positively, our action is orderly when, following that command, we go into the world to make disciples of all nations, to baptize them and to teach them all that has been commanded to the Church. Negatively, it is ordered action when it is unspotted by the corruption and love of the world (Romans xii, 2; James i, 27; 1 John ii, 15). In the light of that double order we discern the confusion which has entered into our church-world relations. On the other hand, going into the world we become disciples of the world so that we import into the Church the corruptions of the world. Then in reaction to our secularism we are tempted to withdraw from the world and to seek holiness in isolation from it. Or, again, our ordered action in making disciples of Jesus Christ becomes the disordered action of those who seek to make converts to themselves rather than to Him and to teach such converts to observe not what our Lord has commanded us to do, but what we command them to do. Thus in our relations to the world we are tempted and often fall into the sins of secularism, of sectarianism, and of proselytism, using that last term to designate the sin which Jesus chastised when He said, "Woe to you, scribes and Pharisees, hypocrites! for you traverse sea and land to make a single proselyte, and when he becomes a proselyte, you make him twice as much a child of hell as yourselves."

The disorder of secularism is perhaps nowhere more apparent in our contemporary Church than in the extent to which we have permitted the order of the world to creep into the order of the Church. Having gone into the world of nations to make them disciples we have often accepted the order of nationalism, so that we not only remained silent before a nation's pretensions to the status of a chosen people, but have even fostered the illusion with our speech, for instance, about an "American theology" or perhaps even an American gospel in social form, or with our confusion of American and Christian "destiny".[1] In other instances we have so confounded Church and nation that we have regarded the former as an aspect of the latter. Again, the secular order and disorder of economic society have been accepted by the Church and been mirrored in its own order. So feudalism entered into the Church only to be displaced there by the capitalist order of a later time; and this in turn may make way for the socialist order. Whatever may be said for such orders of economic society as containing within themselves for their time and in their times elements of a natural order, the acceptance by the parts of the Church of secular gradations of rank, honour and wealth runs counter to its own order of mutual service. That it should carry out its mission to the men in the middle classes of capitalist society is doubtless a part of the Church's order, but that the mission should result in the formation of a middle-class church which defends the secular outlook and interests of that class is an evident corruption. That this disorder should lead to the demand for the formation of workers' churches which are to represent the secular as well as religious interests of another economic class is intelligible; yet the disorder in the latter case would be as deep as in the former. Perhaps the most painful disorder which has resulted and results from our conformation to the world is present where differences popularly and wrongly called "racial" have entered into the organization of the Church, so that worldly, anti-Christian, white

[1] Note: Many specific examples of this disordering action can be given not only from the pages of theological writings, but also from home and foreign missionary appeals. But in an ecumenical Church each national group can best supply its own specific examples.

and Gentile pride disfigures and profanes the assemblies of Christians, by drawing caste lines even in worship services and at the Lord's Table, and by introducing "respect of persons" even into missionary and educational service.

The disorder in our church relations antithetical to this one is the sin of withdrawal from the world we are commanded to enter. It may be less manifest in external conduct in our day than it was in the days before the great series of monastic reforms and the Protestant Reformation. Yet it is present in other forms, as when we confess our faith only to each other's sympathetic ears in the Church and not before the world, or when we withdraw from the conflict with atheism in the world into our cells for the cultivation of our spiritual life, or when we disclaim responsibility for the political and economic disorders and sufferings of men because the Gospel relates us to another world than this one, or when we consent to the statement that "religion is a private matter".

As for the sin of "proselytism", though we may be inclined to regard the statement of Jesus about the making of proselytes as directed to men of another community than ours, we cannot wholly evade the indictment. We are aware that it has been difficult for us to distinguish between making disciples of Christ and making proselytes, between turning men to the Lord whose cause we seek to serve and turning them to ourselves who serve this cause. We have wanted men to become as we are, because we are Christians, and have confused the imitation of ourselves with the imitation of Christ. So in our relations to the Jews we have virtually demanded their acceptance of that Gentile Christianity which Paul freed from compulsory imitation of Jewish Christianity, while in our relations to the nations of the East we have found it difficult to dissociate our Western patterns of life and thought, of ritual and confession, from the pattern of Christ. Hence also we have carried into non-Christian countries divisions relevant to our culture but alien to theirs, and have with the Gospel exported also our spiritual disorders, and our secular, temporal order which for them has sometimes been a source of disorder.

v

In our repentance we are made aware that all our human

wrongness in the Church is related to a disorder in our relation to its Head. On the one hand every unbrotherly act of which we are occasionally or habitually guilty in our relations to other parts of the Church and to the world outside is also, we must confess, an action of disobedience to Him. On the other hand it appears that every such disobedience is evidently rooted in something wrong in our relation to Him. We disobey Him because we do not trust Him. In faith we acknowledge Him as the risen Christ who gives us in our time His order and commandments; in doubt we think Him dead and believe that it is we who must give others His orders. So we arrogate to ourselves the right to rule His Church for Him. In faith we are assured that all power has been given to Him in heaven and on earth and that therefore we can, as we ought, make disciples of all nations; in our doubt of His power we adjust ourselves to all the ruling forces in the world, to the prejudices which hold sway over the minds of men, to their love of life and of status, to their worship of civilization and nation. In this adjustment we shift our faith from Christ to other saviours and other lords, though our tongues continue to confess His Lordship. In faith we accept the possibility and the reality of suffering with our Head and even learn to rejoice in it as a necessary element in our own and the world's salvation; in our doubt we shun suffering and perhaps fear even more to lead others into the fellowship of the cross. Hence our relations to the world are confused and confounded by the fear that we shall suffer if we proclaim and confess Christ before the hard-hearted, the mighty in knowledge or other strength, and by our anxiety that we may lead the humble and the weak into increased or additional sorts of suffering. So we become defensive or withdraw. In our faith we accept His orders to feed His lambs and His sheep in whatever particular situation He has called us; in our doubt we question His justice, fearing that others may receive a more exalted position than we, and, like Peter, we betray our jealousy of each other by asking, " Lord, and what shall this man do? "

Thus it is that in the same sphere in which our fundamental order as a Church appears, our fundamental disorder as members of the Church also becomes evident. Because we are ordered to the Head and by the Head of the Church therefore we are the Church and in the Church; because in this disordered relation we doubt and disobey our Head, therefore, we are disordered in all our parts and in all our relations. Hence our sole but also our sure hope of salvation lies not in giving new orders to ourselves or to one another, but in the ordering which proceeds from Him Who rules us and calls us to ever new responses of free obedience. So we say, "Lord, we believe, help thou our unbelief," and in the measure of our faith do in our present what He commands, turning in sorrow from our disordering actions and in joy to His ordering.

THE CHURCH OF GOD AMID THE
DISORDER OF MAN

(a) HER WITNESS IN OCCUPIED EUROPE

by Arne Fjellbu

D URING the years of persecution, the Church of Norway was faced with a situation quite different from that which the Church in Germany had to face. In Germany the wave of nationalism rolled along outside the living Church; it was directed to a great extent *against* the Church. The leaders of the Confessional Church of Germany found no support in the national movement, which developed in the opposite direction. In Norway, however, the good national powers joined in active support of the Church and drew from her their strength and inspiration in their national struggle.

In Germany the enemies of the Church came from the people. The ideology and view of life of the Nazis had grown out of the native soil of Germany itself, had their origin in *Blut und Rasse* and *Blut und Boden*; these Nazi theories of blood, race and soil were adopted by the authorities of the State and through them pervaded the whole people.

In Norway, the enemies of the Church came forward and made common cause with the intruders who occupied our country and deprived us of our national freedom and independence. Those Norwegians who collaborated with the forces occupying our country, the Norwegian Nazis, were regarded as traitors, and as such they were despised and regarded with contempt by the majority of the people. From the very outset the Church found it, humanly speaking, very easy to assume its attitude towards the disorder of man—an attitude which proved to be fortunate for it. Practically the whole people sided with the Church. This was a new situation. Though the Church of Norway is a national Church comprising ninety-seven per cent of the total population, and in spite of the fact that the whole people, through religious and moral instruction in the schools, were being in-

fluenced by the Christian faith, the influence of secularism had
been felt for some time. The Church had not succeeded in
counteracting these tendencies. In fact, it must be admitted
that they had infected the theology of the Church itself.

Before the second world war serious attempts had been made
in Norway, as in Germany and other Lutheran countries, to
establish relations between theology on the one hand and
philosophical and scientific investigation and cultural life in
general on the other. As far as theology was concerned, the
result had more often been an adaptation than a conquest,
because people had failed to realize sufficiently that the Church
and theology have a character of their own.

During the inter-war period serious efforts had been made to
maintain the independence of theology and the Church in face
of the world and the cultural and national life of Norway. The
price of this independence, however, was the isolation of theology
and the Church. Co-operating with several concurrent forces,
this isolation forced the Church into a " ghetto existence ", which
gave the impression of a sequestered life. When the last war
came, the Church burst out of this " ghetto existence " and was
suddenly standing amidst the people, with a full understanding
of their problems, national, social, humanitarian and cultural.
The Church became associated with the people as never before.
The concerns of the people were those of the Church. Favourable as this position was for the Church, from a human point of
view, it involved a serious problem: did it put the Church of
Norway in a position similar to that in which the *Deutsche
Christen* had been placed when the national ideas overshadowed
the Christian, and the Church became definitely nationalistic
and ceased to be " a Church of God "?

This was not how things turned out in Norway. *Here the
Church associated with the people as the Church of God.* This
was due to the fact that, during the German occupation all the
fundamental human values were at stake. The fundamental
human values, however, are identical with the eternal, absolute
values; and those in question were right and justice, truth,
liberty and goodness, values which Christian influence through
centuries had made the indispensable heritage of our people.

The occupying power did not invade Norway for military
purposes only. The occupants were indeed missionaries preaching a new view of life, a new religion, which they wanted to

force upon the Norwegian people. Once this was realized, a violent awakening made the people conscious of their Christian heritage. And the Christian reasons produced for these values rested on such sound foundations that the secular-humanistic view of life was more or less abandoned. Most people found these values anchored in God. This being so, their victory was assured. That is why the Word of God became a living force for many people. In these circumstances the Word of God became a matter of interest because it held high those values which were at stake.

Of course not everyone saw this clearly. As a matter of fact not a few regarded the attitude and the struggle of the Church from purely national and opportunist points of view. In the struggle against Nazism, the Church proved an important and valuable brother-in-arms. The reasons why the Church entered the struggle were purely Christian ones, vindicated by the Scriptures. The result produced in the situation in question, however, was a good one. When waging war, one is grateful to one's allies, even though one may happen to oppose them at some point or other.

With these qualifications, the characteristics given above are correct. The following declaration by a Communist during the war bears witness to this: " During the war all the ' isms ' will change. None of them will emerge from this war without having been changed, perhaps beyond recognition. There is only one exception: Christianity, the foundation of which is something objective and unchangeable."

From the very first day of the German occupation, the Norwegian Church was anxious to stand only upon ground proper to the Church as such. Any action or utterance from the Church would have to be justified from the Bible and from its Christian confession of faith, from its secure position in the words given us through divine revelation.

At the beginning, this resulted in an action which was unfavourable to the national awakening of the people. In the autumn of 1940 the Nazi authorities decreed that the prayer for the King should be omitted from public worship. The bishops of the country had to yield on this point. The reason why this apparently humiliating and compliant decision was taken was that the Church wanted to avoid a conflict with the occupying power on a matter which touched so closely upon the political problems of the country. During the succeeding struggle against the Nazi authorities, the Norwegian Church again and again emphasized that the fight was not political but ecclesiastical, and that the battle-field was that of the Word. In this connection it may be of some interest to stress that, in its fight against those authorities who had caused the great disorder, the Church derived much inspiration from the writings of Martin Luther. His works became a real arsenal of weapons in the struggle of the Church.

This fact may perhaps surprise many non-Lutherans. Luther is generally understood to have preached obedience and loyalty to the temporal authorities. This view has been derived from Luther's idea of "the two realms"—the temporal (represented by the state authorities) and the spiritual (represented by the Church). This idea has been interpreted to mean that each of these realms has its own master, and that two kinds of obedience are therefore called for. According to this, the leaders of the Church might yield to the demands of the secular rulers in all temporal matters, even in cases where they were ordered to perform sinful acts—even the words of Satan. It was considered satisfactory as long as obedience were paid to God and His Word in matters spiritual. Within the Lutheran Church this interpretation has been used to subordinate the Church to the state in a way that has been altogether horrifying.

During the war Luther was discovered anew. It was proved that though Luther preached the doctrine of the two realms, these were both *of God*. Only as long as the authority of a state *considers God as the highest authority* is it in accordance with the Order of God. Melanchthon, the other great Reformer, expressed the same idea in his doctrine of the "two tables". The special duty of the Church is within the first table. The task of the authority of a state is contained in the seven[1] last commandments: "*Magistratus est vox decalogi*," Melanchthon said. And Luther developed this idea further. Caesar's place is in the second table of the Decalogue. He cannot ascend higher (unless he is led astray by the Devil), but is subject to the commandments of the second table; he is bound to do what God

---

[1] In the Lutheran numbering of the Decalogue, the first two commandments in the tradition of numbering usual in this country are made one whilst the tenth is divided into two. So Anglicans, e.g., would speak here of the six last commandments.

orders, for God alone reigns, and Caesar is not able to alter one single commandment.

Ideas such as these from Luther's writings strengthened the Church of God amid the disorder of man. And imbued with this spirit, the Church felt obliged to maintain the law of God in the face of the authorities, when they trespassed against God's commandments.

In what follows, examples will be given of these fundamental beliefs in the different fields where the Church was faced by the disorder of man.

The first Norwegian institution to break with the occupying power was the Norwegian Supreme Court, the highest legal institution of the country. The members of the Supreme Court resigned as soon as the German intruders usurped the right to appoint members of law courts, in order to make them dependent upon the party then in power, thus violating the independence of justice and the sovereign majesty of the law. There ensued a state of lawlessness in the country. No one any longer felt safe. We were a people whose rulers were no longer a terror to the evil works, but to the good (Rom. xiii, 3). In this situation the Church engaged in a fight of her own for right. and justice, for the social order established by God, the Order of God.

A few months after the members of the Supreme Court had handed in their resignations, the bishops of the country sent a memorandum to the Ministry of Church and Education, in which they asked for an unambiguous declaration as to whether the state accepted and felt bound by the judicial and moral obligations expressed in the basic faith of the Church, i.e. in the Bible and in the Creed. "That the state should feel bound by this is necessary from the intrinsic nature of the Church," the letter from the bishops reads.

In a later memorandum addressed to the chief of the Department for Church and Education, the last paragraph reads: "Everyone who instigates evil is under the judgment of God." And in the document proper, fundamental statements such as the following express the view of the Church on the disorder of man: "The Church does not interfere with matters temporal when she exhorts the authorities of the state to be obedient to the highest authority, which is God" (Luther) . . . "consistent with our calling, we urge the rulers of our society to make an end of whatever may be opposed to the holy Orders of God, as regards justice, truth, freedom of conscience and goodness, and we admonish them to build without aberration on the divine laws of life."

During the whole period of occupation the Church, in the same spirit, carried on her fight against the authorities for law and justice in Norway.

Later, when the attacks were directed *against the Church* itself, it had to fight for *the freedom of the Word of God*, for the right to preach in accordance with the Word and its own conscience. During this struggle the bishops issued several pastoral letters which clearly and concisely pointed out the duties and rights of the Church in face of the disorder of man.

The most classical document from this period is one called the *Foundation of the Church*. Among other assertions in the document, the following points of view are maintained: The servants of the Church can only, through the Church, accept instructions as to how the Word of God is to be preached in an urgent situation. The free preaching of the Gospel must be the salt of God in the life of the whole people. The same pastoral contains the following passage: if one kind of régime tries to obtain the position of ruler over another, this is a sin against God, Who is the Lord and Authority of every Order. It is not the task of the Church to hold a position above the state in secular matters. This would be trespassing upon the Order established by God. Similarly, if the state attempts to tyrannize over men's souls and prescribe what the people shall believe, think and feel, this is a sin against God. For if the state tries to force people's souls in matters of religious belief, this only results in pangs of conscience, fraud and persecution. If this is the case, God's judgment spoken in the Scriptures becomes urgent. When the power of the state is no longer founded upon justice, then the state is no longer an instrument of God, but a demonic power. (Luke iv, 6; John xiv, 30; Rev. xii-xiii.)

In this connection the pastoral letter refers to Luther: "The secular authorities may not rule over consciences. . . . If those holding temporal power encroach upon the spiritual rule and try to imprison consciences, where God alone wishes to hold the sceptre, then they shall not be obeyed."

In this fight the Church, faced with the disorder of man, saw these words shining before it: "The Word of God is not bound" (2 Tim. ii, 9) and "We ought to obey God rather than man" (Acts v, 29).

The next sphere in which the disorder of man was made visible was in the attitude of the state to the children and to youth. In the beginning of 1942 the Act of National Youth Service was passed, the purpose of which was to remould Norwegian children and young people on the same lines as the Hitler Youth in Germany. This gave the signal for a fierce struggle, in which Norwegian teachers as well as Norwegian homes made a tremendous effort to save the souls of the young. In this conflict the Norwegian teachers showed how they felt bound by their conscience, and the firmness of the teachers gave strength to the whole people in their fight for our invaluable Christian heritage.

The Church, of course, took an active part in the struggle and made its views clear to the state authorities, as well as to the people. One of the many declarations by the bishops to the authorities reads as follows: "Whosoever by constraint attempts to remove children from the hands of the parents responsible for them, and to infringe upon the sacred rights of the home, will strain the parents' conscience to the utmost. Every father and mother knows that one day they will have to answer to the Almighty as to how they have brought up their children, or allowed them to be brought up. They must always show greater obedience to God than to man."

When the atrocious persecution of the Jews began and once more showed the disorder of man, the Church again spoke its mind in criticizing the evil-doings of the authorities. A letter to Quisling, read from every pulpit in the country, contains the following passages: "The disregard for the human worth of the Jews is directly contrary to the Scriptures, which, from cover to cover, clearly lay down the fact that all peoples are of the same blood. See especially Acts xvii, 26: 'God . . . hath made of one blood all nations of men.' In fact, God seldom speaks more clearly than in this passage. 'For there is no respect of persons with God' (Rom. ii, 11). 'There is neither Jew nor Greek' (Gal. iii, 28). 'For there is no difference' (Rom. iii, 22)." And first and foremost the letter reminds the authorities that when God through the Incarnation assumed human form, He chose to be born in a Jewish home by a Jewish mother.

"According to the Word of God all human beings have the

same human worth and the same human rights. And these fundamental principles the authorities of our state are by law bound to respect. . . . By virtue of our calling we therefore exhort the secular authorities in the name of Jesus Christ, our Lord, to stop the persecution of the Jews, and to forbid the spreading of racial hatred in our country through the press."

These examples of urgent situations may be sufficient to illustrate, within the limits of a short essay, the attitude of the Church amid the disorder of man.

During these times of lupine savagery the Church stood forth as a united Church. An ecumenical movement originated in the period of persecution, uniting the Norwegian Established Church and the other church communities in Norway. The communities of Dissenters, and on some occasions also the Roman Catholic bishops in Norway, fully supported the views expressed in the letters to the state authorities, as well as in those of the Norwegian people. There was also brought about a unification of the divergent movements within the Norwegian Church. *Ecclesia una sancta catholica* was glimpsed, to the glory of God.

One final experience must be mentioned: how the people gathered to hear the Word and to partake of the Holy Communion. The crowding in the churches was partly due to the fact that the Church stood for the national values, that it expressed what no one else ventured to say in public during these years. It may partly be explained by the fact that the Word of God found wide access to the hearts of men and bore fruit there. The increase in the number of communicants, a more general understanding of the Lord's Supper and its place in the Christian community, unity in Christ and unity with one another experienced by Christians during these years—these are the best proofs of this fact.

These years saw also the growth of a greater social responsibility among Christians. Norwegian Christians felt called upon by God to confront the disorder of man with the Church of God.

Times change. The disorder of man, however, continues to be a menace to the future of the world.

The Church of God knows on what foundation it has been **built**. Valiantly the Church has still to obey God rather than man. The Word of God is not and cannot be bound. But the Church is bound to the Word of God.

And Christ's Promise is heard concerning the Church: "The gates of hell shall not prevail against it" (Matt. xvi, 18).

(b) THE WITNESS OF THE GERMAN CHURCH STRUGGLE

by Edmund Schlink

WHEN an anti-Christian power invades a nation from outside by force of arms, it is a different matter from when it arises within the nation itself, with all kinds of promises which at first it appears to fulfil. In the first case, where it destroys the people's freedom, it is clearly recognized as an enemy; in the second case, where it appears to give the people freedom, its treacherous character is hidden. In the first instance the Christians in their resistance enjoy the comradeship of all who love their country; in the second case the Christians' resistance isolates them from their own people, and they are regarded as traitors to their country. In the first case, resistance is made in loyalty to one's own government against the enemy-invader; in the second case, resistance is directed against one's own government, which has developed into an enemy of Christ, so that painful conflicts break out more and more not only between the orders of these authorities and the commandments of God, but also (as it at first appears) between the divine commandments themselves, i.e. between God's commandment to obey the authorities (Rom. xiii) and the commandment "to obey God rather than men" (Acts v, 29).

Before the Nazis made war on the other countries of Europe, they had already persecuted the Jews and the Church in Germany. They did not do so in open antagonism to Christ, but camouflaged it as "positive Christianity". They did not take action openly as opponents of the Church, but "as protectors of the Church". They did so by using quotations from the Bible, and by claiming to be fulfilling God's commandments. They thus built up an enormous propaganda-machine, which resulted in a general inflation of values, because it sanctified anything it wanted to, so that finally nothing remained sacred. The totalitarian state then went still further and threw its whole weight against the Church, trying to suppress and to destroy it by all kinds of illegal attacks. The Church was not allowed to have any influence on public life, and it was debarred from access to the press and from the use of large halls. Religious instruction in school was either, to a great extent, abolished, or it was robbed of its biblical content. The theological faculties were allowed to atrophy, and the theological colleges were closed. The men and the young people were systematically severed from the Church, and forced into the Party; even the women and children who went to church were watched. The printing of Bibles, catechisms and hymn-books was prohibited, whole branches of church work were forbidden, Christian charity institutions were robbed, church leaders were deprived of their offices, and church order was largely destroyed. Hundreds of Evangelical pastors were taken away from their churches by the state police. Some of them suffered a martyr's death.

The effect of this attack by an anti-Christian power corresponded exactly to what the New Testament prophesies concerning the time during which the Church must undergo persecution.

I

There was a great falling-off among Christians. Many began to be ashamed of the name of Christ, gave up going to church, and instead of baptism, confirmation and Christian marriage and burial, wanted the " dedications " of the " neo-pagan " cult offered by National Socialism. Families were torn asunder: children denounced their parents, husbands opposed their wives, brothers and sisters took opposite sides in the cleavage between faith and error. Love grew cold in many hearts. Its place was taken by delusions and hardness of heart.

This defection occurred not only among the rank and file of church people, but even among the clergy. Many became preachers of the anti-Christian myth and entered the service of the Nazis to replace the loyal pastors and church leaders who had been deprived of office. Many of them became false teachers, and then persecutors of the Church, by proclaiming and denouncing resistance as disobedience to God and hostility to the authorities, and refusing to allow people persecuted by the Nazis to share in the fellowship of prayer and mutual assistance.

But even more shattering than the apostasy, as such, was the way in which it was usually taken for granted, with an easy conscience. When the Nazi philosophy began to influence Christians, many of them did not even notice that all this Nazi talk about "the Almighty" and His "providence" had nothing to do with the Living God, the Father of our Lord Jesus Christ, but that it was directly opposed to Him. They did not notice that the propaganda about freedom, national community, and sacrifice, had nothing to do with God's promises and God's commandments, but that it actually distorted them. It became evident that people were not at all clear about Christian teaching. In many churches, even before the Nazi regime, preaching had become an arbitrary religious explanation of personal destiny and world events. Otherwise, when the crucial moment came, it would have been impossible for a man of our own time to gain such an ascendancy and for him, with his personal philosophy, to become the object of such widespread faith and hope.

At the same time it became clear that the Church had grown much more bourgeois than had previously been realized. People had grown accustomed to regard God primarily as the protector of ordered family life, a help in the education of children, and a friend in the big events of life such as leaving school, marriage and death. He had become the guarantor of national and civic security, in the midst of the insecurities of this world. In many people's minds, Jesus' hard words about what it meant to follow Him had either fallen into oblivion, or had lost their edge. Jesus' challenge to leave one's native land and one's family for the sake of the Gospel, and to choose the way of suffering, seemed strange and remote from modern Christian life. That is why church-goers were surprisingly helpless and unprepared when the persecution started, and they had to choose between abuse, contempt and tribulation for Christ's sake, or rejecting Him altogether. Behind this apostasy stood the failure of Christian teaching which had come to light since 1933, but had a long history; this was why Christians were powerless when the anti-Christian attack set in. To a large extent God's commandments had been severed from the consolation of the Gospel, and were wrongly regarded as autonomous "orders of creation" and political ordinances. The kingdom of this world had become to a large extent either confused with Christ's Kingdom, or else completely cut off from it, instead of the true distinction being made between the two realms both under the dominion of the Triune God. For many people the Church had already become either a function of the state, or a pious ghetto, before the totalitarian state forced it into this position.

So the Third Reich was an apocalyptic experience for the Church and its neo-protestant past, which we shall not soon forget. The breakdown of so many churches was not so much *caused* by outside pressure as shown up by it. The forces at work outside the Church showed up what was real in the life of these churches, and what was only an empty shell. It was impossible to foretell which individuals and which churches would prove to be really spiritually alive in time of persecution, and which would be dead. We found that strong members suddenly became weak, weak members suddenly grew strong; the Church was like a tree, some of whose most healthy branches withered away, while others which seemed almost dead, put forth new shoots.

II

The fact that this apostasy did not cause the death of the Church, but that it received new life, was due to the miracle of divine grace. This renewal began when the Church recognized the enemy's attack as the hand of God, and the unjust encroachments of the state as God's just judgment. The renewal began when resistance to injustice became at the same time an act of repentance and of submission to the mighty hand of God.

Thus through the onslaught of anti-Christian propaganda the Church's ears were re-opened to the Word of God. "It shall be nought but terror to understand the message" (Isa. xxviii, 19). But at the same time God's Word challenged us, questioned the reality of our own religion, and forced us to recognize God simply and solely in His Word. Under the attack of "neopaganism", but especially through the power of God's Word, its promises and its demands, our usual attempts to see God's revelation in other historical events and forms, ideas and words, save in the historic event of God's revelation in Jesus Christ, completely broke down. Now natural theology broke down; it had assumed a great variety of forms and had been preached as the religion of conscience and idealism, as mysticism and *historismus,* as the religious interpretation of the nationalist past and of the socialist future. Jesus Christ, the Word made flesh, was recognized and acclaimed afresh as the sole Word of God. And one of the strongest Bible movements in the history of the Church has taken place during the last few years in the Evangelical Church, through its new understanding of the Old and New Testaments.

People gathered afresh around the sacraments. The number of communion services and of communicants increased. In the midst of all the tribulation and distress there awakened a new longing for the concrete, personal experience of receiving the body and the blood of the Incarnate Son of God Who has given Himself for us. This destroyed the oppressive solemnity of the memorial services, the form in which the communion services had largely been celebrated. By receiving the body which Jesus Christ gave for us on the Cross, we realized that this same Christ gives Himself to us in the sacrament as the Risen Lord, Who will come again. In the sacrament, through sharing in Jesus' death on Golgotha, we realized more and more that, in this same sacrament, we also share in the great Sacrament to which He will call His own from all over the world, to celebrate it with them in God's Kingdom. But looking forward to His return, we already received the foretaste of the future Marriage Feast which the Lamb will celebrate with His bride, the Church, at the end of time, for ever and ever. These communion services echoed the joy of the early Christians, to whom the body and blood of Christ were objects of the greatest joy and praise.

The Church was again recognized as the meeting-place of believers around the Word and the Sacrament. It is the meeting-place of those who hear and of those who bear witness. In the midst of the collapse of the national Church, and the refutation of the belief that the Church *consisted* of the mass of tithe-payers or of people interested in the Church or of those who were still nominal members, the local gathering of Christians " under the Word of God " assumed a fresh significance. People realized, to their strength and consolation, that the Church was not a mere collection of like-minded persons, but a concrete, local reality. Jesus' promise, that when two or three were gathered together in His name, He would be there in the midst of them, proved to be a great force. So during the last few years the name of " brother " blossomed again, both in the home churches and in those which were scattered, in the prisons and at the front. And the discovery of brotherhood was not confined to one's own confession. Brothers were recognized outside our own confession, where we had not looked for them before, and consolation was found in unexpected places. This discovery of brothers in other Christian churches did not remove the confessional differences between them, but the emphases were changed and opposition paled in face of the reality of God, Who is more gracious and merciful than any dogma of grace.

The liturgy took on a new meaning, after a long period of decay during which the order of service and church worship had become very individualistic and subjective. This break-away from the past occurred in many churches at the same time, quite independently of one another, by the common recitation of the Creed during the service. Then came the special prayers for those in exile or in prison, based on identical prayer-sheets which were used in churches all over the country, and many forms of prayer sent to the churches, expressing in the same words the distress and the thanksgiving of Christians. In this way the upholding power of the common prayer of the brethren was revealed afresh. But the Church is not only a fellowship of brothers, but also a fellowship with our fathers. The Church is one and the same, at all times, as well as in all places. As the isolation of the churches and of individuals increased, the stronger grew the belief in one holy ecumenical Church in all. places and at all times; and this certainty sought expression and was strengthened by the increasing use of the ancient prayers of the Church and the psalms, used by Christians at all times. Through these prayers we realized that across all distances and even across the war-fronts, we were *one* people with worshippers in all nations.

The ministry was regarded in a new light. In the local church, it was seen that the first duty, which takes precedence of all other tasks, is to preach the Gospel and to administer the sacraments. But it became especially clear that the Church cannot be led by anything but the voice of the Good Shepherd, as preached in the Word of God. Church government, therefore, must not be left to secular authorities; it is incumbent upon the Church itself, to control its own affairs. The realization that the Church can only be governed in submission to God's Word was preserved in a severe struggle to hold theological examinations, ordinations and visitations, the burden of which fell mainly on the younger brethren (curates and assistant clergy) and their families, who had no security at all. Through these experiences the opposition between the two possibilities of episcopal or synodal order lost its exclusiveness and sharpness. For it became clear that the office of bishop was different from secular leadership, and that real synodal government differed in the same way from political-democratic principles of government. Moreover, it became clear that a purely formal, legal authority cannot really govern a church.

All kinds of spiritual gifts were given by God. As more and more the pastors were taken away from their churches by state expulsions and for military service, the more their congregations had to face the test of being asked: " Do you believe in God's promise? " In this situation many congregations failed. But in many churches things were accomplished similar to those described in Rom. xii and 1 Cor. xii, which had not been taken into serious consideration since those early times. Gifts came to light which may have been present in the congregation before, under a pastor who thought he ought to do everything himself. In some cases the congregation did not receive these gifts until the difficult times began. Many elders then began to understand their task in a new way as that of watchmen. Many who had only listened to the Word before, now came forward to read to the congregation, or to give their own exposition of a passage of scripture. Many, who had never thought of doing so before, accompanied bereaved persons to the cemetery, so that the body should not be laid in the earth without a reading from scripture and a prayer. In addition to the old office of deacon, new duties were assumed; readers, catechists, both men and women, undertook the care of the poor and pastoral work, while young people taught the children. In many places the joyful discovery was made that all gifts can be of service to the community, and that Christ's grace can only be glorified aright through the diversity of spiritual gifts and services.

The Church realized afresh its responsibility for the world. The weaker the Church became, the stronger grew its certainty of the lordship of Christ, the fact that " all power in heaven and on earth " is given to the Risen Christ (Matt. xxviii, 18). The Church began to see the world in a new way, through faith in the ascension of its Lord; the Church can no longer allow any realm of life to be a law unto itself; for over and above all human action in every sphere of life, the Church must proclaim the lordship of Jesus Christ. Under the onslaught of the totalitarian state and its claims, the false conception broke down that obedience to Christ applied only to private life. As the totalitarian state no longer recognized any private sphere, the problem of Christian obedience had to be stated in a new way. Since the totalitarian state made use of every sphere of life for its own arbitrary political objects and its anti-Christian ideology, it became clear that not only in family life and in individual religious life, but in the decisions of the judge, in industry, in economic life, in the doctor's treatment of the sick, in the application of military force, and in all political action, obedience to God was at stake—the Lord Who through His death has made everything on earth His own. Hesitatingly, but with growing confidence, the Church in the Third Reich began to proclaim that in every sphere of life we owe obedience to God in Christ, proclaiming its message in face of the world and helping the persecuted. The Church in Germany carried on its struggle not only for the sake of its own existence, but also on behalf of other oppressed races and peoples, whatever their faith.

All this proved that the Church can only help, in the midst of the disorder of the world, by really being the Church. Its most important duty to the world consists in allowing itself to be re-made by the Word of God. When the Church derives its life solely from the Word of God made flesh, the witness of that word within the Church is bound to have effect in saving and bringing order into the world around. But if the Church bears witness to something other than this Lord, however well-intentioned its advice, warning, help and sacrifice may be, it will only increase the disorder of the world.

III

During the last few years the Evangelical Church in Germany carried on its struggle against the anti-Christian power of the state, as a religious struggle. The Church had to decide between decay and renewal. Denial of Jesus Christ meant decay and death. To confess Jesus Christ means life in the Holy Spirit. What were the elements in the Church's faith, which determined what it said and did throughout these years?

The confession of the Church is public witness to Jesus Christ, the Crucified and Risen Lord, as Lord of lords. Confessing Christians declare before the whole world, "that they belong to this Lord in faith and obedience, and wish to remain His, come what will ".[1]

Through its confession the Church rejects the claims of the world and its self-made gods to have any control over it. Confessing the Lordship of Jesus Christ means at the same time unmasking and rejecting the false doctrines of the present day.

Through its confession the Church makes its attack on the world, its ideologies and its self-glorification. The Church's confession is Christ's weapon in His struggle against the kingdom of Satan.

Confession of the Lordship of Christ means at the same time confessing one's own sins. For the Lordship of Christ is the realization of His grace. But how can the Church testify to His grace, to the world, unless the Church recognizes that it consists of sinners who live on this Grace? The Confessional Movement means a movement of repentance.

The confession of the Church makes the One, Holy, Apostolic Church of all times and places real and actual. To confess with our brethren unites us also to our fathers in the faith. In the struggle of the contemporary confessions against the Third Reich, the confessions of the old Church and of the Reformation period received new life. At the Synod of Barmen, Lutherans, Reformed and United, each being loyal to his own confession, made their united confession of Jesus Christ as " the one Word of God ".

The Church's confession is both a witness to the world and a witness in the sight of God; it is not only addressed to the world for God; it is also addressed to God for His own sake; it is therefore both a hymn and a doxology, giving praise for the mighty Act of God. Thus the idea of confession developed in its original New Testament fulness. The Church's confession is always at the same time a witness to the Lordship of Christ in face of the world, a confession of sin, and adoration and praise of God's majesty. The confession must not therefore be understood in its one aspect only, as a new controversial act, or as a never-changing dogmatic possession, or only as a new form of liturgy, or even as a form of church government. If we isolate the

[1] Confession of the Synod of Barmen

different aspects of true confession the whole confession disintegrates.

Looking back on recent years, the Confessing Church has no reason to feel satisfied with itself. Everything that it did was due to the grace of God. And what at first appeared to be judgment, revealed itself as mercy, as soon as we humbled ourselves before it. The destruction of our earthly supports and securities (which the Church had hitherto regarded as the sources of its own stability) proved to be the grace of God; for we were thrown upon our Lord Jesus Christ. The sufferings of the Church were also God's mercy; for through these sufferings Christ permitted us to share in His glory. He permitted us to experience the greatness of the glory of insecurity, danger, poverty and persecution for the Gospel's sake, and to realize what security is prepared for the insecure, what wealth for the poor, and what safety for the persecuted.

AN ADDITIONAL NOTE

by Reinhold von Thadden (formerly Chairman of the " Council of Brethren " in the Confessing Church)

Professor Schlink's admirable treatment of a vast theme was of necessity so brief as to leave room for two possible misunderstandings. Owing to the slowness of correspondence with Germany, this note is added by one who also took part in the struggle but is now living in Switzerland.

I. It is important to point out that it was not only the Protestants who protested against the pagan views of life and against the wickedness and violence of the Nazis. There was an equally strong opposition from the Roman Catholic Church, as is proved by countless examples of bold outspokenness (e.g. Bishop Count von Galen in Munster), of readiness to accept suffering and martyrdom. But it must not be forgotten that the background and the circumstances of the Roman Catholic Church struggle differed widely from the proceedings in the Protestant camp. The protection of the Concordat between the Roman Curia and the Hitler government delayed the development of events, and it was not all bishops, priests and lay people who were martyrs for their faith. Still in the end there were perhaps among the broad masses of the Roman Catholic clergy and faithful at least as many resisters as among the Protestants.

It was probably the Catholic teaching concerning the Eucharist and the fact, connected with it, that Catholics are accustomed to a life of surrender and sacrifice, which lay behind the constancy and endurance of the Catholic martyrs that often compelled our admiration. The Catholic camp was strengthened by the conception of the existence of "natural rights", a conception which helped the Roman Catholics to nail down the errors of the National Socialist doctrines.

II. A second misunderstanding might arise if it were concluded from Professor Schlink's synopsis of the spiritual fruits of the German Church's struggle that the attitude of the Confessional Church, with its Council of Brethren, was the only witness heard during all the years of persecution in Germany. Here two things must be said:

(1) In the discussions which took place between the Nazi church of the German Christians on the one side and the church resistance movement on the other, there was in fact no other really audible voice which gave the message of salvation in Jesus Christ and of a real divine community on earth equally clearly and with the same readiness to take risks. Neither the large number of neutral clergy nor certain groups among the free churches dared at that time to say openly to their congregations or to the world what ought to have been said, and the fact remains that amongst Protestants almost the only ones to show open opposition were those who had some connection with the Confessional Church and had accepted for themselves the resolutions of the Barmen Synod.

(2) But one must not at once conclude from this that in the whole of Christendom there were no currents or movements, which, apart from the actual combatants, were striving to renew the Church on biblical foundations, and which were realizing their object in the face of growing difficulties and threats from the Gestapo. Here Pietism with its fellowships and its free churches, the German Student Christian Movement, and the novel missionary activity of the German "Protestant Weeks" were as important as the quiet constructive work of the "intact" churches of Württemberg, Bavaria, etc.

We might call this Christian desire to cling to that which
the Bible has taught us a sort of passive resistance, while the
Confessional Church had the task of active resistance. But
in fact it is not possible to formulate such distinctions without
saying something essentially false. So one can only refer to the
tragedy of the strained relations for years between "Dahlem"
and "The Lutheran Council", which weakened the unanimity
of the brotherhood in face of their common foe.

This complex of questions raises the further question how to
explain the fact that in the course of years the work of the Church
became concentrated more and more on cultivating the inner
life. One answer is that every other activity of the Church was
year by year to an increasing extent forbidden by the Nazi
authorities, most closely watched and pursued by the Gestapo.
Finally it was only possible to influence the congregations in the
most intimate circles of the Sunday church services and the
church buildings, and even there only when the pastor had the
courage, as a member of the Confessional Church, to take the risk
of exerting his influence. Under these circumstances it is not
surprising that there was a steady fall in the number of the more
secular listeners on the fringe of the Church.

Further, one must remember that a large majority of the
members of the German Protestant Church hardly saw the
problem of the significance of the Church for the state and the
people as Anglo-Saxons see it, and only extremely rarely took
any practical steps about it. Just for this reason one can only
say that in a sense the Protestant Church contributed materially
to the collapse of the Weimar Republic. Probably in their
hearts most members of the Church held "conservative"
opinions, and were filled with love of their country and loyalty
to the state. But after the First World War the Lutheran,
Reformed and "United" (*Uniert*) members of the Protestant
Church were certainly ready in all honesty to work with the
Weimar Constitution and to take a share in the pacification of
the world from inside Germany. As far as I know there were
no National Socialists in the Church until the moment they
seized power.

III

SIGNS OF HIS APPEARING

———————

Volumes I, II and III in this series, prepared for the World Council Assembly, contain a chapter surveying the evidences, from many countries and churches, of renewal in the aspect of the Church's life with which the volume is concerned. Although Miss Wyon has drawn on correspondents from all over the world, such a chapter as this is bound to seem to those who know any region well to have been arbitrary alike in selection and in omission. Only a far longer process of consultation than was possible could have forestalled such criticism. Even as it stands, we believe the picture given to be broadly true and to present by vivid selection what could otherwise be only lifeless generalization.

EVIDENCES OF NEW LIFE IN THE
CHURCH UNIVERSAL

by Olive Wyon

THE Christian Church is entering an entirely new period in her history. The Great Century, with its unparalleled expansion, lies behind. No one knows what lies ahead. As the Church moves out into this unknown future, can she discern the Signs of His Appearing? We can begin our study with the knowledge that the most recent period of church history (from 1914 to 1944) has been described, by so great an historian as Professor Latourette, as "one of the great Ages of Faith". In spite of two devastating world wars, and the world-wide upheaval that these have caused or intensified, never before has the Church Universal been so conscious of its world-wide character; never before has it struck root so deeply in the life of peoples outside Europe and America; never before has it been so deeply aware of the sin of disunion, and so anxious to achieve real unity.

It is the aim of this paper to record some concrete "signs" of this new life—if it exists. The weakness, deadness and apathy of so much church life at the present time is only too evident. It would be easy to paint a picture of the Church in grey and sombre colours. In a certain European country, where the Church was in a very low state, the people used to say: "For six days of the week our pastors are invisible! On the seventh they are incomprehensible!" But when we look at the Church as a whole, elements which may seem insignificant when seen in isolation, gain a certain coherence when seen as part of a spiritual pattern which is emerging out of the mists of confusion and disorder. So our record will be something like a picture by Rembrandt: the darkness will be pierced at vital points by Light from above. We do not forget the darkness; but we look thankfully at the gleams of heavenly light; for they are a promise and an assurance that we possess a Kingdom that cannot be shaken.

I

(i)

"If we have got the Living Church, it is easy to put up the buildings!" These are the words of a Chinese bishop, speaking of his devastated diocese, after the close of the war with Japan. To him, in this context, the "living Church" means the "local Family of God", the group of Christians living in a particular place, which meets regularly, as a family, to worship God. Here the Word of God is preached; here the sacraments are celebrated; here is the local "colony of heaven". A "living Church" in this local form, however small and humble in appearance, is an oasis of order and peace in the midst of confusion and disorder, and a centre of light and hope for the whole neighbourhood. One of the facts of the present Church situation is that such churches *exist*. The atomistic individualism of the recent past is disappearing, to give place to something nearer to the New Testament meaning of the *ecclesia* in a given place, whether that be Corinth or Rome, Shanghai, Berlin, or Cape Town, or some remote village in India, China, Africa, or in the Islands of the Pacific.

In China, for instance, in spite of a depressing political situation, and the shadow of famine, the Church situation is full of hope. These local churches have come through great tribulation, and in some instances, of course, there have been losses. But the main note is one of courage and vitality. Only a very "tough" and hardy people could have come through such experiences with renewed life, and an almost entire absence of hatred and bitterness for their late enemy. Report after report comes from China in these terms: "The churches seem to be full of vitality, and are expanding, largely by their own efforts." In one of the poorest districts of Fukien the church life is very vigorous. These people are hardy and virile. They "make excellent pirates, and even better church workers!"

Many churches were cut off from the rest of China for years, and were left entirely to their own resources. From place after place come reports of increased life and vigour during these years of isolation. In some instances this meant there was an increase of forty per cent in the membership of the local churches. Here is the story of one Chinese Church during the war years. It is in the little town of Fukow, in a district flooded by the Yellow River. When the missionaries returned they had to walk for three days over dried silt or along the tops of the dykes above the swirling waters which surrounded Fukow on nearly every side. The town had suffered terribly from war and from floods. But when the English friends reached the mission compound they found a gatekeeper in charge, a clean and tidy mission house, a renovated church building, and a flourishing school for poor children. The church leaders were soon discovered; then their Western friends heard the whole story. When the Chinese Christian elders knew that the enemy was approaching, they decided that at all costs they must protect the church and mission compound. So several of them moved into the mission house, with such of their belongings as they could save from the floods. When all outside Christian activity was impossible they gave themselves to prayer and to Bible study. Some of them learned the Acts of the Apostles and the Epistle to the Romans by heart, and they all studied these two books together. As soon as it was possible they restarted the school; but the church building was in a terrible state, so, after much prayer and discussion, these people (who were already in great financial straits) decided to give a tithe of everything they could sell. They set to work to clean and repair and redecorate the church. Then they reopened it; when the English friends arrived they found the Sunday services in full swing and a crowded church, with many new people being drawn towards Christ.

(ii)

"Worship is the key-stone of order": nowhere is this sense of peace, meaning, significance, experienced so deeply as in the act of corporate worship. A living Church offers living worship. The very existence of Christian worship in the midst of an unbelieving world is like a light in a dark place. An Iranian official recently visited a Christian church built in Persian style: "There is something here that grips my soul," he exclaimed. The Christian architect (himself a missionary) says: "It is difficult to over-emphasize the value of a church in a Moslem land like Iran. To enter a church there is to set foot on Christian soil: to pass from one environment to another wholly different.

There is something about a church where devout worship is offered which differentiates it from all other places."

Worship in the young African churches is still at the experimental stage. Separatist African sects, with their drums and dances and curious rites, make a great appeal, and draw crowds to their services. The dangers of such meetings are obvious, but an experienced European missionary remarks, caustically: "Too much heat is not necessarily worse than excessive cold!"

A Protestant missionary points out that "Catholic" worship, whether Roman or Anglo-Catholic, has a great attraction for the primitive African, and for Christians of the first generation. The services in the churches founded by "Evangelical" or non-episcopal churches in the West, usually reflect the state of affairs in the Home Church, only on a still "simpler" level. The revivalist fire which once gave this kind of worship its real power has died out, and in too many places the result is respectability —and dullness. "Is it any wonder", writes a missionary from West Africa, "that our Christians say, under their breath, or openly, 'What a weariness it is!'" But there are signs of a new spirit. In Uganda, for instance, where the Church has been established longer than in many parts of Central Africa, there is a deepening sense of worship, and a growing appreciation of beauty in Christian worship. Worship is becoming more closely related to the daily life of an agricultural people. A new kind of service was recently held at the close of the long dry season and the beginning of the rains. The first part consisted of praise and thanksgiving for rain and for water. The second part was an act of dedication. First of all, various members of the congregation brought offerings symbolic of their daily work: soil, roots, seeds, hoes, and laid them before the altar. Then the whole congregation knelt and offered themselves to God for His service.

The same congregation had a memorable Easter Day. Here the growing sense of worship reached its climax. Easter Eve was spent very quietly as a day of preparation, closing with a service late at night in a bare chapel, where the grey stone fabric of a "tomb" stood before the communion table, its entrance closed by a great stone. During the night, a few men and women prepared the chapel for the Easter communion. When the communicants entered the building early on Easter morning, they found the "tomb" open, surrounded by a mass of glowing flowers; while white frangipani blossoms and tiny candles shone like stars on the floor of the sanctuary. The whole service was an act of praise and adoration of the Risen Lord.

One of the most moving instances of living worship comes from the United States of America, from the bogs of New Jersey. This "church" met in a room eighteen by twelve, in a shack that had been turned into a chapel by twelve cranberry pickers. They had come from Florida, where they had been able to go to church. But here in New Jersey, in this out-of-the-way settlement, there was no church and no possibility of public worship. But these men and women were hungry and thirsty for God. So two families decided to live in one room in order to free the other for the chapel. These two families called themselves "God's committee". They cleaned the room, gathered wood, made rough benches, then found volunteers to carve an altar, and a cross upon it. Then they wrote to New York and asked for someone to take their services. A negro minister, a graduate of Yale Divinity School, heard of their need, came to see them, and promised to help them. Someone who visited this "temple in a shack" says that never had he learned more about the reality of worship than in this little community. Above the home-made altar someone had painted a cluster of cranberries, a sign of the dedication of their daily work in the bogs. The service was simple and informal. Negro spirituals were sung; the minister read and prayed, while the people stood with bowed heads in a silence that could be felt. During the sermon questions were asked, and answered. Then a man came forward with two broken bowls, containing Bread and Wine. The Eucharist was celebrated, and Christ came to His people in the Breaking of Bread. This is a living Christian community, and its worship is a token of the dedication of the whole of life—in its hardness and its poverty and its isolation—to the Glory of God.

The keynote of living worship is joy, a joy which breaks out on great occasions. The recent Church Union celebrations at Medak in South India are a case in point. More than five thousand people were present to rejoice over the birth of the Church of South India. Great crowds marched in procession to the cathedral, to the music of village bands, which were making a joyful noise unto the Lord with drums and flutes and cymbals and pipes, and all manner of musical instruments. As the proces-

sion drew nearer, the Christian Girls' School started a familiar
Telegu lyric:

> *O what rejoicing! O what rejoicing!*
> *Gladness all telling above!*
> *Jesus our Master our sins hath forgiven,*
> *For all is the bliss of His love.*

This lyric has a tune which sets people dancing in their hearts,
and the great procession took it up with fervour. The service in
the cathedral was deeply impressive. And at the close, the
singing of the Telegu lyric:

> *Holy, Holy, Holy, Blessed Lord,*
> *Can the tongues of purest angels*
> *All Thy praise and grace record!*

lifted all hearts to God.

(iii)

New life within the Church is not only manifested in the
regular worship of the local community, or on great occasions.
"A rediscovery of the New Testament Church" is also visible
in the *liturgical movement*, which aims at renewing the worship
of local parishes or congregations within various communions.
It is a striking fact that the same urge to revitalize the liturgical
life of the Church is present in every part of the Universal
Church at the present time: in the Orthodox Church, the
Roman Catholic Church, and in many Protestant churches, with
their differing traditions. In those churches which possess an
ancient liturgy the effort is made to fill the external forms with
meaning, and to encourage the faithful to know themselves to be
part of the Body of Christ in their own town or village. In the
Protestant churches, especially in those which had almost
entirely lost all sense of the meaning of liturgical worship, in
many countries there is a new movement in favour of liturgical
practice.

In France, for instance, the restoration of unity among the
Reformed churches has led to a renewal of liturgical life. A new
love of the Bible has brought with it a desire for greater reality
and beauty in worship. A Commission for the renewal of the

liturgy was set up in 1946, and it has already accomplished much. Space does not permit us to describe the work of this Commission in detail, but one point of great importance must be noted: the Commission is quite clear that henceforth the Eucharist must be given its rightful place in public worship, and no longer be regarded as an "additional" service.

This emphasis in the French Reformed Church on liturgical renewal, and on the centrality of the Eucharist, is part of a renewal of spiritual life as a whole. This renewal has three main characteristics: (*a*) the return of the Church to the Bible; (*b*) a new sense of the Church as a divine organism (not an association merely formed by men); (*c*) emphasis on the centrality of the Eucharist.

A similar movement, entitled *Church and Liturgy,* is at work in French Switzerland. The young French and Swiss pastors who are active in these movements feel strongly that "in re-establishing a liturgical framework in their services they re-discover the great commonplace of primitive Christianity, and, at the same time, without ceding anything of doctrine, they arrange new ways of approach to other communions".

The liturgical movement in the Roman Catholic Church is active in several countries; in Germany and Austria and also in France, Belgium, Italy and Portugal. It has already produced a considerable literature, much of which is welcomed by Protestant readers. Theodore Wedel remarks: "The literature of the Roman liturgical movement reads as if the Reformation had come alive again," for "a New Testament doctrine of the Church, a rediscovery of the meaning of the Church as the Body of Christ, runs through this Movement as a whole".[1]

On the other hand, while there is a definite desire in some Protestant churches to enter into the ancient heritage of the liturgies of the Church, this movement is not a return to the past. Its leaders realize that "liturgy is a community possession", and that "only a Spirit-bearing body can create liturgical worship—and only if it lives a life in time", that is, a life that is fully rooted in the actual life of society, and is aiming at bringing the Rule of God into every part of the life of mankind. Younger men and women in the Reformed churches, in particular, are aware that there is nothing archaic in this renewed interest in liturgy. They see it as an answer to the need of the

[1] *The Coming Great Church,* p. 33.

day for living community, under the guidance of the Holy Spirit. They are fully aware that a new liturgical tradition requires an act of creation. As one of them puts it: "We need a modern worship service, a living one, and, after so many 'venerable' texts, a youthful liturgy."

(iv)

The living worship of the Church springs from the living revelation of God in Christ, mediated through the Bible. The Bible is a searchlight in the life of the Church, for it lays bare its sins and failures; it alone can show whether a Church is alive or not. The Bible, which brings the message of God's love for all mankind, is a fire which burns, as well as a balm which heals.

Through all the recent storms of persecution, enemy occupation, war and upheaval, the Church in many lands has learned that its power to endure, to resist all temptations to lower its standard, come from the Bible.

The Church in Germany certainly found the Bible to be its sheet-anchor during the period of persecution. From 1933 to 1938, each year the sales of the Bible exceeded the sales of *Mein Kampf* by more than 200,000. The sale of the Bible in Germany rose from 230,000 in 1930 to 1,120,000 in 1939. This increase was due not only to the experience of the Confessional Church, but to a similar Bible Movement within the Roman Catholic Church. A vigorous Bible work had been going for some years, but the pace was accelerated by the troubled times through which the Church was passing. One feature of this work was the Bible Conferences for priests in which the clergy were taught how to spread the knowledge of the Bible: in 1943 one hundred and thirty-eight such conferences were held. This increased interest in the Bible also helped to draw Protestants and Catholics nearer together in their time of common strain. At one time joint services were held in a Berlin prison by imprisoned Catholic priests and Lutheran pastors, for "the Word of God is not bound".

A return to the Bible is a characteristic of the renewed life within the Orthodox Church in Greece. "'Apostolic men" like Makrakis and the Archimandrite Matthopulos based their efforts to awaken new life within their own Church on a deep and prayerful study of the Bible. Present movements, like that of

Zoë (Life), owe their inception to these two men. Among many other literary activities *Zoë* also acts as a Bible Society. It prints the Bible in the original Greek; the New Testament reached a third edition in 1938 with 100,000 copies; the Old Testament (Septuagint) has also been issued in a smaller edition. Another movement which is at work within the life of the Greek Orthodox Church is that known as the *Anaplasis* movement. The basis of all its literary and evangelistic work is the study of the Bible led by university professors. In Orthodox Greece to-day there is indeed a "hunger and thirst for the Word of God".

These three examples from Europe could be multiplied over and over again from every continent. In China, for instance, the demand for Bibles has been increasing, in spite of the present difficult situation, and in spite of all the troubles caused by the war with Japan. The life of the Church is being deepened and strengthened by emphasis upon the Bible. All over China new seminaries and Bible schools are being established. In these simple "colleges" the lay leaders of the Church are being trained, while a more advanced theological training is being given in centres of higher education. Roman Catholic scholars are also actively producing Chinese translations of the Psalms and other books; their printing-presses can hardly keep pace with the demand.

In Great Britain, after a period of decline, the tide has begun to turn. There are many societies which encourage the daily reading of the Bible, such as the Scripture Union, the International Bible Reading Association, the Church Bible Study Union (with members in forty countries), and others. One of the best known is the Bible Reading Fellowship, a movement which began very modestly in a London parish (St. Matthew's, Brixton). The clergy and parish workers came together to see what could be done to deepen the religious life of their own congregation. So in January 1922 the "Fellowship of St. Matthew" came into existence, and one hundred people joined it. In two years there were 300 members in the parish. Then three other parishes joined the fellowship, and the membership rose to 500 at the end of 1924. Then came a time of great expansion: by February 1929 there were 20,000 members; in 1939 there were 238,000. By this time the movement had spread far beyond Great Britain. The Monthly Notes were being issued in Mandarin (for China), in Bengali, Tamil, and Arabic.   Australia, New Zealand, and Canada formed their own auxiliaries.   Members are of every shade of ecclesiastical opinion, and although the movement remains an Anglican one, many members and writers of Notes belong to the Free Churches.   During the six years of war there were 98,000 new members.   There are now 6,600 branches and the Monthly Notes go out to 351,000 people.   The leaders can only say with amazement: "This is the Lord's doing, and it is wonderful." They realize that "there are depths of meaning in the Bible that man has not yet fathomed.   The Bible is ahead of the times."

(v)

In life on life the Eternal witness stands,
Enlightenment and freedom in His hands.

These lines from a poem by a Bengali woman suggest the gift that Christ has brought to Indian women.   The actual achievements may not yet be many, but their quality is of a very high order.   From the days of Christian pioneers like Pandita Ramabai, who introduced a ferment into Hindu society which is still at work at the present day, when Indian Christian women are taking a responsible share in the life of their country and of the Church, there can be no doubt that here, in the activity and character of women leaders, is an evidence of living Christian faith which is something new.

In hospitals, schools, colleges, as well as in the directly evangelistic work of the Church, "there is a company of Indian women leaders of quite outstanding ability, devotion and character".   A recent Christian visitor to India says: "Few things in connection with the Church in India were more encouraging and impressive than this."   More and more directly missionary responsibility is being borne by "these Indian women colleagues".   The same writer was impressed by the work of the Biblewomen in South India.   He says: "In many villages I could easily pick out groups of those who have come under their training and influence.   They had a bright and alert bearing that made them quite distinctive."   Women also take a share in "revival" movements: Pennamma Sannyasini, a woman preacher of Travancore, travels about South India and Ceylon, preaching and conducting Conventions.

One of the most recent movements within the Church in India is the establishment of the Missionary Training Centre for Indian Women Workers in connection with the Women's Christian College at Madras. This is a small beginning, but it is full of promise. It " aims at giving women of education and experience a special training that will fit them for the new responsibilities that await them in Church and mission service ". Amidst so much wealth of material it is difficult to choose an outstanding illustration of the work of Indian women in the Church, but a particularly characteristic piece of service is that of the Bethel Ashram in Travancore. This Ashram was begun by two women: one Indian and the other English; it has now grown into a resident community of from one hundred to two hundred women, girls, and little children. This Ashram, which is entirely a women's community, is thoroughly Indian in character. It does much good work of a practical kind, and it exerts a creative influence. This is not surprising when we see how much emphasis is laid on prayer and worship. The chapel is the centre of the Ashram. These women know and live by the truth that apart from Christ they can do nothing.

Similar evidences of the value of the service of Christian women comes from China. " The women will be the salvation of China ", was the verdict of a foreigner in China some years before the recent war. Now that the curtain has been lifted, and we know what has been happening in China, we can see how great a part has been, and is being played, by Chinese women. Here is a typical instance: during the war a Chinese lady was in charge of a Christian hospital in Hong Kong. She had to handle a situation which often seemed desperate: she endured dangers, privations and humiliations; she and her fellow-workers met this situation with great courage and dignity. Crisis after crisis arose which required the greatest wisdom and tact. She took it all as " part of the day's work "; but one who saw her soon after the liberation of the city and district says: " There are not many stories of quiet heroism in the war to beat it, the triumph of Christian faith over fear and difficulty."

Again, in Amoy the Chinese minister of a large and flourishing church was caught in Manila when the war broke out, and could not get back to China. With the help of an evangelist, his wife carried on his ministry, " undaunted by imprisonment and torture at the hands of the Japanese, and not abating one jot of her zeal on account of her sufferings". In other instances, women with little education, but full of love and zeal, spread the faith wherever they are. In a small market town where there is no church yet, a Christian woman has lived and witnessed to such effect that she has gathered a Christian group of fifty to sixty people from eight villages, as well as from her own little town.

In many countries much directly evangelistic work is being initiated and carried on by women: we have seen that this is the case in India; it is certainly so in China; in France some of the most promising efforts of the French Reformed Church are those carried on by women. They are part of a considered plan to create small Christian communities in working-class districts which will grow into local churches. Thus from the beginning, a team, or a group, lives as a Christian fellowship in the midst of a pagan neighbourhood. These groups are based on a Rule of "prayer, poverty, witness, and work". One such team settled in an industrial district on the outskirts of Paris; it was composed of three women, a trained nurse, a midwife, and an evangelist. Between them, they earned just enough to carry them through (the "evangelist" did other work in the summer months to enable her to make her own financial contribution to the common pool). After some months, the friendliness and service of these three women had drawn people to them. Sunday services were held regularly: Bible study groups were being carried on; children and young people were coming to clubs and classes. A local church was coming into being.

Evangelistic work within the framework of the Eastern Orthodox Church was begun in Greece (during the German occupation) under the influence of an educated Greek woman. In 1942, Mrs. Chrysanthi Makrykosta, the daughter of a well-known surgeon in Athens, called together a number of women from the upper classes of society, and several men in influential positions. The members of this group took counsel together for the spiritual welfare of their people; they have now started courses of addresses and lectures which are given in the University of Athens, in the Law Faculty, every Sunday afternoon. The movement calls itself the "Christian Corner"; it has districts; everywhere the effort is made to awaken real religious life within the framework of the Orthodox Church. The members of this movement also do a great deal of pastoral work in the hospitals of Athens, and among the numerous patients in the Leper Colony near the city.

It is not difficult to recognize signs of God's working in the freedom and creativeness of Christian women leaders in different countries; but perhaps the most creative and fruitful work of all—in its actual influence—is that of the Christian women who are never mentioned in "reports"; whose names never figure on any lists; the people whom one scarcely notices, and of whom one never hears. These are the women, often mothers and grandmothers, who live a life of loving thought for others and of unceasing hard work; who train their children in the knowledge and love of God; who lead them into the life of prayer and the love of the Bible.

When the Christian life has almost disappeared outwardly, these women as a matter of course will conduct simple services in their homes for their neighbours and their children. These are the people who keep the flame of Christian faith burning in the secret of the home. These women do more for the life of the Church Universal than anyone can imagine. Throughout the recent war we get glimpses, now and again, of such humble devoted lives. And we know that this hidden life and service of women in their homes is being given freely and unselfconsciously all over the world to-day. Little is ever said about this service, which is almost more important than anything else at the present time; but reading between the lines of the papers sent in from every part of the world on *The Life and Work of Women in the Church*, we can see that behind it all stands this hidden, devoted, creative life.

In a rural district in Africa there is a Christian Women's Guild! At a recent conference nearly all the speaking was done by African women, with a freshness, originality, and sense of drama which were delightful. The whole conference was full of happiness. These women, and their daughters, have a great responsibility. Most of the year the men are away at the mines or elsewhere, and "all really depends on the women—the welfare of country and people, and, most of all, the building up of the Church".

A new movement which is full of promise in several countries is the "Christian Home Movement". The Indian leaders of this movement say plainly "that the Christian home is not the affair of Women's Meetings or Mothers' Unions alone, but that it is the affair of men, women, and children, who, having been placed in Christian families, are privileged to share in the greatest Christian Home of all, the Church Universal ".

An illustration of what these ideals can effect when put into practice comes from South India. In a certain district men and women *together* are co-operating in a spontaneous revival movement. The leaders are a husband and wife from Madras. They work as free-lances, but are glad to co-operate with the churches. "The leaders, husband and wife, work together as one, sharing alike in platform and personal work." Their helpers are being trained on the same lines, husband and wife co-operating in prayer, work and witness. These Indian evangelists lay great stress on the Christian Home. Their work is bearing fruit. " Converts from Hinduism are coming by families ", husband and wife standing together in their new life.[2]

(vi)

A characteristic sign of " new life " is one which is being evoked by the mass paganism of our day. Laymen and laywomen are feeling the need to carry the Christian message and the Christian life into the whole range of their daily life and work. Roman Catholic women are already doing this in a deep and systematic manner through the Grail Movement in Holland and in Great Britain. The new Protestant centres which are springing up in Switzerland (Bossey, Essertines, Geneva), Germany (Bad Boll), France (Cluny), Sweden (Sigtuna), Holland (Driebergen) and elsewhere, for " lay training ", all have the same aim: to proclaim the Lordship of Christ in every sphere of human life, in and through the exercise of one's vocation. Behind all this new movement lies the conviction that nothing but a total Christianity will have any power to combat mass paganism and materialism.[3]

Christian Youth Movements are too well known to need description here. The Oslo Conference of 1947 may be regarded as a symbol of the strength, vitality and promise of these movements which are such a vital part of the life of the Universal Church.

[2] Telegu Baptist Convention.
[3] A brief survey of these laymen's movements all over Europe is to be found in Volume III of this series, *The Church and the Disorder of Society.*

II

One of the abiding characteristics of the Christian Church as a whole is its power of inward renewal. Again and again, when the fire of Christian faith and love is burning low, and the Church seems almost moribund, new movements, led by inspired men and women, have arisen to meet the need of the day. Latourette points out that these unofficial, spontaneous movements, in their turn, stimulate and fertilize the organized church life of the day. To go no further back than the seventeenth century, and to confine our attention to Protestantism, we can trace this line of spiritual renewal from the Puritan movement in England, and in Holland, to the continental movement which may be described by the general term of Pietism, and on to the renewal of the Church of the Brethren, which brought forth the Moravian Church, with its extensive missionary work, and its influence upon Wesley and the Methodist Revival, followed by the birth of the whole modern missionary movement.

(i)

One of the primary forms in which this new life bursts forth is that which is called a "revival" or a "religious awakening", like the Methodist Revival in England at the end of the eighteenth century, or the "Great Awakening" in the Thirteen Colonies of America. The largest revival movements of this kind took place during the nineteenth century, most of them in Anglo-Saxon countries. On the Continent, through the influence of Pietism, a wave of "revival" spread over Western Europe. The result was that "Christianity had a more extensive and a more profound effect upon mankind in the nineteenth century" than ever before.

In the United States of America the influence of these revivals was shown "in the resourcefulness and adaptability of American Protestantism in meeting its varied problems". They also left their mark in the emphasis on the need for personal religion, and in the impulse to social reform which was such a marked feature of American Protestantism in the nineteenth century.

One of the most significant events in the American religious life of the present day is the rise of new sects which "are sweeping across America like a spiritual hurricane". The respectable people in the well-established churches may be "tired of revivals"—especially of a stereotyped and organized kind—but thousands, and possibly millions of people, dissatisfied with the church life to which they are accustomed, and longing for something more vital, have broken away from the larger communions and have founded new sects. This tendency has been intensified by the movements of population during the war. Whenever members of sects from the rural districts moved to cities to earn their living they took their religion with them, and started small groups for worship and fellowship in empty shops or garages or in their own houses. At first the middle-class people in the older churches found this movement difficult to understand, and regarded it as a war-time phenomenon which would fade out as soon as the war was over. Now, however, the movement is being taken seriously, and those who have studied it with sympathy and the desire to understand, see that it bears a striking resemblance to the great evangelical revivals of the eighteenth and nineteenth centuries; they now realize that this is not a wholly new movement, but that it has been growing in strength for the past twenty years or more.

It is impossible to guess how many people are affected by this movement: some would say twenty millions; a careful observer has said from two to three millions. Numbers, however, are less important than the spirit which impels these people, and there is no doubt that there is something vital about them. There is an " eschatological " fervour and glow about these sects. Their numbers grow because they " shout their religion, sing it, pray it, wherever they are—in the factory, field, or on the road ". They print and distribute striking tracts and posters; they spend money on broadcasting and on newspaper evangelism before they think about buildings. In one sect alone (Jehovah's Witnesses) 45,000 men and women give part or full-time each week to evangelism by word or tract or open-air preaching.

Of course this emotional kind of religion is sometimes exploited by unscrupulous people for their own ends. But in the main it is true to say that these people are genuine, and that their religious experience means everything to them; that is why they are so eager to share it with other people. " At their best ", says an American observer, " the sects have an answer for the guilty feelings of millions of people for whom sin is still a consuming problem." The positive results of this type of revival are evident: a love of the Bible; healing of disease; moral improvement; debts paid.

Many of these sects are very small and meteoric, and these are usually the ones with the longest names: " The Apostolic Overcoming of the Holy Church of God "; " Christ's Sanctified Holy Church Coloured "; " The Pentecostal Fire-baptized Holiness Church ". But there is one, called the " Church of God and the Saints of Christ ", which began in the year 1896, when a man called William S. Crowdy, a Negro cook working on the Santa Fé Railway, had a vision in which God " called " him by name, told him to leave his present work and to lead his people into the true religion. He obeyed at once; went to Kansas and began. Nearly fifty years later Crowdy's work survives in some two hundred churches with 35,000 members. Such an instance reminds us of Ruskin's phrase about " this any place where God lets down the ladder ".

The appeal of these sects is mostly to the under-privileged, the poor and the forgotten. These smaller sects are found in the dingy side streets of the great cities, or in lonely valleys among the mountains of Kentucky and Tennessee—or in the heart of a group of Negro shacks far in the South, or on the coast of Southern California. " Not many wise, not many noble . . ." would serve as an apt description " of all the more sober small sects of America ", says Willard Sperry. Here again we see that " the really creative, church-forming religious movements are the work of the lower strata ",[4] for " the sect is born out of a combination of spiritual and economic forces ". In any case, " the sectarian outbreak of religion ", says a careful observer, " is after all a renewal of vitality . . . in religion and in the Church ".[5]

In India, revival movements occur both within the churches —in the form of large and influential conventions—and outside organized church life in free-lance activities. Some " revivalists " form new sects; others—many of them *sadhus*— go about the country-side preaching and often healing. Historically speaking, revival movements in India and Ceylon owe a great deal to the Welsh revival of the present century, to the Keswick Convention, and to the work of men like Spurgeon, Finney, and Moody and Sankey in Britain and America.

To turn to a very different environment, a revival movement —strongly biblical in character—has been going on in China

[4] E. Troeltsch.   [5] H. P. Douglass.

for some years. It appears to have begun about 1926. It continued to spread through many provinces of China until the beginning of the war. The movement spread from north to south: from Manchuria into Shantung, Hopeh, Honan, Shansi, Hupeh, Hunan, and into other provinces as well, including Fukien.

In Manchuria, in 1933, the Presbyterian missionaries said that in several places "flood-tides of spiritual power have swept people out of the complacency of their former lives and carried them on waves of emotional confession and agonizing prayer into church membership". The leaders were Chinese, both men and women. "Bible classes are full, and meetings are crowded. Dead churches have come to life again." In Shantung a missionary writes: "The revival is a work of God . . . the evidence of changed lives; opium given up, idols torn down, quarrels of years' standing made up, village hoodlums turned into humble men of prayer . . ."

When communication between the occupied part of China and the outside world was reopened in 1946 it was found that this kind of revival had been going on—more quietly perhaps—even during the war. In many places the effects are still evident. A recent English visitor to Amoy found the churches there full of vitality, and obviously still carried on the wave of new life which had been brought to South Fukien some time before by Dr. Sung and other Chinese evangelists. Here is an authentic work of God.

This widespread awakening has already had a great effect on the young Church in China. It has given a great impetus to the tendency to make the Church indigenous. All the committees and conferences in the world could not do what this revival has achieved. Now the Chinese Church knows for itself that "God has visited His people"—where they are; and that they have their own place in His purpose.

The characteristics of this movement are to some extent similar to those in other countries: a deep sense of sin; joy of conversion; love of the Bible. The young Church had prayed for a revival, but it came at first in the form of a judgment on the House of God, and, in its initial stages, it was a very grave and difficult experience. Sins of the past had to be acknowledged, confessed, and forgiven; men and women who had previously felt themselves in no need of repentance now knew that they too were sinners—and this not in a general way, but they saw their need of forgiveness for specific sins of omission or commission. It was very personal; each person knew that God was *there*, dealing with him. It is evident that this is the work of *God*; no human power could have such a cleansing, renewing, effect. The genuine leaders were increasingly driven to prayer; they realized that of themselves they could do nothing. Their experiences led them to the conviction that "when God can get hold of someone . . . to do the work of an intercessor, then He can begin to release spiritual forces for the renewal of His Church".

(ii)

"The fact that to-day we have reached an extremity of secularism suggests that we have reached a new point of departure for religion. Christianity itself is eternally true, but Christianity will have to be positively recreated within the lives of individuals, in terms of personal experience." These words may be regarded as a summary of the aims and hopes of the many small and hidden groups which are springing up within the Church in many lands to-day. What is the inward urge which creates such groups? In nearly every case it is the desire for a closer and more sustained contact with God. Closely allied to this is a deep desire to have a closer contact with one's fellows; to enter into a more living experience of human community. Since the one depends upon the other, it is evident that the impulse is a true one.

Such people, before all else, want to learn to *pray*. They are loyal members of their churches; they have usually "said their prayers" all their lives long; they are regular attenders of the services of their own communion. But their souls "are athirst for the Living God", and so the small, intimate group is born. Natural leaders emerge; and in the course of time a group of "seekers" becomes a creative community. Sometimes such a group is a "cell" within a parish or congregation; sometimes its members belong to different churches in the same neighbourhood. In the intimacy of the group and the common search for better ways of praying and living a new unity comes into being. "I used to be a terrible spike," said an English Anglo-Catholic layman one day, "until I heard a Nonconformist pray—and all my spikes fell off."

Groups of this kind exist all over Great Britain. Most of them are small; and most of them are little known, save by those who belong to them. Periodically their experience is pooled in a conference which has the formidable name of *The Advisory Group for Christian Cells*. Its purpose is well stated in the following paragraph: "There is springing up within the Church, and on the fringes of it, a movement of great promise and vitality. No one is organizing it. It has come into being in response to man's need, and we believe that it is a movement of the Holy Spirit. Its distinguishing feature is that small circles of friends gather together at regular intervals in one another's houses. They meet for prayer, intercession and Bible study, and to plan together for common action." The writer continues: "The ultimate aim is to renew the life of the whole Church. The Church will catch fire when there are enough of these 'living coals'. . . ."

Other similar groups carry on a similar activity: there is the *Fellowship of the Holy Cross*; the *Servants of the Spirit*; the *Society of the Companions of Jesus*; the "*Together*" *Groups*; the *Fellowship of Meditation*; the *Associates of the Iona Community*; the list could be made much longer; but these few names give an inkling of the kind of spiritual activity which is working like a hidden leaven within the Church, as well as on its fringes, in Great Britain.

In addition to these informal groups which meet in private houses, or in rooms lent for the occasion, small centres are being established where men and women can come away from their work for a few days to pray and talk and think together, in order that they may return with new courage and vision to their ordinary life. The Retreat Movement in the Church of England is an outstanding example of a spiritual activity of this kind, set at the heart of organized church life. Similar houses to be used for retreats, belonging to other communions, have been founded in the United States. High above the Blue Valley in North-east Pennsylvania stands Kirkridge, which is first of all a centre for religious retreat and study, and also the headquarters of "a group of Christians scattered over America and beyond, living under an agreed daily discipline"; it also represents a movement within the Church "seeking God's revival of the Church primarily through the ministry". Spiritually it has many affinities with the Iona community in Scotland. Trabuco, in the hills of Southern California, is another centre "where the religious life is attempted ". The building stands alone on the summit of a mountain ridge with a vast view over "waves of tawny hills like lions' shoulders in the sun ".

These two centres for retreat and consultation in America are typical of a quiet movement connected with the *Wider Quaker Fellowship* which is fostering the practice of retreats and of serious study of the life of prayer. A paper called *Inward Light* helps to keep the members of this scattered movement together and gives news and results of common experiments. It reports "a growing concern among Friends and others for inner life and growth"; similar movements are: the *Tens* (Methodist) in Mexico and China, and the *Order of the Holy Cross* in U.S.A. At Pendle Hill, the Friends' centre for religious and social study, frequent Retreats are held. A monthly devotional booklet, entitled *The Upper Room*, is produced by the Methodist Church in the United States. Its circulation runs into millions, and it is published in Spanish, Portuguese, Chinese, and other languages, as well as in Braille for the blind.

Permanent centres for Christian life and service which are closely allied in spirit to these Western groups and movements are the Ashrams of India. Here an old Hindu form of religion has been revived and adapted to Christian use. The first Ashrams appeared over two thousand five hundred years ago "as forest dwellings where men devoted to religion lived the simple life, and to which disciples came, not only to receive instruction, but to be trained in the realization of spiritual ideals". Twenty years ago, however, few Indian Christians knew what an Ashram meant. Now they are springing up in many parts of India. Nineteen in India and one in Ceylon are in touch with one another. Six are Anglican; five are Mar Thoma (Reformed Syrian Church); two are Methodist; one belongs to the Orthodox Syrian Church; four are inter-denominational; and one is inter-religious, in which Hindus and Christians co-operate.

(iii)

"Every revival is unlike any other revival. It seems that God breaks out in an unexpected way every time. . . . To those who are watching for the first signs of the coming revival, the omens are convincing, God is going to break out on the land." One of these "omens" characteristic of this "great Age of Faith" is the urge towards Christian unity. This impulse takes many forms and appears in many countries. The first impetus seems to have come from missionary conferences in 1854 and 1860 in New York and Liverpool respectively; the first stage in this movement culminated in the Edinburgh Conference of 1910. The second stage followed, and gathered speed after 1914; its various expressions are usually summed up in the general term, the "Ecumenical Movement", which finally led to the proposal to establish the World Council of Churches: "an organization more inclusive ecclesiastically than any other the Christian Church has ever known" (Latourette).

No great organization, however, will of itself create spiritual unity. Everything depends upon the "seed of unity" being implanted within small groups or "cells" within the local church, and thus working secretly, and often without observation, within the Body of Christ. When such phrases as "the Communion of Saints" or the "priesthood of all believers" begin to glow with new meaning, and to influence the actual church life of a district, this "seed" will grow; it may become a great tree, whose leaves will be for the healing of the nations.

An example of Christian unity in practice, on the local scale, is the parish of St. Matthew Moorfields, Bristol. Here there is "a breath of the authentic fire of Pentecost". The former Bishop of Bristol said once: "People are always asking me to stop things that are going on in Moorfields, but I can't resist the Holy Ghost!" It is indeed largely due to the wisdom and sympathy of this Bishop that this novel experiment has been able to continue. One of its main concerns has been, and is, to carry on the work of the parish as part of a United Front. This means that for the past five years the work of the churches in this whole area of Bristol has been carried on together: two Anglican parishes, three Methodist churches and one Congregational church. Every Tuesday morning, after a corporate Communion Service at St. Matthew's, the ministers of these five churches meet to make joint plans for the work of the Church in their district. This does not mean that differences of outlook and belief are ignored; they are known and respected. But it does mean that "at any and every point where a united witness is possible they try to give it". This is done not merely because it is far more practical and effective, but because the leaders in this experiment "believe that thereby we are living, and can give to our congregations, a Christianity nearer to the mind of Christ than the less dangerous, but not necessarily less sinful, acceptance of the traditional lines of ecclesiastical division".

This group of churches has a United Communion Service once a month, in which, as one of the clergy of the district puts it: "We seek to go as far as we possibly can without abandoning what each denomination has of distinctive value to contribute to the ecumenical Church."

On the large scale, this impulse towards unity has led to a number of actual unions. Several have been in existence for some years; others are being considered. The most recent, and the most striking of these unions is the Church of South India. It is significant because it is the first time that episcopal and non-episcopal churches have united. The fact that "India is a mission-field in which nine of the eleven living religions of the world are found" may have been one of the reasons that has moved the Christian Church in this part of India to lead the way. For a long time past Christian leaders—Indian and European and American—had been accustomed to meet each other every year to confer together about their common task, and to worship together; thus to some extent they had "grown together" before any scheme of union had been launched.

This union is an epoch-making event. It is true, of course, that the act of union ushers in a period of "growing together", and in some quarters has evoked, not welcome, but grave misgiving. A great deal will depend on the success of this venture for the whole future of church unity all over the world.

The ceremony at which the Church of India, Burma and Ceylon, the South India United Church, and the South India Provincial Synod of the Methodist Church, became the "Church of South India", took place in St. George's Cathedral, Madras, on September 27th, 1947. There were 600 people inside the cathedral; outside, a palm-leaf awning had been erected which sheltered another 2,000 persons. At 8 a.m. the first procession entered the cathedral and moved down the nave. The bishops wore simple white rochets with saffron-coloured stoles (saffron is the colour of religious devotion in India). An Indian bishop presided (Bishop C. K. Jacob). The Call to Worship was followed by the singing of the hymn *O God, our Help in ages past*. Bishop Jacob offered the prayer of invocation; then a layman read the seventeenth chapter of John as the lesson. Dr. Wierenga, the Senior Presbyter of the S.I.U.C. (from the Dutch

Reformed Church of America) then led the congregation in a prayer of confession. The Resolutions of the Churches and the Books of Signatures of Assent were then placed upon the Holy Table. There was a deep hush as the three representatives read the resolutions of their churches accepting the Union. Each man in turn went to the chancel steps to read his part. Then each carried to the altar a signed copy of the Basis of Union and the Constitution of the Church of South India. This was followed by a prayer offered by an Indian clergyman. Then Bishop Jacob, standing at the altar, with his pastoral staff in his hand, read the following Solemn Declaration: " Dearly beloved brethren, in obedience to the Lord Jesus Christ, the Head of the Church, who on the night of His Passion prayed that His disciples might be one: and by authority of the governing bodies of the uniting churches, whose resolutions have been read in your hearing, and laid in prayer before Almighty God, I do hereby declare that these three churches . . . are become ONE CHURCH OF SOUTH INDIA . . . in the Name of the Father, and of the Son, and of the Holy Spirit. Amen." The whole congregation sang the *Te Deum*. The work of twenty-eight years had at last come to fruition. A great step had been taken, and " there was great joy in that city ".

The signs of renewal within the Church Universal may not be many, but they are full of promise. In the midst of a world in disorder and despair, these points of light show that God is at work. In the words of Christopher Dawson: " Wherever Christianity exists there survives a seed of unity, a principle of spiritual order, which cannot be destroyed by war, or by the conflict of economic interests, or the failure of political organization." Thus it seems to be the will of God to carry out His purpose of redemption and restoration through "a spiritual nucleus of believers who are the bearers of the seed of unity". The Church does not know whither she is being led. But as she moves out into the unknown future she knows that she has been given an imperishable " seed " of divine life, to cast into the furrows of this world. In this hope she prays: " Awake, O North wind, and come thou South; blow upon my garden, that the spices thereof may flow out ", bringing forgiveness, healing, and new life to the whole family of mankind.

IV

THE ECUMENICAL MOVEMENT

The occasion for the production of this volume was an officially representative gathering of Christians which constituted a new factor in the life of Christendom. So this book ends with a section which considers some of the outstanding questions raised at this juncture in the history of the ecumenical movement. We consider the tension between regional and confessional loyalties within the Universal Church, the growing significance of the Younger Churches in this new fellowship, the causes for the absence from the fellowship of the largest single Christian communion, and, finally, the meaning of this new, permanent organ of the ecumenical movement, the World Council of Churches itself.

1

REGIONAL AND CONFESSIONAL LOYALTIES
IN THE UNIVERSAL CHURCH

by Oliver S. Tomkins

I THE ROAD TO UNITY

WE seek Christian unity. But when we begin to ask how
we reach it from the positions our churches actually
occupy to-day, the answer in practice is that it is either
through the growing together and mutual understanding of *confessions*[1] or through the closer co-operation of Christian bodies
in a region,[1] sometimes culminating in a regional achievement
of church union. It is interesting that, within the ecumenical
movement in recent years, the trend towards unity has expressed
itself in the Faith and Order tradition primarily in terms of
confessions—how does Lutheranism accord with Anglicanism?
Orthodoxy with Calvinism? and so forth. Regional differences
are only of significance here if they coincide with theological
differences. On the other hand, the more practical aspect, which
is symbolized best by the Department of the World Council for
Reconstruction and Inter-Church Aid, has been a great en-
courager of *regional* agreement. Separated churches in the same
area have transcended their differences both to promote the giving and to administer the receiving of practical help—and often
have found, in the process, that their relationships to each other
are being altered at a deeper level. At the point where doctrine
and practice meet—in evangelism—the ecumenical movement
has hardly begun serious activity, partly because at this very
point the tension between confessional and regional loyalties is
most acute. The practice of " comity " in the mission-field was
not a solving but a postponing of the problem. When the continued existence of comity becomes unbearable (as in South
India) and is resolved in a regional church-union scheme, it
precipitates some acute problems for confessional loyalty.

We all profess loyalty to the Church of our own confession,
which may also exist in a world-wide form. None of us can

---

[1] Problems of *terminology* in each of these cases are discussed in what follows.

escape the demand to express Christian unity, so far as we can, in the various regions in which God has set us to live. The purpose of this essay is to set out, as clearly as its short limits allow, the relation of these loyalties to each other.

In the anomalies of a divided Christendom, the word *Church* is used in a variety of senses. New Testament and primitive usage permit only two. One sense is that of the organically one Body of Christ, the New Israel, to be in which is inseparably connected with being in Christ, in which there are no divisions of race or class but which is set in the world as an earnest of the "age" not of this world. The other sense is that of the *local* manifestations of this one body. In Apostolic times it was often very small, "the Church that is in the house of Priscilla and Aquila" (Rom. xvi, 5); or the Christian community in a pagan city, "the Church of God which is at Corinth" (1 Cor. i, 2). The author of the *Revelation* addresses his messages "to the seven Churches which are in Asia". Any other use of the word "Church" is thus scripturally unsound.

But the division of Christendom has produced three other concepts, of which the word "church" is often used, and by those who use it, with a temporary legitimacy, the regional church, the denomination or confession and (in some cases) the inter-national organization of the confession. These concepts must now be more closely examined.

II THE REGIONAL CHURCH

An early extension of "Church" beyond the strictly local is to the regional, or often national, Church. The latter is an elusive concept, because the concept of nation is itself elusive. *Nations* in some sense are co-eval with civilization: what has given "nations" new overtones in recent centuries is the development of *nationalism*. But long before the development of the nationalisms of the fifteenth and sixteenth centuries, "national churches" had begun to emerge. Their history is complicated. It must suffice here to say that the various racial and regional loyalties of the Byzantine Empire quickly produced "national churches"; that the struggle between Eastern and Western Christendom included a struggle over the legitimacy of autocephalous, regional churches as against the centralized catholicity of the Papacy, a struggle in which both sides overstated their case and left in the late Middle Ages a confused heritage, to which the Reformation was heir.[2]

The common assumption of both East and West since Constantine, that the community and the Church were two aspects of a single entity, was carried over into the Reformation with resulting territorial, or national, churches of varying confessions, Lutheran in Scandinavia and in some German *lände*, Presbyterian in Scotland and some Swiss cantons, Anglican in England. It was chiefly through the rise of Independency in England that a new and sharp distinction between Church and territorial community developed. The strength of the Independent elements in early settlers of North America was a major reason why religion in the United States has never had the pattern of regional associations that characterized Europe.[3]

The theology underlying the various forms of regional church is as complex as their history. Here it is possible only to pick out, in bare summary, some of the theological convictions which are relevant to our inquiry.

(1) The *Christian Empire*: the classical doctrine in the West, following the Constantinian settlement, vindicated the relationship of Church and Empire as two aspects of one whole. One body of men had henceforth two aspects and two governments —a secular government in things temporal and an ecclesiastical government in things spiritual. Thus Gelasius I formulated by the end of the fifth century the concept which was to dominate the whole Middle Ages. Its presupposition is a vast political-cultural unity within which regional or national differences are quite secondary. This concept was never formally abandoned even when the Western empire had long ceased to have the posited cohesion.

(2) The *Christian Nation*: in the greater diversity of the Eastern Empire, nations were a more real fact and Eastern theologians gave them a more serious place in their interpretation of the economy of God. With the development of nationalism in the West, many theologians have found for them a real, but limited, place in the order of creation. The Old

---

[2] See especially a valuable short historical study, *National Churches and the Church Universal*, by Prof. Dr. F. Dvornik of the University of Prague (Dacre Press, London, 1945).

[3] For excellent descriptive and interpretive articles on this whole question see the essays in the Oxford Conference volume *Church and Community* (Unwin 1937), especially those by Ernest Barker, Hanns Lilje, Manfred Björquist, Stefan Zankow and E. E. Aubrey.

Testament exaltation of the nation has found some very dubious exegesis, but, more securely, on the basis of the total biblical interpretation of history, nations can be accepted as something "given", but transcended and controlled by the Gospel.[4]

(3) The *National Church*: accepting the nation as a part of the order of God for human living, many church traditions have evolved quite clear-cut conceptions of the vocation of the national church. The idea of the "godly Prince" was an axiom of sixteenth and seventeenth-century Christian thought. The modern mind is startled by the completeness of its acceptance. Buttressed by references to archetypal sovereignty in the Old Testament, it found political expression in *cuius regio, eius religio*. It was simply the transference to a different unit of community of the medieval identity of Church and state. Thus Hooker can quite simply write, "in a Christian state . . . one and the self-same people are the Church and commonwealth". On this assumption, national churches conceived their duty to God. In Lutheran terms, the national church is seen as testifying uniquely to the *prevenient* and *universal* grace of God. As Einar Billing wrote of the Church of Sweden, "The one thing we know about every person in our country . . . is that he too is included in the grace of God. . . . That is why we christen our children."[5]

(4) *Establishment*: having its origin in the concept of the "godly Prince", many European churches developed an official relationship to the state, though the details of the relationship vary widely, whereby the state civil rulers *as such* acknowledge the Christian faith, and the Church as such is reckoned (as well as being a super-natural society) to be part of the civil order. But the theological justification of establishment is still vindicated by some theologians, in spite of a complete change in its political forms. To take only one quotation from England, Professor Leonard Hodgson preaching to the University of Cambridge,[6] vindicated the state-connection by appeal to the Old Testament prophets who "spoke as representatives of the God Whom king, nobles and people all professed to worship". Our Lord and His disciples were not *in a position* to interfere as those prophets were—and adds " . . . the witness of the Bible

    [4] Cf. the essays by Lilje, as a Lutheran, and by Zankow, as an Orthodox, op. cit., pp. 94-114 and 153-159.
    [5] Quoted by Björquist, *Church and Community*, p. 119.
    [6] See the *Cambridge Review* 1942, Vol. lxiv. pp. 11-12.

(is) to the truth that only an established Church is in a position to be prophetic." He goes on to point out that after the Edict of Milan in 313, the Christian Church was henceforth in the prophetic vantage-point.

(5) The *two kingdoms*: although Calvinism too has generally welcomed "establishment" in the sense of recognizing its duty to minister to *all* the people, it has often combined this with an affirmation that the Church stood as a kingdom within a kingdom. Andrew Melville in Scotland and Voetius in Holland both contended for the right of the Church to be considered as a free and distinct corporation, with power to decree the constitution and discipline of its membership. The strong, centralized system of the Reformed churches distinguishes their claim for the autonomy of the Church within the state, or indeed (as in Geneva and New England) to establish theocratic states, from

(6) *Independency*: here the governing notion is that of the *gathered* Church in the *local* congregation. But this conception need by no means imply a sense of irresponsibility for the commonweal. In sharp contradiction to the defenders of establishment, both these last two groups would maintain that only a church which owed no kind of dependence upon the state was free to exercise a prophetic ministry towards it. The history of the heirs of the "gathered Church" is full of examples of their valiant exercise of that ministry.

This over-simplified summary of some basic theological convictions as to the relationship of the Church to the regional community makes no allowance for the myriad ways in which theological attitudes have been influenced by political, cultural, economic and other social forces. But however brief our summary it would be inadequate without some indication of them.

(i) *Language* has perhaps been one of the most potent forces in creating a church coterminous with a particular cultural unit. The use of the vernacular in worship has a profound effect on the mind of the worshipper and so deeply affects the cohesion of the Church. The necessity, on one side, for Rome to enjoin the use of Latin to undergird her conception of universality and, on the other, the stubborn persistence of distinctive community-churches in spite of dispersion, as in the Armenian Church and in countless churches transplanted to the United States, illustrate the cohesive power of language.

(ii) *Caste, etc.* Some churches came into existence in a particular caste or economic class and with difficulty, if at all,
transcend it. The Syrian Church of South India was, and is,
as completely a caste church as the Salvation Army was, and is,
a proletarian movement. Such bases of church-community may
or may not coincide with regional community and they show an
astonishing power of persistence long after the circumstances in
which they originated have changed. Most regional areas possess
one or more church-communities based on such origins which
constitute at least as formidable an obstacle to Christian unity
in that area as any doctrinal differences; and the doctrinal differences are rendered more intransigent by the existence of such,
often unacknowledged, non-theological factors.

All that has been said about caste, can be true *a fortiori* of
race.

(iii) *Cultural disunity.* A regional church presupposes a
quite highly developed degree of cultural unity in the region
of which (in whatever terms) it is *the* Church. Where, because
of the size of the region or the newness of its culture or the destruction of its old culture, there is cultural disunity, a regional
church of any kind is improbable. It is doubtful whether the
United States has yet achieved the cultural unity to make a
"national church" conceivable,[7] quite apart from the diversity
of the churches there and the aversion of many of them to the
idea. We have yet to see the effect of the rising nationalism of
the East, with its attendant re-emphasis upon their old cultures,
upon the desire of Christians there to achieve a *united, regional*
Christian witness. Whilst South India is not a wholly distinct
cultural unit within India, the difficulties attending the emancipation of India were often used as an argument in favour of a
united Christian Church there.

Enough has been said to show that the *regional church* is a
highly complex entity, both in theoretical conception and in
historical fact. But the basic idea is simple. Man lives in communities. The small community, within which men can know
each other personally, is cared for in the parish or local congregation. The community of mankind also has its proper place
in the Christian scheme as the sphere of the Universal Church
militant here on earth. Between the two, man's life is also lived
in other communities, historically variable and intricately com-

posed, but always bearing some relationship to territorial region. The "regional church" is the Christian attempt to bring that form of life, as it must bring all forms of life, under captivity to the law of Christ.

III INTERNATIONAL CONFESSIONS

We must first face difficulties of terminology. We have seen that *Church* has only two fully Scriptural meanings, with "regional church" as a possible legitimate use under certain circumstances. How then are we to describe the various Christian bodies which in fact now exist? Most of them claim for themselves the name of *Church*, some also allowing it to other bodies, according to criteria which vary from the rigour of Rome, which allows it, and then hesitantly, to none but the Orthodox Churches of the East, to the latitude of those who would deny it to none who wish to claim it. But it is certainly used to describe a bewildering range of phenomena. Here we are concerned only to find a suitable word to describe perfectly familiar facts, since to use the word "church" would be a *petitio principii* for many readers. The fact to be described is a community of Christians held together by a common body of doctrine, recognizing a common ministry, having common courts or assemblies for the determination of matters of faith, worship and discipline, in varying degrees having access to common finances, generally (but not necessarily) having a common nationality, the whole bound into a recognizable entity by a common history. This entity we propose to call a *denomination*. Where such a body organizes itself into a relationship, more or less close, with those who share its distinctive theological tenets but are members of other nations, we call it an *international confession*.[8]

The number of denominations in the world is probably uncounted. But since we are concerned here only with the chief

[8] Thus, in the use of words adopted here, the Church of Greece and the Church of Bulgaria are "denominations" but belong to the international "confession" of Orthodoxy; the Church of England and the Protestant Episcopal Church of U.S.A. are "denominations" in the Anglican "confession", the Church of Norway and the Evangelical Lutheran Churches in India are "denominations" in the Lutheran "confession", etc. It is a terminology which will satisfy no one wholly, but wide consultation with others has not enabled me to find a better. It is even more confusing when the thought has to be expressed in other languages also!

manifestations of their inter-national organization, we need only concern ourselves with eight main families. They are: [9]

(1) *The Roman Catholic Church:* organized into some 1,300 dioceses. It is by far the largest centralized Christian body in the world, defined by acceptance of the supremacy of the Papal See.

(2) *The Churches of the Orthodox East:* comprise a family of fifteen autonomous churches, each having its own territorial area and usually comprising an ecclesio-national entity. No full Ecumenical Council has been held since the eighth century.

(3) *The Anglican Communion:* its one effective international organ (though purely advisory) is the Lambeth Conference, normally held every ten years. The first was held in 1867, and the eighth is arranged for July and August 1948.

(4) *The Lutheran World Federation* recently held its fourth international meeting at Lund (Sweden) in July 1947.

(5) *The Baptist World Alliance* was founded in 1905 and held its last Congress in Copenhagen in 1947.

(6) *The Alliance of Reformed Churches holding the Presbyterian System* was founded in 1877 and is holding a council meeting at Geneva in August 1948.

(7) *The Methodist Ecumenical Council* is a consultative and advisory body which held its last meeting at Springfield, Mass., in September 1947.

(8) *The International Congregational Council* was formed in the 1880's; it has recently been reorganized, and its next meeting is planned in 1949 in Boston, U.S.A.

All these "international confessions", in spite of their differences, have in common the fact that they transcend national, regional and racial boundaries, uniting men from every part of the earth in allegiance to certain commonly held convictions as to the nature of Christian truth. Some are more closely bound to regional origins, though even the Orthodox churches are developing in Western Europe and in the United States an Orthodoxy less and less tied to national origins. Some are highly centralized, and all are gaining in sense of cohesion as modern means of communication increase their possibilities of contact. Even those which set least store on their world-wide character, having no interest in exercising dominion over their members'

---

[9] The writer has given up any attempt to provide statistics. There are simply no reliable ones available.

faith, do not neglect any inter-national means of helping their members.

IV THE CONFLICT OF LOYALTIES

The only way in which a Christian, in a divided Christendom, can be a member of the One Holy Catholic Church, his faith in which he professes in the Creed, is by being a member of what, in this essay, we have called *denominations* and *confessions*. For some, their confession *is* the Catholic Church. Roman Catholics and, with a different emphasis, Eastern Orthodox, conceive of Christian reunion only in terms of the integration of others into their Church. All confessions believe that, under God, their tradition witnesses to truths which it is their duty not to abandon. All Christians live in " regions " in which they have a sacred obligation to manifest the unity of the Church and to proclaim the Kingdom of Christ. In almost every part of the world the two duties are hard to reconcile.

In this conflict of loyalties, what are the affirmations which might be made in common by all Christians who participate in the ecumenical movement? The High Priestly Prayer of the Lord of the Church (St. John xvii) suggests the two poles between which the life of the Church must be lived. Christ prays for His disciples " that they may be one that the world may believe ", and almost in the next breath, " Father, sanctify them in Thy truth; Thy word is truth ". The life of the Church is to be a *unity* for the evangelization of the world: at the same time its unity is in the *truth*, this truth is itself the Word to which the Evangel witnesses.

Herein lies the justification, in their own spheres, of regional churches and international confessions. It is of the nature of evangelism to be local, concretely concerned with souls in time and place; it is of the nature of truth to be universal, transcending boundaries of time and place.

It is a truism that the " missionary areas " have set the pace in plans for Christian unity, and such plans are always closely related to evangelistic fervour or to the awareness of Christians of themselves as over against an unbelieving world. To seek unity is an inevitable response to a love for souls, not an abstract " love " but love for *these* souls.[10] Their conversion and their

[10] Cf. the following essay on *The Ecumenical Movement and the Younger Churches*.

sanctification equally demand it. Precisely because evangelism is concerned with definite locality, regional church unity is demanded; because the Church is responsible to Christ for the common social life of all men, the Church must seek corporately and unitedly to carry that responsibility. These principles remain true at every level of corporate human existence, both strictly local and in regard to the larger community. So long as the nation-state is the power it is in men's lives, so long will there be need for the Church to find forms which are fitted to speak to and act in the nation in the name of God.

But at once the contemporary Christian mind reacts with a caveat. Erastianism is an ugly perversion. Nationalism has so often been the bane of our age that *nationalistic* churches are merely the fortification of evil. Only if national churches are seeking to guard nations from nationalism are they true to their calling.

At this point "inter-national denominations" may speak a relevant word. Every denomination believes itself to be trustee of some *truth*, and, because it is a truth, thereby transcends spatial boundaries. It is because members of the same denomination in different nations hail in each other witness to a truth which unifies them, whilst it separates them from others, that they develop their *inter*-national organization. In each of the cases we have listed, that recognition, tacit or implicit, is the justification for their existence. In none of the cases (except Rome) is there any attempt on the part of the inter-national organs to legislate for or to override the autonomy of their local unity, but, in all, a sense of community in God-given truth is present and that sense is a basic condition for the existence of a "church".

As Erastianism is the corruption of national churches, a magnified *sectarianism* is the corruption of inter-national denominations. A community drawn together by recognition of a common truth is prone to become a defensive alliance against all others. The very process of drawing men together from all over the world on a basis of their distinctive convictions is liable to develop a vested interest not so much in the convictions as in their distinctiveness.

As each of these concepts is liable to its own abuse, so they stand, not in a simple but in a dialectical relationship to each other. There are forms of unity which are perversions of truth.

We dare not forget how in Germany and Japan a totalitarian government attempted to coerce Christian unity to serve its own perversion of truth. It is in the light of such a fate that the development of a " national Christianity " bought at the price of dogmatic integrity, is rightly feared.

There are forms of loyalty to truth which are the enemy of unity. Wherever partial truth is elevated into the whole, wherever doctrinaire abstractions distract from the love of souls, there unity is threatened. It is the perpetual peril of the life of the theologian and ecclesiastic that he should substitute the traditions of men for the commandments of God.

But in spite of the possibilities of their perversion, both concepts have a lawful place in the only policy open to a divided Church. Evangelization and social witness which are regional and concrete, demand unity, regional and concrete, a unity of which the regional church is a proper form. So it is only to be expected and welcomed that in almost every part of the world federations, "councils of churches", and plans for co-operation and even for organic unity are going forward on a national basis and developing with increasing momentum.

But, by an inherent dialectic, the development of "international denominations" has coincided with the development of such national movements. Every one of the eight groups we listed (except the Orthodox, for reasons which they are the first to lament) have held or are about to hold assemblies which symbolize their unity—from the Consistory of Roman Cardinals in February 1946 to the International Congregational Council planned for 1949. Although many of them are modest in their claims, all testify to a truth which they believe to transcend the local loyalties of man, of which they are trustees for all Christendom.

Yet neither concept is one in which there is any final resting-place. Above them both stands the One Holy Catholic Church, declared by God, and obscured, even whilst it is professed, by men. Loyalty to *that Church* corrects the errors of the lesser loyalties which are but broken parts of an intended whole. It is not the purpose of this essay to discuss the relation between the " ecumenical movement " and that Church of our faith,[11] but it is relevant to its purpose to point out that in the ecumenical

[11] See the essay on the *Significance of the World Council of Churches*, by Dr. W. A. Visser 't Hooft, pp. 177-193.

movement both these concepts already have the context within which they can most fully be themselves and yet avoid their own perversions.

The World Council of Churches is neither a federation of "national councils" nor yet a federation of denominational federations. It is, deliberately and consciously, a council of *churches* in the sense described in this essay as "denominations". For, in the empirical situation, such are the actual entities of Christian organization from which the other two concepts derive. "Churches" in this sense represent the facts; yet as the Council develops it will rightly stimulate its component units in national and regional areas to develop their own co-operation at ever-deepening levels, though in a context in which merely national viewpoints are checked and enlarged, whether among older or younger churches, among established or nascent nations. At the same time it will provide (even in its constitution) for the corporate contribution of the great distinctive Christian traditions, not in order that they may harden into rivalry but that they may be mutually enriching. Truly regional churches are needed, and will be needed for so long as men's lives are lived under strong regional influences of whatever kind; international confessions are needed until their limitations are transcended in a wider unity, and such truths as they guard are universally recognized. But such loyalties ever live under the threat and the promise of the Living God Who calls us to unity in the truth.

2

THE ECUMENICAL MOVEMENT AND
THE YOUNGER CHURCHES

by Paul David Devanandan

IT is too early in the day to assess the extent of the influence
of the ecumenical movement on the life and thought of the
younger churches. During the fateful period of the war, the
World Council of Churches was still in formation; and its direct
impact had to be limited to the nearer reach of the older
churches in Europe and America. In the meantime, several
events of far-reaching importance have taken place in the
countries of the younger churches. Japan is no longer the first-
class power that it was; China is still recovering from the ravages
of war and internal discord; India is now divided into two
dominions which are not yet reconciled to each other; the island
peoples of the Far East have been quickened to new self-consciousness.

Altogether in the younger churches, the period of the war set
back progressive Christian undertakings which were directed
towards objectives inspired by the ecumenical spirit. For one
thing, many projects for expansion and consolidation for which
we had counted on resources of strength in men and money
from abroad had to be shelved. We had to make the most of
what we had, with whatever foreign help that was still available
in addition.

These very adverse circumstances, at the same time, provided
opportunities for inter-church and inter-mission co-operation on
an unprecedented scale, especially in areas where orphaned
missions continued to work. In places where missionary leaders
were forced to leave, on account of enemy action, native lay
leaders carried on. By necessity they kept on in total disregard
of denominational differences, in the larger interests of maintaining the unity and the fellowship of the faith. In some areas the
sudden turn of political events brought compulsion on the
Church, sometimes by state action, to close its divisions and form
one organization.

Local conditions in the various younger churches of the East differ widely. Even in the same country, the Church is at different stages of development in different areas. What is attempted in this paper is a review of the situation mainly with reference to conditions prevailing in India. A good deal of what is said about the younger church in India may be, to an extent, true of younger churches in general, at least by implication.

One thing must be stated at the outset. It may well be claimed that the modern concern for Christian unity in Protestantism acquired a new momentum when confronted by the practical needs of the missionary enterprise in non-Christian lands. At any rate, as the International Missionary Council took shape, and the vision of world-evangelism at Edinburgh (1910) inspired men and women in the different mission-fields to undertake co-operative action through what later came to be known as the various National Christian Councils, an added justification and urgency was given to the growing desire for Christian fellowship, as well in the life and work of the Church as in its faith and order. If Oxford and Edinburgh (1937) registered the approval of Christian thought in the older churches, Madras expressed the desire of the younger churches, that it was time for us as a world-community to recover and possess that ecumenical oneness which is God's design for His people. All this is a matter of history, but it is not always recognized that the missionary enterprise and the ecumenical movements are closely inter-related.

What the younger churches have given to the movement is little, indirect and pragmatic rather than positive and ideological. The reason is not far to seek. We are still young; some of us are still in the "mission-stage" of infancy; not all of us have come of age. Perhaps our contribution to the ecumenical movement is still to be made. Before we discuss the possible nature of what we of the younger churches are likely to contribute to the movement, we may pause to consider what the immediate effects of the movement have been so far on our life and experience.

One remarkable difference between the Jerusalem and Madras meetings of the International Missionary Council was the emphasis rightly placed on the Church. On the mission-field we had not always recognized in our preaching that the Church formed a fundamental feature of the Gospel, that to invite non-Christians to accept the Christian way of life necessarily implied an invitation to join the Church. "Is the challenge of the Gospel to India fully declared unless all the time it is presented as including, in the directest possible way, a challenge to join the organized Church of Christ?" asks Dr. A. G. Hogg in his recent study on *The Christian Message to the Hindu*. "And must not the command 'Follow Me' have as an intrinsic part of its meaning a summons to join His New Israel—that Church of which He . . . selected the first leaders?" And Hogg goes on to add, "Whether or not this note was insufficiently stressed in the preaching and teaching of my contemporaries on the Indian mission-field, I have to make regretful confession that it had very little place in my own teaching. This was because, until almost the end of my missionary career, the idea of the Church was no intrinsic part of my conception of the Gospel."

It can be said with little fear of contradiction that what makes the primary difference in outlook between the leaders of a previous generation in the younger churches and those who are the leaders of to-day (both local and foreign) is that they perceive no mere "consequential relation" between Gospel and Church but a relation which is both "integral and constitutive". Undoubtedly this changed understanding is due to the influence of the ecumenical movement on our thought-life. In the early days of the movement towards church union in South India the dynamic came from two sources: one was the practical necessity for co-operation, forgetting our differences, so that we may more effectively and economically carry on the evangelistic task; the other was the drive of a blind sentiment based on the swell of impulsive feeling which refused to admit that Christian unity can permit differences.

As the negotiations for union in South India proceeded, the ecumenical movement in the older churches gathered force. We profited by your studies and conferences. We came to a fresh understanding of the biblical basis of the Church, of the historical traditions connected with various denominational views concerning the ministry, and we realized the significance of the symbolic rite of the sacrament of the Lord's Supper as a ratification of the essential unity of all believers in fellowship with one another and with the Head of the Church.

Now that the Church of South India is an accomplished fact, we look back with thankfulness that in all our travail to interpret locally in the life of the Church in South India the ecumenical oneness of the World Christian Community, we had kept the following ideals firmly in view: (1) The unity of the Church is organic. (2) It comes about in the actual process of growing into unity. (3) It is possible to comprehend and include all that is valuable and worth preserving in the different denominational traditions. (4) A transitory period of adjustment and "irregularity" is inevitable.

In both the younger and older churches there has been a manifest desire to work for unity. But while we talk in terms of "unity" in the hope of a future good to be realized, you of the older churches invariably think in terms of "reunion", with your minds retracing the past history of divisions hallowed by the memory of saints and martyrs. This seems to be a fundamental difference in outlook. It is responsible for your emphasis on a "federal basis" of union while our insistence is on "organic" union. In the immediate years to come, as the younger churches grow in strength and influence and as they become more and more independent of their connection with the older churches, this difference in outlook and objective will become pronounced.

Paradoxically enough, one of the blessings of the ecumenical movement in the older churches is the fresh discovery that many devout men and women have made of the significant values contained in the traditional teaching of their various denominations. It is true that there has been a clearer conception of the Church. But alongside of this there is growing self-consciousness of the denominational churches too, and in some cases Christians of a denomination with large membership in different countries have come together to form world federations and ecumenical conferences. To us of the younger churches, it is passing strange that with the spread of the ecumenical movement, and frequently as a direct consequence of it, many smaller sects and sub-denominations have now become prominent and active participants in the national councils of churches in countries like Britain and the United States.

This revival of denominationalism concerns us vitally. Many small missionary societies from the lands of the older churches, sponsored and supported by some one or other of these minor denominations, feel justified in starting evangelistic work in areas where the younger church is moving towards organic unity. They tend to counteract what seems to us progress towards unity.[1] This anomalous situation can be very distressing in areas where "missions" supported by funds from abroad and "churches" directed by local leadership exist side by side.

As indicated in a previous paragraph, the younger churches are in various stages of development, even in the same country. In the "mission-stage", where the primary emphasis is on evangelism of the non-Christian and the nurture of the infant community of converts, denominationalism has no place whatsoever. One of the important lessons of missionary history is that as evangelists we cannot afford to be denominational. It is in the "church-stage" of missionary history that we tend to become conscious of denominational teachings. The evangelist's message is universal; the minister of a church instructs his congregation concerning the special teachings of his denomination. We look to the ecumenical movement to help ease the transition in our development from the "mission-age" to the "church-age"—and it seems so clear to us that only if we keep in view the hope of a church organically one can we effect a right transition from "mission" to "Church".

In South India, for instance, another complication arises. Not only do we have denominational churches in this area, but also a fairly large section of the Eastern Orthodox communion in Travancore, referred to in general as the Syrian Church. They are a sadly divided community. Apart from the Uniat-Syrians, there are two main sections of the Syrian Church—the Orthodox Syrian Church and the Mar Thoma Syrian Church. Within the Orthodox Church there are two main parties—the Patriarch's party, which owes allegiance to the Patriarch of Antioch, and the Catholicos' party, which recognizes a local Catholicos as its administrative head. Besides, there is a section of members of the Syrian Church which forms part of the Anglican diocese of Travancore and Cochin, which was one of the four dioceses to be included in the Church of South India.

At the time negotiations were started for union in South India, the Mar Thoma Syrians were thinking of joining in the scheme as it took clearer shape. The spread of the ecumenical idea did not only effect a revival of a healthy denominationalism (like everything, liable to be abused), but also a new interest in Eastern Orthodox churches. The many Orthodox communions

[1] Cf. the preceding essay on *Regional and Confessional Loyalties in the Universal Church*.

in Europe and the Middle East were thus quickened to a new sense of importance. To us of the younger churches it is very clear that these Orthodox communions will not easily give up their separate identity even within the ecumenical fellowship. In India, on the other hand, it seems unfair to encourage these Orthodox communions of the Syrian Church to persist in division. They might have eventually formed part of the new united Church if it were not for the revived consciousness of separatism that the ecumenical movement has paradoxically enough engendered.

There is one important point concerning the significance of the ecumenical movement about which the younger churches would desire clarification. A good deal of confusion is caused by the easy way in which the term "ecumenical" comes to be applied. Any inter-denominational undertaking, for instance, is described frequently as "ecumenical", especially where the project is taken up by several denominations, each retaining its separate identity, and yet all working together for a common end. No one can quarrel with such a use of the term, for it does connote that outlook of fellowship and sense of unity which characterizes the coming together of churches of different denominations.

But it is also true that the term "ecumenical" denotes a number of churches of different lands, each with a culture all its own. So that the world community of Christians in their ecumenical oneness would bring together in multiform grandeur, into a single rich mosaic, the varied culture-patterns characteristic each of the national and racial groupings into which we Christians of the world would seem to be divided by the very order of creation. To us of the younger churches the national expression of the common faith is a precious possession. Not a little of our energy in the infant church in our midst is employed in exploring ways and means of making it indigenous to the soil. We hope some day that the younger church, each in its own land, will prove worthy of its cultural heritage and national genius.

The ecumenical movement which seeks to unite the Christian peoples of the world into a sense of togetherness ought to be both inter-denominational and inter-national. To us of the younger churches it is the inter-national nature of our faith that strikes the imagination; to you of the older churches it is the inter-denominational character of ecumenical Christianity that compels admiration. After all, you do not differ so widely among yourselves culturally, and your present history has drawn you all so much more closely together that there is a vague fear (why not be frank about it?) amongst us of the younger churches that in a World Council we may lose our national identity and cultural uniqueness, being dominated by the sheer weight of your collective strength and cultural homogeneity.

Perhaps this is one reason why we have greater loyalty and affection for the International Missionary Council than for the World Council of Churches at this stage in the progress of the ecumenical movement. To us it is vital that ecumenical Christianity be both international and missionary. We are concerned seriously with the fact that church-consciousness and mission-consciousness have not always kept together in the recent development of the older churches. The ecumenical teaching in regard to inter-denominational fellowship evokes great enthusiasm. But the challenge of the missionary cause as an ecumenical task does not seem to meet with the same response.

Earlier in this paper reference was made to a signal contribution that the ecumenical movement has made to the younger churches. It brought us the conviction that the relation between Gospel and Church is not merely consequential, but integral and constitutive (to borrow the telling words of Dr. Hogg). What the ecumenical movement has not yet brought home to the older churches is this same truth, only expressed in terms of relation between Church and Gospel. Interest in missions is not derived from enthusiasm for the Church; both proceed from fidelity to the Gospel, the faith once for all committed to the saints.

Many leaders in the older churches are already conscious that if the ecumenical movement is to make a real impact on the life and thought of Protestant Christendom everywhere, it ought to keep in view the ultimate goal of the organic unity of the Church universal and catholic; it should be increasingly alive to the international and inter-cultural nature of the ecumenical faith as it is to the inter-denominational and inter-church nature of the world community of believers; it should quicken ever anew the missionary nature of the faith so that the integral and constitutive nature of the relation between Church and Gospel is pressed home to the Christian conscience.

This contribution is written from the background of the author's own situation, that of the Church in South India. Other areas might have stressed other aspects of the relation between the ecumenical movement and the younger churches. Space prohibits a truly representative survey of the outlook of the younger churches unless it were to be of a very vague and sketchy kind. We have preferred to let a single representative speak in concrete terms of the situation he knows best, though it has meant omitting interesting material from other areas.

EDITOR.

3

THE ROMAN CATHOLIC CHURCH AND THE
ECUMENICAL MOVEMENT

(a) by K. E. Skydsgaard

I

THE most difficult front in ecumenical work is beyond any doubt the relationship to the Roman Catholic Church. One might be tempted to say that the difficulties here are so great that any relationship at all is rendered impossible. It is an ever-recurring sentence when the ecumenical movement is under discussion, that "all church communities are represented *with the exception of the Roman Catholic Church*". Is it therefore possible, when talking about the relationship between the Roman Catholic Church and the ecumenical movement, to say anything else than that there is no connection whatever between the two?

The purpose of the following pages is to show that the matter is much more complex than is generally supposed.

In the ecumenical movement we may distinguish between three tendencies. The foundation for any kind of ecumenical activity lies in the acceptance of the bitter and tragic truth that the unity of all Christians in one visible body has been shattered and that, instead of their common cohesion in one outwardly visible Body, many Christian bodies do in fact now exist, not only side by side, but often in fierce opposition to one another. It is just because the various communities are beginning to realize that this separation is a sin and an affliction, which is obviously contrary to the will of Christ, that there is to-day an ecumenical movement. In this bitter recognition of facts all churches agree—including the Roman Catholic Church, which perhaps feels a deeper grief over the disunion and dismemberment than many other churches.

This basic recognition is the first point. The second trend is a divergency in the interpretation of the unity of the Church, an interpretation which naturally also has a practical influence upon ecumenical work. In the non-Roman Catholic churches the interpretation varies and may lead to conflicts. We only need to mention the interpretations of the Church and its unity by the Greek Orthodox, the Anglican, the Lutheran, the Reformed, and other Protestant churches. But the differences of opinion on this question between these churches have not been able to prevent them, on the whole, from joining in the common ecumenical movement during recent decades, culminating in the setting up of a World Council of Churches.

For there is also this third feature of the ecumenical movement, that the churches are moving out of their isolation into active co-operation, not only in matters of practical concern, but also in order to get closer to one another in questions of faith and teaching. In many cases the different points of view give rise to conflicts and difficulties, but behind it all there is a common will for mutual understanding and thorough discussion of the problems which are the cause of the difficulties. It is here that the Roman Catholic Church has felt that it must call a halt. It shares in the grief over the divisions among Christians and it is deeply interested in the unity of the Church, but its own interpretation of this unity not only differs so widely on important points from that of the other churches that it is not able to join in the efforts, but must even insist upon a definite and uncompromising "No". We only need to mention the encyclical *Mortalium animos* (1928) in which Pius XI definitely prohibited any Roman Catholic from taking part in ecumenical meetings. "Thus, Venerable Brethren, it is clear why this Apostolic See has never allowed its subjects to take part in the assemblies of non-Catholics."[1]

Protestants often accuse the Roman Church of narrowness and sectarianism, of ecclesiastical arrogance, and spiritual imperialism. And it cannot be supposed beyond question that such factors have not played a part in the attitude adopted by the Roman Catholic Church, both on the part of individual theologians and of papal proclamations down the ages. It is often an impossible problem to reconcile the words, and also the spirit, of the official proclamations with the ecumenical leanings and sympathies of many individual Roman Catholic theologians.

However, it would be a serious mistake to content oneself with

---

[1] *True Religious Unity*, Engl. trans. of *Mortalium animos*, p. 20 (Publ. by the Catholic Truth Society, 1928). See also *Codex juris canonici*, Can. 1325, para. 3.

such a reaction to the position of the Roman Catholic Church. It would, in spite of every difficulty, constitute a far too cheap and easy solution for the non-Roman churches. The attitude of the Roman Catholic Church must be explained from far deeper and more essential factors, as is now being realized much more widely than previously. When Rome contends that the unity of the Church is not a goal lying ahead, but something which *has* already been made manifest in the Roman Catholic Church itself, because this alone is the Holy Catholic Church, and thus alone the Church of Jesus Christ, and when it further contends that true reunion can only take the form of a reintegration or reincorporation into this unity,[2] this is not, on her part, the expression of some kind of spiritual imperialism, but the expression of a particular conception of the nature of the Church and its unity. If, therefore, we are to come to a real understanding of the unsympathetic attitude of Rome to the ecumenical movement we must try to probe into this basic point of view.[3]

But even though we want to try to penetrate into the deepest motives lying behind the refusal of Rome to join in the ecumenical movement, and by doing so, to respect and perhaps also understand its attitude, will not the result be, nevertheless, the same as before, that between the Roman Catholic Church and the ecumenical movement there can never be any connection? Shall we not, in spite of consideration and sympathy, be forced to say that *here* the ecumenical movement has reached its absolute limit?

The question is this: Are the other churches to be content with the answer officially given by Rome, and consequently to regard all ecumenical efforts from Roman Catholic quarters as irrelevant private efforts which have no foundation in the Church itself and which must therefore be regarded with the greatest reserve? The answer to this must be an emphatic "No!"

So far as I can see it is not sufficient in these matters to abide by the more or less official statements, both previous and contemporary. The papal decrees, even where they are most

---

[2] "There is but one way in which the unity of Christians may be fostered, and that is by furthering the return to the one true Church of Christ of those who are separated from it" (*Ibid.*, pp. 20-21).

[3] A very clear explanation of this view is given by M. J. Congar, O.P.; *Chrétiens désunis. Principes d'un Oecuménisme Catholique*, 1937, pp. 63-148; Engl. trans. (Bles, 1939), pp. 48-115.

explicit, do not express the whole attitude of the Roman Catholic Church on this question, just as, for instance, the condemnation of a Protestant doctrine does not contain the *whole* attitude of the Church to Protestantism.[4]   Therefore: the exclusive study of the *Mortalium animos* would not be sufficient to obtain a really clear conclusion, as it is chiefly directed against the ecumenical movement in its first inadequate and groping attempts, an inadequacy which is now also felt by many leading theologians in the other churches.   That Encyclical is definitely in opposition to the ecumenical movement which found its expression at Stockholm in 1925 and may not be—and actually is not, even in the Roman Church—taken as covering everything which the Roman Catholic Church has to say in this matter.[5]

Here, as always when we are trying to understand the nature of Catholicism, it is not enough to study only official documents, but we must force our way into the living theological and ecclesiastical tradition as expressed in the whole spiritual life of the Roman Catholic Church.

We cannot set our minds at rest with the thought that this problem has been solved once and for all.   It is obvious that the ecumenical question is not seen in the same light by the Roman Catholic Church as it is by the other churches; this does not mean, however, that it is of *no* consequence whatever to the Church of Rome.   It is also true that the ecumenical movement here actually reaches a boundary line, but it does not mean that this boundary is to be absolute—only that in this case other methods must be employed.   What would be the sense of an ecumenical enterprise which had not at least the intention of including the largest of all the Christian communities?   If it had not, it would instantly cease to be ecumenical.

The question then is this: How is ecumenical co-operation between the Roman Catholic Church and the other Christian bodies possible to-day?   And: How does the Roman Catholic Church itself regard the possibilities of such co-operation?   The reply to these questions is closely connected with the relationship between Rome and the other churches.   And here we must make a distinction.   Its relationship is not the same to the Greek Orthodox, to the Anglican, the Lutheran and the Reformed

[4] See, for instance, L. Lambinet, *Das Wesen des katholisch-protestantischen Gegensatzes*, 1946, p. 208.
[5] Cf. Congar, pp. 179ff. (Engl. trans., pp. 116-144); also an article by Charles Boyer, S.J., in *Unitas* (Vol. II, No. 4; Dec. 1947; publ. in Rome).

churches, not to speak of all the other larger or smaller church communities. The order in which these churches are mentioned signifies an increasing degree of difficulties in mutual relationship. In the following pages we will primarily consider its relationship to the Reformed churches, more especially the Evangelical-Lutheran Church.

I am well aware what influence this limitation in point of view will have on the value of the present paper. Thus it will hardly be possible to avoid the difficulty that, for instance, American readers will find very little which bears upon their problems, just as members of the Anglican, not to speak of the Orthodox, Communion may be justified in feeling that their attitudes have not been expressed. However, it will be difficult for any member of a particular church to express adequately the problems of other churches. For each individual church has its own, often very complex, problems in this field. I hope it will be possible, even from this more limited point of view, to minimize the "limitation" by treating the matter in such an inclusive and general way that it may be of interest also for others than members of the Lutheran Church.

II

During the course of the centuries an essential change in the relation between the Church of Rome and the Evangelical Church has taken place. It is best understood by contrast with two attitudes which, although still to be found, belong essentially to the past. The first might be called the attitude of *confessional polemics*. At this stage, each side assumes that it fully understands what the other side means and is only concerned to refute it. Although the motive was the defence of truth, the method of assault from embattled positions led to polemics rather than to mutual respect. By reaction, there next emerged the attitude of *confessional irenics*,[6] which also assumed that positions on both sides were known and fixed, but that they merely represented a beneficial variety of outlook within the infinite range of truth. The works of Schleiermacher admirably illustrate this relativist attitude.

[6] I here take the word " irenics " in another sense than the one in which it is used in the " irenical method " as described by Dom C. Lialine in *Irenikon* (IV, 1938, p. 4). On the contrary, the thought expressed there corresponds in several ways to the third standpoint which I describe.

But theology is a question of *truth*, not of points of view. Although at many points widely apart, these two attitudes are paradoxically alike in one regard, they both assumed that the relationship between the two confessions was known and unalterable. So both are fundamentally non-ecumenical.

In opposition to these two attitudes, there is now a third, which is finding new ways and is opening up new perspectives; this view will undoubtedly have a more and more decisive influence on future developments.

In order to understand it I must draw attention to individual factors which have contributed to the fact that Roman Catholicism and the other churches have moved nearer to one another. I shall mention three, the first two of a more historical, the last of a more theological nature.

In the period following the Reformation, Catholicism and Protestantism were separated from one another, not only religiously, but also politically and culturally. To be a Catholic or a Protestant meant not only that one had a different faith, but also that one had a different political opinion, and a different culture. *Cuius regio, eius religio.*

Later a change took place. Both the Age of Enlightenment and Romanticism brought the two parties closer together, not in faith, but on the purely humane-cultural level. In the Romantic Period a cultural sphere was created, supported by Catholics and Protestants alike. The difference between these two Confessions became more and more a purely religious contrast. From a merely external, sociological point of view, Catholicism and Protestantism are to-day compelled to live side by side in the same sphere where both Roman Catholic, Protestant and atheistic forces make their influence felt, in spite of the fact that Catholicism to-day still strives to create its own cultural and political sphere. It is a fact that the relationship between Catholicism and Protestantism varies very greatly in this common sphere. There are places where the relationship may be rather strained, not least where a politically defined Catholicism attempts to make its influence felt, and at times exerts strong pressure on an Evangelical minority. The relationship may also be difficult where Catholicism exists as a missionary church in countries with a predominantly non-Roman Catholic Christian population.

On the other hand, it must be emphasized that Roman

Catholicism and Protestantism have been drawn closer together, by common struggle and distress, into a common front against the anti-Christian powers of our times. We are in the midst of one of the great decisive epochs and transition periods in the annals of humanity, a period in which old things are dying and new are being born, a period in which everything is characterized by anxiety and pain, dissolution and a watching for the new which is to come. At such a time it is not strange that the Christian churches should draw nearer to one another and should be more intent upon what they have in common than upon what is separating them. When there is danger and distress things may happen of which smug self-sufficiency does not feel any need. When one's house is on fire one does not feel like continuing an old quarrel.

At such a time there is a possibility for ecumenical work for which the previous ages did not give occasion. One is simply forced into it. It may prove that behind greatly dividing formulations there is, nevertheless, a unity both in regard to the view of man and his relationship to the various earthly spheres of life in which he has been placed, and with regard to essential points in the Christian Faith. There can be no doubt that developments during the past few years in the Western countries have played a very great part in the change of relationship between the Roman Catholic and the Evangelical churches. We only need to remember the relationship of the two churches under Nazism.

The Evangelical Church also has its history. It will hardly be possible to maintain that the history of the Evangelical Church is a blameless one. The Reformers denounced the Roman Church for having muddied the pure waters of Revelation with the traditions of men. Now Protestantism must confess that the philosophy of liberalism and the conclusions of biblical critics, in their extreme and irresponsible form, sometimes betray the principles of 'the Reformation.

In this respect the theology of Karl Barth has had a decisive influence. His uncompromising attitude towards the Roman Catholic Church has not prevented him from regarding it as a very serious challenge to the Protestant Church. " Here ", he says, " in the Catholic Church there is an ecclesiastical substance, a knowledge that the Church is the house of *God*—corrupted, unrecognizable substance perhaps, but nevertheless not lost substance."[7]

Finally a third and last reason should be mentioned for the changed relationship between the Confessions. To the same extent in which Protestant theology again turns towards the Reformation and in renewed sincerity enquires into its mission, to the same extent we shall once more come face to face with Catholicism, and the latter with us. As long as we only met Catholicism with the accusation of being a religion of hierarchical authority or a mystical, magical sacramental religion, Catholicism probably heard nothing but the questions of modern emancipated culture. It was a query *from outside* only, not from *within,* i.e. from a church which declared itself to be standing on the ground of the Bible and the Creed. It was not the same question as was set out in Luther's 62nd Thesis: *Verus thesaurus ecclesiae est sacrosanctum evangelium gloriae et gratiae Dei.* The new hope in the situation to-day is that the Catholic-Evangelical discourse is now possible as a real theological and ecclesiastical discourse.

III

We have now come to the point where we may repeat the question already previously asked: How is ecumenical co-operation between Roman Catholics and Evangelical-Lutherans possible to-day?

Students of Catholic-Protestant relations differ in their estimate of the relationship between the official utterances of the Vatican and the more co-operative attitude of certain Catholic groups and individuals. But Catholics of the latter kind would emphatically deny that their action implies any kind of disloyalty to the Holy See. Perhaps the soundest interpretation of the discrepancy is to see a distinction within the Roman Church between what can be safely said *coram populo,* which is always extremely reserved and, indeed uncompromising, and the liberty of action which authority is content to allow to groups and individuals whose fundamental principles are judged to be wholly sound and reliable. The Roman Church *as such* is wholly uncompromising and yet, where more flexibility appears, it is no less truly part of the life of the same Church.

[7] See *Der römische Katholizismus als Frage an die protestantische Kirche, Zwischen den Zeiten,* 1928, pp. 224 onwards.

It is of very great importance that the ecumenical movement should realize this standpoint and act accordingly. Thus great misunderstandings and difficulties can be avoided. The meeting between Roman Catholicism and Evangelical Christianity can only be a meeting between individuals or groups of individuals from the different communities. It is here that the ecumenical work between the two parties must take place, but on the other hand, it is here that it is possible. *This* is where, for the time being, the effort must be made.

The most important part of this work is *prayer*: "*ut omnes unum sint*"—"in such a way and at such a time as God wills it", as it is phrased in the literature of the *Octave of Prayer for Unity*, that remarkable movement associated with the name of the Abbé Couturier of Lyons. Earnest prayer on both sides must be the basis for all ecumenical work.

There is, further, *active co-operation in practical matters*, e.g. co-operation on social questions, and in opposition to wrong political interference in education, the family and the professions, which has been definitely encouraged by the Popes in recent years.[8]

Added to this comes the *study of the Bible*. It is remarkable to note how widely Catholic and Protestant scholars have come to agree in their interpretations of Holy Scripture during the last twenty-five years, and a widespread movement to encourage Bible-reading is in progress in the Catholic Church.[9]

Finally, the *common theological discussion* of controversial matters, in periodicals like *Catholica* (which is temporarily suspended), *Irenikon, Dieu Vivant, Unitas* and others, and through personal contact. This last approach has been practised to a great extent in the *Una Sancta* movement, which became very widespread during and after the war, especially in Germany, where theologians and often also laymen gather together for frank and fraternal discussions of questions concerning faith and order. The great material which very likely is to be found here should be made the subject of thorough investigation. This new co-operation is based upon two points: First, the two parties are both included in the *Una Sancta*. This sen-

[8] See especially the Pope's Christmas Broadcast, 1941; the Foundation of *Unitas*, announced by Vatican Radio, 11th July, 1945, and the Encyclical *Quemadmodum*, 1946, appealing to all *Christians* to help children in distress after the war.
[9] See the account of it in Suzanne de Dietrich, *Renouveau biblique* (Edition Oikumene, Geneva, 1945), pp. 271ff.

tence will be understood differently by Roman Catholics and Protestants, but it is, nevertheless, possible that the two parties can acknowledge their oneness in this common assertion: "On both sides we are included in the Church of Jesus Christ."[10] To deny this would be to deny the reality of Baptism. The condition for a real ecumenical co-operation is that the two sections of Christendom do not begin by denying this fellowship, this one-ness in *Una Sancta*, visible in our common Baptism and, in spite of all, in our common Creed: *Credo in Iesum Christum, filium Dei unigenitum, Dominum nostrum.*" This unity is something which is bigger and stronger than all differences and contrasts, because it does not originate in something human but in God Himself.

But secondly: In this very unity the differences become evident, differences which are not of peripheral importance, but are concerned with the most vital part of the confession of the common faith. A difference which does not penetrate to the very core of the matter is of no importance. The acceptance of this difference on vitally important points is a condition without which ecumenical discussion will lack sincerity and reality.

In admitting the tension between these two poles—one-ness in faith in Christ on the one hand, and the contrast in matters of faith of vital importance on the other—all ecumenical work must be carried on. This tension must be endured and not be neutralized by false compromises or be neglected through the one party feeling superior to the other in self-sufficiency.

The question then is *how* this work is to be done. What is needed first and foremost is that this radical change of heart on both sides, now confined to a few, should become general.

It is one of the great misfortunes, due to long separation, that a widely differing mentality has been created. The contrast between the two churches is not only a contrast in the way in which the great Christian questions are being answered, but also in the very manner in which these questions are being asked. In the course of time certain established and almost insurmountable prejudices have grown up on both sides which assert themselves with the certainty of an axiom whenever Catholics and Protestants speak, either about one another or to one another.

---

[10] As to the interpretation of this sentence on the Roman Catholic side, see, for instance, Congar, p. 278, and Rademacher; *Die Wiedervereinigung der Kirchen,* 1937, pp. 15 onwards.

There is here a feeling of resentment which must be energetically stamped out.

On the basis of such a change of mentality, a new discussion must and can take place between Roman Catholics and Evangelicals where the fundamental issues may be debated, not as "controversial matters" where it will once more—although perhaps in a more friendly manner—be a case of defining what is truth and what is heresy, but in such a way that the two parties may state their position to its fullest limits and as concisely and copiously as possible, and in such a way that the other party will actually *listen* to it.

In order to achieve this it is necessary that the two communities study one another's theology, and try to find out the principal and central motives. This will have the result that the theological discipline called "symbolics" will receive a new aspect. It will not, as hitherto, be only polemical, nor merely a descriptive historical science, although it must always rest upon thorough historical studies, but it becomes the theological discipline in which the individual Confession, so to speak, leaves its own sphere of living and enters into a direct contact with the other Confessions. In this way "symbolics" becomes the self-critical conscience within the individual Confession, in which it regards itself in the critical light of the other Confession, while at the same time feeling the necessity of its own questions relative to the position of the other party.

A further important feature of the spirit of impartiality in which such a discussion must take place is the *demand for truth*. It must not for one moment become a matter of obscuring all that which each side has accepted as being the truth, and there can be no thought of working out a more or less artificial formula of unity on any point. An accepted point can only be abandoned when that which a church has been teaching, or has neglected to teach, proves to be in disobedience to Christ Himself. This is to state that both Catholics and Protestants must place themselves under the authority of the prophetic and apostolic teaching. They must both be under the sovereignty of the revelation of God as found in Holy Scripture. When the individual churches begin to ask themselves if this or that teaching is truly in accordance with the Word of God, ecumenical work has already begun. For in so doing, a spirit has been created which does not agitate for its own infallible opinions, a spirit which is not obstinate and quarrelsome in sticking to its own, once-for-all adopted opinions, and which is not ashamed, when the occasion arises, to let itself become convinced by clear reasoning, because truth is greater than opinions and personal pride.

Now the objection may be made that this spirit may *perhaps* be possible in the Evangelical Church, but that it is impossible *on principle* in the Roman Catholic Church. The Evangelical Church may possibly accept a question from the Roman Catholic Church directed to itself, but the opposite is unthinkable beforehand. From a Roman Catholic point of view, a discussion must always aim at proving to the Protestant the inner untenability of his whole perception. It is beyond any doubt that great difficulties will arise here and, nevertheless, we on the Evangelical side must be aware of various signs which clearly indicate that on the part of Catholicism also a new attentiveness is awakening, an inner investigation, a self-criticism, not of the Church as such, but of the exact form which the Roman Catholic Church has taken in the course of its empirical development, in which restrictions and prejudices have occurred, so that truly Catholic thought (which in this connection means the whole and undivided Christian truth) has had an incomplete development. The same is the case when it is said that the Roman Catholic Church, in order to be truly catholic, lacks something which now exists outside its limits in the other Christian bodies. Protestantism possesses genuine elements of truth which have not found expression in the Roman Catholic Church. And even though the latter may add that what Protestantism contains of actual "catholic" matter can only find its true and complete expression in being transplanted into the bosom of the Roman Catholic Church, there is in this view a self-criticism, a frankness, and a responsiveness which at first sight seems astonishing to a Protestant who has already long since formed his final opinion of the Roman Catholic Church.

If we study Catholic theology to-day,[11] dealing with these questions with an open and attentive mind, we should be startled time after time by the frank willingness to admit that "catholic" was often turned into "catholitical", and that often the opposition to one or the other controversial opinion forced Roman

[11] See, for instance, Congar, pp. 30 onwards; Lambinet, pp. 207 onwards and Rademacher, pp. 39 onwards. Collate also R. Grosche: *Pilgernde Kirche*, 1938, J. Lortz: *Die Reformation in Deutschland*, and O. Bauhofer: *Einheit im Glauben*, 1935.

Catholic theology into a one-sidedness, not only with regard to the individual theologian, but also in the ecclesiastical definition of doctrines as evidenced in *Enchiridion symbolorum*. Catholicism is something far greater than the anti-Protestantism which is threatening to become the all-deciding factor in post-Reformation Catholicism and to make of the Roman Catholic Church "a fortress almost as much as a Church" (Congar). From the Evangelical side we must not misunderstand this, and must not draw light-hearted conclusions from it, but on the other hand we must not be ignorant of the fact that here something is happening, and must refrain from giving it a false and unsympathetic interpretation based on preconceived ideas.

In this new mentality and this new objectiveness the present view on the relationship between the Roman Catholic Church and the Evangelical Church differs widely from both the polemic and the irenic standpoint. In this spirit the discourse demands a real effort and study of the great fundamental issues: Holy Scripture and Tradition, Church and Ministry, Word and Sacrament, Justification and Sanctification, the real meaning of the Gospel and of faith in Christ. The more the two churches, each in its own sphere and according to its own light, probe into and live according to the truth about Christ, the more we may hope that the final and surviving unity will emerge *in spite of all*.

IV

I began by saying that the most difficult front in ecumenical work was the relationship to the Roman Catholic Church. The thoughts put forward on the previous pages have not aimed at weakening this assertion. On the contrary!

Ordinary ecumenical co-operation between the churches must go on without the participation of the Roman Catholic Church and probably also be the subject of much criticism and antagonism from many quarters in the Catholic Church. The Pope's Encyclical with its definite refusal to join in this work still holds good.[12] Nevertheless, something new is emerging. Therefore

---

[12] On this point it is interesting to compare what two commentators, one from Evangelical and one from Catholic quarters, think about this question.

The Evangelical commentator: "*Mortalium animos* represents not only the official doctrine, but the working policy of the vast machine, and, while I am most eager for every kind of personal understanding with persons, I suggest that

the result must be that even here on the most difficult front,. where apparently irrefutable reasons speak against it, an ecumenical activity is at work—perhaps in a way different from that manifest in other places, but equally important.

To the above, which has been only briefly outlined, it might with good cause be asked, as it actually has already been asked, "What is the value of these contacts between Roman Catholics and other Christians which are essentially contacts between religious individuals and groups, meeting on a common plane of mystical experience?" The answer to this question must in the first instance be the not very positive one: Of how great or how little value this co-operation will be it is impossible to-day to determine with certainty. Everything is still in its beginning. But it should be emphasized that that which to-day takes place quietly *may* some day break through and be of an importance at which we at this moment cannot guess.

Meanwhile it is imperative to work, to watch and to pray for the unmistakable signs which, in spite of all preconceived opinions, nevertheless have appeared on both sides.

Finally we must realize that, even though it may be considered beforehand to be a rather "impossible" enterprise, it is nevertheless certain that it is the road which we must follow at this moment, although the way ahead may seem dark and obscure. Often a traveller must follow a certain path without knowing exactly where it may take him. He must do it because he knows that, in spite of everything, this is the path *he* must take at this point. Thus it is also in the relationship between the Roman Catholic Church and the Evangelical churches. Even the contrasts in all their profundity will in God's good time illuminate the eternal truth.

---

the World Council should, in general, rest their relations with the Vatican on the assumption that *Mortalium animos* represents their view and policy still."

The Catholic commentator: "To tie up with *Mortalium animos* is not advisable, nor to *Codex juris canonici Can., 1325, par. 3,* which forbids religious discourse with people of other faiths. The widespread *Una Sancta* movement in Germany shows that since Pius XII this canon is evidently no longer in force." The commentator thinks that the encyclical of Pius XII *Mystici corporis Christi* (1943) gives a far better basis for a real dialogue.

(b) A Supplementary Note by a Roman Catholic Writer:
Fr. Maurice Villain

W HAT does the Roman Catholic Church think of the ecumenical movement? What is she doing, and what is she capable of doing on its behalf? Such is the question.

The classic reply is well known. The encyclical *Mortalium animos*, of whose decisive conclusion Professor Skydsgaard has reminded us, would seem finally to preclude Catholics from any active collaboration in the work of reconciliation between Christians such as is conceived by the ecumenical movement. Rome, it is said, has once and for all condemned, even in principle, pan-Christian conferences.

We are grateful to Professor Skydsgaard for having interpreted this document of the first importance with a more discriminating eye, and also for having generously exonerated Rome from the charges of pride and imperialism which on this account are so often directed at her. The attitude of Rome is, as a matter of fact, governed by her own conception of the Church. Her consciousness of being the authentic visible society established by Christ has always been part of her faith; she professes that the ecclesiastical body united to Christ since Pentecost has never been able to renounce Him, in spite of the stages of its development (which are precisely the law of its life), in spite of the very grave crises through which it has passed in the course of centuries, in spite of the moral failures of its leaders and of its members. Its apostolicity is a historical gift; its personality—and consequently its internal unity—cannot in any circumstances be lost. That is why the Catholic Church, in her official documents, regards the unity of Christians as being a step of re-admission into her fellowship; that is why she is seen to distrust the compromises which seem likely, in however small a degree, to stand in the way of the constitutional principle which is her flesh and blood. Hence her severity towards the pragmatic ideas of Stockholm (this is said with full recognition of the nobility of the enterprise of N. Söderblom, who was, moreover, extremely far-sighted, and made more dogmatic claims than the bases of the *Life and Work* conference would lead one to suppose); hence her reserve, now as in the past, towards a congress which seeks gropingly the " body " in which the spirit of unity, in labour everywhere among non-Catholic Christians, may ultimately become incarnate.

Many are astonished, many are shocked. For my part I shall simply confess that I have more than once asked Protestant friends: " If, in the face of such tentative efforts, and, up to now, of such uncertain results, you had been Rome, what, then, would you have done? " There has been an instant's reflection, followed by the hesitant but unmistakable reply: " We would probably have waited. . . ."

This Professor Skydsgaard perfectly understands. And how grateful we are to him for having made his readers feel the extent of the tragedy which this dualism of positions involves for the future of Christian unity: for showing them how painful it is for the Roman Church to be unable to overthrow the barrier of her own constitution (and of her faith) in order to go to Christians who—as many besides herself know—positively need her if their labour is not to be in vain. Who, henceforth, having weighed the extreme gravity of this point of conscience, can speak in irony?

Yet Rome is acting.

Her silence, to begin with, which is itself a witness, carries with it its own efficacy. I do not speak in paradox, but because that is my conviction after having studied the rising tide of big conferences. Has not Rome's silence played a part in directing the ecumenical movement towards dogmatic essentials which could not be clearly perceived in the engagements so nobly and generously entered into at Stockholm? From the first appearance of *Faith and Order* at Lausanne, it orchestrated—if it may be put so—the demands of Anglicans and Orthodox for a more constructive theology of the Incarnation and the Sacraments; it stimulated Protestant researches into the structure of the Church as an apostolic-hierarchical institution; and what doubt can there be that one day it will pose this very serious question as being one of primary importance?

But furthermore, Rome brings to the ecumenical movement above all the collaboration of her prayers. When in 1908, in the Episcopal Church of America, the *Octave of Unity* was instituted, bishops were to be found among us who adopted it. Moreover, it was a French priest who, in 1937, effectively extended its audience to world-wide dimensions, in the new formula of the *Week of Universal Prayer for Christian Unity*. Discretion prevents me from being more explicit, but one would do well to reflect on the spiritual contribution made by the little tracts of Lyons which, each year, stimulate the intercession of Christians, both Catholic and non-Catholic. Between the feasts of the Chair of St. Peter and of the Conversion of St. Paul (January 18-25) they are all bidden to kneel together, to repent together, with one voice to ask of the Father of all " the Unity which Christ wills, and as He wills ". Our appeal was heard, the cry " Awake " has little by little reached all the corners of Christendom, and no more is needed but to draw the net tighter by a combined and persevering effort. The World Council is assuredly the first body to profit by these earnest supplications; besides, has it not admitted as much since the *Faith and Order* movement joined in observing this Week of Prayer? And it is in truth in this perspective that we must see the message of Mgr. Charrière, Bishop of Lausanne, Geneva and Fribourg, to the World Council in February 1946 through an intermediary, the Swedish Lutheran Bishop Ingve Brilioth; we read there this sentence: " While you are met together at Geneva to concern yourselves with this essential problem (Unity) my prayer goes up with yours, in union with the one which Jesus made on the eve of His Passion . . ." Is this not the sign of a new spirit?

How, after that, could our Catholic activities, steeped in an atmosphere of such spiritual density, fail to find what Father Congar calls the " ecumenical dimension "? True, all ages are not propitious to it. At the beginning of the twentieth century, for example, the Modernist peril, which the Church was not yet prepared to master, forced Pius X back on a narrowly traditional position. But this very concentration made possible the germination, in the following age, of many prophetic seeds whose flowering we are witnessing to-day. In this general task of " taking stock of our resources " of which the pastoral letter of Cardinal Suhard, *Advance or Decline of the Church* (1947), is one of the most authoritative and optimistic testimonies, I should like at least to stress, as falling exactly within our subject, the renewal of biblical studies. If Rome's silence seems to our Protestant brethren to raise the question of the Church as a community, their attitude to Rome seems to raise for Rome the question of the Word of God. Now to this fundamental question the

biblical renewal is an active answer. The task will be a long
and exacting one, because it is not enough to possess scholars
trained in the best disciplines; we need in addition and above all
a clergy so conversant with the Scriptures that the whole range
of its teaching is nourished by them, and that it is zealous to
communicate to the faithful the taste for them and their daily
practice. Not until then, to use a happy phrase which pastor
Arnold Bremond has made his own, will the Mother Church
have discovered anew her "biblical milk".[1] Besides, the
encyclical of Pius XII *Divino afflante Spiritu* makes this a duty
of the clergy, and outlines the methods to be used.

There remains a long series of facts and indications which
taken together can help us to pass a judgment on certain profound trends, virtual rather than clearly declared, of the Catholic
Church.

A book could be written tracing the graph of Rome's attitude
towards the Orthodox churches, but I must for lack of space
confine myself to a bare enumeration. We can first of all
record a progress, within the last eighty years, in the papal
documents: from Pius IX who was content strictly to recall the
rights of the Roman Church—to Leo XIII, who was the first
to advocate the study of Eastern history and theology—and to
Pius XI above all, who laid stress on the obstacles of a psychological nature which history had piled up in the path of
rapprochements; and on this matter he allowed it to be understood that the Catholic Church had to examine its conscience
and to admit reforms. We might also note the creation, in the
last twenty-five years both in and outside Rome, of technical
institutes—universities, colleges or monasteries—for the study of
the languages, theology and liturgies of the East, and the
establishment of an annual *dies orientalis* in all seminaries, in
such a way that now the spirit of Orthodoxy is present in the
Catholic Church. In another connection, centres such as the
priory of Amay (at Chevetogne in Belgium) or Istina (at Paris)
are extremely valuable for meetings of theologians. But how
much we regret, on both sides, that political pressure constrains
the Patriarchal Church of Russia to decline the advances of the
West!

Although it is here much more reserved, the attitude of the
Roman Church towards the Reformed churches is not at all

---

[1] *Edifier l'Eglise*, Delachaux and Niestle, 1945, p. 102.

the systematic refusal that one might imagine. Witness the colloquies, which are becoming more and more numerous and well attended, between Catholic and Protestant theologians—spiritual meetings in the form of retreats, intellectual meetings, or better still both at once, when study is illumined by prayer; meetings which are never secret but always authorized by the diocesan bishop or by the superiors of the religious orders; meetings which are no longer tentative, as are those which occur at the outset of such a difficult experiment, but properly conducted, here and there at least, by a precise method, put to the test in specialized groups (for the Catholic theologian has now at his disposal an approach appropriate to researches of this nature). Here are loyal exchanges of views on all subjects, including the extreme points of our divisions; a unique field of investigation for the understanding of mentalities; detailed information on the principles, the constituent parts, the vocabulary of our respective religious traditions; constructive essays grounded in the original sources and dealing with the true pivot of problems, so often unbalanced by " this besetting fever which the spirit of the Counter-Reformation has imposed on Catholic thought";[2] times of recollection, of fervent resort to the Spirit when, at sore points, cries of *Non possumus* are uttered.

Such is our modest work. It is in truth only laboratory work, limited to relatively restricted groups; but we believe ourselves able to affirm that it goes deeper than does the work of large official meetings, and that these meetings will themselves one day benefit by it.

Is there any need to recall also that an ecumenic literature, already quite important, has appeared among us, springing either from the general stream of theological studies, or from more particular experiments of which I have just spoken, or on the occasion of Weeks of Prayer. To the articles quoted above, let me add the following reviews, which are wholly concerned with questions of reunion: *Irénikon, Russie et Chrétienté, Catholicité, The Eastern Churches Quarterly, Unitas,* etc., and the collections: *Unam Sanctam, Ad Unitatem, Théologie, Sources chrétiennes,* etc. We owe, finally, a special reference to the *Una Sancta* movement, taken in hand by the conference of German bishops at Fulda.

[2] A. M. Roguet, O.P., preface to *La Clef de la Doctrine Eucharistique* of Dom Vonier, Lyons, 1943, p. v.

The objection may be made that the Catholic Church is absent from these labours, since she does not commit herself by any official step. This is to fail utterly to appreciate her behaviour. As Professor Skydsgaard well understands, the action of the Catholic Church goes beyond her own documents (which are, especially on this subject, very rare, and show moderation, for the use of the flock whose faith they seek to preserve); it includes in reality the whole area of her tolerations and safe-conducts. We must remember that we are here in the midst of prophetism. Prophetism ordinarily appears in the peripheral rings of the Church, which does not, however, mean that it is necessarily independent or adventurous, since in any case we have just shown that it is, in the circumstances, permitted and controlled by the hierarchical authorities. Before the prophet's word is fully endorsed by the pronouncement of an official decree, there is for him an uncertain period in which he feels himself to be isolated, in which perhaps he suffers at the hands of the very Church that he serves with his whole heart: but all the same, the permission he is given to go ahead is in effect firm ground under his feet: henceforward he knows that he is not working in vain for the development of the *Una Sancta*, even though his action may, once or twice, be checked and mortified; after all, his confidence will increase, in that he feels himself to be carried on the waves of a universal prayer. He is not toiling outside the Church or on her farthest boundaries, but in her and with her—from which we may be allowed to conclude that the Church is present in his action.

These facts, big with possibilities, cannot fail to affect the viewpoint of *Mortalium animos*. Not that the fundamental principles of this encyclical can be modified, since they are part of the very structure of the Catholic Church, but it is not impossible that their application may be, if it is established that the facts of the ecumenical problem have changed.[3]

In view of the pragmatic starting-point of Stockholm—a mistaken departure, even in the opinion of many Protestants, as Professor Skydsgaard has remarked—Pope Pius XI showed clear-

An encyclical, which is an act of the *ordinarium magisterium* of the Pope, does not imply, in itself, doctrinal infallibility. It is not infrequent for an encyclical to complete, elaborate or even to correct an earlier encyclical: compare *Quadregesimo anno* (1931) and *Rerum novarum* (1891); and compare *Divino afflante* (1943) with *Providentissimus Deus* (1893) and *Spiritus Paraclitus* (1920).

sightedness by his vigorous and alert response. But since then, especially since Edinburgh, the doctrinal trend of ecumenism has righted itself and become firmer. Even if the Edinburgh Conference does not seem to have registered a very important positive result—we think rather that it came up against dialectically insurmountable dilemmas—it did at least propound the true dogmatic problems, and, in a most humble recognition of human weakness, it gave unanimous expression to the desire for " the fullness of unity " based on " a common understanding of truth as it is in Jesus "—which implied the resolution to adopt other methods and to transcend, at all costs, the plane of dilemmas, without abandoning the least portion of Christian truth in a compromise. We acknowledge the same supernatural confidence in the preparations for future meetings.

To speak now of Amsterdam is beyond my competence, and what I will venture to say commits no one but myself. It is clear to all, after what has been said, that the Roman Church cannot be officially represented in the World Council in the sense of sending delegates to Amsterdam; besides, we know she would not be invited. Does it follow that Catholic theologians could not, if invited to, bring to the conference a real and positive collaboration, in which they would emerge from the never very attractive role of silent observer? For my part I see no objection to this, I see even a form of duty which it would be ungracious for us to shirk; it would be a question of generous and utterly disinterested brotherly aid, by writing or in speech, on questions related to the programme. This unofficial witness would be an authentic expression of Catholic doctrine, which must of necessity be heard in a conference of this kind, and it would at least be one manifestation of a presence which it seems to us impossible any longer to ignore.

We fear that these few pages, too superficial a guide, will be incapable of effectively suggesting our purpose. We have tried to show that between the Ecumenical Movement and the Roman Catholic Church a convergence is not only possible, but is gradually taking place. On the one hand, we have affirmed our confidence in the progress of the Ecumenical Movement towards total solutions (by purification, the reconciliation of complementary dogmas, progressive renewal in the waters of the authentic Christian tradition), in the absence of which it risks a hopeless breakdown. But on the other hand, we do not believe ourselves to be contradicting the principles of the Catholic Church when we affirm that she too is beginning (by purifications, internal reforms, a reintegration of Christian values which are well preserved in separated confessions) to pass beyond the stage of development which she has reached at the present time. The opposition between "catholic" and "catholitical" of which Professor Skydsgaard makes use well expresses what I am hinting at here. Without becoming other (dissimilar to herself) in her personality and faith, the Catholic Church will have taken on other features, different behaviour, which will call forth a vital reintegration (not an absorption, not a submission pure and simple) of the Christian churches, whose renewal will make them ready to rediscover " their Mother ".

It is a slow advance, hidden, if only one isolated movement at a time is considered, by its blunders and frequent set-backs; but nevertheless a forward advance, from the standpoint of a historian who observes it even in the relatively recent past, or from the standpoint of a sociologist who scans the horizons of the future.

Will the road not end until the return of the Lord, or in the event of sudden changes? Only the Spirit of God knows, Who is the master of the fortunes of the Church. What is certain is that in our own day we are present, in wonder, at a concert hitherto unknown in History: just as the sacred voice of an organ fills a whole cathedral, even to the very smallest chapels, even to the corners of the tiniest carved ornaments, so the Spirit of God breathes through the whole living Church, the young and fresh song of hope in Christian Unity.

4

THE SIGNIFICANCE OF THE WORLD COUNCIL OF CHURCHES

by W. A. Visser 't Hooft

I INTRODUCTION

THE plan of forming a World Council of Churches was conceived in 1937. The draft constitution was elaborated in the following year. The invitations to the churches to participate in the formation of the Council were sent out in the winter 1938-1939. Then came the war, during which thorough theological discussion between the churches proved impossible. It is, therefore, not astonishing that the fundamental questions concerning the nature of the Council and its function have not yet been clarified and that we approach the first Assembly without having arrived at a clear common conception of the precise nature of the body which we are setting up together.

It should be said at the outset that this is to some extent inevitable. The type of relationship between the churches which the World Council represents is a new phenomenon in church history. The Council and the member churches will only discover gradually just what this unprecedented form of interchurch fellowship does and does not mean. Room must be left for the guidance of the Spirit, and too much definition at this early stage might prove a hindrance rather than a help to future development.

On the other hand, there are reasons why the conversation about the nature of the Council cannot be postponed any longer.

The internal life of the World Council itself makes clearer definition of the Council's nature imperative. Many decisions which the Assembly or other organs of the Council have to take involve a conscious or unconscious conception of the character of the Council. Unless it proves possible to elucidate certain basic principles, these decisions will be taken in a purely pragmatic way and the Council will be in danger of becoming an opportunist body in which momentary considerations of expediency rather than the Word of the Lord dominate the situation.

The Council cannot, of course, adopt one specific ecclesiology as its basic conception of the nature of the Church and of church unity. If such a generally acceptable ecclesiology were available the ecumenical problem would be solved, and there would be no need for an ecumenical "movement". The present situation is characterized precisely by the fact that churches with very divergent conceptions of the Church seek to live and work together in spite of their differences. But while it is impossible to force this situation, it is equally impossible to go forward without some tentative principles and definitions concerning the nature of the new body which the churches together have decided to set up.

In drawing up its Constitution, in deciding on the criteria of membership, in defining its functions, in fixing the manner of representation, in planning its activities and in many other areas the Council gives in fact an implicit answer to the question concerning its own nature. And whenever the World Council speaks to the churches or to the world—through its Assembly or through its responsible committees—it expresses in one way or another a conviction concerning its own significance.

It is then not surprising that the question: "What is the World Council?" is being raised in different quarters, sometimes in a tone of expectation and sometimes in a tone of suspicion.

Already in 1935 Dietrich Bonhoeffer, who since proved by his witness and death how deeply his life was rooted in the Una Sancta, had warned the ecumenical movement that the struggle of the confessing church involved a decisive question for the ecumenical movement: *Ist die Oekumene Kirche?* The Church is only there where men witness to the lordship of Christ and against His enemies. And there is no true unity where unity in confessing the faith is lacking. Has the ecumenical movement that unity? Does it seek *that* unity? And if not, is it truly the Church of Christ?[1]

There is also to-day, in many circles, a very strong expectation concerning the work and the message of the World Council. Again and again it is stated that now at last the Protestant, Anglican and Orthodox Churches can speak with a common voice. The frequent use of the expression "The World Church" suggests directly or indirectly that there now exists

---

[1] *Evangelische Theologie*, August 1935; see also *Some Quotations from Comments*, p. 195, by Dr. J. H. Oldham.

an organ through which the churches which have agreed to join will regularly proclaim what is the mind of Christ with regard to the great spiritual, social and political problems of our time.[1]

But there is also a good deal of suspicion. Some wonder whether the Council, with its representative and official character, will ever be able to give a true lead in proclaiming the Christian witness with regard to the great issues of our time. Others are afraid that the opposite may happen and that the Council may become a centralized administrative body which will commit the churches without their consent to decisions which they are not ready to take, or that it may even become a super-church which will try to dominate the member churches.

It is then time to define more clearly than has been done so far what the Council is and what it is not. Are the high expectations justified? Is there good reason for anxiety?

II BACKGROUND

It may be useful to begin with a short summary of ecumenical developments leading up to the formation of the World Council.

As a result of the untiring efforts of a small group of pioneers the ecumenical conferences of Stockholm and Lausanne are convened. For the first time in centuries the churches meet together. But what do these meetings mean? Are they intended to demonstrate the oneness of the Church of Christ and to declare the common faith? Are they a visible representation of the Una Sancta? In trying to answer these questions, we are confronted by a fundamental dualism in the definitions and statements which these conferences make and which are made concerning them. For on the one hand both conferences deny (in different ways) that they intend to speak on behalf of the churches and to represent the Church Universal. But both speak to the churches and to the world in such a way that they are inevitably regarded as claiming to represent, though in a very provisional and imperfect way, that unity which in New Testament language is the unity of the one Body, the one Church of Christ.

Thus the Stockholm Conference says quite clearly that its resolutions will not in any way be binding on the Christian communions represented at the Conference, unless and until they are presented to, and accepted by the authorities of each com-

[1] *Ibid.*

munion. It says also that it desires "all Christians in the region
of moral and social questions to begin at once to act together,
as if they were one body in one visible fellowship". In these
two ways it makes it clear that it does not claim to be the authorized and representative voice of the Church, as the visible fellowship of the one body. But in its "Message" it says: "We
realized afresh our common faith, and experienced as never
before the unity of the Church of Christ." In emphasizing this
unity of faith and in addressing the world on the basis of that
unity, the Conference becomes in some manner a voice of "the
Church", and its message can be understood only as a first
attempt to express the common mind of the Una Sancta which
here begins to manifest itself again. This shows that "Stockholm" understood itself on the one hand as a conference *about*
church co-operation in a particular realm (the realm of Christian
ethics), but on the other hand as an occasion to demonstrate, at
least in part, the unity of the Church.

The Lausanne Conference was characterized by a similar
dualism. Its leaders explained that, while it was summoned to
consider matters of faith and order, "its object is to register the
apparent level of fundamental agreements within the Conference and the grave points of disagreement remaining", but that
"it is emphatically not attempting to define the conditions of
future reunion". In other words, its intention is not to achieve
Christian unity or to declare it, but to study the prospects of
reunion. But here again the inner dynamic breaks through, for
the Conference receives unanimously a "message of the Church
to the world" which is a statement of the main contents of the
Gospel and which is widely publicized. It is inevitable that
Lausanne is, therefore, regarded, not merely as a conference
which discusses church unity in faith and order, but also in
some way as an attempt to confess the faith of the churches in the
measure of unity already attained.

Now this dualism has remained characteristic of the ecumenical movement. At times it has spoken of itself as an agency
of the churches to prepare the way for unity; at other times it has
acted as an organ which declares the unity already achieved.
This is even more clearly seen in the Oxford and Edinburgh
Conferences. For the Oxford Conference spoke in its message,
in its substantial reports and in its word to the German Church,
much more definitely as a voice of "the Church" than the

Stockholm Conference had done. In its message, it declared clearly that "God has done great things through His Church", and that "one of the greatest" is that "there exists an actual world-fellowship", so that "our unity in Christ is not a theme for aspiration; it is an experienced fact," of which the Conference itself is an illustration. Similarly the Edinburgh Conference in its "Affirmation of Unity" goes further than the Lausanne Conference in defining the nature of the unity which already exists and "which is deeper than our divisions". In the opening service of the Conference, the President (Archbishop Temple) said: "The occurrence of the two world conferences in one summer is itself a manifestation of the Una Sancta, the holy fellowship of those who worship God in Jesus Christ." But both conferences maintain the principle that they do not speak authoritatively for the churches and do not, therefore, speak as the Church Universal.

It is necessary to keep these matters in mind if we are to understand the origins of the World Council of Churches. It entered into the inheritance of the Stockholm and Lausanne movements. And as in this way the ecumenical movement found more definite shape, the duality to which we have referred also became more pronounced.

For on the one hand the creation of the Council means that for the first time since the divisions of the Church took place a permanent body is set up which represents the churches directly and officially. The World Council differs from all other ecumenical bodies which have existed or exist to-day in that it is *de jure* and *de facto* a Council of *Churches.* Its member churches will wholly determine its policy. It has no being apart from the churches.

But on the other hand the proposed constitution makes it abundantly clear that the Council is in no sense a super-church. The Constitution says: "The World Council shall not legislate for the churches", and the official explanatory memorandum comments: that the Assembly and Central Committee "will have no constitutional authority whatever over its constituent churches" and that the Council exists "to serve the churches, not to control them". The two emphases appear again side by side in the statement which the Provisional Committee of the World Council issued in April 1947. That statement declares that the Council owes its existence to the desire of its member churches to express their unity in Christ, but underlines that it does not usurp the functions which belong to its constituent members and disavows any thought of becoming a single unified church structure dominated by a centralized administrative authority.

III WHAT THE WORLD COUNCIL IS NOT

This short summary of the background of the World Council has shown that it is possible to consider the World Council from two different angles. The emphasis in the title can be placed on *Churches* or on *Council*. By exclusive emphasis on the first one arrives at the conception of a body which demonstrates and so makes effective the unity of the Church, in so far as that unity exists already. By exclusive emphasis on the second, one arrives at the conception of an organization which works for unity, but which does not itself speak or act as an embodiment of the Church Universal. In the first case the World Council is itself the Church, though the sense in which it is the Church needs further definition. In the second case it is an association which serves the churches without itself representing " the Church ".

Now it is quite clear that neither of these views of the Council meets the case. The Council cannot claim to *be* the Una Sancta or a partial embodiment of the Una Sancta, because it lacks the essential *notae ecclesiae*. If one measures the situation within the ecumenical movement by the various definitions of the Church in the confessional standards of the churches, one finds that the World Council does not correspond to any of these definitions. And if one goes back to the Bible and compares the fellowship which the churches have in the World Council with the *koinonia* of the Acts and the Epistles, one finds that essential aspects of that *koinonia* are lacking to-day, namely, the full common witness and full sharing in the sacramental life.

It is true that the ecumenical conferences have been able to give expression to a common mind, but the scope of their witness has been very limited. And the fact remains that the teaching of the churches in the Council is not a common *kerugma* with different aspects or emphases, but in many respects a confusion of tongues. The churches contradict each other on points which they consider, and must consider, as essential parts of their message. In joining with churches of other confessions in the fellowship of the Council they recognize that Christ is at work in these other churches, they accept, therefore, the duty of discussion and co-operation with these churches, but they continue to look upon these other churches as churches whose teaching is incomplete, distorted or even heretical. It is impossible to claim that this provisional and tentative relationship between the churches is itself the Una Sancta.

Moreover, the impossibility of complete fellowship in celebrating the Holy Communion together is a clear sign that the churches in the World Council dare not pretend to be a *koinonia* in the biblical sense of that term. Indeed our inability to meet together at the Lord's Table reminds us more insistently than anything else that the unity which has been granted to us is only a shadow of that full unity which characterizes the Body of Christ.

Again a body representing the Una Sancta would have far greater authority than that which the churches are willing to entrust to the World Council. At the present moment the constitutional limitations of that authority are probably more rigid than those placed on any other representative church body in the world. Now these limitations are inevitable and even desirable under present conditions. To demand greater authority at this stage would be to ask more than the real ecumenical situation warrants. But that fact by itself shows that the World Council is by no means a first preliminary edition of the Una Sancta.

It is, however, not only in the realm of these easily observable conditions of its life, but in the less tangible realm of the spiritual situation that one discovers strong reasons why the Council should not make too exalted claims for itself. The churches are at the moment not able to manifest the Una Sancta in a way which corresponds to the reality of its nature. The unity which would be seen, if the issue of unity were forced now, would be far too much a unity of compromise. There is still in much of our present ecumenism a strong element of relativism and of lack of concern for the truth of God. And so our unity would not be the biblical unity *in truth*. There can be no real representation of the Una Sancta until the churches have turned in a new way to the Word of God, until they have discovered their sickness, until they have found something of that clarity and certainty of preaching and witness which characterized the New Testament Church, until they are truly "becoming the Church" and meet each other on the level of that *metanoia*. In the providence of God signs are not wanting that some of these things are beginning to happen. But we are yet far away from the time of harvest. Until that time it will be well for us to be very modest in our claims.

Is the World Council then just an organization? If it cannot be considered as a visible representation of the Una Sancta, must it be considered as a man-made organ which may have a very noble and useful function to perform and which may render great services to the cause of the Church but which is not itself an expression and representation of "the Church"? Should the World Council look upon itself as one of the many Christian organizations which undertake specific tasks on a temporary basis and until such time as the Church can undertake these tasks itself? Is the World Council just a matter of conferences, committees and secretaries, or of information and philanthropy?

It is a fact that the World Council is often presented in such purely organizational terms. Thus, many "practically minded" supporters of the Council speak of it as just an agency of collaboration in concrete tasks. Now the Council is certainly such an agency, but its origins show clearly that it cannot be satisfied with that role. However grateful we may be to the pioneers of Stockholm, we cannot and dare not go back to the "as if" theology which demands that we shall act "as if" we were one in faith. We have discovered that our witness to the common faith is our first and foremost duty to the world and that without that witness our unity in "life and work" is impotent. When churches meet together they cannot leave on one side the question of their common confession of allegiance to their common Lord. It is not by accident that the ecumenical conferences have borne that witness in spite of all canonical obstacles to their doing so. The inner dynamic of the Church forced them to do so.

The same applies to the view that the exclusive purpose of the Council is the fostering of common study. Study is indispensable and common study on an ecumenical level is one of the great needs of the hour, but a Council of Churches cannot possibly consider study as an aim in itself. In the setting of the Church's mission study can have meaning only as a preparation for action, that is, for decisions of faith. When this is forgotten study may even become a danger, for study without decision fosters a theology-for-the-sake-of-theology rather than for the sake of the Church. If the ecumenical movement meant that all possible Christian standpoints were to be set permanently side by side on equal pedestals, it would become a museum and cease to have any relevance for the living Church.

The World Council cannot be content to be a federation of bodies, each of which watches jealously over its own sovereignty. A fellowship of churches which know that there is no sovereignty save that of their common Lord must differ essentially from a pragmatic combination of sovereign states. The gathering together of the churches can have spiritual relevance only if these churches desire in some way to become members of the one Body, and if, even in the early stages of their meeting, they give evidence of that desire. But if 'they do so, their relationships cannot possibly remain of a purely organizational character.

The World Council cannot be a mere organization simply because it is a Council *of Churches*. For the Church in the churches insists on asserting itself. Wherever two or three churches are gathered together, the Una Sancta is in the midst of them and demands to be manifested.

IV. WHAT THEN IS THE WORLD COUNCIL?

We have seen that the World Council cannot claim to *be* the Una Sancta. We have also seen that it cannot be satisfied to be a more or less permanent conference about church unity or an organization for practical purposes. On the one hand it dare not minimize the very real disunity within its membership; on the other hand it may not refuse the gift of unity which the Lord has actually given and gives to the churches, when He enables them to speak and act together. The Council may not anticipate that unity which belongs only to the truly reunited Church,[2] but neither can it refuse to follow the call to speak with one voice and to act as one body whenever that call is addressed to it. The Council cannot create the Church out of the churches, but

[2] One critic, who speaks for many of similar outlook, wishes to reject the word "re-union", holding that, historically, there never has been a wholly united Church, and that the use of this word obscures the fact that something *new* is now being wrought by God.

neither can it stand aside as an observer when the Church in the churches affirms and expresses itself.

This is the dilemma which dominates the whole existence of the Council. Its member churches are as yet unable to *be* together the one Church of God, but they are no longer able to regard their fellow-members as being outside the Church of God. They cannot unite, but neither can they let each other go. They know that there is no unity outside truth, but they realize also that truth demands unity.

Is there any way out of this dilemma? Only a way of faith. Only a way which takes its point of departure not in man-made syntheses or theoretical schemes, but in the simple truth that the unity of the Church is the work of the Lord of the Church. This truth has been clearly expressed at both the Oxford and Edinburgh Conferences. The Oxford Message says: "The source of unity is not the consenting movement of men's wills; it is Jesus Christ whose one life flows through the Body and subdues the many wills to His." And the Edinburgh Affirmation says: "Thus unity does not consist in the agreement of our minds or the consent of our wills. It is founded in Jesus Christ Himself."

In his opening sermon at the Edinburgh Conference, Archbishop Temple said:

"It is not we who can heal the wounds of His Body. We confer and deliberate, and that is right. But it is not by contrivance and adjustment that we can unite the Church of God. It is only by coming closer to Him that we come nearer to one another. . . . Only when God has drawn us closer to Himself shall we be truly united together; and then our task will be, *not to consummate our endeavour, but to register His achievement.*"

Karl Barth puts the same truth in a different way. He states that: "all efforts towards unity depend altogether on an act of recognition by the Church", namely, the recognition of the fact that this particular unity is willed by God. When this is really the case "we must obediently do our share so that we do not contradict on earth what is God's will in heaven".[3]

And is not this also the true significance of the basis of the World Council? It means that the living Christ—God and

---

[3] *Evangelische Theologie*, April 1935.

Saviour—alone can create the unity which we seek. Thus it gives the Council the indispensable foundation for its existence.

Unity is *received*, but that does not mean that man's rôle is purely passive. We are to look out for it and to be constantly ready to receive it. The unity which is given to us must become visible and effective in our midst.

Archbishop Temple wrote in 1939:

"The full unity of the Church is something for which we must still work and pray. But there exists a unity in allegiance to Our Lord, for the manifestation of which we are responsible. We may not pretend that the existing unity among Christians is greater than in fact it is; but we should act upon it so far as it is already a reality." (Letter of Invitation to membership in the World Council.)

The way out of our dilemma is, therefore, to consider the World Council as a means to manifest the unity of the Church, whenever and wherever the Lord of the Church Himself gives that unity: a *means* and a *method* and no more. The World Council *is* not the Una Sancta, but a means and a method which have no other *raison d'être* than to be used for the building of the Una Sancta. Therefore, it is far more than a movement about unity, and far more than an organizational innovation.

The World Council must, therefore, not pretend that it represents the Una Sancta, but it may and it must claim that it is the body in which and through which, when it pleases God, a foretaste of the Una Sancta is given. As an institution, it has no authority, not even as much authority as its member churches, which can take their stand on the basis of their respective confessions of faith and whose authority within their own sphere of action is unchallenged. From a horizontal viewpoint it remains just a council of dissimilar churches which disagree about important matters of faith, order and ethics. But from a vertical viewpoint, it is the place where the *koinonia* in the one faith may become (and has become) at least partly visible. When that happens, then indeed it has true authority. Then the confusion of tongues ceases for a moment, and the disunity of the many churches is overshadowed by the unity of the one Church of Christ.

Who shall say when this is the case? Certainly not the World

Council itself. For as we have seen, it can only try to express the mind of the Una Sancta, but not claim to *be* the Una Sancta. Rather it is open to any member church, and indeed to every church member to decide whether, in each given case, it recognizes in the World Council a manifestation of the one Body which fulfils the will of the Head. The World Council does not claim any authority for itself. But it must realize that it may, *Deo volente*, suddenly take on the formidable authority of an organ of the Holy Spirit.

Its whole life must be a constant counting with that possibility and a constant watching for that intervention from above. If it lives in that attitude, it will not become a mere ecclesiastical bureaucracy and will have true relevance for the life of the churches.

V   THE WITNESS OF THE WORLD COUNCIL

That witness consists first of all in the *fact* of praying, living and working together. The very existence of the World Council proclaims the good news that Jesus Christ unites men of all churches, nations and races. But that witness is incomplete if it does not lead on to a clear common proclamation of the Lordship of Christ in all realms of life. In this sense the original "Stockholm" tradition must remain alive in the World Council. Our basis in which we affirm the Lordship of Christ (for the words "God and Saviour" mean that we acknowledge Him as divine Lord in the radical biblical sense) is not merely a doctrinal formula, but the answer of the Church militant to the decree of mobilization issued by its rightful Head.

The demand that the churches as gathered together in the World Council should speak out and take a clear stand in relation to the idolatries, the crimes and temptations of our chaotic age, comes with all the more insistence now that a number of churches have, after a very long period of silence, realized again that the Church has a prophetic ministry to perform. This insight must permeate the whole ecumenical Church. Such common testimony has an especial significance for minority churches or for churches suffering isolation. But the world also needs to hear a clear united voice which confronts it with the reality of God's judgment and God's grace.

But though it is clear that the churches *ought* to speak together, it is not so clear that they *can* speak together. The

particular churches speak on the basis of their confessions and
(or) their confessional theologies. Their witness is an application of all that their members have heard and learned in their
common effort to live by the revelation of God in Jesus Christ.
Within these churches there may be considerable divergences
and tensions, but there are nevertheless common "traditions"
which enable each of them to speak in one voice.

Now the World Council has no such background. It has
nothing but its basis, which is interpreted in different ways. It
has no common spiritual language. The meaning of witness and
confession is understood differently by different churches. And
while they are all at one in recognizing the authority of Holy
Scripture, there are deep divergences between them as to the
actual significance of that authority for the life of the Church.
Dare the World Council speak as long as it has to stand on so
uncertain a foundation?

Before we answer that question we have to look at another
aspect of the problem, namely: who is to speak *as* or *for* the
World Council? As we have seen, the World Council is not a
union, not even a federal union, of churches. It is only a *council*
for specific purposes and with strictly limited authority. It consists of churches which are opposed to any delegation of power
to officers of an ecumenical body, some because they are against
all hierarchical forms of church order, others because they believe that such an order can only exist in fullness in a truly
reunited church. It is therefore out of the question that one
person could speak officially on its behalf.[4]

This is not merely a matter of canon law. It is an inevitable
consequence of the present situation. For every one of the
officers of the Council is a churchman who stands somewhere in
one of the particular churches. Not one of them is a supra-
confessional person. Every one of them represents *a* voice *in* the
Council rather than *the* voice *of* the Council. And even if one of
them should try to speak for it, no one who knows the realities
of the ecumenical situation could possibly regard his voice as
being the voice of the fellowship as a whole.

But if the World Council is neither spiritually nor legally

[4] An Anglican critic writes, " . . . some churches are opposed to delegation
of power to officers of an ecumenical body not for either of the two reasons given,
but because they are *supporters* of an hierarchical form of church order and
believe that it exists in the churches possessing the apostolic episcopate. I think
for completeness, it is important that this third reason should be stated."

entitled to speak out, should it then remain silent? At this point we have to remember the paradoxical character of the World Council. If the World Council looks inwards at its own situation, it cannot possibly speak. For it will then become obsessed with the difficulties of its own internal life and postpone the day of witness to the Greek kalends. But if it remembers that it is not merely an organization which has to take account of the empirical realities of its own life, but that it is an instrument offered to the Lord of the Church to be used as He wills, then it will hope for and pray for the miracle of its receiving authority from God to speak.

A true miracle! For the World Council can only speak if the very heterogeneous group of its leaders is suddenly transformed into a homogeneous fellowship of witness. The many individual voices which speak from somewhere in the divided Church may become the common voice which speaks from the centre of the one and undivided Church. A miracle—and, therefore, not something to be forced, but something to be received.

What is the weight of such a common word? It cannot commit the churches in the World Council. It carries no official character. It is a defenceless utterance which may be challenged from almost any quarter. It is simply the word of men who say: "We have no canonical authority. We have no right to speak for all the Christian churches, not even for all non-Roman Christian churches. But we are leaders of a council in and through which the churches seek to re-establish the *koinonia* which they had lost. We cannot, therefore, refrain from praying and working for the manifestation of that *koinonia*. And we cannot remain silent when God answers our prayer and gives us a word of common witness. It is for each church to decide whether it recognizes in our witness the genuine voice of the Una Sancta."

The World Council must then always be ready to be used as the voice of the Una Sancta. And it must prepare itself for this task by eliminating all conditions which keep it from witnessing and which it is in its power to eliminate. Thus it must get rid of all fear of the political and organizational consequences of a clear witness, and of many other human, all too human, considerations. It must be ready to speak out whenever there arises an issue of decisive moment for the cause of the Church in the world. Very often it will fail. In the future, as on several occasions in the past, it will happen again and again that, though there is a willingness to speak, no agreement can be reached as to the content of the message to be proclaimed. And, if it does speak, it will have to be prepared to meet with severe criticism and to be repudiated as a voice which does not represent the conviction of the churches. All that is inevitable and belongs to the risks of the ecumenical adventure.

Everything depends finally on the fundamental readiness to be used. If the World Council refuses to act as the organ of the Una Sancta, it has no promise. But if it is founded on an absolute willingness to be used, even its failures will finally prove to be blessings.

VI IMPLICATIONS OF WORLD COUNCIL MEMBERSHIP

What does it mean for a church to become a member of this World Council? What we have said about the Council means that the acceptance of membership is more than a matter of practical strategy. Participation in the Council must be based on a willingness to collaborate with other churches and on a readiness to share in serious common study concerning the witness of the Church to the world and concerning church unity. But there is more. Entrance into the World Council presupposes willingness to manifest together with other churches that measure of unity which is now granted to the churches in the Council and to strive with them for the manifestation of the full unity of the Church of Christ.

This does not mean that a church entering into the Council automatically recognizes the claims of all other churches in the Council to be in the full and true sense of that word parts of the Church Universal. Such recognition is most desirable, but it is the goal, not the beginning of the ecumenical process. We need the World Council as an emergency solution just because the churches are not at one in their convictions concerning the true faith and the true order of the Church. It must be, and indeed is, possible to enter the World Council without compromising on any fundamental confessional points of faith and order. Participation in the World Council does not imply a relativistic attitude concerning the essential and indispensable characteristics of the true Church of Christ.

But membership in the World Council implies that each

church should recognize at least in its sister churches in the Council the *vestigia ecclesiae*, that is, the fact that in some sense the Church of Christ exists also in them and that the Lord of the Church is at work in their life. It has been well said (by Professor Herrmann Sasse) that the creation of the World Council of Churches means that for the first time the churches accept the consequences flowing from the classical doctrine, taught by practically all churches in the Council, according to which the Church of Christ includes all those who confess His name, even if their confession is incomplete or mixed with error.

But if it is recognized that Christ is at work in other churches, it is the duty of each church in the fellowship to listen to the witness of these churches, to open itself to the truth of God which it may learn from them, and to be ready to let its own faith and life be enriched or corrected by this fraternal contact.

Churches cannot treat each other as if they were sovereign states which defend the integrity of their rights and territory. They must on the contrary rejoice when the ecumenical situation leads to constructive battles and beneficial invasions. The members of the ecumenical family cannot adopt the principle of non-intervention. They let themselves be questioned by their fellow members. They exhort each other to greater faithfulness and to renewal of life. They call each other back to the Apostolic witness. They are their brothers' keepers, and whatever concerns the churches confessing the same Lord, is their concern. If the World Council should do nothing else but set in motion this process of constructive and mutual challenge, so that the churches cease to be on the defensive towards each other or to behave like rival states, and that they let themselves be transformed in the give and take of a common struggle for the truth of God—that alone will justify its existence.

But the purpose of it all is the healing of the Church. All churches need the same physician. As together they turn to Him, together they will be healed.

VII   INSTITUTION OR MOVEMENT?

All that has been said so far can be summarized in the statement that the World Council has no future if it does no more than reflect the empirical reality of the *churches as they are*, but that it has a promise, if it is and remains a willing instrument in the hands of the Lord, Who is the power of God. It is specially true in the ecumenical realm that to stand still is to go backward. If the ecumenical movement becomes an ecumenical institution, its days are numbered.

But does the official institution of the World Council at the time of the Assembly not mean that the danger has become much greater? Are we not precisely at the point at which a pioneering movement in the life of the churches is transformed into an official and representative ecclesiastical body? Are we not attempting the impossible, if we make the churches with their immobility and ineradicable conservatism the pillars of an ecumenical fellowship which can only live if it remains on the move?

These are real questions. The risk is indeed considerable. There is a real possibility that a church-centred ecumenical body will prove to be so static, so inhibited, that it will tend to "freeze" the ecumenical situation and become an obstacle to advance. Church history is full of examples of movements of the Spirit which have ended up as bureaucratic organizations without true spiritual power.

But we have no choice in this matter. The ecumenical movement has discovered with increasing certainty that its aim is not a unity of individuals but the unity of the Church. And the Church is not to be found in the realm of abstract ideas or of inward sentiments, but in the historic and visible churches. At the present moment ecumenical advance means precisely the determination to carry the witness to the Una Sancta into the daily life of the churches, to give up the mirage of an ecumenical movement above or outside the existing churches and to make the churches themselves the pillars on which the ecumenical structure rests. The transfer of responsibility to the churches themselves is the direct result of the convictions which have been forced upon us in our ecumenical discussions. The principle that the churches alone will determine the policy of the Council is, therefore, fundamental in its structure and in its work.

But this principle can be applied in different ways. It might be taken to mean that the Council will be wholly in the hands of the clerical leaders. That interpretation is, however, rejected by the Utrecht Constitution which states that the Assembly and the Central Committee shall consist of both clerical and lay persons, men and women. For the churches in the Council believe that the laity (men and women) have a creative rôle to play in church life. None of the functions which the Council sets out to fulfil can be performed unless the whole membership of our churches participates, directly or indirectly, in its life. If this insight is taken seriously, it will go a long way to save the Council from excessive clericalism.

But there is more to be said. As the churches accept their ecumenical responsibility, they should remember that in the carrying out of this task they will need the continued assistance of those forces which in the "pioneering" and the "provisional" stages have given the real impetus to the ecumenical movement. Now some of these, although they are *of* the churches and *in* the churches, are not "official" and "representative" in the more technical sense of the term. It must not happen that important groups which are devoted to their churches and to the ecumenical cause suddenly find the doors closed to any active participation in ecumenical life simply because they are not in official positions of church leadership. While it is clear that the governing bodies of the Council must consist of men and women directly chosen by their churches, it is not only desirable but quite indispensable for the healthy development of the Council's life that it should make the fullest possible use of the services, the contributions and also the criticism which come to it from "unofficial" quarters. This is particularly true with regard to those Christian thinkers, theologians and men of many other professions, who have given substance to the programme of ecumenical study and through it to the preparation of the world conferences. It is also true with regard to the workers in the field of interdenominational co-operation, of missions and of inter-church aid. It should become increasingly true of the women of the churches. And the ecumenical youth movement must be given its rightful opportunity. Ways and means should, therefore, be discovered by which in the work of the commissions, the departments, the conferences under the auspices of the Council, the present participation of all such forces is not only maintained but strengthened. Thus alone can we escape the danger of becoming institutionalized, and remain a movement sensitive to the dynamic influences of the Spirit.

Is it possible to build a World Council which is truly rooted in the life of the churches, but which corrects and completes its own official character by welcoming spontaneous contributions from groups and individuals who are in another and significant sense members and spokesmen of the Church Universal? Is it possible to give the prophetic voice a place in a priestly structure? Whether it is possible or not, the attempt must be made. For we go forward in the name of a King Who is both prophet and priest. Where His Kingship is acknowledged, and there alone, the priestly and the prophetic are seen to be aspects of the same reality, which is His Church.

SOME QUOTATIONS FROM COMMENTS

Owing to the importance of this paper, not only for the Assembly for which it was written, but for the whole current discussion within the Ecumenical Movement, the writer of the paper and the Commission producing this volume both wish it to be supplemented by extensive quotation from a few of the critics who read it in its first and second drafts. It is thus made unmistakably clear that the essay does not profess to give a final answer but to initiate a discussion in which many voices, in many churches and countries, must take part.

1. *Dr. J. H. Oldham (Christian Frontier Council, Great Britain)*

Experience has shown that, provided the fundamental principle is loyally adhered to (i.e. that the Council has and claims no *ecclesiastical* authority) and *in proportion as* it is universally recognized and confidence is created through such adherence, action can be taken over a wide field by such bodies as the International Missionary Council, the British Council of Churches, and presumably also by the World Council of Churches—*but only on one condition.* That condition is that at meetings which authorize such action there are present leading representatives of the churches, who in giving their approval have reasonable confidence that if the action in question is challenged in their respective church assemblies they can successfully defend it. I should like to see this point, which in my view is an immensely important one and quite fundamental to the working of interdenominational bodies, brought out much more strongly and clearly in the memorandum.

2. Dr. F. E. Mayer (Lutheran Seminary, St. Louis, Mo., U.S.A.)

It is imperative that the question as to the nature of the Council be clearly defined. While some believe that the World Council is an expression of a common faith and an experience of the unity of the Church of Christ, there are many others who believe that the Council can at the present time only "register the apparent level of fundamental agreements within the Council and the grave points of disagreement remaining".

The author correctly points out that the World Council, "cannot claim to *be* the Una Sancta or a partial embodiment of the Una Sancta, because it lacks the essential *notae ecclesiae*". I fully agree with the author, that the *koinonia* of the New Testament is not present in the World Council because essential aspects of that *koinonia* are still lacking to-day. I believe that many Christians were suspicious of the World Council because its leaders apparently identified the outward union of churches with the New Testament *koinonia*. We are glad to note that this treatise does not view the *koinonia* as a *fait accompli*.

Since only the living Christ can establish the New Testament *koinonia*, the foremost problems to be solved are: Who is Jesus Christ? How does He establish the unity? What is the Word? What is the essence and which are the marks of the Church? In fact, it seems to us that, as Dr. 't Hooft points out, the paramount and basic problem is: To what extent is Holy Scripture final or does the experience of the churches modify or supplement this Word? We believe that this problem is basic, and therefore suggest that a study of this problem be included in the agenda of the Amsterdam meeting.

3. Prof. Dr. H. Sasse (Erlangen, Germany)

The churches which are joined together in the Council are separated not only because there are legitimate differences between them, but also because they cannot acknowledge the heresies which one discovers in the other. The Baptist doctrine of baptism is a heresy for Anglicans and Lutherans. The *sola scriptura* is a heresy for the Eastern Church. The denial of the *sola fide* is a heresy for Evangelicals. We cannot avoid acknowledging this, and therefore there is no intercommunion amongst the churches of the World Council. But what is it that unites these churches? Is it Christian love? Yes. Because of love they cannot ignore each other. Is it their common needs and tasks? Again yes. But it is more. All these churches are united by the great creeds of the Old Church, by the *consensus quinquesaecularis*, by the "great articles of the divine majesty", by the trinitarian and the christological faith, those articles of which Luther said that, in the controversy with Rome, there could be "no quarrel or disagreement" about them. It is the task of the ecumenical movement, and therefore also the task of the World Council of Churches, to show for the first time in the history of the Church, that this common possession makes possible a real, even if not complete, unity. That is why the Lausanne statement of the common creed is so important. This consensus makes it possible for Catholic and Protestant churches to work together. It keeps the door open for Rome, and we must keep this door open if the Council wants to be "ecumenical". It is the task of the World Council of Churches and of the churches who are united in it, to show the world what fellowship in the faith in the tri-une God and in the God-Man creates amongst Christians and churches, but it is a condition that what divides the churches, where they still have to pray and work together for the illumination of the truth, is just as honestly stated.

But should it be said that this double relationship of unity and division is not possible, the answer is: Since the decision in the controversy about baptism of heretics in the third century against Cyprian and the African Church, and since the fight of Augustine against Donatism, it has been recognized in the dogma of all Christian churches that also amongst heretics there are at least the *vestigia ecclesiae*. The Lutheran Church has never—not even at the time of the strictest orthodoxy—denied that the Church of Christ was to be found in the church of the Abyssinians or in the mission churches of the Jesuits. Yes, she has believed that even in the Arian churches of the early centuries the right faith in the true divinity of the Son had not been completely extinguished. It is the task of the ecumenical movement to draw the consequences out of these facts of church history. In it the denominations are brought into a new relationship. The World Council of Churches cannot do more than this. When it does, and only does, what it can do, then God will do what He alone can do.

4. *Principal N. Micklem (Mansfield College, Oxford, England)*

The paper seems to imply that there are two kinds of authority. One is proper canonical authority which the World Council does not claim. The other is such authority as the World Council may carry by its own wisdom. This is expressed on page 190 by saying that the World Council does not claim any authority for itself. This, I submit, is to misrepresent the nature of authority in the Church. Canonical authority is relative to the rules which the various churches have adopted—this is legal authority, not spiritual authority. The World Council would properly claim no authority for itself in regard to its own wisdom, but when a representative group of Christians of varying points of view meet together and after prayer and discussion are led to a common agreement and common assurance, and are given a common word, they may say in all humility " it seemed good to the Holy Ghost and to us ". That is not to claim authority by their own wisdom, but is, as page 188 says, an instance of the formidable authority of the Holy Spirit. There is no other authority in the Church, as distinct from the denominations. This is not a second-rate and weak kind of authority. It is the authority of the Spirit commending itself to the minds and conscience of Christians.

5. *The Bishop of Chichester (England)*

The fundamental fact is that the World Council is a body without any ecclesiastical authority in itself, or any power by itself to commit any of the churches which are represented upon it. It is important to emphasize this at the start and to secure its acceptance as a governing principle. This, however, does not mean that it can have no spiritual influence, or that it cannot do or say things of importance to Christianity. In this connection it may be of interest to recall that the Lambeth Conference (though limited to Anglican churches) is based on the same principle. Thus, when the Lambeth Conference was first assembled in 1867, the Archbishop of Canterbury (Longley), before issuing the invitations to Bishops of the different Anglican Provinces, took special pains to declare " I should refuse to convene any assembly which pretended to enact any Canon, or affected to make any decisions binding on the Church ". And the latest

Lambeth Conference (1930) spoke again of " its strict adherence to purely advisory functions ". Nevertheless, successive Lambeth Conferences have issued statements (as well as advice to Provinces) which have been of service by their own weight in guiding thought; the test of acceptance being the consent of the hearers.

6. *Dr. Samuel McC. Cavert (Federal Council of Churches, U.S.A.)*

The Council should carefully refrain from assuming an authority over the churches which the Constitution clearly denies to the Council and which the Council could not, in fact, exercise even if the Constitution sanctioned it. The more explicit the Council is on this point, the greater will be its actual influence on the life of the churches.

We should not conclude that because the churches have not delegated any authority to the Council at the beginning, they will never be willing to do so. It is entirely possible that if the sense of need for a more united Church increases and if the Council commends itself strongly to the churches by the way in which it fulfils its present limited functions, the time may come when the churches will desire to assign certain responsibilities to it and to confer on it a constitutional authority in certain specified matters.

We should not allow the problem of "authority" to become a sort of "bogey-man" frightening the World Council from doing what the occasion requires. The tendency to be timid and hesitant lest the Council should exceed its "authority" will probably need to be resisted.

MEMBERS

OF ASSEMBLY COMMISSION I

ON

" THE UNIVERSAL CHURCH IN GOD'S DESIGN "

(This list includes those members of the Commission who were appointed before the end of 1947 and who therefore were able to participate in the preparation of the volume.)

The Rt. Rev. Bishop Gustaf AULÉN, *Strängnäs*, CHAIRMAN
Professor Clarence Tucker CRAIG, *New Haven, Conn.*, VICE-CHAIRMAN
The Rev. Oliver S. TOMKINS, *London*, SECRETARY AND EDITOR

Professor Karl BARTH, *Basel*
President Conrad BERGENDOFF, *Rock Island, Ill.*
Professor S. F. H. J. BERKELBACH VAN DER SPRENKEL, *Utrecht*
The Rt. Rev. Bishop Angus DUN, *Washington D.C.*
Professor George FLOROVSKY, *Paris*
Professor Georgia HARKNESS, *Evanston, Ill.*
Professor H. A. HODGES, *Reading*
President John MACKAY, *Princeton, N.J.*
The Rev. Canon R. A. MANUEL, *Calcutta*
Professor Richard NIEBUHR, *New Haven, Conn.*
Professor Regin PRENTER, *Aarhus*
Professor A. M. RAMSEY, *Durham*
The Rev. Kenneth RICHES, *Oxford*
The Rev. Hébert ROUX, *Bordeaux*
Professor Béla VASADY, *Debreczen*
President Francis C. WEI, *Wuchang*
Professor Ernst WOLF, *Göttingen*

INDEX OF SUBJECTS

Amay, Priory of, 172
Ashrams, in India, 120, 130

Barmen, Synod of, 105, 107
Bible, renewed love of, 101, 107,
    108, 117-119

" Cell " movements, 129
"Christian Home" movement,
    120, 122-123
Church:
  and Bible, 22ff., 75
  as Body of Christ, 19, 20, 39-42,
    46, 49-51, 53-54, 59-60, 82
  as Communion of Saints, 21,
    47-48, 61
  and Creeds, 65
  doctrine of,
    in New Testament, 33
    in Old Testament, 32
  as *ekklesia*, 33, 44ff.
  and Kingdom of God, 33ff.
  and *koinonia*, 18ff., 35, 46
  and Lay Ministry, 103
  and Local Congregation, 67ff.,
    73
  and Message, 55
  and Ministry, 27ff., 37ff., 51ff.,
    62ff.
  and Pentecost, 48ff.
  and Sacraments, 22ff., 36, 47,
    49
  and Unity, 28ff., 51, 60-61, 66,
    170ff., 173, 176

Church—*continued*
  in China, 111ff.
  in France, 121
  in Germany, 97ff., 100ff., 107
  in Greece, 117, 121ff.
  in India, 132, 133, 148ff.
  in Norway, 94ff.

Ecumenical Conferences, 179-181
Encyclicals, Papal, 53 (n.19),
    156, 158, 168, 172, 174
    (n.3)
Erastianism, 144

Lambeth Conferences, 198-199
Liturgical movement, 102, 115-
    117

Retreat movement, 129
Revivals: Methodist, 124ff.
  in Europe, 124ff.
  in U.S.A., 124ff.
  in China, 127
  in India, 126

Una Sancta movement, 163, 173

Women, service of, 119-123
Women's Christian College,
    Madras, 120
World Council of Churches, 146,
    156
  Reconstruction Department of,
    135
Worship, 63ff., 113

INDEX OF NAMES

Adam, Karl, 51 and n.18.
Aquinas, St. Thomas, 43
Augustine, St., 50, 51 (n.14, n.15),
    54 (n.23), 197

Barth, Karl, 161
Billing, Einar, 138
Bonhoeffer, Dietrich, 178
Bremond, Arnold, 172
Brilioth, Bishop, 171

Cavert, S. M., 199
Charrière, Mgr., 171
Chichester, Bishop of, 198
Chrysostom, St. John, 50
Congar, Father, 171
Couturier, Abbé, 163, 170ff.
Cyprian, 197

Dawson, Christopher, 133

Galen, Bishop von, 106
Gelasius I, 137
Gregory of Nyssa, 43, 48 (n.7)
Grosche, Robert, 44, 44 (n.2)

Hermas of Rome, 53 (n.20)
Hodgson, Leonard, 138
Hogg, A. G., 149

John of Damascus, 43

Khomiakov, 53 (n.22), 54 (n.24)

Latourette, K. S., 110, 131

Leo XIII, 172
Luther, Martin, 92, 93, 94, 162

Mascall, E. L., 53 (n.21)
Mayer, F. E., 196
Melanchthon, Philip, 92
Melville, Andrew, 139
Mersch, E., 53 (n.19)
Micklem, N., 198
Moehler, 53 (n.22)

Oldham, J. H., 195
Origen, 43

Pius IX, 172
Pius X, 171
Pius XI, 156, 172, 174
Pius XII, 172

Quisling, 95

Ramabai, Pandita, 119

Sasse, H., 192, 196ff.
Schleiermacher, 159
Söderblom, N., 169
Suhard, Cardinal, 171

Thadden, Reinhold von, 106
Turrecremata, Cardinal, 43

Voetius, 139

Wedel, Theodore, 116

REPORT OF SECTION I

"THE UNIVERSAL CHURCH IN GOD'S DESIGN"

Received by the Assembly and commended to the churches for their serious consideration and appropriate action.

I. OUR GIVEN UNITY

GOD has given to his people in Jesus Christ a unity which is His creation and not our achievement. We praise and thank Him for a mighty work of His Holy Spirit, by which we have been drawn together to discover that, notwithstanding our divisions, we are one in Jesus Christ.

We speak, as Christians from many lands and many traditions, first of all to thank God for His goodness. We come from Christian churches which have for long misunderstood, ignored and misrepresented one another; we come from lands which have often been in strife; we are all sinful men and we are heirs to the sins of our fathers. We do not deserve the blessing which God has given us.

God's redeeming activity in the world has been carried out through His calling a People to be His own chosen People. The old covenant was fulfilled in the new when Jesus Christ, the Son of God incarnate, died and was raised from the dead, ascended into heaven and gave the Holy Ghost to dwell in His Body, the Church. It is our common concern for that Church which draws us together, and in that concern we discover our unity in relation to her Lord and Head.

II. OUR DEEPEST DIFFERENCE

It is in the light of that unity that we can face our deepest difference, still loving one another in Christ and walking by faith in Him alone. It has many forms and deep roots. It exists among many other differences of emphasis within Christendom. Some are Catholic or Orthodox in clearly understood senses; some are Protestant after the great Reformation confessions; others stress the local congregation, the "gathered community" and the idea of the "free church." Some are deeply convinced that Catholic and Protestant (or evangelical) can be held together within a single church. Yet, from among these shades of meaning, we would draw special attention to a difference to which, by many paths, we are constantly brought back. Historically it has been loosely described as the difference between "catholic"[1] and "protestant,"[2] though we have learned to mistrust any over-simple formula to describe it.

The essence of our situation is that, from each side of the division, we see the Christian faith and life as a self-consistent whole, but our two conceptions of the whole are inconsistent with each other.

It is impossible to describe either tendency or emphasis briefly without doing it an injustice. Each contains within it a wide variety of emphasis and many "schools of thought." But in each case we confront a whole corporate tradition of the understanding of Christian faith and life: We may illustrate this by saying that the emphasis usually called "catholic"[3] contains a primary insistence upon the visible continuity of the Church in the apostolic succession of the episcopate. The one usually called "protestant"[4] primarily emphasizes the initiative of the Word of God and the response of faith, focussed in the doctrine of justification *sola fide*. But the first group also stresses faith, and the second also stresses continuity of the visible church in some form. Moreover this difference of emphasis cuts across many of our confessional boundaries. Conversation and understanding between these traditions are often made even more difficult by the presence in each of many who are accustomed only to their own forms of expression, are ignorant of others' traditions and often hold beliefs about their separated fellow Christians which are a travesty of the true situation. Yet even when the conversation is between those who deeply trust and understand each other, there remains a hard core of disagreement between different total ways of apprehending the Church of Christ.

Each of these views sees every part of the Church's life in the setting of the whole, so that even where the parts seem to be similar they are set in a context which, as yet, we find irreconcilable with the whole context of the other. As so often in the past we have not been able to present to one another the *wholeness* of our belief in ways that are mutually acceptable.

[1-4] *Note:* Clearly "catholic" is not used here to mean Roman Catholic, and "protestant" in most of Europe is better rendered by "evangelical."

III. COMMON BELIEFS AND COMMON PROBLEMS

It is not possible to mention all the points which have been raised in our discussion together, still less to mention those which have been discovered in other fields of work on Christian unity, especially the work of the Commissions of Faith and Order. All that we do here is to indicate certain points to which we have given attention, and some of the ways in which we believe they can be pursued in the ongoing work for Christian unity. We consider that the book *The Universal Church in God's Design*, which was written in preparation for our studies, contains much helpful material and we commend it to the serious attention of our churches as they face these problems.

We group our agreements into those which concern the *nature* of the Church and those which concern its *mission*, each followed by some disagreements which are revealed by a closer examination of the agreements.

A. *We all believe that the Church is God's gift to men for the salvation of the world; that the saving acts of God in Jesus Christ brought the Church into being; that the Church persists in continuity throughout history through the presence and the power of the Holy Spirit.*

Within this agreement, we should continue, in obedience to God, to try to come to a deeper understanding of our differences in order that they may be overcome. These concern:

1. The relation between the old and new Israel and the relation of the visible church to "the new creation" in Christ. It appears from our discussion that some of our differences concerning the Church and the ministry have their roots here.

2. The relation, in the saving acts of God in Christ, between objective redemption and personal salvation, between scripture and tradition, between the Church as once founded and the Church as Christ's contemporary act.

3. The place of the ministry in the Church and the nature of its authority and continuity, the number and interpretation of the sacraments, the relation of baptism to faith and confirmation, the relation of the universal to the local church; the nature of visible unity and the meaning of schism.

B. *We believe that the Church has a vocation to worship God in His holiness, to proclaim the Gospel to every creature. She is equipped by God with the various gifts of the Spirit for the building up of the Body of Christ. She has been set apart in holiness to live for the service of all mankind, in faith and love, by the power of the crucified and risen Lord and according to His example. She is composed of forgiven sinners yet partaking already, by faith, in the eternity of the Kingdom of God and waiting for the consummation when Christ shall come again in the fullness of His glory and power.*

Within this agreement also, we should continue, in obedience to God, to try to come to a deeper understanding of our differences in order that they may be overcome. These concern:

1. The relation between the Godward vocation of the Church in worship and her manward vocation in witness and service.
2. The degree to which the Kingdom of God can be said to be already realized within the Church.
3. The nature of the Church's responsibility for the common life of men and their temporal institutions.

We gratefully acknowledge these agreements and we seek the solution of these disagreements. God wills the unity of His Church and we must be obedient to Him.

At many of these points, our problems cut across confessional boundaries, and we are grateful to God for the way in which we continually learn from our fellow Christians and for the way in which He is making Himself more clearly known to us through our fellowship with one another. In some parts of the world and to some of our members, issues which we have discussed here do not seem important or even relevant. Yet, because they are vital to some, they ultimately concern all. Among others whom we represent, many of our difficulties seem either to have been overcome or are on the way to solution. We thank God for all that lights the path to visible unity.

IV. THE UNITY IN OUR DIFFERENCE

Although we cannot fully meet, Our Lord will not allow us to turn away from one another. We cannot ignore one another, for the very intensity of our difference testifies to a common conviction which we drew from Him. The Body of Christ *is* a unity which makes it impossible for us either to forget one another or to be content with agreement upon isolated parts of our belief whilst we leave the other parts unreconciled.

Yet we have found God, in His mercy, penetrating the

barriers of our fundamental division and enabling us to speak, in the common language of the divine revelation witnessed to in the Scriptures, about the points at which we find we meet. Wherever we find ourselves thus speaking together of our unity, we also find ourselves faced by some stubborn problems. In dealing with them, we discover disagreements which are to be traced back into our different ways of understanding the whole and, beneath those disagreements, we find again an agreement in a unity which drew us together and will not let us go.

V. THE GLORY OF THE CHURCH AND THE
SHAME OF THE CHURCHES

The glory of the Church is wholly in her Lord. In His love, He stooped to redeem her and to crown her as His bride. We praise God for continually renewed signs of His love for the Church. In recent years, it has been given to many of our fellow Christians to rediscover what it is to be a "Church under the Cross." There they discovered new life, found the Bible as a living, contemporary book, made a good confession of their faith and saw the Church come to life in the steadfastness of thousands of humble Christians. We praise God for many signs of awakened life in the churches in many lands. Christ is moving many to a more sacrificial identification with the homeless and desperate, to a more vigorous evangelism and to a deeper theological seriousness. In many parts of the world, He is drawing long-separate Christians towards a closer approach to unity. Some notable unions have been achieved. For the courage, enterprise and vision which inspired them, we give thanks to our one Shepherd.

Although genuine convictions and loyalty to truth itself have their part in the making and perpetuating of divisions, we confess that pride, self-will and lovelessness have also played their part and still do so.

Within our divided churches, there is much which we confess with penitence before the Lord of the Church, for it is in our estrangement from Him that all our sin has its origin. It is because of this that the evils of the world have so deeply penetrated our churches, so that amongst us too there are worldly standards of success, class division, economic rivalry, a secular mind. Even where there are no differences of theology, language or liturgy, there exist churches segregated by race and colour, a scandal within the Body of Christ. We are in danger of being salt that has lost its savour and is fit for nothing.

Within our divided churches it is to our shame that we have so often lived in preoccupation with our internal affairs, looking inward upon our own concerns instead of forgetting ourselves in outgoing love and service. Our churches are too much dominated by ecclesiastic officialdom, clerical or lay, instead of giving vigorous expression to the full rights of the living congregation and the sharing of clergy and people in the common life in the Body of Christ.

We pray for the churches' renewal as we pray for their unity. As Christ purifies us by His Spirit we shall find that we are drawn together and that there is no gain in unity unless it is unity in truth and holiness.

VI. THE WORLD COUNCIL OF CHURCHES

We thank God for the ecumenical movement because we believe it is a movement in the direction which He wills. It has helped us to recognise our unity in Christ. We acknowledge that He is powerfully at work amongst us to lead us further to goals which we but dimly discern. We do not fully understand some of the things He has already done amongst us or their implications for our familiar ways. It is not always easy to reconcile our confessional and ecumenical loyalties. We also have much to gain from the encounter of the old-established Christian traditions with the vigorous, growing churches whose own traditions are still being formed. We bring these, and all other difficulties between us, into the World Council of Churches in order that we may steadily face them together. Because it is a Council of Churches, we must discuss them in a full sense of responsibility to those who send us, not pretending to agreements which our churches as a whole would repudiate.

The World Council of Churches has come into existence because we have already recognised a responsibility to one another's churches in Our Lord Jesus Christ. There is but one Lord and one Body. Therefore we cannot rest content with our present divisions. Before God, we are responsible for one another. We see already what some of our responsibilities are, and God will show us more. But we embark upon our work in the World Council of Churches in penitence for what we are in hope for what we shall be. At this inaugural Assembly, we ask for the continual prayer of all participating churches that God may guide it in His wisdom, saving us both from false claims and from faithless timidity.

MAN'S DISORDER AND GOD'S DESIGN
Volume II

THE
CHURCH'S WITNESS
TO
GOD'S DESIGN

THE
CHURCH'S WITNESS
TO
GOD'S DESIGN

AN

ECUMENICAL STUDY

PREPARED UNDER THE AUSPICES OF THE

WORLD COUNCIL OF CHURCHES

VOLUME TWO

CONTENTS

List of Contributors

I THE CHURCH'S COMMISSION 13
  1 A World Task—*Hendrik Kraemer* 14
  2 The Duty and Authority of the Church to preach the
    Gospel—*Lesslie Newbigin* 19

II OUR UN-CHRISTIAN WORLD 36
  1 Rival Secular Faiths—*Wilhelm Pauck* 37
  2 The Disintegration of Society in Christian Countries
    —*Paul Tillich* 53
  3 The Church's Failure to be Christian—(i) *Frank Bennett*;
    (ii) *S. C. Neill* 65

III SOME AXIOMS OF THE MODERN MAN 80
  1 Axioms by Emil Brunner 81
  2 From Great Britain 81
  3 From America 82
  4 From Germany 82
  5 From France 84

IV THE GOSPEL IN ITS RELEVANCE TO THE
                              PRESENT TIME 85
  1 *Walter M. Horton* 88
  2 *Pierre Maury* 98

V THE GOSPEL AT WORK IN THE WORLD 113

VI THE APPROACH TO ADHERENTS OF
                              OTHER FAITHS 168
  1a Aspects of the Modern Situation in India—*S. W.
    Savarimuthu* 169
  b The Approach to Adherents of a Primitive Religion
    in New Guinea—*George F. Vicedom* 178
  2 The Approach to Israel—*The French Committee of
    Witness to Israel* 190

VII IS THERE A PROBLEM OF EVANGELISM? 200

  Membership of the Commission 207
  Index 209
  Report of Section II

CONTRIBUTORS

BENNETT, Frank, Rector of Wigan, Lancashire, England.

BRUNNER, Emil, D.THEOL., Professor of Systematic Theology, Zurich. Author of *The Mediator, Justice and the Social Order*, etc.

HORTON, W. M., PH.D., Professor of Theology, Oberlin. Author of *Can Christianity Save Civilization?, Our Christian Faith*, etc.

KRAEMER, Hendrik, D.TH., Director-general of the Ecumenical Institute, Geneva; formerly Professor in the History of Religions, Leiden; Missionary in Indonesia. Author of *The Christian Message in a non-Christian World*, etc.

MAURY, Pierre, D.D., Professor of Dogmatics, Protestant Faculty of Theology, Paris; Vice-President Reformed Church of France. Author of *Trois Histoires Spirituelles, Le Grand Oeuvre de Dieu*, etc.

NEILL, S. C., Assistant Bishop to the Archbishop of Canterbury; Co-Director Study Department, World Council of Churches; formerly Bishop of Tinnevelly. Author of *Christ, His Church and His World*, etc.

NEWBIGIN, J. E. Lesslie, Bishop in Madura, Church of South India; formerly Missionary of the Church of Scotland. Author of *The Reunion of the Church*, etc.

PAUCK, Wilhelm, D.THEOL., Professor of Historical Theology, Chicago. Joint author of *The Church Against the World*, etc.

SAVARIMUTHU, S. C., Church of Sweden Mission, Chidambaram, S. India; formerly Professor, Lutheran Theological Seminary, Madras.

TILLICH, Paul, D.D., Professor of Theology, Union Theological Seminary, New York. Author of *The Religious Situation*, etc.

VICEDOM, G. F., Missionsinspektor an der Missions-Anstalt, Neuendettelsau; formerly missionary in New Guinea. Author of *Die Mbowamb, Die Kultur der Hagenberg-Stämme im östlichen Zentral-Neuguinea*.

THE CHURCH'S COMMISSION

PREFACE

The scope of this volume is to some extent determined by its length. The compilers, faced with the alternative of either attempting a comprehensive survey, in which each section would have to be so short as to exclude all illuminating detail, or of taking merely a selection of relevant material to illustrate problems and enterprises which could not be described in detail, without hesitation chose the latter course. This volume is no more than an introduction to the study of contemporary evangelism. The reader will at once become aware of omissions. For instance, in section VI, nothing is said of Islam or Confucianism or of several other great religious systems. Even the three sections which are printed deal only with a small part of their subject. One of the reasons for the adoption of this method is that, although ancient religions manifest a large measure of stability, much change is going on within them, and no fair statement can be made about the real religious significance of these systems at the present time, without deep research into materials not easily available. But equally in the sections dealing with the Western and partly Christian world, the study has been episodic rather than thorough, and all that has been attempted has been to give glimpses of deep-rooted problems and of evangelistic enterprises which show that the Gospel has not lost its old power to win men and to transform them.

Nevertheless, this is in some ways a pioneer volume. For the first time it has been recognized that the problems of the proclamation of the Gospel in East and West are fundamentally the same, and that old distinctions are out of date. The effect of this book may be rather to raise questions in the mind of readers than to answer them; if so, its real purpose will have been achieved, since this volume is only one of the first stages in a continuing process of study of evangelism in the modern world, in which all readers of the book are invited to participate. It is hoped that a more thoroughly documentary study may later be published in the series Ecclesia Militans, *edited by the Study Department.*

A WORLD TASK

by Hendrik Kraemer

WITHIN the scheme of the general theme: " Man's Disorder and God's Design " of the first Assembly of the
World Council of Churches, Commission II is assigned
the task of treating as its part the subject: "God's Design
and Man's Witness." In other words: evangelism, the proclamation of the Gospel to all men, in all lands, in all situations and
civilizations, in all conditions and circumstances, to and in all
spheres of life; witnessing to God's redemptive order in Jesus
Christ, by word and deed, in the situation of the revolutionary world of to-day. This is literally a task of world-wide
dimensions.

The sixteenth century witnessed a rise of the great missionary
movement, that rose from the Roman Catholic Church in accompaniment to the first wave of political and economic penetration
of Europe in Asia and America. In the eighteenth century
began the great missionary movement of the non-Roman
churches, which has been one of the characteristic marks of
modern church history, one of the saving features amongst the
many weaknesses and failures of the Church in its reactions to
the revolutionary changes of modern society. It cannot be said
that this growing missionary enterprise, although an expression
of the essential apostolic nature of the Church, had its real roots
in the churches. It was mainly carried on by groups of people,
who were gripped by the vision of the missionary obligation
towards the unevangelized world. William Carey, the cobbler,
wrote in 1792 his " Enquiry into the obligations of Christians to
use means for the conversion of the Heathen", proclaiming to
his fellow-Christians the self-evident duty of the Church in terms
of a new message and a new appeal. This missionary movement
of the eighteenth and nineteenth centuries was the response of a
band of men and women to the appeal that came to them from
the increasing widening of the geographical, cultural and
religious horizon, resulting from the growing contact between
east and west. In other circles it aroused a vast intellectual

curiosity, but in those Christian men and women it called forth
a deep evangelistic fervour, kindled by imagination, vision and
a passion for self-sacrifice for Christ's sake. The most universal
and pointed expression of this attitude is to be found in the
words, ascribed to Wesley: "The World is my Parish." In the
mouth of the great pioneers of the eighteenth century, this
dictum was the terse formula of their faith, hope, love, and
obedience, of their spontaneous understanding of the essential
nature of the Church.

If ever there was a time to live and act by the vision laid
down in these words "The World is my Parish", then it is
undoubtedly the time in which God has placed us. It is simply
forced upon us by the dramatic contemporary situation. We
are not living in the age of discovery of new continents, civilizations and religions, which were at the first contacts stable and
static bodies and structures of life. We have grown into a close
and fatefully interrelated world-unity and have passed from
static stability into a universally revolutionary situation. Primitive tribes, ancient oriental civilizations and societies, the modern
Western world in all its parts and aspects, are at present living
through crucial conflicts, tensions and anxieties, which are world-
wide in character, extending to all phases of human life,
mutually conditioning and influencing each other, for good and
for evil. Everywhere the unity of life is shattered to the core
because of the collapse of old certitudes and the throwing away
of old bondages. Everywhere there is a restless and painful
searching for new foundations on which a new integrated unity
can be constructed. The clash of these endeavours for reintegration results in an unimaginable amount of strife and suffering.
The universal disintegration of society and its ensuing
demoralization releases everywhere demonic forces, leading to
terror and wanton oppression. Everywhere rival faiths and
secular gospels, in the East as well as in the West, are competing
for the allegiance of man, or want to make him their subservient
instruments. Everywhere the problem is or becomes acute:
is religion relatedness to a world of transcendental realities and
values, a necessary part of human life, or is it an antiquated
stage in the evolution of the race? This question lurks behind
modern secularism, behind the pretension of science as a competitive force and triumphant substitute for religion; also
behind the ideal of a man-made "Good Life". At the same

time dreams about the necessity and possibility of a new humanism, which is really universal, resulting from the meeting of the great cultural traditions, embracing the whole of mankind and constituting the basis of world-understanding, are dreamt by some of the most representative and sensitive minds from the East and the West.

This staggering and seething humanity of to-day, in its perilous quest for the reintegration and unification of life, challenges the churches all over the world. On account of it the Christian churches find themselves in an unparalleled missionary situation, not only in the " non-Christian " world, but as emphatically in the so-called " Christian " world. In comparison with the eighteenth century, the new feature is that as a result of the *élan* of the missionary movement of the nineteenth and twentieth centuries, the Church has become a body which, according to its nature, is not only *related* to the whole world, but is also *represented* all over the world. Older and younger churches, notwithstanding their different'cultural, religious, and social backgrounds, and atmospheres, are virtually in the same position and dealing with a common situation. It is a well-known experience in international gatherings of Christian leaders, when they meet at present out of their common concern for the responsibility of the Church in the world of to-day, that they instantly discover this essential unity of their problems, hopes, and anxieties. The term " world-wide " is therefore fully justified. It has an urgency and depth as never before. The churches everywhere face the task of evangelizing a world in every respect in revolutionary transition, of proclaiming its message and asserting its peculiar character in environments, partly hostile, partly indifferent, partly open-minded.

That there is a world task confronting and waiting for the churches is a plain fact. Far more important is the question *whether* and *how* the churches will respond to this challenge. This stupendous task cannot be met, as in the eighteenth century, by far-sighted individuals and by groups whose heart is afire. It will only be taken in hand and carried out when the apostolic nature and obligations of the Church are grasped realistically and effectively understood and loved as the given privilege and task of every member of the Church, of every church and of the churches together. In all three respects we are still in the stage of initial discovery of those truths and requirements, which are essential and self-evident marks of Christianity and the Church. We begin to understand that the vast multitude of lay-members of the churches is the greatest potential force the churches, humanly speaking, have, in carrying out their commission to witness to the power of salvation and renewal of life that is in Jesus Christ. We begin to understand that only rarely as yet are the churches as churches really shouldering their missionary privilege and responsibility towards their peculiar environments and towards the world at large. The consciousness of this inescapable duty is growing. There are springing up in many places endeavours to embody this new awareness, which have to be acknowledged with great gratitude. This growing awareness impels many minds towards the necessity of searching for a new understanding and a fresh interpretation of the biblical message of God's design for man and the world. God in His mercy is using the perplexingly confused state of the world to awaken in the Church the anxiety for the rediscovery of its own nature and its *raison d'être*. Yet, on the whole, the churches *as* churches still remain far more complacent about their own situation and the situation of the world than they have any right to be. This complacency in itself is a sign that the churches sorely need a new awakening to the revolutionary character of the Gospel. They cannot exercise any spiritual leadership in the present revolutionary world if they do not manifest a readiness constantly to reform their own ways and attitudes, in obedience and openness to the revolutionary forces that emanate from the proclamation of God's estimate of human standards and human conditions. The coming Assembly, in confronting the churches with the world task that is pressing upon them, will have to seek ways and means in order to impress upon the churches the inescapable duty of assuming, humbly but confidently, this world task. This certainly will not happen if the prevailing complacency and self-centredness are not felt as a capital sin against God and the world.

We hardly begin to understand that the only adequate response—adequate to the essential nature of the Church—to the task of the proclamation of the Gospel by word and act, by prophetic guidance and sacrificial love, in this disrupted world, is that the *whole* Church is responsible for the whole world. The unprecedented call to world-wide evangelism, showing that God's purpose in saving the world means affirming His Lordship over all conditions of life, and therefore demands from us Christians the readiness to pioneer in entirely new directions —this call is at the same time an urgent appeal to the churches to start a fierce battle for victory over the too readily accepted ecclesiastical provincialism in which they are moving and living. It is a mighty call towards "endeavouring to keep the unity of the Spirit in the bond of peace", towards envisaging the task as a common task, as a God-given opportunity to become awake to the obligation of discharging this task as a manifestation of the ecumenicity of the Church in the world.

If by God's Grace the coming Assembly is the beginning of a resolute, realistic and obedient facing and assuming of the world-task by the Church, still one essential condition has to be fulfilled, without which all our intentions will appear in the end as confidence in our own human powers of decision, wisdom and courage. This essential condition is that God may grant, through the Assembly, an awakening of the spirit of unceasing prayer through the churches all over the world. "With God all things are possible", the renewal of the Church and the performance of a humanly speaking impossible world task; provided we sincerely and humbly believe that prayer is the greatest and most efficacious power that God in His mysterious wisdom has entrusted to us. It is the sole legitimate Christian answer to the feeling of impending disaster, that dominates the minds of men at present, and threatens to create a sense of unreality in talking about a world task in a world that, seemingly, hastens to self-destruction. God only knows whether the time for the Church to fulfil its task will be short or long. Our speculations and forebodings, however justified they may be by the trend of world events, never can be the right point of orientation for the behaviour of the Church. It is only to be found in the identification of the Church with God's solicitude, for the world, Who so loved the world, that He gave His only begotten Son, that whosoever believeth in Him should not perish, but have everlasting life.

2

THE DUTY AND AUTHORITY OF THE CHURCH
TO PREACH THE GOSPEL

by Lesslie Newbigin

I INTRODUCTORY

THIS paper has the strictly limited purpose indicated by its
title. Preaching the Gospel is not the whole duty of the
Church to the world. The Church has the duty to do
everything which is summed up in the command "Thou shalt
love thy neighbour as thyself". That duty is inherent in the
nature of the Church no less than the duty to preach the
Gospel. The Church—acting corporately and through its individual members—has to go out to men where they are, in their
need and pain and bewilderment, to get under their loads and
help to bear them, to find men where they lie wounded, bind up
their wounds and bring them home. It has also to do what is in
its power—corporately and through its individual members—to
bring all the common life of men, their economic and political
systems, their family life and their social customs, under obedience to Christ. And the Church has to do these things, not with
an eye upon possible conversions, but because these are the
things love must do. The present paper does not deal with these
things, simply for the reason that the subject of the paper is
"The Duty and Authority of the Church to preach the Gospel".

It is true that these two elements in the Church's duty to the
world must not be separated; the preaching of Christ will be
vain if it comes from men and communities in which the signs
of Christ and love are lacking. But equally they must not be
confused. When they are, two results follow: the distinctive
work of telling the good news of a redemption wrought for men
in Christ is obscured; attention is deflected from the evangel to
the evangelists. On the other hand, the Church's works of love
lose something of their spontaneous and disinterested quality
and come to be assessed primarily for their value in winning
converts. I would plead that we shall understand and discharge
both parts of our duty better if we are willing to think as clearly

as we can about each part separately. This paper deals with one part only.

But while the word "evangelism" has become in current use too broad a term to describe the subject of this paper, "preaching" is perhaps too narrow. In normal use it describes only the act of speaking in public before a congregation. It has also acquired—in English at least—a strong flavour of moral exhortation. Let it be said at once that we are not called upon to consider either the duty of every Christian to be a public speaker, or the duty of the Church to provoke to good works. We are to consider that part of the Church's duty which is described in the New Testament by the words *kerussein*—to proclaim, or herald, the good news of God's act in Christ—the *euangelion*. The most characteristic and vivid form of this activity is the public speech of an evangelist before an audience of his fellow-men; but only a false view of Christianity argues that the duty of proclamation laid upon the Church is in this precise form laid upon each member. "Are all evangelists?" asks the Apostle. All are not, and are not meant to be. And yet the duty of evangelism is a duty laid upon the whole Church. It follows that there is a duty laid upon every member of it to take his proper part in that task. There is obviously room for discussion about the relation of the duty of the individual Christian to the duty of the Church in this matter. But the primary purpose of this paper is to exhibit the source and nature of the duty and authority given *to the Church* to preach the Gospel.

II   THE SOURCE OF AUTHORITY IN THE WORD MADE FLESH

The duty and authority of the Church to preach the Gospel derive from Christ, and from no other source. If we are asked "by what authority?" we can only answer—in the last analysis —"In the Name of Jesus."

In the Incarnation of the Son of God the story of revelation moves forward to its decisive chapter. Here we have no longer only the prophetic word bearing witness to God, but God Himself present among men in a life, death and rising again which perfectly reveal His nature and effect His will. Yet even here, and from the very beginning, the preaching of the word is at the heart of His ministry in the flesh. At the very outset of the Gospel according to St. Mark, we read that "Jesus came into

Galilee preaching the Gospel of God, and saying, 'The time is fulfilled and the Kingdom of God is at hand: repent ye, and believe in the Gospel.'" There is no point—even at its very beginnings—where the Gospel is something other than a thing preached, a *kerugma*. The preaching of the first Apostles was the continuation of that which was the beginning of the Gospel, namely, the fact that Jesus came into Galilee preaching. It was the continued burning of a fire which, from the moment of its first kindling, possessed the quality of fire—namely, that it burns. "The Church exists by mission just as fire exists by burning" (Brunner). It is not only that the Word became flesh and that the Church was commissioned to proclaim that fact: it is also that the characteristic act which ushered in His ministry in the flesh was the act of preaching—of heralding the gracious act of God. When Jesus sent out the disciples as apostles to preach the Gospel, He was sending them not to begin something new, but to continue what He Himself was doing.

The question of authority arose at the outset. He spoke " as one having authority " (Mark i, 22). His teaching was contrasted with that of the scribes. We know how they taught: they spoke "from the authorities ", quoting tradition and precedent. Jesus spoke " as one having authority " in Himself. By the form (e.g. Matt. v, 21-2, 27-8, 33-4, 38-9, 43-4; vii, 29; xix, 8-9; and many passages in St. John) and content (e.g. Matt. x, 32-40; xi, 25-7; xviii, 19-20; xxv, 31-46; xxvi, 64; Mark viii, 38; ix, 41-2; xii, 1-12, 35-7; xiv, 24; John v, 16-18, 19-27; vi, 28ff.; viii, 12ff.; ix, 35-41; x, 9ff.; xi, 25ff.; xv, 1, etc.) of His teaching, by His works of healing (e.g. Matt. xii, 28; Mark i, 27; iii, 11; iv, 36-40; Luke vii, 2-7, etc.), by His acts of forgiveness (e.g. Mark ii, 1-12; Luke vii, 48-50) and by His calling of men to follow Him (Matt. xi, 28-30; Mark iii, 13ff.; John vii, 37ff.), He revealed the consciousness of possessing an authority derived from no human source but committed to Him by His Father. By so doing He confronted men with the necessity of deciding to accept or reject it. One who speaks " from the authorities " does not confront men with such a challenge: he requires no more of them than that they should test what he says by the standards which they already recognize as ultimate. But Jesus confronted men with a new ultimate: they had to decide for or against *Him*.

The duty and authority of the Church to preach the Gospel spring from this authority which was in Jesus Himself. This is not to deny that we have to do much preliminary work in order to make men feel that the Gospel is for them. In approaching any particular group of people with the Good News we have to relate our presentation of it to the place where they stand. We have both to state the Gospel in the language of the hearer and also to show his precarious foothold. Later chapters in this volume will attempt this task. But the basis of our authority to preach the Gospel does not lie in the fact that we can demonstrate—at least to our own satisfaction—that Christianity is superior to other forms of belief, ancient or modern. If we ourselves approach the Gospel, or encourage others to approach the Gospel, as the best among possible cures for human ills, we are bound to misunderstand it. The Gospel is news of God. It is not something offered to man for scrutiny and comparison with other ways of salvation. It is something much more formidable than that; it is the message to men that their Creator has come to them in judgment and mercy, to lay hold of them and make them His in the perfect fellowship of His eternal joy. The Gospel can only answer the needs of twentieth-century man if the Church which is entrusted with it recovers the sense that the Gospel is not primarily the answer to men's needs. Whatever is said in the proper place about the strategies by which we seek to bring home to men this tremendous message of God's saving acts, we must be clear that the mission which we have —its obligation and its authority—comes to us from that meeting with God in Christ and from nowhere else. Our purpose is not to deal with the immediate practical issues of evangelistic approach to twentieth-century man in East and West, but to explore the Gospel itself in order that by facing Christ Himself afresh we may hear and understand anew His command to go and make disciples of all nations.

We have to avoid the error of citing the authority of Christ after the manner of the Scribes and Pharisees, and so using His Name but reversing His method. By refusing to cite "authorities" and by confronting men with His own unique authority, He placed upon men the terrifying responsibility of discerning between truth and falsehood. "Why even of yourselves judge ye not what is right?" He asked (Luke xii, 57). He assumed that, by God's Spirit, they could recognize Him for themselves, and the evoking of that recognition was in a sense His supreme task. For the Church merely to cite His command to preach the Gospel is, therefore, not enough: it must in each new generation so learn Christ that it may feel the constraint and hear the command afresh through the Spirit, and that it may know with what authority it faces a world whose rules obstinately question its right to speak.

III WHAT IS THE GOSPEL?

In the New Testament the earliest and simplest statement of the Gospel is " The time is fulfilled and the Kingdom of God is at hand ". To understand these words we have to look both before and after. We have to take account of God's dealings with Israel, recorded in the Old Testament, and of the marrow of Jesus' words, unfolded in the record of His teaching, acts, death, resurrection and ascension, and of the coming of the Holy Spirit. If we neglect the Old Testament background, we shall read into the words of Jesus the meaning they have for us in the twentieth century. If we focus our eyes on the Old Testament we shall be blind to His eternal meaning. While Jesus necessarily began with the words His hearers knew, His message so far exceeded the limits of their understanding and expectation that they finally rejected Him as an impostor. We have to go on from this first bare announcement—" The time is fulfilled and the Kingdom of God is at hand "—to see what manner of fulfilment God gave to the cherished hopes of His people, and what manner of kingdom it was that had come near. For this we have to turn first to the preaching of the Apostles in the earliest days (e.g. Acts ii, 14-36; iii, 12-26; iv, 8-12; viii, 32ff.; x, 34-43; 1 Cor. xv, 1-8) when, filled with the Holy Spirit (the authentic sign of the new age), they were at last able to read all the strange experience which had befallen them since they were called from their nets to follow the new Teacher. We find here the essential pattern of the Gospel preaching, and we can trace the same pattern in the " Gospels " in which the record of Christ's words and works has been preserved for the use of the Church, and in the later creeds in which the Church has sought to crystallize the Gospel message. When we study this early preaching and these records, we see that the Gospel is the proclamation of a series of events in history which have been—from their first dawning—proclaimed to be decisive for human history and for every individual. " The time is fulfilled . . . Repent and believe."

Presupposed in these words of our Lord there are at least these three fundamental doctrines: the doctrine of God as Creator and Lord of the world and of time, Who has power to announce the end of one age and the dawning of a new; the doctrine of men as His children, made in His image, yet ranged in a common rebellion against Him; and the doctrine of the election of Israel as His people, and their long preparation for the fulfilment of His reign. Christ's own announcement, as wrought out in His words and deeds, can be described as that of something accomplished and of something impending, of something to be received and of something to be hoped for, of redemption and of consummation. Under these five heads then —Creation, Fall, Election, Redemption and Consummation— we shall seek to make clear the sources in the Gospel of the duty and authority of the Church to preach it.

A. *Creation.* The message with which the New Testament opens presupposes the firm monotheism of the Old. When Jesus spoke and acted as He did, it was plain that the Kingdom of which He spoke was the Kingdom of the one Creator of all things and all men, the Almighty, the Eternal, the All-Holy. What also became plain was that Jesus Himself claimed to be the King. In the context of a pantheistic or polytheistic religion, the manner and matter of His words might have been interpreted as the manifestation of religious genius or sainthood. as these are understood in these contexts. But in the world in which He lived and moved, no such interpretation was possible. He confronted those who heard Him inexorably with the alternatives of calling Him blasphemer or else of acknowledging that in Him the Creator Himself, Very God, had indeed come among men. The Old Testament has no place for demigods, and Jesus can accept no such place. The authority with which He meets us is the authority of our Creator, imperiously demanding unconditional surrender. Yet unlike the absolute claims made in the name of men or of human institutions it does not destroy the frail yet priceless treasure of our rational and moral integrity. He leaves us free to reject Him if we will. The absolute surrender which we know ourselves bound to make to Him is not extorted. And when we give it, we know that we have not lost our freedom but gained it. These things are so just because Christ's authority is the authority of our Creator Himself, the authority upon which our rational and moral integrity rests. It is because we have been made by Him and for Him that our hearts and minds can find rest in Him alone.

But if this be true for us, it is true for all men. It is an integral part of that doctrine of creation which the words of Jesus presupposed, that man is made in God's image. Without pretending to explore this doctrine, we may assert that man has been so created that he finds his true self only in a free response to God. This is the note of humanity everywhere and always, marking off man from the rest of creation. When therefore we say (as we must) that Christ's authority is that of our Creator, we are saying that it is as true for all men as it is for ourselves, that they can only recover their true humanity by a free surrender to Christ. If we deny this (either by our theory or by our practice); if we think and behave as though there were any created person to whom the Gospel message is not relevant, we deny the deity of Christ and treat Him as though He were but a sectional or tribal demigod.

This point is central if we are to claim the right to preach the Gospel, from civil governments which deny it. It is not simply that we believe Christianity to be the true religion and therefore desire to propagate it. Others have the same conviction about their own religions and have deduced that a minority has the right to demand freedom to preach because the state ought not to prohibit the propagation of truth, and a majority in power has a right to put obstacles in the way of other religious communities because the state ought not to encourage error. In so far as Christians fall into this error, and use the political power available to them to deny freedom to religious minorities, they forfeit the grounds upon which they can rightly claim freedom when they are themselves in the minority. These grounds are the belief that all men are so created in God's image that they can only find their humanity in a freely given obedience to Him, and the belief that in Christ the Creator of all men has come among men in order that through His redeeming work all men may be enabled freely to give that obedience. Jesus Himself, in the days of His flesh, placed upon men the responsibility of themselves making the ultimate decision about their destiny —the decision of faith. He scrupulously protected men's freedom to reject Him. These facts ought to be a perpetual reminder to the Church of the true grounds for her claim that the state should respect the freedom and responsibility of every

man to make the decision of faith.[1]   There are times when the
Church can only assert her claim by the witness of her martyrs.
But she disastrously compromises her claim, and casts away what
her martyrs have won, if she uses political power to deny to
men their freedom to reject the Christian revelation.

B. *The Fall*.   At the heart of the Old Testament revelation,
which is the presupposition of Jesus' first announcement, lie the
twin doctrines of Creation and the Fall (Gen. ii, 4-17; iii, 1-19).
Man is what he is because he has refused that for which he was
created.   That "there is none righteous, no, not one " (Ps. xiv,
3; Rom. iii, 9ff.) is the common conviction of the Old and New
Testaments.   That is not to say that the distinctions which we
properly draw between good men and bad men, between just
causes and unjust causes, are obliterated.   On the contrary, they
are felt with the deepest intensity.   But over all, over humanity
as such, over all men and all their works is written " dust thou
art and unto dust shalt thou return ", and this sentence is traced
to a primal rebellion against God the Creator, a rebellion in
which man and his whole history are therefore involved.   Among
ourselves we may distinguish better and worse; in relation to
our Lord and King we rank as members in a gang of rebels.   The
fissure that runs right through our human nature between what
we are and what we ought to be is the result of our denial of that
responsibility to God in virtue of which alone we are human.
Our predicament is set vividly before our eyes in the Passion
story, where we see the Son of God utterly alone, tried, condemned, cast out, crucified; and ranged against Him, not the
rabble only, but the chosen leaders of the noblest religion and
the most august political order which the world had known.
The whole human race is represented in the drama of Calvary.
There all men without distinction stand condemned as enemies
of the Most High.   There, for the same reason, they stand as
objects of His grace Who so loved *the world* that He gave His
only begotten Son.

But this, it must be repeated, does not mean that distinctions
are obliterated.   There are bad and good men under every sky.
There are higher and lower religions.   There are nobler and

---

[1] I do not forget that there are many forms in which the issue of the freedom
of the individual *vis-à-vis* the state is being pressed on our world.   I speak here
only of the freedom of religious minorities to profess and propagate their faith.
Where this specifically religious freedom is denied, all other forms of freedom
are in danger.

baser elements in every religious community. These distinctions are real. Otherwise the Crucifixion of Jesus would be a meaningless episode. The power to recognize goodness and its constraint upon the conscience are at least part of what is involved in our creation in the image of God; they are the heritage of all men in every time and place. What, then, is the relation of the Gospel to goodness as it is found in men apart from Christ? By what right do we preach the Gospel to men who are—it may be—better than ourselves?

So far as the answer is covered by the doctrine of the Fall of man, the clue is found in St. Paul's analysis of the relations between Law and Gospel:

(a) Whenever the Gospel is preached, it is preached to people who are already in some sense under law. If there were a people to whom the distinction of right and wrong was unknown, even in its most corrupted and debased form, it would be impossible to find in the language of that people words in which to preach the Gospel. But where there is a distinction between right and wrong, there is the knowledge —however dim—that right is what *ought* to be done.

(b) The Gospel, while it presupposes the law, is not built upon it. Law rests upon a true apprehension of the Will of God, but the attempt to fulfil the law leads men into deeper estrangement from God. This paradox is the measure of human sin. Man, while refusing to accept that utter dependence upon God which Creation connotes, is haunted by the knowledge of that for which he was created. This knowledge drives him to the attempt to realize the purpose of his creation under conditions of his own, not God's. This attempt drives him into still more profound estrangement. The Pharisee becomes the arch-enemy of the Christ. The publican and the harlot go into the Kingdom first. The Gospel of a reconciliation with God which is free because no righteousness could earn it, is a scandal to those who have most zealously sought a righteousness which could. The good men in every religion, those most sensitive to the perfection of Jesus, are often at the same time the most bitter opponents of the preaching of the Gospel.

(c) The Gospel fulfils the law (Matt. v, 17). That is to say, it produces the moral fruits which the law demands but which dutiful obedience can never produce. All duty is summed up in the duty to love God and our neighbour, yet we cannot love as a matter of duty. That we should love God and our neighbour is indeed God's perfect will for us. That we apprehend that will as a command going counter to the inclination of our own nature is the measure of our rebellion against God. When we make it our business to fulfil the law of love, we end in the tragic impasse of pharisaism. God's perfect will is fulfilled in us when love—spontaneous and self-forgetting—becomes the inmost law of our being, when we can say "I am crucified with Christ, yet I live, yet no longer I but Christ liveth in me"; when—in other words—we are re-born in Christ and He is formed in us. This new life is the fruit of the Gospel—a life lived in faith, "the faith which is in the Son of God who loved me and gave himself up for me" (Gal. ii, 20. Cf. Rom. x, 4-9).

The relation between Law and Gospel is thus not simple. The good non-Christian is both nearer to God and farther from Him than others. The duty and authority of the Church to preach the Gospel to every creature rests on the fact that it is in Christ alone that God has provided the mercy-seat where man's total rebellion is judged and pardoned. The Church disastrously obscures this fact, and compromises her missionary claim, when she permits within her own life ways of thought and devotion which encourage reliance upon anything other than the full, final and sufficient sacrifice of Jesus Christ upon the Cross. She has to be perpetually on her guard against the very natural and human tendency to put traditions of piety, dogma, and ritual into the place which belongs to Christ alone. When she does this, she assimilates Christianity to the world religions, and obscures the uniqueness of the Gospel with which she is entrusted and by which she lives. Her inner life has for ever to be tested by the apostolic warning, "Far be it from me to glory, save in the Cross of our Lord Jesus Christ" (Gal. vi, 14), and her missionary effort by the word, "We preach not ourselves, but Christ Jesus as Lord" (2 Cor. iv, 5). There is ample need for deep shame and humility as we face the task of preaching Christ to men better than ourselves. There ought to be no room for doubt as to our obligation to do so.

C. *Election.* It is the common teaching of the Old and New

Testaments that Israel is the people of God, chosen from among all the nations of the earth to reveal and effect His will for all mankind. It is the teaching of the New Testament that the Christian Church is the re-constituted Israel. Even at the height of his polemic against those who sought to bind upon the Church all the ordinances of the old Israel, St. Paul never forgets the continuity of the Church with Israel. He speaks of Gentile Christians as slips of wild olive grafted "contrary to nature" into a good olive tree—that "green olive tree, fair with goodly fruit" which is God's Israel (Jer. xi, 16; Rom. xi, 13-24). It is only in the light of God's revelation in Christ that the real meaning of His calling of Abraham and of Israel is made clear (cf. Eph. ii, 11; iii, 10). The Church alone is the true Israel, the seed of Abraham (Gal. iii, 29), in which Israel's history is understood and Israel's calling fulfilled. The preaching of the Gospel is indissolubly linked with the existence of a people called and set apart by God to be its bearers.

This unbroken link between a Gospel claiming to be the final and universally valid truth of human existence and a particular human society, a particular strand chosen out of all the complex web of human history, is offensive to the majority of those in our time who rightly seek to understand human history as one whole. It seems to involve an intolerable confusion between the particular and the universal. Yet we have to insist that this element of particularity is integral to the Gospel message. To demand that the doctrine of God's universal love be dissociated from the history of a particular people is to expect it to conform to the pattern of general propositions or laws which are typical of human reasoning. To demand that the knowledge of God's universal love be available to all men equally is to expect that I should know it without the actual experience of meeting my neighbour. General propositions even with regard to the love of God do not take a man one step outside the circle of the self. It is possible to combine enthusiasm for the doctrine of universal brotherhood with inability to live in brotherly concord with anyone. Profound mystical experience is compatible with profound egotism. But love is a relation between persons which breaks that circle of egotism. It involves commitment to and dependence on another. It is thus not chance but inner necessity of love's nature, that the Gospel of God's love should reach us in the form of an invitation to join a particular human fellow-

ship. God's purpose of love must be worked out through election. The Church is not something which we create to embody
our response to God's love; it is God's Israel, the body which
finds us and brings His love to us. If we believe that God is
love, we must believe this; if we resent it, we make the history
of the human society on earth ultimately meaningless.

We may thus say that the Church, simply because it is the
Church, has the duty and authority to preach the Gospel. It has
this duty and authority because God has chosen it for this thing.
He might have chosen some other race to be His Israel, some
other persons than us to be His Church. But in fact He has
chosen us. If we fail to preach the Gospel to others we flout the
purpose with which He chose us to be the unworthy bearers of it.

This is not to deny that God is at work in manifold ways outside the bounds of the Church—every missionary knows in what
wonderful ways men are prepared for their meeting with Christ
in His Church (cf. Acts x, 1-8)—but it is to assert that the clue
to all God's dealings with His human family is to be found in
the Church, the particular, visible, historical society in which
men and women are bound together in the communion of the
Holy Spirit, and which grows through history by holding up
Christ before men in Word and Sacraments, and by ministering
His love to them in its common life. Reconciliation with God
is at the same time reconciliation with His reconciled children
(cf. 1 John iv, 20). Incorporation in its life is incorporation in
the divine life which the Son shares with the Father and the
Holy Spirit (Eph. ii, 11-22; John xvii, 20-3).

Of course the churches as we know them are far from answering this description of the Church. While it is of the essence of
the Church to be a distinct, visible, historical society existing
alongside other human societies, it ought not to be a society
marked by any particular human characteristic, but simply
humanity reconstituted by its redemption in Christ. The only
peculiarity of the Church among human societies ought to be
this relation of its members to God in Christ. The stumbling-
block of the Cross ought to be the only stumbling-block with
which it confronts the outsider. Churches are particular
societies in the wrong sense. Every addition to the Church's
creed beyond what is strictly required to safeguard the truth
of the Gospel itself adds one more stumbling-block and further
obscures its true character. Disunity is both the effect and the

fruitful cause of the erection of such stumbling-blocks. Each denomination becomes marked by peculiarities of its own and weakens its claim to be the new humanity in Christ offering reconciliation to God through Him. I do not forget that these divisions have arisen, in part at least, precisely out of men's desire to safeguard the truth of the Gospel, or that reunion can only come by a common return to that truth. My purpose is to emphasize the connection between the duty of evangelism and the duty of reunion. The Church, because it is the Church, has the duty and authority to preach the Gospel. The Church's disunity is a contradiction of its own nature and the abdication of its authority to declare to all men the Gospel of redemption.

D. *Redemption.* The Gospel announces an accomplished redemption. The Church has the duty and authority to preach it because it is the redeemed community. The Church's evangelism is not only its obedience to the command of the Lord, it is the passing on of that divine life which it has received from Him. The duty and authority to preach the Gospel are implicit in that sharing in the divine life through the Holy Spirit which is the constitutive fact of the Church's existence.

The Church's life, the life hid with Christ in God, is a sharing in the divine life. The New Testament speaks of the Church as "a colony of heaven" (Phil. iii, 20—Moffatt's translation). Its citizens have been "translated into the kingdom of the Son of his love" (Col. i, 13). They "taste the powers of the age to come" (Heb. vi, 5). They are "justified by faith". But the Church does not enjoy all these blessings as a possession apart from God; it enjoys them in that, and in so far as, it lives by faith in the Gospel. It is when the Gospel is heard and believed, when the redemption accomplished on our behalf on Calvary is the sole ground of our confidence, that the love of God becomes the law of our being. When a man understands what it means that Christ died for him, he cannot any more live for himself. The life he lives is a gift of God's mercy. He has no ground of hope save in the death and resurrection of his Lord. The citadel of egotism has fallen and all the defences men erect against their Creator are down. Then alone is a man's soul laid fully open to the presence and power of God's Holy Spirit. Then alone, therefore, he receives the life for which God created him —a life of freedom and fellowship with God and with His children. The Church, just in so far as it lives by faith in the

Gospel, truly shares in the divine life and tastes the powers of the age to come.   Because this is so, the Church's duty to preach the Gospel belongs to its very nature.   " One died for all " (2 Cor. v, 14).   It is of that constraining love that the Church is born and lives, and the same constraint must necessarily lay upon the Church an ambassadorship for Christ to all for whom He died.   The Church cannot stand under the Cross without accepting an obligation to share with all men the redemption which was there won for it.   It cannot evade that obligation without cutting itself off from the divine life by which it lives.

The Church is the bearer of the Gospel in two distinguishable senses.   It is the bearer of it as the guardian of the apostolic witness to those historic events in which our redemption was wrought out.   It is the bearer of it as being the redeemed community in which the love of God shed abroad through the Holy Spirit is bringing forth the fruit of good works and holy lives. As the redeemed community the Church will be marked by freedom from selfish concern for its own salvation, and by wholehearted self-committal to men in all their needs and sorrows and perplexities.   It will necessarily concern itself with all men's concerns, for this is what love does.   At the same time it will point unceasingly to the secret of its own life, to the facts of God's work in Christ, to the one Name given under heaven by which we must be saved, to the judgment and mercy under which those within and those without alike stand.   When these two activities are set over against one another the Church betrays its trust.   Preaching divorced from concern for all men's needs will be words set against deeds, for men will not believe the message of God's grace if they do not see signs of that grace in the messengers.   Service of men divorced from preaching will be but mocking men with false hopes, for there is no place other than the Cross where men may be reconciled to God, and every man must go there himself.

Evangelism is the activity of the redeemed community seeking to share with all men the joy of redemption, and to welcome all men into the fellowship of those who share that joy.   Much harm has been done in this matter by a wrong kind of individualism.   The human agent in evangelism must be the fellowship. Whether the immediate agent at any particular juncture be the oratory of a great preacher, or the simple act of a group of Indian villagers going out for their " week of witness ", or a word spoken

in personal talk which bears witness to Christ as Lord, evangelism must surely always be recognizably the witness and the
invitation of the fellowship of Christ's people. It is the Church
which must be the "mission". It is upon the *Church* that the
authority and duty is laid to preach the Gospel, for the Church
is the redeemed community which itself lives by the Gospel.

E. *Consummation.* An incomparable note of urgency sounds
through the first preaching of the Gospel. "The time is fulfilled and the Kingdom of God is at hand: repent ye and believe
in the Gospel." The urgency lies in this, that it is the announcement of something which has happened and which at the same
time points to something about to happen. God does not sleep.
The promises are not forgotten and they are not idle dreams.
History is not a meaningless repetition of cycles; it is real and
moves to a real climax. There is not an infinity of time either
for the race or for the individual. The Master of the house is at
the door and the servants are summoned to awake "while there is
yet time" (Luke xii, 35ff.). There is no time to stay and argue
with those who will not give heed to the message; the messenger
is to leave only the dust of his feet as testimony that the Kingdom
of God has verily come near (Luke x, 10-11). The good news of
the Kingdom is to be preached in the whole world for a
testimony to all the nations, and then shall the end come (Matt.
xxiv, 14). Christians are therefore called upon to throw themselves into this task with the energy born of good hope, looking
confidently for the day of Christ's glorious return. The Church
has the duty and authority to preach the Gospel because the
Gospel is the message that the eternal Lord of history has
revealed Himself in history in order to confront man with the
final issue of his life on earth.

God's revelation of Himself in Christ is the revelation of the
meaning of history as it is in the counsel of God, and those who
by faith apprehend the revelation look for the end of history
when the secret of God's purpose shall be apparent to sight.
This element of expectation is necessarily involved in the possession by faith of redemption through Christ. "Your life is hid
with Christ in God. When Christ who is our life shall be manifested, then shall ye also be manifested with him in glory" (Col.
iii, 3-4). To the New Testament writers this expectation was
vivid and immediate. The fact that we can now look back on
two thousand years of further history ought not to dull the vivid-

ness of our hope but to deepen our sense of God's forbearance. The Gospel brings every generation face to face with the end of history; therefore any true apprehension of the Gospel will lay upon the believer an urgent sense of responsibility to open the eyes of all men to the crisis in which they stand.

There is revealed in the Gospel the meaning and end of history both for the individual and for the race. The one is not exhausted in the other. Both are to be fulfilled in the Kingdom of God. The individual is brought by the preaching of the Gospel face to face with his Creator and Lord, and is compelled to face the issues of his life. The offer to him in Christ of complete and final salvation is inevitably at the same time a revelation to him of the possibility of complete and final damnation. The decision of faith is made in this tremendous context. It is not possible rightly to believe the Gospel except with some awareness that these awful issues are concerned in it. It is not possible so to believe it without awareness of its equal urgency for every human soul. Our Lord discouraged speculation on the question, "Are there few that be saved", but He made the question an occasion for stressing the urgency of the issues involved in discipleship (Luke xiii, 23f.). It is not possible to be true stewards of so tremendous a message and at the same time to be dilatory in handing it on.

The Gospel is at the same time the revelation of the meaning and end of history as a whole. It is the revelation of God's age-long secret, His purpose to sum up all things in Christ (Eph. i, 10). Of this purpose the Church is the first fruit and the agent (e.g. Eph. iii, 10-11). The Church lives now by faith, and it is only to the eye of faith that it appears as the Body of Christ and therefore as the centre of world history (cf. Eph. i, 22-3). But faith eagerly awaits the day heralded in Christ's first preaching when faith shall be lost in sight and the Kingdom of God shall be revealed in glory. Until that day the Church must confess before the world the faith by which she lives, and so play her part in hastening that day's dawning. History moves to a real climax, away from the social equilibrium which belongs to man's natural inheritance, and towards the final crisis where heaven shall stand nakedly revealed and men must enter on their heavenly inheritance or perish. The Church is bound by her own faith to take history seriously, and in this hour of history when on the one hand the sin of man threatens the utter destruction of human life, and on the other the Church has been granted a new vision of her world-wide unity, Christians will look up in hope knowing that their redemption draws near. This is an hour when the Lord is forcing us to see the whole destiny of the human race in the light of His eternal purpose, and when there is laid upon the Church, through which He has willed to make His purpose known, the duty and authority to proclaim to all men His saving acts. "Behold, now is the day of salvation."

II

OUR UN-CHRISTIAN WORLD

PREFACE

*For some years it has been clear that the Church has been losing
hold in the ancient Christian lands, and that its losses here have
not been compensated for by the gains in lands of the younger
churches.*

*Why has the Church thus lost ground? Perhaps because it
has come to rely on other things than the presence and power of
its Master—security, property, the support of secular powers.
Perhaps also because it has forgotten that it is always face to face
with an urgent evangelistic task, and that the Church cannot
survive unless each generation as it arises is brought to the knowledge of Christ.*

*When Christian faith fails, the mind of man does not remain
a vacuum. Man is an idol maker; if he ceases to worship the true
God, it is certain that he will make other gods out of his own
imagination. One chapter in this section tries to depict some
of the gods worshipped by modern man, systems of thought
which have taken to themselves something of the passion and
power of religious faiths. But deeper than these consciously held
doctrines are obscure convictions on the level of the half conscious and subconscious; these may be, and often are, contrary to
the Christian conception of God and man, and toughly resistant
to them.*

*In face of a world entrenched in its own conceits and unwilling
to be won for Christ, only a genuinely Christian Church can be
effective. The tragedy is that the Church itself has often been
infected by the worship of false gods and the spirit of the world,
thus making its proclamation of the Gospel ineffective. If the
world is much less Christian than it ought to be, much of the
responsibility can be laid at the door of the Church itself.*

1

RIVAL SECULAR FAITHS*

by Wilhelm Pauck

THE International Missionary Conference, meeting at Jerusalem in 1928, sounded the warning that, as all over the world religion was confronted by secularism, Christian missionaries should recognize that the Christian Gospel must be proclaimed in a world where the validity of every historical religion was being challenged. Since then the echo of this warning has been heard wherever the churches have discussed their evangelistic task.

The present plight and temper are read in terms of a "crisis of religion". Everywhere people have become alienated from the historical religions. The "modern" spirit of western civilization is regarded as the chief cause. The scientific world view and the feats of scientific technology in the conquest of natural powers and resources entail a gradual estrangement from the Christian Faith. Since the beginning of the nineteenth century, first the educated classes and then the masses tend to leave the churches or to ignore them. The expansion of western science and technology throughout the world has corresponding influence in non-Christian civilizations.

Many who concern themselves with the problem assume that they are face to face with a movement of mass-atheism. They think that when people left the churches they became godless and that in their godlessness they live and die without any concern for their own salvation or for the salvation of mankind. But this is not so. Though alienated from the churches, modern secularists are not necessarily irreligious. From the Christian point of view, their "religion" must be judged idolatrous. But it expresses itself in an earnest quest for a coherent understanding of man and the universe and for the meaning of life. Indeed,

* This paper is based on discussions held by the *Chicago Ecumenical Study Group*. Several sections taken from papers by members of the group have been incorporated in it. The final draft of this article was prepared by Professor Wilhelm Pauck, the chairman of the group. It should be stated that the group as a whole could not be convened in order to approve this *résumé* of their discussions.

"secularized" modern man is in search for a faith upon which human existence can be staked and which can direct human destiny. Certain world views, which promise the realization on this earth of the age-old human hope for the good life, have already found millions of ardent adherents. Proclaimed and taught as "realistic" analyses and interpretations of the world as it actually is, they engender a loyalty which is often stronger than that by which Christians are attached to the Gospel of Christ.

Thus in confronting secularism, the Christian Church in fact meets "secular faiths" which claim to be its rivals. It would be going too far to say that Christianity is challenged by "rival secular gospels", for these secularized movements do not appeal to their followers in the name of "good news" to be declared as the hope of salvation. But it is right to consider them as alternatives to the Christian Faith, for they carry the conviction that life can be so ordered that everyone will be able to live well and happily.

In a brief analysis of the most influential of these "faiths", we shall not attempt to trace their historical origin or to evaluate them critically, either on their own presuppositions or in the light of Christian doctrine. It will be our purpose so to describe them that their attraction for so many can be understood.

In order to prevent possible misunderstandings, we should point out that some of the world views we are about to characterize are not in all respects incompatible with the Christian faith. However, we are here not concerned with the problem of the inter-relation between the Christian Faith and the world views. We shall therefore discuss the "secular faiths" not in the light of the question to what extent and under which conditions the world views represented in them are reconcilable with the Christian Faith, but we shall analyse them solely in the light of the fact that they are held by many people of to-day, who, having been estranged from the Christian Church, embrace these "faiths" as alternatives to the Christian Gospel.

I

Most of the secular faiths are, in one way or another, humanistic: they centre all that is worthy of loyalty on factors or aspects of the human world. But because humanism is a movement in its own right and because its world view is widely advocated, we must treat it specifically.

Several kinds of humanism have flourished in western civilization. All of them were inspired by the ideal of *humanitas* first developed in classical antiquity. The contemporary movement is not unrelated to historical humanism, but it derives its primary impetus from the modern scientific spirit. It is, therefore, commonly referred to as *scientific humanism*.

In so far as modern humanists are concerned with ends, they assert, like their predecessors of old, that the goals of human life must be found in the nature of man. In so far as they are concerned with the means by which these ends can be realized they affirm that they are available in the natural abilities of man and in the energies and resources of nature which can be made accessible to these abilities. On the achievements of the natural and social sciences they base their hope that at length men will overcome all those frustrations which have dogged their search for happiness.

Scientific method applied to the processes of nature and to human society, so the humanists believe, has demolished the main tenets of Christianity. Especially the supernatural and other-worldly features of historical Christianity are superstitions to be buried in the cemetery of human errors with other myths that in the course of human evolution and development have rightly been exploded. The science of man will provide in the course of time not only objectively tested knowledge about all human capacities of body and mind, but techniques for their full development. What biology, physiology, anthropology, psychology, sociology, and particularly the science of medicine, have already accomplished in interpreting man's nature and its possibilities as seen against the background of evolution must be broadcast by scientific education, that all may share in the benefits of scientific human culture.

Humanists pin their hope on the further development of technical skill, which they regard as an extension of the scientific spirit. The technological progress of the last two hundred years proves that scientific knowledge will enable men really to achieve the greatest good of the greatest number. Modern machines have made it possible to provide all with the necessities of the good life. For the first time in history an economy of abundance instead of an economy of scarcity is in sight; the good life, a life free from poverty, drudgery, disease, ignorance, fear, and misery is now within the reach of multitudes; a future of universal peace and happiness is no longer a Utopian dream.

Already a general improvement of morals and manners has been accomplished wherever the scientific-technological spirit has been permitted to mould human life. Where machines have produced abundance, in western Europe and North America, people have become cleaner, more gentle, more reasonable, and more friendly. There cultural opportunities abound and millions can take advantage of them. These nations are the most powerful, the most enlightened, the wealthiest in the world, as the envy and emulation of other countries demonstrate.

To be sure, it seems that technological progress has in part served to aggravate the ills of mankind. The frightfulness of the two world wars was enhanced by the horrible efficiency of mass destruction. That these wars broke out at all must apparently be explained by the economic convulsions into which the nations were driven by the technological needs of men and markets. In the age of atomic energy, inaugurated by the annihilation of large cities by two small atomic bombs, future holocausts may destroy all civilization.

But the humanists contend that these conflicts were due to the fact that the nations have not yet learned properly to use their new power. The dangers inherent in atomic energy will disappear if men will accept a planned economy and a planned political order comprising the whole world. For thus the destructive possibilities of released atomic energy can be forestalled and its immense promise of good developed and distributed.

Civilization is about to enter a new age. It is the dead weight of the past that still paralyses the intelligence of men in every part of social life, but particularly in religion, morals and education. The inertia of traditional ideas, habits, and value-judgments holds up the building of a scientific culture. So too often political and economic decisions do not conform to the one world of technological progress in which men do exist and must exist. As there is no substitute for intelligence equipped with scientific method and technical skill, men must work patiently and methodically to explore the maladjustments and disorganizations of society. They must exercise imagination and creative daring to perfect the fabulous possibilities for good offered to them in the man-controlled technological world.

II

The *democratic faith*, the working creed of many church members in the U.S.A., Great Britain, the British Dominions, and the Scandinavian nations, represents a modification of the humanist faith. Its outlook is determined by the confidence that man is able to master himself and his world. In this respect they share the general conviction of the humanists concerning ᵗʰe character and promise of scientific-technological civilization. But it is the cause of democracy that elicits their primary loyalty and is the source and substance of their hope; a political actuality and an ideal not inconsistent with Christianity. They hope, all over the world, to build a house to shelter the activities and decisions of the common life on a basis of equality, with freedom of enquiry, of criticism, and of action.

These ideals have developed historically on the soil of Christian civilization. Indeed, the majority of modern Protestants regard the system and order of democracy as more easily reconcilable with the Christian ethic than other political forms of government and social order. We are dealing here with secular "democratic faith" and not with the Christian interpretation of democracy.

"Democracy" may be a term used by particular national states or groups within these states as the ideological symbol cloaking the pursuit of special interests. Yet the ablest and wisest defenders of this faith see democracy as the one political and cultural means of checking national and group interest and achieving a genuine freedom and equality under law for all groups and peoples. Originally an individualistic faith, expressed in economic, political and ecclesiastical theory and practice, democracy has increasingly envisaged a more organic doctrine of society in which responsibilities and collective functions are stressed as fully as individual rights.

Democracy can adjust itself to new situations and new demands. Politically, democracy has always involved some type of constitutionalism with legal guarantees of the rights of individuals and minorities, provision for free discussion and free elections in which the will of the majority (with proper safeguards) determines the decisions of the group. Yet the demo-cratic faith cannot be limited to the practices of democratic governments, the forms of election and parliamentary and judicial institutions. It insists that the right to criticize those in power must be preserved and all purely arbitrary authority rejected.

This aspect of the democratic faith presupposes a certain view of human nature, namely that "the greatest natural resource of any community is the latent intelligence and good will of its members; and it seeks those forms of society which run a certain risk of preliminary disorder in order to elicit that resource".[1] With this belief in the latent good will of the people, and supplementary to it, must be ranked the restraints in systems of checks and balances set up as barriers against the abuse of power. So Walt Whitman defended democracy: "I do not put it (democracy) on the ground that the People, the masses, even the best of them, are in their latent or exhibited qualities essentially sensible and good, nor on the ground of their rights; but that, good or bad, rights or no rights, the demo-cratic formula is the only safe and preservative one for coming times."[2]

Those who believe in democracy not only as a form of govern-ment but as a faith depend heavily on the spread of knowledge, particularly upon the methods of scientific enquiry as offering the model and the chief resource for the increase of intelligent co-operation. One strong group says: "The democratic faith is in essence the belief that human resources may become adequate for human needs wherever freedom of enquiry exists and co-operative techniques are developed."[3]

This group holds that questions about the *ends* and *values* of life are open to such enquiry, and the problems concerning them are soluble by this means, if at all.

To sum up, the democratic faith is essentially a faith in the worth of every person so that each individual is equal before the highest demands of the moral order; it is a faith in the capacity of men through intelligence and good will to relate themselves to one another in search for a co-operative solution of

---

[1] W. E. Hocking, *The Lasting Element of Individualism.*
[2] Walt Whitman, *Democratic Vistas*, Viking Press anthology of Whitman, p. 413.
[3] *The Scientific Spirit and the Democratic Faith*, N.Y. Kings Crown Press, p. xi.

their common problems. Its programme is: give the people a chance, through education, which provides the methods and information by which truth may be discovered; through institutions, economic, political or social, which encourage freedom and co-operation; through public discussion of differences; and through the methods of disciplined scientific enquiry. So they will achieve whatever good life in a world community may be possible in this not wholly pliable nor yet wholly intractable universe.

III

The "democratic faith" assumes that individual freedom of opportunity guaranteed by freedom of religion, freedom of speech, freedom of the press, freedom of assembly, etc., will produce a co-operative society of men who will also enjoy freedom from fear and want. To these freedoms must be added that of "free enterprise". Indeed, the democratic faith described is the outlook of the Western world of the capitalistic bourgeois.

Critics of democracy point to the tensions engendered by capitalism. Freedom of opportunity is so far from being guaranteed, that the good life cannot be attained until society is rebuilt, and until the principle of capitalistic free enterprise in particular has been recognized as irreconcilable with the democratic faith in the freedom of all men.

Socialism has found millions of adherents all over the world, but particularly in Western society, by spreading this criticism of capitalism among the working classes. The outlook is humanistic and democratic, but radically distinguished from that of the scientific humanists who believe in the productivity of unfettered human intelligence, and from that of the democrats who put their trust in the latent good will of free men. Socialism advocates a social-economic revolution. Some socialists (e.g. the British Labour Party and the Social Democrats of continental Europe) hope to effect this revolution gradually within the framework of the modern constitutional states, but the *communists* (now organized in the International Communist Party under Soviet Russia) look for the violent overthrow of all non-communist governments in order that a dictatorship of the proletariat may be established.

The communists regard themselves as the true representatives of the doctrines of Karl Marx who was the first to proclaim the modern socialist programme. This programme is based on certain fundamentally simple economic theories which can be easily understood, and have become the basis of the communist faith.

The marxist-communist criticism of the "democratic faith" and, indeed, of all "humanistic faiths" is that they are not based on a realistic knowledge of the processes of social change. According to Marx, the basic feature of any civilization is the system whereby the people in that civilization produce clothes, houses, and all the material goods which they need. This system must necessarily be determined by those who control the means of production. As long as society is divided into classes, that class will be in power and rule the other classes, which controls the means of production. Moreover, because human life is determined by economic productivity, all so-called values of civilization (e.g. religion, art, philosophy) are nothing but a superstructure erected upon the economic order. As long as economic power is in the hands of one of the classes of society, civilization will therefore be necessarily distorted. It cannot reflect the good of the whole. As a matter of fact, all historical civilizations produced as they were by societies divided into the unequal classes of masters and slaves, property owners and dispossessed workers, must be interpreted as designs by which those in control endeavoured to justify their possession of power and to perpetuate it. Especially religion has been used persistently (primarily by virtue of the alliance of the priests and clergy with the ruling classes) to hoodwink the under-privileged. Its teachings and its practices must therefore be suspected of being nothing less than the opium of the people.

A just order can come into being only by the abolition of social-economic classes. Only a classless society can guarantee true human freedom, where all will have the opportunity to realize material prosperity and cultural well-being. Only such a social order can develop an honest and free human civilization.

Modern bourgeois society is dominated by the owners of capital, the chief means of production in an industrial society. An ever-increasing number of the members of society are deprived of economic control (thus becoming more or less identified with the proletariat) while the possession and control of capital is more and more concentrated in the hands of a few.

These processes make it possible to organize the natural class struggle in such a way that the proletariat can be prepared to seize power and to establish a dictatorship whose task it must be to inaugurate the classless society on the basis of a complete socialization or collectivization of the means of production.

This programme cannot fully succeed unless it is put into action all over the world. The establishment of a communist state in one nation can and must be only the beginning of a world revolution. It is therefore necessary that the workers of the world unite. They must be made class conscious and aware of their responsibilities in the class struggle. In particular, they must be immune to the narcotic influence of capitalistic ideologies, through knowledge of the economic determination of history and the philosophy of dialectical materialism. Moreover, they must be taught to accelerate the irresistible process of decay to which capitalism is subject, by undermining the working of the capitalist order from within. Finally, they must be prepared to seize power at the opportune moment.

To-day, the communist faith has adherents all over the world. Under the leadership of the Communist Party of Soviet Russia, which has succeeded in establishing a proletarian dictatorship and maintaining it against enemies from within and without, they prepare themselves for the day of freedom from capitalistic oppression which, they firmly believe, will inevitably come. They are united under the strict discipline of their party and are ready for all the sacrifices that may be demanded of them. Dogmatically confident that their faith will change the world for the better, they stand ready to challenge all other faiths.

IV

Interpreters of Russian communism have often noted that its leaders did not unite the Russian people in the war against Nazi Germany under the banner of the communist world revolution, but by appealing to their national consciousness and to their love of " Mother Russia ". At the end of the conflict, Stalin decreed that the victory over Hitler should be commemorated for ever as " The Great Patriotic War, 1941-1945 ".

Those who are convinced that *nationalism* is the faith which determines human destiny, see in this fact a proof of the validity of their conviction.

Nationalism does not pretend to be a universal faith. It is avowedly pluralistic. It does not claim to unite men in a programme of world transformation and human betterment. It is a faith that arises from the recognition that human destiny happens to be so ordered that different groups, societies and states are held together by the bond of membership in specific nations. By virtue of the working of an almighty providence, each of these nations is endowed with a common spirit that manifests itself identically in all stages of the national historical development and thus binds all individual members of the national community into a unity which transcends the past, the present, and the future. As it is the fate of each individual to be born into a specific nation, to live well and responsibly means to identify himself with its life.

The nationalist does not hesitate to accept the lesson of history that nations rise and fall; but he asserts that as no man can choose to which nation he shall belong, conscious cultivation of membership in the nation must be the fundamental law of everyone's life—whatever the strength or weakness, the youth or the age of his nation. Each nation has its own particular task to perform—a task which can be learned from history and from the study of the national genius. Every man must live for his nation.

The spirit of nationalism is akin to that of patriotism. Indeed, it feeds upon the natural attachment to the home and the home-land. But if it is not seen in connection with the historical background from which it has arisen, it cannot be understood as "modern man's other religion" to use Edward Shillito's words. Nationalism has become an attitude of mind marked by the readiness to place the nation above every other interest. In two world wars nations compelled to fight for their survival demanded complete and unquestioning support. War propaganda was developed along nationalistic lines. It had the effect of determining the decisions and affections of millions of men in such a way that their nation was given priority over anything else.

The Nazis exploited all this to the utmost. What others did in fact, but without openly demanding a transvaluation of conventional values, they dared to proclaim as the first commandment to be followed by all Germans: Germany is eternal—therefore all other values are secondary to and derived from this primary one. All over the world a similar spirit prevailed, but German nationalist absolutism was unique because it was so thorough-going.

Historically it is no accident that nationalism became man's other religion, for it developed in close connection with the Church, and, in the course of the nineteenth century, it became the Church's successor as the chief guarantor of social unity within the limits of a given national state.

Since the days of the Roman Empire, indeed since the beginning of political history, religion has been regarded as the surest cement of the social group. For centuries all states followed the rule that peace and concord could not prevail among their citizens or subjects without religious or ecclesiastical uniformity. When the modern national states arose—at the time of the Renaissance and the Reformation—they, too, relied on religious conformity to maintain social unity and strength. All Europe hailed political success and expansion as religious achievements and regarded ecclesiastical conformity as a national-political requirement. Thus, most modern nations grew up in dependence upon the social unity maintained primarily by the churches. Everywhere, national self-consciousness was saturated with ecclesiastical motives and loyalties.

Nationalism as a political maxim, entailing a nation's right to independence and expansion, emerged only in the nineteenth century. At first, it was a reaction of Europeans to Napoleonic imperialism: the "nations" must be free from the yoke of the emperor! Later on, it inspired constitutional restraints on royal absolutism: the "nation" must determine its destiny! Finally it became the chief motive of that economic expansion which accompanied the rise of industrial capitalism: the "nation" must have a place in the sun!

At the same time, the ideals of the American and French revolutions spread. Democratic rights and liberties were gradually established all over the western world. Foremost among them was the freedom of religion. Thus the age-old requirement of religious conformity as the basis of unity was abolished. The modern states adopted ecclesiastical neutrality, granting the right to free religious association. At last the churches ceased to serve as the main instruments of social and political conformity.

However, the need to cultivate cohesion in political communities continued. It was satisfied by means of nationalism. In all western nations—and soon almost everywhere—national history was made one of the chief subjects of study in primary and secondary schools. Historical research into national traditions flourished. Commemoration of the anniversaries of national heroes fostered the spirit of nationalism and bound communities together in the bonds of a common destiny.

By the beginning of the twentieth century nationalism had everywhere grown so strong that neither the Christian churches nor international organizations of labour and other interests could prevail against it. Even after the second world war, which was fought to break a party which exploited nationalism to the utmost, it survives, for everywhere multitudes are persuaded that unless nationalism can provide solidarity, the historical states and communities of the world will be dissolved in chaos. On this spirit all those popular movements thrive which are organized to enable special interest groups in society to gain their ends. Our own generation has witnessed the phenomenon of a totalitarian régime like that of Mussolini, designed to exploit the weak and disintegrating Italian nation for the purpose of satisfying a demagogue's dreams of grandeur, able to maintain itself for two decades, because it was based on the nationalistic loyalties and memories of the Italian people. And if it were not a tragic fact, it would seem incredible that the whole world became involved in the bloodiest of all wars because a " revolution of nihilism " like that of Hitler and his party succeeded in legitimizing itself in the eyes of the proud and cultured German people by appealing to its nationalistic spirit and by causing its youth idolatrously to worship the German nation as if it were divine.

v

There is nothing unusual in the fact that different programmes of action in pursuit of the good life vie with one another for support from the people of our time. But it is most extraordinary that the movements we have been describing are supported by many who believe that the programmes of these movements are valid substitutes for Christian teachings or that they represent a religion of their own. None of these movements originated in a religious concern. Their founders, if they had any, did not intend to inaugurate new religions. That they have nevertheless become pseudo-religions and as such rivals of the Christian faith is the most disconcerting fact of our time. How can this be explained? We shall not attempt to assess the responsibility of the Christian churches. It must suffice that the question why secular enterprises and programmes have become "faiths" cannot be answered rightly if the failure of Christians to live up to the demand and the promise of the Gospel is evaded.

The fact with which we are all confronted, whether we are Christians or not, is that the fundamental sanctions on which Western civilization has been founded have disintegrated. For this is the crisis of civilization, that when people desire to justify the character of civilization they find themselves standing before an abyss of meaninglessness! When they enquire into the ultimate motives of their actions, they discover that there is nothing that they really believe in, or that convinces them as ultimately trustworthy. Thus they give themselves with frantic and absolutist devotion to concrete programmes that seem to them to promise a reconstruction of the cultural life. Philosophical or social-political programmes originally designed to deal with specific problems of the cultural life are embraced as if they were gospels. It is for this reason that humanism, democratic idealism, communism, nationalism have become religions for many modern men. To elude the futility that threatens the cultural life, they sanctify the world views that underlie these programmes by an idolatrous perversion of the true character of these movements and of true religion as well. One must, therefore, suspect that this pseudo-religiousness is not really an escape from futility, but a concession to it.

This suspicion is supported by the fact that fanatical nihilists have again and again exploited the pseudo-religiousness of secular programmes for their own ends. The leading Nazis were such nihilists, and they found followers by fanning the flames of a perverted nationalism and a perverted humanism. There are other nihilists who exploit the religious fanaticism of some communists for their negative ends.

The danger of this association of nihilism with pseudo-religion is that when the creed is reduced to the status of a temporary programme of action, the disillusionment of its victims is so radical that they identify themselves with nihilism itself. They conclude that it is better to hold frankly to a stark nihilism than to cover it with the cloak of pseudo-religiousness.

The most terrible aspect of the life of contemporary civilization is that this is precisely what is happening. The total destruction which "total war" has heaped upon millions of persons
has entailed also the dissolution of all faiths. Loss of family,
home, work, the collapse of all conventional order, the failure
of artificial programmes, the spectre of continued and un-
relieved hunger and poverty, and the apparent hopelessness of
the future have caused many to view life as if it were nothing
but existence in the abyss of meaninglessness.

Thus it has come about that the prophecy of Nietzsche, who
was himself tempted by nihilism, has come true, the prophecy
which he formulated in the following terrible words:

"Is it not inevitable that men will finally renounce all that
is comforting, holy and healing, all hope and all faith in the
hidden harmony of the world, in future bliss and justification?
Is it not inevitable that men should renounce God and that,
out of cruelty towards themselves, they should worship the
stone, that which is stupid and heavy, fate, nothingness? To
sacrifice God for nothingness—this paradoxical cruelty has
been kept in reserve for the generation about to rise; we all
know something about it."[4]

Nietzsche hardly foresaw, even in his darkest forebodings, that
this prediction would be fulfilled in the nihilism of our own
time. He wrote these works interpreting the cultural mood of
his day which he understood more profoundly than most of his
contemporaries.

Many of the features of this mood are still alive in contemporary literature, but now its nihilistic implications have become
fully apparent. We conclude our analysis of the secular faiths
of our time with a brief description of the spirit of negation that
is voiced in much modern art and literature.

A variety of nihilistic moods have emerged. They reflect the
progressive alternation of traditional beliefs and "mythologies".
One feature of the Romantic Movement was the fact that the
human being was "left alone, seeking the visible world" (Wordsworth), deprived of other symbolic supports. The effect of the
successive impact of "realism" and "naturalism", of the social
sciences, and psychology down to our day, has been that even

---

[4] Friedrich Nietzsche, *Jenseits von Gut und Böse*, Leipzig, 1906, p. 79.

such spiritual support as the Romantics would assign to the soul, to man, and to nature has been cut off (Marx, Darwin, Freud). Then the machine and the pressure of factory life, insecurity due to the impersonal concentration of economic power, and the enticements of money or luxury, have broken the mould of older loyalties, community forms and ceremonies. No longer persons, men become neurotic. Thus suffocation of the individual and personal life has called forth violent reactions, including both revulsions against older faiths, and new irrational cults.

Sophisticated expression of nihilism may be found all the way from the Satanism of certain of the characters in Dostoievsky and the moods of Nietzsche down to the tenets of the logical Positivists and to Bertrand Russell's theme of "building on the foundations of an unyielding despair". Yet the most significant instance of nihilism is perhaps that of the practical man in the street, the lost modern man, who believes nothing and who lapses into sheer debauchery. It sways many young people in the off-hours from factory or from military duty at home or abroad who recognize no claims other than those of coercion or pleasure. They do not say, "I think this is good", but "I like it", or "I want to do it". The argument of such people is that all alleged moral authorities are hypocritical, that science and historical studies have exposed ancient credulities, and that economic life, free enterprise or collectivism, is an arena of "dog eat dog". In this attitude some of their most powerful impulses and desires are inexorably blocked and thwarted. This induces acute suffering, and disenchantment turns to cynicism.

In contemporary neo-mysticism and irrationalism explosive repressed vitalities come to the fore, asserting a positive "gospel" in esoteric and æsthetic forms. They are to be distinguished from nineteenth-century romantic or vitalistic mysticism since they are not founded upon the conceptions of the soul or of nature. They build upon the archetypes and myths designated by contemporary psychology, or, more significantly, upon the sense of the creativity in being itself. Maritain has pointed out, in connection with a discussion of the modern movement in poetry, that the denudation of the modern consciousness of all its older supports has encouraged experiments in "immediacy", in "the creative contemplation of the depths".

Denying, on the one hand, all rational and idealist systems and such conceptions as reason, nature, substance, and, on the other hand, all social authorities, patterns and conventions, Existentialism in its atheistic form comes out with a *tabula rasa*. This "philosophy" which after the war, and as an outgrowth of the war experience, has come to the fore in France, and has found a response among certain members of the intelligentsia of America and Great Britain, is not a complete nihilism. . . . It is not a complete nihilism, because a form of personal consciousness is still acknowledged as real. The category of "existence" is accepted and the category of "essence" is denied. In a world that is absurd man must not proceed on the basis of the certainty "I am" or "I think" or "the world is", but on the basis of the awareness "I act" or "I suffer". The one thing that remains is the will, but in an antinomian field. Emphasis is placed upon the reign of the arbitrary, capricious, the *acte gratuite*. Thus, freedom in a radical way is stressed, carrying with it a sense of emancipation from all ethical systems and tyrannies. But an "ethic" of some sort grows out of it, since it is logical to accord to others that "freedom" which is the ultimate fact about human existence.

These are the "rival secular faiths" which to-day challenge the Christian Faith. No Christian evangelism can be "effective" within our world that does not take the fact into account that the people who are emancipated from the Church have yielded in some way or other to the appeal of these "faiths". And no "witness" to God's "design" offered in the Gospel can be true that has not been chastened by the repentance induced by the criticisms of Christian creed and works revealed in the teachings, programmes, hopes, and moods of the "secular faiths".

2

THE DISINTEGRATION OF SOCIETY IN CHRISTIAN COUNTRIES

by *Paul Tillich*

An integrated state of society is one in which creative forces are held in balance by the power of an embracing and determining principle. When this principle is lost, balance is destroyed, and the society disintegrates. Disturbances of social equilibrium are, of course, unavoidable, because the dynamics of every life process involve tension between elements which are static and others which drive ahead. Such tension includes the risk of conflicts, defeats and partial destruction. It is a sign of power and strength when a life-process can stand many deep tensions without disintegration. But there is a limit which cannot be exceeded, and this limit is the preservation of a uniting and balancing principle.

In most Christian countries contemporary society has lost such a principle; it has either fallen into a spiritual vacuum or it has accepted principles which are disrupting instead of uniting. This is the general predicament of our period and the causes of its predominantly self-destructive traits. And the same development which has deprived our society of an embracing and determining centre has to a large extent made it inaccessible to the Christian message. In the past Christianity has furnished the uniting principle; but it has been so infected by the general contemporary disintegration that many now regard it as incapable of reintegrating secular society within Christian countries. Therefore when evangelism undertakes to conquer secularism within Christendom it faces an ambiguous situation. On the one hand, the secular mind is deeply moved by the conscious or unconscious quest for a new spiritual centre. On the other hand, it does not look to the Christian message as the answer to its quest; it regards Christianity as a well-known and well-refuted part of disrupted Western culture. Consequently the evangelist must ask two main questions: First, through what development has Christianity lost its power to be the uniting centre in the life of Christian countries? Second, how can it become again, in the present situation, the spiritual centre of Western civilization? The following analysis is concerned with these two questions.

I DETERMINED AND AUTOMATIC BALANCE

It is obvious that every society represents a "balance of power"—political, social, intellectual, spiritual. Even the most conformist society, primitive as well as developed, involves actual and potential diversities which call for continual integration into the whole of the life-process. The question immediately arises as to what furnishes the balance; and two fundamentally different answers can be given.

In the first case equilibrium is attributed to a determining centre. This "centre" holds together political, cultural and spiritual elements in strict interdependence, and it constitutes an over-arching, all-supporting authority which is acknowledged spontaneously by the "common sense" of the society it unifies.

In the second case equilibrium is attributed to a self-regulating process. Here there is no visible, centralizing authority. Political, cultural and spiritual differences of a fundamental kind can even be accentuated without being looked upon as disruptive, because of faith in an uncentred automatic harmony.

Modern society has made a slow but irresistible transition from the first to the second type of structure. Loss of the determining principles of the European past and maximal acceptance of automatic adjustment of social processes has been the great theme of the recent centuries of Occidental history. The process has been slow, and it has never completely reached its goal; conversely, the centrally determined society of the past was never entirely lacking in divergent elements. But in history the predominant trend is decisive.

The state of contemporary Western society (and, through world-wide repercussions, of Eastern society in some measure) shows that belief in automatic balance is justified only so long as remnants of the first type of structure are consciously or unconsciously co-determinative. When the latter disappear entirely and automatic adjustment is the only means of regulating divergent political, cultural and spiritual tendencies, a process of rapid disintegration sets in, and the need for a new centre is passionately felt. The success of all so-called totalitarian attempts is due to the fact that they seem to fulfil this need. These attempts are dangerous—and ultimately weak—because the centre they furnish is so biassed that it must be imposed on dissenting groups through terror. Thus the reaction against uncentred automatic balance has led to the complete destruction of balance and to profound disruption in every sphere of human existence. But this reaction must not be evaluated in purely negative terms. Like ancient tragedy, it has a revealing character; it reveals the human situation in the light of the eternal, and it can give to present-day Christian evangelism a point of contact which has been lost sight of for centuries.

II THE PRINCIPLE OF IMMANENCE AND ITS DILEMMA

"The principle of immanence" is employed as a technical phrase in this article. It is intended to refer to view (a) which finds meaning, value and reality exclusively within natural and human processes, and (b) which therefore rejects the belief that these processes (and their meaning and value) depend upon a transcendent ground. As such, the phrase covers pantheistic views like Bruno's and Spinoza's; but it also includes modern naturalism. Criticisms of "the principle of immanence" offered in the following pages should not be misunderstood. as directed against belief in the immanence of (the transcendent-immanent) God.

Furthermore, in this article, the phrase "spiritual centre" is used to stand for the determining centre of society as a whole. Such terminology is justifiable because a centre cannot be established in either the cultural or the political realm without a spiritual foundation from which it derives (spontaneously acknowledged) authority. Even the totalitarian systems have recognized this, despite the fact that they have been anti-spiritual and one-sidedly political in character. They have identified their political organization with the ultimate meaning of life, and they have used quasi-religious symbols in thought and action for the establishment and maintenance of their authority. Thus they have become rivals of those groups, especially the churches, which have preserved a spiritual centre from the past.

Unless a "centre" is basically spiritual, it cannot unify society.

On the other hand, a spiritual centre is not real and has no power to furnish balance unless it is embodied in a political group and expressed in cultural forms. Even the most anti-political and anti-cultural religious ideas cannot escape the latter fact. "Spirit" is the meaning *and* power of communal and personal life, not their meaning alone.

The loss of a spiritual centre in modern society coincides with the rise of the principle of immanence. The causes of this rise are "material" as well as "ideal", and the effects are political and cultural as well as religious. But whenever the principle has gained ascendancy, it has destroyed the spiritual centre of personal and communal life.

The principle of immanence reduces existence to a sum of finite life-centres and their inter-relationships. Each finite centre of being, value, meaning and purpose is conditioned by others; all are transitory and ambiguous in their significance. None is suited to represent an ultimate concern, to evoke an unconditional devotion, to become a spiritual centre determining and balancing all the others. There is no balancing principle in the totality of the finite; there is no power of ultimate integration in the "world".

Thus modern society has been driven into an insoluble dilemma. Either it must rely on the supposedly automatic balance of the finite centres, or it must establish one of them as the all-embracing and supreme power which controls all the others. If it follows the former alternative—ostensibly in the interests of freedom—it is driven into patterns where human values are subjugated to impersonal "laws" of economics and politics. If it follows the latter alternative, it arbitrarily regiments all other finite interests by investing one particular centre (or centres) with absolute power; and when the source of order thus becomes tyrannical, human life is disrupted through either revolt or enslavement.

In our period the second alternative has followed the first, revealing the real depths of the disintegration which attends belief in the principle of immanence and the consequent loss of a spiritual centre. An outstanding contemporary example of the dilemma is seen in the split between American and Russian centres of world power. Everyone recommends a balance between them, but since a spiritual centre which transcends both is lacking, each takes one step after another in the direction of a "monolithic" structure of world-organization. Confidence in an automatic harmony between finite centres breaks down as soon as any important decision has to be made.

A less spectacular but perhaps even more significant example of the lack of a spiritual centre is to be found in the family. The function of the modern family has become almost entirely utilitarian. It makes provision for sexual relations; it constitutes the smallest economic unit; it guarantees the introduction of the younger generation to some traditional patterns of life; it creates a protective community of comradeship, friendship and love. In all these respects the family still makes an effective contribution towards preserving present-day society. But it has to struggle against great odds. And where there is no uniting principle which transcends utilitarian considerations, the life of the family is at the mercy of the strength or weakness of the factors just mentioned; sexual satisfaction, economic success, mutual sympathy, social protection and adjustment. Since these factors are subject to the tremendous oscillations and insecurities of a competitive society, the cohesion of the family becomes weaker every day. No "enlightened self-interest" on the part of its members is strong enough to resolve automatically the conflicts that arise—especially those which originate in the unconscious.

This leads to a third example: the disintegrating effects of the principle of immanence upon the individual personality. Here the conflict between various unconscious strivings, each of which tries to conquer the centre of consciousness, presents the basic problem of integration. An influential school of modern psychological thought believes that personal integration is possible by an automatic balance of the various personal trends; it assumes something like a pre-established harmony between them. Psychologists recognize that this harmony has been disturbed by external influences, especially in early childhood. But they believe that if the structural effects of these early disturbances are therapeutically removed and the personality is "set free", an automatic process of balancing will begin and the conscious centre will be able to make free decisions unaffected by the compulsive power of morbid strains. From this point of view, a determining spiritual centre is not only superfluous, but even dangerous. It is claimed that the "spiritual centre" in innumerable cases has been a means of internal

oppression and a source of compulsions. That certain theological ideas have been and still are employed repressively is an
undeniable fact; *vide* hopeless feelings of guilt before the wrath
of an arbitrary Deity, fear of Hell, belief in double predestina-
tion, etc. Moreover, the authoritarian, oppressive character of
earlier transcendent principles is partly responsible for the
movements in modern history which have replaced a spiritual
centre by an automatic process. It was the domination of the
centralized late-medieval Church which brought about the reaction of the nation-state with its stress upon absolute political
sovereignty and reliance on the balance of power. It was the
abuse of paternal authority and its ritual consecration by the
churches which brought about the reaction, first of the wife and
then of the children, against domestic tyranny. An inflexible
and unimaginative attitude towards sacred marital laws and
the social conventions they safeguard has played a part in
fomenting rebellion against monogamy. Finally, the false
identification of religion with legalistic demands has contributed to an explosive reaction against repression, and to
reliance upon automatic psychological balance, for the liberation
(autonomy) of personality. In view of these developments, one
can understand why much modern psychotherapy is very suspicious of attempts to re-establish a spiritual centre for personal
life. Knowledge of the devastating consequences of religious
authority in the past leads to the assumption that such authority
will always be arbitrary and repressive. What contemporary
psycho-analytic theory largely overlooks, however, is the fact
that even the "liberated" personality, like every other, needs a
directing and supporting centre. Even when oppressive patterns
have been overcome, new forms of servitude—anarchic and
eccentric, perhaps, instead of compulsive and conformist—are
likely to replace those which have been eradicated. Everything
depends upon whether the new centre is partial, and consequently destructive, or whether it is universal, and consequently creative. Only an "ultimate" concern can balance
the various conditioned concerns of our personal life. Psychotherapy can help men to reduce internal conflicts, anxiety and
hostility; but by itself it cannot furnish goals and values that
are free from the distortions of purely personal or cultural pressures. To-day mental disease is most widespread in lands where
a strong repressive tradition has been followed by an *uncentred*

secular culture. Psychotherapy has contributed to the removal of repressions, but it cannot remedy, and in some respects it even aggravates, the lack of a spiritual centre.

All these developments are supported by changes in the relationship between man and the realm of "things". This relation constitutes the fourth example of the loss of a spiritual centre under the principle of immanence. It is so obvious, that it has received a major share of attention from interpreters of our time. It can be described as the perversion of means into ends because of the disappearance of an ultimate end. An ultimate end necessarily transcends all preliminary ends; it makes the latter means for something beyond themselves. Thus it is a spiritual centre towards which all dealings with "things" can be orientated. When religion, by presenting an ultimate end in an "other-worldly" way, deprives preliminary ends of their significance, it leaves unused the infinite and almost miraculous means given in the structure of nature and in man's power to understand and control nature. For thousands of years, including centuries of Christian history, the transcendent end prevented the free development of immanent ends and the infinite means for their fulfilment. The victory of the principle of immanence, however, has changed the situation radically. It has liberated man from an animal-like slavery to nature. The discovery of new means has created new ends in turn; and there is no discernible limit to this discovery of new terrestrial "goods" through science. At the same time, however, the criterion of the value of an end has been lost. Man is engulfed in a continuous stream of ends which become means and means which become ends; the waves of this stream come and go without expressing anything unconditional, and without being related to a transcendent criterion. One of the most expressive symbols of this situation is the way in which money can transform itself from a means into an end—the all-pervading end for innumerable people. Man himself becomes a means in the service of "things", and he becomes empty in the process of pursuing one provisional end after another without any ultimate end. Therefore he is ready to accept any ostensibly ultimate goal which is presented with passion and convincing power. But under the principle of immanence no end can really be transcendent and unconditional, though it may appear to be so. And in the struggle to enforce the acceptance of some finite end as absolute, the immensities of the technological means discovered by science are used for an immensity of destruction. The belief that expansion of scientific control over nature is accomplished by an automatic balance of finite ends breaks down, just as the theory of automatic balance has broken down in politics and economics, in family and community life, and in the psychology of personality.

Out of the break-down emerges the quest for a new spiritual centre which is truly transcendent, unconditional and universal. Evangelism should show the way to an answer.

III IMMANENCE AND INDIVIDUALITY

The principle of immanence has an implication which deserves special discussion, namely, the "unordered" rise of the individual as individual. Individualization has an ambiguous character. It intensifies, but it also separates. At the human level, the individual possesses freedom and capacity for self-transcendence; thereby man stands at the top of the scale of being. At the same time, human individuality is completely self-related, isolated and lonely. (Self-relatedness is a structural, not a moral-or-immoral, characteristic of man.) To be sure, man as an individual self has a capacity for reunion, love or communion, which is lacking in every sub-human being. This power of reunion, however, is dependent on a reality which transcends the individual self without dissolving the structure of self-relatedness. This reality has been called "Grace" or "Love" (*Agape*) or "the New Creature". It has been the main content of Christian preaching, and it is supposed to overcome the ambiguity of individual selfhood.

Christianity has always acknowledged that the individual self is the bearer of the divine image; but it has not always understood the significance of the individual as a unique mirror of the divine life and as the realization of a unique eternal destiny. Christianity has used its reuniting power for the rejection of the claims of the individual self, and thus it has unintentionally produced the individualistic reaction which characterizes secularism. Secularism, in turn, has lost the spiritual centre in which the individual is liberated from isolation and loneliness. Estrangement of individual from individual characterizes life within the Christian nations. The word "individualism" is not only outworn, it fails to touch the real point, namely, the tragic isolation of the individual because of the loss of a trans-individual uniting centre.

The individual is strong as long as he lives from a communal spiritual substance, of which he is a unique expression. He loses his power in so far as the spiritual substance is wasted or lacking. Then the following process starts: The individual falls prey to the mass; he becomes an atom within a mass, normalized, standardized, driven by the forces of mass-psychology. The lonely individual hides himself under the pattern of his group. He has no power to resist it. He has no spiritual standard by means of which he can judge the group (and himself). When this happens the situation is ripe for the rise of a few powerful individuals who determine the pattern of the life of every individual in the group of which they have become leaders or dictators. The standardized individuals subject themselves to those who represent their standardized, often unconscious, ideals. Then a collective situation can be created in which the individual loses his temporal as well as his eternal significance. He is not lonely any more, because he has surrendered his individual self and because there is no life-content left in him by means of which he could separate himself from the collective. The anxiety of isolation and loneliness is overcome, but the price paid is sacrifice of individual personality. The rush towards standardization and collectivization within modern society is an indirect quest for a spiritual centre. But the path which is being followed leads to an extinction of the individual as individual, and therefore to a demonic, sub-personal structure of life. This is a tragic consequence of the loss of Christianity as the spiritual centre of the " Christian " nations. The reaction against an empty individualism leads to a demonic collectivism.

IV POINTS OF CONTACT FOR EVANGELIZATION IN THE LIFE OF WESTERN SOCIETY

The general point of contact for evangelical apologetics is the (conscious and unconscious) quest for a new spiritual centre on the part of Western society. Christian evangelism in its application to the needs of man in our disintegrated Western world must show that Christianity is able to furnish a transcendent and unconditional centre, and at the same time to balance the concrete, divergent elements which enter into our present social, political and spiritual existence. The Christian churches can seek to demonstrate these things, first, by their very existence, second, by their evangelistic witness, and third, by their apologetic power. In order to succeed, Christian faith must liberate itself from those distortions which have made it participate in the disintegration of the Christian nations. This in turn involves two things. First, Christian faith must conquer in itself the principles of immanence and of empty individualism. Second, Christian faith must not again become authoritarian (heteronomous) in an oppressive and arbitrary way.

The disintegration of society within the Christian nations closes one way and opens another for Christianity. It closes the traditional way of the Christian churches and it opens a new way which is not yet fully visible but whose direction can already be discerned.

The first requisite action is one of dissociating the Christian order from disintegrated Western society. No "religion" that is merely part of the process of disintegration can become a healing power; only something which transcends the process can give it a new spiritual centre. The Christian order can dissociate itself only through the power of that Foundation which is at the same time its Judge: The New Being, manifest in Jesus as the Christ. The prophetic note (not the theological system) offered by Barth and his friends must be understood in terms of a movement to dissociate the Christian order from the Christian nations and their disintegrating culture. Barth points to the absolute transcendence of the absolute, the unconditional character of the unconditioned, the divinity of the divine. These seeming tautologies are the theme of every prophetic message, of every dissociation of the healing power from what it is supposed to heal.

If this dissociation is carried through, the possibility of a new spiritual centre appears; the principle of immanence is broken, and with it the vicious dilemma between an automatic and a tyrannical organization of social life. The transcendence of the spiritual principle guarantees that it is not identical with any conditioned, finite centre. On the other hand, however, it does not simply abandon human life to its automatic, compulsive and self-destructive patterns. The voice calling for dissociation—in Jewish prophetism, in the New Testament, in the Reformation, in Neo-orthodoxy—never sanctions the establishment of a new idolatry; but men, of course, quickly misunderstand it and identify the new spiritual centre with an absolute nation, an absolute Church, an absolute creed or an absolute theology. Whenever this misunderstanding occurs, the dissociation merely leads to another, often a more tyrannical, attempt to claim that some conditional form of life is unconditional.

Dissociation of the Christian message from disintegrating Western society requires a true conception of the relationship between transcendence and immanence. The orthodox supra-naturalistic version of this relationship is disastrous; it regards the transcendent as a second objective " realm " of miraculous events, and heavenly individuals (including God) beyond the natural, historical world. So long as the issue is conceived in such a manner, naturalism is always right in refusing to acknowledge this transcendent realm. The creative ground, the judging power and the fulfilling meaning of all finite centres and events is not a second " realm " of reality; it is the source, structure and ultimate meaning of the *one* world in which finite centres and events are found. It has been and always should be the intention of the Christian Church to point to this ultimate ground of life and experience, and thus to lead every generation to *the* spiritual centre of its own existence. The Christian Church should perform this task for " the Christian nations " of the present age.

Hence the true dissociation of the Christian order from the disintegrating Western world includes a true association with Western culture and with every other part of our world. Supra-naturalism, because it is incapable of a true dissociation of the unconditional from the conditional, is also incapable of a true association of them. It seeks to control and suppress from outside the finite centres of meaning and being, instead of permeating and affirming from within. Yet association and dissociation are interdependent in a precise way, and each must be complete. It was the glory of the Jewish prophets that they reached completeness in both respects; by distinguishing the righteousness of God from all finite human aims, they pointed to the restoration of a right relationship between the two. Similarly to-day the Church, by differentiating its message from the shattered assumptions and illusions of Western culture, must *be* the spiritual centre for a re-integration of human life. It must become a spiritual centre for healing the neurotic mind of the individual and the split consciousness of the masses. It must become a spiritual centre for children in relation to their parents, and for parents in relation to each other and to their children. It must become a spiritual centre for the relation of man to nature and to the machine, to money and to the competitor. It must become a spiritual centre for the self-accusing scientist, and for the educator whose task has become empty because he (and his culture) has no stable scale of values to offer a younger generation. If the Christian faith, through the Church, is unable to furnish a new, all-embracing, non-tyrannical spiritual centre, then it has nothing serious to say to our time; and it will perish in the West as one finite centre of life and meaning in the vast disintegration of the Western world. Christianity is either healing power from the ground of human existence, or it is one contributing factor, among others, to the personal and social sickness of our period, and will perish with it.

The problem discussed in this article thus leads inevitably to the fundamental question about Christianity's healing power. In so far as Christianity is merely one cultural phenomenon among others, it is enmeshed in the forces that are destroying Western society. It can resist disintegration only by furnishing a spiritual centre which transcends the patterns of Western culture; and it can furnish the basis for a new integration of life only by replacing the principles of immanence with a principle which reunites all finite concerns—political, communal and personal—with their ultimate ground. Of course, it is not possible to assert that Western society can be saved. Still less is it possible to assert that God's plan for the world depends upon its salvation and that of the Western churches which have been associated with it. This paper is written from the conviction that Western civilization has in the past incorporated great spiritual values, that it is worth saving if it can be saved, and that the only means by which it can be saved is the recovery of the Gospel of Christ as the power which can heal the sickness of society from within, from the ground of its own being. Even if all this were destroyed, the Gospel would still be the Gospel, and God's purpose would go forward through other men and in other ways.

3

THE CHURCH'S FAILURE TO BE CHRISTIAN: I

by Frank Bennett

IT has become fashionable to describe this present age in the West as post-Christian. It would be more accurate, though cumbersome, to call it post-Constantinian. For to speak of the state of affairs that history has lately been leaving behind as Christian is, to say the least of it, question-begging. There has been falling to pieces the particular relation between the Church and Society in general which the conversion of the Roman Emperor brought about. That such an approximation between them is unknown to the New Testament does not condemn it, for the providence of God did not cease to act at the end of the first century. But it means that mimetic recognition of Christianity by the public and the now diminishing ethical assets which have followed from it cannot be regarded as fundamental by the New Israel. Thus the undiscriminating use of the term, post-Christian, covers up what has been happening under a generalization. It evades the whole question of Constantine.

Constantine has been acclaimed as a triumph and deplored as a disaster. What is certain is that his conversion meant a revolution. To Tertullian the very idea of a Christian emperor had seemed grotesque; the Christian was an outsider and he gloried in it. There were also many who in the event were driven into the segregated strictness of the Egyptian desert by the effects upon the Church of imperial favour and in various forms their protest has continued. Yet it is difficult to see what else the Church could have done. It could not write above its portals, "Emperors not admitted". One must believe that God was calling His Church to this risk, that it was He Who brought it to this point and made this demand, for the course of history is in His hands. But risk there undoubtedly was. "Lead us not into temptation" might well have been the most fervent prayer. In point of fact the Church succumbed in due course to every temptation.

But now, with Constantine in reverse, the voice of God would seem to be calling us through new circumstances to a reorientation—to rediscovery—and it is the Church itself that we are being called upon to rediscover. Certainly there can be no antiquarian reconstruction of the primitive—no return to what was—though the latter days may find much that is significant in the first. But history is not a slate that can be wiped clean, nor in any case may the Church write off the responsibility placed upon it through Constantine and still more in the Dark Ages. A new relation will be very far from meaning that the Church can wash its hands of society. On the contrary, it must steadfastly set itself to do for an again disintegrating world all which that world will allow it to do without encouraging· delusions. Nor may Christians disparage the State. Rather they must seek to confer upon it a sense of its God-given status and responsibility. But it will be of the first importance to observe the drastic nature of the change which has taken place in the relation of the whole Church to the Western environment. Far more is involved than any mere question of state-connection. Churches which have never had that advantage or disadvantage, whichever it may be, now find themselves none the less profoundly affected by the new attitude of the society within which they exist. The first need will be to clear away what has become débris, and much of it is fit subject for repentance.

We can thank God among the ruins and accept for our purging the chàstisement of the awkward situation in which the disappearance of ill-founded success has placed us. But our temptation is to content ourselves with the last relics of it and, most of all, to preserve the state of mind which it induced. We have been a power in the land. We have wielded a power very different from that which Christ promised to His Church. Not that the Church can fail to reckon with power; idealistically to suppose that power does not count is to live in a dream world. The Church may often be required to manipulate power in the interests of the moral law, but the Church must beware of power. Actually it has grasped it with both hands, and this has been true of almost every part of the Church, for the immaculate have with a few notable exceptions lacked opportunity rather than desire.

Stretched out over centuries of church history is the secular arm. Very considerably by means of it an immense and imposing structure was built up. But it was not fitting that the sword and the threat of the sword should be employed for building on the foundation of the Apostles and prophets with surely a tortured Christ, given into His people's hands, as head corner-stone—and now we are paying the price. For the sins of the fathers are visited upon the children. We are solid with the continuing Church in its sins as well as in its graces, and the least Erastian churches have not always been loath to eat of the forbidden fruit. But the Church did not merely use the world; it sank neck-deep into the world, and that, not to seek and to save, but to manage. Here again it is difficult to see what else it could have done in the initial stages of the process. Almost overnight the Church found the world on its hands. How in the crisis of imperial disintegration could bishops have refused the magistracy which charity itself thrust upon them? Yet aberration threatened. Pastors would be swallowed up in prelates after the manner of Byzantium and the proper tension between Church and State assume unbecoming feudal forms. Already Avignon with its hard-headed bureaucracy loomed on the horizon. When and where the "godly prince" ousted the Pope, there was no real change of heart, but by that time the decline of ecclesiastical greatness, which has become so steep of late, had already set in. Then one might have expected that God's Church would with a sigh of relief have loosed its hold on earthly governance which once it had been compelled to undertake. Not so! By now it had acquired a fatal inheritance—a position to keep up. For management had led to self-aggrandizement and, not least among dissidents, to a flair for intrigue, so that still what is apt to seem most important is that the Church, or some part of the Church, should be advantaged.

Now certainly the Church cannot live outside the world, for God has put it into the world. It was inevitable and, up to a point, most proper that it should reflect the culture and civilization in which at any given time it found itself. To-day it reflects only too accurately the absence of a culture. But it became not only in the world but of the world and, if some of this story is ancient history, it is this ancient history which, deflected by God, has placed the Church in its present predicament. It is the aftermath of this history which provides present temptations. Blatant power may have fallen from the hands of the Church, but Satan becomes only the more cunning. Still we manœuvre where we can no longer control; we set up secretariats; we prefer organization to faith. Most of all, we remain obsessed with our heritage of apparatus. The basilicas of Old and New Rome set a fashion which has bequeathed buildings many and some of them great. The favour of kings and lords and early capitalists peopled Europe with a numerous clergy. Thus the Church now finds itself like some indigent nobleman who must make a show of preserving the family mansion and retainers, lest he should seem to have become less noble. This becomes his life work; it absorbs him. So the Church is under temptation to be absorbed in maintaining itself and to compromise the Gospel in order to entice those who will have none of the Gospel but who have the money. Not the preaching of Christ crucified is presented as the objective, but something entitled "spiritual reconstruction", "spiritual values" or whatever it may be. Once it was pardons and faked relics; now it is "spiritual values". The pardons and relics sold better than the "spiritual values", but both have proved useful to a Church feverishly striving to keep up its former position in a changed world. For in such circumstances the Church has to choose between a measure of prosperity and the life which can only come by death and resurrection. The latter is the choice of faith. Israel must come out of Egypt.

Now indeed the process of coming out must be most painful. One loses caste; one invites a taunt song; one is despised. They may be happy who find this done for them by a revolution. Shearing by a Gestapo is attended by physical suffering, but psychologically the severest test may be a lingering decline. It is notable that the confessing churches have succeeded in interpreting their distresses dynamically, theologically. The voice of God has been heard speaking in the fire. Not that those areas of the Church which have undergone persecution have been brought to perfection. The unpersecuted have expected too much of the persecuted, and have been surprised to find them, not perfect, but exhausted. But the persecuted have also been apt to expect of those who have remained in comparative ease that which they of all people were the least likely to possess. They have expected them to retain and redistribute an *élan* which has everywhere been lost, but most of all among those to whom the same struggle has presented itself in an utterly undramatic form. These last are the most subject to illusion and its attendant depression. On the one hand, they are able to go on expecting that what is being irrevocably, but in their case gradually, shattered will be restored. They do not recognize the Shatterer. On the other hand, repeatedly and increasingly disappointed expectations sink them deeper in the trough. Called, smitten in mercy, pointed to salvation, they still look for a conjuring trick or seek to devise one. Thus those churches are already a stage ahead which have been humbled to the uttermost, though for them too it is still possible to resist God's will. In the churches as yet least touched, and that by decline rather than by cataclysm, it is often the struggling congregation, not the still apparently prosperous one, that is in the vanguard. It begins to take to itself the insights of adversity.

This is not to say that we should turn iconoclast; it is not a case of wildly abandoning everything. Faithful work has been done and has maintained a body of the faithful bearing the marks of apostolic heredity. There is a Church which lives— sometimes in spite of the Church—and it is not invisible. The first step is always humbly and thankfully to accept that which God presents, not *de novo*, but out of the past. He presents companies of sinners with whom their fellow-sinners must seek incorporation. But to accept will be something very different from complacency. There is that which has to be sought, which has to be recovered after centuries of identification with Mesech and Kedar, and it is elusive. It cannot be defined, but will emerge from common life in the Spirit. Thus both the arrogance of the revolutionary and the sleep of the traditionalist are to be avoided. The new is new and yet it must take shape hidden in the infected womb of the old.

There are quiet stirrings, there are patient experiments among humble Christians up and down the world, which will be bearing fruit when the heralded movements have been forgotten. There the new comes to birth where the Body of Christ is being built up, for there a People comes into being and not a mere machinery. The tragedy is that so much of the thought and energy of the Church goes into undertakings which, because they are unrelated to the humble places where the life is lived, result in little but a piling up of more dry bones. To tell the truth, there is much unconscious despising of the little ones. They are left outside the councils where theologizers make so bold as to discuss them. This is ominous, since again in this the Church follows the trend of the world. Yet they think of things among the sycamore trees of Tekoa which are hidden from the wise and prudent.

What is most necessary now is that the Gospel, disentangled from a perfectionist confusion of Gospel with the Sermon on the Mount, be again lived in the thoughts and ways of the local churches. For there its content and application were originally worked out, not in the schools, but in the emergencies of day-to-day church life. The most glowing doctrinal passages of Scripture have to us a surprisingly occasionalist background. The meaning of redemption was discovered even in the squabbles. But we have let the Gospel become irrelevant to the life of the Church. For now the hopes of the Church are apt to be quite other than the hopes of heavenly citizens who "look for the resurrection of the dead". Often they are little more ·than the fashionable hopes of the moment put into ecclesiastical dress. Again, we pray for "The fellowship of the Holy Ghost" and rely on mere cameraderie. We preach justification by faith and ourselves justify by works giving and desiring continual human commendation in our churches. True, this is for the most part in the little things, yet it is exactly in the little things that the whole thing is either Christian or sub-Christian. Where else? It is exactly in the small event, the casual word, the detail of administration, that the Gospel is or is not proclaimed.

Scripture must permeate and govern the everyday life of the Church. Here there is need for much thinking but also for patience. The rediscovered Bible has as yet scarcely penetrated beyond a narrow circle, nor need this surprise. Hardly have pastors and teachers digested what has to be relearnt; still less have they found a medium for reconveying it. But this medium will be discovered, not in conferences, but in the persevering converse of the pastor with his people. There has come to be an un-Christian haste about the Church, a haste which is something very different from a sense of urgency. God does not ask us to be alarmed for Him, but then it is for our position in the world that we are alarmed, for we are more than half persuaded that His honour is bound up with its maintenance. Constantine's legacy remains the Kingdom of God to us, while we preach that it is not. It is not even the Church.

It is a Tower of Babel—progress run to pride—and Nemesis overtakes it. The Church erects its Towers of Babel too—inevitably, for the Church is involved in fallen terrestrial existence. But the Church should by faith be able to forsake them and move on. With the Bible in its hands it should be in a position to interpret, to accept, to use that which the hand of God does to it. Have we perhaps been more forward in interpreting the distresses of secular society than those of the Church? Have we proclaimed the end of the Renaissance age in the history of Europe, and failed to observe the end of the Constantinian phase in the history of the Church? But now it is " Farewell, Byzantium ". God strips His Church of the spoils of its former victory that it may be driven back on Him. He undermines its security that it may learn to live by faith. He baffles it that it may be brought to see that all things are possible with Him. Most of all, He removes occasions of glorying other than " in the cross of our Lord Jesus Christ ".

For it is only faith that is going to move mountains. Such faith must find expression in the quality and action of corporate life—" Ye are our epistle ". And this corporate life will only be "fellowship in furtherance of the Gospel ", when it is grounded in an apprehension of the Gospel and is in Him Who is the Gospel. The Christian hope of salvation, resurrection, attainment, by incorporation in and through Christ, must be recovered, for apart from that there is no good reason for expecting anything to happen—at any rate through us. As to that most excellent gift of *agape*, this will be the fruit, not of exhortation, but of a Church which reaches out hands to Pentecost.

It is then time for " finis " to be written to discussion and for each man to sink himself in the dedicated life of some part of the royal priesthood whose totality is Christ. For here is the key to the future—maybe a distant future to be patiently looked for but the only future that is going to count. At present the Church in its hurry speaks not only to a vacuum, but from something very like a vacuum. The Word makes no impression because the Church behind the Word makes no impression. When the world declares that the Church is not Christian it means for the most part that the Church is not perfect. It disparages earthen vessels. But the world points its finger at the inexcusable when it notes that the Church is so largely indistinguishable from the world. It is of the world alike in calibre and outlook, and in part this is because it has been absorbed where it should be holding aloof. Certainly we need continually to be reminded that it is for the world that Christ has died and risen again. We need to regain the vision of the consummation set forth in the first chapter of Ephesians. Yet the Church has also to stand over against the world, and that, for the sake of the world. For what the world most needs of the Church is neither diagnosis nor advice, but the word of God prophetically spoken, and for that the Church must learn to live again by faith.

THE CHURCH'S FAILURE TO BE CHRISTIAN: II

by S. C. Neill

IT is easy to criticize the Church and to point out its failures. But we have a right to ask the critics to state what it is that in their estimation the Church has failed to be. Very often we shall find that the Church is being judged by some purely human standard, that the critic is objecting because it has failed to be or to do something which it never set out to be or to do, and that he has failed to take note either of what the Church is divinely intended to be, or of the supreme difficulty of the task which has been set before it by its Creator. The Church is to be the body of Christ. The principle of its life is that of the incarnation. It is to manifest the life of God among men. Each of these elements, *the life of God* and *among men* has to be emphasized; if the Church is to be faithful to its vocation *as Church,* each has to be maintained in its due proportion. If the manward side is overstressed, the Church is in peril of becoming so closely identified with human projects and ideas as to lose its capacity to be what God intends it to be, the critic and the judge of all human purposes that develop themselves in independence of God. If the Godward side receives a one-sided and exclusive attention, the Church tends to lose its power to be the salt of the earth and the light of the world. To maintain the exact proportion is to walk on an extremely narrow path. The sinlessness of Christ is manifest exactly here, in His inerrant judgment of the path that He is to follow, so as to be at the same time wholly at the disposal of the Father Who sent Him, and also to be wholly at the disposal of men so as to be their Saviour, without allowing either aspect of His work to encroach on the other, or, through conflict between them, to introduce an element of uncertainty into the directness and decision of His activity. It is the maintenance of this tension that constitutes the inevitability of the Cross. To enter into the life of men with the promise of salvation arouses the expectation that salvation will be given in terms of their all too human hopes and desires; the absolute refusal of these hopes and desires demanded by loyalty to the divine purpose cannot but call out the enmity of those who feel that they have been cheated out of the very thing that they have been led to count on, and so leads them to destroy that in which they had begun to trust. From the point of view of the world, the Church is always in the ambiguous position of the Christ; it seems both to promise and then to deny the very thing which it had promised; in the life of the Church, therefore, as in the life of the Christ, the Cross is an inevitable element. But this Cross is inevitable only if the Church, like the Christ, maintains the fulness of its vocation, both in absolute loyalty to God and in absolute serviceableness to men.

The essential failure of the Church will be found in its failure to do justice to both terms of its vocation. On the one hand, the Church may so withdraw itself as to be no longer deeply concerned in the affairs of the world, and may purchase peace at the price of loss of effectiveness. The great monastic movements were in their day a necessary protest against the tendency of the Church to become so much involved in the world as to lose its sense of distinctness and divine vocation. The monasteries did render incalculable service to the Christian cause by the preservation of much in the heritage of the ancient world that would otherwise have perished, by their missionary enterprise and the civilizing work that they were able to do among peoples newly Christianized, and by their unfailing witness to the primacy of prayer and worship in the Christian life. Their weakness lay in a withdrawal from the world such as our Lord Himself never practised, and in the belief that the world, as the Kingdom of Satan, is utterly irredeemable, so that a man's only hope of salvation is to come out of it entirely, abandoning it to the destruction which is its destiny, and in which a man, if he remains in it, cannot but become involved. When the opponent of the Church criticizes it on the ground of its other-worldliness, this criticism may be misplaced; but also it may have in it an element of truth, since genuine Christian other-worldliness consists not in the abandonment of the world to the powers of darkness, but in the ceaseless demand that the Kingdom of God should come here on earth, and the recognition that salvation can come not from within the world, but only by the descent upon it of the divine as it was manifest in Jesus of Nazareth.

In other times and circumstances, the Church has taken the path of identification with the world. This has been a perilous path, but one which could not have been refused. The Church has the power, divinely implanted, to be the fashioner of the life of nations. Only those who have lived long in a country which has never been Christian can appreciate the extent to which the Church was successful in imposing on Christendom the Christian pattern of living, and how even in lands where secularization has gone furthest, the mind of a Western man still moves within the Christian categories and the Christian framework of thought. It is impossible to regret the immense labour of education undertaken by the Church in the past and to some extent still undertaken in the present, or to regard as wholly misconceived its involvement in plans for social reform. Yet the partial Christianization of the secular world had its Nemesis in the partial secularization of the Church. When we have allowed for a certain bitterness and unreasonableness in the critics, we may yet find much to learn from them, since the basis of their criticism may be a dim and perhaps not more than half-conscious recognition that the claim of the Church to be a divine society is not valid, unless it is recognizably a society different in kind and in operation from the secular societies which it is its task to educate and to judge.

The achievement of Jesus was the creation on earth of a new kind of life, a life in which the fellowship with God made possible through redemption cannot but become articulate in a new fellowship among believers different from that of any other society. The Church is the place in which the Word of God is proclaimed continuously both in judgment and in mercy. It is the place in which the believer learns to translate the principles of divine revelation into applications to the ordinary concerns of daily life. It is the sphere in which he is assured continuously of the reality of the forgiveness of God. It is the fellowship in which, if it is true to its nature, the intractable problems of personal relationships, of money, of work, of leisure, of race, are solved, both as a rebuke to the world which has failed to solve

them and as an example which the world can in a measure
follow. It is in the Church that man learns to apply to all the
affairs of time the judgments of eternity, and so to live in that
perspective in which alone it is possible for him to be aware of
his true greatness without falling into the sin of Adam and desiring to assert his independence as against God. The world is
vaguely aware of its need of such a society. The deep root of the
neurosis so widespread in all the countries of the West is man's
uncertainty of being loved, and the failure of ordinary love to
penetrate to that deepest level where men really live and where,
if they are starved of love, they can have neither security nor
peace. In a society in which the love of God is constantly
mediated by the unfailing and assured love of the brethren, man
can find himself at home and at peace: there is no other place
of healing for his sickness.

If we consider the serious criticisms of the Church, those, that
is, which are made from other motives than jealousy or pique,
we shall find that many of them resolve themselves into the
objection that the Church just is not what it claims to be, and
lacks those qualities without which it cannot be the body of
Christ.

Most educated men in the world to-day have some knowledge
of the Gospels, and some mental picture of the character of Jesus.
They realize, perhaps better than many professing Christians,
that the only true criterion of Christianity is likeness to Christ.
The heart of their complaint, though perhaps they would be
hard put to it to frame it in words, is that they do not see in
Christians and in the Church that likeness to Christ which they
have a right to expect. Real holiness is impressive and attractive; if the Church has failed to hold the respect of the ordinary
man, may the cause not be, in part at least, that the children
of the Church have failed to set before the world the challenge
of unmistakable holiness after the manner of Christ?

One criticism is made not infrequently by the convert from
a non-Christian religion. In many parts of the world the convert has to abandon the whole of the life and tradition in which
he has grown up, and must depend only on the fellowship of
believers for all that is represented by family and community.
Even where the break is not as complete as this, the convert has
jettisoned all the thought-forms by which previously his life
has been determined, and has made the adventure of embark-

ing on the unknown sea of the Christian life. Far more than
any " convert " in a quasi-Christian country, he is in need of
trust, affection and guidance from those among whom he is now
to find his home. Again and again the complaint is heard that
the Church is not a welcoming body, and that the atmosphere
into which the newcomer enters is cold and suspicious. It must
be recognized that the convert in a non-Christian country is
an unknown quantity. His conversion may have been quite
genuine; yet in the field of Christian experience he is a child;
on a great many subjects he is uninformed and unaware of the
Christian way of doing things. He makes many mistakes, and
sometimes offends his Christian friends by his erratic ways.
There is always the possibility that he may fall away and return
to his non-Christian faith. This is a point which is not often
mentioned in missionary magazines and books, but it is one
which has to be taken seriously. The most difficult point of all
is that of marriage; the stability of a young convert depends as
much as anything on his finding a true Christian partner, with
whom he can begin to build up as he desires a genuinely Christian home. But parents are naturally suspicious, and are more
likely to desire for their daughters a safe marriage with an
established Christian than the uncertain adventure of a partnership with a convert. The anxiety is natural; yet how can the
new convert grow unless he is taken at once into a fellowship
of real trust and confidence? Even in Western lands, those who
have come out of a non-Christian environment have been known
to complain that they have missed in the Church the warm
fellowship which they had previously found in the public-house
or the athletic team.

Another objection which, it has to be admitted, does lie
against the Church as it is, is that secular motives enter far more
into its life than is right. Within the fellowship of love, there
should be no place for ambition, rivalry or intrigue. But it is
obvious—more perhaps to the outsider than to the member of
the Church, who may have become all too used to things as they
are—that these evils do enter in. They began very early to
corrupt the Christian society; in the fourth century, at the election of Pope Damasus, the Church where his followers had met
in armed conflict with those of his rival Ursinus was strewn with
the bodies of the slain. In modern times, party passion within
the Church does not perhaps go to such extremes; but it may still

happen that elections to offices in the Church are accompanied by the same kind of lobbying, canvassing and intrigue as are manifest in the operations of secular politics. The worth of a minister is sometimes assessed in terms more appropriate to a skilful company promoter than to a follower of Jesus Christ. Indeed, the Church only too readily takes the colour of the world, whose god is success.

A third criticism is that the Church, so far from transcending class and social distinctions, has in fact stereotyped them. There are not many churches in which it is possible for Christians of all social strata and levels of education to feel at home together and to worship as one fellowship. This difficulty is far less felt in Roman Catholic and Orthodox than in Protestant countries. Even there the difficulty cannot wholly be avoided; a French Roman Catholic writer has recently pointed out that the atmosphere of the ordinary Parisian church is bourgeois, and that it is almost impossible for the proletarian, used to an entirely different kind of life and environment, to recognize it as his spiritual home. The greater difficulty felt in Protestant countries seems to be closely associated with the character of Protestant worship and its special emphasis on the sermon. Intellect divides; on the emotional and intuitive level men are much more nearly akin. The sermon is aimed at minds of different calibre. The Eucharist is a service of levelling; there may be immense differences in spiritual apprehension, but at the climax of the service, rich and poor, educated and unlearned, all do the same thing. Except in unusual circumstances the sermon has but rarely the same universal appeal. Any minister who has been faced with the task of preaching to a mixed congregation, such as is still to be found in villages where the tradition of church-going has not been lost, is familiar with the problem of knowing what to say to the congregation. What will appeal to the better-educated will be unintelligible to the ploughboy; what will go home to the heart of the ploughboy will be tedious to the instructed Christian. Part of the problem of proclamation is the adaptation of the Gospel to the hearer; even to his vocabulary. The result is seen in the stratification of churches in cities. Even where there are not such special difficulties as lead to the separation of white and Negro congregations in the United States and South Africa, there is a tendency for congregations to follow social groupings, for the richer and

poorer to worship in separation from one another, and so for
the concept of the Christian family to be obscured by the fortuitous operation of social and economic factors.

A radical challenge to the Church comes from the working
class. Where does the Church stand in relation to the working-
class movement of the last century? It claims to be the champion
of the oppressed and disinherited. Even the most conservative
of Christians must admit that a century ago the working classes
in all European countries were oppressed and disinherited; few
would be likely to deny that the working-class movement has
been, at least in a measure, a claim for justice and liberty such
as are declared in the Gospel to be the birthright of every man
made in the image of God. This is not to deny that the movements of the left, like all other human enterprises, have been
tainted with selfishness, unfairness to others and corruption.
But have the churches ever had the courage to say openly and
unitedly that they stand for the principles of justice, that they
can be relied on to support any movement which tends to improve the lot of men, and that they are unequivocally against
privilege divorced from responsibility? Much more has been
done by Christians than the critics of the Church may recognize.
It has also to be borne in mind that social and political progress
can never be the primary concern of the Church. Yet when all
this has been allowed for, it is still true that for the alienation
of the working classes from the Church, the Church itself must
bear some measure of blame. There is an inevitable tendency
for the Church to become bourgeois; the virtues of honesty, diligence and thrift which ought to be practised by all Christians
raise men in the social and economic scale; those who have themselves most hardly won security are not always the most ready
to share it with others; it is all too easy to identify the Church
with the *status quo*, to believe that its prosperity depends on the
maintenance of things as they are, and so to be suspicious of any
movement for extensive changes.[1] This attitude, so common as
to be almost normal among Christians of the West, is a denial
of the true nature of the Church. In every age, oppression and
wrong reconstitute themselves, and there is no Utopia this side
of the coming of the Kingdom of God with Power. The Church

---

[1] In 1879, when the first organized strike took place in Sweden, the strikers
wished to have morning prayers, and invited a clergyman to take these for them.
The clergyman not merely refused, but notified the police, who called out the
military to compel the strikers to come back to work.

is pledged, by its loyalty to Jesus Christ, to fight every form of oppression and wrong. Unless it is a revolutionary Church, it is not a Church at all. This does not mean that the Church is bound to be revolutionary on terms fixed by the makers of a contemporary revolution. Far from it; the Church must stand aloof and retain its freedom to proclaim the Word of God in judgment and condemnation on reactionaries and revolutionaries alike. The deification of the proletariat in the Marxian system is a mythical, mystical and irrational element with which the hard-headed common sense of Christianity can make no terms. But independence must not turn into indifference; that wrong is not all on one side must not be taken as an excuse for silence when the situation demands plain speaking. On the whole, it has to be admitted that the churches have been marked by timidity rather than by courage; they have been more ready to appease the aggressor than to risk their own position and possessions by any bold challenge.

The recognition of failure is the first step towards success. If the Church has failed to be Christian, its failure cannot be due to any adverse circumstances or difficulties consequent on its passage through time. It can only have come through failure on the part of the Church to understand its own vocation as the body of Christ. What the vocation is was plainly indicated by St. Paul in his exposition of the meaning of the Eucharist; as the many grains are gathered into one loaf, so the many members of the Church by drawing near to God are made into one bread, one body. But the grain is gathered into one only in order that the loaf may be broken and given for the life of men. The life of the Church is not for itself. In that life there must always be these three elements: constant drawing near to God through Christ, the experienced fellowship of love through the presence of Christ in His body, the self-giving of the Church for the life of the world, after the example of Him who came that men might have life and might have it abundantly.

III

SOME AXIOMS OF THE MODERN MAN

———————

PREFACE

The section which follows is obviously different in character from the rest of the volume.

At one of the preliminary meetings, Professor Emil Brunner of Zurich pointed out that man's thinking is to a considerable extent determined by inner convictions not consciously thought out or clearly expressed, taking the form of Axioms of contemporary proverbial wisdom, and that part of the difficulty in evangelism to-day arises from the contradictions between most men's Axioms and the general structure of biblical thought and ideas.

Professor Brunner was asked to formulate a brief statement of some typical Axioms of the modern man; and his list of Axioms is here printed, though he himself would not wish it to be regarded as final or exhaustive. A suggestive paper by Mr. C. S. Lewis of Oxford on this same subject had previously been circulated, and groups in various countries prepared lists of Axioms, a selection from which is here printed.

The compilers of this volume well understand that no Axioms can be fully representative; but it is believed that this method of study can be very profitable, and that others may find it a useful exercise to draw up similar lists of Axioms representing the mind of those groups with which they are most closely in touch.

1

AXIOMS

by Emil Brunner

1. Everything is relative.
2. What can't be proved can't be believed.
3. Scientific knowledge is certain and the standard of truth; matters of faith are uncertain.
4. Beyond death nobody knows.
5. "Real" means seen and handled.
6. The big things are the great things. Because man is so small in this big universe he is so little.
7. I cannot help being what I am.
8. Freedom means doing as I like.
9. Justice means equality.
10. To put religion first is religious arrogance.
11. Laws of nature determine everything.

2

AXIOMS FROM GREAT BRITAIN

1. There may be a God—but what does it matter?
2. Man needs education—not redemption.
3. A sense of sin cramps your style.
4. Christianity's all right—if it worked.
5. It's only human nature after all.
6. Science displaces dogma.
7. At all costs keep an open mind.
8. I just couldn't care less.
9. There is nothing good or bad, but thinking makes it so.
10. What I believe matters little—it's what I do.
11. "Just the art of being kind
    Is all this sad world needs."

AXIOMS FROM AMERICA

1. Truth is established only by proof, and ultimate truth is unknowable.
2. Look out for number one. If you don't, nobody else will.
3. Human nature is fundamentally sound, but needs guidance and correction to achieve its fulfilment. " Sin " is just another name for ignorance or correctible imperfection, or biological lag.
4. There is progress in history, but society may yet destroy itself if the discoveries of science are not controlled.
5. There always have been wars and there always will be. You can't change human nature.
6. " God " is really a projection of man's ideals.
7. A man's religion is his own business and every man has a right to his own belief.
8. Other-worldliness is dangerous because it distracts attention from the effort to gain freedom, security, and justice in this life; and anyway we know nothing about what happens after death.
9. Jesus was a good man. What we need are a lot more people like Him. Now, take Lincoln . . .
10. Do a good turn when you can—but don't be a sucker.

4

AXIOMS FROM GERMANY

1. Komme mir keiner mit grossen Ideen! Es ist ja doch alles Betrug—oder bestenfalls Selbstbetrug, vor allem in der Politik! Traue niemandem!
2. Ich glaube nicht, dass es noch irgendetwas Dauerhaftes gibt. Und mit dem Tod ist sowieso alles aus.
3. Es hat keinen Sinn, sich für grosse Dinge einzusetzen, denn jeder Einsatz bleibt vergebens, und man selbst ist nur der Dumme dabei (überhaupt: wenn ich das Wort " Einsatz " höre, wird mir schon schlecht).
4. Bestimmte Leute tragen die Verantwortung für unser Schicksal; sie sind offenbar gewissenlos und erfüllen ihre Aufgabe schlecht; aber ich kann das nicht ändern.

5. Wieso soll ich schuld sein an dem Unglück der Menschheit? Mag man die Schuldigen suchen und bestrafen—ich möchte endlich meine Ruhe haben.

6. Wir haben es so lange schlecht gehabt, nun sollen es "die andern" (Herr x und Herr y, meine Nachbarn) auch mal zu spüren bekommen (das Axiom des Denunzianten).

7. Wenn man satt ist, kann man wohl Pläne für die Zukunft schmieden oder von Moral und Religion reden—wenn man hungrig ist, fällt das alles aus. Das gilt für die Einzelnen wie für die Völker.

8. Niemand hilft mir—warum soll ich andern helfen? Mehr als man mir bietet gebe ich nicht her.

9. Vielleicht wird es doch eines Tages wieder besser werden— aber wann? Es kommt darauf an, dass man sich so lange eben noch über Wasser hält.

10. Es scheint, dass Gott im Leben gewisser Leute eine Rolle spielt. Leider bin ich selbst über dies Stadium hinaus.

11. Wenn es einen Gott gäbe, dann . . .

12. Ich will von Vereinen und Organisationen und somit auch von der Kirche nichts mehr wissen, sondern will mein eigenes Leben leben. Eine Beitrittserklärung unterschreibe ich nirgends mehr.

ENGLISH TRANSLATION

1. Don't talk to me about your wonderful ideas! They are all lies. Or at least you are self-deceived, especially in politics. Don't trust anyone!

2. I don't believe anything stable exists. And when you're dead everything is finished, anyhow.

3. There is no sense in bothering about great causes, for every attempt to support such things is utterly useless, and you are just left holding the baby!

4. Certain people bear the responsibility for our destiny: it's obvious that they have no conscience at all and that they do it badly. But *I* can't alter that.

5. How can *I* be guilty of the misery of humanity? Find the guilty and punish *them*! But I want a little peace.

6. We've had such a bad time for so long, it's time that someone else had a taste of it! (Mr. A and Mrs. B for instance.) (This is the type of person who "informs" against his neighbours.)

7. When you've had enough to eat, it's all very fine to talk about morals and religion, but if you are hungry nothing else matters. This applies to individuals as well as to nations.

8. Nobody helps *me*—why should *I* help other people? I'm not going to give people more than they give me.

9. Perhaps one day things will get better—but when? Everything depends on keeping one's head above water.

10. It seems as though God plays a part in the lives of certain people. Unfortunately I myself have got beyond this stage!

11. If there's a God, then . . .

12. I don't want to join any more societies or organizations, but I want to live my own life. I'll never sign any more membership forms.

AXIOMS FROM FRANCE

Prouvez-moi Dieu, j'y croirai.
Tout est relatif.
Toutes les religions sont bonnes pourvu qu'on les pratique.

Je n'ai pas besoin de religion pour faire le bien.
Les chrétiens ne valent pas mieux que les autres.

Si c'est Dieu qui donne la croyance, qu'il commence. Ce n'est pas ma faute si je ne crois pas.

La religion, c'est pour les riches. Ils ont le temps de s'en occuper.

Dieu pardonnera, c'est son métier (Voltaire).

Qu'est-ce que j'ai fait au Bon Dieu pour être si malheureux?

Si Dieu existe, je ne le félicite pas.
Il n'y a pas de Bon Dieu.

Je ne crois que ce que je vois.
Quand on est mort, on est bien mort!

ENGLISH TRANSLATION

Prove to me that God exists, and I'll believe in Him.
Everything is relative.
Every religion is good, provided you really believe in it.

I don't need to be religious to do good!
Christians are no better than anyone else.

If it is God Who gives us faith, let Him get on with it! It isn't *my* fault if I don't believe!

Religion is for the rich! *They* have time to bother with it!

God will forgive; that's what He's there for (Voltaire).

What have *I* done to deserve this?

If God exists, I don't think much of Him!
I've no use for God!

I only believe what I can actually see.
If you are dead, then you *are* dead!

IV

THE GOSPEL IN ITS RELEVANCE TO
THE PRESENT TIME

PREFACE

The Faith of the Church does not vary with the changing climates of human thought, but the Gospel as preached, if it is to find its way to the hearts of men, must be adapted to their capacity for understanding. In this section, we have tried to show both aspects of this paradox.

The Confession of Faith here printed was drawn up at the Tambaram (Madras) Meeting of the I.M.C. in 1938, by a group drawn from many countries and churches, and was adopted by the whole Assembly. It is a reaffirmation of the Faith by which the Church has lived since the beginning.

The other two chapters in this section consider the approach to modern man in his perplexities, points at which he is most accessible to the Gospel, and some at which he specially needs to hear its message. One chapter considers the Gospel as the response to needs of which man is conscious; the other presents it rather as the message which man needs to hear but is unwilling to listen to. The Gospel must always proclaim that message, which is most unwelcome to natural man, that the wages of sin is death.

THE FAITH BY WHICH THE CHURCH LIVES[1]

WE live by faith in God, the Father of our Lord Jesus Christ.

Above all and in all and through all is the holy will, the creative purpose, of the Most High. The world is His and He made it. The confusions of history are in the grasp of His manifold wisdom. He overrules and works through the purposes of men, bringing to nought their stubborn and rebellious lust for power but building their fidelity into the structure of His reign upon earth.

Man is the child of God, made in His image. God has designed him for life in fellowship with Himself, and with his brothers in the family of God on earth. Yet in the mystery of the freedom which God has given him, man chooses to walk other paths, to seek other ends. He defies his Father's will. He seeks to be a law unto himself. This is the deepest cause of the evil and misery of his life. Alienated from God he seeks his salvation where it cannot be found. Impotent to save himself, he stands ever in need of conversion, of forgiveness, of regeneration.

Who then shall save? God saves, through Jesus Christ our Lord. "God so loved the world that He gave His only begotten Son that whosoever believeth on Him should not perish but have everlasting life." This is the heart of the Christian gospel, the gospel which we proclaim.

God in His infinite love has acted for men's salvation. He has come among them in Jesus of Nazareth, His Word made flesh. In Him, He has conquered the power of sin and death. Jesus Christ in His teachings and life of perfect love recalls men to that which God would have them be, and brings them to shame for their betrayal of His expectation. Through His faith and perfect obedience they come to trust the only true God. His suffering and death on calvary bring them to see the exceeding sinfulness of sin and assure them of God's pardon. His resurrection is the victory of holiness and love over death and corruption. Through His risen and living presence, men who dedicate their wills to Him become with Him partakers of eternal life.

[1] Affirmation reprinted from *The World Mission of the Church*: Findings and Recommendations of the meeting of the International Missionary Council, Tambaram, Madras, India, December 12-29, 1938.

In the strength and joy of forgiveness, daily renewed at the foot of the Cross, they are made more than conquerors over every evil.

For Christ, the Kingdom of God was central. He called His followers to seek first God's Kingdom and His righteousness. Through acceptance of His call to suffering love and through trust in divine help, men are summoned to be co-workers with Him for the increase of justice, truth and brotherhood upon earth. His kingdom is both within and beyond this world. It will be consummated in the final establishment of His glorious reign of love and righteousness, when there shall be a new heaven and a new earth where death and sin shall be no more.

To the gift of Christ, God has added the gift of His Holy Spirit in the Church. Christ's true Church is the fellowship of those whom God has called out of darkness into His marvellous light. The guidance and power of the Spirit are given to this Church that it may continue Christ's saving work in the world. It seeks to build up its own members in the knowledge of Christ, challenging them anew with the message of His redeeming love, comforting them with the assurance of God's forgiveness in Him, teaching them the way of love through service for their brethren in Christ.

For those that are without Christ the true Church yearns with the love of its Master and Lord. It goes forth to them with the evangel of His Grace. It practises His ministry of compassion and healing. It bears witness against every iniquity and injustice in their common life. It bears their sorrows and heartache on its prayers. To it is given the solemn privilege of entering into the fellowship of the sufferings of Christ.

In spite of all the weakness and shortcomings of our churches, Christ's true Church is within them; and our hope for the redemption of mankind centres in His work through them. Through the nurture and discipline of the Church, Christian life comes to completion; in glad service within the fellowship of the Church, Christian devotion is perfected.

1

THE GOSPEL IN ITS RELEVANCE TO THE
PRESENT TIME

by Walter M. Horton

THERE is a hunger in the world to-day for good news. Most news is bad news. To read the morning newspaper at the breakfast-table is to risk getting indigestion, if one reflects too deeply upon the implications of what one reads. Year after year, our minds and our hearts have been battered and bruised with bad news. Who will show us anything good?

The Christian Gospel is "good news". But people hungry for good news are for some reason not reaching out eagerly for the Gospel. The word has an antique flavour; its meaning has been forgotten. And the contents of the Gospel, as ordinarily presented, do not sound like news; they sound irrelevant to the present hour; they do not speak to men's condition.

The *Gospel itself*, of course, is not something to be discovered by analysing contemporary conditions, and attempting to improvise an answer to modern problems. The Gospel *has happened*. As the Tambaram Confession reminds us, "God in His infinite love *has acted* for men's salvation . . . *has come among them* in Jesus of Nazareth, His word made flesh . . . *has conquered* the power of sin and death." The news that God has thus acted must therefore always be essentially the same news, "yesterday, to-day and for ever".

The duty to *preach* the Gospel is likewise an invariable duty, derived primarily from the impact of the Gospel itself, not from the state of the world. Those whom God has "visited and redeemed", those whom He has released from the powers of darkness and brought over into light and peace, cannot possibly keep the news to themselves. Gratitude to God, plain justice to those not privileged as yet to hear and know of God's graciousness in Christ, require that the news be told, whether men hear or whether they forbear. But the Gospel is not told in love, unless every effort is made to relate it to the actual condition of contemporary men.

There is no easy short cut to the preaching of the Gospel to-day. What is required, if the Gospel is to go home to the hearts of the people, is a work of theological reflection which will effectively relate the perennial affirmations of the Christian Faith to the actual questions and the felt needs of the present generation. Because God has made man in His own image, we know that we can count on the fact that there *is* some correspondence between man's need and Divine Grace.

In our own time this correspondence evidently exists at four points: (1) between the universal longing for *security* and faith *in God the Father Almighty;* (2) between the world-wide hunger for *peace and fellowship* and faith in *Christ the Reconciler;* (3) between the general *weariness and mental lassitude* with which our age is afflicted, and the *inward refreshment and sustaining power of the Holy Spirit;* finally, between the *despairing hope* which makes our contemporaries clutch at straws, and the *hope-beyond-despair* which enables Christians calmly to steer through rough waters by the pole-star of *God's everlasting Kingdom.*

I SECURITY AND ALMIGHTY GOD

Our world is insecure, and knows it. It looks backward with nostalgic regret, knowing that the ordered, stately stability of nineteenth-century society is gone for ever. It knows that multitudes of our contemporaries have been bombed out of their homes, torn from their families, driven from their native lands, herded like cattle into great huddled masses of lostness; and sees no adequate assurance, in any existing scheme of " collective security ", that a similar fate, or worse, may not overtake anyone now on earth, any time, anywhere. It knows no defence against the atomic bomb, feels no confidence in any nation's promise not to do indefensible things in self-defence.

" Freedom from want, freedom from fear "—how eagerly our world responded to these slogans! Economic security and political security were dreams that kept many living on, through the hardships and multiplied insecurities of war, in hope of the final day of liberation. Now that " liberation " is accomplished, it has become clear that the post-war world is still famine-ridden and fear-ridden, fundamentally less secure than the world of 1939, and must be expected to remain so for an indefinite length of time. Where is safety, where is shelter, where is there any impregnable stronghold in such a world?

The Christian answer is, *"In God the Father Almighty, Maker of Heaven and Earth."* Just before the outbreak of war, in a world already "shaken to its foundations", the Tambaram Confession enunciated this basic faith in God the Creator in words that still sound prophetic and pointed in this post-war era: "Above all and in all and through all is the holy will, the creative purpose, of the Most High. The world is His and He made it. The confusions of history are in the grasp of His manifold wisdom. He overrules and works through the purposes of men, bringing to nought their stubborn and rebellious lust for power, but building their fidelity into the structure of His reign upon earth."

In such a God, Ruler over all because He is the primal Source from Whom all being and all power are derived, many have found secure refuge in these stormy times, and many more would welcome the good news that there is such a refuge, if the way to a living trust in the Almighty Father could be clearly pointed out to them.

But even an utterly convincing experience of God's protecting power quickly becomes unreal to the person who has had it, or is perverted into superstitious magic in his mind, unless he finds adequate interpretation for it. It is the Christian Church's great privilege and duty to interpret all such experiences as evidences of the constant sustaining power of One Who is no mere private protector of a few miracle-men, but the universal Father of all His creatures; One Who disciplines them severely when they go counter to the law He has written in their hearts, but delivers them as often as they turn to Him for help: But the Church must also make clear what *kind* of "deliverance" is promised; she must keep the way open to a durable trust in the Almighty God by a sober, credible doctrine of divine Providence, that squares with the tragic facts of life; still more by her own steadfastness and unwavering confidence under hardship and persecution, "looking unto Jesus, the author and finisher of our faith, Who for the joy that was set before Him endured the Cross, despising the shame".

In its interpretation of the meaning of trust in the Almighty Father, the Church must not stress God's *power* at the expense of God's *love*. At bottom the modern hunger for security is a hunger for love, for feeling "at home" somewhere—cared for and understood by someone who will "never let you down". In our increasingly depersonalized society, such love is cruelly hard to find. Where will a Negro or a Jew look to find it among his fellow-men? Men join power-blocs and follow dictators because it makes them feel less alone, less lost, less defenceless; but there is no final security in loveless, ruthless power. Uneasily, men realize that the power which protects them while they are useful may at any moment trample them under foot, if they become more of a burden than a help. In such a world, it is good news that there is One Whose name is Father, not only as Primal Source and Supreme Power, but as the eternal redemptive Love that will not let us go. To believe this is not easy. Christian preaching needs the support of Christian loving and Christian living, if it is to make a real impression on humanity to-day.

II PEACE ON EARTH, AND CHRIST THE RECONCILER

Every Christmas, when the story of the birth of the Saviour is read in the churches, and echoes of it resound in the press, an almost audible sigh[1] of longing arises in response to the angel's proclamation of "peace on earth". Modern men do little conscious praying; but they pray unconsciously for peace with their whole being, as trees pray for rain in time of drought, or animals for food in time of famine.

The Christian answer to this prayer is *Christ the Reconciler*. "For He is our peace, Who hath made both one, and broken down the middle wall of partition between us." Even in our churches, whose testimony is weakened by their unhappy divisions and their many worldly entanglements, the work of Christ has actually brought about a state of peace and reconciliation between recent enemies, to which there is no analogy in the world of nations.

At the Stuttgart meeting of church leaders from many nations in 1945, Martin Niemöller's candid words of confession at once brought forth acknowledgment of complicity in guilt from his fellow-Christians; and on the basis of mutual forgiveness peace

---

[1] I heard a literally audible sigh arise from a Parisian audience at a performance of James Hilton's *Lost Horizon* in 1937. When the first caption was thrown upon the screen, and the idea of Shangri-la—a place free from the threat of war—was set before their minds, the whole audience sighed in unison.

was sealed between them.   Let Niemöller himself express this Gospel in his own words:

> "His name, 'Prince of Peace', is not His name in vain.   If He has come to bring forgiveness of sin, He has come to bring peace between God and mankind and at the same time He brings peace between men.   That is the one peace which really can be established and cannot be overcome, the peace which may exist between those who know about the forgiveness of sin and who, as sinners who have been forgiven, become brethren and sisters in Jesus Christ."[2]

Niemöller is only one conspicuous instance of Christ's work of peace and reconciliation in our time.   From the opposite end of the earth come the following words, in a letter from a Japanese friend: "We, all Japanese, are awful sinners.   While we think about war, we are fallen into a deep and strong suffering that is of sin. . . . Not only that your people treat us very kindly.   We are facing the greatest opportunity to repent under the Cross of Jesus. . . . I have much and strong pain about it. . . . I pray the profound and real peace of the world.   The whole world ought to come beneath the Cross.   The Lord's prayer shall be realized."   How can I rightly answer my friend in Japan, except by saying that we Americans, too, have great sins to confess, and by praying with him that our whole world may find "profound and real peace . . . beneath the Cross?"

Between Christians, mutual forgiveness is natural and seldom misunderstood; in the world at large, it is generally confused with weakness.   Because of this common confusion, it is not easy to pass from the accomplished fact of Christ's peace among repentant Christians to the general "peace on earth" for which the world still longs in vain.   The modern world wants peace, but is it willing to bend beneath Christ's yoke, and learn of Him?   Apparently not yet.   But if the Church can go on being a little oasis of "profound and real peace" in the midst of universal strife and confusion, some day the world may be willing to pay the price of admission to that charmed circle.

What the world *needs* and what the world *wants* are, of course, not the same thing.   The world *wants* something negative—

[2] Speech at Cleveland, Ohio, reported in *Current Religious Thought*, March 1947.

peace in the sense of absence of conflict, permitting everyone to pursue his interests undisturbed. The world *needs* something more positive—real fraternity, real community, real fellowship, which would so unify men's interests in allegiance to one Chief End that they would no longer clash. Real fellowship is God's great gift to the Church, renewed as often as Christ the Reconciler brings His followers to active, positive, joyful peace with one another after each breach of right relations. Only God can finally quicken man's need for fellowship into an active sense of *want*, but the Church can at least avoid scandalizing people by quarrelling in public, and at best exhibit the kind of family feeling that makes people wish they belonged to that family.

III MENTAL LASSITUDE AND THE HOLY SPIRIT

Our post-war era is not only tormented with a sense of insecurity and an unsatisfied longing for peace and fellowship. It is oppressed with a feeling of *mental lassitude* alternating with feverish, ineffective activity—something akin to a collective neurosis. Every war is followed by a period of mental and moral reaction, and this is proving no exception. To be sure, there is nothing quite parallel to the complete disillusionment and cynicism that followed the First World War. This time, our idealism in fighting the war did not fly so high, so it could not fall so low. No one expected this war to cure all our ills; it was popularly described as "a dirty job that had to be done". Yet if the extreme reaction of the "twenties" is not being repeated, there are many signs of the weariness, exhaustion, peevishness, indifference, mental confusion, and moral inertia which weigh down men's minds and dull their consciences after every great effort.

Average men are magnificent when their backs are against the wall, and hearth and home are at stake; they lapse into triviality and slackness when the immediate danger is over. Having no inward dynamo to keep them going, they simply "go dead" when the external current is cut off. More than one war veteran has found civilian life such a "let-down" after the excitement and glamour of war that he has taken to his bed, and refused to get up. While such cases are extreme, our whole population is suffering from mental and moral "let-down". Life seems "flat, stale and unprofitable".

The Christian answer to this prevailing state of mental lassitude is not an argument, not a doctrine, not even a method of treatment, but *a power*; the regenerative, re-creative, re-directive, refreshing and sustaining power of the *Holy Spirit*. The Apostle Paul knew this power well, and he knew its moral fruits: "Love, joy, peace, long-suffering, gentleness, goodness, faith, meekness, temperance," dispositions diametrically opposed to the mood of lassitude. It was this power, proceeding from God through Christ, residing in the Christian *Koinonia*, and "falling upon" many, on their first contact with the Christians, like a sudden shock from a high-voltage current—it was this power, received probably through the conductive medium of the martyred Stephen, which had transformed the Apostle from a divided and distracted man into one with a clear mission, and an inexhaustible inward source of strength and joy. Sometimes he refers to this inward source as Christ-possession, sometimes as Spirit-possession, but both terms refer to the same phenomenon. In his famous testimony, "I can do all things through Him who inwardly empowers me" (Phil. iv, 13), either Christ or the Spirit may be referred to. After all, "The Lord is the Spirit." The Holy Spirit is not just any power that may take possession of man—as for example Friedrich Nietzsche and Adolf Hitler were sometimes visited by an imperious sense of inspiration that lifted them out of themselves. It is specifically that Spirit of Jesus that led Him to Calvary for our redemption. Courage to live and to die in the strength of that Spirit. What does the world need more than that!

It has often seemed as though the power of the Spirit had died out of the Church. It *has* died out in certain churches, and they have withered like sapless branches of an otherwise fruitful vine. But somewhere at all times in the many-branched vine, even in the coldest winters, the life of the Spirit has continued; and from time to time this life has risen again with startling force. The prime condition for such a spiritual awakening seems to be a *worshipping fellowship* of devoted Christians, an intimate "cell" group of some sort, deeply convinced that "they that wait upon the Lord shall renew their strength, they shall mount up with wings as eagles, they shall run and not be weary, they shall walk and not faint". Such groups are sources of life in many local congregations at the present day.

If the jaded lassitude of our discouraged times is to be overcome by a new wave of spiritual vigour and moral renewal, it cannot be done by simply pointing to the testimony of Scripture. Rightly or wrongly, to the men of our time the Bible seems far away and long ago. If the Bible comes alive to them, it will only be because they see that it is essential to the life of a group that makes an immediate testimony to the power of the Spirit. As an instance of such living testimony, consider the following letter written by the members of a metal-workers' union to the members of the Community of Cluny, a Protestant religious order in Eastern France:

"Our opposition and indifference towards the bourgeois Church made us dubious of contacts with Christians.

So our first encounters with the Community of Cluny were full of curiosity and scepticism.

But in the course of regular meals and conversations, we came to understand that there were Christians who wished to have all things in common. This first point made us abandon our scepticism. Then the fact that the urgency of profound social and economic reforms was felt on both sides, drew us still closer together.

It was only much later that we asked to be instructed in the truths of the faith and understood that this also had meaning for us."[3]

It is deeply significant that many Christian groups in various lands and different communions are now springing up, dedicated to worship, study and fellowship, aiming to live out the meaning of the Gospel in their common life as the Spirit shall reveal it to them, and then to apply the laws of Christian fellowship to the solution of the social problems of our time. In these experimental movements the power of the Spirit is beginning to be poured out afresh, for the renewal of the life of the Church.

IV DESPAIRING HOPE, AND GOD'S KINGDOM

It is often remarked that the best evangelistic approach to modern men is through their intense concern for social problems, and their desire to get closer to the root of social ills than any secular programme of reform can bring them. This is true,

[3] Roger Schutz, *Introduction à la Vie Communautaire*, p. 10.

but there is one great difficulty with this approach: our contemporaries are losing interest in social problems, because they
are losing hope of their solution in any form; they are in a state
of near-despair, clutching eagerly at straws, only to cast them
bitterly aside and resolve not to be duped again.

A certain kind of Christian optimism has no "word" for
men in this mood—American "activists" of breezy Utopian
type would cut no ice among people in acute distress in Europe
and Asia. Nor would the European Christians who preach
the "Gospel of despair" be any help either. We must be
grateful that the contrast between Christian "optimism" and
"pessimism" is much less than formerly. Both together are
drawing nearer to the real answer: the promise of God's
Kingdom, which alone can save the world from its present
despair.

The Christian hope of the Kingdom, as found in the New
Testament and echoed in church history, is neither Utopian nor
pessimistic. The modern hope of progress through scientific
and technological mastery of Nature is now generally seen to be
Utopian. Communist hope is Utopian. Christians know that
all such hopes are deceptive; they have seen what men of power
did to their Lord.

But Christians have also seen their Lord rise victorious over
the men of power who thought they had disposed of Him; and
they have seen Christ's "little ones", the humble and meek to
whom He addressed His Beatitudes, show remarkable resilience
and staying power in quiet, patient resistance to the efforts of
many strong rulers (from Nero to Hitler) to break their stubborn
loyalty. This realistic hope, which has passed through and
beyond despair, delivers them from pessimism, and gives them
a pole-star by which to steer through all the vicissitudes of history, even those terrible ones that now beset us: the ultimate
triumph, at the end of history, of the God Who revealed His
power and glory as well as His merciful justice at the turning-
point of history, in the humble and majestic figure of Jesus.

In thought, in teaching and in *action*, Christian hope-beyond-
despair will prove its power to answer and correct the false,
despairing hope that deludes and tantalizes our generation. New
Testament eschatology and apocalyptic are not expressed in
language which our age can comprehend—though our mood is
really an apocalyptic mood, which with a little encouragement

might understand the darkest enigmas of Daniel and Revelation. Such understanding must come from groups of Christians who through steadfast hope outlive and outplan and outmanœuvre all their adversaries; who work steadily on when others succumb to mental lassitude and despair; who undertake constructive projects when the world is going to pieces all about them; who hopefully plan and build to the glory of God when human wisdom would counsel not to waste the effort.

Almighty God the Creator, Christ the Reconciler, the Holy Spirit our Comforter, and the hope of God's everlasting King-dom—these Christian affirmations not only answer the needs of our time, but constitute the perennial framework of our faith. None of these affirmations is finally to be separated from any of the others. There is a redeeming love as well as creative power in the Almighty Father, security as well as peace in Christ the Reconciler, fellowship and hope as well as inspiration and courage in the work of the Holy Spirit. But these affirmations sum up between them the four great acts of God—three already enacted and one yet to come—wherein the whole biblical drama of human history is comprehended. The One God revealed in these four great acts is, we believe, the source from Whom all blessings flow, the answer to every human need, the complete and final cure for the modern sense of the *meaninglessness of existence*—if only men will meet the conditions He lays down. The Christian evangelist knows that the divine conditions and terms on which true security, peace, fellowship, courage and hope are to be had, are *bad news* to the natural man—bad news, which in loyalty to the God of truth must not be concealed. But he hopes that the richness of the divine blessings, the adequacy of the divine answers, the meaningfulness of the new life in God, may overcome the resistance of man's lower nature, since they correspond to deep hungers God has implanted in all His creatures. It is one of the main tasks of good evangelism to make these correspondences specifically clear, in terms of the specific mood and temper of our time.

2

THE GOSPEL IN ITS RELEVANCE TO THE PRESENT TIME

by Pierre Maury

THE Gospel message is the life-blood of the Church. Every society draws upon the ideal which it embodies and expresses. In a far deeper sense, Jesus Christ founded the Church to be first of all missionary. Take away the missionary message, and the Church has lost its *raison d'être*.

The proclamation of the message certainly involves the creation of a community. And this community is not merely—like other communities—an association whose members share the same conception of life and conduct. Its very existence constitutes the *mystery* of a supernatural unity, what St. Paul called the "mystery of the Church" (Eph. v, 32), the Body of the Christ, risen and seated at the right hand of God. But the life of this Body is continuously maintained by those who are grafted into it, by its new members. The Church is concerned with *all* nations (Matt. xxviii, 19). Not indeed for reasons of earthly power nor in the proselytizing spirit of great human organizations or movements; but because Jesus Christ offers Himself as the Saviour of *all*. He "gathers together in one" (Eph. i, 10) in His own person and His own work "all things which are in heaven and on earth". Without the Church's witness, the Lordship of Christ is not exercised according to His will. Unless the good news of Christ is announced *to all*, the world is lost in fatal ignorance and can only follow paths which lead nowhere.

Hence the preaching of the Gospel is the central problem of the Church's life—not a technical problem, but a question of life or death; not a modern problem, but a perennial demand and a perennial difficulty.

.　.　.　.　.　.　.　.

This problem involves two equally intrinsic elements: the *truth* or rather the fidelity of the Church's preaching—what the

New Testament calls the "uncorruptness and gravity" of "sound speech, that cannot be condemned" (Titus ii, 8)—and its *intelligibility*. Unsound, or in a sealed book, the Gospel is equally idle.

In other words, the Church has to speak about the God of eternity, and about the age to come, to men who are dwellers in time, living according to the fashion of this transitory world. If the Church has nothing to say about eternity, it had better say nothing at all. And if it speaks about eternity as if it were already there and out of touch with history—no one will listen. In either case Jesus Christ will be betrayed.

Now this twofold condition represents a twofold test for the Church; in Bible language a twofold *temptation*. Sometimes, with its eyes on the age in which its message is given, the Church adapts itself to the present and confines itself to relative truths as ephemeral as the people who hear them. Sometimes, knowing that its message goes beyond the changes and chances of history, the Church talks a "timeless" language which is a foreign tongue to the world, and its message becomes bloodless and abstract. In one case it spoils its preaching with inept apologetics; in the other it dooms itself to cryptic mysteries. (In every age of history it would be easy to illustrate the Church's halting between the two duties laid upon it by God; has it not sometimes been possible to accuse it of Byzantinism—even when it was affirming the eternal nature of the mystery of Jesus Christ over against a perishing world; and at other times to reproach it for such subservience to the age that its message became a "philosophy of enlightenment"?)

Still a clear distinction should be drawn between the two demands which the life of the Church can never escape. These demands are not of equal importance, or rather one is subordinate to the other. In the summary of the Law, the second commandment is like the first and should be equally obeyed, but only on condition that it *follows* the first; in just the same way the Church's preaching is only true to man's need if it is *first* true to Jesus Christ. To man in his concrete situation, the Church tells the truth about himself and his destiny only if it speaks to him about Jesus Christ " the same yesterday and to-day and for ever " (Heb. xiii, 8), i.e. only if its language is not that of " *the present age* ". The Gospel explicitly claims to be " a mystery and a hidden wisdom " which no man knows until there are proclaimed to him things which " eye hath not seen, nor ear heard, neither have entered into the heart of man" (1 Cor. ii, 9) —in theological language, to be a *revelation*. Any preaching which discards or discounts this note of its witness is doomed to failure in obedience and loyalty.

But if so, the question suggested by " The Relevance of the Gospel to the Present Time" implies a precise answer. The Church has no obligation to exhibit, between the present age, modern man and contemporary civilization and its own message, such harmony and concord as would ease its task in bringing to them the Word of the Gospel. Far from it, the Church must expect that the Gospel—to-day as always—will proclaim something *different* from what modern man says and demands. Often there will be *contradiction* rather than agreement between the Word of the Church and the words of the world. Just when the Church's message contradicts the thought of modern man it will really fulfil his deepest expectations. For what man really desires is not what he thinks or imagines that he desires; it is what, according to the will of God, he *needs*. The greatest service that the Church can render will be to tell people not what they can quite well tell themselves, but what they do *not* know and yet unconsciously seek and ensue.

Hence the one problem for the Church, now as always, is to uncover that ignorance of God which the wisdom of the day hides: to witness to that Revelation, foreign to humanity, of which she is the ambassador, in terms as plain, precise and up to date as they are strictly faithful to the truth.

What are the truths which the world to-day repudiates, and the Church must proclaim in language that the world can understand? Evidently those to which the Church has borne witness ever since the days of Christ on earth. For the ways in which men go astray are fundamentally the same, and so is the content of Revelation. There is no more real novelty in heresies and idolatries than in orthodoxy.

This obstinacy of error, and this identity of truth, is briefly comprehended in this, that, while God claims to be adored, loved and served, Himself Alone in what He is, what He has done, what He is doing and will do, the sin of man will always consist in refusing all or part of this adoration, love and service in order to apply them to his own ends. But this self-deification of man takes different shapes at different times, and the Church must penetrate every disguise, so that its eternal message may be God's Word for to-day.

In our diagnosis, we should not be satisfied with the obvious symptoms of the sickness of society. For instance, man is plainly afraid and in search of security; he is proud of his unprecedented technical achievements and absorbed in his material successes. This being so, it is clear that in proclaiming the goodness of God in creation and redemption—His Providence, or in reminding man that "he does not live by bread alone", the Church will speak to his condition. Nevertheless, the Church needs a deeper reading of present realities if it is to discover afresh and to preach the Christian message in terms of the day.

To me personally it seems that the sin of modern man, and his wretchedness, are shown in three special fields: *modern man believes in history, he knows nothing of forgiveness, and is fumbling after a working morality.*

It is to this man, the worshipper of his special idols and the victim of his own illusions and terrors, that the Church must speak about the God Who throws down idols and frees men from despair and from death. As the Church has never any other message than the name of Jesus Christ, we may say that to-day it must publish His name as *Judge, Saviour* and *Lord.*

MODERN MAN'S FAITH IN HISTORY AND CHRIST THE JUDGE OF HISTORY

The signs of modern man's blind confidence in history are manifest. At one and the same time he imagines that he is making history and knows that he is determined by history. Thus the pride, typical of our epoch, is matched only by its fatalism. People talk about creating a new civilization, even a new humanity, different from any hitherto known and yet feel helpless to avert the destruction of the human race by their technical inventions. For example, it is striking to see side by side, sometimes in the same person, the basic optimism of the communist and the apocalyptic terror inspired by atomic power. Thus our civilization sways between the intoxication of its own creative power and craven surrender to extinction by the work of its own hands.

But a deeper uncertainty underlies this paradoxical inner

conflict. *Above all, our world suffers from having no Judge.*
To give worth to its efforts and its destiny it has nothing but
itself. It is only from an earthly future that it expects any
verdict on the present. So a master of French politics entitles
his diagnosis of the contemporary scene, " History will judge "—
a standard formula for the modern mind. Pragmatism of the
nursery! Historical results can furnish no yardstick. First because " results" imply some external measure of their creative
value. Even so, their value vanishes in the evolutionary process in which they occur. No effort can be warranted by its
success, for success is relative to the judgment which assesses it;
and no success is the last of the series. The recognition that
progress is a myth has long ago taught us that trust in the verdict
of history is an illusion. But our age, though it no longer believes that evolution is necessarily beneficent, is more than any
other age subject to the fascination of the future. In the depths
of its spirit, it is stirred by Messianic hopes; its eyes are always
on the future, not only to quicken its activities, but as the sole
reward of toil.

There are two catches in this relative thinking. First, selfless-
ness little short of absolute is demanded of the individual. The
makers of history are never to hear the verdict, which will be
delivered when they are in their graves. That is not the worst.
If nothing but history is real, then there will be no verdict at
all. History cannot cry finis to itself, and the human adventure
indefinitely prolonged has no goal and therefore no sense. The
astringent wisdom of the Preacher proclaiming the vanity of all
which ends only to begin over again was not " new under the
sun ". What marks our age is the blind folly of its ambitions
and dreams. The Great White Throne was for Western civilization until the nineteenth century a certainty: in the Middle
Ages an obsession. It therefore had a standard of moral judgment as well as hope and a mission in life. Our age has no rules
left, and no real trust in the future.

It is this modern man, the victim of his own vain trust in
history, that the Church addresses. It can only meet this
idolatry by preaching this essential element of the Christian
message: *the world and history have an end:* they are moving
towards it as well as limited by it. And this *end* is not a date
like any other—the end of the world, the last event in history.
It is a *verdict* pronounced by the ever-transcendent Creator of

the universe. History judges nothing; it is subject to its Judge. History will be stopped one day, not by arriving at its end, but by the decree of Another. This is what we are told by the Preacher at the end of his lucid, sceptical confession. His real meaning is shown in the last verse of his book: " Fear God, and keep his commandments: for this is the whole duty of man. For God shall bring every work into judgment, with every secret thing, whether it be good, or whether it be evil " (Eccles. xii, 13-14).[1]

In order to preach this message, the Church is not called upon to elaborate philosophies of history. These would be just as arbitrary—even if they called themselves Christian—as when they are invented by experts who take no account of God. Nor should the Church preach a Gospel of the Beyond, which disparages human history and its vicissitudes. Above all, it should not promise compensation in heaven for the miseries of earth; Eternity, thought of as a reward or as an indemnity, would be only a vain extension of the vanity of Time.

The Church must re-learn the meaning of history. This means that it must first of all heed everything that happens in time and treat it seriously, from the most trivial events to sweeping collective movements, from personal decisions of faith or scepticism to the great battles which the Church has had to fight. " God will bring every work into judgment." But above all the Church must announce God's activity in history, which in Jesus Christ and His Incarnation gives Time its divine value. The Church must also respect history, because it knows that since the Death, Resurrection and Ascension of Jesus Christ the meaning of every period of history has become clear (has been " fulfilled " to use the language of the Bible), and now the world only awaits the visible manifestation of this fulfilment. We have arrived at the final stage of history. We are living in " the last days " (Heb. ix, 26; 1 Cor. x, 11; 1 Pet. i, 20). Hence our attitude to history is that of *expectancy*, watchful, active and ardent; expectancy of history's final goal.

More than this, the Church, aware that it is living in " these last days ", must speak in a way apt to this particular epoch; and this epoch is the interval between the Ascension of Jesus Christ

---

[1] It is interesting to note that when Paul wanted to preach the Gospel to the pagan Athenians, he spoke to them *first* about God's judgment in Christ (Acts xvii, 31).

to the right hand of God and His return in glory. The Church always expresses the same truth; but not always in the same way at all times. The Prophets of the Old Testament and the Apostles of the New say the same thing of Christ, Who is the same yesterday and to-day and for ever (Heb. xiii, 8), but not from the same angle. So the Church to-day must preach the same message as ever, but matched to the hour. What distinctive features of this "Interval" mark its basic difference from other ages? Let us say simply that the Gospels (Matt. xxiv and parallel passages) specify outwardly an increase of great catastrophes (wars and cosmic cataclysms of a more and more terrible nature), and within the Church an increase in infidelity and apostasy, and love grown cold; but at the same time they foretell that the Church, even though greatly reduced in strength (Matt. xxiv, 12-14), will be more missionary than ever (Matt. xxviii, 19). Then the Church must neither be surprised at its own apparent failure nor discouraged; on the contrary, it will be the time for sure hope and watchful expectation; the time of the antichrists, but also the time immediately preceding the glorious and unmistakable return of the Son of God.

The fact that the Church of to-day is speaking during this particular period of history ought to give her message a special emphasis and certainty. She should be fearless when everything seems to deny and to repudiate her message.

.   .   .   .   .   .

The Church must therefore preach the truth of the Bible eschatology—in a way suited to the times. Thus the message will assume an urgency and effect which it has too often lost. Thus she will preach with confidence and hope. And thus without artifice or accommodation to human ideas, she will meet the real desires, unavowed and often unconscious, of modern man. For if modern man no longer dreams of Paradise Lost but of a future Golden Age, it is because without this future he has nothing left to choose, to do or to expect. It has often been noted that the main attraction of the totalitarian mysticisms, especially the mysticism of communism, is found in the promises which it makes to the men of to-day. Those who understand this tremendous modern religion best are clear that it is the idealism of historic materialism (though the contradiction in terms is formal) which gives it its drive. Only a Christian eschatology, quiet and confident, can stand up to this messianism, can make life worth living again for the prisoners of a hope which is mundane and built on sand.[2]

This is not the time or place to recall the central elements of this Christian eschatology. We shall merely say that it must be expressly *totalitarian* and not individualistic, it must be cosmic and not tepidly humanist. The return of Christ to judge the living and the dead, and by His verdict to inaugurate the Kingdom of God, must be trumpeted with all St. Paul's and St. John's glory in the splendour of Christ, the Christ by Whom and for Whom *all things* were made. On these heights any pettiness, any churchiness becomes impossible, and the actual relations between the Church and the world can be made clear. Eschatology (and not any doctrine concerning the Orders of Creation) is the one thing which can restore the Church's freedom in face of the world, and its sure expectation that this world will be brought to judgment.

MODERN MAN'S IGNORANCE OF FORGIVENESS AND JESUS CHRIST OUR SAVIOUR

It is not surprising that modern man, who places his faith in history, repudiates the idea of *forgiveness*. For history does not forgive. History deals with what *has happened* and is therefore beyond repair and pardon. Hence those who place their confidence in history alone can no longer grasp the essentially Christian reality of the *remission of sins*. From this it follows that the tragic *motif* of our atheistic age turns about an *unsatisfied need for justification*.

In every age, indeed, man has refused to be a "miserable sinner". In every age the "hatred of grace"—the true form of original sin—flares up in man's passionate desire to assert his innocence as well as his rights. In every age man repeats, like Adam, "It is not my fault", thus showing that self-justification is the very heart of sin. And in every age this assertion of one's own integrity is naturally paired with imputations against others (Adam accuses Eve, Eve accuses the serpent). Excusing one's self always leads to accusing others. . . . But this per-

[2] I recall the significant revolt of a young communist who protested only against one of my Christian affirmations, that of the Last Judgment. "By what right do you dare to announce this event," he said, "which if it took place would change the whole of ethics and the whole of human faith?"

manent tendency in human nature appears to-day in a special form.[3]

First, it is no longer exclusively or chiefly related to the individual obsessed by personal failure. It is expressed in the public utterances of parties, nations and classes. For instance, it is significant that the communist religion loudly proclaims the moral *innocence* of the proletariat and the impeccability, even the infallibility, of the " Party"; and at the same time it persistently assails other economic systems and other classes, conveniently regarded as incarnate in America or some other nation. Our age is relentless in the hunt for scapegoats. Hitler's antisemitism is only the most monstrous example. But, underneath the surface of his self-justification, modern man—including the communist—believes in his own natural goodness. According to him the imperfections of civilization (suffering, injustice, war) are entirely due to non-human factors, such as the uneven distribution of wealth.

This feature of our age should not surprise us. It always emerges when calamities and impending disaster come to disturb man's naïve confidence in his own powers. And the stresses of our civilization may be measured by the violence of the reproaches hurled at one another by parties, races, nations and classes.

Nor need we wonder that modern irreligion often takes the form of an accusation directed first against God and secondly against the Church. When the atheist repeats, " if there were a God . . ." or " it is the Church's fault ", he is really asserting his own innocence and trying to believe in it.

But the misery, and doubtless the real agony, of this man is that, for all his imputations against others, he does not succeed in reassuring himself. The more he proclaims his innocence, the less he succeeds in convincing himself of it; so that our time has been called with some justice " the age of the guilty conscience ".[4]

[3] This revolt against the idea of sin, this assertion of innocence, has never been expressed more violently nor more logically than by Nietzsche (for instance " Sin, the supreme form of the corruption of humanity ", *The Anti-Christ*, fragment 49). It is indispensable to read and meditate upon this brilliant forerunner of modern thought, if we want to understand contemporary Western civilization, which derives most of its main ideas from Nietzsche.

[4] For instance, it is striking to read the last letters written by French communists who were shot during the Resistance. With impressive monotony they all repeat in effect, " I have nothing to reproach myself with. I die with my head high. . . ." I do not know of any more harrowing confession of inward

In face of this tragedy, what should be the message of the Church? First, and above all, the Church must cease to be "conformed to this world" (Rom. xii, 2), as too often in the past two centuries, by allowing itself (more or less consciously) to water down the essentials of the biblical Revelation. The Church must give up confusing evil with imperfection, and sin with mistakes and weakness. It must cease from turning salvation into a merely ethical problem, the problem of "right action", and it must give up every kind of justification by works—those types of Christian atheism and of man's uneasy impiety. In other words the Church must admit God's *accusation against* man, and against herself first. The Church must not try to justify herself by citing her virtues and successes, or by blaming the sin and incredulity of the world.

But this "fear of the Lord, which is the beginning of wisdom" for the Church (Ps. cxi, 10), this humility in which it should live and speak, is no adequate definition of her present duty of witness. The Church must learn once again to speak of *free pardon*. For it is futile, nay harmful, for the Church to speak of sin against God unless it also speaks of the *forgiveness of this sin*. It is futile, nay harmful, for it to speak of the insulted righteousness of God unless it also speaks of His justification freely offered. One of the Church's gravest mistakes is undoubtedly to *preach about sin* before proclaiming the remission of sins; in theological terms to *preach the Law before the Gospel*. By this fault the Church lays itself open to all kinds of misunderstanding and provokes nothing but indifference or rebellion.

Thus, as in all great epochs of its history, the Church fulfils her responsibility only by proclaiming *before all* else Christ Jesus and Him crucified. This is the Church's responsibility; it is also her only chance of making herself heard and believed. For outside the Church who proclaims to modern man, tormented by his guilty conscience, God's offer of forgiveness? Who else offers this forgiveness in its reality, as the end of the guilt from which modern man is trying in vain to struggle free, as the opportunity to begin life completely afresh and to have real peace within? Who else offers this deliverance either to individuals or to nations? The world's crown of sorrows lies

anguish than these letters. In the same way the whole of " existentialist " literature fails to conceal this fear. The doctrine of " the absurd ", i.e. life has no meaning at all, is only a supreme effort at self-justification for a life which is falling in ruins.

in the fact that no word is heard of God's forgiveness—nor of man's forgiveness of man. Hence the violence and despair which overwhelm men's lives and bedevil their relations. Hence also the impossibility of any real justice. For justice can never be restored if it is conceived as nothing more than a perpetual balancing of accounts.

. . . .

But if this message of *God's righteousness* is to be heard (that righteousness which justifies through forgiveness in Jesus Christ), the Church must not utter stereotyped and unintelligible formulas. It must constantly re-learn the concrete content of the promise made by Jesus *"Seek ye first the Kingdom of Heaven and its righteousness, and all these things shall be added unto you"* (Matt. vi, 33). The Church must not believe in this promise alone: but it must *really* believe in it.

THE SEARCH FOR AN ETHIC.   JESUS CHRIST IS LORD

This brings us to the third subject which must be included in the teaching of the Church to-day: the moral teaching for which our modern world is seeking and hoping.

The signs of this search are obvious. Far from making us doubt it, the moral chaos in which we live should, on the contrary, be regarded as the visible evidence of this need. For it is not only the grim consequence of the cataclysm of the two world wars. It is the child of the earthquake that has shattered civilization itself.

It may perhaps be said with truth that the end of the age of individualism has brought with it the end of the individualist ethic typical of that age, and has revealed the need for a social morality. The bourgeois of the eighteenth and nineteenth centuries saw his duties as almost exclusively concerned with personal relationships. They demanded primarily personal honesty, charity and morality. Social conditions, political attitudes, international relations did not belong to the sphere of ethical obligation. This limitation of morality to private life led on the one hand, in the secular world, to the actual denial of moral obligation (the inevitable result of the unconscious egoism of bourgeois civilization), and on the other hand in Christian thought to a more or less puritanical pietism. The birth of a collective age or, to put it briefly, "the birth of the masses" (according to Ortega y Gasset's classical phrase) has forced on our attention the problem of social justice and, above all, the moral problem raised by the existence of the proletariat. Thus the demand for a wider code of ethics has been born again in the modern conscience.

But as the range of ethics has been extended the *absolute validity* of ethical standards has been called in question. Not only have the world deluges which have not yet abated undermined the belief of modern man in the existence of permanent, indubitable "values", and in the possibility of applying them to a reality which appears too complex or too recalcitrant; but the reactionary or revolutionary philosophies of power have led him to regard success as the one and only moral touchstone. "The end justifies the means." This old adage has come to be the accepted wisdom of the greatest movements of our time. It is a fatal one: for when the means are morally indifferent, the end itself cannot preserve the sanctity ascribed to it.

But here again we discover the same inner tragedy which we noted above. Modern a-moralism does not satisfy those who profess it. Never have moral professions been so frequent. Every political speech smacks of a sermon. Every international discussion stalks behind the swelling phrases of the Pharisee. Doubtless despair (which is universally recognized as the dominant note of our generation) throws into relief this vast masquerade. Man to-day longs for the "good" life; he longs for society to be "just", for the nations to cease doing "evil" to one another. He longs for all this. But he no longer believes that these ideals can be real.

What message should the Church give in the midst of this moral yearning, chaos and despair? It is lost labour sadly to bemoan the evils of the time. The Church has too often believed that the sternness of its message consisted in enumerating—with sorrow or anger—the wickednesses of the world, or in exhausting itself in moral exhortation. Needless to say, also, the message of the Church in this sphere would be completely irrelevant and idle if it confined itself—through timidity or acquiescence—to reciting the precepts of individualist morals, on the pretext that no collective change is possible, valid or real, without an individual change of heart.

Here again the Church must learn to "discern the signs of

the times" and "to judge the spirits" (Matt. xvi, 3; 1 Cor. xii, 10), i.e. to recognize, even in the miseries, revolts or nightmares of the world, an urgent appeal that it should be true, in its preaching, to the Gospel of God.

Again, it is impossible here even to sketch what would have to be included to-day in a code in tune with the biblical revelation. But bearing in mind what has been said, we would point out that this ethic must be:

(a) An ethic which is *true to history*, i.e. true to the *whole of life*, both individual and collective, taking full account of the whole of concrete reality, and giving this reality the importance conferred on it by the "creation of all things in Christ Jesus" (Col. i, 16) and the incarnation of Christ—but equally true to the *end of History*, that is, to Christian eschatology.

(b) An ethic which is *true to the demands of justice*, both individual and collective, manifested by the uneasy conscience of modern man; but which is also true to *that other limit*, set by Divine Justification to any claim of man to be able to fulfil the demands of absolute morality: i.e. a personal and social ethic which has a place for *free pardon*: God's forgiveness of man and man's of men.

This specific declaration on moral questions is doubtless the point at which the Church encounters the greatest difficulty in making its message acceptable or even intelligible to the world. In order to overcome this difficulty, the Church needs both courage and vision. It must realize that it will always be accused either of Bolshevism or craven conservatism. It will be criticized by turns as other-worldly and as this-worldly. And above all, it will be criticized for those Christian reservations, which make it impossible to propose for this world an ideal which is final, practicable and adequate. But this difficulty and these criticisms should not deter the Church from endeavouring patiently to discover and to uphold the concrete forms of society in which the outward *signs* of the Lordship of Christ should be visible.

The ethic preached by the Church will never consist of anything but provisional rules, applicable to a transitory world. This ethic will always be characterized, in a double sense, by its *expectancy of the Kingdom*; negatively by rejecting the dream of an ideal to be realized here below; positively by affirming that faith in the coming of the Kingdom is not really faith unless it changes the conduct of those who are sure of its coming. In

other words, the ethic preached by the Church will be equally
far removed from the dream of a Christian civilization identified
with the Kingdom of God, and from a religion which retires
from the world and passively hopes for a heaven reserved for the
blessed.

In these remarks we have often used the expression " the Message of the Church ". Of course, this includes both the spoken
message and the message " incarnate " in the life of the Church
and in that of each of its members. It is only too evident that
the reason why people do not believe what the Church *says* is
often due to what the Church *does*, and especially to the undeniable ineffectiveness of its message upon its own members. What
is the use of the Church speaking, if people can always point to
the contrast between " the worth of Christianity and the un-
worthiness of Christians " (Berdyaev); if they can mock at the
spectacle of a Church entrenched in private piety, afraid to venture out on the quest for a social morality, mumbling formulas
without experiencing the joy and power they contain; if people
can point on the one hand to divisions within the Church tolerated with an easy conscience simply because they are inherited
from the past, and on the other hand, to the ignorance of and
indifference towards *the real Christian significance* of those questions on which the great Christian confessions have taken their
stand in opposition to one another; above all to the spectacle of
so many parishes which are incapable of being real *communities*
and are divided by internal differences, selfishness and political
and social distinctions stronger than their professed unity.

In conclusion let me say that, if these are some of the features
of the Church's message for the world to-day, and if the
" relevance " of this message to the world is this *contradiction*
between the " present age " and the " age to come ", the Church
must not expect its message to meet with much success. But
the modesty of its earthly hopes should not discourage the
Church. For when the Church puts its trust in its own earthly
success, it is really playing a losing game. The Lord of the
Church did not promise the little flock that when He returned
He " would find faith on earth " (Luke xviii, 8). But seeing that

the Church has sure and certain hope for the future of the whole world, its message will always be "good news". And, until the end, there will always be some who are ready to listen to it as the good news for all men. Jesus Christ Himself has promised it (Matt. xvi, 18; xxiv, 12-14).

V

THE GOSPEL AT WORK IN THE WORLD

Synopsis: Preface – The Ecumenical Approach – The Lay Apostolate – Tensions in Evangelism – Mass Movements – Individual Seekers – Evangelism in the Parish – Evangelism in the Orthodox Church – Revival Mass Meetings – University Missions – The Moral Rearmament Movement – The Need for Fellowship in Evangelism – Religious Films – Religious Broadcasting – Religion in German Schools – Evangelism in Professional Life – The Lost Community – The Iona Community – CIMADE – Industrial Chaplains in Scotland – *La France, pays de Mission?* – Post-Christian Paganism – The Recovery of Community – The Return of the Intellectual *Élite* – An Illustration from Greece – The Conventional Christian – Evangelism, an Ecumenical Task

---

PREFACE

With a view to the compilation of this chapter a questionnaire was sent out to leaders of evangelistic enterprises in many countries, many friends were approached personally with a request to furnish accounts of what were known to be striking experiments in evangelistic work, and two scholars, one in England, and one in U.S.A., were asked to draw up statements on the present situation of the evangelistic enterprise.

After a great mass of material had come in, the Secretary of the Commission was asked to select what seemed to be the most significant experiments, and to draw up this chapter, not as a catalogue of many different types of work, but by the method of choosing significant illustrations from different countries, confessional areas and strata of human life.

It is believed that the reading of this chapter will prove encouraging, since it does make manifest that in many ways and many spheres the Gospel is actively at work. But the reader is warned to bear in mind the conclusion that nowhere in the world at present is there any sign of such great movements towards a living Christianity as have marked the greatest epochs of history in the Church in the past.

THE GOSPEL AT WORK IN THE WORLD

THE evangelistic programme of the early Church was extremely simple. Assured that in Jesus Christ God had spoken His final word to the world, the Christians took it for granted that this word was to be spoken to all nations throughout the world. The outpouring of the Holy Spirit on the day of Pentecost was the initial fulfilment of the Old Testament promise *I will pour out my spirit upon all flesh* (Joel ii, 28), and the representatives of many peoples gathered in Jerusalem on that day were regarded as the first-fruits of the harvest which was to be gathered in from all nations. Analytical criticism of the text of the gospels may question the exact relationship of certain recorded sayings to the words of Jesus Himself; such criticism enhances rather than reduces the weight of the evidence as to the views and convictions of the early Church afforded by such passages as: *All authority hath been given unto me in heaven and on earth. Go ye therefore and make disciples of all the nations, baptizing them into the name of the Father and of the Son and of the Holy Ghost: teaching them to observe all things whatsoever I commanded you: and lo, I am with you alway even unto the end of the world* (Matt. xxviii, 19-20).

At a time when eschatological expectation in the form of daily waiting for the *Parousia* was extremely strong, the sense of world mission, apparently contradictory to the eschatological foreshortening of history, was firmly held and no acute discordance was felt between the two. As a recent writer has expressed it: " This intensity of the numinous realization of the Manifestation of God in Christ, which keeps it from being too closely measured by external events, and so lifts the presence above history, is itself the source of a larger Christian hope for history. Christianity finds itself unable, with all its certainty regarding the ultimate outcome of events, to foreclose the course of history. Whatever happens in the external world, and whatever divine judgment on men and events thereby comes to light, no occurrence, however critical in the human historical sense, not even the Fall of Jerusalem, not even the later collapse of Rome and the Empire, could be regarded as writing *Finis* to the historical process. And the reason comes from within the Christian experience itself. There is the Christian mission to the world to be gone on with; and this, as it succeeds, expands the horizon of Christian hope. The ' Not yet the End ' of early Christian prophecy, which cannot regard any foreseeable event as putting a term to the course of the mission, opens ever new possibilities for the life of the world. So Christianity retains the passion and the ultimate hope of the apocalyptic, but transcends its impatience and its pessimism, its consistent principle ' Go on with your work, whatever happens', is not without significance for us to-day, when, sometimes in despair of history, we are tempted to relapse into apocalyptic moods."[1] *This Gospel of the kingdom shall be preached in the whole world for a testimony unto all nations; and then shall the end come* (Matt. xxiv, 14) represents the sober and matured experience of the two first Christian generations. The apocalyptic expectations kept alive in the Church the sense of urgency: the time is short, the Gospel must be preached to all nations; therefore there can be no dallying with the task. But at the same time, the sense of the world-wide task tempered the at first intemperate expectation. The experience of the growing Church led men to see that God's plans were larger than they had at first supposed, and that they would take longer on the historical plane to mature than the ardent hopes and longings of the first generation had admitted.

The association of the apocalyptic emphasis with missionary zeal is a recognizable feature of church history in all ages. Whenever the emphasis has been on the static or evolutionary aspects of the life of the Church, the world task of the Church has taken a subordinate place in its theology and its practice. It is to this fact that we must look perhaps for the explanation of another recurrent phenomenon that in all ages, except the first, the task of world-evangelization has been the preoccupation of the few —and not of the main body of the Church. No Christian body, except perhaps the Church of the Moravian Brethren, has ever been engaged in its totality in the work of the evangelization of the world. It is not difficult to see why this is so. The life of the Church is a state of continual tension between the institutional and the prophetic, between that which conserves the precious heritage of the past and that which reaches out to claim in the name of Christ the new and as yet undiscovered. The

[1] W. Manson, in *Journal of Theological Studies*, July-October 1947, pp. 145-6.

nature of man is acquiescent rather than adventurous; the prophetic therefore always maintains a precarious existence in the Church, the institutional tends to become the means for the suppression, not for the expression, of new life. In these days, it is still true, as in the past, that the world-mission of the Church is the concern of the few; the majority of practising church members would probably not deny in theory the proposition that the Gospel is to be proclaimed throughout the world, and that this is a continuous obligation of the Church until the end of this age; but the urgency of this task has not entered the range of their thinking, or become an integral element of their experience of Christ as the Lord of the Church and as the Lord of history.

The problem of the Church's world mission is the crisis of the ecumenical movement. If an ecumenical movement is not primarily a strategy of world-wide evangelism, then it is nothing but an interesting academic exercise. The development in separation of the International Missionary Council, and of the other great movements Life and Work and Faith and Order may be indicative of a dangerous dichotomy in the Church's thought. The historical and confessional preoccupations of Christian thinking tend always to a static point of view. There are as yet very few signs of ecumenical thinking in the writings of theologians. Ecumenical thinking is that which not merely is aware of the revolution in the state of the Christian Church brought about by its spatial extension in the nineteenth and twentieth century, but also takes seriously the Gospel as that act of God which cannot be understood except as His proclamation of salvation for the whole world, and as that word of God which awaits, for its final interpretation, the contributions to be made by all the nations of the world as they are gathered into the one fellowship of the world-wide Church of Christ. At this point as at so many others, the Church can be the Church only by a return to the New Testament and by the recovery of New Testament perspectives and categories of thought.

The emphasis here laid on the Church as the means and the sphere of evangelization is itself an integral part of New Testament theology. Nowhere in the New Testament is there any suggestion that the Gospel can be thought of out of relation to the Church, the Church itself is an essential part of the Gospel. The message and the mission of Jesus cannot be rightly understood unless we recognize the real continuity, in His mind, between the old Israel and the new Israel which He was calling out through the covenant in His blood, and the emphasis in His thinking and planning on the community which was to incorporate and also to proclaim the fruits of His redeeming work. Nowhere in the New Testament is there any suggestion that it is possible to be a Christian outside the Church. In the true sense of the words, *extra ecclesiam nulla salus* is sound New Testament theology. St. Paul treats faith and baptism as the inner and outer aspects of the same experience; to him the question whether salvation depends on faith or on baptism would have appeared meaningless.

It is true that there was a simplicity in the early days of the Church which it is difficult to recover to-day. We are called to deal with two classes of persons, to whose status the New Testament directs no attention—infants baptized but not as yet able to make that response of personal faith without which membership of the Church cannot reach its fulness; and those who though baptized are content with such a remote and rudimentary allegiance to the Gospel that it is difficult to apply to them the glowing terms in which the early Church spoke of the relationship of the redeemed man to God. In neither case are we called to deny the reality of membership in the Church which baptism conveys; we are compelled to allow for the blurring of New Testament simplicities which has come about in the centuries of the Church's life. At this point, the experience of the younger churches comes to our help. The real significance of baptism is much more fully understood by the convert, and even by the non-Christian, where the Church stands over against a non-Christian faith and manner of life. The non-Christian system is a totality. It does not on the whole concern itself greatly with the inner beliefs and convictions of the individual, but it lays its hand on every aspect of his activity in the family and society. It can tolerate interest in the Gospel of Jesus Christ and even the profession of inner faith in Him. But baptism is the great and tragic reality. It involves the rejection of one totality and acceptance of another. It puts the individual beyond the possibility of compromise. He has died to the old in order to embrace the new. The real nature of evangelism can be understood when we apply to the quasi-Christian world the insights gained in the non-Christian world. Nominal Christianity itself is a non-Christian or even anti-Christian system. It is a total way of living which is centred in man and not in God, and therefore is not subject to the will of God, neither indeed can be, all the more dangerous because a measure of conformity to Christian ethical standards may conceal the basic difference between such a position and the reality of Christian faith.

In the Roman Catholic Church there has been a tendency to stress so strongly the outward and corporate as to overlook the necessity of the personal act of will and decision by which the member of the Church becomes a living member. By reaction against this, the Protestant evangelist may fall into the opposite error of proclaiming Christ in detachment from the life of the Church as the Christian reality in space and time. In this case, it is difficult to avoid one or other of the distortions, which come about when Christ is presented as a historical figure in the past, adhesion to whom falls within the category of memory, or as an intellectual ideal or idea, which can be grasped by intellectual apprehension. Neither of these is an approach to the reality of what the New Testament means by faith. Christ is not known until He is known also in His incorporation in the Church. Membership in Him remains unreal, until it is tested by willingness to accept membership in His visible body in all its division and weakness and unattractiveness. The aim of making men Christians must recognize as a necessary part of itself the aim of making them churchmen.

THE LAY APOSTOLATE

Another aspect of the evangelistic strategy of the early Church demands mention. It was taken for granted that, though there would be whole-time evangelists, who were entitled to "live of the Gospel", yet every member of the Church would be by vocation a witness and an evangelist. We read in the Acts *they therefore that were scattered abroad went about preaching the word* (viii, 4). Professor Telfer has recently emphasized the importance of this aspect of the life and ministry of the primitive Church. ' Have those little ones no share of apostolate? The greatest act of discretion under Christ in the whole history of the infant Church, to wit, the admission of uncircumcised Gentiles to salvation by faith in Jesus Christ, took place neither on the initiative of the Twelve, nor of their delegates, but on that of private Hellenist brethren fleeing the persecution at Jerusalem.

After much taking of counsel, and confirmation through the experience of St. Peter, with yet more confirmation from the vocation of St. Paul, St. Luke represents the apostolate-by-title as ranging itself behind the apostolate-by-fact on this supremely important issue."[2] It is well to note what is involved in his apostolate-by-fact. It does not depend on any commission or authorization by the Church. Its motive force is simply the sense that Christ must everywhere be preached, and pity for the intolerable tragedy that any man should die in ignorance of the glorious Gospel that Christ has died for all. It is taken for granted that every Christian will have such a knowledge of the truth as to be able to give a reason for the faith that is in him, to defend that faith when it is attacked, to set it forth persuasively when opportunity offers, to present that challenge to personal decision without which the hearer, even when attracted by the Gospel, may escape its implications for himself, to carry that infectious sense of joyfulness and victory, which in the majority of cases is the generative power of conversion, and to guide the neophyte through the difficult stages of temptation and dis-heartenment, which nearly always follow on the acceptance of the gift of God in Christ.

The attempts now being made by many churches to recover the lay apostolate, and the enthusiasm with which some success-ful attempts at its recovery have been greeted, indicate the dis-tance which the churches have travelled from the total commit-ment apparent in the records of the earliest time. Even in bodies which have not gone so far as the Roman Church in making a sharp distinction between the *ecclesia docens* and the *ecclesia discens*, there has always been a strong tendency towards prelacy, that is, the assumption by the ordained ministry of the functions which belong to the body of Christ as a whole. This has a two-fold Nemesis; in the first place, it tends to paralyse the activity of the ordinary members of the Church, and so to stunt their spiritual growth; and secondly, it has the result that, when the lay apostolate is in some form restored, it is most difficult to counteract the inveterate tendency of the lay apostles to abandon the advantages of their amateur status, either by joining the ranks of the paid servants of the Church, or by assimilating them-selves, perhaps half unconsciously, to the manners and traditions of the professional ministry.

[2] *Journal of Theological Studies*, July-October 1947, p. 226.

TENSIONS IN EVANGELISM

The starting-point for all study of evangelism to-day must be the lamentable truth that, in the year 1948, the evangelistic task of the Church has, in many parts of the world, yet to be begun. It is obvious that the greater part of the world is as yet non-Christian, in every sense of that word. Yet that is less than the truth. Precise statistical information is naturally unobtainable. But it can be said with some approximation to the truth that of the people now existing in the world, one third has never so much as heard the name of Christ, and another third has never heard the Gospel so proclaimed as to be intelligible and a possible object of faith. If Christ really died for all, it cannot be the will of God that His Gospel should be so long and so widely unproclaimed.

The ecumenical movement has grown out of the movement which led sixty years ago to the foundation of the Student Volunteer Missionary Union and the World's Student Christian Federation. The slogan of those days was, "The Evangelization of the World in this generation." That phrase is now often discounted as the expression of youthful enthusiasm and visionary ardour. It was not felt as such at the time; it was an attempt to put into a few words a sense both of the purpose of God and of the potentialities existing but as yet largely unrealized in the existing churches. The progress of the movement of world evangelism in the past two generations, in spite of the disasters of wars and the collapse of empires, suggests that the phrase was not after all so visionary. The world as a whole is much more accessible to the Gospel than it was sixty years ago. Modern methods of communication, exploration, modern techniques such as the radio and the films, the mastery of disease, the reduction to writing of all the main languages of the world, have between them eliminated most of the obstacles (except such as are presented by the human limitations of the proclaimers and the hearers of the Gospel) in the way of the missionary enterprise. It is the considered opinion of many Christians well qualified to judge, that, if the churches would return to the Bible and to New Testament Christianity, it is not impossible that, within the next fifty years, the Gospel should be brought within the hearing, if not of all, at least of the great majority of the people now living in the world. Political conditions have closed certain areas to the work of evangelism; but it is not certain that those doors will remain for ever closed, and in the meantime other immense areas have been opened up, and are accessible without hindrance to the advance of the churches.

At this point, we must not overlook the tension between outward spread and inner strengthening, which is a constant element in the life of the Church. It is impossible that the Church should be healthy, if it has not at all times a strategy and a passion for world-wide evangelism. But its most immediate duty is to evangelize itself. There is not, and never has been such a thing as a completely Christian Church. There was ground for the somewhat petulant outburst of a scholar who cried out for someone to write a book "debunking" the early Church as Dr. Coulton has "debunked" the Middle Ages. There is a tendency to idealize the apostolic Church, and to suppose that all its members lived all the time on the highest level of Christian experience and martyrdom. The early ages of the Church were marked by a dynamic power of expansion never equalled in later centuries. But the truth about them, though less edifying, is much more consoling than the stylized picture drawn by the hagiographer. The early Christians were not by any means all saints; they had in them a large admixture of human weakness and passion. It was through their weakness that God was pleased to perform the miracles of the foundation of His Church and its preservation through the days of the persecutions. But the Church of the Fathers was not a perfect Church; nor need we too much regret that there is no perfect Church to-day.

But even if there were, it would not long remain perfect. The Church can never escape the obligation of reconverting itself. This is due not only to the corrupting influence of man's sinful nature even in the temple of God, but also to the obvious fact that a new generation is all the time succeeding to the old, and that that generation in its turn needs to be converted. To have been born in a Christian family is indeed an advantage, the greatness of which can hardly be imagined by those who have never worked in a non-Christian country. But the predisposition to faith is not the same as faith. In times of stability, it is possible for the Christian tradition to be handed on almost automatically, so that, without any special efforts of evangelization among the young, each generation is only slightly less

Christian than the one which preceded it.   But a sudden time
of testing not infrequently reveals that what had been taken for
faith was really no more than conformity, and had not the inner
strength to stand against the rough testing of persecution or of
a changed intellectual climate.   History shows that it is possible
for a Church which is not experiencing year by year the renewal
of the Holy Spirit to become completely desiccated and in the
end to collapse and disappear.   Almost all the churches in
Europe are finding themselves under the condemnation that
they had taken their own stability far too much for granted, and
that their present poverty in man-power and in influence is due
in part at least to the failure to realize the urgency of the continuous task of inner evangelization.   Conversely, some of the
most encouraging evidences of evangelism which will come
before us in this study concern the renewed sense in many
churches of the primary importance of this very task, and of
the serious and enterprising way in which steps are being
taken to repair the consequences of long-continued neglect in
the past.

Another tension in the evangelistic task is that between the
claim of the individual and of the group.   An individual is, in
a sense, a separate entity, with his own incommunicable and
secret life.   On the other hand, an individual only reaches the
level of personal being through relationship, through membership in a group and a society, by which his thought and actions
are at every point conditioned.   What is the object of evangelism?   Is it to detach the individual from the social group in
which he has grown up and to transplant him to another, in
which for a long time he will remain an alien, suffering all the
disadvantages of being torn up from the soil in which he was
naturally rooted?   Or is it to touch the group as a whole, so to
permeate its life with the spirit of the Gospel that gradually it
is possible for the individual to find his Christian faith within
the group, the family and the society?   The contrast between
these two approaches must not be made too absolute.   On the
one hand, the appeal must be sooner or later to individual decision, and there can be no substitution of a corporate movement for that final personal choice.   On the other the aim of all
evangelism, even if it involves disrupting the original group, is
to give the convert a home in a new society.   Yet this contrast
of emphasis will meet us at many points in our study.   It pre-

sents one of the most interesting problems in the whole field of evangelism and one to which no simple, perhaps no final, answer can be given.

MASS MOVEMENTS

This study will concern itself mainly with evangelism in lands which are already partially or nominally Christian. But the distinction between Christian and non-Christian countries, between older and younger churches, is increasingly felt to be artificial. The work of evangelism is one; every part of it throws light on every other. It would be a mistake to disregard the light which can be thrown on problems in the West by similar problems in the East, where they are likely to present themselves in sharper and simpler forms, and where therefore the main issues tend to stand out unconfused by secondary considerations. It may be valuable at the outset of our study to take two illustrations, from Eastern lands, of successful evangelism at the opposite extremes of the evangelistic approach.

In modern missionary history, the so-called Mass Movements among the depressed classes in India present the most spectacular developments.

The character of the movements is determined by the peculiar social structure of India. The different castes in a village, though mutually interdependent in innumerable ways, are separated from one another by a rigid system of rules and barriers. But this segregation externally is balanced by an intensely strong corporate sense within the caste, not merely in a single village, but over wide areas, linked together by intermarriage and relationship. Within the group, life in every aspect is determined by group feeling and the sense of corporate responsibility to an extent which was probably familiar in the small village communities in medieval Europe, but disappeared in the West with the breakdown of feudalism. To be sure, even within such a system, the individual remains an individual still, with his own particular character, hopes and desires. But individual initiative and enterprise are not encouraged, and for an individual to make a decision contrary to the general mind of the group requires qualities of independence which are rare in any society. Inevitably, the Christian movements have followed the social structure. One caste over a wide area may have been deeply stirred, without any effect at all having been produced on any other caste.

It has often been said that missionaries turned their attention first to the depressed classes, among whom most of the great movements have taken place, thinking that they would be easier soil to work than the more privileged classes. On the whole history does not bear out the charge. The movements among the poor and the disinherited were neither foreseen nor planned. In many areas the beginning of them was almost fortuitous, following upon long and unsuccessful attempts to find access to those to whom the world had been kinder. But once the movements started, they increased in range and numbers, until the inrush into the Church began to resemble an avalanche.

The progress of the movements has in almost every case been the same. The subject of a change of faith would be introduced to a village group by one person who had become interested. For months the subject would be talked over in the village, principally by the elders, but in that freedom of discussion in the open air, which is almost universal in tropical countries. One of the considerations which would weigh most heavily with the old and wise would be the absolute necessity of avoiding a breach in the harmony and integrity of the group. Be the advantages of Christianity what they may, they are dearly purchased by a group which has lived from time immemorial in the security of group life, if the result of the change is the permanent disruption of the existing unity. It has to be admitted that in the minds of these very poor and backward people, the appeal of the Gospel is very far from being limited to spiritual considerations. Desire for fuller life, the hope of education, the possibility of protection from powerful adversaries, all play their part. One of the responsibilities of the evangelist is to see to it that, so far as is humanly possible, no group is accepted for Christian instruction unless there is recognizable at least some element of spiritual desire.

The extent and strength of the movement may be gauged by the fact that in one area of one mission, the Church increased in thirty years from 30,000 to 135,000 adherents. In the Telugu-speaking part of India, considerably more than a million converts have been gathered in.

Critics of the Mass Movements, both Christian and non-Christian, have not been lacking. To the non-Christian, the whole movement tends to appear as the result of an intense desire on the part of the Christian community at all costs to increase its numbers and its influence in a country more and more governed by democratic methods and by the counting of heads. The criticism of the Christian is on rather different grounds; he is concerned about the purity of the Church, and disturbed by the effect on it of the importation of vast numbers of backward and illiterate people steeped in superstition and in non-Christian ways. The converts are ignorant and superstitious; unless it is possible to provide them over a period of thirty years, that is, until a generation has grown up which has never known heathenism, with constant teaching and pastoral care, it is unlikely that they will ever grow up into a living Church.

On the other hand, the supporter of this method has much to say on his side. No such movement is ever carried through to success without bitter and sometimes long-continued persecution of the new Christians; their willingness to endure persecution is one of the best possible evidences of their faith. A careful study of the make-up of the Indian Church at the present time shows that perhaps eighty-five per cent of its members, including some of those now furthest removed from Mass Movement conditions and in the most important positions, owe their origin as Christians to Mass Movements of an earlier period. But the most important consideration is that relating to the environment and social setting of the convert. An individualistic Christianity is an impossibility; the believer must have a Christian milieu, in which his faith and charity can expand. The provision of this milieu is one of the greatest problems. From every country and from almost every type of evangelistic work comes the same complaint: the existing churches are so unwelcoming, they do not provide the kind of atmosphere in which a convert can breathe; they are so stereotyped that for him the effort of adjustment is almost intolerable. With the Mass Movement convert it is otherwise; he brings with him his social environment. When a large group comes at one time to join the Church, it brings with it its whole pattern of relationships and social integrations. This is conditioned through and through by the non-Christian past; it needs to be completely worked over and recast in the light of Christ and His word; the Christianizing of an environment is often a more difficult task than the Christianizing of an individual or a family. But there is no stage at which the convert is *déraciné*. His roots are here; this is the soil in which he has grown up; if this soil can be refertilized by the word of Christ, he can continue to grow in it as a Christian with a natural and characteristic growth, and not as a mere imitation of his European guides.

These remarkable movements in a non-Christian country raise in an acute form many of the problems that will confront us in many different countries. But the root question of all is the relation of the working of the Spirit of God to mass activity and the psychology of the crowd. Why is it that men, apparently shut off in their own separate existence as individuals, become susceptible at levels below the purely rational to strains and movements of the Spirit, are taken out of themselves and swept on ways that seem to involve a complete change in their nature and activities? What we should call highly civilized peoples seem as subject to such movements as the very simple from whom our main illustration was taken. The movements in themselves seem to be almost neutral, capable of becoming an instrument in the hand of God, but capable also of being turned most neatly to serve the purposes of the devil. What was it in the mental configuration of England in the eighteenth century that made it so ready a field for the work of the Wesleys? How far is the Church right in trying to produce such widespread movements? Should it rather wait for them, and be ready to turn them to the purposes of the Kingdom of God when they manifest themselves? Or should the Church always be suspicious of the large movement, believing that the work of God is best done in the quiet of the individual spirit? These are questions which this study is written rather to evoke than to answer.

INDIVIDUAL SEEKERS

Let us now turn to a piece of evangelistic work as different as could be imagined in every respect. In China, one of the most familiar figures is the wandering monk. Among this fraternity are to be found as many varieties of character as among the wandering friars of the Middle Ages in Europe. A few are rogues, some are charlatans, but many are deeply religious men, with a real inner quest for light and peace. Rather more than twenty-five years ago, a Norwegian missionary was led to give special attention to men of this class and to seek means to win them for Christ. The wandering monk is essentially an individualist. Even though he should spend part of his time in a monastery and accept the discipline of a closely corporate life, it is an individual quest for salvation which has driven him out to leave the intimacies of home and family for the endless way. His migratory life makes him inaccessible to all the ordinary methods of preaching the Gospel. After some years of experiment, the attempt to evangelize the monks took shape in the Christian Institute of Tao Fong Shan, " the Mountain from which the Christ Spirit is blowing": On a beautiful mountain near Hong-Kong has been built what may be called a Christian monastery. The Buddhist pilgrim who comes there will find nothing that jars upon him or seems unfamiliar; everything is in Chinese style; the buildings, the gardens, the whole rhythm and mode of life speak to him of that which is familiar. Yet there is a difference; there is no attempt to conceal the Christian element in that outwardly Chinese life. The emblem of the monastery is " the opened lotus flower, which in the east is the symbol of the soul of man that has opened itself to the influence of the divine and eternal "; but it is the lotus flower out of which arises the Cross, the divine answer to man's quest and his questionings. Here the wandering monk can come and stay as he will, think and meditate, question and read, and then move on as he will. Of the success of the method, to use a word which is never appropriate to any kind of Christian activity, there can be no doubt. Since the beginning of the work, more than 8,000 monks have passed through Tao Fong Shan; more than a hundred have found there the answer to their question and have been baptized. Several have been ordained to the ministry of the Church.[3]

This enterprise, and others like it, such as the many Christian Ashrams which have come into existence in recent years in India, raise urgently the question of the relations between the past of the seeker after Christ and his future. To become a Christian at all, he must become a new man in Christ. But how much does that require him to put off of what he had before he came to know Christ? Is there anything that can be retained, or must he start again afresh and acquire the whole of a new world in which to live? Was God at work in his old beliefs, or are they

[3] Information supplied by the Rev. K. L. Reichelt.

to be repudiated as wholly of the devil? Is his new faith in Christ to be regarded in some way as a development from or as the perfection of his old? Or is it a new and foreign power which condemns the old and shows up its worthlessness? These are questions that have perplexed the Church all through the centuries. If any finally satisfactory answer could be given, it is probable that it would have been given ere now and would have been universally accepted. As it is, opinion tends to swing from point to point. Generally speaking, the tendency of converts themselves is to take a very severe view of their own past; others believe that in Christ, old things are not abolished but are taken up into the new life and transformed, just as in the new man in Christ, the old man is not abolished, but is still visibly present, and not merely as the legacy of sin.

This second point of view is always in danger of syncretism, through allowing the old to determine the content or at least the shape of the new. The Cross may be shown arising out of the lotus; but if by any chance the lotus should determine the form of the Cross, then what would be presented would be not the Christian Gospel, but some hybrid, with no real power in it to save. From a very early date in the history of the Church, we can see this process at work. All the Gnostic sects arose from the attempt to reshape the Christian Gospel according to the presuppositions of the Hellenistic world; the Church which was successful in expelling Gnosticism was not so successful in putting the contribution of Greek thought in its right place in subjection to the Word of God. The success of Tao Fong Shan in avoiding this type of syncretism seems to be due to its determination to keep the Word of God and His message as the measure and the rule of all things. It is His Word which determines how far use can be made of the Chinese tradition of beauty and an ordered life in order to make plain for the Chinese the way to Him; it is not the Chinese tradition which determines the form of the presentation of the Gospel to the Chinese.

This single illustration, again, raises deep problems, which recur in every attempt to win men for Christ. The heart of the problem is the relation between the old and the new, or to put it in other words, between sameness and difference. Is the Gospel to be presented to men as the thing essentially familiar, because they have always known it in their hearts already, and therefore appealing to them as the truth which leads to the home long since known though only dimly discerned? Or is it to be presented as the absolutely new, the truth so paradoxical and startling as to call out Tertullian's *Credo quia absurdum,* and to pass the sentence of condemnation on every human striving as misdirected and irrelevant?

EVANGELISM IN THE PARISH

We have first gone far afield, in order to set forth in the most challenging form possible some of the problems that come up whenever and wherever men try to present the Gospel. For the rest of our study, we shall be on more familiar ground, considering various ways in which men have tried to solve these basic problems, in countries which have had a long Christian history, and where the challenge is to restore to life a Gospel which has ceased to mean anything to most of those who are dimly familiar with it.

From a very early date, the unit of the organization of the Church has been the parish, the area within which a family of Christians lives. One of the most momentous steps in the development of the Church was the change from the assembly to the parish, from " the Church that is in thy house " to the area in which the Christian family lived. Once the principle of the parish has been established, as it has been to some extent even by those communions which believe most strongly in the " gathered Church "—the fellowship of believing people—the natural mission-field for the Christians of the parish is the non-Christian or non-believing element in its area. Even in so-called Christian countries, the actual state of the parish in all towns and in many rural areas is that it consists of a small nucleus of church-goers and a very much larger mass of the occasional conformists, the indifferent and the hostile. The natural activity of the Christian ought to be, and usually is not, that which is described by the expressive French word *rayonnement.* In the parish setting, evangelism ought not to be a matter of occasional special efforts, but a permanent element in all Church activities, and that for which the whole worshipping community recognizes that it is being trained. The evangelizing agent is not the ordained minister, but the whole Christian fellowship.

One Methodist Church in America has made a very successful experiment in parish evangelism. After a careful and business-like survey of a given district, a team of Christian people was trained for individual visitation. During less than four years this Church recorded an addition of 1,043 new members, more than half of whom had been won by this special "lay" effort.[4]

The varieties of parish evangelism are very many. No method can be transplanted from one area to another, and great scope has to be allowed for individual gifts and enterprise. One leading minister has been able to build up a large congregation almost entirely on the basis of very careful preparation of couples coming to him desiring to be married, and by individual spiritual care of them after marriage. But in all such efforts, the principles set forth in the one example here described will be found essential—that the spearhead should be the witness of lay people, who have a word to say of what Christ has done for them, and that there should be a welcoming community into which the newcomer can be brought, and in which he will find it possible to live, to worship and to serve.

EVANGELISM IN THE ORTHODOX CHURCH

At the opposite extreme from the carefully systematized methods of American evangelism are the spontaneous movements which from time to time spring up among simple people, without the leadership of authority or the direction of specially gifted people. We are glad to have received from an Orthodox source a detailed account of the movement which grew up in Yugo-Slavia between the two wars. The ethos of this movement is so different from anything familiar in the Western churches that the brief extracts, to which we are limited by consideration of space, deserve the careful attention of all students of evangelism.[5]

"After World War I there emerged in the Balkans two religious movements; one in Greece and another in Serbia. In Greece it was called Zoë (Life), and in Serbia Bogomolzee (God Worshippers). They were the same in spirit but different in origin. The Zoë was founded upon the theophilosophy of a notable Greek thinker Makrakis, whereas the Serbian

---

[4] Information supplied by Professor E. G. Homrighausen.
[5] Information communicated by the Rt. Rev. Bishop Nicolai Velimirovic, of the Orthodox Church of Yugo-Slavia, now resident in America.

movement Bogomolzee sprang from the personal spiritual experiences of the common Serbian men and women during the awful years of war sufferings.

"They were singing, those Bogomolzee, singing almost continually, not only at their meetings but also while working in the fields and in houses or travelling in trains or on foot. The worldly songs almost disappeared from among them; they sang spiritual hymns and psalms.

"'Sing, brothers, sing. Rejoice and be exceedingly glad. For we were blind and now we see. We have found the truth, and we know now whose children we are. We know our Saviour and the path of our salvation. Sing, brothers, sing.'

"The hymns they sang were composed by themselves. But they circulated anonymously. Most of the hymns were published in either their monthly magazine *Missionary* or in separate booklets, but very rarely signed by the authors. There is a very great number of hymns and songs. If they all were published in book form, there would be several books as large as the present Hymnal Book of the Episcopal Church. Of course they are not all of literary value, but many are. Before that movement, we in our church did not have any Hymnal in popular tongue. This was a novelty which moved thousands of human hearts. Even the Moslem children in Bosnia used to sing them in the streets and fields.

"External miracles caused conversion, repentance, thanksgiving, heart rejoicing and singing. Yea, the miracles produced a fundamental change of the inner man, of the 'hidden man of the heart'.

"This happened to many of the Bogomolzee and Zoësts during and after War I. Before their striking experiences they were—as they afterwards publicly confessed—either indifferent to religion or lukewarm or even hostile to it. The practical consequence of each of these attitudes was the immoral conduct. Their public confessions, together with their changed life, drew to the Movement many of those who listened but did not have a spiritual experience of their own.

"Similar cases in war and peace time are innumerable. But there were also cases witnessed by crowds of people. In one single monastery of St. Naum on the shore of Ochrida Lake, the records were published for three years. Each year showed between 130 to 163 healing cases, some of extreme gravity like lunacy, paralysis, skin disease, epilepsy and others. Personally, I was an eyewitness of several such cases. Here is a very strange instance. A young man, lean and emaciated, was brought, hands bound with a rope. At the door of the church the demoniac became suddenly very violent. He broke the rope like a straw and attacked six men who tried to bind him again. With a fury he knocked them down, and they retreated scared, and left him alone. I was wondering about such a giant's strength in such a frail creature. After a month of continual prayers for him, he became perfectly sane and reasonable, but very weak and exhausted. I asked him whether he remembered what he had done in the monastery, and he answered: 'I remember everything. I am sorry but it was not I who offended and hurt the people. I tried to speak politely but somebody in me stopped me and he spoke slandering words. I tried to cross myself because I knew I was in St. Naum, but he stiffened my right hand. Not I, but he knocked the six by my hands, and my hands pained me terribly. I was his plaything. When I wanted to speak as a man he barked through my mouth like a dog.' "

Our Orthodox Church teaches that miracles mean God's intervention in human life and affairs. If God's interventions are denied, then our prayers to God are of no avail. To believe in God, however, and not to pray to Him means to believe in an *unemployed* God who uninterestedly and powerlessly is looking from heavenly galleries down to all miseries of men. If God were an unemployed God, He would not be a living and loving God but an idol. On the other hand, to pray to God means nothing else but to expect His intervention, His miracles, be it directly or indirectly. It is certainly a paradox to deny God's miracles and yet to say the Lord's Prayer as some of the Church's antagonists do. For in that prayer we are asking for bread, forgiveness, deliverance from evil. That is to say, we are asking God's miracles.

"Our new spiritual movement added nothing to our old theology. Its contribution to the Church, however, has been remarkable in three points:

1. In a great accumulation of individual spiritual experiences in harmony with age-long Christian experiences, with accentuated moral obligations;
2. In creating a huge religious poetry as a moving expression of our faith.
3. In accentuating especially the dogma of God's Providence, in its deepest and largest sense.

"A Russian ' starez ' gave us an additional counsel:
"Turn neither to the right nor to the left, as the Lord said to Joshua."

This advice is very precious, especially for our times when some Christian theologians and priests have been confusing their flock by introducing the political terms—rightists and leftists— into the Church and religion. This division has nothing to do with Christ's revelation. There are no leftists and rightists in our Lord's teachings. For it is more exact than mathematics. Therefore, the Orthodox Church, even in the countries ruled by the extreme leftists, has gone not an inch away from the inherited Faith and Order and Liturgics, neither to the left nor to the right.

"Our brothers in the movement eagerly read the Revelation and whisperingly conversed about the last-time mysteries.
"The reading of Christ's eschatologic sermons and of the Book of Revelation produced in human souls a wholesome fear. Among the Bogomolzee that was not fear of what is to come, but the fear for one's soul. It was indeed purifying fear of God. But the joy of the final victory of the Lamb over the beasts was the top feeling. They sang many hymns regarding Christ's victory over the beasts and Christ's second coming in glory.

> *Behold the Lord is coming with His host*
> *Let His enemies tremble and not boast,*
> *The earth is quaking, the stars in flight,*
> *Hail, brothers, the Lamb victorious*
> *Meet your Bridegroom at midnight."*

REVIVAL MASS MEETINGS

At an earlier period of evangelistic enterprise, the great and classic method was the campaign of large meetings, held for a number of days together by some outstanding evangelist. There are men still living who can remember the great days of Moody and Sankey, and the extraordinary and permanent results brought about by their work in many churches and many lives. It is the common view that the day of such campaigns is past. Certainly the spiritual atmosphere has greatly changed from what it was in the days of Moody. The task of the evangelist was to get his hearers to take seriously the things which they half-heartedly believed, and to assure them that there was in Christ the power to live the kind of life which their own conscience assured them to be right. Now all that has changed. The spiritual capital of the West has been dwindling at an alarming rate. Although a recent Gallup poll revealed that ninety per cent of the Americans questioned returned an affirmative answer to the question whether they believed in God, for the most part ignorance of the Christian Faith and what it demands, relativity in morals, the general scepticism which questions whether anything can be truly known unless it can be made the object of scientific investigation, have made the task of the Christian evangelist much more difficult. But if more difficult, surely much more interesting, since he is dealing with questioning minds, and finds himself not merely challenged to give of his best, but has the assurance that, if he is successful, he will be adding to the Church those who can give an independent witness of greater value than that of the merely acquiescent believers of earlier times.

But evidence from many countries shows that the day of the mission campaign and the mass meeting is by no means over.

Perhaps the most remarkable of all the reports that have come in is that concerning the great series of public meetings organized by French Protestants in the days following the liberation in 1945. Protestants in France, as one of their own reporters frankly remarks, have suffered from a minority complex since the days when Henry IV forbade Protestant worship in Paris, and since for a hundred and fifty years Louis XIV and his successors harried them with fire and sword. So it was a gesture of no small importance when the small Gouvieux team,

alone and without any support except that of prayer, decided to
hire the Wagram Hall in Paris for the public proclamation of
the Gospel. This great meeting of 5,000 auditors was followed
up by similar great gatherings in other parts of Paris. Never
in the history of French Protestantism have such manifestations
of enthusiasm been seen. Questioned as to the actual value of
such gatherings, our reporter retorts: " Eh quoi? Comptera-t-
on pour rien d'avoir placardé dans tout Paris, à milliers d'exem-
plaires, le nom du Christ et l'appel à lire son évangile? "[6]

France is not alone among the Latin countries in having had
experience of such mass evangelism. In Italy, the position of
the small Protestant communities, the largest of which is the
historic Waldensian Church, is more difficult by far than that of
the Protestant churches in France. Yet here, too, the spirit of
courageous witness has been at work. Preachers of those
churches have ventured out into the open air, have hired
cinemas and other public halls for meeting with no other object
than the straightforward preaching of the Gospel. And to their
surprise they have found crowded audiences and a ready hearing.
The Roman Church, too, has launched its great campaigns of
evangelism, with many signs of success. As one of our inform-
ants told us, " Italy is a religious country. Secularism has not
penetrated the soul of the people as it has in France. Italians,
even when they are anti-clerical, are not anti-religious." In the
main this description seems to be true.[7]

Not unnaturally America seems to be the country in which
the large-scale campaign still seems most to prosper. In spite
of all that has been done between the wars by the more unwise,
commercially minded, even immoral promoters, to discredit this
type of evangelism, it still flourishes and claims its great successes.
That which has acquired the widest publicity is the " Youth for
Christ " Movement. This started with Saturday night meetings
for youth in New York; but it quickly spread across the continent and even beyond the limits of the United States. " Its
programme consists of mass meetings on Saturday nights, in
which Gospel singing periods, testimonies, special musical
presentations and a Gospel message are presented in the style of
a radio broadcast conducted by a master of ceremonies." Its

---

[6] *Enquêtes sur les Valeurs spirituelles à Paris:* Editions Oberlin, Strasbourg
1947, ff. 196-7.
[7] Information communicated by the Rev. P. Eynard, T. Vinay and C. Brutsch.

theology is conservative, and its piety "pietistic". Even the critics of the movement readily admit that its leaders are actuated by a genuine desire to win the young for Christ and to link them up with the work and worship of the regular churches. "This movement seems to be getting a response from both youth and adults because it presents Christian experience as something so meaningful that men are willing to express concern and joy over it. There are many who believe that it secures its following because the churches have somehow failed to minister to the basic emotional needs of youth in a spiritual way." The operative word in this statement is joy.[8] We have received a personal testimony from one who received through the work of Youth for Christ in Holland the vital experience of the knowledge of Jesus Christ, that it was the unmistakable joy of the leaders and of those taking part in the meetings which made real what had previously been only intellectually known. By contrast, the worship and life of the churches seemed solemn, and to lack that personal appeal without which youth cannot easily be won.

Movements not dissimilar to Youth for Christ have been operating in England and Ireland, and filling some of the largest halls in the country. All these movements, however they may differ in detail, seem to be marked by the same strength and weakness. Those who have professed the experience of conversion at such gatherings tend to embrace a sect-type of Christianity without a strong sense of social responsibility. Inevitably the organizers of the meetings have not themselves a strong programme of follow-up; they would say, perhaps, that this was not their business, and that it was left to the local churches to do that part of the work; if the local churches fail to corral the sheep expertly driven towards them, who is to blame for that? To this the local churches might answer that, if young people are taken by an emotional experience out of the natural fellowship in which they ought to be growing, it becomes all the more difficult to make them at home again after the breach of continuity.

The most serious question, however, has reference to those who attend these great meetings. From what class are they drawn? Exact statistical information cannot be obtained; but the impression obtained by those who have gone into the matter most fully is that usually ninety per cent of those present are

[8] Information communicated by Prof. E. G. Homrighausen.

already at least occasional attenders at some Christian place of worship, and that the majority are in fairly close touch with some Church and its organizations. This is not necessarily a condemnation of such movements. Many acquiescent church members need just such a stimulus to bring their Christian life out of the chrysalis stage into active life. And, if no more than ten per cent of those present belong to the alienated class, to have got even so many together under the sound of the Gospel is by no means a contemptible achievement. It is important, however, that neither those responsible for the organization of the campaign nor the responsible leaders of the churches should be deluded by imagining that what is happening is different from what in reality it is.

UNIVERSITY MISSIONS

Before leaving the subject of campaigns and large-scale movements, some space may be spared for two movements of more than marginal importance, touching a class of person rather less closely associated with the Church than those reached by Youth for Christ and similar organizations.

The practice of holding University Missions has shown considerable revival both in America and in England. The older generation of Christian leaders can remember the great campaigns of the last years of the nineteenth century, when the life of whole universities was shaken and hundreds of lives were touched. A feeling had grown up that the day of such efforts had passed, and that, if such missions were held, the results would be, in the slightly cynical but not untruthful remark of an exceptionally acute observer, that the benches " would be occupied by the godly, who had come to set a good example to the ungodly who were not there ". The experience of recent years has shown clearly that there is still a place for University campaigns well prepared and rightly led, and that they will have their influence not only on the students, but also on members of the staff.

We may take as an example the remarkable Mission to Oxford University in February 1947. This was preceded by a very long campaign of preparation, during which Christian groups were formed in all the colleges, and trained in the work of prayer and witness. The chief missioner was supported by twenty assistant missioners, men and women, who lived in the colleges and were available the whole time for personal work among the students. Evening meetings were held every evening for a week, not, as had been customary, in a church, but in the Sheldonian Theatre, the official meeting-place of the University. Expectation was far exceeded. The theatre was well filled each night, more than filled for the concluding meeting. The hearers included many students who had previously had no connection with any religious organization. During the week, the Mission was the main subject of conversation in the University. All emotional appeal was rigidly excluded, yet throughout the week there was a growing feeling of intensity and expectancy. Two features in the Mission were specially notable. First, important as were the evening meetings, the work of the chief missioner proved to be of secondary importance compared with that of the assistant missioners in smaller groups, college meetings and personal work. Secondly, at the end of the week of meetings, there was not, as there usually is after such special efforts, a feeling of exhaustion and collapse. The Christian groups, reinforced in many cases by new members, set themselves quietly and practically to the task of making the University more Christian. Nine months later, a well-placed observer was able to write: "I feel that for the first time in at least ten or twelve years, the tide is very strongly with us."[9] All who were in any way associated with the Mission were agreed that its remarkable success was due, under God, to the long period of careful preparation, and to the fact that the Mission was a corporate enterprise of almost all the Christian forces in Oxford.

THE MORAL REARMAMENT MOVEMENT

The second movement which deserves consideration is that which now calls itself Moral Rearmament, but it is still frequently known by its earlier name, the Oxford Group Movement. Moral Rearmament has been the object on one side of extravagant adulation, on the other of unusually venomous criticism. It is therefore a little difficult to assess its real place in the Christian scene at the present time. The movement stands for the direct application of the absolute standards of the Gospel to practical daily life. It believes in the direct guidance

[9] See Supplement to *Christian News Letter*, June 1947.

of God as available at all times to every believer. For years it has worked on the method of holding house-parties, at which, by the exchange of experiences and by a spirit of intimate, perhaps it is not unfair to say hearty, fellowship, the new-comer is drawn into the realities of Christian life. The movement has set itself to reach a class of wealthy and worldly people, whom the ordinary churches had largely failed to touch, and may therefore justly claim to have broken new ground in the evangelistic field. In recent years M.R.A. has also done important work in industrial centres.

The criticisms directed against the movement are many and well known. Some have felt that its financial methods might be improved by a little more openness. Others find disturbing its slightly childish methods of publicity, and its delight in the exploitation of famous or well-known names. More serious is the objection that the seeking of guidance, as practised by the groups, may easily claim the sanction of the Holy Spirit for the promptings of autosuggestion. The constant, and unanalysed, use of the word democracy suggests the uncomfortable and slightly ludicrous picture of a line-up of the Oxford Group with the Pope and American big business on the anti-communist front. Those who know the movement from within, however, claim that "Moral Rearmament raises the vital question of the ideological basis of true democracy". Its leaders lay stress on the need for a spiritual basis of democracy—in other words, that God should be recognized as the Supreme Authority and Creative Power in the daily life of mankind.

But when the worst has been said, the movement may claim to have rendered signal services to the Christian cause in the depressed period between the wars. A considerable number of those who are now convinced Christians owe to the Group their first contact with the Christian Faith as a live and challenging force. Many, who had been Christian for years, and not all of whom have remained within the circle of the movement, will bear witness that through their contact with the Groups they were delivered from complacencies and inhibitions which were hindering their Christian usefulness. No one can spend a day at a Moral Rearmament House Party without experiencing the charm of an exuberant and sometimes naïve cheerfulness and friendliness. The comment of a German visitor, after his first experience of the fellowship, was, "These people really think it is possible for something to happen," no bad thing in a world where the Church is perhaps a little too much given to bewailing its lost opportunities and to confessing its sins in public. If the cheerful expectation of the Groups that the Kingdom of God is just round the corner is eighty per cent due to a youthful zest for life as yet unbroken on its roughnesses, it is possible that the other twenty per cent draws its strength from a genuine and unbreakable conviction of the reality of the miraculous working of God in the drab and disheartening twentieth century.

THE NEED FOR FELLOWSHIP IN EVANGELISM

In all the activities so far described, there is an element, psychologically important, to which we shall have occasion to refer again. Modern man, at least in the industrial West, is oppressed by a sense of loneliness and pettiness. Torn up from many of his natural roots, and not feeling intensely that there is any place where he belongs, he is seeking, albeit subconsciously, for fellowship. Conscious of his smallness, as an atom in a mass society, he desires to compensate for that smallness by belonging to something great. In war-time, this compensation is for many achieved by the anonymity of uniform, by the spirit of the regiment or ship and by a sense of the greatness of the cause. In peace-time, the old irksome sense of triviality sets in again. It is clear that some forms of Christian evangelism on a large scale owe their success to their appeal to just these two needs of men. This is not to disparage them. The needs were planted there by God, as a part of the natural inheritance of man. They cannot find their full satisfaction anywhere except in the family and the city of God. Our concern is only that it should be the family and city of God in which the satisfaction is offered, and not in some transitory and ephemeral home of the emotions.

RELIGIOUS FILMS

As we pass further away from the central nucleus of regular church membership, the problem of the evangelistic approach to those who stand aloof from the Church becomes more difficult. Such people will not ordinarily come to church, or to a religious meeting. How then are they to be reached?

The development of the modern techniques of the radio and

the film have opened up possibilities of which the churches have been rather slow to see the significance. It may be said that people who have no interest in religion will not listen to a religious broadcast, and will not go to see a religious film. The facts are against this supposition. Expert collection of evidence shows that in countries which have regular religious broadcasts, an astonishing number of non-church-goers do listen to them, many casually, some of set purpose; and that if a religious film is good enough, millions of people will flock to see it.

The Roman Catholic Church has been very fortunate in the appearance in quick succession of four films of considerable merit and widespread popularity—*Going My Way*, *The Bells of St. Mary's*, *The Song of Bernadette* and *The Keys of the Kingdom*, in each of which religion in its Roman Catholic form has been presented as interesting, attractive and even exciting. It must not be supposed that others have been idle in the matter. Religious and biblical films are being produced, and there has been a steady rise in the technical quality of the films produced. But this enterprise is still in its infancy, and time will be required before religious films can compete on the grounds of excellence and interest with the best productions of the secular world. This matter is of urgent importance, since in the modern world the tendency is for man to learn through eye and ear together, and to be far less impressed by what touches the ear alone than by what appeals to several senses simultaneously.

RELIGIOUS BROADCASTING

On the air the situation differs very much in different countries. In England, the British Broadcasting Corporation, a Government-sponsored organization, allocates a considerable amount of air-time each week, on several distinct programmes, to religious services, lectures and discussions. Great care is taken to make sure that all the main denominations have a share in the time allotted, and that speakers representative of many different points of view are chosen. Events which combine religious and national significance, such as the Coronation of the King, are usually broadcast. Complaints have been heard from various quarters that the B.B.C. tends to be rather colourless. There may in the past have been just grounds for this complaint. But the religious department of the B.B.C. is launching out on a more adventurous programme, adapting its messages to the needs of different types of hearers, and giving opportunity for frank discussion on the air between Christians and non-Christians. It is hard to measure the value of radio-evangelism in England. But the diffused effects of the religious programmes on literally millions of listeners are by no means negligible as a factor in the evangelistic situation.

Very different is the picture in the United States. Here responsibility for the proclamation of the Gospel over the air is shared by churches, or federations of churches, with individuals who feel a special vocation to this ministry and sponsor their own programmes.

One of the largest and most influential agencies is the National Radio Religious Commission of the Federal Council of the Churches of Christ in America. The Council sponsors seventeen weekly broadcasts on the three great religious networks, apart from broadcasting minute prayers for the United Nations, special Holy Week services and other features. These programmes, being sponsored by a joint organization, have no denominational emphasis, and therefore according to one witness "are instructive and pastoral in nature, but not arresting and demanding in their claims". Precise evidence as to the extent to which they are listened to, and as to the effect produced by them on their hearers, are not in the nature of the case available. Yet it is noteworthy that not long ago 14,000 copies of a single sermon were distributed to listeners who had asked for them.

We have received somewhat detailed information of an outstanding individual effort, in which a preacher who is also an able theologian preaches every Sunday, and reaches an audience which is computed to reach the staggering figure of fifteen millions in many lands. Twenty-five thousand letters reaching his office every week are some measure of the interest aroused. These sermons are definitely evangelistic; they present to the hearers the Christ of the Scriptures and demand a personal response. The following statement, though rhetorically expressed, is an indication of the enormous possibilities of the radio as a means of mass evangelism: " Lighthouse-keepers . . . rangers in lonely forest lands . . . inmates of hospitals and prisons . . . head-hunters in New Guinea . . . West Indians

. . . Indians near the isthmus of Panama . . . soldiers in the Aleutians . . . shipyard workers in California and down in Baltimore . . . all tell how they found Jesus as Saviour as a result of this vast, worldwide broadcast every Sunday morning."[10]

In the lands of the younger churches, the use of radio as a means of evangelization is scarcely as yet in its beginnings. Yet there are striking exceptions. The ordinary observer, if asked to put his finger on that spot on the map of the inhabited world where we should be most unlikely to find a missionary radio station, might well point to the top of the Andes Mountains in South America. But it is precisely there that one of the most remarkable modern missionary enterprises is to be found. Tune it on the right wave-length, and at almost any hour of the day or night you may find yourself listening to the Voice of the Andes from Quito in the Republic of Ecuador. When the pioneers chose this location for their Gospel radio station, they did not know that a place on the Ecuador 10,000 feet above sea-level was about the most perfect place in the world from which to secure good and clear transmission.

The " Voice of the Andes " was initiated by North American enterprise. Its theology is what would ordinarily be called fundamentalist. But its promoters were wise enough to realize the need of a right identification with the life of the country and of the continent in which they had chosen to work. Those who are not familiar with the Latin-American point of view tend to forget the almost Messianic self-consciousness of the Latin-American peoples, their conviction of the superiority of their culture to that represented by the United States, and their belief that South America is the continent of the future. The " Voice of the Andes ", recognizing all these factors, set itself from the start to be not a selling agency for a foreign and in many ways uncongenial culture, but the expression of an existing culture which needs to be criticized and deepened by a new apprehension of the Gospel of Jesus Christ. Those who work for this enterprise do so from profound conviction of the truth of its central religious message. They are a team of evangelists, regarding the non-religious part of their programmes not as bait, or as marginal to the central issue, but as part of the total evangelistic programme. The station now broadcasts in seventeen languages. Its programmes are heard very widely throughout

[10] Information communicated by the Rev. E. G. Homrighausen.

the world, and letters from many countries give evidence both of its technical efficiency and of the effect of the words spoken over the air.[11]

In many parts of the world, the development of religious broadcasting presents what appear at present to be insuperable difficulties. Yet it is clear that there is no point at which the combined resources of the churches can be brought to bear more profitably than this. It has been suggested, for example, that a strongly equipped radio-station somewhere in the neighbourhood of the Iron Curtain, and broadcasting in the languages of all the peoples behind the curtain, would be one of the few means available to the churches for surmounting that division between East and West in Europe, which seems day by day to be becoming more absolute. Another proposal is for the establishment of such a station in a position from which the Gospel could be broadcast to all the countries of South-East Asia.

RELIGION IN GERMAN SCHOOLS

One of the greatest evangelistic opportunities of the churches is religious instruction in schools, in countries where something of the Christian tradition in national life has been retained. There is here a great field for study. Here we can do no more than give an indication of the way in which, in certain circumstances, Christian teaching in schools can be used as a means for making contact with almost wholly de-Christianized sections of the population.

Under the present régime in Berlin, religious teaching can be given in the schools to children whose parents desire it, but this is wholly the responsibility of the churches, and not of the education department or of the controlling authorities. It is the business of the churches to find, train and pay those who will give religious teaching, the conditions under which they do so being controlled and guaranteed by the secular authorities, but without interference with the actual religious teaching given. The churches at once organized a great campaign to secure both the teachers and the scholars; provision had to be made for about 300,000 children, and for each child requiring religious instruction a written application from a parent or guardian was needed.

An active campaign was set in motion to secure the applica-

[11] See Clarence W. Jones: *Radio, the New Missionary*, Chicago, 1946.

tions. Announcements were made from the pulpits in churches. For a fortnight, large posters were displayed in Berlin. Notices appeared in the papers. In spite of all this effort, in some quarters the returns were very few. Personal visits to parents were found to be essential, and these, when tactfully undertaken, proved to be most efficacious. One teacher has recorded her experience as follows: The holidays were devoted to visits to the homes of 239 children, all of the working class, whose names and addresses she had obtained. In almost every case, the reception was courteous. Some parents replied: " Give the children something to eat, and don't bother us about teaching them about God." Others agreed that religious instruction is a good thing for children as part of a general education. As a result of 505 personal visits, in the course of which three families could not be seen in spite of five separate visits to each house, eighty-five per cent of the children were provided with the necessary applications and were added to the classes for religious instruction in their schools. It happens that this was also the proportion for the whole of Berlin. In some wards, even those most strongly influenced by communism, the proportion of children for whom application was made reached as high as ninety-five per cent. In the majority of cases, the parents proved to be largely or wholly alienated from the Church, but did not wish to be considered pagans; for the Church as an institution they had little good to say; of religion as a factor in the life of men they were not unappreciative.

Of the results of this personal contact with homes and of the religious instruction provided for the children, it is too early as yet to speak. It is possible already to indicate the immense possibilities of contact with family life on this level, as a means of building a bridge over the chasm which, not only in Berlin but in almost all the great cities of the industrial west, divides the Church from the places where men and women really live.[12]

EVANGELISM IN PROFESSIONAL LIFE

At the opposite extreme from these great endeavours at mass approach, we have received most encouraging reports of what is beginning to be known as the professional approach, the attempt to make contact with men and women more or less dissociated

[12] Information communicated by Pastor Lökies, Berlin.

from traditional and organized religion, at the level of their professional life and occupation, helping them to understand the meaning of the Christian Faith by setting it forth to them in its relevance to man in his daily life and in the place where he works.

One notably successful effort of this kind is reported from the North of England. It brought together in conference about two dozen men from four large factories each employing 2,000 workers. Those concerned included representatives of management, office staff, shop stewards, foremen and younger men who were possible future leaders in some capacity. The aim was " to get first-class lecturers to describe what the Christian Faith and life actually is, to tell the story of Christ through the ages and suggest the application of Christianity to industrial and other spheres of life ". The Conference came into being only after long and thorough discussion with both managements and men; in some cases the members of the Conference were actually chosen by the workers as their own representatives. The programme appears to have manifested that peculiar English combination of sobriety, allusiveness and fun and games, which is so perplexing to those not born between Land's End and John o' Groats. Those attending the Conference were asked to bring towel, soap and ration book, and an open mind. After each lecture discussion was fast and furious, but " the interesting thing was that after the first night their minds were far less on industry than on their intense desire to find out what this Christianity was about ". Those who had been present went back to their work charged with the responsibility of telling their mates all about what had been going on. Letters received from them were both moving and illuminating. " In the workshop it's an easy and pleasant job to discuss the conference with its many absorbing points: the majority of the chaps want to know about something and appear interested. The actual lessons I have learned, however, will be much more difficult to explain. You see, the men have not the atmosphere in a factory in which to think of such things." . . . " You anticipated our having to stand up to a mixed reception and I assure you I got it. We are a pretty mixed lot in the factory as you can guess, and believe me some of them haven't made life a bed of roses this last week or two, but the more taunts and criticism I received the more' determined I became to stick to my guns. Mind you, many of the chaps were genuinely interested, and their appreciation has helped considerably in keeping me to my resolution."[13]

The United States provides fascinating information of an experiment still in its early stages of development, but so significant as to challenge the closest attention. Here the approach was not to the industrialist and the worker, but to the professional man in the narrower sense. Of those who found spiritual help in the groups now to be described, all were graduates, some teachers, others lawyers or business men and women. One who was intimately connected with the work states modestly that " it is what any evangelical with some imagination would do if groups asked him to do it "; the information is offered, however, with the caution that though it may serve as a challenge, it will not provide a model. " I have seen failure after failure to use the model. Chiefly I think because most of us have not learned to listen to the people long enough to be able to speak to them, and still think there is some way to speak to them *en masse*. There isn't yet, that is for people in the middle classes. They are all over the lot and must be spoken to as they wander around, not as being in one place all the time."

These groups started from a liberal and humanistic attitude and were deeply interested in social justice. Three-quarters were originally antagonistic to any form of classical and institutional Christianity. Beginning with discussion on current subjects, the members found themselves driven back to basic study, especially of Christian doctrine. After a time, two groups fused to set up a Christian University for laymen, which met in the basement of a residence, with Seminary Professors as lecturers and long discussions after lectures. The course started with Adam (not Smith, the one in the Bible), and ended with Archbishop Temple, much time being given to the classical Christian writers, St. Paul, Augustine, Calvin and Luther. Results were so satisfactory that the course has now been regularized and is on the way to becoming permanent. The standard of work expected is indicated by the note that some of these laymen had read in the course of their studies the second volume of Dr. Niebuhr's Gifford Lectures, Cochrane's *Christianity and Classical Culture* and the one-volume abridgement of Arnold Toynbee's *Study of History*.

Of all the results of this experiment, the most important from

[13] Information communicated by the Rt. Rev. the Lord Bishop of Woolwich.

the point of view of this study is the changed relationship of the members of the groups to the organized Church. After some years of work, fifty per cent of those attending the groups were regular in attendance at church services, many of them taking responsibility for parish activities, and those who had themselves become convinced Christians were fired with the missionary spirit, and constantly bringing others within the charmed circle of the groups.[14]

It is obvious that such methods cannot be used, except where there is a group of educated lay people, anxious for knowledge and willing to take trouble to obtain it. But it is possible that the failure of the Church to hold the laity has been due in part to the fact that it has asked too little of them. Men who earn their living in the cut-throat atmosphere of industrial life must be alert and have their wits about them. They take infinite trouble over the perfection of a technical process. It may be that they are much more ready than is often supposed by the clergy to take the same sort of trouble in their quest for religion. The astonishing increase in many countries in the demand for first-rate music is perhaps an indication of a thirst for reality that will see its way to satisfaction, when confronted with first-rate religion for sale at top prices only.

Post-war Germany has been the scene of similar enterprises, with the characteristic differences to be expected with so different a climate and background. Worse almost than any crime of the Nazis against the lives and bodies of men was their systematic and largely successful attempt to destroy the spiritual and cultural bases on which European man has built his life for more than a thousand years. Consequently, after the Nazi *débâcle*, an immense number of men have found themselves inwardly torn in pieces, without principles, without guiding lights, without intellectual or spiritual security. The situation in Germany is different from that in other countries, since it has come about not only through the slow disintegration of the Christian idea, but by a violent breach of continuity. For the traditional ideas of the *corpus Christianum* has been forcibly substituted a different set of ideas, based on contemporary valuations and not on any abiding principles. With the collapse of these ideas, those subjected to their influence have found themselves in a state of terrible mental confusion, in which despair is one of the

[14] Information communicated by the Rev. Robert S. Bilheimer.

strongest ingredients; and for them the way back to Christian conceptions may be long and doubly arduous. It has been the task of the Evangelische Akademie at Bad Boll in Württemberg, and other homes of the spirit which have sprung up to extend its work elsewhere, to gather together thoughtful men of many types, and to help them to think through their problems honestly and in the light of the word of God. Bad Boll has entertained lawyers and doctors, leaders in industry and workers, farmers, poets, artists, journalists, civil servants, churchmen and teachers.

For all, the problem is in its main lines the same. They have lost their way and have to be helped to find it.

The leaders of the Akademie have found that any merely intellectual discussion soon becomes wearisome to the non-Christians. The threefold emphasis of the Akademie is on Christian teaching, exposition of the Bible, and living testimony from within the life of the Church. Many of those who have attended the sessions have gone away with a renewed Christian conviction. But what is to become of them when they go home? If they find an unwelcoming Church, a pietistic atmosphere so intent on the affairs of the world to come as to be unaware of the urgent pressure of the affairs of this world, speaking a remote and unfamiliar language, how are they there to find a spiritual home? We are reminded yet again, not merely that all evangelistic work must be done in closest contact with the life of the Church, but that no evangelistic work can ultimately be successful until the Church itself is both the home of the saints and also the evangelizing body.[15]

At a distance from the centre of ordinary church life, little greater than that of the Evangelische Akademie, we may place such an enterprise as St. Michael's House, Hamburg. It requires very little imagination to realize the difficulties involved in the running of such a home by an English priest in the British occupied zone of Germany. The natural suspicions are so strong as to raise initially the question whether any useful work at all can be done under such conditions. The only answer is that the experiment has worked. For more than a year, very carefully selected representatives of different levels of society in Germany have been brought together for courses at St. Michael's House. The Christian Faith has been set before them in an atmosphere of fellowship, and in a way which to many of them has proved

[15] Information communicated by Dr. Eberhard Müller.

entirely fresh. The old presentation, and the biblical language used by some of those who have spoken to them, have left them entirely unmoved; but the presentation of the Gospel as a way of life relevant to every concern of man, including his social problems, his art, his recreations, has given to many a sense that here is something which at least deserves investigation. Testimony has been borne by a most distinguished German visitor to the astonishing atmosphere of fellowship which he found in the House. Among those who have attended courses have been some who not merely were not Christians, but whose minds had been deliberately and systematically de-Christianized by special Nazi training. Even among these, some have become ardent Christians, and even helpers in the work of the House. Many others have found a home in their local churches. The secret of the work has been the life in common. After all, it was by living with the disciples that our Lord educated them; in the fellowship of a life lived out in mutual trust and service, what were once no more than intellectual categories come to life, and are seen as the revelation of the love of God.[16]

THE LOST COMMUNITY

So far we have been writing mostly about work among those who, though now alienated from the Church, have at one time or another had some connection with it, and retain at least some memory of the Christian Faith. But beyond this circle, there is another circle, and a very wide one, of those who are completely alienated from Christian ideas and traditions, and constitute a mission field in the strict sense of the term. It is among the "proletariat" of the great cities of the West that most representatives of this class are to be found; but there are countries in which the *élite* is more pagan than the masses.

What is to be done about these spirits, which will not come when you do call for them? Of what spiritual needs, if any, are they still conscious? What access can the Church find to the lost sheep, which shows no marked consciousness that it is lost?

From all quarters comes the cry that the great evil wrought by industrialization is the destruction of community. Many of those most concerned about the welfare of the Church put the

[16] Information communicated by the Rev. S. Goodchild and others.

recovery of community in the very foreground of the evangelistic plan.

THE IONA COMMUNITY

Best known of all these modern communities is that founded in 1938 on the island of Iona in Scotland, from which in the sixth century Saint Columba carried the Gospel to the mainland. To this we can give only a little space, not because it is unimportant, but because it is already well known and information about it is available in many places.

The founder, a leading minister of the Church of Scotland, was moved by three considerations—deeply experienced and felt—that the Church has almost entirely lost its hold on the working classes, that it has done so because its ministers speak to that class from outside, and that the breach can be healed only as those who are to be ministers of the Gospel learn to live and work with working people. Members of the community, consisting half of theological students or young ministers, and half of artisans, spend the summer months on Iona, leading a life of discipline and prayer, and engaged in the rebuilding of the ruined medieval abbey. In the winter they return to their ordinary work. The simple rule of the community lays stress on three points—prayer, the use of time and the use of money. There can be no question, as with a regular community, of common possession of goods; but each member is expected to accept a standard rate of expenditure, to keep careful accounts and to justify any personal expenditure beyond the generally accepted rate.

During the winter months, the work of the community spreads out in many directions in the parishes. One of its most important activities is the Community Home in Glasgow. Here the Christian Faith is taught, not as an intellectual abstraction, but as something which is related to man in society. The young people are taught to think politically, as responsible members of a society, and industrially, as workers with others in great enterprises. They are shown that, as children of God, they have rights of which perhaps previously they were unaware, and that a new order in industry can be brought into being, if employers and workers together can see their tasks as part of their Christian obedience to God.

At one burning point, Iona is tackling the problem of communication. It is becoming a commonplace among evangelists that those of the younger generation are less susceptible than their fathers to the influence of the spoken word. This raises the question whether the Church has not to learn again from its own experience in the Middle Ages, and to use the drama far more than it has done for centuries as a means for imparting a religious truth. What is important in the Iona experiment is that the young people interested do not act plays written by other people for their benefit, they write and act their own plays out of the heart of their own conviction and experience. The same method is followed by the group called " Religion through Drama ". Experience has confirmed the initial conviction that men are most willing to take the trouble to explore the meaning of the faith, when they want to do something and to express something.[17]

CIMADE

" Cimade's " greatest originality is the way in which it was born and grew as an emergency organization with no definite method or limits and just one aim: to bring the Gospel to the most stricken among the victims of the war.

In the autumn of 1939 the five Protestant Youth Movements of France decided to do something together for the evacuees from the East of the country dispersed in the West, and the first teams set at work during the winter. War events put an end to this work in May 1940.

In the autumn of that same year terrible rumours began to spread about the conditions of the concentration camp of Gurs, where 15,000 to 20,000 Jews and foreigners lived crowded together in barracks surrounded by barbed wire. Cimade had no money, only good will and a great determination that something had to be done. Madeleine Barot, after weeks of daily struggle with the director of the camp, got permission to occupy one of the barracks. Two members of the Cimade settled within the barbed wire camp, organizing Bible study and worship and a circulating library. They made clear from the beginning that they were " l'Assistance protestante " and that they came to share what they had: the Gospel. As time went on they were used by several relief agencies but kept always their evangelistic pur-

---

[17] Information in the *Coracle*, the magazine of the Community, and in other works published by its members.

pose. As months and years passed by, the work was extended to other camps; hostels for refugees were created; during the tragic period of the deportations the young teams of Cimade workers battled day and night to save as many lives as they could, and helped hundreds of men and women over the Swiss and Spanish borders. Those who saw them take such risks wondered why they did it, and were told that it was done in the name and for the sake of Christ. This was for many the point of departure of a personal decision for Christ.

In the post-war period work was started in the bombed areas of Northern France, Normandy and Alsace. The prisoners in the camps were freed, but needed help to readjust themselves to life; homes were created to receive them. Their place in camps and jails was taken by their former persecutors: they, too, needed the Gospel and Cimade set to work amongst them. The government having decided to try to reform its penitentiary system, the Cimade was asked to co-operate. It now has in twenty-seven stations, eighty-four full-time workers and one half-time worker. About a third of these are foreigners (American, Swiss, Swedish, German, Roumanian), and belong to different churches (Lutheran, Calvinist, Methodist, Baptist, Orthodox), so this has become a true ecumenical piece of work in personnel as well as finances.

What are the characteristics of this work?

1. First it is not so much an organization as a living body of people, ever ready to experiment and meet emergencies.

2. It is made up of young people (the average age is twenty-five) who for two years or more leave their professional work or their studies to consecrate this time to Evangelism.

3. These are generally untrained workers, a small number only coming from Theological schools or women's schools of training for religious workers, who come to Cimade before entering into their life's work as Pastors or church workers.

4. They work always in teams of two or more, so as to be the nucleus of a community in the *milieux* in which they live.

5. They share as much as possible the conditions of life of the people to whom they bring their witness: during the war they lived in concentration camps, they are within the walls of prisons, they plant their barracks among ruins in devastated areas. The problems, the hardships of material conditions of those they approach, they bear also.

6. They keep in mind the fact that the Salvation given by our Lord is for the whole of man, therefore they must be ready to serve human beings in all aspects of life, material, moral and spiritual.

7. Enough initiative is given to the workers to find for themselves the method of evangelism which will be best suited to their specific work. No set rule is given for them to follow except to be faithful to their witness.

8. Cimade tries to be a community where each feels spiritually responsible for the general work, and where all are associated in its development. This is made possible by biennial meetings when all the workers come together for a period of eight to ten days to unite in worship and Bible study, to discuss together the various aspects of their work and to make plans for the future.

INDUSTRIAL CHAPLAINS IN SCOTLAND

If the working man will not come to listen to the parson where he preaches, can the parson go to the working man where he works? The Church of Scotland has proved that in many cases he can. During the war, the experiment was made of attaching Industrial Chaplains to great works, where managements and men were willing. From a small beginning, this has grown to a great enterprise. To-day there are more than 250 such chaplains, almost all of whom are parish ministers, who voluntarily undertake the care of this "other parish". What the working man appreciates above all is absolute sincerity and simplicity; where these are found, it is only a matter of time for the chaplain to find his way into the confidence and respect of the workers. Usually it takes time, quite a long time, before factory services and discussion groups can be instituted. But long before that, the chaplain finds himself consulted on personal problems and difficulties. And contacts made inside the walls of the factory can be followed up outside it. It cannot be said that great results have as yet been attained in increased church membership, but there is already the beginning of a changed attitude to the Church. The workers know that the Church of Scotland desires to be the Church of the Scottish people.[18]

---

[18] Information communicated by the Rev. William Bodin.

An ex-Moderator of the Church of Scotland says: "In speaking to these men, I never approached them as though they were heathen. Almost all of them have been baptized or have had their children baptized; on the whole they prefer to be married in church. The connection with the Church may be only very remote. But that is our starting-point; we must help them to realize the meaning of the thing that they are dimly and half unconsciously holding on to." He was speaking of Scotland. There, though the process of secularization has gone far, it has still left a certain Christian temper and outlook, the last relic of that deep penetration of the Scottish spirit by the theology of Calvin and of the Shorter Catechism. But there are other countries in which the secularizing process has gone much further.

LA FRANCE, PAYS DE MISSION?

A good deal of attention has been drawn lately to a book called *La France, Pays de Mission?*,[19] a penetrating and serious study of the religious state of France coming from a Roman Catholic source. This is only one of a whole series of similar studies, Roman Catholic and Protestant, which probably give us fuller and more reliable information about contemporary France than about any other country. But, with certain modifications for local conditions, a great deal of what is written in these books can be applied to other countries also. From the point of view of the churches, the picture is far from encouraging; it reveals a state of things in which very much less than half the population has any regular connection with any Church or any place of worship, and in which the stratum furthest removed from the Church lives in what really can be described as paganism. One survey reckons the following external marks as indicative of this pagan condition—that the children remain unbaptized, that civil marriage rather than religious is the rule, and that moral restraints, if any, are social and not religious in their sanctions. In some areas, the mental climate is conditioned by anti-Christian ideologies, such as communism, or by traditional anti-clericalism. Even where this is not so, suspicion of the Church is deep-rooted, and any approach by the Church to these classes has to meet with many initial difficulties. Reports from all quarters indicate that at no point

[19] By H. Godin and Y. Daniel, Paris 1943.

and in no country has the Church been able to make a break through on a large scale into this lost country.

One of the difficulties is that the Church presents itself to the working class as incurably bourgeois. In a way this is inevitable; the bourgeois virtues of diligence, thrift, sobriety and caution are also Christian virtues. When the outcast is converted, he begins to take on the habits and colouring of the Christian society in which he has begun to move. So when the visitor from the non-Christian zone happens to make his way to a church, he finds himself at once drenched and dismayed by a bourgeois atmosphere, which he dislikes and distrusts and in which he cannot find himself at home.

An acute French Roman Catholic observer deplores the separation which results: "We priests have a culture which is bourgeois. From whatever origin we may come, our studies in the minor and major seminaries, our studies of philosophy and theology rapidly transport us into another climate, which is not exactly that of the bourgeoisie, but is closely related to it. The Abbé Godin, who came from the working classes, used to relate that when he returned from the seminary and renewed contact with his old friends, they made him realize, to his sorrow, but as he realized rightly, that he was not like them, that he was no longer one of them." The same writer continues by analysing the causes and the nature of this subtle difference: "The man of education reasons about his actions; at the lowest, he has made himself a little philosophy of existence with the help of some principles accepted by his intelligence. The world of the people acts on impulse, in which sentiment plays the principal part. The world of the people in the great cities of the present day acts according to certain materialistic aphorisms, which for it represent wisdom: 'Must take your chance when you can.' 'There aren't many good moments in life; it's silly not to enjoy yourself when you can.' Materialistic but also revolutionary, the latter type being summed up in the phrase 'You've got to defend yourself'. The man of education is proud of his critical spirit; he likes to discuss what he hears or what he reads; the last thing in the world he wants to do is to think like everyone else. The world of the people, on the contrary, thinks collectively. The opinion of the great world is its opinion and it acts accordingly. . . . The true description of this is absence of personal ideas, absence of principles, and therefore conformity to the manner of thinking current in a man's surroundings, whether it be his place of work, or the place where he spends his spare time or the sphere of his political activity. . . . Man does not possess a clearly marked personality of his own. . . . The man of education, in making judgments, starts from certain absolutes, which serve him as criteria. In the world of the people, everything, including morality, is a matter of opinion. 'Everyone has his own ideas' is the most common formula. Furthermore, ideas have no validity; you act as you can or as you like; 'after all, a man's free, isn't he?' This instinct for liberty comes partly from the revolutionary temper, but partly from the teaching of the secularized schools, which had no universal basis . . . there remains the confused idea that everything is true or false according to the point of view, and finally that 'it's all rot, anyway'."[20] This analysis could probably be confirmed from many sources. One correspondent, who has recently exchanged the life of a university student for that of a factory hand, informs us that the thing that troubles him is the incapacity of his fellow-workers to think or to reason. It is possible to be convinced that what has brought the West to disaster is its over-emphasis on intellectual values, its desertion of biblical realism for the intellectualism of the Greeks, and among the Greeks its preference for Aristotle as against Plato, and yet to feel that the complete divorce of the great mass of the people from any strictly intellectual process is a great hindrance in the way of its recovery of Christian conviction and Christian standards.

POST-CHRISTIAN PAGANISM

All those who have striven with this great mass of post-Christian paganism are agreed that it can be reached only from within. The failure of the Church has been in incarnation; it has not been the body of Christ among the poor and downtrodden; the Gospel has not been preached as good news to the poor. For this the Church cannot be held altogether to blame. The blizzard of the Industrial Revolution swept upon it at, from the Church's point of view, the worst possible moment. During the eighteenth century, while the Industrial Revolution was gathering momentum, the Church in every country was sunk in a lethargy of complacency and spiritual ineffectiveness. The

[20] Paroisse, Communauté missionnaire, by Père Chéry O.P., Paris 1945.

great revivals of the late eighteenth and early nineteenth century came in time to palliate the evil, but by that time the secular revolution had travelled far ahead of the religious. The organization of the Church was medieval and rural; in the countryside of Brittany and the Tyrol, it has held its own. But it had no machinery suddenly to change over to meet the demands of the enormous aggregations of men, displaced persons we may almost call them, in the new industrial cities. In circumstances such as these, it is not surprising that the great masses of the working class lost all touch with the Church, that enterprises such as the Salvation Army and the MacAll Mission in Paris could not do more than touch the fringe of the problem, and that our fathers and grandfathers have left to us a burden under which the most apostolic spirit may well stagger. Now, a hundred years too late, the Church has to learn afresh the meaning of incarnation, to follow Christ in the desperate adventure of His complete self-identification with the sons of men in their poverty, sinfulness and alienation from God.

The first step in self-identification is understanding, and that understanding cannot be won outside the world of the alienated. What this means is illuminated for us by the noble words of one, a distinguished evangelist, who has set forth for us his experiences of what it meant to put himself alongside those whom he desired to win for Christ. "Understand that, at the same time as I was holding, in all sincerity, as the word of God, the truths commanded to be held by the strongest faith, I was also, by methodical doubt, pushed by an act of will to the point of the absolute abandonment of that faith, endeavouring to weigh the value of the moral or religious attitude of those whom I was meeting. I put into the effort all the sympathy I could draw from my fellowship with Jesus Christ. . . . I will not deny that I had bad times. It cost me nothing to get rid of the mental and moral habits of the bourgeoisie, and to adopt attitudes nearer to the mentality of the working class and to the demands of justice; that cost nothing but remorse that I had not done it earlier, and anxiety lest even now I was not carrying it sufficiently far in practice. It did cost me dear to withdraw myself, even provisionally, outside the world of the faith in order to think from other points of view, to submit myself to other lordships than that of Jesus Christ, to put out the light of the Gospel and to see the world as a pagan sees it, thus finding myself without hope because without God in the world. . . . This kind of double existence . . . had the effect of setting up in the depths of my soul the conflict between the world and the faith, between paganism and Christianity, of dividing me, and threatening me with ruin."[21]   Others who have made the same experiment have not found the same forceful words in which to express their experiences; but the experiment of mental adjustment is one which has to be made by every true missionary.   Without becoming as a Jew, it is impossible to win the Jew; but the becoming is always costly and indeed perilous.

This identification in sympathy does not involve necessarily identification with a particular party or with one single programme of social action; it reserves to itself the right to criticize the very people that it desires to win, to see their follies and weaknesses as clearly as their virtues.   There are Christians who have felt it right to join political parties of the left or near-left; others have found this incompatible with their loyalty to Christ. The true attitude of the Church is that expressed by the Whitby Conference of the International Missionary Council—complete identification with the needs of the people, and complete detachment in relation to their desires.

The problem of evangelism may also be expressed as that of natural contact.   To know the workers, it is necessary to live among them and to love them.   Some have found that the best way is to work with them in the shops and factories as ordinary workers, earning their own living just as others do, perhaps at the first concealing their Christian faith and their clerical character.   A number of Roman Catholic priests in France have served in this way with the approval of their bishops.   One Capuchin brother, who, after a considerable time in the factory and after being fully accepted into the workers' fellowship, revealed to his companions the fact that he was a monk, received the not unfriendly answer: "Oh, well, why not?   Everyone has the right to be an idiot in his own way."   It may be taken as almost certain that there are fields for evangelization to which access is impossible in any other way.   On the other hand, it is clear that this cannot be the vocation of everyone, and there is perhaps a growing consensus of opinion that anything which suggests concealment may arouse in the workers, who have their own special sensitiveness, a resentment, a feeling of having been

---

[21] *Enquetes sur les valeurs spirituelles à Paris*, pp. 116 et 117.

got at, which may take away all the advantage gained by natural-
ness in contacts at the start.

From the slums of Marseilles comes a moving account of the
work of two priests, living in poverty and in the closest proximity
to the life of the very poor:

"For some time I have had a companion, a brother in
religion, who finds himself very quickly at home in the life of
the alley. . . . My companion goes to work in the docks, and
is seen alternately in his white robe and in overalls. No one
is astonished. One neighbour explains to the others: 'You
see, my dear, the little Father (as he is called to distinguish
him from me) has finished his studies, and now he wants to
work in order to understand the miseries of the poor.' Taking
advantage of the extensive liberty granted during the period
of war, the Father has obtained the Bishop's permission to say
his Mass in the evening. Several times already I had said
Mass in my room. If too many people were expected, the bed
and the stove were put out into the courtyard, and the Supper
of the Lord was celebrated on the table at which my neighbours and I regularly took our meals. . . . Whether you
approve or not, how near all felt themselves to the Jesus of the
Gospels! But I had never celebrated my Mass at home as
regularly as my companion, since it is quite impossible for
him to celebrate in the morning before leaving for his work.
In the evening, however, a few people always drop in, and
sometimes those who for one reason or other do not feel themselves worthy to take part in the sacrifice send their proxies
in the shape of flowers which they have bought expressly for
the purpose, beautiful real flowers from the flower-shop. But
more beautiful than the flowers are the genuflections, correctly made but laborious, of this priest, who has worked hard
all day in the docks, and whose gestures bear the mark of all
the loads that he has carried."[22]

In such an enterprise we feel ourselves very near to the heart
of the original Gospel. Before we can hope to see results on
the large scale, we must look for the multiplication of such small
groups of those who are able to live, to learn and to love within
what has been so long a closed land to the Church. The break-

[22] M.-R. Loew: *En mission prolétarienne*, Paris.

through is slow and costly. Is any other method available by which it can be achieved?

THE RECOVERY OF COMMUNITY

Many people in many countries are enquiring about the right method of presentation of the Gospel to the de-Christianized proletariat in the post-Christian West. The answer is that no one knows. Methods of evangelism in the non-Christian world have been intensively studied for a hundred and fifty years. The study of this new and difficult mission-field has scarcely begun. All that can be reported at present is the experience of some pioneers, with their insistence that the first duty of the Church is to listen before it speaks, and to understand the nature of the soil in which the Word of God is to be sown before it launches out on extensive sowing.

If the break-through is achieved, even on a small scale, it ought to result in the formation of a Christian community, in the place where people live, and within the framework of the natural community. Chaplaincy work in shops and factories is useful and admirable, but it can never take the place of the parish, the Christian community based on the natural links of propinquity, common interest and mutual trust. And where is that basis to be found in the modern industrial town, or, still more, in the suburbs inhabited by the respectable class of the clerks and the better-paid artisans, a class almost as de-Christianized as the proletariat, though in a different way? Yet even in the most atomized human society, there are vestiges of community. If it is no more than by going week by week to the same grocer's shop, people do become aware of one another, and do begin to establish some kind of relationship; there must the Church begin to find its opportunity. As in the mission-field, traditionally so called, so in the modern mission-field, the great danger lies in taking the Christian out of his environment. The one criticism we have received of the great Roman Catholic movement, Jeunesse Ouvrière Chrétienne, is that the interest of its members tends to be found in their branch of the movement and not in the place where they live and work. So begins the process of detachment, of bourgeois adaptation, which may make the young Christians admirable Christians, but renders them so much the less useful as evangelists to their fellows.

The absolute necessity of a Christian community, conscious of itself as a family and in the place where its members live, has been well set forth in the classic work on the subject *La France, Pays de Mission?* (pp. 147-8):

> " If in a garrison town, one collected the Christians from a dozen regiments or barracks, distributed according to the letters of the alphabet in a dozen communities, one would have Christian communities which might become extremely fervent and produce saints, but they would not become in each environment a radiating nucleus, because they would not correspond to natural communities. One would have strong and victorious Christian personalities, helping certain brothers, but seen from the interior of the barracks, they would present a certain appearance of Protestant individualism. . . . It seems that the task of a genuinely Catholic popular mission would be to discover all the natural human communities which exist, and to form in each of them, with the aid of a priest, a Christian nucleus which would become a radiating community."

In a Protestant setting, a few words and phrases of this account might have to be altered, but has not the statement of the problem and of the method by which alone it can be solved a certain right of reality and truth? In so far as the Church can be said to have been successful in the recovery of lost ground, it seems to have been by the rebuilding of the sense of community through a Christian group, which was in the first place a worshipping community.

THE RETURN OF THE INTELLECTUAL ÉLITE

We should lose perspective in this survey if we allowed it to be supposed that the very poor are the most extensively de-Christianized class. Our Lord said that it was hard for the rich to enter into the Kingdom of Heaven, which is a very different thing from saying that it is hard for them to become respectable. They do, but that does not make them citizens of the Kingdom of Heaven. In the last resort it is the intellectual *élite* which makes the mind of a nation, though it may take long for the thoughts of the *élite* to penetrate the mind of the common man. One of the most serious factors in the Christian situation for many years has been the almost complete isolation of the intellectual world from the faith and practice of the Church. For some time, there have been welcome signs that a change is taking place. One well qualified to judge has hazarded the opinion that " as the *élite* were the first to go, perhaps they will be the first to come back ". It is not possible for man to live for long on nihilism. As we saw, the almost desperate question of the young educated people of the world is: " Is there anything else except nihilism? " If the Church, especially through the voice of laymen, can show plainly that there is something else, and that it has been won as painfully, and with as desperate determination to know nothing but the truth, as any modern ideology, then there is good hope that some at least of the younger generation will be found ready to listen and to embark on the dangerous adventure of taking the Christian Faith seriously.

AN ILLUSTRATION FROM GREECE

The separation of the intellectuals from the faith tends to be at its apogee in countries where the Church is served by an uneducated priesthood and the schools and universities have been secularized. To a large extent both these conditions have been experienced in Greece. The village priesthood, faithful as it was in its vocation, had had little chance of theological education, and in many cases knew little more than the ritual and the music of the Mass. Schools and universities had been under a dominantly secular and unbelieving influence. One of the most remarkable evangelistic enterprises that has come to our notice is the statement on the relations between science and religion put forth by a body of Greek men of science. Put in crude language, the burden of this document is that it is not necessary to be an ignoramus in order to be a Christian. This is a discovery which has been made in other countries also, but in Greece it came with the force of a new revelation. Many thousands of copies of the document have been circulated, both in Greece and in Cyprus, and there is no doubt that its effect on the minds of many readers has been profound. These Greek scientists naturally owed much to the writings of their colleagues in other countries who were Christians. But their effort was independent and not called forth by any impetus from without; much of its value resided in its completely non-clerical character.

To the intellectual world it is nearly always the layman who can speak with the greatest force and the greatest power of carrying conviction.[23]

THE CONVENTIONAL CHRISTIAN

Last of all, what are we to say of that large class, the nominal Christians who know the Gospel but have never experienced it as regenerating love, who have the form of godliness but deny the power thereof? In an earlier document sent out by our commission, this class is spoken of in terms on which we find ourselves unable to improve:

"These are the people who have made terms with the Gospel, without surrendering to its demands, who satisfy themselves that they are Christians by observing its outward forms and evade its more embarrassing requirements by careful attention to those which can be fulfilled without moral unheaval. These people are not merely most recalcitrant to attempts to show them the vanity of their religion in the eyes of God, but are also the greatest obstacle in the way of the evangelization of those who are outside the churches. The unattractiveness of Christianity as seen in them is taken by those outside to constitute the final condemnation of Christianity in all its forms."

We must not yield to the temptation to exaggerate in our condemnation of these conventional and lifeless Christians. After all, the strength of their position lies just in the fact that their claims for themselves are so largely true. It is their regular attendance at Church which has kept the structure of the Church in being, where otherwise it would have disintegrated. It is their financial support which has enabled the Church to struggle on, at least to maintain a ministry and regular worship as a witness to men that there is a reality beyond the visible world. Within the rather narrow limits of what they regard as obligatory, they have maintained a remarkably high ethical standard; their virtue is not all hypocrisy, their profession of loyalty to Christ is not all affectation. It is much more the reality of their goodness than the perfection of their hypocrisy which

[23] Information communicated by Prof. G. Bratsiotis, Athens.

makes them almost impregnable against the assaults of the real Gospel of Christ. It is far harder for the pride of fallen man to accept the forgiveness of God for his virtues than to submit to God's judgment on his sins.

And after all, the congregations are very much what the clergy have made them. For the most part, the clergy have been content to preach traditional dogma unrelated to the pressure of contemporary perplexities, or a moralism severely conditioned by the accepted standards of a quasi-Christian society. In neither case has the Gospel as preached by them borne much relation to the explosive variety proclaimed in Galilee and sealed on Calvary. Our complacent Christian congregations would be very gravely disturbed by the thought that God might really put down the mighty from their seat and exalt the humble and meek. They find it hard to imagine that anyone can take seriously the proposition that a man's life consisteth not in the abundance of the things that he possesseth. In the Protestant churches, they have not had too many examples before their eyes of those who venture all on taking the Gospel seriously. Even in Roman Catholic countries, where the existence of monasticism might serve as a daily challenge to consider what the Gospel really demands of men and women, the tendency is to suppose that the monk and the nun have made their sacrifice not in order to challenge ordinary Christians to make the perfect surrender of themselves to Christ in the terms and under the conditions of their own vocation, but just in order that, sacrifice being concentrated as it were by proxy in one part of the Church, the other part might be exempted from the disturbing necessity of accepting the totalitarian demands of Christ.

EVANGELISM, AN ECUMENICAL TASK

Without the conversion of the Church, world-evangelism cannot be more than a name. If anything has stood out clearly in the course of this long study, it is that evangelism is weak, when it depends on the devotion and initiative of a gifted individual. It is unfruitful until it has incarnated itself in a community. It can be effective according to the will of God only where it is the Church itself, the whole company of faithful people, which is the evangelizing instrument, since it is only the whole Church which can bring the Gospel gloriously out of the church building and the cloistered calm of the sanctuary into every corner and crevice of that world which, by the grace of God, has already been redeemed through Christ, and has to be brought in fact and in reality into the realm of that redemption.

The Church cannot become the evangelizing body until it recovers New Testament Christianity. What that would mean is the business of this whole volume, indeed of all the Assembly volumes, to set forth. Here attention may be drawn, in the context of evangelism, to two points which might in other connections be overlooked.

The early Church was ecumenical in its outlook. It took it for granted that this Gospel was to be preached throughout the world, and that where Christ had given so clear a command, He could be relied on to supply the means. But it also recognized that ecumenical Christianity meant the acceptance of the local Christian brother across all the difficulties and divisions of race, habit and background. The effort was so great that it strained the grace of God to the utmost and nearly broke the Church in two; but in the end the Jewish Christian did what he had thought impossible and accepted the Gentile as really a brother in Christ; and the Gentile got over his horror of circumcision and was willing to sit at the table of the Lord with the Jew. The Christian of New Testament times took it for granted that where he went the local fellowship of Christians was his home and that he must seek for no other. Modern Christianity has not even begun to be ecumenical. The ordinary worshipping congregation in a European city does not consciously rejoice in the fellowship of the Eskimo and the Sea Dyak; in fact, if the Eskimo or the Sea Dyak, in natural attire and bringing with him his characteristic atmosphere, were to come in and sit down beside it, the congregation might show signs of perturbation and distaste. The Christian stranger in a foreign land does not take it as a matter of course that he will seek out whatever Christian fellowship may happen to be there and make it his home, even if it involves sitting on the ground with humble African or Indian Christians. It must be emphasized that until acceptance of the fellow-Christian and self-identification with the fellow-Christian, whatever his race or habits, and still more difficult, whatever his denomination, is taken for granted, we have not really begun to be Christian; we have not reached the standing-ground from which evangelism becomes a serious possibility.

Evangelism is the proclamation of the death of Christ. It would be well if the churches would take seriously the apostolic teaching as to the place and the means by which the Lord's death is principally and indispensably to be proclaimed. *As often as ye eat this bread and drink the cup, ye proclaim the Lord's death till he come.* Holy Communion every Sunday for every Christian, except those formally excommunicated, was the rule and practice of the Church. Proclamation of the Gospel on any other basis was unthinkable. One of the great Reformation insights was the recovery of this principle. The Reformation broke on the obstinate adherence of the people to the medieval deformation of Christian worship, and their refusal to be guided by the Word of God. To-day there is no Church in the world (except some of the smaller pietistic bodies) which can claim that it is showing forth in doctrine and practice anything that even faintly resembles New Testament Christianity. Recovery of New Testament doctrine and New Testament order are highly important things, and rightly engage the attention of the learned. But perhaps we have got the order wrong; perhaps a little experiment in New Testament obedience might not be out of place. If the churches were to make the few simple changes in their order which would be involved in this return to the New Testament, and would accept the universal obligation of the sacramental proclamation of the Lord's death every Sunday by His Church, the results might be surprising. The churches might discover that, without knowing how, they had again become the body of Christ. They might find that the hidden forces of evangelism had broken through, and that it was once more within their power to show forth Christ as the Saviour of the World.

VI

THE APPROACH TO ADHERENTS OF OTHER FAITHS

PREFACE

As has been indicated in the preface to Section I, the old distinctions between the Christian and non-Christian world have largely broken down. Yet there is a difference in the approach to the man who has never heard of Christ at all, and that to the man whose outlook has to some extent been conditioned by upbringing in a partially Christian country. In this section we have attempted to indicate the problem of approach in three widely different religious areas.

The approach to Israel is the standing challenge to the Christian Church. Do Christians who have Jewish neighbours expect and desire that these Jewish neighbours will become Christians? If not, have they any right to claim an interest in evangelism elsewhere? The problem of Israel in God's purpose and of the future of the Jews in the world are controversial in the extreme, and on many matters there may be legitimate difference of view among Christians. But if we hold that Christ died for all men, and that His Gospel is to be preached to all nations, the proclamation of the Gospel to Israel stands out as an absolute obligation from which the Church must not try to escape.

1

(a) ASPECTS OF THE MODERN SITUATION IN INDIA

by S. W. Savarimuthu

THIS paper has been written in Sweden, after an absence of more than six months from India. In the swirl of change statements here made may already be questioned: and a picture true to-day may "date" before the Assembly of the World Council of Churches in August, 1948. We can but try to indicate some permanent elements in the approach of the Christian evangelist to adherents of the higher religions in the modern world.

I THE EFFECT OF NATIONALISM AND INDEPENDENCE ON CHRISTIAN PROPAGANDA

"Propaganda" is a good Christian word lately corrupted in secular use. It is better to regard our task as "evangelism" rather than as "propaganda". "Evangelism" is biblical, Christian; as comprehensive as Christianity itself.

Again the word "Evangelist" in certain sections of the "mission-field" has come to mean the paid agent of a particular mission, more or less qualified for the task, who speaks to a small or large group for some time and is then at liberty to do other jobs. What he does elsewhere should not, he desires, be mixed up with what he means to say in his evangelistic message; and the group he addresses, he feels, is a loose crowd who should be taken as individuals and nothing more.

This is, in fact, a veritable inflation of the "coins minted in the New Testament". Evangelism is the "preaching", the *kerugma*, of the word of faith by a representative of the Spirit-filled community to men and women who are not yet "united by faith with them that heard" (Heb. iv, 2).

It follows that the work of the evangelist is part of the total impact of the Christian community on the entire environment of men who have not yet accepted the evangel in faith.

Similarly, the adherents of the higher religions are first of all men and women, individuals, centres of consciousness. But they live and move and have their being in a circle that includes, within its ambit, aspects which seem incongruous and inconsistent, but are taken into a living unity. They are a people, an historic society, with "a local habitation and a name", a language that both conserves and expresses their thought and life, religious, social, and political.

Nationalism in India is another complex whole. It is as broad and deep as Indian life in general. Now one aspect, now another comes to the conscious level, but at bottom it is a unity in variety. The emphasis, in increasing intensity, has long been on the political struggle to express itself against British Imperialism. Since that struggle has won its legitimate victory, other phases of the national urge begin to manifest themselves, clearly or vaguely, gently or with violence.

The religious revival, which has been long pent up, occasionally spurting out, is now gaining momentum as it takes step after step. The ramifications of this religious nationalism can be traced by the vigilant eye in almost every aspect of Indian life.

In education, for instance, English, which was the first language and the chief medium of instruction, is now fast giving place to the mother tongue, even up to the university standard. When Tamil becomes the medium of instruction, it brings in its wake all that the Tamils have stood for, politically, socially, culturally, and not the least in religion during four or more millennia. There was a time when the Christian boys of a mission school complained, after a period in Tamil language, that the Tamil pandit was saying things which went directly against what the Christian master had taught them in the preceding Scripture class. Now, not only the English language, which both conserves and expresses Christianity, is pushed into the background, but its place is "occupied" by Tamil.

Roughly it may be said that what English is to the Britisher, Tamil is to the Tamilian. Those who know the two languages with some real understanding will be able to gauge the depth and significance of the effect of replacing English by Tamil on Christian evangelism. What has been vague during the days of nationalism is now effectually achieved and enforced as a result of political independence; and scripture teaching is steadily being banned from the regular school hours.

A reverse process is at work. Most of the place names in South

India which were wrongly pronounced and ill spelt by the Englishman changed their pronunciation and spelling: e.g. Tirunelvaly became Tinnevelly, Nagapattinam became Nagapatam. Now there is a return to the beautiful old and meaningful names. This may be regarded as a sort of paradigm for almost everything that concerns evangelism in independent India.

Education in general and women's education in particular has been largely the outcome of the pioneer work of the Christian missionaries. Time was when missionaries and Indian Christians were the leaders in all educational matters. The pioneering work of Christians has awakened the non-Christians to such an extent that they are not merely in the vanguard but would scarcely, if ever, give room for Christian leadership.

The religious revival, cultural renaissance, and social revolution set in motion by the direct or indirect impact of the Christion enterprise in India have gone so far that many would not only discount their debt to Christianity, but also assert that they could very well do without it. The Harijan Movement started by Mahatma Gandhi may be traced, with some justification, to his fear of the dangerous possibility of the masses of the oppressed and depressed classes of India moving away from Hinduism and into the Christian Church as they were already beginning to do in hundreds of thousands. Most of the social and economic disabilities of these castes are fast being removed by the government now in power both in the provinces and in the Centre. The Christian who was once an untouchable is led to think that his present position is not after all any better, materially, than that of his social compeer outside the Church. A few have been reconverted to Hinduism with the help and approval of men of higher castes and positions.

The religious resurgence has been such that they not only study and imitate the missionary methods of the Christians but they seek to improve on them. Formerly the Danish Mission Reading-Room and the Kellett Institute were the only two public halls in Madras where lectures on religion and social subjects were delivered. Speakers aspiring to a public hearing sought the favour of men in charge of these halls for trying their mettle in the art of public-speaking. But to-day there are more than ten such places where regular meetings are held on various subjects by men of ability. And it is hard to get these men to speak in our halls, and few attend such lectures when delivered under our auspices.

They study, imitate and improve upon the Christian and literary societies, issue books of all sorts and prices. If the Christian issues a diary with a Bible verse for each day, the Tamilian issues a diary with a Kural couplet for each day! Examples could be multiplied. The Annammalai University in Chidambaram is eclipsing the Nataraja temple in the town by aspiring to become the cultural centre of the Tamil country.

Enough has been said to show that the dormant spirit of nationalism, awakened and confirmed by political independence, is now expressing itself in many ways. This is bound to hamper those who seek to approach the adherents of the higher religions with the Word of the Gospel.

II JESUS THE TEACHER

Educated Indians and adherents of higher religions, have doubtless evinced a keen interest in, and a deep appreciation of, "the teaching of Christ". Multitudes in India, as in Palestine, have been "astonished at His teaching". But they did not go even so far as the Jews did when they knew that "He taught them as one having authority, and not as the scribes".

Adherents of higher religions in India, perhaps elsewhere, too, have not recognized the compelling authority of the Master, because they have not been taught to contrast His teaching with the ethical codes of their own law-givers—a Thiruvalluvar, a Manu or a Chanakya. In other words, they have not been taught to proceed from the "teaching" to the divine-human personality of the Teacher, Who teaches with authority, and *not* as their scribes, a Yajnavalkya, a Shankara or a Ramanuja. The good in this case, as in others, has been the enemy of the better.

Excessive concentration on the teaching of Christ has led them to believe that they could have the Law without the Gospel, ethics without Faith. From their pre-suppositions it is not surprising that they not only "compared" Christian ethics with their own but even asserted that theirs are better. It is only natural that to them Christ *is one among the many*. The decisive challenge of *the One* still remains to be faced. Both Christian theology and evangelism and the characteristic Hindu view of religion have been responsible for this result. Christ, or rather,

Jesus of Nazareth may be acclaimed as a Mahatma, a superman, a religious genius, or an Avatar. He may be even a god, but he cannot be worshipped as " My Lord and my God ".

This phenomenon may be viewed from another angle. When Christ is presented as the moral teacher, the Hindu refers to the high morality of the *Kural* of Thiruvalluvar. When Christ is presented as the *Bhagavan* or the Lord who is worthy of our *bhakti* or faith he refers to the *Thiruvasagam* or the *Tevaram*, the *bhakti* literature of the Tamils. The *Kural* looks mainly at the horizontal relationship between God and man without any vital reference to God. (It is open to serious doubt whether the first chapter of the *Kural*, which does contain references to God, is really one with the body of the treatise.) On the other hand, the *Thiruvasagam* and the *Tevaram* are concerned mainly with the vertical relationship between God and man without any living relation to the fellow-man. In Christ the relationship is neither purely nor exclusively horizontal or vertical. When a man is in Christ, he is vertically in contact with God, and horizontally in a relation of loving service to his neighbour. The truth of the relationship is not merely God and I: nor I and my neighbour, but God, I and my neighbour. This is the Law and the Prophets.

From this point of view, one could go on to say that Jesus Christ is the fulfilment of both the *Kural* and the *Thiruvasagam* simultaneously. Nor could one stop there. He is their fulfilment after fulfilling them both together, shattering each in its dangerously one-sided emphasis and pointing to the higher synthesis that is Incarnate in Himself.

An insight into the ethical and religious literature of a particular social group like the Tamils might give us the cue to the kind of religious and theological research which could develop a Christian apologetic, negative and positive.

III " THE AREA OF CONTACT "

The question of the area of contact is as important as it is difficult. Various opinions have been held and as often criticized. One may perhaps be cheered by the reflection that the earlier missionaries established better contact when they were not hampered by stiff theories. But one could presume that they would have been happier to get some working theory which would confirm their practice and in some measure guide their daily work.

It is legitimate and necessary to find points of contact with those whom we want to evangelize. We are certainly nearer to the adherents of the higher religions than to the materialists, or the Lokayatas as they were called in India.

The first point of importance is the fact that all evangelists and hearers are the creatures of God. "O God, Thou hast created us unto Thyself, and our hearts are restless (or unquiet) until they find rest in Thee" (Augustine). Again, "Be comforted, thou wouldst not seek Me hadst thou not found Me. Thou wouldst not have sought Me unless thou hadst possessed me" (Pascal).

Let us try to understand the first statement of Augustine. The relation spoken about is that between the Creator and the creature. The Creator is not only the cause of our restlessness but also its cure. Could we not perhaps restate the sentence somewhat as follows: "O God, Thou hast created us unto Thyself: Thou dost keep our hearts restless until Thou givest us rest." The restlessness of the human heart is not so crudely anthropocentric as is suggested in some quarters. God the Creator is concerned in restoring fallen humanity to its "rest" in Himself. To those of us who have been met by God in the Incarnation of His Son, this fact of God's concern comes with refreshing clarity. "If there is any meaning in it, it means that God wants, even passionately wants, contact with man, and thus through the act of His revelation shows His belief in the possibility of contact. Stronger argument than this for the existence of this point in man there cannot be. The apostolic nature of God's revelation in Christ presupposes it."[1]

A patient and scientific study of the life and writings of more than one non-Christian saint from different religious atmospheres reveals the fact that there is a common humanity, a common capacity for moral and religious experience, effort, achievement and failure, common aspirations, needs and dreads. Nay more, there is not only seeking but also finding, the joy and exultation of having been found of the Lord. It is here that the Christian evangelist must evince an "untiring interest in the religion, the ideas, sentiments and the institutions—in short, in the whole range of the life of the people among whom he works, for Christ's sake and for the sake of the people."[2]

---

[1] H. Kraemer, *The Christian Message*, etc., pp. 130ff.   [2] *Ibid.*, 140.

It is essential to realize a fact of major importance. All the time the Christian evangelist is seeking to establish points of contact with the non-Christian, he is also seeking and finding points of contact with the evangelist and his evangel *in his own way*. It is common experience of those who have attempted to preach the Gospel in India to the adherents of higher Hinduism, that at the end of a talk someone comes to us and says: "Thank you for the message: we have the same idea or truth in our scriptures. So-and-so has said like this," and gives a quotation. The danger lies in the evident conclusion that he has drawn: "All the religions are the same: there is nothing after all so different from mine in yours."

Here, then, the area of contact turns out to be an area of conflict from the "radical" "apostolic" Christian point of view. Every point of contact is surely a beginning only, for the contact may lead to further contact, or it may develop into conflict. From the time the seed is sown to the time of its harvest there are many stages, at any one of which the growth may be thwarted by Satan, by tribulation, or by thorns (Mark iv, 14-20). And it is in one or more of these stages that the "totalitarian" aspect of the religion to which the man belongs conflicts with the total claims of Christ and the system of Christian thought and life. And it is just here that it is most important to remember that, although the man belongs to a religious system, he is still and continues to be a thinking, deciding human being. And with this understanding the Christian should lead him into the wrestle between his personality and that of his Saviour.

Dr. Kraemer makes the missionary the point of contact.[3] "The missionary" should not be made to mean the person sent from Europe or America to India or the East, but the "man with the message" or "the man with the Word". Even so, he should not be considered as an individual, pure and simple. Every Christian is, or ought to be, a source of contact: *actually* he may be—as often he is—a bad ambassador for Christ. But with and beyond the individual Christian, there is the community of Christian believers, the Church, the Body of Christ, of which we are all members.

The task of evangelism and of the evangelist is to be the ambassador for Christ, through the Church, in "announcing" the Gracious Word, to bring the 'hearer into fellowship with

[3] H. Kraemer, *The Christian Message*, etc., p. 140.

God and the faithful. In other words, the real missionary is the Christian Church in which Christ lives and reigns with His saving grace of forgiveness. It is the life of this "fellowship" in joy and in suffering that draws in those outside.

The evangelist who is a member of this fellowship may be used of God to mediate Him to the others. It is essential to realize the humbling fact that we Christians and Christian evangelists more often *hide* God than *reveal* Him. It is our comfort to know that because this treasure is put in earthen vessels, God reveals Himself in our "hiding" Him, so that the glory might belong to God alone.

Contact is, therefore, a work of the Spirit of God. The Holy Spirit always works in a community: "Where two or three are gathered together in my name there am I in the midst." In any case, the Spirit works in more than one person simultaneously. The Spirit moves not only a Cornelius but also a Peter: not only a Saul but also an Ananias. Thus contact is an act of the Spirit of God between two or more persons.

This aspect of the fellowship may be pushed further: In a country like India where the Ashram life has been in practice for several millennia, a Christian Ashram may become a growing point. It is a small group of Spirit-filled Christians, of more than one nationality, perhaps, seeking to live a life of fellowship and to develop a corporate personality, and demonstrating it in life, thought and word, in prayer, meditation and study. It is a church within the Church, growing out of her, supported by her, and serving her as a centre of experiments and demonstrations of the Christian corporate life and seeking to influence the world outside.

The life of the Christian is the Bible of the non-Christian. The life of the Christian Ashram may be the Bible that he who runs may read.

IV THE POINT OF STRESS

The Gospel is one, unchangeable and indivisible. It is committed to us, deposited in the Church, witnessed by the Apostles. We cannot, nay, we shall not add to it or subtract from it. We can only receive it in faith and obey it. And we must go on preaching it.

But the Gospel is too great for us. We with our little minds and lesser hearts could see it only darkly as in a glass. And therefore we could take for ourselves only such aspects or elements of it as we are capable of receiving. It is therefore but natural that in the history of Christian apologetics, now one aspect and now another has been grasped and communicated to others. There is thus a twofold limitation: the limitation of the evangelist, on the one hand, and that of the hearer, on the other.

The stress in the India of the early decades of the present century has been, as has been shown above, on Christ the Teacher. Perhaps that was what the evangelists of the time considered to be the essence of the Gospel or what would "appeal" to the Hindu. The result has been nothing short of disaster.

The point of stress for the preaching of the Gospel in the world of to-day is faith in the Resurrection of Christ, by "God the Father, who raised Him from the dead".

The Hindu or the Moslem has, outside the special revelation in Christ, "understood by the things that are made His eternal power and godhead". This is, indeed, the opening door when the Christian evangelist speaks to him of the God of Power, the God Who raised Christ from the dead. For the non-Christian will or must raise the question: Why from the dead? Then the evangelist presents his Gospel as it developed historically in the life of the Church. From the faith of the Risen Lord backward to the fact of the crucified Saviour—the causes or the events, the purpose that led Him to the Cross; later His miracles and teaching—and lastly the stories concerning His birth. (The Hindu has had no great difficulty in the virgin birth, nor has it been a matter of major theological difficulty to Indian Christians, except for those who have inherited the problem from Western theologians.)

Is not this the order in which the gospels came to be written? Is not the Resurrection the faith of the primitive Church? Is it not here that the Apostle Paul has laid the stress—Faith in the Risen Lord?

When this approach is made there follows in natural sequence, the stress on the Church, the Spirit-filled community, the Society of the forgiven.

The Holy Spirit is the Spirit of the Risen Lord and of God the Father. After His resurrection, Jesus lives and reigns everywhere, but chiefly and dynamically in His Body, the Church. Or, conversely, where Christ is with forgiving grace, there is life and bliss, that is the Church.

M

It is the Church where this faith is to be made dynamic in acts of love (Gal. iv, 6). Wherever this faith is directed inwardly towards God and outwardly towards our neighbour, we are in relation both with God and our neighbour: our "neighbour" includes both those that are of the household of faith and those that stand outside.

(b) THE APPROACH TO ADHERENTS OF A PRIMITIVE RELIGION IN NEW GUINEA

by George F. Vicedom

THERE is no single missionary method which can be applied at all times and in all places. Primitive peoples differ greatly from one another, both in their original characteristics and in their disintegration due to the impact of Western civilization. Missionaries come from various churches and schools of thought, and their missionary methods are often determined by their theology and by the customs of their church at home. In this paper, therefore, I can only describe some experiences of my own among the very backward peoples of New Guinea, in the hope that they may also be of use to missionaries working in a different setting.

I

The following obvious principles of missionary method are, of course, presupposed:

1. The missionary is an ambassador of Christ. Primitive peoples judge the Christian message, and God Himself, by what the missionary says and does. His responsibility is therefore immense.

2. In the person of the missionary primitive people meet a world which is entirely foreign to them. The first thing the missionary has to do, therefore, is to establish a right relation between himself and his hearers. He must meet them on the plane of our common humanity, just as God became man in His Son in order to bridge the gulf between Himself and us.

3. The missionary tries to do this by learning their language as fully as possible, and in his life by trying to adopt their laws and customs as far as the Gospel will allow him to do so. In this way he will become familiar with their way of thinking, and this will enable him to express the Christian message in a way that touches their hearts.

4. He can only apply his message aright, if he himself has thoroughly studied the life and religion of his hearers, and has set them in relation to the Gospel before he begins to preach.

5. In his preaching he must not take 1 Cor. i and ii as his starting-point. These chapters must be understood in the light of chapter xv, 3-4, where we read that Paul's preaching was "according to the scriptures", i.e. was based on the fundamental preaching about God.

6. In all conversions mixed motives play a certain part, especially in the case of mass movements. But God uses even such conversions for His own purpose; and He entrusts His messenger with the task of turning a superficial conversion into something inward and real. There are no real conversions apart from repentance and amendment of life.

7. The missionary must be an "Ambassador of Christ", and not a social reformer. Among primitive peoples bad social conditions are all linked up with their religion. Thus their whole mind and outlook must first of all be transformed by the Word of God; then their elevation in the social scale will follow as a matter of course.

II

The actual problem of finding a point of contact arises first of all in the preaching itself, for the message is strange to the man who hears it. The missionary should begin with something which his hearers already understand, in order to make the new idea comprehensible to them. In making the point of contact, however, there is always the danger that the new message may be understood in the old, heathen terms. The better a missionary learns the language the less danger will there be of this kind of misunderstanding. A further danger is that of making a premature attack upon pagan abuses. This is bound to provoke opposition, because primitive peoples only acknowledge the authority of the particular god to whom they are bound by their origin. "Your God has nothing to do with us! " Further, every "point of contact" is wrong which uses the pagan religion as a logical proof of the rightness of the Christian message. Primitive people instinctively reject this kind of argument. They are guided, not by their heads but by their hearts. The best method is always a simple, sincere, and positive presentation of the message.

Why is this so? It is because God is already in contact with every human being. The missionary can build on what God has already implanted within the human heart, especially the two facts of the religious sense and conscience. The missionary must ask himself: What is the attitude of primitive man to the Numinous? How far is he aware of his "creatureliness"? Has he a certain sense of dependence on the gods? How does he express his sense of need for communion with the higher powers? If we study these questions among primitive peoples we make the surprising discovery that they only have religious contact with those supernatural powers with which they are causally connected, i.e. with the spirits of their ancestors and with the creator-god. Their relation to the other supernatural powers in their religion is more or less confined to magic. So here the missionary has found an important starting-point: he can show his hearers their connection with God, in order to bring them into a religious relation with Him. The more the message is psychologically attuned to the religious attitude of his hearers, the more successful the missionary will be.

Every religion is expressed in conduct, i.e. through the conscience. The missionary must therefore try to touch the conscience of his hearers. This is especially difficult in the case of primitive peoples. There are anthropologists and missionaries who say that these people have no conscience at all, because they can do all kinds of things without any apparent effect upon their conscience, and they behave as if they were innocent lambs! This judgment is mistaken. Their religion only determines their right attitude to their god, and not to men in general, and only to those who are connected with their own god. On the other hand, among primitive peoples there exists a proof which is important for the Christian message. Among all primitive peoples we find commandments which are not unlike the Decalogue. These would not exist unless people had a certain glimmering of moral obligation to their neighbours as well as to their god. Since the lawgiver has been forgotten, the ancestors have become the guardians of these commandments, and that is why they are only kept by their descendants. If we succeed in convincing the conscience of these primitive people that God is the Lawgiver, we have found a second important point of contact.

The commandments are only valid within the tribe. The individual members are so closely related by blood, that they can only take a decision in agreement with the tribe. According to the commandments they are responsible for one another and bound to help one another. Here therefore we have to do with a collective tribal-conscience. Personal freedom and personal decisions exist among primitive peoples only outside the tribe. Anyone who takes a decision against the tribe is expelled from the community united by the tie of blood. This applies also to religious matters. Crimes committed by individuals are regarded as sins of the community. The tribe purifies itself from these sins, if necessary, by driving out the sinner. The worship of primitive peoples is always an affair of the community. Therefore among primitive peoples individual conversions can only take place if the individual leaves his family-clan. In so doing he loses his rights in the primitive community. Mission work among primitive peoples has always suffered from this fact.

The history of modern missions shows us that this difficulty need not exist. Great successes have been achieved when the preaching has been consciously addressed to the collective conscience of the tribe, i.e. when an attempt has been made to convert the tribe as a whole, or when the whole tribe has been brought to God through the witness of individual converts. We can trace this trend in all mass movements among primitive peoples. The Christian message touches the tribal conscience and not so much the conscience of the individual. On the other hand, on Nias, for instance, we can trace a certain arrest in the mass movement, because there the experience of God did not spread from the individual to the conscience of the community.

The missionary approaches the task of restoring the original connection between his listeners and God, by telling them the story of the Creation. This story has proved of inestimable value among primitive peoples. The more fully it is believed (and this soon happens, because God speaks here as Creator), the more the pagan religion is shaken. Primitive people are here confronted by the One God, Who, as Creator, is the Lord of all things, and especially the Lord of man. Through God's act of creation all peoples are of one blood, hence the ancestors and local gods lose their significance. The soul comes from God, so there is no frightening ghost which goes on living among the spirits of the ancestors. God had made all things good—so the old traditions were lies. God as Creator and Lord is the supreme revelation to primitive peoples. In New Guinea I have experienced again and again how His name spread like fire from village to village, and how the story of the Creation became the general topic of conversation among the population.

Through this preaching the primitive idea of God undergoes a fundamental change. The deistically conceived creator-god, far removed from this world, is replaced by the Creator-God and Lord, Who is near and living, Who has become not only the Creator of primitive society but also their Father in Jesus Christ. It is the Fatherhood of God which first of all makes the greatest impression on these primitive people. But this change in their idea of God brings with it a change in their sense of sin. Just because they are so deeply impressed by God's Fatherhood, they realize that their right relation with Him is determined by their right relation to their brothers—sin against one's brother is also sin against the Father. Thus the sphere of conscience is greatly extended; the content of conscience is deepened by the Word, and its standard is given absolute validity by God.

When this change in the idea of God has taken place in the conscience of primitive peoples, the time has come to use the antithetical point of contact. There are plenty of points of contact, of which only a few can be mentioned here. All religions try to solve the problem of death. Primitive man attributes the cause of death either to the spirits (in which case he resigns himself to his fate) or to evil men—in which case he tries to appease the spirit of the dead by revenge, and thus to root out the evil. His need for salvation is eudaemonistic, and is confined in a self-centred way to this world. Here the story of the Fall, taken in connection with the Gospel of Jesus Christ, works in a redeeming way: for death is the result of sin, of the broken relation between man and God. In this way primitive peoples begin to get some idea, for the first time, of the ultimate depths of sin; although they are still too much involved in their previous ideology to grasp at once redemption as a whole. They think that they will be saved from death if they live a sinless life.

Nevertheless the Message concerning Jesus Christ is very important for them. The fact that God has restored the relation between Himself and the human race through His Son, is of great significance for their tribal way of thought. Jesus becomes their brother, and thus brings them into touch with God again. In this way He becomes their Friend and Helper, Who shows them the way to the Father. Here a completely new religious world opens up to primitive people. The blood-feud disappears; they can live in peace. As God forgives our sins for Jesus' sake, so we must forgive one another. God does not ask for any sacrifices, as the spirits did; anyone may call upon His Name with impunity, even women, and everyone may pray to Him and tell Him all that is in his heart. God does not shroud Himself in mystery, but permits His Word to be proclaimed to men. They find they can rejoice in God, something which they could never do in their pagan days.

III

The assimilation of the Christian message and the deepening of people's understanding of it, depend essentially on the right way of preaching and applying it. We give four examples of the right way of presenting the message:

1. The message must always be addressed to the congregation as a whole.

2. The message must always be one of good tidings. Primitive people are already suffering quite enough from the pressure of the law; the burden should not be made heavier. They do not want to hear what God demands of them, but what God has done for them.

3. The Law and the Gospel must therefore be applied in the right way. This is done by placing the God Who acts (on the basis of the Bible stories) in the very centre of the message. Here the Law and the Gospel are united. On the basis of the Bible stories the full content of the message can always be presented. In them the hearers can see how much God cares about men— the trouble He takes over them, how men decide for or against Him, and His attitude to their decision. So the figures of the Bible serve as examples for primitive people.

4. Out of consideration for his hearers, too, the missionary should not preach on a different subject every time, but should keep to one subject until it has been understood. Different stories from the Bible may be used as illustrations every time, but the fundamental ideas must be the same. If something is still not clear to his hearers, he can resort to parables and the language of symbolism.

Once the contact between God and man has been established, it is not very difficult to see that the message is carried out in action, so long as the missionary takes care not to place the Christian Gospel on the same level as the pagan religion, which would encourage hypocrisy. For example, when the Mumeng in New Guinea continued to commit pagan misdeeds even after they had been converted to Christianity, the missionary took away their catechists and teachers. " You don't need any more assistance! " he said. " First of all do what God has already told you! " The effect was astonishing. The whole tribe discussed the situation, and then decided to make a thorough clearance of all their pagan practices; then they said: " Give us our helpers back again! When they left us, God went away. We cannot live any longer without His Word! " If the missionary upholds the honour of God, such a radical change takes place in the life of the tribe that it is like a miracle. The more successful the primitive people are in their new life, the more they regard it as a proof of the truth of the Christian message. The words of John vii, 17 come from their hearts. They know God in obedience.

Conversion does not take place without a struggle. The Gospel must renew the whole of life. On Mount Hagen in New Guinea at a meeting of the tribe, the missionary was offered some pigs if only he would go away and take his God with him. For while he was there they felt they could not go on practising their pagan customs. But some of the young men replied: " It is impossible to send this God away again. He lives in our own hearts. As soon as we want to do something, a voice asks whether it is right before God. And we don't want Him to go away. We don't want to return to paganism." The struggle swayed from one experience to the other. Months later ten tribes at a big tribal gathering decided in favour of God. The pagan customs were expressly forbidden, and their decision for God was publicly and solemnly celebrated. For the first time Christianity was accepted by the whole tribe, and the individual Christian was no longer confronted by the antagonism of his tribe.

In all their struggle to lead a new life, in spite of all their joy in the life which God has given them, a certain discontent gradually creeps in. The people realize that in spite of all their honest intentions, evil cannot be completely eradicated. In their pagan religion, if they acted in the prescribed way, they had a feeling of security—a feeling of being in the favour of the god. The Christian Gospel does not give this guarantee. Illnesses and accidents occur, in which the hand of God is recognized, and which are traced back to human sin. At first their eagerness to fulfil God's will is all the stronger. But they cannot attain their object. They cannot rely on their own "works". Here the Christian message is faced by a dilemma. Even in the case of faithful preaching the idea of sin cannot be deepened, and the need for salvation cannot be further awakened through preaching the Cross. Here the missionary is helped by the practice of the Apostles. They placed the Resurrection and the Second Coming of Christ in the very centre of their message. This actually shows us how to lead primitive people to a further stage in their religious experience. In such a situation, at an Easter festival, I preached about the Resurrection of Christ—which I had already done before—and finished the sermon by saying that the Lord will also raise us up, when He returns to judge all men. The effect was astonishing. Even the old men asked, "What shall we do to be saved?" For the first time their life, their salvation, had a new object: eternal bliss. But now their sins stood in the way. It was essential that their sins should be forgiven. This was the moment when the word from the Cross was understood as the message of God's mercy. Now they knew that we cannot save ourselves, but that God in His mercy has saved us. If I see the matter aright, then, the Christian message to primitive people takes the form of an ellipse, whose two focal points are the Creation and the Resurrection and Advent of Christ, but at the point where the lines intersect stands the Cross.

IV

When we now turn to the last question—how can the life of the people be permeated with the spirit of the Gospel?—the paradoxical reply is: through individual decisions. Quite apart from the fact that the Gospel is always forcing primitive man to face the need for decision, God gives him two special opportunities of bearing witness: first of all, when the tribe is awakened and the members who have been convinced are baptized. In the case of the conversion of a whole tribe, individuals come forward and win more and more of their fellow-tribesmen through the power of their own conviction, until finally the majority are on their side. The conversion of the tribe is therefore preceded by the conversion of the individual. But as there will always be some people who only take part in the tribal conversion because they go with the stream, the individual is again faced by a decision when he is baptized. This is where the really convinced members of the tribe stand out from the rest. The conversion of a tribe never results in mass baptisms, but in the founding of a Christian Church within the tribe. However great may be the power of baptism to draw people together into a community, it must nevertheless be preceded by individual conviction. This is especially the case where baptism is preceded (as used to be the custom in the early centuries) by thorough instruction and by a private confession of sin. Before baptism everyone confesses his sins personally, and receives personal forgiveness. At baptism he personally renounces the devil and all his works, and is received into God's Covenant of grace by receiving a new name. The whole group of people who have been personally called forth from the tribe forms the Church. It is their task to impregnate their tribe with the Gospel. Secondly, the Church influences the life of the tribe by the mere fact of its existence, since it is like a city set on a hill. If the tribe has been converted, the members of the Church become the leading personalities in the life of the tribe. And those who have not been baptized imitate the habits of the church members. It is the Church which determines and fixes customs and laws, on the basis of its Christian judgment, in agreement with the people. It sees that the decisions are carried out. The conscience of the Church can only remain alert if it can take action as an independent body, and if its decisions are also recognized by the missionary.

The dynamic power of the Church can only develop when the Christian message is part of the life of the people. It is not a question of introducing strange customs, but of purifying those that already exist and of deriving them from God's purpose in

Creation. This can only be done by the Church. For instance, the members of the clan remain attached to one another, but the clan no longer acts according to the principle: " Everything is good that serves the purpose of the clan," but according to the commandment to love one's neighbour, which includes all men. Marriage is preserved, but for the sake of God it becomes monogamy, based on loyalty, in which the woman is regarded equally as the child of God, and therefore has the same rights as the man. So every sphere of life is placed under the judgment of the Word, and emerges in a new form, just like the individual. Through the Church the Christian message becomes the order of life for the people.

Thus the Church can only exercise a dynamic influence on the people if it is itself constantly struggling against evil, and training its own members to be pure in their own hearts. Its missionary power varies in proportion to its self-discipline. So long as the life of the Church is in order, the pagan members of the tribe feel a great longing to be permitted to join it. But if the life of the Church is hollow and insincere, its message will have no meaning for the life of the people. It is fairly easy to carry out this discipline in a Church in a primitive tribe. The sense of mutual obligation and responsibility, which is already present in the tribe, comes to full fruition when it is filled with power from the Word of God. The tribe of God has come to birth. All Christians therefore in the New Guinea Church do pastoral work. Lukewarm Christians are visited and warned. If the admonitions of individuals are not effective, these Christians are then brought before the village church or the church of the district, which realizes its responsibility for every member. The unbaptized members of the tribe therefore realize again and again how earnestly God seeks for every individual soul, through the Church. Sins of the individual are regarded as sins of the community. The community purifies itself by admonishing the sinner publicly in its religious services, and if necessary, by expelling him. The community as a whole repents with him. If the sinner repents, the Church rejoices that it can accord him forgiveness. Unbaptized members of the tribe are treated according to the reformed native law, which is influenced by the Gospel. Pagans are deeply impressed by this struggle against sin.

In addition to discipline, there is the missionary service of the

Church. Where missionary work has been rightly carried out, this "native evangelism" will seem perfectly natural. Mass movements only occur if the pagans who have heard the Word pass it on to their fellow-tribesmen as a matter of course. This impulse to bear witness should not be hindered because it is "unofficial". Once a Christian Church has come to birth, it must be consciously tended and fostered. The individual members have ample opportunity to proclaim the Word of God to their fellow-tribesmen. They can do so in the midst of their ordinary life, but also in church services. In New Guinea all Christians are free to speak in church services. The communal morning and evening services in the villages, which all the members of the tribe attend, are conducted by the Christians in turn. The congregation takes part in the sermon by question and answer. The sermon may also be amplified by individual Christians. After the services the Christians often discuss for a long time how to apply what they have heard to the life of the community. This produces a common desire for a purer community life which influences the whole people.

An important method of evangelism, and of permeating the life of the people with the Gospel, is the school, for which the Church has the full responsibility. Its main service is to educate the people, and especially the young, in the Christian way of life. How seriously this task is regarded in New Guinea may be seen in the fact that, in villages or communities where the school is not properly attended, the local churches forbid the baptism of children. It is then quite clear that children may only be baptized if they are going to be brought up as Christians. But the Church is also called to work among those who are pure pagans. Where a mission to primitive people has understood that evangelism must be done by the members of the tribe itself, it has not only achieved its greatest successes, but the Christian Church itself then becomes truly "indigenous". This method will be all the more successful if missions avoid the old mistake of treating these mission-workers as their own "employees". They are working for the Church, and the Church therefore has to provide for their support. If the Church is given the opportunity, it will also gladly accept the spiritual responsibility which this involves. The more a church is allowed to fulfil its own tasks and to organize its own work, the greater is its joy in service and sacrifice. The churches in New Guinea do not receive any money from the mission, although every native church has its own mission-field in which its men are working. In 1939 the Christians in New Guinea (some 45,000 in number) had over 800 mission-workers in their service. In connection with this mission-work it is evident that the more strongly the Church can support its mission-work and the nearer it is to it, the more effective that work becomes; and that the farther the mission-station is from the church, the more difficult it is to carry on the work. This is another proof of the responsibility of the Christian Church for the penetration of the whole life of the people with the Christian message.

In all this, however, we must take care to avoid the great danger by which the churches at home are faced. In the Christian sense there can never be a national church, which includes all the members of the nation. Once this takes place, the Church has lost its unique position. But we can try to Christianize the people through the Church, whose members will influence the rest of the community.

The many problems which arise—the problem of the second generation, or of the relation of Christians to their government (which is a particularly burning one among the natives of Africa) —cannot be developed at greater length here. The one thing that matters is always: decision for God. The more the Christian message has gained an influence over men's consciences, the easier it will be to attain this. The task of this paper is to show how this can be achieved.

THE APPROACH TO ISRAEL

Contributed by the French Committee of Witness to Israel

O NLY blind optimism could have expected the Jewish tragedy to vanish at the end of the war with the Nazism which had forced it to the front of the stage. We know now that, here as elsewhere, the war settled nothing. On the contrary, although the position of the Jews to-day in Europe and the world is less tragic than it was in the years when every day threatened thousands with extermination, it is perhaps even more desperate, because all the hopes the survivors hugged have been cruelly dispelled. Except in some countries, including France, in which, although anti-semitism is certainly more active than before the war, it is not definite enough to forbid their existence—the Jews of Europe are living parked in the camps in which the Germans had concentrated them, or else they are being ill-treated by the liberated populations. But the evolution of Zionism is leading to an apparently insoluble dispute with Great Britain and ranging against Jewry even those who flew to arms against the totalitarian *régime* of their murderers.

The Church of Jesus Christ, which could not tolerate the Nazi persecution of the Jews, cannot remain indifferent to their present plight. Not that the Church needs to intervene in the political problem that the Jews want to settle in Palestine and that the British refuse to let them do so; but because the Church, as the " New Israel ", must not forget that it is bound up with Israel according to the flesh, whose name it has inherited. Karl Barth has just reminded us that " from the Christian point of view the most serious aspect of the nihilist revolution was the struggle against Israel and hence against the mystery of the Incarnation of the Word of God."

It is not a question, therefore, of the Church adopting a position inspired by what unbelievers so easily call " Christian charity ", but of being bound to solidarity in its attitude and in its action. It is not a question of " pitying the Jews ", but of basing our Christian attitude and our Christian action on the certainty that our destiny is linked up with theirs.

First, our attitude; for our salvation and theirs is at stake. Persecution of the Jews condemns us, and indifference to the salvation of the Jews condemns us no less. The cry of Paul, " Woe is me, if I preach not the gospel! " (1 Cor. ix, 16) includes, in the Epistle to the Corinthians, and throughout the history of the Church, preaching the Gospel to the *Jews*.

Then, our action, which should flow from this attitude. In our dealings with the Jews we must never weary of showing solidarity with them. The Church must not relax when the concentration camps are closed. Moreover, we must never let such action dispense us from the duty of preaching the Gospel. We must not reflect that conversions are considerably encouraged by the giving of relief; but neither must we admit for a moment that if the people relieved have a spiritual life which satisfies them and a magnificent religion, we should confine ourselves to helping them physically or morally.

On the contrary, we must remind ourselves of the appeal of Calvin, which was the outcome of his meditation on " The Similarity of the Old and New Testaments ":

" Who then dares to represent the Jews as destitute of Christ, them with whom we are informed the evangelical covenant was made, of which Christ is the sole foundation? Who dares to represent them as strangers to the benefit of a free salvation, to whom we are informed the doctrine of the righteousness of faith was communicated? "[1]

Yet a religious newspaper, following upon a controversy between a Christian writer and a historian, recently published an article on the sources of Christian anti-semitism. There are passages of St. Thomas Aquinas and of Luther which are shocking on this point. But when Christian churchmen do not intend to be hostile, when they are dealing with the Mystery of Israel, their language is so technical that its meaning escapes not only the Jews whom they wish to address, and whom they unintentionally wound, but a whole mass of people who cannot understand them, and may interpret their writings as an encouragement for their own tendencies.

[1] Calvin, *Institutes*, Book II, Chapter X, Section IV.

THE BLOOD FALLS

However serious these verbal misunderstandings may be sometimes, they are not the only ones which must be avoided and put right. A Jew who has been stricken in body and soul by the trials of the last few years will tend to make no difference between an anti-semite like Hitler—who declared he was fulfilling the will of the Almighty by annihilating the Jews—and the men who explain, or even excuse, the persecutions by saying that they are God's answer to the cry of the Jewish people: "His blood be on us, and on our children" (Matt. xxvii, 25). This notion of the blood falling on the heads of the Jews must be faced; we must not evade it in order to avoid wounding anyone's susceptibilities. We cannot prune the Word of God to meet the needs of evangelism.

Yes, the blood is falling. Yes, the Gospel says, "*All the people said, 'His blood be on us, and on our children.'*" And according to the interpretation given by the Old Testament, the blood falls as a punishment (see especially Joshua ii, 19). This seems to play into the hands of the religious and secular extremists who say to the Jews: "You asked for it! You are responsible for your own persecution!" Even the Church allows itself to be betrayed into extravagant language, interpretations and actions which condone or encourage persecution, and so to participate in it. The Jews then reply that this expression is found only in the Gospel of Matthew, who was the most anti-Jewish of the Synoptic writers, and they point out that Jesus was put to death by the Romans under the pressure of a powerful minority in one City: Jerusalem.

There would appear to be ground for the assertion on both sides. Yet, if the Bible is regarded as God's Word, both must be driven out of court and their strange blindness rebuked.

In our view, the curse was invoked in the name of the whole Jewish people, just as Pilate condemned Christ to death in the name of all Gentiles. But Jesus replied with a Word of blessing, valid for all Jews and all Gentiles: "Father, forgive them, for they know not what they do" (Luke xxiii, 34).

This Word is for the whole Jewish People and for all men: "For God hath concluded them all in unbelief" (unbelief which culminated in the crucifixion of His Son, for which both Jews and non-Jews are responsible) "that He might have mercy upon all" (Rom. xi, 32). This mercy was manifested by His death, which was an act of redemption for all men.

Through that death the New Covenant was sealed in His blood. The blood which falls, then (in accordance with the Jews' invocation) is "the blood of sprinkling, that speaketh better things than that of Abel" (Heb. xii, 24)—and this sprinkling exceeds the sprinkling made by Moses at the Passover (Heb. xi, 28) to which the Jews nevertheless owed their deliverance.

Peter, the Apostle of the Jews, preached nothing else to them at Jerusalem (see his sermons in Acts ii and iii) than their responsibility for the death of Jesus, in accordance with "the determinate counsel and foreknowledge of God" (Acts ii, 23), although he knows "that they did it through ignorance, as did also their rulers" (Acts iii, 17). He added: "Unto you *first* God, having raised up His Son Jesus, sent Him to bless you, in turning away every one of you from your iniquities" (Acts iii, 26).

There are two dominant affirmations in Peter's preaching which ought to form the basis of a message to the Jews to-day: "The promise is unto you" (Acts ii, 39) and "Neither is there salvation in any other" (Acts iv, 12).

"THE PROMISE IS UNTO YOU"

Israel is a Chosen People, in virtue of God's own promise, and in order that that promise may be fulfilled. Upon this promise St. Paul took his stand when, at Antioch in Pisidia and elsewhere, he proclaimed in the synagogue Jesus "raised by God according to promise", raised up "in fulfilment of His promise" (Acts xiii). So the Gospel for the Jews should be able to stand simply on what the Old Testament says about them. It is always a matter of lifting the veil which Jesus Himself lifted at Emmaus, of explaining the Scriptures as the deacon Philip explained them to the Ethiopian eunuch.

But Israel has been unfaithful to this promise. In the Old Testament this unfaithfulness consists essentially in their refusal to recognize the One, True God, and to consecrate themselves to Him, i.e. in a form of idolatry. The punishment for this idolatry comes in the shape of the trials and sufferings God permits Israel to endure. But the Gentiles, who made them-

selves the instrument of this punishment, are in their turn condemned and overthrown for having attacked God's People.

The Church to-day must return to the attitude and the
message of the prophets, for Israel, for the Jews, and for its own
members. It is a message of repentance and of hope.

To the persecuted people, the Church must say that their
sufferings are not God's vengeance for the death of Jesus, but an
appeal to conversion and to turn from their unfaithfulness. It is
obviously very hard to use this language to the survivors of the
Nazi massacres. But Christians cannot attempt to proclaim the
Gospel to the Jews unless they begin by affirming that Jesus
really is the Christ, the Son of God, and that their unfaithfulness
consists in their refusal to recognize Him as the Messiah foretold
in the Prophets. In this connection, it is essential to explain the
exact significance of the doctrine of the Trinity, which Orthodox
Jews represent as the worship of several gods, and therefore as a
betrayal of monotheism.

To the people who pray, "Blessed be His glorious Name for
ever", Christians must say that this Name, which the Jews do
not know, and which they represent by the sacred Tetragram,
this Name which God refused to reveal to Moses (to whom He
only said what He was)—this Name has been revealed in Jesus
Christ. "Neither is there salvation in any other; for there is
none other name under heaven given among men, whereby we
must be saved" (Acts iv, 12).

To anti-semites, on the other hand, the Church must proclaim the judgment which is meted out to those who attack
God's People. In no case can anti-semitism be justified by
Israel's unfaithfulness; anti-semitism is always, in the last resort,
self-righteous justice. Persecution of the Jews is always harmful
to the Church, just as the unfaithfulness of the Jews is only the
reflection of the unfaithfulness of Christians.

THE WALL OF SEPARATION

This then would be the basis for an organized campaign if
the Jews were on their side a coherent body attached to their
faith and worship: if there were not between most of them and
the main body of Christians a mass of prejudices, sometimes justified, but generally due to the fact that they completely misunderstand one another. We must see how they can be cleared away.

In view of these prejudices, Christians should not reproach Jews for the mote which is in their eye, but give heed to the beam in their own. Above all they should not lose sight of the immemorial tradition of persecution which has developed defensive reflexes, quickened to acute sensitiveness by the horrors they have lived through during the Nazi régime. There are reproaches which we can no longer bring against them, even if we think them just; and searching examination is called for before we accept for ourselves the most legitimate. In particular all hope of a successful mission goes by the board if we start from the premise that Jews cannot be assimilated; and that is far from proof in the social, even if it is plausible in the theological world.

Moreover, we should not expect to overcome these prejudices apart from Christian faith. Rather, for Jewish converts and for the Christian in his approach to the unconverted, Christianity ought to get behind them, and they will collapse of themselves.

Anti-semitism is far more than one such prejudice. For anti-semitism, "to be or not to be" is the basic question in our relations with the Jews. It is essential that Jews and Christians should drive it out of the field in alliance, not with uncoordinated arguments on different fronts. So long as a Jew can suppose that Christians as a whole are anti-semitic, or that the Church does not fight anti-semitism in every shape and form, there will inevitably be a movement of repulsion, turning Jewish eyes away from the Gospel which their sincerest friends in the Church want to lay before them.

It follows that, unless we are to be at cross purposes, a clear distinction should be drawn between anti-semitism and the anti-Judaism which is involved in every summons to conversion, and concerns the Church too, for the Church has constant need of conversion and a constant tendency to Judaism. All suggestions that as a Christian one is really a Jew are special pleading. The aim of general conversion cannot be anything less than the spiritual destruction of Judaism. There we meet a "rock of offence", for the sincerest Jews regard themselves as a Remnant necessary for the preservation of the world and, in this world, of the Law of Sinai. But Christians, even when they tell them that the Remnant is unfaithful, cannot forget that the preservation of Israel until the last days is one of God's mysteries.

To shrink from this anti-Judaism—whose eschatological quality certainly takes the edge off the reactions it is liable to provoke—means admitting that there are Jews and Greeks within the Church, admitting that God (or at any rate His unfaithful Church) has respect of persons, and recognizing the possibility of separate Jewish-Christian churches.

Moreover, as long as the anti-semitism of certain Christian groups forces Missions to the Jews to contemplate the possibility of creating such communities, we may wonder who needs the Gospel first, and ask ourselves whether we are not putting the cart before the horse in accepting such a necessity. For if we do so the wall of separation is not broken down.

This is our message to the people which is not like other peoples, which suffers even while it glories in its separation: the wall is broken down. It has been broken down in Jesus Christ.

"NEITHER IS THERE SALVATION IN ANY OTHER"

There is none other name whereby we may be saved; nor whereby they may be saved.

In fact, the problem of the attitude to adopt towards the Jews and of the efforts to convert them, all comes back to the general problem of converting the world, and of the Christian life. " For in Christ Jesus neither circumcision availeth anything, nor uncircumcision, but a new creature " (Gal. vi, 15).

Nevertheless we meet different reactions among converted Jews, and so among those we hope to convert. These differences make it essential to vary the message which is to be addressed to them.

Some have come to the Gospel because they have seen in it the fulfilment of the message spoken by the Prophets. Most of the Jews who have come from Liberal Judaism are naturally among these. To them the Christian message must make it clear that Jesus Christ is not "one of the prophets", nor even the greatest of the prophets. Otherwise we shall be acquiescing in their changing over from a Liberal Judaism to an equally (or still more) Liberal Christianity which is disloyal to the Lordship and the Divinity of Jesus Christ. That Jesus was one of the prophets was, as we know, just what even the Jews who had Him crucified were ready to accept.

Some Jews have come to the Gospel, or may do so, from a break, spiritual or social, with their old world. They often fall into a dualism, opposing the vengeful God of the Old Testament to the Gospel's God of Love. They refuse to recognize any Christological meaning in their scriptures, which they discard. They find themselves in agreement on this point with many Gentile converts and many who have been brought up as Christians.

Some Jews brought up on the Jewish scriptures are in the same position as the first disciples at Emmaus and the Ethiopian eunuch; they confess that the real meaning is revealed to them and see how the Law is fulfilled. These above all should be encouraged. But to all the others, even if we begin by coming down to their level because " children need milk ", we must in the end without fail preach this real Gospel.

Their very silence will remind us that this message of the Cross fulfilling the Law is a stumbling-block to the Jews (1 Cor. i, 23). What was true in the first days of the Church (even for Peter, the first confessor) is always true. That explains the two varieties—the over-simple fulfilment and the complete break-away—which we have already reviewed. But we have no other message.

Still, it was this very stumbling-block in which the Jew, Paul, and the Jewish apostles believed, and which they preached. The Jews must be made to realize that they are the pivot of the salvation brought by the Messiah of Israel, the King of the Jews, which was addressed first to Jews, and received first by Jews. It was Jews, it was Peter, who were the first to reply to the vital question: " Whom say ye that I am? " (even if they did not yet accept the scandal of His death and resurrection): " Thou art the Christ, the Son of the Living God " (Matt. xvi, 16).

We must then bring it home to the Jews that not only the Old Testament, but also the gospels and the epistles, are *Jewish scriptures*, and that it is these Jewish scriptures in which we Christians believe. There again, for all men, salvation is of the Jews.

Finally there is the largest group, the Jews who are completely indifferent to their traditional beliefs. Among these we must again distinguish between those who hardly realize that they are Jews, or do not admit that being Jewish implies a real difference and separation, and those Jews who insist on their own special position—their race—without basing themselves upon any spiritual reality: the indifferent and the Zionists, to make a rather arbitrary distinction.

The first thing which we must say to the Zionists is that the salvation of the Jews, and their personal salvation as Jews, lies not in Zionism but in their Saviour Jesus Christ. This is the most difficult, if not the most repellent, thing that could be said to them from the human point of view; because by faith alone comes conviction.

To the oppressed in the depth of their distress, the prophets announce that God has not abandoned His People, and that He will provide for their salvation. It is of their salvation, and not of any material advantage, that we must to-day speak to the Jews, including the Zionists.

While men are crying out that God is dead, the world is a prey to systems which claim to bring temporal security, and which all result in slavery or despair. Communism, Nazism and the existentialism of Sartre all attempt to save man from his chains, which grow heavier and heavier. Nationalism, too, is, for Jews, a desperate attempt of men who hope to save themselves by material means.

The Church cannot avert her eyes from the significance of Zionism for Israel, the world, and the Church herself. But she must also declare to Jews, as well as to communists, existentialists and internationalists that there is no salvation in any other than Jesus Christ.

There still remain the indifferent, who are undoubtedly the most numerous. It is hard to know whether the best course is to remind them of their double infidelity: the general infidelity of Judaism first, which has failed to recognize its Lord and Saviour, and then their infidelity to Judaism; or whether we should not simply speak to them in the same way as to any other paganized or post-Christian "Gentiles" in the modern world.

Though this analysis may appear to enter into details, it is still only an outline. In particular, it omits to take into account the different problems which arise according as our message is addressed to Western Jews or to refugees from the closed communities of Eastern Europe. It says nothing about the masses of opportunist converts, modern Moriscos, many of whom have only asked for baptism in the hope of escaping persecution. This should remind us that evangelization (of Jews as of all others) should not address classes of men, but individuals. For the call of God, which it can only echo or carry, is absolutely personal.

In fact we again discover that there can be no device or prescription for the evangelization of Israel, since the liberty of God's Word makes nonsense of our prescriptions, our devices, and the techniques of which we are so proud.

On the other hand, concern for the message to be preached to the Jews, like concern to meet the attacks which through them are directed against the mystery of the Incarnation of the Word of God, will always have the merit of making the Church take its stand on the unity of the biblical revelation and the indivisibility of the two Testaments.

The mode of presenting the Christian message may vary with the Jews with whom one is dealing: orthodox, liberal or non-practising; but the essence cannot vary. Certain preliminary conditions are, however, indispensable. First, the people who undertake this work must *love the Jews*, not *in spite of* the fact that they are Jews (because they are wretched) but *because* they are Jews (and wretched). The second condition, which follows from the first, is that they should know them and—more precisely—should know the extraordinary variety of the cases with which they may have to deal.

Finally, we fully realize that all men's efforts will be vain unless God, through His Holy Spirit, enables those whom we wish to evangelize to respond to His grace. All efforts for evangelization should, therefore, begin with constant intercession. " Brethren, my heart's desire and prayer to God for Israel is, that they might be saved " (Rom. x, 1).

VII

IS THERE A PROBLEM OF EVANGELISM?

THE repeated use of the phrase *the problem of evangelism* suggests a point at which our volume may meet with sharp criticism from certain quarters. There are Christians who hold that there is no such problem. The Christian Faith, they would say, is not a human contrivance but a divine revelation, given once for all in Jesus Christ; the Church has therefore nothing to do but proclaim continually the truth it has received, and all will be well. This statement, though true, is by its oversimplification essentially misleading.

The Gospel is the final Word of God to men. But revelation is not static; it has to be apprehended afresh in every generation, and the scribe instructed in the mysteries of the Kingdom of God is bidden to bring forth from his treasures things new and old. The Lord of the Church bids His people hearken to what the Spirit *saith* to the churches. The Bible is therefore also the contemporary utterance of God to His people, speaking to their condition through words which, though written long ago, have an inexhaustible power of renewal as the approach of the living God to man in his changing needs and situations. The Church lives both by the Word and by the Spirit; not by the Word without the Spirit (the way of scholasticism), nor by the Spirit without the Word (the way of illuminism). But the Church can live by both Word and Spirit only in so far as it is the listening Church, attentive and eager to hear the Word of God to-day.

To listen to the Word of God is not enough. The Church is called to listen also to the confused voices of men. There is a perpetual change of intellectual climate. Words change their meanings and their connotations. Problems which are of burning significance for one generation become marginal for the next. Its word must be to men, in their common speech, and in unmistakable relevance to their needs, both those needs of which they are conscious, and those to consciousness of which it may be that they need to be awakened. Evangelism is perpetually a task not only of proclamation but also of translation.

It is obvious that the task of evangelism has its perils. The Church, by loyal faithfulness to what it has received, may make its message meaningless. By excessive concern for the contemporary relevance of its utterance, it may be betrayed into unfaithfulness to the Gospel of God's judgment and God's mercy. But to say that a path is perilous is not the same as to say that it is not the path appointed by God for His Church to follow. The problem of evangelism is just the perpetual rediscovery of the narrow way on which alone the Church can be faithful to its twofold vocation of faithfulness to God and service to His creatures.

HAS THE CHURCH FAILED?

As churchmen, we believe in the Church as the Bride of Christ, not having spot or wrinkle or any such thing. Yet we are confronted by grim and disturbing realities. In almost every country of what was once called Christendom, the Church is losing ground.

Why is this? Is it because of the growth of anti-Christian forces? There have always been such in the world. Is it due to persecution? The past and the present give evidence that persecution can revive the Church. It can continue to be a living Church only if it sets itself consciously and deliberately to live every day in dependence on its living Lord and on nothing else. A Church well settled and established tends almost inevitably to rely on the permanence of the *status quo*. And, where it is prosperous and at peace, it tends to forget that its task is always evangelistic and can be nothing else. Conformity, even sincere and devout conformity, is not faith. The Church has too much accepted as its purpose something other than that single purpose by which it is God's will that it should live—the bringing of every man individually under the judgment of God in order that every man individually may become partaker of the salvation wrought once for all by the death and resurrection of Jesus Christ.

Nothing is to be gained by frequent public confessions of guilt and failure on the part of the Church. But a sober and well-founded recognition of failure is a necessary preliminary to recovery. The Church is not dead, and the feeling that the Gospel no longer has anything to say to modern man is baseless. The evidence assembled in Section V points in another direction. Yet these new experiments in evangelism are only stars in a very dark sky. The world at large regards Christianity and its message as definitely belonging to the past. The problem of evangelism is how to awaken in modern man a consciousness of the perennial relevance of the Gospel.

EVANGELISM AND THE UNITY OF THE CHURCH

The weakness and limited success of contemporary evangelistic effort raises in an acute form the question of the continuing divisions of the Christian churches and the acquiescence of the vast majority of Christians in them. The only valid argument for the union of the churches is theological, a belief that unity is the will of God for His Church, and that the Church as the Body of Christ ought to represent on earth the mysterious unity of the Godhead. Can we afford, as things are, to continue divided? Is not fellowship in evangelism one of the points at which we can realize our unity in the essential oneness of the Gospel, and so grow towards fuller fellowship in church life and organization?

Most of the efforts chronicled in these pages are the isolated enterprises of single churches. All the more important for this reason are the attempts which have been made to join the Christian forces, either permanently or for one single, large-scale evangelistic adventure.

This is the significance of the so-called Commando Campaign in London during the year 1946. The enterprise was Methodist in origin and inspiration, but clergy and workers of many denominations took part in this well-planned and carefully prepared attempt to stir the whole of London with the consciousness of the Gospel as a living force. It is too soon, perhaps, to assess the lasting effects of the Campaign. It is certain that in many places access was found to large bodies of men and women ordinarily out of touch with any form of Christian witness. Many clergy and congregations were roused to new hope and activity.

But in fairness, the opposite side of the picture has also been presented. Those who hold a strongly sacramental and corporate view of the Church and its life do find it difficult to work in fellowship with those whose emphasis is more on individual conversion. And what is to happen when people are converted and wish to enter the fellowship of the Church? To which body are they to give their allegiance? This is a problem which has long perplexed all inter-denominational missions. To face the problem frankly is not to despair of the solution. Fellowship in evangelism may not result in solving the problem of solution, but it certainly will foster an acute consciousness of the scandal of division.

WHAT IS EVANGELISM?

At what point can evangelism be said to be effective? In setting forth the various experiments which have come under our notice, we have attempted to deal with them critically and objectively. In order not to delude ourselves into false imaginings, we must be aware that no evangelism is effective, however impressive may have been its manifestations at the time, unless its results are permanent. The meaning of permanence may be considered in three connections:

1. *Evangelism and Church*

Belief in Christ is imperfect, unless it includes recognition of the obligation of membership in His visible body, the Church. To many who have come to love and trust in Christ, this is a severe test; the Church as it manifests itself in many places is so unattractive, its fellowship so cold and uninviting, that it is hard to believe in the reality of its connection with the Gospel of life. Yet to admit that there can be any separation between the Lord and His Body is a fatal abandonment of New Testament Christianity. Allegiance to Him must mean acceptance of the Church, whatever its weakness or unattractiveness may be.

Even among Christians there is a tendency to underestimate the importance of the Church and its ordinances. At their best, these outward things are means of grace; at their worst, they are the divinely appointed instruments for that continuity of the Church in time without which the proclamation of the Gospel cannot be assured. Unless the Church is utterly apostate, we must take hold of the fact that it has within itself the possibility of renewal through Word and Sacrament.

2. *Evangelism and Society*

The purpose of evangelism is not the redemption of human

society; but unless the Christian fellowship is a redemptive influence in society, it may be taken as certain that it has failed to apprehend the fulness of the Gospel. If a man is brought into living fellowship with Christ, his whole relationship to God undergoes that change expressed by St. Paul in the classic phrase *Thou art no more a servant but a son*. But with this changed relationship to God must go a new relationship not only to the other members of the Christian group but to all men generally. The world is too often content with the attitude of Cain, *Am I my brother's keeper?* For the Christian, such cynicism is impossible; he knows, if he has understood the Gospel at all, that he is responsible for the welfare of all men.

In his family, and in his place of work, the Christian must be known as a model of integrity, consideration for others and willingness to serve. He must stand courageously for what is right, regardless of his own interests. In society, the Christian group must be known to stand for the common well-being of all, for that sense of obligation to all men which springs from belief in God as Creator and in Christ, Who is the King of all spheres of life.

The extent to which an individual or a Christian group can affect the environment is conditioned by many factors outside the Christian life. But recent history has shown with startling clarity the results which can be achieved by a small but determined minority. The withdrawal of the Christian group into itself, so that it appears at best as a mutual assurance society, is a denial of the vocation assigned to it by its master to be the light of the world, the leaven that leaveneth the lump. The world in passing its judgment on the Church is perfectly entitled to turn against it the word of the Master Himself: *By their fruits, you shall know them*.

3. Evangelism and Witness

If a man is a true Christian, he does not need to be stimulated to win others for Christ, though his zeal may need to be corrected by the wider experience of those who have gone further than he in the Christian way. Every true Christian understands from within the meaning of St. Paul's "Woe is me, if I preach not the Gospel". The treasure he has found hidden in the field is so immense that it is impossible for him to keep it to himself. The lay apostolate is the hope of the Church in the modern world.

It stands to reason at any time that only a very small fraction of the Church's evangelistic work can be done by the paid servants of the Church. If a study were made of the human instruments by whom men have been won for Christ, it would probably be found that comparatively few had been won by the clergy, and that far more had been brought in by their own parents, or by their companions in work, than by any other means.

The work of the lay apostolate is one in which every Christian, however simple, can take part. The heart of it is the ministry of intercessory prayer, the ceaseless pleading for individuals before God. The second element is the living before the eyes of men in their ordinary places of resort of an unmistakably Christian life. The third is a quite new way, *vid.* to find out patiently how in this modern world the Christian view of life can be brought to bear on the various spheres of life in which the member of the Church fulfils his vocation.

In this modern world with so many conflicting "gospels", there is often a great uncertainty amongst church members about what they have to proclaim. In order to exercise its evangelistic task properly, the Church will have to find ways in order to enable her members to give a relevant witness in word and deed.

At certain great crises, the uncertainties of Christians yield before the demands of a situation in which circumstances force on the Church the choice between life and death. In the struggle of the German Church, some of the issues of the Gospel stood out in stark clarity. Is Jesus the only Lord of the Church, or has it any other? If it is claimed that He is the only Lord, Who then is this Jesus, Who makes such uncompromising claims, and will not tolerate any division of allegiance among His followers? In face of this challenge, the Word of God awoke. The questions of the hour and the answers to them were proclaimed from the pulpits and found an echo in the hearts of the hearers.

The Church is always in a state of crisis. Its conflict is always against principalities and powers, the rulers of the darkness of this world. Sometimes these powers seem to sleep; but in reality they are always active, malevolent and destructive, never more dangerous than when they seem to sleep. Real evangelism means that the Church in all its ranks is constantly aware of the ever-present crisis.

The Gospel does not promise to the Church what, measured

by human standards, can be called success. It does give the assurance that the Gospel is the power of God to salvation to everyone that believeth, and that this power will never wear out. It does lay upon the Church an inescapable duty to preach the Gospel to all men to the end of time. When the message of redemption is preached, humbly but with burning conviction, and lived out, it will not fail to find a hearing. Those who hear with faith may be few. But God keeps the issues of the world's history in His own hands; His working is mysterious, and much of it lies out of the sight of men. If the Church is faithful to its task, it may be sure that God will not allow anything of its love, its service to be wasted, but will use it all for the establishment of His Kingdom. The Church must live always by faith, not by sight. But faith is not a second best. It is the human aspect of the faithfulness of the unchangeable God, and has always in it the divine promise. This is the victory that overcometh the world, even our faith. According to your faith be it unto you.

MEMBERS

OF ASSEMBLY COMMISSION II

ON

" THE CHURCH'S WITNESS TO GOD'S DESIGN "

(The list includes those members of the Commission who were appointed before the end of 1947 and who therefore were able to participate in the preparation of the volume.)

Professor Hendrik KRAEMER, *Geneva,* CHAIRMAN
The Rt. Rev. Bishop Stephen NEILL, *Geneva,* SECRETARY

The Very Rev. Professor John BAILLIE, *Edinburgh*
The Rev. R. S. BILHEIMER, *New York*
Professor P. BRATSIOTIS, *Athens*
Professor Robert L. CALHOUN, *New Haven*
Professor P. D. DEVANANDAN, *Bangalore*
Miss Suzanne de DIETRICH, *Geneva*
Professor John FOSTER, *Glasgow*
Professor Walter M. HORTON, *Oberlin, Ohio*
Professor Kenneth S. LATOURETTE, *New Haven, Conn.*
The Rt. Rev. Bishop Hanns LILJE, *Hanover*
Professor Pierre MAURY, *Paris*
The Rev. D. T. NILES, *Ceylon*
Dr. Miguel RIZZO, *Sao Paulo*
Miss C. M. VAN ASCH VAN WIJCK, *Zeist*
President Vi fang WU, *Nanking*

INDEX

(a) Subjects

Ashram movement, 176

Baptism, Significance of, 117

Christ, Authority of, 20ff.
  Lordship of, 17, 18, 110
Church:
  Bible and the, 70
  as the Body of Christ, 34, 69, 72
  Class distinction in, 77
  and the Dark Ages, 66
  Failure of, 65ff., 72ff.
  Labour and the, 78
  and "other-worldliness", 73
  and Roman Empire, 65
  as a Royal Priesthood, 71
  Secularization of, 74, 76ff.
  as "True Israel", 29, 30, 117
  Unity of, 35
  World Mission of, 115ff.
  World-wide character of, 16
Creation, Doctrine of, 24ff.

Democracy, as a creed, 41ff.
Disintegration, Evangelism and, 62ff.
  Totalitarianism and, 55

Election, Doctrine of, 28, 29
Evangelism:
  America and, 135
  Anti-Semitism and, 194ff.
  Apologetics in India and, 172ff. 177ff.
  Ashrams and, 127ff.
  Broadcasting and, 141ff.
  Buddhism in China and, 127

Evangelism—*continued*
  Challenge to the Church, 16
  Christian Unity and, 202ff.
  of the Church, 121
  Cimade and, 152ff.
  Eastern Orthodox Church and, 130ff.
  Ecumenical Movement and, 120
  Films and, 140ff.
  France, and, 155ff.
  French Reformed Church and, 134-135
  Great Britain and, 136
  in India, 169ff.
  Industrial Chaplains and, 154
  Intellectuals and, 162ff.
  Iona Community and, 152
  Israel and, 190ff.
  Kingdom of God and, 34
  Laity and, 118ff., 145ff.
  Mass movements and, 123ff.
  Moral Rearmament and, 138ff.
  Need for, 15
  in New Guinea, 178ff.
  Oxford Group Movement and, 138ff.
  Parochial, 129ff.
  Permanent results of, 203ff.
  Religion in German Schools and, 144ff.
  Revival Campaigns and, 134ff.
  in Roman Catholic Church, 14
  Task of the Whole Church, 17, 32, 165ff.
  Universities and, 137ff.
  Urgency of, 33

Evangelism—*continued*
  Waldensian Church in Italy
    and, 135

Fall, Doctrine of the, 26ff.
Family life, disintegration of, 57

Gospel, and Forgiveness, 105ff.
  a *kerugma*, 20, 21
  Law and, 27ff.
  Man's need of the, 89ff.
  Message of the, 23ff.

Harijan Movement, 171
History, meaning of, 33, 34, 101
Humanism, Modern Science and,
  39ff.

Immanence, Principle of, 56
International Communist Party
  (Russia), 43ff.
International Missionary Coun-
  cil, Jerusalem, 1928, 37
International Missionary Coun-
  cil, Tambaram, 1938, 85, 86f.

Labour Party, British, 43

Nationalism, as a Creed, 45ff.
  Italian Fascism and, 48
  and National Socialism, 46-47
Nihilism, Present Crisis and,
  49ff.

Parousia, 114
Personality, disintegration of, 57
Prayer, Renewal and, 18

Redemption, Doctrine of, 31

Socialism, as a faith, 43
Society, Classless, 44
  disintegration of, 15, 53

Transcendence and Immanence,
  True relation between, 63

World Council of Churches,
  Assembly, 17, 18

(b) Names

Abraham, 29
Ananias, 176
Aquinas, St. Thomas, 191
Aristotle, 157
Augustine, St., 147, 174

Barot, Madeleine, 152
Barth, Karl, 62
Bennett, Frank, 65
Berdyaev, Nicolas, 111
Bilheimer, Robert S., 148
Bodin, William, 154
Bratsiotis, G., 164
Brunner, Emil, 21, 80, 81
Bruno, Giordano, 55
Brutsch, C., 135

Calvin, John, 147, 155, 191
Carey, William, 14
Chéry, Père, 157
Cochrane, C. N., 147
Columba, St., 151
Constantine, 65, 66
Cornelius, 176
Coulton, G. G., 121

Damasus, Pope, 76
Daniel, 97
Daniel, Y., 155
Darwin, Charles, 51
Dostoievsky, 51

Eynard, P., 135

Freud, Sigmund, 51

Gandhi, Mahatma, 171
Gasset, Ortega y, 109
Godin, H., 155, 156
Goodchild, S., 150

Henry IV, 134
Hilton, James, 91n.
Hitler, 45, 94, 96, 106, 192
Hocking, W. E., 42
Homrighausen, E. G., 130, 136, 143
Horton, Walter M., 88

John, St., 105
Jones, Clarence W., 144

Kraemer, Hendrik, 14, 174, 175

Lewis, C. S., 80
Loew, M.-R., 160
Lökies, Pastor, 145
Louis XIV, 134
Luke, St., 119
Luther, Martin, 147, 191

Makrakis, 130
Manson, W., 115
Maritain, Jacques, 51
Marx, Karl, 44, 51
Maury, Pierre, 98
Moody, D. L., 134
Müller, Eberhard, 149
Mussolini, 48

Neill, Stephen, 72
Nero, 96
Newbigin, Lesslie, 19
Niebuhr, Reinhold, 147
Niemöller, Martin, 91, 92

Nietzsche, Friedrich, 50, 51, 94, 106

Pascal, Blaise, 174
Pauck, Wilhelm, 37 and n.
Paul, St., 27, 29, 79, 94, 98, 103n., 105, 117, 119, 147, 176, 177, 179, 191, 193, 204
Peter, St., 119, 176, 193, 197
Philip, deacon, 193
Pilate, Pontius, 192
Plato, 157

Reichelt, K. L., 126f.
Russell, Bertrand, 51

Sankey, I. D., 134
Sartre, Jean Paul, 198
Savarimuthu, S. W., 169
Schutz, Roger, 95
Shillito, Edward, 46
Spinoza, 55
Stalin, 45
Stephen, St., 94

Telfer, W., 118
Temple, William, 147
Tertullian, 65, 129
Tillich, Paul, 53
Toynbee, Arnold, 147

Ursinus, 76

Velimirovic, Bishop Nicolai, 130
Vicedom, George F., 178
Vinay, T., 135
Voltaire, 84

Wesley, John, 15
Whitman, Walt, 42
Woolwich, Bishop of, 147
Wordsworth, William, 50

REPORT OF SECTION II

THE CHURCH'S WITNESS TO GOD'S DESIGN

Received by the Assembly and commended to the churches for their serious consideration and appropriate action.

I. THE PURPOSE OF GOD

THE purpose of God is to reconcile all men to Himself and to one another in Jesus Christ His Son. That purpose was made manifest in Jesus Christ—His incarnation, His ministry of service, His death on the Cross, His resurrection and ascension. It continues in the gift of the Holy Spirit, in the command to make disciples of all nations, and in the abiding presence of Christ with His Church. It looks forward to its consummation in the gathering together of all things in Christ. Much in that purpose is still hidden from us. Three things are perfectly plain:

All that we need to know concerning God's purpose is already revealed in Christ.

It is God's will that the Gospel should be proclaimed to all men everywhere.

God is pleased to use human obedience in the fulfilment of His purpose.

To the Church, then, is given the privilege of so making Christ known to men that each is confronted with the necessity of a personal decision, Yes or No. The Gospel is the expression both of God's love to man, and of His claim to man's obedience. In this lies the solemnity of the decision. Those who obey are delivered from the power of the world in which sin reigns, and already, in the fellowship of the children of God, have the experience of eternal life. Those who reject the love of God remain under His judgment and are in danger of sharing in the impending doom of the world that is passing away.

II. THE PRESENT SITUATION

Two world wars have shaken the structure of the world. Social and political convulsions rage everywhere. The mood of many swings between despair, frustration and blind indiffer-

212

ence. The millions of Asia and Africa, filled with new hope, are determined to seize now the opportunity of shaping their own destiny. Mankind, so clearly called even by its own interests to live at peace, seems still rent by a fanaticism of mutual destruction.

The word "faith" has acquired a new context. For most men, it is now faith in the new society, now to be founded once for all, in which the "good life" will be realised. Even in the present-day confusion, there are still many who believe that man, by wise planning, can master his own situation. Such men are interested not in absolute truth, but in achievement. In face of many religions and philosophies, it is held that all truth is relative, and so the necessity of a costly personal decision is evaded.

A formidable obstacle to Christian faith is the conviction that it belongs definitely to a historical phase now past. To those who know little of it, it seems merely irrelevant. More thoughtful men, who hold that it enshrines some spiritual and cultural values, regard it as no longer honestly tenable as a system of belief. And yet there is an earnest desire for clearly formulated truth. The religions of Asia and Africa are being challenged and profoundly modified. In the period of transition, the minds of millions are more than usual open to the Gospel. But the tendency in these countries to press an ancient religion into service as one foundation for a politically homogeneous state already threatens the liberty of Christian action.

So the Church sees the World. What does the World see, or think it sees, when it looks at the Church?

It is a Church divided, and in its separated parts are often found hesitancy, complacency, or the desire to domineer.

It is a Church that has largely lost touch with the dominant realities of modern life, and still tries to meet the modern world with language and a technique that may have been appropriate two hundred years ago.

It is a Church that, by its failure to speak effectively on the subject of war, has appeared impotent to deal with the realities of the human situation.

It is a Church accused by many of having been blind to the movement of God in history, of having sided with the vested interests of society and state, and of having failed to kindle the vision and to purify the wills of men in a changing world.

It is a Church under suspicion in many quarters of having used its missionary enterprise to further the foreign policies of states and the imperialistic designs of the powers of the West.

Much in this indictment may be untrue; but the Church is called to deep shame and penitence for its failure to manifest Jesus Christ to men as He really is. Yet the Church is still the Church of God, in which, and in which alone He is pleased to reveal Himself and His redemptive purpose in Jesus Christ, in whom and in whom alone the renewal of man's life is possible.

It is a Church to which, through the upheavals of the modern world, God cries aloud and says "Come let us reason together" (Isa. 1, 18).

It is a Church that is, to millions of faithful people, the place where they receive the grace of Christ and are given strength to live by the power of His victory.

It is a Church awaking to its great opportunity to enter as the minister of the redemption wrought by Christ into that world with which God has confronted us.

It is a Church that today desires to treat evangelism as the common task of all the churches, and transcends the traditional distinction between the so-called Christian and so-called non-Christian lands.

The present day is the beginning of a new epoch of missionary enterprise, calling for the pioneering spirit, and for the dedication of many lives to the service of the Gospel of God.

III. THE CHURCH'S TASK IN THE PRESENT DAY

The duty of the Church at such a time can be expressed simply in one sentence—it is required to be faithful to the Gospel and to realise more fully its own nature as the Church. But fulfilment of his duty involves a revolution in thought and practice.

A. *Worship and Witness.* Worship and witness have sometimes been held in separation, but they belong inseparably together, as the fulfilment of the great command that men should love God and should love their neighbour as themselves.

When the ordinary man speaks of the Church, he thinks of a group of people worshiping in a building. By what that group is, the Church is judged. Effective witness becomes possible only as each worshiping group is so filled with the joy of the risen and living Lord that even the outsider becomes aware that, when the Church speaks, it speaks of real things.

But a worshiping group of individuals is not necessarily a community. It is essential that each group become a real fellowship, through acceptance by all of full Christian responsibility for mutual service, and by breaking down the barriers of race and class. It is intolerable that anyone should be excluded, because of his race or colour, from any Christian place of worship.

The world to-day is hungry for community. But to many it seems that the fellowship of the churches is much less satisfying than that which they find in their own secular or religious organisations and brotherhood. This cannot be put right, until the churches more recognisably bear the marks of the Lord Jesus, and cease to hinder others, by the poverty of the fellowship they offer, from coming to Him.

B. *A People of God in the World.* The Church must find its way to the places where men really live. It must penetrate the alienated world from within, and make the minds of men familiar with the elementary realities of God, of sin and of purpose in life. This can be done partly through new ventures of self-identification by Christians with the life of that world, partly through Christians making the word of the Gospel heard in the places where decisions are made that affect the lives of men. It can be done fully only if, by the inspiration of the Holy Spirit, the Church recovers the spirit of prophecy to discern the signs of the times, to see the purpose of God working in the immense movements and revolutions of the present age, and again to speak to the nations the word of God with authority.

C. *The Ecumenical Sense.* Each Christian group must be conscious of the world-wide fellowship of which it is a part. Each Sunday as it comes, is a reminder of the innumerable company throughout the world, who on that day are worshiping the same Lord Jesus Christ as God and Saviour. It can attain to fulness of Christian life only as it accepts its place in the great purpose of God that all men shall be saved, and takes up the responsibility for prayer, service and sacrificial missionary enterprise involved in that acceptance.

IV. MISSIONARY AND EVANGELISTIC STRATEGY

The evident demand of God in this situation is that the whole Church should set itself to the total task of winning the whole world for Christ.

A. *Lay Work and Witness.* This is the day of opportunity for the lay membership of the Church. The work of God requires that every member of the Church, ordained and lay, be an active witness. The layman has his duties in the Church in worship and stewardship. He is charged also with a task in the world outside. The most obvious sphere of witness is the home, the place in which the Church of the coming generation is to be built up. Some are called to special ministries of preaching or intercession. For most people the field of witness lies in the place where they do their daily work. The way in which they do their job or exercise their profession must be unmistakably Christian. But also they are called to bear courageously, as God gives the opportunity, that witness in word through which others are confronted with the challenge of the Living Christ. Christian service is to be conceived in the widest possible terms. The variety of forms of witness is just the means by which God can make known the fulness of the Gospel as His answer to all the needs of mankind.

B. *Co-operation in Evangelism.* The churches may find a denominational framework too narrow for its work today. Most evangelistic work is carried out by denominational agencies in separation. In many situations this is the natural way. But there are places where the work can best be done through co-operation in evangelism. Many difficulties may have to be faced. It is important that the constituent churches of the World Council of Churches seek comity among themselves in all matters relating to evangelistic effort and to their respective spheres of responsibility. But it is God Himself who is showing us the inadequacy of those things to which we have been accustomed. The churches are called today to be much more flexible in organization than in the past. They must deal with every situation in the light of the total task.

There are parts of the world where the Church is holding on under great difficulties, and where its liberty of action is restricted or denied. Its witness is carried out more by suffering than by preaching. Such churches rightly claim that within the fellowship of faith they shall be supported by the prayers and succour of every member of the world-wide Church.

In other areas, God has set new opportunities before the Church. Millions of people are ready to listen to the Gospel, and are already considering whether it is their only hope. Such areas should be considered the responsibility of the whole Church, and not only of those at present engaged in work in them; adequate resources in personnel and money should be made immediately available to the local churches, so that what needs to be done can be done effectively and without delay. The younger churches are crying out for the help of Christian colleagues from the West. Churches older and younger alike call urgently for the dedication of lives to the ordained ministry, and other full-time vocations of service to Christ in His Church.

C. *The Problem of Our Divisions.* If we take seriously our world-wide task, we are certain to be driven to think again of our divisions. Can we remain divided? St. Paul told his Corinthian converts that he could not give them solid food, because their divisions showed that they were still carnal. God gives the gift of His grace to churches even in their separation. We are persuaded that He has yet additional gifts to give to a Church united in accordance with His will. The pressure for corporate unity comes most strongly from the younger churches; the older manifest greater caution. The path to unity is always beset by many difficulties. But the ecumenical movement loses significance, unless all its constituent churches bear ceaselessly in mind the prayer of Christ "that they all may be one; as thou, Father, art in me, and I in thee, that they also may be one in us: that the world may believe that thou hast sent me" (John XVII, 21), and are prepared to move forward, as God guides them, to further unity in Faith, in fellowship, at the table of the Lord, and in united proclamation of the word of life.

V. "NOW IS THE ACCEPTED TIME"

As we have studied evangelism in its ecumenical setting we have been burdened by a sense of urgency. We have recaptured something of the spirit of the apostolic age, when the believers "went everywhere preaching the word." If the Gospel really is a matter of life and death, it seems intolerable that any human being now in the world should live out his life without ever having the chance to hear and receive it.

It is not within the power of man alone to create a new evangelistic movement. But the Holy Spirit is at work in men with men. In the past He has from time to time quickened the Church with power from on high. It is our earnest hope and prayer that He will do a mighty work in our day, giving the Church again wisdom and power rightly to proclaim the good news of Jesus Christ to men. We rejoice that the World Council of Churches has included evangelism in its programme of development. Already we are seeing signs of renewal and fresh life.

Now, not tomorrow, is the time to act. God does not wait for us to be perfect; He is willing to use very imperfect instruments. What matters is that the instrument should be available for His use. The results of our efforts are not in our hands but in His. But He has given us the assurance that "it is required in stewards that a man be found faithful," and that where that faithfulness is found, He is able "to do exceedingly abundantly, above all that we ask or think."

NOTE: In this short statement, it has not been possible to indicate in any detail the new problems in evangelism that have to be solved, and the new methods of work that are available to the Church to-day. There is a great field of research open in such matters as the use of radio and television, and in the application to local conditions of principles generally agreed upon. We venture to refer readers to the preparatory volume of our section *The Church's Witness to God's Design,* and to the Report of the Whitby Conference of the International Missionary Council *The Witness of a Revolutionary Church,* and to the printed volume of the speeches delivered at that Conference, in which will be found much fuller discussion both of principles and of applications, and evidence of the power of God at work in the world to-day.

MAN'S DISORDER AND GOD'S DESIGN
Volume III

THE CHURCH
AND THE
DISORDER
OF SOCIETY

THE
CHURCH AND
THE DISORDER
OF
SOCIETY

AN

ECUMENICAL STUDY

PREPARED UNDER THE AUSPICES OF THE

WORLD COUNCIL OF CHURCHES

VOLUME THREE

THE
CHURCH AND
THE DISORDER
OF
SOCIETY

AN
ECUMENICAL STUDY
PREPARED UNDER THE AUSPICES OF THE
WORLD COUNCIL OF CHURCHES

VOLUME THREE

CONTENTS

List of Contributors

I GOD'S DESIGN AND THE PRESENT DISORDER OF
CIVILISATION Reinhold Niebuhr   13

II TECHNICS AND CIVILISATION J. H. Oldham   29

III THE SITUATION IN EUROPE Jacques Ellul   50

IV THE SITUATION IN ASIA—I M. Searle Bates   61

V THE SITUATION IN ASIA—II M. M. Thomas   71

VI THE SITUATION IN U.S.A. Reinhold Niebuhr   80

VII PERSONAL RELATIONS IN A TECHNICAL SOCIETY
Kathleen Bliss   83

VIII THE INVOLVEMENT OF THE CHURCH John C.
Bennett   91

IX NEW BEGINNINGS IN THE RELATIONS OF THE
CHURCH WITH SOCIETY E. C. Urwin   103

X A RESPONSIBLE SOCIETY J. H. Oldham   120

XI THE STRATEGY OF THE CHURCH C. L. Patijn   155

XII AND NOW? Emil Brunner   176

Membership of the Commission   181

Index   183

Report of Section III

CONTRIBUTORS

BATES, M. S., Ph.D., Professor of History, University of Nanking. Author of *Religious Liberty*.

BENNETT, J. C., D.D., Professor of Christian Theology and Ethics, Union Theological Seminary. Author of *Christian Realism, Christian Ethics and Social Policy*, etc.

BLISS, Mrs. Kathleen, Editor, *The Christian News-Letter*.

BRUNNER, Emil, Dr. Theol., Professor of Systematic Theology, Zurich. Author of *The Mediator, Justice and the Social Order*, etc.

ELLUL, Jacques, Docteur en Droit, Professor in the Faculty of Law, Bordeaux. Author of *Le Fondement Théologique du Droit*, etc.

NIEBUHR, Reinhold, D.D., Professor of Applied Christianity, Union Theological Seminary, New York. Author of *The Nature and Destiny of Man*, etc.

OLDHAM, J. H., D.D., formerly Editor of *The Christian News-Letter* ; Senior Officer, Christian Frontier Council ; Secretary, International Missionary Council. Joint author of *The Church and its Function in Society* ; author, *Christianity and the Race Problem*, etc.

PATIJN, C. L., Doctor of Law, Counsellor to the Ministry of Economic Affairs at The Hague.

THOMAS, M. M., Secretary, World's Student Christian Federation ; formerly Youth Secretary of the Mar Thoma Syrian Church of Malabar.

URWIN, E. C., General Secretary, Social Welfare Department, Methodist Church of Great Britain. Chairman, Social Responsibility Department, British Council of Churches. Author, *Religion in a Planned Society, Can the Family Survive ?*, etc.

I

GOD'S DESIGN AND THE PRESENT DISORDER OF CIVILISATION

Reinhold Niebuhr

I

OUR civilisation has been engulfed in obvious and wide-spread political and social confusion since the second decade of this century. One world war has followed another ; and the second conflagration has left the world in even deeper distress and less assurance for the future than the first. While western civilisation has been the centre and source of the world's disorders, the social confusion and political tumult has spread from this centre into the whole world.

The most immediate cause of our distress could be defined as the inability and unwillingness of modern men and nations to establish and re-establish community, or to achieve and to reconstruct justice under conditions which a technical civilisation has created. We know, of course, that no human society has ever been free of corruption, of injustice and domination. As Christians we are particularly aware of the fragmentary and imperfect character of all human communities. But there are periods of history in which conflicting and competing social forces reach a state of comparative equilibrium and nations arrive at comparative concord. While we cannot, from the standpoint of a Christian interpretation of history, make too sharp a distinction between these periods of calm and of tumult, it is nevertheless important to consider the specific causes of the more explicit forms of disorder from which our generation is suffering and see how they are related to the general and perennially operative causes of injustice and confusion in the human community.

The favourite Christian interpretation of our present distress is to attribute it simply to the secularism of our age. It is an interpretation to which Catholicism is particularly prone but which many Protestants also make. According to this thesis the world fell into confusion when modern civilisation disavowed faith in God, an apostasy which had the moral consequence of destroying the authority of God's law over the recalcitrant and competing wills and interests of men and of nations. While it is worth noting that the sanguine hopes of a humanistic age have been cruelly disappointed in the harsh realities of our own day, we must resist the temptation to throw the whole responsibility of our present distress upon " secularism."

The fact is that the " Christian " mediæval civilisation against which modern secularism revolted had not so simply achieved " God's order " as it pretended. It was in fact incapable of making place for the forces and interests which a commercial civilisation had developed ; and its own uncritical identification of the ambiguous moral realities of a feudal society with the will of God was one of the causes of the secularist revolt. Furthermore, modern secularism was not primarily involved in the moral nihilism of denying any law beyond human interests. It was blinded by another error. It believed that it would be a comparatively simple matter to define the laws of justice by which human affairs were to be regulated, and an even simpler matter to achieve an accord between competing and conflicting human wills and interests.

A truly Christian interpretation of our present distress must be able to appreciate the necessity, or at least the inevitability, of revolts against the pretensions of so-called " Christian " civilisations even while it seeks to correct the illusions which led modern secularism astray. We must beware lest we fall into the sins of the elder brother in our Lord's parable, by gloating over the discomfiture of the Prodigal Son, who is not yet prepared to return to the house of his Father, but who has certainly wasted his substance in that " far country " in which he hoped to achieve independence.

The interpretation of our present disorder which attributes it primarily to the evils of secularism is usually also involved in the error of assuming that it is possible to define the order of God in detailed and specific laws and rules of justice. But God's order can never be identified with some specific form of social organisation. It is very important to arrive at concepts of justice which draw upon the common experience of mankind and set a restraint upon human self-interest. But it must be recognised that, in so far as such principles of justice are given specific historical meaning, they also become touched by historical contingency.

There are basic conditions set by God to which human life must conform. But these cannot be identified with any particular social or political organisation. For these are all tentative and ambiguous methods of preserving a tolerable harmony of life with life, sin presupposed. Among man's God-given gifts are his unique freedom which enables him to create human communities, wider and more complex than those which natural cohesion prompts. In so far as man is a limited creature his forms of social organisation are determined by natural compulsions. He lives in communities in which the kinship of family and tribe and geographic limitations set the bounds of his society.

In so far as man is a unique creature who can break the bounds and transcend the limits of nature, forms of communal organisation and structures of justice are subject to endless historical elaboration. The natural limits of geography, language and ethnic affinity always remain as one factor of cohesion in the human community ; but they are determinative only in the negative sense. Positively the law of human existence for man as free spirit, who transcends natural limitations, is the law of love. Only in the free giving of life to life and the uncoerced relation of personality to personality can full justice be done both to the unique individuality of every person and the requirements of peace for the whole community. Various schemes of justice must be devised to give the law of love practical effect amidst the complexities of human society and to approximate under the conditions of human sinfulness its ideal harmony of life with life. But all such structures and schemes of justice must be regarded as relative; for they embody egoistic and sinful elements in the very structure, intended to set bounds to sin. For the Christian the love which is revealed in the suffering and self-giving life and death of our Lord, is the only final and authoritative definition of the " order of God."

Our actual human communities are always shot through with disorder and confusion ; for the same freedom which enables man to build wider and more complex communities also gives him the power to make his own will, whether individual or collective, the perverse centre of the whole community, whether the whole community be defined in national or international terms. The domination of the weak by the strong and the conflict between various wills, interests and forces are the inevitable corruptions of human self-seeking in all historic communities, though tremendous differences may and do exist between forms of justice which preserve a tolerable degree of harmony and those which embody domination or conflict.

II

While there is thus no perfect peace or order in any human community there are times and seasons when a tolerable justice, hallowed by tradition and supplemented by personal discipline and goodness, gives society a long period of social stability. There are other times when the sins of the fathers are visited upon the children ; and new social forces rise up as the " vengeance of the Lord " against traditional injustice. We are living in such a time.   This is a period of judgment in which the structures and systems of community which once guaranteed a tolerable justice have themselves become the source of confusion and injustice.

We are witnessing, and participating in, the decline of a European civilisation, together with a wide confusion in a world community.   The immediate occasion for the social and political confusion of our day is the progressive development of technics.   Technical advance first created a commercial civilisation which could not be contained within the static forms of the agrarian-feudal economy of the mediæval period.   Subsequently a further development of technics created an industrial civilisation which could not achieve or maintain a tolerable justice within the liberal presuppositions which a commercial civilisation had complacently accepted.   These same technics increased the possibilities of world community ; but the first impetus of a technical society toward world community was an imperialistic one.   The European nations, armed with new technical-economic power, used their power to establish their dominion in Africa and Asia ; and came in conflict with each other over the spoils of their imperial thrusts.   More recently the African and Asiatic world has risen in rebellion and opposition to this dominion. Their first resentment was against economic and political injustices, resulting from this new expansion of European power. More recently they have felt the pretension of ethnic superiority which the white races expressed in establishing their power, even more keenly than the economic and political injustices.   The missionary enterprise, emanating from the Christian portion of the white world, has been, on the whole, a counter-weight to this evil. But this enterprise was seriously embarrassed by the fact that the European world (in which we must include America and the British dominions as well as other nations with a European heritage) was not only the source of the Christian missionary impulse but also the basis of the thrust of imperial dominion.

Thus the development of new technical power created a potential, but not an actual, world community. The new power was exercised too egotistically to establish world-wide community. Some of the imperial powers gradually developed a sense of imperial responsibility which mitigated the exploiting tendencies of imperialism. Nevertheless the total effect of the expansion of technical power has been to give international tensions a world-wide scope and to involve the world in two conflicts of global dimensions.

The introduction of technics into the various national economies also tended to destroy the more organic and traditional forms of community on the national level. Urban life produced atomic individuals who lacked the social disciplines of the older and more organic societies and industrialism substituted dynamic inequalities and injustices in place of the more static inequalities of an agrarian society. The new liberal society which developed with modern commerce and industry did establish many individual rights and liberties which did not exist in the older society. It created democratic political institutions, extended and even universalised popular education, prompted many genuine humanitarian reforms, granted the rights of citizenship to women, and used many new scientific technics for alleviating human misery.

But all these gains could not hide the fact that modern industrial society was unable to establish a tolerable justice or to give the vast masses, involved in modern industry, a basic security. Consequently a virtual civil war between the new industrial classes and the more privileged and secure classes of landowners and owners of industrial property destroyed the unity of industrial nations. The healthiest modern nations are those, who either (like America) have been sufficiently privileged to have been able to avoid a desperate struggle between the industrial and middle classes ; or who (like Britain and some of its dominions and some of the smaller nations of northern and western Europe) have been able to mitigate this conflict by religious and moral resources of a special order. Nevertheless the total effect of the rise of modern industry has been the destruction of community on the national level and the extension of conflict on the international level.

III

To attribute the social confusion of our era to the introduction of technics is, however, to give only the negative cause of our discontent. The more positive cause has been the failure of men and nations either to desire or to achieve a tolerable justice within the new conditions created by expanding technical power. This moral failure cannot be attributed merely to ignorance and sloth. Everywhere there are evidences of the positive thrust of the sinful pride and will-to-power of old oligarchies and new social forces, of old cultures and new ideologies. Every one of the social, cultural and religious forces involved in the readjustments of modern society has contributed to the failure of modern society. We must seek most rigorously to avoid the temptation to interpret our disaster as the consequence, primarily, of the sins of the classes, nations and forces with which we are not allied.

Amidst the vast social and cultural movements of modern life it is possible to isolate and define three broad forces, each of which must bear a portion of responsibility for our present situation. The first is the old power of the landlord. who dominated the agrarian society ; the second is the newer commercial and industrial owners ; and the third the rising industrial classes. The Catholic faith had historic affinities with the first class, though in some predominantly Protestant nations established or state churches tended to maintain as intimate an embrace with the older agrarian aristocratic classes as did Catholicism. This affinity gave the Catholic Church a certain freedom from the prejudices of the rising commercial-industrial culture which sometimes enabled it to establish contact with, or maintain the allegiance of, the new industrial labourers. This was an achievement which was beyond the moral and religious competence of most Protestant groups. But this affinity also placed Catholicism in frequent alliance with feudal-agrarian conservatism and in opposition to both the liberal-democratic forces and marxist-labour forces. The political situation in Spain and some South American countries exemplifies this

tendency with particular vividness. Sometimes efforts to reconstruct the older authoritarianism under modern conditions betray
Catholicism into active alliance with fascism, as in Italy, Spain
and Austria.

Furthermore, Catholic moral and political theory, which
makes a " natural law," with fixed and specific content, the norm
of political and economic justice, is an inadequate guide for
regulating the complex relations of a modern industrial society.

In general, churches, both Catholic and Protestant, are
inclined to prefer the social forms of an established order and fail
to recognise that new conditions may change an old justice into a
new injustice. Thus they are heedless of the divine judgment
which challenges every historic social order in so far as it incorporates injustices. Thereby they tend to give religious support
to the moral complacency of established and privileged classes.

The new commercial-industrial society was informed partly
by secular-liberal and partly by Protestant religious and moral
viewpoints. The modern liberal culture assumed that a free
expression of all forces and interests in society would automatically make for justice. In its most consistent form modern
liberalism believed in a pre-established harmony in society, akin
to the harmony of non-historical nature which would guarantee
justice if only governmental controls were reduced to minimal
terms. This *laissez faire* theory did not realise that human
freedom expresses itself destructively as well as creatively, and
that an increase in human freedom and power through the
introduction of technics makes the achievement of justice more,
rather than less, difficult than in non-technical civilisations. The
liberal culture of our era believed, either that the egoism of
individuals, classes and nations was limited and harmless, or it
hoped that the expression of self-interest was due to ignorance
which could be overcome by growing social and political
intelligence. This optimism misread the facts of human nature,
as they are known from the standpoint of the Christian Faith and
as they are attested by every page of history. It therefore led to
pathetic illusions which have been refuted by contemporary
history. Thus the political principles which were to guarantee
justice actually contributed to ever greater concentrations of
power in modern society and to resulting injustices.

While some Protestant churches capitulated to the moral
sentimentalities of this secular creed of progress and became

uncritical allies of the commercial and industrial oligarchy in modern society, others failed to preserve a prophetic independence of modern middle class culture, even where they maintained a more Biblical faith.   Sometimes (and this was the special temptation of Lutheran churches) they sought to be a-political because they recognised that all political positions are morally ambiguous.   But they failed to recognise that an ostensibly non-political position tends to become political by supporting the established, against the advancing or challenging social classes.   Also they did not always see that, though it may be impossible or unwise for the Church as such to engage in the political struggle, it is the duty of Christians to engage in it.   For the political struggle is the means of achieving a tolerably just social order.   However morally ambiguous every political position may be, Christians cannot disavow the responsibility of making political choices and decisions.

Sometimes (and this was the particular temptation of Calvinist churches) the new problems of justice in a technical society were approached legalistically.   The Biblical legalism was frequently irrelevant to the issues raised and tended to support an uncritical individualism against the urgent demand for community in an industrial society.

Both the Catholic and the Protestant forms of the Christian Faith were thus involved in the decay of our civilisation and were partially responsible for the rise of new secular religions, which promised the establishment of a more integral community and which rose in revolt against both the Christian and the secular forms of the liberal society.

Every form of community in human history only approximates to the obligations of the love commandment; for communities are kept in order partly by power and partly by natural impulses of cohesion, such as a common language, a geographic limit and a common history.   But the achievement of a tolerable harmony of life with life is always related to the love commandment. Historic Christianity failed to implement the moral imperatives of the love commandment under the new conditions of a technical age.   Thereby it helped to give rise to political religions which sought either cynical or utopian methods of achieving community.   Traditional Christianity expressed that side of the Christian truth which appreciates the perennially fragmentary character of all historic achievements and realises that our final fulfilment is possible only through God's forgiveness. But it neglected the possibility and necessity of achieving community under the new conditions which each age sets and which were particularly challenging under the new conditions of a technical age. The new political religions on the other hand had no sense of the divine judgment and the divine fulfilment which stands against and over all human history. They promised the fulfilment of life either in an idolatrous national community or in an international classless society, conceived in utopian terms.

IV

The two forms of political religion which have aggravated the social confusion of our day, in their very effort to arrest it, are remarkably different in principle. The one is morally cynical and the other morally sentimental and utopian. The one worships force and the other hopes to establish an anarchistic millennium by using revolutionary force to eliminate the need of force in a pure and classless society. The one worships a limited national community. The other hopes for world-wide international community. That they should turn out to be so similar in practice is one of the most instructive aspects of our contemporary situation. It proves that the self-righteous fury of a consistent marxism may be as dangerous to the establishment of community as the cynicism of a consistent fascism. This similarity in practice, despite differences in principle, can only be understood from the standpoint of a Christian interpretation of life and history ; for only from that standpoint is it possible to see how quickly human virtue turns to evil when men forget the sinful corruption in every expression of human interest.

It is nevertheless important to emphasise the differences in principle between the two. Fascism was immediately responsible for plunging the world into the second world war. Its consistent moral cynicism destroyed all moral restraints and disciplines of a Christian and a humanistic culture. It developed forms of cruelty and inhumanity which plumbed hitherto unimagined depths of evil and sowed seeds of vindictiveness from which European civilisation still suffers. Marxism, on the other hand, when stripped of its religious illusions and of its false promises of redemption may well contain proximate solutions for the immediate problems of social justice in our day. It is

wrong to regard the socialisation of property as a cure-all for
every social ill ; but it is no more wrong than to regard such
socialisation as of itself evil.

There is even now no possibility of bringing social stability
and a measure of justice to an impoverished world if this conflict
between Christianity and marxism is not resolved. In the whole
of Europe there are forms of socialism which dread and abhor
the totalitarian consequences of a consistent communism. They
do not always recognise that this totalitarianism may be, not so
much a corruption of the original marxism as the inevitable
consequence of consistent marxist principles.

The socialism in the western world, which abhors the
totalitarianism of communism, has difficulty in achieving a
pragmatic attitude toward the problem of property because
remnants of a utopian religion still infect its thought. But a
conservative Christian culture bears a large measure of responsibility for this confusion. It also has not freed itself from a too
dogmatic negative attitude toward socialisation. It is significant
that the healthiest western nations are those in which this conflict
was mitigated by various cultural and religious influences. In
these nations the impulse to achieve justice through socialisation
was partly generated by the Christian Faith and was therefore not
in opposition to the whole Christian heritage. In some of the
smaller continental nations, particularly in Scandinavia, the
socialist impulse stands in competitive, but not uncreative,
relation to the more traditional Christian culture. In Britain
marxism was always qualified by Christian perspectives. Therefore a pragmatic form of socialism gained political victory without
any obvious rent in the national community or in the texture of
an historic Christian culture. In America, on the other hand,
the technical achievements and the natural wealth of the nation
have prevented the socialist impulse from achieving any success.
This fact prevents sharp social conflicts but it also places the
nation in the grave peril of a too uncritical devotion to the
principles of classical liberalism. Therefore it may deal too
tardily with the problem of adequate moral and political control
over the dynamics of a technical society.

The problem of how to maintain freedom under the intense
and complex forms of social cohesion in modern technical society
and how to achieve justice when freedom is maintained cannot
be solved by any neat principles. It must be approached

pragmatically from case to case and point to point. We know that it is possible to buy security at too great a price of freedom ; and to maintain freedom at too great a price of insecurity for the masses involved in the modern industrial society. The Christian Faith as such has no solution for this problem. It ought, however, to be possible for a vital Christian faith to help people to see that both freedom and order are facets of the love commandment to which we must approximate; and also that such approximations under conditions of sin and law are bound to be imperfect in all human history. The conflict between order and freedom is perfectly resolved only in the Kingdom of perfect love which cannot be completely realised in history.

V

The possibility of avoiding another international conflict depends to a large degree upon the measure of health which can be achieved in that part of the world which is not under the dominion of the communist totalitarianism. ' Such health in turn requires a new and more creative relationship between the Christian Faith and the problems of justice and community in national life. But the peril of international anarchy is broader than the dangers thus far discussed. The internal confusion within the life of nations has aggravated, but is not solely responsible for, the new situation which we face in the community of nations. Even without the particular forms of social chaos in European culture previously analysed we would have faced the difficult problem of organising the global community, which modern technical civilisation had created by the new interdependence of modern means of transport and communication. Contrary to the assumption of our secular culture that this new interdependence would automatically create a new international accord, the increased intimacy of nations actually accentuated the evils of both imperial dominion and international conflict. Modern technics have, in short, created a potential, but not an actual, world community. Nor have the hopes of our secular culture been realised, that the fear of mutual annihilation would persuade nations to adjust their institutions and loyalties to the wider ends and responsibilities which this world-wide interdependence requires. Furthermore, the hope, expressed by many secular utopians, that the peril in which we stand would persuade nations to create a world government out of whole cloth, has also proved false. We have seen how the fear of mutual annihilation through atomic destruction is easily transmuted into the fear that the foe may annihilate us.

On every side we see in the life of nations that it is more difficult for man, particularly for collective man, to do the things he ought to do than modern secularism had imagined. All human actions betray the fact that though "we delight in the law of God after the inward man, there is a law in our members which wars against the law that is in our mind." We see, furthermore, that even the most terrible judgments do not quickly shake men and nations from the paths of self-seeking or from vindictive passions, which aggravate the evils caused by war. The words of the prophet Jeremiah apply to our generation : "Thou hast stricken them but they have not grieved ; thou hast consumed them but they have not received correction" (Jer. v, 3). The general tendency of men and nations is either to minimise the depth and breadth of the crisis in which they stand, or to be driven into hysteria by it. As St. Paul observes: "For they that sleep, sleep in the night, and they that be drunken are drunken in the night" (1 Thess. v, 7).

In this situation the first task of the Christian Church is to interpret our sorrows and distresses, the agonies and pains through which the world is passing, and to recognise the hand of God in them. We must, as Christians, neither fall into complacency by evading the gravity of our experience, nor into despair and hysteria by interpreting the distress of our day as merely confusion without meaning. There is a divine judgment upon our sins in this travail of the nations and in this fall of nations and empires, in this shaking of historic stabilities and traditions. If this divine judgment is perceived it can transmute the despair (the sorrow of this world which leads to death) into the "godly sorrow which worketh repentance" (2 Cor. vii, 10).

The prophets of Israel saw no possibility that the entire nation would thus interpret the vicissitudes of history. They hoped that the renewal of life would be possible through a "saving remnant" which would understand them from the standpoint of faith. St. Paul rightly insisted that the Church had become the "Israel of God," the saving remnant, with this function in society. But the Church, too, must not presume that it has this redemptive relation to society unless it fulfils the conditions of contrite faith. The measure of our creative relation to the perplexities of our time depends upon the knowledge of our own involvement in the guilt of the nations. It is not our business to defend a " Christian " civilisation which was never Christian in ethical achievement, or to justify ourselves against the mistakes of secularists and utopians. We must, of course, bear witness against the illusions of a secular culture which have developed from the rejection of the Gospel of Christ. But we must also know that " judgment " begins " at the house of God," and that the judgment of God is upon all the institution and traditions of religion as well as upon the political and economic arrangements of the nations.

While we must inevitably make careful and considerate judgments upon men, nations and institutions according to the relative degree of justice and community which they embody, we cannot afford to make such judgments final. Neither the Christian Church nor a Christian civilisation is called upon to judge the world, but to mediate divine judgment and grace upon all men and nations and upon itself. However terrible the evils which the Nazi rebels against civilisation achieved, our resentment against these evils must not obscure the common sin and guilt of all nations, out of which this specific evil emerged. This insight of Biblical faith must persuade the Church to bear testimony against the vindictiveness of nations towards their vanquished foes. They foolishly imagine that their victory is the proof of their righteousness and therefore vainly imagine that the destruction of an evil foe will eliminate evil from human society. Thus, heedless of the truth our Lord taught in the Parable of the Unmerciful Servant, they accentuate evil in trying to overcome it.

This Gospel warning against self-righteous vindictiveness is as relevant to our relations with possible competitors of to-day as with the fallen foe of yesterday. A democratic civilisation will take the wisest possible steps to prevent the new spread of totalitarian creeds ; and if it is truly wise it will know that economic and political health is a better barrier to the spread of totalitarianism than purely strategic measures.

VI

The Christian Faith is, of course, unable to promise, as do secular creeds, some final historical redemption from all social evil. The revelation of God's judgment and mercy in Christ negated both the pre-Christian and the post-Christian expectations of an earthly paradise ; and has taught us to look " for a city which hath foundations, whose builder and maker is God " (Hebrews xi, 10). The Kingdom of God always impinges upon history and reminds us of the indeterminate possibilities of a more perfect brotherhood in every historic community. But the sufferings of Christ also remain a permanent judgment upon the continued fragmentary and corrupted character of all our historic achievements. They are completed only as the divine mercy, mediated in Christ, purges and completes them. Our final hope is in " the forgiveness of sins, the resurrection of the body, and life everlasting."

Applied to our present situation this means that we must on the one hand strive to reform and reconstruct our historic communities so that they will achieve a tolerable peace and justice. On the other hand we know, as Christians, that sinful corruptions will be found in even the highest human achievements.

We ought as Christians to strive more, and not less, earnestly for the peace of nations. We ought not to be indifferent to the problem of what technical-political instruments are best suited to maintain a tolerable peace and to express man's obligation to his neighbour. On the other hand our faith ought to supply us with a resource which secular idealism lacks. We must learn to do our duty in the peace of our security in God, which is not disturbed by the alternate furies of unjustified hopes and unjustified despair. Knowing that "neither life nor death ... can separate us from the love of God which is in Christ Jesus our Lord " we will not be surprised to discover that all historic securities are imperfect.

There is a tendency among Christians, as well as non-Christians, to retire to the security of law, and to forget that even the best laws may become the servant of interest and sin, and that even the most hallowed institutions must be submitted to the test, whether they achieve the best possible accord between a man and his neighbour under prevailing conditions. The rapidly changing conditions of a technical society require that our sense of obedience to law shall be expressed primarily in terms of our obedience to the law of love. We have been tempted to forget not only St. Paul's warning against the impotence of law (Romans ii, 17-23) but also our Lord's warning that our righteousness must exceed the righteousness of the law. Unless divine grace flow into the heart, men will not only fail to obey the law but will use it as an instrument for their own advantage. Christian legalism has helped to sow confusion into the chaos of our day. The cure for modern lawlessness is not more emphasis upon law or efforts to define specific laws more sharply. The cure of modern lawlessness is to bring the idolatry and self-worship of all men and nations under divine judgment and to free men from both law and sin so that all things may be theirs if they are Christ's. In that spirit they can create not an anarchistic millennium but communities, and constantly renew and refresh them by the spirit of love.

Whether the nations and empires, the cultures and institutions of our day will bring forth fruits meet for repentance and thereby escape the wrath which overhangs them we do not know. Our business must be to mediate the divine judgment and mercy through Word and Sacrament so that men may know God as the author of both their death and their new life, of both the judgments under which they suffer and the new health which they may find as men and nations by His grace.

VII

In this volume we are seeking to illumine various facets of the great problem of the relation of the Christian Church to the crisis of our age.

Our first purpose is to throw some light upon the character of the crisis. Our chapters on diagnosis are meant to relate the insights of the Christian Faith to the best knowledge of our day, in seeking to understand the effect of technics upon the problems of human brotherhood in the various dimensions of human relations. We believe that it is as important for Christians to understand the particular causes of the particular disorder which characterises contemporary history as to know what are the perennial sources of perennial sinful corruptions in human society.

We have also given some attention to the involvement of the Church and the churches in various sins and corruptions of modern society, whether these are expressed in racial pride, nationalistic idolatry, or economic and political imperialism. The Church, as well as the individual Christian, must see in the distress of our day the judgment of God which calls it to repentance and to a renewing of its mind.

We believe that, though we have no reason to be proud of what has been accomplished, it is nevertheless apparent that in many areas of Christian life genuine fruits meet for repentance have been shown forth, and we have sought to give some account of these " new beginnings " in the life of the Church, in its relation to the social and political issues of our day, and in its guidance of Christian lay activity.

We have, furthermore, sought to draw some conclusions from the evidence on the social tasks which claim the special interest and service of the Church, and on the right strategy which the Church should pursue in seeking to conform to the injunction of our Lord to be a light to the world and a leaven in the world.

While it is not possible, even in an ecumenical study, to do full justice to the varying aspects of the Church's tasks and problems in various parts of the world, we have sought to make this study as world-wide as possible. We have given account of regional deviations and peculiarities in both the diagnostic and in the more affirmative approaches to our task. We are conscious of the fact that the world crisis has its centre in the European world but that its effect may be even more shattering in the Asiatic and African world. It is very important that European and non-European Christians should see the issues each from the viewpoint of the others, so that the world-wide character of the Church should become a means of grace to all of us in more fully apprehending the meaning of the universal Christ, who speaks to each and to all nations and peoples.[1]

[1]Most of the problems with which we deal are considered more fully in the reports and findings of the Oxford Conference on Church, Community and State held in 1937. Many of the problems have, of course, been sharpened by the fact that the Oxford Conference only anticipated, while we look back upon, the world catastrophes of the past decade. We therefore recognise a depth and breadth in the world crisis which could not have been fully anticipated. It is important, nevertheless, to recognise that the Oxford Conference gave many important directives to the mind of the Church for dealing with the problem of its relationship to the social order, which have not been sufficiently studied by the Church at large, but are in our opinion still valid. It is particularly important to note the general strategy which informs the Oxford directives. The Oxford Conference sought to find a middle ground between a Christian view which offered no general directives to the Christian for his decisions in regard to social and political institutions, and the view which tried to identify the mind of Christ too simply with specific economic, social, and political programmes. For the ecumenical movement, in the opinion of many, this middle ground is still the proper basis of approach.

II

TECHNICS AND CIVILISATION

J. H. Oldham

I. INTRODUCTION

OUR object in this chapter is to examine more closely the changes which modern science and technics have brought about in the life of man and society. There can be no real understanding of the predicament of society without a profound awareness of the revolutionary nature of these changes. In the five or six thousand years of recorded civilisations the range of man's powers, the reach of his arm, the speed at which he could travel, the rapidity of communication remained relatively stable. Up till the latter part of the eighteenth century the possibilities of men in these respects did not differ greatly from those of classical antiquity. From that time the curve of technical development began to rise sharply and has become steeper and steeper. A stage has now been reached at which the nature of the process has become fully clear. Men have learned not only to invent but the technique of invention. The result is that invention follows invention with bewildering speed. There may be, indeed there certainly are, limits to what men can achieve, but they are not fixed or clear. The frontier of science and invention is open country. Through these advances the whole structure of human existence is undergoing a huge change and reorganisation, marking one of the great turning points of history.

The technical advances which began in the eighteenth century, and in the nineteenth broke into a gallop, have resulted in the complete conquest of space. Instantaneous communication by speech has become possible with any part of the world. The most remote places can be reached to-day in travel more quickly than the citizens of a single nation a century and a half ago could visit one of the more distant towns in their own country.

The new scientific knowledge which has made these changes possible has had a similar revolutionary effect on the minds of men, giving them a new picture, or rather a succession of new pictures, of the nature of the universe, and a new conception of the powers and potentialities of man. Not only has there come about a fundamental change in the external conditions of men's lives, presenting them with new problems in their relations with one another, but the spiritual foundations of western civilisation have been loosened. The basic convictions and largely unquestioned assumptions by which the life of western society has in the main been guided, and to which appeal could be made in Christian preaching, have been thrown into the melting-pot.

No conception of the task of the Church in society is adequate that is not suffused with an awareness of the scale of these changes. It is to men who have passed through these experiences and been moulded by them that the Christian message has to be proclaimed to-day. The Church is still far from having come to terms with the new knowledge and its practical consequences. This is one reason why it is so little able to speak convincingly to the mind of the age. New zeal in proclaiming the Gospel will achieve little unless it is accompanied by a no less determined effort to *understand*. When we speak of the renewal of the Church, it must never be forgotten that what is needed is not only a change of heart and conversion of the will but a far-reaching renewal of the mind and imagination.

II. THE ADVENT OF THE MACHINE

Attention will be focussed in this chapter in the main on the coming and effects of the machine. But the development of technics cannot be considered in isolation. It has taken place in close and inseparable connection with other factors, which are necessary to an understanding of its impact on society. In the discussion which follows we need to distinguish and to keep clearly in view four influences which, in combination and in mutual reaction on one another, have given shape to the world which exists to-day.

The first is scientific discovery, method, and theory, which seek to unlock the secrets of nature.

The second is applied science, technology and invention, which turn knowledge to practical uses.

Thirdly, there are the human purposes which these intellectual processes are made to serve, such as the creation and acquisition of wealth, the increase of power and the prosecution of war. Modern science and technics have developed in the closest association with capitalism and the modern state, and it is these three powerful forces working together and re-enforcing one another that have made the world what it is to-day.

Fourthly, there is the general way of looking at things characteristic of modern man, the temper or philosophy of the age, to the shaping of which all the forces that have been mentioned contribute and which in turn determines the purposes they shall serve.

It may be worth while, before proceeding further, to recall to our minds the broad course of modern technical development, taking as our main guide the account given in Mr. Lewis Mumford's *Technics and Civilisation*,[1] which is the most comprehensive general survey at present available.

Mr. Mumford distinguishes three overlapping and interpenetrating phases in its history.

The first phase, which may be regarded as extending from the tenth century to the middle of the eighteenth, can be described in terms of its characteristic materials and sources of power as the period of wood and water. In it began the significant process of the separation of the production of energy from its application. There was a progressive development of the water-mill and the windmill. The immense expansion of the textile industries in the eighteenth century was achieved not by the steam-engine but by water-power. Among the inventions of this period which laid the indispensable foundations of all that was to come later were the advances in glass-making, changing the whole aspect of indoor light, improving eye-sight by the aid of spectacles, and placing at men's disposal the invaluable instruments of the telescope and microscope ; the perfecting of the clock, which as the first real instrument of precision set the pattern of accuracy for all other instruments and became, even more than the steam-engine, the key machine of the industrial age ; and the printing press, without which the rapid expansion of knowledge would have been impossible. In this period also lies the emergence of the factory, or, as it was called in the beginning, the mill, in which in a central building, divorced from the home and the craftsman's shop, large bodies of men were assembled for co-operative industrial production.

The second phase of technical development, which may be

[1]Routledge. 1934.

regarded as dating from about 1750, was based on coal and iron. Already by that time the foundations of the industrial revolution, which transformed men's ways of thinking, means of production and manner of living, had been laid. What the second revolution did was to " multiply, vulgarise and spread the methods and goods produced by the first." Products of the mine determined the characteristic inventions and developments of this period. The feverish rush for wealth, the degràdation of human labour, associated with the exploitation of mineral resources contaminated the whole of industrial activity. The increase of power and the acceleration of movement were the dominant objectives. Production and more production became the absorbing goal. Outstanding among the inventions of this period were the railway and the steamship, which began the revolution in transport that has led to the conquest of space and the unification of the world.

What is, perhaps, of chief significance in Mr. Mumford's survey is his recognition and description of a third phase, beginning in the first half of the nineteenth century and rapidly gathering momentum in the twentieth, which differs markedly from the preceding phase. It interpenetrates but has not displaced the phase of coal and iron. The ideas and motives of the earlier period still persist and dominate the industry and politics of the western world, but beneath the surface far-reaching changes are in progress. Perhaps the most outstanding among these is the development of electricity as a fresh source of energy. It brought into the industrial field its own specific materials, the new alloys and the lighter metals. A new series of synthetic compounds came into existence. Lightness and compactness acquired a new value. Mathematical accuracy, physical economy, chemical purity, surgical cleanliness are among the attributes of the new period The growing interest in biology has made itself felt in the technological field. The old unquestioned faith in the machine has been undermined by the organic conception of *life* which is slowly and imperceptibly transforming men's outlook in all directions.

Since Mr. Mumford wrote atomic fission has opened up a new source of power. There is not room in this chapter, nor would it be profitable at this stage, to speculate about the changes which its use for industrial purposes may bring about in society, but they will certainly be far-reaching.

III. THE BENEFITS OF THE MACHINE

We may consider first those effects of the machine on human life, which have been in the main beneficial.

The most obvious service of the machine has been enormously to heighten man's capacities.

Benefits of this enlargement of human capacity are undeniable. Science and technics have enabled men to overcome obstacles that stunted their growth and hemmed their lives within narrow limits. They have improved health and extended the span of human life. They have emancipated men from deadening drudgery, and opened up endless new possibilities of cultural growth.

The achievements of the machine and the human powers which have produced them are among God's good gifts to men. Unless we are clear about this at the start, the picture which emerges from our discussion will become distorted. We must neither be afraid of the machine nor seek to escape from it.

We must give full weight in our thinking to what scientific discovery and the advent of the machine have done in widening men's horizons and enlarging their imagination. The modern age began in a spirit of wonder closely akin to worship. As Mr. Philip Mairet says in a penetrating essay on " A Civilisation of Technics,"[1] " in the great European scientists and naturalists up to and including the early nineteenth century, there is to be found such a love of the creation, united with such intelligence, modesty and finely schooled perception, as is recorded of no other place or time." It is that spirit and temper that has given to the modern age such elements of greatness as it has possessed. " Should we have been able," Mr. Mairet asks, " to proceed as far as we have towards a mechanised economy, unless men felt, even if vaguely, dimly and uncertainly, that our society was doing something *great* in this age of progress, and that the technical miracles were themselves, in some sort, a collective achievement worthy of human life and love ? Perhaps even the machine workers have more than half believed that in this phase of history men were doing what men are for—not indeed doing it well enough, nor unmixed with baser purposes, yet on the whole giving expression to something inherent in man and his world-position—fulfilling a possibility that ought to be fulfilled."

[1] *Prospect for Christendom.* Edited by Maurice B. Reckitt. Faber & Faber. 1945.

Secondly, technical development has created new conditions of association and co-operation in work. For the work of the individual craftsman, who produced a finished article by his own efforts, it has substituted a process in which each individual has a hand in making only a small, perhaps infinitesimal, part of the final product. This distribution of activity in carrying out a common task deprives men of the satisfaction which a craftsman takes in the work of his own hands and of the education which he gains in perfecting his own skill. But there is no reason to regard modern forms of production as providing on the whole a less worthy form of human life or one less rich in possibilities of human growth. Technical production places men in relations of dependence on one another and assigns them a share in a joint undertaking. It creates conditions in which men can develop powerful loyalties to the common enterprise and find opportunities of working and, if necessary, of sacrificing themselves for the common good. The technical sphere, as has been said, possessed " an ethos of its own which is bound up with the ideas of common work, grading and anonymity, but also with those of service, responsibility and a sense of solidarity which may even lead to a genuine readiness for sacrifice. It is just here that the forces can be found by which the temptation to a misuse of technical power can be overcome."[1]

Dr. Niebuhr has already indicated that there has been a notable connection between technical development and the growth of democratic institutions. Factories and industrial towns brought people into association with one another and stimulated thought and political activity. The trade union movement is in the main a development among industrial workers, and the co-operative movement had its birth in industrial centres. The history of trade unionism, which was born among " the dark, satanic mills," is a long record of initiative, purposiveness, comradeship, loyalty, and triumph over all kinds of difficulty.

In Great Britain, in particular, which led the way in the industrial revolution, and where many of its worst evils became manifest, there has grown up (largely under the inspiration of religious non-conformity) a genuine industrial culture. In its industrial towns, especially in the north of England, as Mr. W. G.

[1] *Frankfurter Hefte.* December, 1947.

Symons has shown,[1] there is to be found a whole structure of working-class institutions and activities, including the vigorous life of trade unions, the great trading and productive institutions of the co-operative movement, the organs of adult education, the friendly societies, orchestral and choral societies and hosts of other clubs and societies of working men. Though some help was received from outside, by far the greater part of all this was the creation of working folk themselves.

Thirdly, we may consider the effect of the technical age on human character. Man's adventures with machines have made exacting and continuous demands on his courage, resource, endurance, persistence, skill, precision, judgment and decision. In those who deal with machines at the higher levels—skilled craftsmen, technicians, administrators—their daily work develops a strength and toughness of character. The language of the machines to those who use them is : " If you make a slip in handling us you die." The management of a factory demands not only knowledge of a variety of technical processes, but ability to deal with men and the capacity to overcome every kind of unexpected difficulty.

Perhaps the change of which the Church has to take account in the fulfilment of its mission to-day is the new temper of respect for fact which science and technics have created in those who have to do with them. We cannot better the description of this given by Mr. Lewis Mumford. " Whereas the mediæval man," he says, " determined reality by the extent to which it agreed with a complicated tissue of beliefs, in the case of modern man the final arbiter of judgment is always a set of facts, recourse to which is equally open and equally satisfactory to all normally con-stituted organisms. The technique of creating a neutral world of fact as distinguished from the raw data of immediate experience was the great general contribution of modern analytic science. . . . The concept of a neutral world, untouched by man's efforts, indifferent to his activities, obdurate to his wish and supplication, is one of the great triumphs of man's imagination, and in itself it represents a fresh human value."[2]

This settled habit of acknowledging a neutral world of fact to which all have to submit has far-reaching social and political consequences. It opens up wide fields of practical co-operation

[1] *The Christian News-Letter*, No. 92, July 30th, 1941.
[2] *Technics and Civilisation*, pp. 360-2. Routledge. 1934.

in which religious differences and questions of ultimate belief can for the time being be left on one side.   People who differ widely in convictions and tastes can by submitting in common to technical requirements successfully co-operate in running a railway or factory, in administering health services and a host of other social activities.   Over a wide field tolerance becomes an accepted and normal attitude.

In a limited, though wider, area the fraternity of scientists offers the outstanding example of a " free " society.   Every one is not only permitted but expected to form and express his own independent judgment.   If he believes others to be in the wrong he says so.   With equal readiness he submits his own opinion to the judgment of his fellows.   All alike are confident that in due course a collective judgment will be formed which will meet with general acceptance.

This attitude and temper is, however, by no means confined to scientists.   It extends to far wider circles where men co-operate to meet the requirements of an objectively determined situation. We must not allow the darker side of the industrial picture, with its cut-throat competition, ruthless exploitation, acute tensions and seemingly irreconcilable conflicts to blind us to the wide range of co-operation and goodwill that exists in the industrial field.   A well-placed and reliable observer of industrial conditions in England can write : " As I travel about the country I find in the men I meet sympathy with other men, love of justice, desire that all should have a chance, mutual respect, hatred of arrogance, acceptance of sensitive responsible ' meeting ' as the proper relation of man with man—attitudes which I believe have never been found so highly developed among human kind."   The conditions described exist, no doubt, in very varying degrees in different countries, and in different areas and sections of the same country, but they are a real element in the actual world, and the picture will be out of perspective if they are forgotten.

There is no reason to doubt that, just as machines evoke in those who have to do with them personal qualities of grit and skill, so a technical society can be a means of fostering social qualities in those who respond to its demands.   A striking illustration is provided in a small volume by Sir Oliver Franks on *Central Planning and Control in War and Peace*.   A philosopher by trade, and now British Ambassador to the United States, during the war Sir Oliver Franks became the Civil Service head of the Ministry of Supply, where he had an exceptional opportunity of observing the operations of British industry as a whole. Reviewing his experience, he makes it clear that the Ministry of Supply was not simply a machine set in motion by the receipt of orders from the appropriate authorities in the Government and emitting a host of detailed instructions to producing firms. The processes of effective planning and control are more *dialectical*. If the operations are to proceed with certainty and success there must be a meeting of minds and a unity of purpose established among the responsible participants. The Ministry was full of intellectual energy and the clash of competing ideas. All claims on limited resources were subject to ruthless cross-examination by interested parties. This argumentative process was an essential condition of success. This story, told in detail by one who had part in it, presents a vivid picture of the possibilities of human co-operation in a technical society.

It is essential that we should not merely acknowledge intellectually but allow ourselves to *feel* the benefits which the machine has brought to humanity. If we fail to do this, the picture of technics which we form will be out of focus. The world of the machine is, at any rate, the world in which a large proportion of the members of the Church have to live. It is a world in which many of them (including workers as well as managers and technicians) find it possible to live a human life in relations with other human beings that are on the whole healthy and satisfying. If this is true, as it unhappily is, only of some parts of the field, there is no decisive reason why with goodwill, intelligence and determination the opportunities should not be brought progressively within the reach of widening circles.

IV. EVIL EFFECTS OF THE MACHINE

But the ascendancy of the machine in modern life has also a darker and more menacing side. Its effects may even be catastrophic.

No study of the machine would tell the truth about it, if it failed to emphasise the intimate association between the machine and war. War has been one of the chief stimulants of invention, as the last war amply demonstrated. Throughout modern history, military forces have absorbed a substantial share of the products of industry. War is the ideal consumer in the rapidity of its consumption.   There has been a close connection between the regimentation of the army and the regimentation of industry.

To-day, as never before, scientific research and technical invention are controlled and deflected with a view to the eventuality of war.   There could be no more convincing or startling evidence of the distortion of the true purposes of life from which we are suffering to-day than the extent to which in all countries, scientific research is under the direction of the military authorities.   In a widely discussed article[1] Professor Ridenour ventures the guess (exact figures are not available) that the expenditure on research by the American army and navy totals $90,000,000, which is three times the amount available in 1940 for scientific research in all the universities of America.

The development of technics has been intimately bound up not only with the practice of war but with the forces of capitalism, imperialism and the growing power of the modern state.   It is association with these forces that has given to technical development its furious pace and demonic quality.   In increasing immeasurably the power at men's disposal, it has stimulated their power-loving impulses and fostered the belief that there is no force that they cannot harness and no object that is beyond their reach.

The callousness to suffering and brutal contempt for human life which characterised the industrial revolution in its beginnings may have been no greater than in earlier periods, but they found new hideous forms of expression and affected vast populations.   The barbarism which disfigured the early days of industrialism—the ugliness and squalor, the reckless pollution of air and streams, the creation of slums, the shocking inhumanities, the conscienceless exploitation of the labour not only of men but of women and children—need not be regarded as inevitable results of the coming of the machine.   These evils are still with us, but in the more progressive countries they are in process of being overcome by factory legislation and other protective measures, by housing schemes, by town and country planning, by the spread of education, by the rise to power of trade unionism and by the changes to which attention has already been called, within technology itself.   There is still much to be accomplished, even in advanced countries, in the emancipation of human life

[1] In the *American Scholar*.   Reprinted in the *Bulletin of Atomic Scientists*, August, 1947.

from the ravages and deformities caused by the machine. But it would be wrong to ignore the progress that has been made. The present task is to build on foundations that have already been laid.

The abuses which have been mentioned are due not to the machines themselves, but to the ambition, avarice, short-sightedness, lack of imagination and absence of a sense of social obligation in those who used them. But there are dangers inherent in the process of mechanisation and the large-scale organisation which is its inevitable accompaniment. Man himself may be subordinated to the requirements of the machine and be deprived of his humanity. He may be reduced to performing a particular function in a mechanical process. He may be assigned tasks which call for no exercise of his intelligence nor for any responsible decision. There is a sense in which this applies not only to the workers but also to managers. They also are victims of the division of labour and the impersonal nature of economic activities, which in the form of precise instructions, rigid formulas and fixed techniques restrict within the narrowest limits the possibilities of creativeness and the development of the human faculties.

Monotonous, repetitive work is the daily routine of multitudes of industrial workers. The work which a man has to do is one of the decisive influences on his character, and if his natural purposiveness is constantly thwarted he will become less of a man and lose his power of initiative and sense of responsibility. In proportion as men lose the sense of meaning and value in their work the will which sustains a technical civilisation must break down.

It has been proved that, where there is the will, much can be done to mitigate the disadvantages of, and to provide the necessary compensations for, the monotony of machine minding. Investigations undertaken over a period of years by the Research Department of the School of Business Administration at Harvard University, have been inspired by the conviction that the prime cause of the evils which threaten to destroy our civilisation is that the extraordinary advances in technical skill in recent centuries have not been accompanied by any corresponding advance in social skill. By social skill is meant the capacity to enter into genuine communication with other persons, to understand their point of view, to respond to their way of looking at things, and so to enlist them in willing co-operation in a common task.   The series of investigations conducted in the Hawthorne works of the Western Electric Company have shown the remarkable results which follow from the exercise of such skill.   These experiments have proved, for example, that many of the common assumptions about incentives are nonsense, and that the satisfaction of the desire for human association can be a more powerful factor in the increase of production than material conditions and rewards.   They have provided practical demonstration—a fact of the highest social significance—that the factory itself may be made a stabilising force and become a centre round which men can develop satisfying social lives.   They have shown that even under modern conditions it is possible for industrial administrators to create within industry itself a partially effective substitute for the old stabilising force of the neighbourhood.[1]

The whole question of the educative significance of *work* has begun to engage the serious attention of educators, and there are many instances of co-operation between industrialists and educators in attempts to find the right solutions.   But these are only the first beginnings in a herculean task.   Men can be delivered from slavery to the machine only by a revolutionary change in the accepted scale of values, in which a primary concern for the growth and welfare of persons takes the place of demonic concentration on technical efficiency and the material product.

We have been concerned thus far with the effects of machines on those who work with them.   But the machine age exerts an influence also on the whole of social life.   People may become so occupied with the products of machines that they have no mind or leisure for anything else.   Their attention is continually taken up with some new toy or gadget.   Machines with their multiplying novelties may drive out of life all the values that lie outside and above the mechanical.

Oliver Goldsmith in the eighteenth century wrote :

> When lovely woman stoops to folly
> And finds too late that men betray,
> What charm can soothe her melancholy,
> What art can wash her guilt away ?

[1]Mayo, *The Social Problems of an Industrial Civilisation.*   Harvard University, 1945.

Mr. T. S. Eliot in the twentieth century writes :

> When lovely woman stoops to folly and
> Paces about her room again, alone,
> She smooths her hair with automatic hand
> And puts a record on the gramophone.

The difference is not due simply to a change in lovely woman but also in large measure to the fact that she has got a gramophone. One of those who have contributed material to this chapter writes :

" There seem to be two distinct things contributing to the same result—our power over our environment, and the fact that we always have at hand plenty of objects with which to distract ourselves. The result is an insensitiveness to tragedy, which brings with it an insensitiveness to religion. What I am thinking of is a certain almost constant power of the mind to find one idolatry after another as a defence against God. It is seldom that we see ourselves in a position in which Christianity can offer us any sort of release. And if, through continual frustration in the management of our personal lives, we do see ourselves in that position, we can go to the pictures and re-absorb, through the comfort of the plush seats and the distraction of the film, the sense that, after all, there is not very much to worry about and hasn't it all been rather morbid ? I think that all this for the Christian is really a more important characteristic of our age than most—more important, for instance, than monotonous and repetitive work, of which I suspect there has always been plenty. I mean the extent to which our imaginative field is limited in this way, so that to believe in tragedy requires for us a strong effort of will."

V. SOCIAL AND PSYCHOLOGICAL TECHNIQUES

The success which has attended men's efforts to gain control over physical nature and make it serve their purposes has been so impressive that they have proceeded to apply the methods that have proved fruitful in the physical sphere to wider areas of life. If the patient investigation of nature has yielded such results, what may we not hope for if similar methods are applied to the study of men and society ? In the anthropological and social sciences machines fill a smaller rôle, but the new lines of investigation may have effects on the future of mankind as profound and far-reaching as the discoveries of physical science.

From the study of inorganic nature investigation has gone on to the study of the processes of life. The progress of biological science has yielded remarkable results in the breeding of plants and animals. Recent discoveries have made it possible not merely to produce new types by a skilful combination of inherited qualities but to modify these directly by bringing about physical and chemical changes in the chromosomes. It may be long before science makes it possible to control at will the human biological inheritance, but that is the direction in which we are moving. As knowledge is gained, it will undoubtedly be applied to man. Already the practice of artificial insemination has been extended to human beings.

It is not merely biological processes that are becoming subject to control. Knowledge is rapidly increasing of the way in which the human mind works and of the means by which it may be influenced. We are learning from psychologists more and more about the effect of circumstances on individuals and groups. The use in schools and factories of a frankly behaviourist technique gives us an unprecedented insight into common practices. The work of Freud and his followers has opened up a whole new field of understanding of human nature by the discovery of hidden mechanisms which determine the adjustment of the self to its environment at deeper levels than the conscious life. Modern psychologists, pursuing the laudable purposes of studying human behaviour and of curing those suffering from mental maladjustment, are beginning to foreshadow the control of character in a way just as significant as control of the biological inheritance.

The present century has witnessed the growth of a whole network of social investigations, in which the attempt is made to understand the individual not only in himself but in the setting of his social environment and in his relation to other persons. Even to enumerate the social surveys of all kinds by governments, research institutes and private agencies would fill many hundreds of pages.

The development of the social sciences has been prompted in the main by the desire to promote human welfare. They are intimately linked with medicine, education, and the promotion of social welfare. But the new knowledge of human behaviour can be used to serve bad ends as well as good, as we can see in the crude use made of it in large-scale advertisement and various forms of mass-propaganda. In totalitarian states the new techniques have been employed to mould the ideas and feelings of the entire population in accordance with the desires of its rulers.

The late Professor Karl Mannheim held that the emergence of the new social techniques at the disposal of governments, including both the new science of human behaviour and the new means of communication through Press, radio, telephone and telegraph, with the power of new weapons behind them, is a fact more fundamental to society than either its economic structure or its social stratification. These latter can be changed, through the use of the new techniques, by an organised group that succeeds in seizing and retaining power.[1]

VI. SALVATION BY KNOWLEDGE

Science and technics had their origin in man's legitimate desire to understand the world, to control it for his own purposes, to add to his knowledge, wealth, and power. The success which has attended them has stimulated and hypertrophied the self-assertive side of his nature. Man has come to conceive of himself as essentially explorer, conqueror, architect. He not only regards these ends as his primary concern, but he has created means of achieving them, so large in scale and so massive in their operation that he is swept forward on an irresistible tide. Science and technics determine the whole ethos of modern life. They create the atmosphere in which we live. They dictate the prevailing ideas and attitudes of modern society.

The modern period began with the realisation that " knowledge is power." The dazzling discoveries of science and the plainly visible results of technical activity flatter the power impulses of men. The cult of power has become part of the modern consciousness and affected the ideals and standards of people generally. Science has become an instrument of power, and the disinterestedness of the thinker and the spirit of contemplation of former times have given place increasingly to the drive of the organiser and promoter.

The temper of the modern age is thus uncongenial to

[1] *Diagnosis of our Time*, pp. 2-3. Kegan Paul. 1943.

Christianity. The things that, in the Christian view, are of primary concern lie on the circumference of the interests and activities of society. The great majority of those who set the pace in human affairs have made up their minds to run the world in accordance with their own ideas and are confident of their ability to do so. God in these circumstances has become superfluous. Men no longer see any need for Him.

There are always in history tendencies contrary to those which are in the ascendant. The pursuit of knowledge and skill may awaken wonder and produce, as it does in many scientists, a spirit of reverence and humility. There is no doubt that in the scientific world the self-confidence and dogmatism of an earlier period have given place to a new openness of mind in regard to ultimate questions.

Men's belief in what science and technics can do for them has been shaken, more particularly on the continent of Europe, by the experience of two world wars. It would be a mistake to suppose, however, that there has been a fundamental or widespread change of attitude. The great majority of men do not know on what they should rely for an improvement of human conditions except the advance of knowledge. Communism is inspired by a fanatical belief in the ability of men to create an earthly paradise by science and technics. In America and Britain the predominant mood among the leaders of thought and action is that with the increase of knowledge men will find a means of overcoming their difficulties and creating a happier world. In Asia many turn envious eyes to the astonishing transformation of Russia that has taken place within a generation, and believe that the utilisation of modern knowledge will enable their peoples to make similar advances.

The important fact is that, whether pessimistic or optimistic philosophies prevail, scientific investigation and technical development go steadily forward. There is no slackening of the pace. The number of scientific workers is being rapidly increased. Research institutes, private and governmental, with vast sums of money at their disposal, are conducting inquiries into every kind of human problem. By the untiring labours of an immense and growing number of investigators there is steadily being accumulated a great body of knowledge about human beings, both in themselves and in their social relations. As the knowledge is acquired it is used in direct and indirect ways to mould their lives, thoughts and feelings and to shape their environment, which in its turn is a powerful factor in determining their mental and emotional life. Society, it is true, has always aimed, consciously and unconsciously, at influencing the lives of its members in accordance with an approved pattern. What is new is the immeasurably more powerful instrument that is now available as a result of the new knowledge and techniques. This instrument is being employed to give direction to the minds, feelings and purposes of men—that is to say, in a field which is the pre-eminent concern of the Church. It was possible for the Church in its ministries to disregard the mounting control of man over physical nature. It cannot possibly be indifferent to the powerful forces that are now being directed to influencing the minds and souls of men. The widespread belief that the chief hope of restoring order to society lies in an increase of knowledge and skill is the most formidable rival faith which Christianity has to meet in the world to-day.

VII. SCIENCE, TECHNICS AND CHRISTIAN FAITH

What, then, is the Christian attitude to the scientific and technical society in which our lot is cast. It must obviously be a two-fold one.

The Church must clearly take full account of the relevance of the new knowledge and skills to the fulfilment of its own evangelistic and pastoral mission. It must enlarge its conception of the meaning of the redemption of human life to include the aids which can be provided by social techniques. The work of the Christian ministry in modern society cannot be pursued in isolation, but will call for alliances with a whole variety of social agencies that are engaged in dealing with different aspects of individual and social behaviour and need.

Again, Christian thinking must do full justice to man's responsibility for the ordering of his own life and the life of society. Trust in God can easily be made, and too often is made, an excuse for shirking responsibility. Over against many forms of mistaken Christian resignation, the scientists and technicians who have set themselves with courage, persistence and devotion to lift burdens from men's shoulders and confer benefits on humanity are in the right.

Further, there is in the world of science and technics a discipline and realism, which establishes standards that the

Church cannot afford to ignore. In religious activities " easy-goingness " and low standards are not visited by the immediate penalties which attend such shortcomings in the technical world, and this fact offers many temptations to slovenliness of mind and action, the substitution of glib phrases for painstaking investigation, and facile judgments on complex and difficult questions, which alienate those who in their own work are guided by higher standards.

While there is much that the Church has to learn and to assimilate, is there no critical judgment also from the standpoint of Christian faith that has to be passed on the temper and practice of the technical age ?   There most certainly is.   It is quite another question, however, whether the Church to-day is capable of pronouncing such a judgment and of making it effectively heard and understood.

We cannot simply concentrate our minds on the truth we have to proclaim and leave out of our reckoning the standing and reputation of those who utter it.   The Church is known ;   it has a record.   All that it says will be judged by what it is known or supposed to be.   Where men have come to distrust the speaker, speech may only harden their opposition.

Again, the great danger that besets any attempt to give a Christian answer to the questions raised by a technical society is that the answer, as we give it, will be too simple and superficial to count for much.   The task with which we have to wrestle is not to formulate on paper or in speech a Christian answer to the perplexities of society but to put enough content into the answer to give it real power.   What is needed to-day is not a doctrine which is impeccable as theory but a faith by which men can live and find guidance for their actions in the thick of the conflicts of society.

With these cautions in mind we suggest three crucial points at which the outlook and temper of modern society is challenged by Christian faith.

The first is that the scientific and technical standpoint has its own inherent limitations.   The trouble to-day is that so many are unaware of these limitations.   In science and technics men set out to solve *problems*.   The " I " that is seeking the solution stands outside the problem.   The wise man, of course, in dealing with a human problem, will include himself with his individual limitations and faults in the picture of the problem that has to be solved. But when he has done this, there still remains a self that is seeking to solve the problem and that is not involved in it. Over against this realm of the problematical—that is to say the entire field with which science and technics are concerned—there is a wholly different realm in which the " I " becomes aware of a situation in which it is itself wholly and inextricably involved. The French philosopher M. Gabriel Marcel, who has devoted much attention to this crucial distinction,[1] has called this sphere the realm of *mystery*. It is in this sphere that the ultimate issues of life are faced.

The standpoint of science and technics has acquired such dominance in the modern world that men are apt to make it the sole approach to the interpretation of themselves. They think of themselves as objects rather than as persons, and the whole realm of mystery in which the self itself is engaged, and for this reason cannot be grasped by the investigating mind, becomes obliterated. Man is thereby deprived progressively of his humanity.

By assuming that the standpoint of science and technics is the only possible standpoint men are prevented from discovering the real sources of the evils from which they are suffering. In investigation the self is taken for granted. All the evils are assumed to lie outside it in the field which it is investigating. A whole new world of experience is opened up when we become aware of an evil in which we ourselves are inextricably implicated.

It is precisely at this point of a moral revolt against the horrors which a technical civilisation has made possible that we may, perhaps, detect an awakening sense of the inadequacy of a purely scientific and technical approach to life and its problems. The fact that technical advance has made it possible to carry out universal massacre stares every man in the face. Men are shocked by the fact that civilised governments are able to mobilise the resources of science to perform acts which make the worst deeds of criminals of little account in comparison. While in a world from which God has been banished it is difficult to find rational grounds for believing in the sacredness of life, a natural piety extending far beyond those who profess any positive religious beliefs condemns such inhumanities as violations of the law of man's being. In this realisation, however vague and inchoate,

[1] Cf. an article on " Technics and Sin " in *The Changing World*, Summer, 1947. Harvill Press.

of an evil in which they are themselves somehow implicated, men reveal an awareness of that realm of mystery, which M. Marcel distinguishes from the sphere of objects and problems with which science and technics are concerned.

The second point at which the modern outlook is open to serious challenge is its failure to understand the profound difference between the study and manipulation of things and the meeting with persons. In the activities of science and technics the observer himself remains unquestioned and unchallenged. For the purposes in view that is right and inevitable. But to regard what can be learned from this detached position as comprehending practically all that matters in life, as many do to-day, is a profound error. The truth is that the most important part of life has been left out.

We do violence to the nature of persons, when we attempt to bring them wholly within the scope of the organising intelligence. In our relations with them we have to acknowledge their immutable otherness and to be ready to live in continuous and fruitful tension with them. It is through the meeting of persons with persons and the fructifying contacts of groups with groups, each preserving his or their unreduced individuality, that men mutually educate one another and grow in stature. By its very nature technics can create only a solitary world, in which one directing mind, one ruling group, one single point of view dominates the whole. It cannot create community, which always requires the existence of two or more different points of view, each of which renounces the claim to have the final, decisive, over-riding word.

There can be no remedy for the present disorder of society unless the present absorption of interest in the technical mastery of things gives place to a new wholeness of thought and living which includes a true understanding of the relations of persons and of human groups. The Christian faith that the greatest thing in the world is love, remote as it may appear from all present realities, is at once the damning judgment of current practice and the clue that can lead mankind out of its present predicament.

The third point at which the assumptions of contemporary society need to be challenged is the question whether any final meaning for life can be found without belief in a spiritual reality transcending the world of time and space with which science and technics are concerned.

The question is being raised from the side of science as, for example, in the Riddell Lectures by Professor Michael Polanyi,[1] in which it is argued that the scientific tradition presupposes that such a thing as truth exists. If there is no truth, it is vain to search for it. Where belief in transcendent truth is surrendered we are left at the mercy of sheer power. There is no alternative except that the strongest will shall decide what is to be done. Those who have abandoned belief in spiritual realities can raise no valid objection to being directed by a totalitarian state.

What is here said about the foundations of science is true also of social and political life. In these spheres too men live by the strength of a common spiritual tradition and by loyalty to a transcendent truth. No human society can exist without government. The relations between those who issue orders and those who have to obey them can be saved from degenerating into tyranny only by the acknowledgment by both of a law to which both alike are subject, of an over-riding truth, justice and charity to which the allegiance of all is due. The relationship between governed and governors is free from any taint of servitude only when there exists between them a genuine understanding. Where there is no belief in a transcendent truth and no acknowledgment of transcendent standards, understanding is no longer possible. There remains only the arbitrary fiat of the ruler.

The Christian critique of our modern technical civilisation is one which goes to its very roots. But any attempt to preen and flatter ourselves for possessing as Christians the clue to the disorder of society is at once held in check and corrected by the realisation how little can be achieved by presenting this criticism in words. Its proclamation by the Church may even have the effect of hardening men's hearts. There is in wide circles a profound distrust of the Church to be overcome before those outside will hear.

What has to be changed is a deep-rooted attitude to life. Christians are themselves entangled in the confusions and misled by the false values of the age. We are swept forward by a restless activity and have no time to pause and face the need for a radical change in ourselves. Yet until we have done this we are powerless to minister to the needs of others.

[1] *Science, Faith and Society.* Oxford University Press. 1946.

III

THE SITUATION IN EUROPE

Jacques Ellul

THE aim of the present chapter is not to give a general picture of the state of European civilisation but merely a description of the elements of disorder—the symptoms of the malady from which Europe is suffering. Of course, most of the elements in this diagnosis are to be found also in other parts of the world. But we shall deliberately omit what applies specifically to the rest of the world, and shall emphasise only what applies to Europe.

THE LACK OF BALANCE

Our first task is to state this disorder as a lack of balance between the values of traditional European civilisation and economic and social conditions to-day.

It is not a question of divergent doctrines. The opposition between the old and the new doctrines is either superficial or of little interest. The *malaise* in Europe to-day is not due to conflicting doctrines, even if we bear in mind the national socialist and fascist doctrines on the one hand, and the communist and materialist doctrines on the other. These doctrines are really only a symptom of the deep-seated malady from which Europe is suffering ; the chief characteristic of this malady is that there is really no doctrine which accounts for the concrete European situation and tries to direct its course.

European civilisation was formed around certain values which have given it meaning and have resulted in the formation of ways of life, social and political structures, and cultural expressions. It is obvious that the two currents which run through the history of European civilisation are, on the one hand, *Christianity*, and on the other hand, *reason* ; these two elements are not contradictory if " reason " be understood in its broadest sense, not in its rationalistic sense. These two elements form the basis of the values which have formed the background of our civilisation— values derived from the Christian ethic (which have become secularised, such as liberty, fraternity and solidarity), values derived from the Græco-Latin conceptions which have helped to maintain a balance of justice. The conditions of life have been dependent upon these values.

From the beginning of the twentieth century, and after a long preparation during the nineteenth century, the conditions of life have changed. The social, economic, and political structures have diverged along independent lines, each one following its own logical course. We see European civilisation breaking up into anarchy before our eyes, because the economic, social, and political forces have developed freely without regard for one another. The traditional values of civilisation are no longer moulding civilisation to-day ; they are no longer taken into account. There is, therefore, a serious lack of balance, and we have reached a definite crisis.

In Europe the efforts to discover new values of civilisation which would polarise all the anarchical forces of our time are called national socialism and communism. The conflict between these doctrines is illusory, since they both contain the very same fundamental principles (dictatorship, economic supremacy of one class or one race, " the end justifies the means," creation of a mass-civilisation) and employ the same methods. The problem is to know whether these doctrines are able to construct, not a powerful state (which they obviously can do) but a *new* society founded on *new values*. Neither national socialism nor communism seem able to produce a new form of civilisation. All they can do is to organise a society in an elemental and inchoate form.

In face of this situation (which is felt more or less obscurely by everyone), it is comprehensible that people should try to hold on to the old values (and it is significant that even communism appeals to the traditional European values when it comes forward as a protagonist of civilisation), such as liberty, patriotism, humanism, justice, etc. These ideas are no longer clear ; they are no longer the straightforward expression of real sentiments— either of the people, or of their rulers. These ideas are no longer related to the material facts of our age, and they are only retained as a façade in an adulterated form. Finally, these ideas are confused with social forms which are, or should be, condemned (*e.g.*, freedom is confused with capitalism, patriotism with nationalism, etc.).

Our European civilisation is suffering, because it has lost the authentic values which would be capable of co-ordinating and guiding the forces which are evolving in anarchy and are tending towards a new civilisation, the characteristics of which are not yet determined, and may never materialise. It is not a question of a political or economic doctrine. Great Britain has shown that it is quite possible to live without adhering to rigorous political doctrines. And we are not called upon to think out a new doctrine. Our task is much deeper ; it is to discover values of civilisation which—with the material elements of our world— will enable us to build up a civilisation. Our present values are quite unsuited to our epoch, and are no longer recognised by the majority of people as being universally valid. The problem is really to discover moral and spiritual values which are in accordance with the material and intellectual conditions of life, which are accepted by the majority of men (consciously or unconsciously), and enable men to lead a balanced life (even in difficult conditions), and to invent new forms of civilisation.

It is characteristic of the Roman Catholic Church that it is far more concerned with doctrine and political action than with fundamental questions. This attitude is perfectly useless, in spite of its external appearance of effectiveness. The Catholic political parties are once again compromising the Church by engaging in a political conflict of the worst kind, which involves the spiritual mission of the Church in a political connection of a very dubious character. The social doctrine of the Church is to a large extent out of date ; it is really only a by-product of socialism, which itself—as a doctrine—can no longer keep pace with the events of our age.

Now, it is possible that a new, authentic civilisation may not materialise. Anxiety on this point arises from the acknowledged fact that the material forces of our time which are developing to an unlimited extent, tend to occupy the whole picture, to crowd everything else out, and to organise themselves in such a way that no new values of civilisation can be created. This organisation tends to be made in accordance with the necessities of development of material forces, and not by subordinating these forces to a higher end. Our problem is : Will it be possible to regain control of these forces ?

THE MATERIAL FORCES DOMINANT IN EUROPE

The State. We do not deny the value of the state. The state is willed by God, and has its own part to play in God's plan of salvation. Without it, an ordered life in society is impossible. But the state may fall a prey to demons, if the power which it represents refuses to recognise the supremacy of God. At the present time we are faced by an extremely dangerous type of state in every country in the world. This must not be regarded as an isolated phenomenon (*étatisme*), which could easily be overcome. For the present evolution of the state is due to economic and technical developments, and has taken place with the consent of the larger part of mankind.

More than in the rest of the world (even in Russia) it seems that the dominant element in Europe is the state. Even if there is no authoritarian doctrine of the state, we are forced to admit that the power of the state is perpetually growing through the development of its administration ; that its sphere of action is continuously expanding ; that in itself it tends to become the criterion of good and evil (the supreme crime in Europe to-day is high treason—that is, crime against the state) ; that it tends to absorb the life of the nation completely, and to form a nation in which the state is the dominant factor ; that it is becoming increasingly abstract—that is to say, that it obeys its own laws, and ignores régimes and persons ; that everyone in Europe assumes that the state provides the solution for all problems. This is true even of democrats and liberals : what they want is a different kind of state, but they do not want to change the nature of the state in its technical form (police, finance) which actually determines everything else. All the European states have not reached the same point of development, but they are all moving in this direction ; Great Britain is an excellent example of this overwhelming predominance of the state in a democratic and semi-liberal form.

Production. Here again, as in the case of the state, we must be on our guard. It is not a question of rejecting production as the outcome of human labour. Nor can we put the clock back and lament over the past. I am not thinking about production in itself, nor do I say that it is a bad thing. But we must look at the present problem in relation to our present disorder, and to the general attitude to production. Now the whole of Europe is haunted by the idea of production. From one point of view this is comprehensible : the necessity of repairing war-damage, and the effort to re-establish a possible standard of life. It is clear that if we are to achieve stability in Europe production is essential.

But this tendency, actually a sound one, is not temporary ; it is permanent, and forms the very basis of the economic systems (whatever they may be) which are developing in Europe. Liberalism and socialism agree on this principle : " production governs all." They disagree only about methods and distribution. The underlying tendency is to subordinate everything to production, including man, who becomes merely an instrument of production (and not only the workers, but the staff, the directors, etc.), and including spiritual values, whose mission is becoming more and more simply that of providing pretexts in favour of production (*e.g.*, the ideology of economics). It does not occur to anyone to challenge the idea that man exists in order to produce more and more. Contrary to socialist theory, the most active factor in proletarisation is not the existence of private property but the fact of this primacy of production. Hence this is one of the most burning problems of our civilisation, and for this reason : if we wish to make a serious analysis of our economic difficulties and of the breakdown of humanist civilisation, we must bear in mind that one of its essential causes is this assumption that " production must come first." I do not mean that " over-production " is the cause of the crisis. It has nothing to do with it. But if the law of production be allowed to take precedence of all other values—which is characteristic of our own time—it is a catastrophe, and no human civilisation can possibly make this law its starting-point.

I will not go into the general problem of technics in civilisation and its moral and political repercussions, since I have already described this several times elsewhere. I shall not, therefore, discuss the question whether technics are good or bad, but only that aspect which concerns the European crisis.

Technics. Possibly this material force plays a less important part in Europe than in the United States. Most Europeans have lost faith in progress, science, and technics, and are no longer hopeful that everything will be solved by these means ; whereas in the U.S.A. and the U.S.S.R. technics still reign supreme. But this is one of the characteristics of the problem in Europe ; fresh technical systems are imposing themselves upon us and invading the whole field of human activity. In certain cases Europe is tending to become an experimental laboratory for new technics, especially in the political sphere (propaganda, concentration camps, displaced persons, political and social realism, Eastern democracy, and the one-party game, etc.). In other cases technics of American origin are being applied to Europe, and are open to the usual contagion. But Europe as a whole no longer believes in these technics—and no longer has the strength, nor the spiritual elevation, nor the social organisation required, to enable it to control the technical instruments which it is being induced to employ. Thus Europe is being led to follow a path which is no longer its own.

On the other hand, in Europe the unifying power of technics is tending more and more rapidly to standardise political, social and economic conditions, and to turn the continent of Europe into a solid *bloc*. Now this is taking place at the very moment when the continent of Europe is divided politically into two zones of influence, and when the last traces of " European civilisation " are disappearing—that is to say, at the moment when the spiritual structure of Europe is breaking down. Thus this unifying tendency of technics is causing a crisis, owing to the political obstacles which it encounters and the absence of any spiritual foundation.

A final element in the political and social world of Europe is *war*. During the last century war has changed its character. It is no longer an accident, a breakdown of peace, as it has always been during the course of history. War has become one of the permanent elements in our society. We have now reached a culminating point in this transformation : European society is entirely built up on a war basis (in this direction Europe has gone farther than the rest of the world which is moving in the same direction). The disharmony between the old ideas and the new facts comes out very clearly at this point : we are still using the methods of diplomacy which proved useful in the days when war was still an " accident," to try to prevent the kind of war which has now become part of our social structure. Moreover, it is not only war between nations which—by becoming totalitarian—has helped to change the idea of war, but also class war which is a permanent element in the life of Europe alone. These different tendencies force us to recognise a society which will be completely subject to them when they are fully developed, and in which it will be impossible to create a human civilisation.

THE POSITION OF MAN

Confronted by these forces, the situation of European man is desperate. First of all, from the material point of view his position is impossible : he is suffering from the disastrous results of an inhuman use of power by the state, of the primacy of production, of an extreme development of technics, without reaping any of the undoubted advantages connected with the latter process : Europe is not wealthy. The following facts must be borne in mind : the growth of large and crowded cities, with its evil consequences for the life of their inhabitants, from the moral, psychological, and physiological point of view ; the fact that labour conditions become increasingly severe, coupled with uncertainty of employment ; the disintegration of family life, due to economic and industrial conditions, and to the pressure of state control ; the disappearance of the middle classes from European society, which is becoming increasingly proletarian, owing to the actual situation in the economic and social sphere. These facts mean that European man cannot rise to the height required to set the standard for a new civilisation.

This is confirmed by the grave fact that in reality there is no further question of measuring and basing the new civilisation on the real man, as he actually is. To-day man is subordinated to *things* and the coming society is a society made for these things and not for man, conceived in terms of things and not of man. This primacy of the *thing* is the highest note of triumph of technics and production. Man must subordinate himself to the necessity of things, or be considered as a thing himself—a fact easily accepted by modern science and utilised by modern politics. Two significant facts stand out : European culture is now centred on the physical and biological sciences and no longer on the " humanities " ; and European politics are becoming mass-politics, based on the supposition that man is a thing (cf. propaganda, etc.).

This leads to the attempt to create a definite type of man. But here emphasis must be laid on the special place of Europe. All over the world to-day societies are trying to create artificially the ideal type of man to fit into this society, *i.e.*, to create the thing with which society can do what it likes. The United States are tending to create this type of man, simply through social milieu and conformity. The U.S.S.R. is trying by every means to create a type of man in conformity with Marxist doctrine. In Europe, owing to the dominance of political life, the tendency is for man to be the tool of the state, but this is not general throughout the twentieth century nor in all countries. It is a sporadic tendency, but nevertheless a very vigorous one. It was this which created the typical radical Frenchman of the Third Republic, and the German national socialist. This tendency to create artificially an average type of man for the service of the state is one of the deepest signs of Europe's decadence, and the abandonment by man himself of his dignity and responsibility.

Undoubtedly there is a growing tendency to create another type of man, who stands out above the masses : that is, the man who shoulders all the responsibilities and makes all the decisions. He corresponds to Burnham's " manager." It is the technician who dominates and directs society in every sphere. But this man is not a superman, in spite of his powers ; he himself is closely dependent on, and subject to, the technics which he has to apply.

This type of man has not yet been developed very far in Europe, in spite of the prominent part it played in national socialist Germany. But it is probable that as organisation increases this new " nobility " will emerge.

This tendency has been made possible by a phenomenon which it is most important to recognise as characteristic of our western world : dissociation of thought and action. This process of dissociation is taking place simultaneously on the following planes : on the psychological plane (man acts for reasons which are not " his own," and, inversely, he no longer expresses his thought in an act ; here are two examples : in the first sense, the influence of publicity ; in the second sense, artistic surrealism) ; on the social plane (for instance, the intellectuals have lost contact with the rest of the nation, and no longer have any influence on society. Increasingly, the masses influence the common life, and when we speak of the " masses " in this sense we mean action which has not been willed but is due to sociological reactions) ; on the political plane (an increasing tendency to use all political doctrines as " counters " in the political game and in the sphere of action—conflict between the state and the administration—the use of political myths).

The deep spiritual cause of this dissociation can be summed up in a phrase : modern man no longer has any *spiritual cohesion*. The relation between God and man, like the relation between man and the world, has been distorted by secular influences, so that man no longer sees himself, or the world, in the true light.

THE TOTALITARIAN NATURE OF THIS SOCIETY

This kind of society, which tends to be constituted by a mere combination of material forces, and thus denudes man of significance, is totalitarian, even if no explicitly totalitarian doctrine is invoked. Socialism has tried to subordinate man, as a whole, to the state, and to use him for its ends ; but French or English democracy wants to do exactly the same. Society will not accept the man who refuses to work, nor the man who refuses to insure himself against unemployment and illness (social security) ; man is becoming more and more part of the social mass—and it is the *whole* man who is involved.

This society is totalitarian in a second sense : it tends to unify the whole of life. In the effort to raise the standard of living, from the economic point of view, it has been necessary to take large-scale action (man has been forced to merge his identity in large groups and, in extreme cases like communism, to lose his individual consciousness) and to " rationalise " the conditions of life. In Europe this attempt at rationalisation is carried on very unequally : very actively in France and Germany ; slowly but surely in England and the Nordic countries ; hardly at all in Spain, Switzerland, and Holland.

At this point we must also emphasise the fact that what we have stated so far varies very much in different countries and' different parts of Europe, when we look at them in their present situation. For instance, the presence of " intermediate " groups which are vigorous in certain countries (Switzerland, England, Holland) makes the power of the state less direct, and the totalitarian nature of society less apparent. But when one is examining an illness one must try to foresee how it will develop. Here we are trying to diagnose this development, and we then perceive that in this respect the difference between the countries of Europe is no longer a difference in kind but a difference of degree ; they are all moving in the same direction, but are at different stages. And they will pass through these stages all the more quickly when the European *bloc* has taken more definite shape.

Finally, this society is totalitarian because it embraces the known means of action and thought, and utilises everything, or rather turns it to its own advantage. Every attempt to break the circle results only in closing it more firmly ; the social security plan, the Beveridge plan, etc., make the individual still more a mere cog in the larger unit, and force him to give up more of his personal life.

Leisure-time pursuits (the cinema, sport) only lead to a still greater social conformity, and aid man to adapt himself more willingly to non-human conditions. A remarkable example of the creation of a totalitarian society by the organisation of " leisure " is provided by England, in the phenomenon of Butlin's holiday camps. All this seems still stranger when we reflect that the war against national socialist Germany has led all its enemies to adopt its methods (total war, concentration camps, state interference with private life, etc.).

THE FAILURE OF THE CHURCH

In our diagnosis of the disorder in Europe, we cannot ignore the failure of the Church. This is seen clearly in the following fields :

The Church has left the care and the protection of man to others. In the intellectual sphere the Church has left the protection of man to science and philosophy ; in the economic and social sphere it has left his protection to socialism. And the Church has made serious compromises with those who control finance. This explains why the Church is so conventional and why it allows man to fall into the hands of those who can only lead him astray.

The Church has left to others the responsibility for revolution. The Church exists in order to insist on constant change in society and civilisation, in order to bring them more into conformity with the order of God. This is a mission of " permanent revolution." But the Church has completely lost sight of the fact that an order of God exists, and it has accepted the

established order of things. Hence instead of representing values
of transformation and judgment (justice, freedom, etc.) founded
on Jesus Christ, the Church has merely stood for conservative
values, and has left the revolutionary function in the hands of
political parties.

The Church has left to others the responsibility for the
spiritual life of the peoples. The Church has become intro-
spective and has forgotten that the Gospel must be present *in the
midst* of the people, and that this can only be achieved by constant
movement, by great movements of evangelisation which, even
if they do not lead to the conversion of all, do draw the spiritual
life of the nation towards the Gospel. The Church has restricted
its work almost exclusively to individual witness and private
conversion, and has left the nations of Europe to seek their
spiritual food elsewhere ; the state with its myths gave them what
they required. In the public sphere the Church, especially the
Catholic Church, took up a political position, and not a spiritual
one, with the same result.

It is evident that this threefold failure of the Church is not
intentional. The Church has never willingly renounced its
influence in the world. But it is an actual state of affairs due to
many causes : the Church's subservience to the State, the
Church's attachment to a given economic form, namely
capitalism (which has led the Church to conform to the prevailing political and social system), division and hostility between
the Churches, misunderstanding of the Church's rôle which made
it act as a political force (through political parties). All these
causes have been effective only in so far as the Church had no
clear view of its divine mission, and was not constantly on the
alert to hear God's message.

As God always preserves a " remnant," the Church's failure
has not been absolute. But it is only through loyalty to the will
of God revealed in Scripture, and through repentance, that the
Church can re-discover its threefold responsibility towards the
world.

IV

THE SITUATION IN ASIA—I

M. Searle Bates

INTRODUCING ASIA

THE present studies tend to be based in the Atlantic region, here to be called "the West." Such centring can be justified, even in seeking a world view, because the West, by predominant economic and military power, by political and cultural influence, has set the "modernising" course for the rest of the earth. Our immediate purpose is not to attempt an independent analysis of the problems of the Asiatic peoples, which are among the universal human problems. It is rather to point out, within cruel limitations of space, some points in which they differ, at least in degree or in setting, from the problems of the West. Large common elements are taken for granted.

The greatest bodies of population apart from the European-North American culture area, and the most strongly established patterns of markedly different social structure, lie in the mass cultures from India eastward and north-eastward—the region often termed "the Orient," or the Far East. The population of China is equal in numbers to that of all Europe save Russia, and that of India is practically so. The Japanese or the Indonesians are as many as the Germans. Korea, the Philippines, Indo-China, Thailand, and Burma are lands each with more human beings than the whole of Scandinavia or than Canada. Indeed, the entire region contains almost exactly half the population of the six continents, the global earth.

That leaves aside the Russian lands to the north and west, with perhaps thirty millions on the continent of Asia ; and also the Moslem countries stretching from Afghanistan to the Red Sea and the Mediterranean, some sixty millions set off from the dense bulk of oriental farmers by their sparse peopling of stony highlands and actual deserts, till one reaches cities at the outer gates of Europe. Important as are these Moslem states, seven large and others small, all of them combined have fewer people than Japan or Indonesia. We therefore attend to the Asia of concentrated masses on the oriental plains and adjacent islands.

They live, indeed, in social patterns varying more widely than those of Europe. It is acutely difficult to be concrete, yet truthful in necessary generalisation, when considering the whole range from primitive hill tribes to the cultured milieu of Peiping and to the industrial technicians of Osaka ; from Tibetan lama to Kagawa, or from Benares priest to Mao Tzetung ; from the unlettered, spiritually coffined peasant of the Ganges or the Yangtze to Nehru, emancipated heir of two worlds.

PROBLEMS NOT OF INDUSTRY, BUT OF RURAL POVERTY

The issues of modern industry and its urban life are faced directly by only small minorities of the Asiatic peoples, except in Japan. True, India has a significant place in statistics of the world's industry, and there are pockets of industrialisation elsewhere. But India's industry is centred in the use of farm products ; and the land is not dominated by the coal, steel, and chemicals of the western machine age. By and large, the mineral resources of Asia are meagre compared with the enormous populations that need to employ them.

The great masses of Asia live by agriculture. A large share of the grain production—and in Asia cereals are life itself—is due to human toil, without even hearsay of machines, with only a minimum aid from draft animals, usually confined to shallow ploughing. Rice culture is prominent, with its peculiar demands upon manual labour, its peculiar resistance to machines, its limited toleration for the buffalo alone. In fact, the requirements of men throughout most of Asia leave little food and little place for animals.

POPULATION MASS AND ASIATIC MATERIALISM

Population crowds upon subsistence with unrelenting pressure. A flood, a plague of locusts pushes below the harsh line of survival vast numbers of bodies normally undernourished. New crops, improvements in transportation, as in Indonesia or in India, have quickly added tens of millions of mouths in a single country.[1]

[1] The people of Java were multiplied from five million in 1816 to forty-one million in 1941. For the past two decades or more, the population of India has been increasing at a net annual rate of fifteen per thousand—now some five million seven hundred thousand per year—and at that rate would practically double within the remainder of this century. Recent rates of increase in the Philippines, in Formosa, and in Indonesia are above those of India. Adequate comparisons should guard these figures from the opposite extremes of startled inference and of casual dismissal.

These leaps in population mark no change in the birth rate, but simply the delivery from starvation and fatal disease of those who would otherwise have perished in weakness. The added multitudes consume the potential gains ; the increased mass is just as weak, just as miserable, as before. Whatever may be the true cosmic judgment upon numbers of humankind, population here and now is excessive in ratio to production. The peoples of Asia do not know the luxury of unemployment, for they have never known employment. Despite the exhausting labour of legions in the crises of planting and harvest, whole countries are covered with hordes of farm folk who crowd their tiny plots, without real outlet for their productive powers—an under-employment or " concealed unemployment " stupendous in magnitude and in social consequence.

Wearing, grinding poverty in such mass as to crush all likelihood of remedy in our time for more than a select few—that is the materialism of the Orient, from which escape is less frequent and less easy than sentimental exaltation of " the spirituality of the East " has often suggested. Due anxiety over the materialism of the machine in the Ruhr or at Pittsburgh should not blind us to the more primitive, more prevalent materialism of the absence of the machine in mass hunger and the insecure toil of human backs—toil not sufficient to ensure even an animal life for many who have known no better. Burdened and darkened in the world's most comprehensive poverty, Asiatic peasants are beset with disease and superstition, demons within, demons without. They have too little part in the treasured higher culture of India and China, too little benefit from modern achievements in Japan.

INFLUENCE OF THE INDUSTRIAL WEST

This is not to say that Asia remains outside the contemporary world, sheltered from its currents of power and of gain, of new knowledge and of new peril. Some peasants, even, are brought in part within the sweep of industrialism—the Japanese requiring chemical fertilisers in their rice-plots ; some Indonesians and others organised in plantation systems to supply world markets. In several lands the advantage of cheap cotton cloth from machines is bought at the price of displacing village crafts and the domestic or off-season work of farm families, the reliance of millions.   Mining proceeds, too often, by exploitation of human bodies.   A considerable society is built upon modern ports and foreign trade.   Wars, depressions, drastic shifts of economic policy in western states which act for their own interests and their own workers, now force irrationally, now halt disastrously, the weak segments of Asia's livelihood which are linked to the West—with tragic effects partly obscured in the absorbent masses of rural poverty.

Japan and Korea experience western military occupation and economic direction, the latter nation with the cruel division familiar to Europe.   The stripping of modern equipment from these countries and from Manchuria follows upon the dislocation and destruction wrought by war throughout eastern Asia.   The terror of the atomic bomb has actually been experienced not in the West but only in Japan.   (Candour must say, however, that the immensity of destruction by other means, the urgency of starvation and other mortal problems leave the Japanese less occupied with the horror and the portent of atomic weapons than are those peoples who have the means, the leisure, and the ironic security to make them.)   China and some other lands deeply fear, perhaps in natural exaggeration arising from their own weakness, the signs of world-wide rivalries which extend to Asia power contests that arise elsewhere.   Not merely India and Indonesia, but several other countries in less startling forms, are undergoing radical reorganisation of political control as western imperialism falters or retracts.   The shift to Asiatic responsibility is undoubtedly right in direction, but the process brings injuries to common folk—at best, damaging uncertainties ; at worst, decades of grievous disorder.

NATIONALISM AND THE AUTHORITARIAN STATE

With the exception of pre-war Japan no Asiatic state has reached the extremes of nationalism and of totalitarianism which give pause to Christian interests in the western world.   But the difference lies more in the degree of technical efficiency than in the spirit and direction of movement.   Asia has no established tradition of individual or group rights guaranteed against arbitrary authority, no sound basis for democratic organisation on a national scale, despite recent imitation of western liberal forms in the Philippines and elsewhere.   Indeed, historic despotism and paternalism fuse with contemporary change to forge a centralised, authoritarian state. Conscious of previous tribalism, social particularism, and political localism under the loosely used authority of the old régimes, present leaders press for greater power to organise the masses, to construct, to tax, to police, to arm. They want to increase the tangible strength of their respective states as against western political and economic control, and by imitation of western states.

These present leaders have thoroughly grasped the demonstration of experience : the one Asiatic state to achieve substantial modernisation in economic and technical phases of its life, was authoritarian Japan. Centralised Germany long appeared to accomplish more in ratio to its actual resources than any other state in the world ; while the democratic accomplishments of the British Commonwealth and the United States have been discounted as the comfortable products of uniquely superior resources, which are thus outside what is practicable for others.

THE RUSSIAN UTOPIA

The attraction of Soviet Russia is tremendously compounded of fact and propaganda, influencing millions even of those who fear and oppose Russian policies, while providing a complete blueprint of community life for other millions who look thither in admiring devotion. To the Asiatic who finds in the ways of past or present no possible escape from individual or national poverty, Russia offers a sharp, confident analysis of the hell he is in, a social saviour with all the plausible advantages of omnipotent system. Because poverty is more completely dominant than in the West, because no alternative has been adequately experienced and established in Asia, because there is so little understanding of the harsher features and the limitations of the Russian régime, so little of the European realisation that socialism is not identical with communism and communism is not identical with Stalin's state, the communist faith and parties daily win converts in Asia. These gains occur despite the open opposition of most governments and the unspoken opposition of peasantries not easily stirred.

The Asiatic in his actual plight is deeply moved by the picture of a handful of Bolshevik leaders able in a scant generation of our own time, against the general hostility of the capitalist-colonial and of the fascist powers, to turn disastrous invasions into well-advertised victories ; to wipe from their vast country the very name of landlord and the very possibility of exploitation by wealthy individuals ; to turn an Empire built upon discrimination into a union of varied peoples boasting freedom from racial, religious, and national prejudice ; and to transform mass illiteracy into the reputation for universal education and practical mass culture ; above all else, to create by their own wills, out of sad rural poverty, an industrial society with strength to withstand Germany and with an earnest of infinite power, security, welfare, comfort—in the name of those who toil.

This picture in certain aspects is grossly misleading. *But the picture prevails.* It has elements of truth. It is presented with assurance and persistence. It is good news to those who are captives of hunger and oppression, those who have seen no other vision of release unto abundant life. All this tends toward acceptance, whether reluctant or enthusiastic, of the omnicompetence, of the drastic collectivism, the oligarchy of one party and its dread police, to be found in the Russian system. Old customs of local autonomy and loose administration, some nuclei of genuine liberal principles, work in certain areas of Asiatic life against totalitarianism. But much of the organised opposition to communism is unlovely and inspires no support ; for it is based upon self-interest and class-interest, repelling the free-spirited and the young.

It must be reiterated that in Asia even communism does not rival nationalism, still driven by the impetus of protest and fresh ambition, the greatest single emotion socially effective. The majority of conscious citizens in the Asiatic states desire increase in the authority of those national states. The passive masses are habituated to social controls. Liberty for individuals, for voluntary groups, for mind and spirit, is not widely nor resolutely cherished.

ASIATIC CULTURES IN THE FACE OF CHANGE

The cultural problem in Asia is notably different from that of the West. Prevailing illiteracy or meagre education, with the partial Japanese exception, exists beneath and alongside mighty cultures of distinctive quality. The literatures and thought-systems of China and India, with their socio-ethical and artistic accompaniments, rank beside the Mediterranean culture as the three major creations of the world in all time. For reasons not simple, the remarkable early triumphs of these eastern cultures were less open to modern development than was the western complex. By way of important example, Confucian teaching was strongly set for the maintenance of the old clan-family of the upper classes in early agrarian feudalism. Indian speculative philosophy, Indian as well as Chinese concern for human relationships, were less devoted to comprehending the physico-biological environment than were the unique series of Greek, early modern, and recent scientific inquiries.

The Asiatic cultures have been till now essentially conservative in their distinctness and in their almost ethnic character, not easily blended with the western culture recently brought into effective contact with them. There are important cases of stiffening or reinvigorating the indigenous cultural factors, convulsively to resist change, or constructively to adapt to the new day. More frequent is the partial rejection or disintegration of old cultural patterns, because they do not match contemporary experience and newly felt needs, or because of the various advantages and attractions of modern ("western") techniques, education, and social habits. Mechanical transport, machine-made goods, the newspaper and the cinema film are forces of cultural change more prompt, more cogent, than conscious judgment of values on the plane of philosophy, religion or ethics. Education tends to follow, lagging and unsteady, the newer outlook of the ports and cities.

Needless to say, the confusion of cultural and educational direction is serious beyond expression. The old, with its mixture of admirable and otherwise, could confront to-day's world only by radical restatement—which is not in sight of practical achievement. The new has all the problems of western culture, plus those of reception, conflict, or adaptation in Asia. Moreover, Asia naturally tends to reach for and to adopt those obviously profitable and pleasing " goods " that can be seen, handled, utilised with no effort of spirit and little of mind. The cinema film carries everywhere its glamour of modern life and technical achievement, in convincing " authenticity " which the untrained eye cannot possibly doubt.

RELIGION IN CHANGING ASIA

The cultures of Asia, whether in their social expression or in their thought-world, are bound up with religious or quasi-religious complexes. Apart from the crude animism that dominates various tribal peoples and underlies the peasant life elsewhere, there are four great complexes which affect more than 200 millions each : Hinduism ; Confucianism ; Buddhism in China, Japan, Thailand, and elsewhere ; Islam in India, Indonesia, and elsewhere. It is impossible here even to mention the significant differences among and within these vast systems, much less to describe and to evaluate them. Let it be remarked, however, that : (1) Here in Asia are found in their impressive, historic strength all the important religions of the world save Christianity. (2) These religions are closely identified with old social and thought systems now in difficulties. (3) All these religions, and the very concept of religion itself, are considered by many intelligent Asiatics to hinder, through conservatism and superstition, the social and intellectual advancement of mankind. (4) These religions, formulators and custodians of the major spiritual values and ethical standards of the Asiatic peoples, are set to oppose innovating forces of a material or intellectual type, *a fortiori* to confront innovation attributable to external forces, *fortissime* to resist *spiritual innovation* that comes from without. It follows that change in Asiatic societies and cultures tends to be at the cost of established spiritual values and ethical standards, as well as of superstition or primitive conduct. Such painful, dangerous adjustments are now in progress, too vast, too delicate, too intricate for any human mind to grasp.

CHRISTIANITY IN WEST AND IN EAST

As fully shown in other studies of the present series, Christian thinkers in the West have come to realise that important elements of western society and culture, assumed to be Christian, are now overborne by utter secularism and by pagan totalitarianism. Nevertheless, Christianity in the West has great resources of tradition and of present organised numbers ; and part of its anxiety is a new awakening to responsibility and opportunity. In the Asiatic countries we are considering—with the questionable exception of the Philippines—there never was a Christian tradition of society and culture, even of the diluted type familiar in the West. Rather, the largest peasant masses of the earth, the immense and socially integrated non-Christian religions of Asia, have formed, and continue to form, a difficult field for Christianity.

Although there is genuine hope and promise in the Christian communities scattered throughout Asia, whose combined numbers may surpass those of Christians in the time of Constantine, their strength relative to the non-Christian society engulfing them is much less. Protestants report in Asia some six million communicants, Roman Catholics some twenty-five millions, of whom nearly two-thirds are in the Philippines. These thirty millions or so, counting with reckless generosity, are scarcely influential among 1,100 millions, of whom they are less than three per cent. (Philippines aside, one and one-half per cent. ; Protestants alone, a scant six-tenths of one per cent.). The leaven is still hidden. Only a mind blind to human actuality or possessed by supreme faith can believe that the Asiatic mass will be fully leavened. Moreover, the present Christians of Asia have become Christians only by detaching themselves to some degree, in India and elsewhere, from the powerful systems of caste, tribe, clan-family, ethnic or culture-bound religion. To a notable extent their immediate ability to influence others remaining within those systems is reduced by that detachment. This difficulty Christian effort in the modern West has largely been spared, because it strives *within* the main tradition of society and culture.

SUMMARY CONCLUSION

Human nature West or East, in varying economic and cultural situations, offers to Christianity the challenge of low achievement and high potentiality. Emphasis upon the problems of mechanised societies should not result in neglecting the interests of important peoples whose daily lives are neither dominated by the machine nor greatly served by it. Disturbed by modern industry and by world-wide forces military and ideological, Asia has her own problems of mass and of overwhelming poverty, which condition her whole outlook. Asia is susceptible to concentrated nationalism and to totalitarianism, and lacks traditions that would secure liberty. Established cultures and religions falter before present changes, but are not displaced. The scattered cells of Christianity are minimised by the surrounding

mass and by powerful climates of custom.   They bear also
the handicaps brought with Christianity of western form, and the
burden of Asiatic reaction to the manifold pressures of Europe
and America upon the Orient.   It is not for us to doubt what the
Spirit of God may accomplish in the heart and life of man, East
or West.   But God's terrifying gift of freedom has permitted man
throughout the earth a response to His Spirit both tardy and
feeble.

V

THE SITUATION IN ASIA—II

M. M. Thomas

THE West has been the bearer of world history in the modern period, and the meeting between East and West is the history of modern Asia. Therefore Asia has not, and cannot have, a diagnosis of her own social disorder apart and different from the diagnosis of the disintegration of western society. But what the Asian would demand of any diagnosis of the western situation is that it should be true ; which means that it should take into the scope of its interpretation the fact of the meeting between East and West, with all its many consequences. Though that meeting is the history of the modern East, it arose out of the nature, and within the development of western society, and must be considered an integral part of it. At the present day, any attempt to diagnose the European situation apart from contact with Asia is as futile as the effort to understand modern Asia in isolation from Europe. The attempt of the West to see western society and its disorder in isolation from Asia has necessarily falsified every interpretation of the crisis in the West.

THE PROBLEM OF THE MACHINE AGE

Christians in the East have been deeply stirred by two events, happening within a few years of each other—Tambaram 1938 and Hiroshima 1945. These two events symbolise the two types of meeting between the East and the West. On the one hand the meeting of the International Missionary Council at Tambaram brought together Christians from sixty nations representing a supra-national divine world community, and they declared their oneness in Christ ; this is the result of the modern missionary movement. Most of the Christians in the great lands of Asia have heard the good news of Christ and His Church in this modern epoch. Even the ancient Christians in these lands received from the modern missionary movement the " open Bible " which has given them a new lease of life. On the other hand, the atom bomb, and the total annihilation of two Japanese cities, of man by brother man, is the symbolic representation of the harsher political relations which include the story of western imperialist exploitation and the rise of Asian nationalism in resistance. Both the missionary and the political contacts are made possible by what is peculiar to the modern period, namely, science, the machine, and technological progress. Therefore, in whatever way one interprets the machine age and its disorder in the East or the West, it should take account, on the one hand, of the supreme tragedy in terms of human poverty, political slavery, and spiritual despair it has caused in Asia, and on the other hand, of the way in which God has been pleased to use it in Asia, to build up His Church. The machine has been instrumental both to man's disorder and to God's design.

THE MACHINE AGE

In Asia the machine age has meant that an order of society whose main features seemed to us unchanging has been blown up with extreme violence. It has been compared to an earthquake, and this is in no sense an exaggeration.

It is incorrect to speak of pre-modern Asia as feudal. The typical Asiatic economy contained within it the remains of primitive communism in the village below and the despotic government above, which promoted irrigation and public works as well as war and plunder. Tennyson was right in his emphasis on the changelessness of the Asiatic scene, when he wrote " Better fifty years of Europe than a cycle of Cathay."

It is the foundation of the traditional Asiatic society that has been shattered by the impact of the West. It is " the only *social* revolution ever heard of in Asia." But it differed fundamentally from the victory of bourgeois society over the feudal order in Europe in that the destructive process was not accompanied by any corresponding growth in technical society. The machine did not go to Asia, but remained in the West, although its long arm " broke up the hand-loom and destroyed the spinning-wheel," and dynamited the " domestic union of agricultural and manufacturing pursuits " which was the foundation of Asiatic society. The modern revolution not only destroyed the old manufacturing towns of Asia, driving their population to crowd the villages, but also destroyed the balance of economic life in the villages. From this arose the desperate over-pressure on agriculture, which has continued to increase right down to the present day, and has made superficial observers talk of over-population as *the* problem of Asia, even while statistics have made it very evident that the density and rate of increase of population have been low compared with the majority of European countries.

Thus, under the sway of imperialism, Asia has in large measure become the "agricultural farm" of the West, producing raw materials for the machines in the West, and absorbing their finished goods. Along with this, feudal land tenure and a heavy tax-system was introduced or strengthened, thus creating new burdens for the peasant. Famine Commissions have all unanimously agreed that the extreme poverty and increasingly frequent and acute famines of Asia in the modern period are due to the fact that "agriculture forms almost the sole occupation of the mass of the population."

It must be evident from this short analysis of the situation that the primary problem set by the machine age for Asiatic society to-day is the reverse of the problem of Europe. The de-humanisation of man is seen in the fact that the peasant who had his organic relations in an intimate village community, where he knew his station and his duties, has become "atomised"; he is tending more and more to the condition of having no other status than that of belonging to a "mass" society, whether communal, national, or class, given over to an impersonal fate. The landless labourer, the starving peasant, the rotting un-employed and the starving beggar, as well as the moneylender, the tax-gatherer, the feudal landlord and the imperial servant—these are some of the products of the machine age, who have lost all sense of community and whose personality has as a consequence been cramped or crushed. It is no wonder that in such an environment the few large factories and estates created both by imperial and by national capital have manifested the worst de-humanising effects of mechanisation. See the peasant or the labourer in Asia, and "One instinctively asks oneself," says an eye-witness, "is this a human being or am I conjuring up some imaginary creature without a soul from the underworld?"[1] Asian nationalism arises out of and as a protest against this state of affairs imposed upon Asia by the imperialist machine.

[1] A. E. Mirams, *Evidence before the Industrial Commissions*, p. 354.

THE MACHINE A PERSONAL REALITY

The greatest tragedy in the Asiatic situation is the absence of any sense of *tragedy* among the interpreters of the situation. Modern history is regarded as following an inevitable course set to it by a natural law of social process. This naturalism, which seeks to diagnose every event in history ultimately in terms of natural necessity, denotes the absence of any conception, let alone the reality, of personal responsible existence as the destiny of man.

The sense of the personal did not exist in the Asiatic society which has been destroyed. In spite of a certain measure of organic wholeness which ancient Asian society possessed, Karl Marx says that it could " quietly contemplate the massacre of the population of large towns with no other consideration bestowed upon them than on natural events " ; that it was " contaminated by caste distinctions and by slavery ; that it subjugated man to external circumstances instead of making man the master of circumstances ; that it transformed a self-developing social state into an unchanging natural destiny, and thus brought about a brutalising worship of nature."

The individualism of the bourgeois society which has been the driving force of western imperialism and Asian nationalism also did not know the meaning of responsible personality. Based on Voltaire's assertion that " the only gospel . . . is the book of nature," it affirmed the dignity of the individual in his own absolute right by nature, and destroyed the basis of his responsibility to his neighbour, and of personal community.

Marxism, which is the basis of the Left nationalism of Asia, has repudiated the conception of personal responsibility as a mere " ideology," and considers man as the product of his conditions. Marx says : " Inasmuch as I conceive the development of the economic structure of society to be a natural process, I should be the last to hold the individual responsible for conditions whose creature he himself is, socially considered, however he may raise himself above them subjectively."[1]

Thus imperialists, nationalists and communists appear to agree in their total rejection of a *personal* interpretation of social reality. Even the ancient religions of Asia now rejuvenated by

[1] See Marx's Introduction to *Capital*. For a fuller discussion of marxian anthropology see *The Christian Understanding of Man* (Oxford series on *Church, Community and State*).

nationalism find themselves able to graft the current inter-pretations of social disorder in terms of natural necessity on to, or to accept them alongside of, their religious thinking, because at the core they too, in their mysticism, moralism, humanism, or relativism, are impersonal.

It is here that the protest of Luther against a purely empirical and rationalistic interpretation of man must be voiced by the Christian Church. " Whosoever considers the essences and operations of creatures rather than their aspirations and expecta-tions," says he, " is without doubt stupid and blind and knows not that creatures are *creatures*."[1]   Man is only known as a responsible being when he is seen as a creature in his relation to God.   But to-day the Church is incapable of making this protest, because a great deal that goes under the name of a " doctrine of creation " in the Church is really derived from rational surveys of " the essences and operations " of man in social history ; the same is true of a great deal that is said about man's " calling " and " vocation."   We may take two illustrations from the Protestant world, devastating in their effects on the Asiatic nations and coloured races.   There are many Dutch Christians in South Africa who find in the doctrines of calling and creation a justification for their policy of racial segregation ; and Christian political parties in Holland take their stand on the doctrine of calling in defending the continuance of imperialism in Indonesia. Perhaps it is not too wild a generalisation to say that the mis-sionary movement itself has sometimes sought to derive its vocation from a rational survey of the history of its so-called civilising mission, so that in some measure the criticism of the rational historian of Christian Missions as an " appendage of imperialism " is justified.

The Church needs to recapture its true doctrine of creation, of man as man, deriving it from the redeeming Word of God and the community of His grace.   Only then can the Christian diagnosis of the machine age be personal.   In such a doctrine, the machine, in so far as it is part of social history, will be declared as a personal reality ; and our disorder will be interpreted as due to the false meaning given to things by *man*, his idolatry which is basic to the creation and manipulation of the machine.   This is not to deny the elemental forces of necessity in any given

[1] See paper by W. M: Horton in *The Christian Understanding of Man* (Oxford series on Church, Community and State).

situation ; but it means an affirmation that the responsible decision of the creature with respect to the Creator, is basic to what appears to-day as natural necessity, and to the way in which that necessity is grasped now to create the present and the future. Not necessity, but the dialectic of a human freedom poised between divine grace and natural necessity will be declared as the clue to the understanding of the modern disorder of man. Thus the situation will be seen to be worse than any interpretation in terms of organic maladjustment makes it out to be—namely, as real tragedy.

THE GREAT NEW FACT IN MODERN ASIA

All talk of a personal interpretation of modern social reality remains on the ideological plane, without releasing power necessary for dynamic action, save as it arises out of the visible reality of a personal community in society, which would remain a scandal to the rationalists who seek to interpret history in less than personal terms. I submit that the missionary movement, and the small congregations of the Christian Church founded in different parts of Asia, whatever they may appear in the eyes of the rational historian, are in their *essence* the one personal reality in all Asia. Proclaiming the gospel, and confronting every man with a responsible decision to repent and enter the historical community of the redeemed, the Church in Asia stands as the one community of persons. Knowing every man as a " brother for whom Christ died," and as destined to a personal destiny beyond the natural order in the order of grace, the fact of the Church is the clue to a personal understanding of man and his history.

This view of man has created a permanent historical tension in Asia between the Church and society. So far as Asia is concerned this tension is as new as it was to the ancient world of Rome. Ancient Asiatic society never knew anything of the sort. The ancient religions of Asia were based on a " primi-tive "[1] apprehension of reality, which regarded religion and the social organisation of the people as one. At its best all it knew was a tension among the different functional castes within the social hierarchy, which might have been creative at one time, and which in its creative aspect Mahatma Gandhi at one time

[1] For the exact meaning in which this word is used here, see H. Kraemer : *The Christian Message in a non-Christian World.*

seemed to wish to revive in free India, by converting the Indian National Congress into a national spiritual aristocracy, in order to keep the state in free India from misusing power or from becoming totalitarian. " I had imagined," says Jawaharlal Nehru, " that the Congress as such would automatically cease to exist with the coming of freedom. He (Gandhi) thought that the Congress should continue, but on one condition, that it passed a self-denying ordinance, laying it down that none of its members could accept a paid job under the State, and if one wanted such a post of authority in the State he would have to leave the Congress. I do not at present remember how he worked this out, but the whole idea underlying it was that the Congress by its detachment and having no axe to grind, could exercise tremendous moral pressure on the executive and other departments of the Government and thus keep them on the right track."[1] But even in this noble conception Gandhism is not able to conceive anything beyond the *moral*, because it does not know the *personal* dimension, transcending even the moral, and uniting the moral and the immoral into one community of the penitent and forgiven ; so the aristocracy is seen only as one element in the functional hierarchy of society and does not contain any power whereby the self-righteousness of the upper caste can be prevented from becoming tyrannical.

The tension between Church and society is also foreign to the real creators of modern Asia. The rationalism imported into Asia from the West did not know anything of a tension between Church and State as a permanent element, because it was based on a " utopian " apprehension of reality, which denied the reality of man's ends and loyalties beyond the social sphere. Thus both imperialism and nationalism reject any idea of a tension between Church and State as a scandal for their reason, and a weakness for their programmes. This is the reason why they seek to integrate the Church with the State.

Strange to the modern West, and foreign both to the ancient and modern East, the costly tension between Church and society, Church and State, introduced by the Word from beyond, made flesh in the social history of Asia, is the one basis for a personal interpretation of social reality to-day, and the one guarantee of the emergence in the future of the free and responsible society. If the missionary movement and the Church in Asia continue to

[1] See Jawaharlal Nehru's Autobiography.

proclaim the transcendent Word of God and to be a community of grace in tension with the political, economic and social orders of Asia to-day and to-morrow, it will be the greatest contribution they can make to Asiatic society.

THE SPLIT IN THE ASIAN CHRISTIAN SOUL

There is no doubt in the mind of Christian Asia that if the dialectic between the Church and the general community which is the basic condition of a free and responsible society, is to be maintained in Asiatic society, Christians in Asia should be closely related to the Churches of western Europe and North America, whose history in some measure for quite a long period reveals this dialectic at work. It is also clear that the preservation of the elements of personal freedom embodied in the Anglo-Saxon and western European political forms is of vital concern to the future of Asia. But the realisation of responsible government in the national sphere and the creation of tolerable conditions of existence for the peoples, which is essential to the realisation of a responsible society, require of Asian Christians in the present state of international politics an entirely opposite orientation. They demand of the Christian as full a participation as possible in the struggle against the above-mentioned countries. In certain countries like Indonesia and Indo-China it means active participation in armed conflict against the Western European powers ; in the rest of Asia the war is no less real though not so open.

Add to this the fact that the U.S.S.R. and the communist parties of Europe appear to be on the side of Asian nations struggling for their freedom, and the nature of the political orientation demanded of the Christian may be imagined. He finds the Anglo-Saxon alliance behind the policy of racial segregation of General Smuts and is told by the Asian delegations to U.N.O. that they find the Soviets more " liberal " on almost all questions regarding Asia than the Anglo-Saxons. Under such circumstances it is only natural that the Asiatic Christian should view the political forms of western European and North American countries as being capable of being maintained only at the cost of keeping over half the population of the globe in the position of a mechanical impersonal mass, and he will ask his Christian brethren in these countries to examine whether there is not a fundamental contradiction within the system of their corporate life which necessitates the imperialist domination of nations, and the segregation and suppression of races other than their own.

The maintenance of this double orientation of life may be the contribution the Asian Christian community is called upon to make towards the building up of a free and responsible society in Asia and the establishment of peace in the world. The tension is creative in so far as it does not create a " split personality " in the spiritual sense. In a situation which is already becoming intolerable, any call to recognise an *absolute* opposition between communism and the free society produces a " split " of this sort. It must be recognised that it is not easy for the average Christian in Asia to maintain a tension of this sort in the present international situation. Many a politically conscious Christian youth has faced it and finding it intolerable, has either consciously rejected the Christian Faith, or has given up politics. This has perilous consequences, both for the missionary and the political task of the Church in Asia. The tension involved in this double orientation should not be aggravated by the western Churches if they are concerned with the future of Church or society in Asia. Many Christians, like the writer himself, see in the united front and the coalition programmes of the Asian nationalism of the Left, the only sane *political way* out of civil war, communal riots, political domination and intolerable living conditions of the mass of the people. And they are convinced that a world peace based on the unity of the great powers within the U.N.O charter is the only step that to-day will save Christian Asia from a final " split " in its soul, and lead ultimately to a responsible society in Asia. If, however, this peace breaks down, as it may, the area of Christian witness in the political life of Asia, in which any creative tension between Christian charity and the necessities of politics could be maintained, will be reduced to a minimum, or even to nothing at all. The opposition between the champions of justice and the saints of God will have become almost irreconcilable.

The supreme need of the hour is the witness, and if necessary the martyrdom, of an " order " of lay political workers, who " being bound and freed in Grace," and " emancipated from both law and lawlessness," are able to maintain in their lives a costly and tragic tension between ultimate Charity and necessary Justice within the dust and heat of the conflicts of the political world. When speech has lost meaning, life alone speaks.

VI

THE SITUATION IN U.S.A.

Reinhold Niebuhr

SINCE America belongs in general to the European world in terms of both its culture and the economic and political institutions of its civilisation, there is no need for a separate full discussion of the American situation. But North American life, including both Canada and the United States, deviates in some marked respects from Europe. The most important deviation is to be found in the stronger hold which the creeds of older classical liberalism have upon political and economic theory in America than in Europe. In Europe this creed has been challenged explicitly by the marxism of the industrial workers, while in America even the most vigorous section of the labour movement is devoid of marxist beliefs. In Europe the state has achieved a growing control over economic process and the idea of achieving justice through the automatic operations of economic life is practically extinct. In America, however, it is still a live option. There are at any rate large sections of the population who regard it as such.

There is, as a matter of fact, more political control of economic and industrial life in America than is commonly recognised. This is a current misinterpretation for which Americans themselves may be responsible. For there are many Americans who describe American democracy in purely libertarian and *laissez faire* terms not so much because the realities correspond to this ideal but rather because they hope it will be possible to return to it after what seem to them to be the aberrations of war-time disciplines. Yet it is significant that such a return should be thought possible in America.

The strong libertarian tendencies in American thought and life, as distinguished from European life, may be due to a multitude of causes, of which a few deserve special mention:

Both the United States and Canada conquered a continent in the heyday of the commercial and industrial period of modern civilisation. They are strangers to the feudal agrarian and more organic community which furnished the background in Europe for the modern liberal society. They are therefore also strangers to the mediæval political theories which assumed the necessity of a strong political and moral control over economic life. Thus classical liberalism came to America in a more undiluted form than in Europe. The possibility of the older and newer theories of the political control over economic process meeting, as they have in Europe, particularly in Britain, was precluded in America.

The wealth of American nations, as compared with the relative poverty of European nations and particularly as compared with the post-war poverty of these nations, makes it less necessary, or at least makes it seem to be less necessary, to establish the kind of controls by which European nations seek to extend or to restore justice. This wealth is partly derived from the abundance of natural resources upon the American continent and partly from the advantages of a continental economy, freed from the irrelevancies of national trade barriers within the continent domain. It may also be derived from the special technical efficiency which Americans have developed. This efficiency has in turn been frequently attributed to the competitive rivalry which the so-called " free enterprise " of America has encouraged, though there is little ground for believing that proficiency in the use of technics is really very much greater than in the more advanced industrial nations of Europe. Some of the efficiency is probably due to the possibility of using mass production methods for supplying goods for a mass market.

The breadth of individual opportunity in nations which had a constantly advancing frontier until a very recent past, was bound to create a more fluid society than in Europe. In this society it was assumed that individuals could advance according to merit and diligence. The class conflicts of Europe were, until recently at least, dissolved into more individualistic competitive striving.

Even Americans who are critical of the undue libertarian emphasis in American political thought and life will probably discern some advantages in these American characteristics which Europeans are inclined to disparage. It can hardly be denied, for instance, that American life is characterised by a high degree of social freedom and equality, however much it may lag behind some European nations in the achievement of political and economic security.

It is probably true, however, that the conditions which

created a peculiar American political philosophy have a rather short-range efficacy, and that in time America will have to learn that the maintenance of both freedom and order, of both liberty and equality is just as difficult as the European nations have found it to be. The illusion that the American nations have found an easier and more satisfying answer to the problem of freedom and order than has been vouchsafed the European world may yet cost the American world very dearly. It might be tempted to cling too desperately to the belief in an automatic harmony of social forces and thereby fail to take such steps in time as are required to manage the vast and dynamic forces of a technical society in the interest of justice and stability.

It must be observed in conclusion that the conditions of a technical society which make the problem of freedom and order a vexatious one for modern man are, in some respects, developed on the North American continent with an even greater degree of consistency than in Europe. There are, in other words, fewer organic and traditional restraints upon economic life than in Europe. This creates a problem which the great productive power of America may ease or even obscure for decades but not in the long run. Ultimately, in short, the task of creating community in the framework of a modern technical civilisation exhibits remarkable similarities throughout the world, whatever may be the superficial differences on this or that continent.

VII

PERSONAL RELATIONS IN A TECHNICAL SOCIETY

Kathleen Bliss

A COMPREHENSIVE survey and evaluation of the effects of technology on personal living would fill many volumes. Here the subject can only be treated in barest outline, and the only justification for including such an outline in this volume is the importance of the field of personal relations in the life and witness of the Church.

It will make for simplification if the main types of personal relationship are blocked out in the following way :

A—RELATIONS BETWEEN THE SEXES

Men and Women at Work

One of the marked characteristics of a technical society is the wide and increasing range of work shared by men and women. The technical society has emerged from a bourgeois society, in which there was a marked differentiation between men's and women's work. In such societies, roughly speaking, women do what is consistent with a continuous cycle of conceiving, childbearing and nursing and men do the rest. Nobody who has seen women ankle deep in mud bending for hours a day in blazing sun to transplant rice seedlings, will hold the theory that in primitive societies Adam delves and Eve spins. Modern technical society is much more like most primitive societies in this respect than it is like the bourgeois society from which it has evolved. Men and women can, and increasingly do, work at the same jobs and share the bonhomie of common work.

This co-operation in work ranges from the intellectual co-operation of men and women in the laboratory or the operating theatre to the casual association of driver and conductress on a bus. The industrial revolution swept men and women and children into factories. So awful were the conditions in most

cases that reformers worked to remove women and children from
factories. In many cases where women remained in industry
(*e.g.*, in textiles) there was a specialisation of function. Their
wages and those of the men were commonly so low that only a
combined wage of man and wife would support a family. Working
men have opposed the entry of women into industry both from
fear of a depressing effect on wages, which would compel their
wives to work, and from fear that employers might replace male
by cheaper female labour. Now the picture is changed. The
increasing application of machinery, which decreases the amount
of heavy and dirty work, the use of light metals and plastics,
the decentralisation of subsidiary industry into small factories
built near to housing estates (made possible largely by electricity) all help to draw women into industrial work. Women
are better organised and better paid. During the war women
showed that they could do many men's jobs not by arguing
but just by doing them. They entered in considerable numbers
agriculture, engineering and transport, and with marked success.
Only the heavy industries and heavy transport remain almost
100 per cent. male industries.

But this steady infiltration of women into industry alongside
men is only one side of the picture. Equally important with the
introduction of machinery in a technical society is the application
of the *principle of organisation* to wider and wider fields not only
in industry but in the wider sphere of society. The office is as
much a typical working unit in a technical society as the factory.
Without it the complex organisation of labour, materials and
capital on which production depends could not function. The
office has received less attention from the social thinker than the
factory. Here is an occupation which is virtually a feminine
monopoly—that of shorthand typist. The shorthand typist is
the type *par excellence* of female labour in a technical society : she
is not only what a great many girls *are*, but what a great many
more girls would like to be—and the appetite of the technical
society for her services is insatiable, for every new activity needs
an office staff. This form of employment offers small chance of
promotion to responsible administrative posts : it is a profession
made up almost entirely of girls and young women—not only
because of their nimbleness of finger but because they do not
expect to make a life work of typing but find it a clean and fairly
rewarding way of earning a living before marriage.

The principle of organising institutions and categories of labour to deal with every department of life has spread throughout society. The child, who used to learn at his mother's knee or at his father's side as he worked, now goes to school : the sick go to hospital. The technical society alone of all the societies which the world has seen can make such economies in the proportion of its population employed in productive tasks that it can afford not only to keep all its children out of productive labour till early adolescence, but also to retain a large teaching force to teach them. Similarly a technical society can afford to look after its sick and to set aside categories of persons to care for them. Public opinion then begins to expect rising standards and demands that what men of science discover to be *possible* shall be *available* to all. So more and larger categories of persons to deal with first one and then another branch of human welfare are constantly created, and teachers, nurses and doctors are joined by hospital almoners, factory welfare officers, staffs of clinics, house property managers, youth organisers, to name only a few. But the most startling fact is that a very large proportion of those employed in these services for the education, health and welfare of the community are women, not merely because women are available but in most cases because they have the qualities which make them good at the work. These tasks demand long training and experience adds enormously to effectiveness. They are in fact life professions. Every year a large amount of skill and training is removed from the direct service of the community when skilled women marry.

It is important that this problem of the technical society— its need for women's work and the conflict between that need and its need for intelligent and responsible mothers, should be approached from the end of society, since it is usually handled by Christian writers from the opposite end, of the needs of the individual. From that point of view the demands of society for women's labour are looked upon as a threat to home life, a rival claim and loyalty, to be dismissed all too often with the catch phrase " a woman's place is in the home " and a far too easy identification of a woman's God-given vocation with her biological function. Such an attitude does less than justice to the large contribution made by women to the closing of the gap between the standards of nutrition, health and education in the homes of the richest and the homes of the poorest—a task only practicable in a technical society and only possible in one where social justice is a constant aim and where women are free and willing to take their share.

Relations Between the Sexes—in Marriage

The association of men and women in work and the need of the technical society for ever-increasing numbers of women in production and office work and of skilled trained women in education, health and welfare, have profound results on marriage. Here it is possible only to indicate a few in the broadest outline :

(i) The tendency of the technical society is to lay stress upon the likeness of men and women. They work together. Women at work wear, as men do, slacks, dungarees and uniform. In some places they have achieved and in others are demanding economic equality. Men and women also share the same leisure activities—sports, hiking, bicycling, swimming, etc. All this serves to mask the fundamental difference between the sexes, a difference which runs through every cell of the human body. Marriage is based not on likeness but on difference. Many a husband finds himself confronted a few months after marriage by a woman perplexingly different from the companion and good friend whom he first knew.

(ii) The technical society has such a voracious appetite for goods and services that there is a continuous demand for women's work. Work in a technical society has given to women an economic independence unknown elsewhere. Work provides a routine of living, companionship, a sense of belonging to a social unit. It greatly widens a woman's standards of comparison as she sees how other men behave outside her family circle and immediate social group. The young wife often feels lost without her work, and economic dependence and a reduction of personal expenditure often produces frustration.

(iii) A woman who had a satisfying career feels not only the loss of income, satisfaction in work and so on, but she also knows that her services are badly needed by society, that there are too few nurses and too few teachers of experience. She knows also that when her children are older time will hang heavily on her hands, but that by then technical progress will have produced new techniques in her profession of which she will be ignorant.

But the technical society is not only moulding women's attitudes and calling for their services, it is present within the home, pushing the woman out.

The technical society has invaded the home and altered the pattern of its life. The organisation of time no longer obeys internal rules based on the natural needs of the family for sleep, food, leisure, etc. Factory hooter and school bell dictate. But the actual layout of a home also has been changed by technology. The hearth used to be the centre of all but the aristocratic home. The cooking was done at it, clothes dried by it, meals eaten and leisure taken in its warmth. So long as the old-fashioned range prevailed someone had to be at home and keep the fire in. Gas and electricity make the fire-tender unnecessary. The modern kitchen is a workshop, and the woman can do her job in shorter hours and with less fatigue. Further, as more of the work of the kitchen becomes a matter of manipulating gadgets, men find it more interesting and take a share. It is not in the homes of the better-off, where technical development only just replaces the domestic servants now gone off to be factory hands and typists but in the lower income homes that the change is felt. That some families have pioneered in exploiting the opportunities which this technical development in the home affords and others have found the added leisure insupportable, is only too obvious.

The modern home is a sort of operational base from which the members go out into the larger community to be educated, to earn their living and to find many of their social satisfactions. Many marriages are coming to grief because partners find they have nothing to hold them together but the biological function of sex, and they find that sex for all its powerful cohesive qualities is essentially vagrant if isolated from all the other factors in human relationship. An outstanding problem of some modern marriages is the reconciliation of woman's biological function in the home (which can never be performed by anybody else) with her God-given aptitudes and skills which society needs. Another outstanding problem is almost the opposite—that of the woman who finds time hang heavy on her hands and does not possess a skill or lacks the will or ability to take full part in any social group outside her home.

A whole generation is looking for a new meaning in marriage. Biological function and social necessity are no longer the powerful forces of family cohesion which they used to be. The meaning has to be found in terms of a committal of whole person to whole person. Here the Christian Gospel has a searching and a saving word.

B—RELATIONS BETWEEN THE GENERATIONS

The technical society has by the discoveries of science, the skill of doctors, the efficiency of health propaganda and the general raising of the standard of living increased the expectation of life at birth by nearly forty years in the course of a century. It is impossible even to mention in this volume the social effects of this gigantic achievement.

Parents and Children

It is not now necessary for parents to produce half a dozen children in order to be reasonably certain that two will live to maturity. Planned parenthood in some form has become a practical necessity for most parents. Since there are fewer small children in a technical society they are regarded with more concern. The dissemination throughout society of knowledge of effective methods of feeding, clothing and caring for small children has been a remarkable fact of modern propaganda. But very subtly the attitude of the young mother is influenced by the general attitude of a technical age. Children, she feels, ought not to be a trouble if you know how to organise and manage them. Put in the right food and the right psychological handling, etc., and you will get the right results. That is a typical *technical* approach, but it can be a denial of relationship. Many successful young mothers do not learn to regard their small children as fully persons, and the children frequently become little individualists expressing their egos at everybody's expense.

Many parents are deeply perplexed by their inability to make any mental contact with older children. They can neither bind them to obedience nor understand them. The present insecurity of the world perhaps leads to an exaggeration of the self-regardingness which is always present in adolescence. But, like children, adolescents are scarce compared to old people in the present stage of development of western society. Employers seek them eagerly, educators and psychologists tend to their needs. Perhaps their very scarcity puts their souls in jeopardy. The

Church has followed secular society in concentrating attention on this group in youth clubs, etc., and whether this makes for better or worse personal relations between this age group and others is a moot point.

Young and Old

The achievement of technical society in expanding the span of life has brought about a new balance of age groups.   A greater number of old people has to be cared for by the work and service of a smaller number of younger people, and this creates problems in personal relations within families.   In any Chinese family (old style) grandma would be reckoned by all infinitely more important than the youngest baby, partly, of course, because there is only one grandma and plenty of babies.   The general drift of opinion in a technical society, which is always thinking of progress is that " it is the future that counts."   On a Christian computation of things, *is this really so?*   Or do we need to re-think our values?   A technical society sets no store by wisdom, the unique possession of the aged, so it has no place which can be filled by the aged and by them alone.   Instead it sets store by the " know-how " of the latest mechanical device.   Furthermore, the pace of modern development has been so fast that older people have been even less able in this than in previous ages to adjust themselves to a new mental climate, and the proverbial impatience of the young is further exaggerated by the fact that two devastating wars in Western Europe have left many old men in authority.

C—RELATIONS BETWEEN NEIGHBOURS

One of the characteristics of " organic " society is that men and women who live as neighbours also work together.   The revolution in communication has divided working and living. Only a tiny minority of people " live over the shop " and the rest have two sets of companions—neighbours and workmates.   It is easy to idealise the organic community of the· past.   In actual fact a great deal of family loyalty was bolstered up by jealousy of other families, craft guilds frequently became cruel monopolies, and villages, far from being cosy communities, derived much of their gusto from envy and spite.   A technical society has brought losses in personal living—restlessness, insignificance, yet for all that, is it not true that in modern technical society with its generally higher standard of living, shorter hours of work, and less keen and bitter struggle against the embattled forces of hostile nature, there is more kindliness and tolerance than there was in most village communities ?   It is far easier to practise the civilised graces of courtesy, bonhomie and good humour with a large number of people than with a very few.   On the negative side, the division of working from living and the comparative ease with which he may pass from one job to another enable a man almost indefinitely to put off fundamental confrontal in human relationships.   He gets on best if he cultivates the art of " getting by."

Perhaps men and women are only capable of sustaining a few genuinely personal relationships, and being compelled by modern life to be associated with many people, they shove off the insupportable burden by depersonalising a large number of relationships.

A plurality of communities and the possibility of passing from one to another is an essential of cultural growth—that was the glory of the old Europe.   It ought to be possible to say that a technical society has vastly enriched the opportunities for exchange and brought more people to participate in it.   In fact, it has created *impersonal* categories, groupings and interests under the names " capital," " labour," " consumers " and the like, and threatens to fall apart into self-interested groups which the state must attempt to hold together.   The great question is how the sense of membership one of another, expressed in the community of neighbours, can infuse the complicated interdependent parts in the technical society, so that the vastly enlarged community which it postulates and presupposes can become a living reality to the ordinary man.

VIII

THE INVOLVEMENT OF THE CHURCH

John C. Bennett

IT is unbecoming for churchmen to speak of the disorder of society without recognising the part that the Church has played in that disorder. It goes without saying that the churches as institutions and communities are involved in the social tendencies that make for disorder described in this book, for otherwise they could not exist in the world, but it needs to be emphasised that often churches give a false sanction to those tendencies and hence they aggravate the disorder. It is one of the most hopeful facts about the contemporary Church that there is probably more rigorous self-criticism within it than ever before.

One presupposition for any discussion of the relation between the Church and the social disorder is that no doctrine of the Church as the Body of Christ should be allowed to obscure its weakness and its sin as a human institution or community. How the divine and the human aspects of the Church are to be held together, without allowing either of them to cancel out the other, belongs to the discussion of the doctrine of the Church to which another volume in the present series is devoted. This dual nature of the Church is itself the source of its most distinctive temptation. More than other institutions or communities that make no claim to represent God, the Church is in danger of confusing the special interests and policies that in a given situation seem important to its leaders, especially to its clergy, with the divine purpose. The repeated manifestations of anti-clericalism in many lands may often be unjust and excessive in detail, but usually the Church has provoked them by this confusing of its claim to represent God with its institutional interests. Its response to such external threats should always begin with self-scrutiny.

The New Testament shows us how to deal practically with the high claims and the human weaknesses of the Church. We need to preserve at the same time both the exalted view of the Church that is presented with greatest power in the Epistle to the Ephesians and the criticism of particular churches that is most searching in First Corinthians.   We need to see the Church as the people of God, as the Body of Christ, and in the light of its true nature examine the concrete forms of the involvement of churches in the disorder of the world.   It is doubtful if we can say anything more devastating than Paul's words to the church at Corinth : " I do not commend you, because when you come together it is not for the better but for the worse " (1 Cor. xi, 17).

It should be understood at the outset that the involvement of the Church in the world's disorder is in part a by-product of the acceptance by the Church of responsibility to bring the whole people of any nation into its sphere of influence and to transform the life of the world in as many ways as possible. There is a permanent dilemma confronting the Christian Church because *involvement* is the other side of *responsibility*. Either the Church will go out and win the nations and attempt to influence the institutions of society or it will seek to remain a very select body of committed Christians.   In the first case it runs the risk of being overcome by the world that it seeks to win, and in the second case it is in danger of becoming a self-righteous sect that has lost opportunities to win souls and to raise the level of civilisation.

We shall consider in what follows some of the consequences of the involvement of the Church in the social disorder. Testimony from several different national or regional situations that has been supplied for the purpose of this chapter will be incorporated. The writer will introduce some material from his own experience as an American churchman in order to give concreteness to the presentation.   When references are made to particular churches outside of the United States the words of representatives of those churches will be used as much as possible so that this chapter may be one of confession rather than of condemnation.   In order to keep this discussion within manageable limits it has been necessary to omit treatment of the more intangible involvement of the churches in the contemporary culture, their frequent absorption of the assumptions of prevailing secular philosophies, their tendency to be bearers of a " western " manner of life, their accommodations to the æsthetic taste of their communities.   It is difficult to draw the line in this area of cultural involvement between that which falsifies Christian faith and that which is a sign that the Church is indigenous and is able to speak the language of the people.   The apostle who said : " For I decided to know nothing among you except Jesus Christ and him crucified " (1 Cor. ii, 2) also said : " I have become all things to all men, that I might by all means save some " (1 Cor. ix, 22).

INVOLVEMENT IN NATIONALISM

Most churches are organised nationally even when they have close confessional relations with churches in other nations and all are subject to national governments. This has long seemed to be the most obvious form of the Church's involvement in the conflicts of the world. The rise of Protestantism coincided with the rise of modern nations and so Protestant churches became closely linked with the aspirations and the interests of particular nations. Professor George Florovsky writes of the Orthodox churches that while their national character " brings them obviously into a closer contact with the life of the people and gives them an opportunity of influencing the current life of the nation," it " circumscribes them in a narrow field of a national provincialism." He says that " the churches are estranged one from another, their unity is dangerously obscured, co-operation is rare." He points out that one reason for this nationalistic emphasis in Orthodoxy is that it was " up to recent times the religion of the oppressed minorities in the non-Christian (Turkish) empire."[1]

One major result of the ecumenical movement to date is that it has caused the churches in the nations to realise that they are a part of an ecumenical fellowship that transcends nationality. The second world war proved the capacity of churches to avoid the militaristic nationalism that has been familiar within churches in other wars. The churches did not often lend a religious sanction to the passions of nationalism nor did they often encourage hatred and vindictiveness toward national enemies.

Churches that are national churches or state churches have in many cases won for themselves a high degree of spiritual freedom. Alec Vidler is probably right when he says of the Church of England : " I think that the Church of England would now be able to exercise as much spiritual freedom as it wanted —but it is inhibited from taking fundamental decisions by the divisions within it."[2] In the Anglican system the parson's

[1]From memorandum for this chapter by Professor Florovsky.
[2]From memorandum prepared for this chapter.

freehold gives to the clergy exceptional freedom from control by the state, by higher ecclesiastical authorities, or by the local congregation. The appointment of bishops by the government is often said by Anglicans to be indefensible in theory but better in practice than other methods of choosing bishops and, so far, free from the kinds of abuse which threaten the independence of the Church. The English experience of a State Church is profoundly affected by the presence in England of strong Free Churches, which on the one hand make it natural for the State Church to emphasise a limited membership, and, on the other hand, have preserved within the nation a tradition of Christian freedom.

As a general rule we can say that the external form of the relationship between church and state does not seem to be the decisive factor in determining the freedom of the Church from national or governmental pressures. And yet a church that has no membership apart from the total number of baptised persons in the nation is peculiarly vulnerable to the temptation to become an instrument of the national interest. Also, such a church will in the long run have difficulty in defining the Christian Faith in its fulness and in its claims upon the church and the believer over against the culture of a nation that is largely secularised. A national church cannot fulfil its vocation by acting through its clergy as a venerable structure that provides sermons and sacraments for a " Christian nation." Its function must be to evangelise the nation and to keep the policies of the nation under criticism, but the performance of these functions requires a *body* of lay members that constitutes a Christian community, distinguishable from the national community as a whole.

In nations where there is separation of church and state these problems take a different form, but it cannot be said that they are solved. In the democratic denominations in the United States which are so largely controlled by laymen, and where the membership is entirely voluntary and distinguishable from the total community, Christianity, as it is understood, is often a rather provincial American faith. There are many degrees of this distortion of Christianity and often it is avoided, but the local Free Church, especially if it lacks the corrective that is provided by liturgy and a strong tradition, is at times little more than a club that reflects the local culture.

It remains to be seen what the long-range influence of the

new nationalisms of Asia and Africa will be on the churches in those continents. At one time the younger churches of mission lands seemed to be outposts of the civilisation and of the imperialistic thrust of western nations. There followed a tendency on the part of the missionaries and the churches in some lands, perhaps most of all in China, to identify the Christian movement with nationalism. " The church in India, partly under foreign missionary leadership, has never been able to raise unequivocal protest against the abuses of foreign and alien rule. On occasions it did appear that some misguided missionaries felt that loyalty to Christ and the British power were almost identical. This earned the suspicion and contempt of nationalist forces in India for the church."[1] Quite generally, nationalism that represents a protest against imperialism and against exploitation by the western powers, has a moral prestige that the older nationalisms of the west have lost, and this moral prestige is recognised to-day by Christians in the west as well as in the east. There is a subtle danger here, and the churches may not discern it early enough to avoid making the same old mistakes that western churches made when they allowed themselves to become instruments of national power and interest. Links between the younger and the older churches, through participation in the World Council of Churches, and through co-operation of missionaries who have come to transcend their own nationalism with the younger churches, can do much to keep the vision of Christianity in these churches from being narrowed by nationalist influences.

INVOLVEMENT IN SOCIAL DIVISIONS

The churches have made less progress in recent years in delivering themselves from involvement in the social divisions within nations than they have in the case of the influence of nationalism upon them. The churches in many nations long ago came to represent the interests and perspectives of particular classes. Though this is to-day more pronounced in the case of " free churches " than it is of national churches even the latter were identified through their leadership with centres of privilege and power in the nations. There is a long history here and there could be much argument as to which of the great traditions— Catholic, Orthodox, Anglican, Lutheran and Reformed—have been the worst offenders. There is one fact that representatives

[1]From a memorandum by Professor V. E. Devadutt.

of all the traditions would admit and it is perhaps the most fateful fact in the history of modern Europe : *the working people and the democratic forces in Europe came to believe that the Church was against them.* It is this fact which underlies the depth of the social struggle on the European continent where the break between classes became, among other things, a religious conflict. This is one example, perhaps the most important, of the way in which the Church has aggravated the social disorder.

There have been eleventh-hour attempts on the part of churches or significant movements within churches to undo the harm that has been done and to show that Christians are concerned about social justice and that Christians reject both feudal and capitalistic forms of oppression. These attempts have usually been sincere, and they represent a new stage in the understanding of the churches of their social responsibility, but they have come very late. The conflict was already too far advanced and the new ideologies of the working class became substitutes for religion and closed too many minds to the claims of Christianity.

Jacques Maritain tells the truth about all the churches, both Catholic and Protestant, when he admits the responsibility of Christians for the atheism of communism. He asks : " What is the cause of this ? " and answers : " It is, I hold, because it originates, chiefly through the fault of a Christian world unfaithful to its own principles, in a profound sense of *resentment*, not only against the Christian world, but—and here lies the tragedy—against Christianity itself. . . ."[1]

A German scholar, Dean Friedrich Langenfass, has written about the failure of German Protestantism in this regard in a memorandum prepared for this chapter. He believes that this failure grows out of a misinterpretation of Luther's doctrine of the " two realms," a misinterpretation that was encouraged by Luther's appointment of the rulers of the various states as " emergency bishops " of the church. In its later history German Protestantism, Dean Langenfass says, " became increasingly identified with the world by an even closer connection with the wealthy bourgeois class and with the nobility." As a result " a gulf opened between the fourth class and the Church, which became wider and wider." This judgment is confirmed by a remarkable statement of the Fraternal Council of the Evangelical

[1] *True Humanism*, p. 33.

Church in Germany (E.K.D.) published on August 8, 1947. The Council said : " We went astray when we began to set up a ' Christian front ' against certain new developments which had become necessary in social life. The alliance of the Church with the forces which clung to everything old and conventional has revenged itself heavily upon us. . . . We went astray when we failed to see that the economic materialism of Marxist teaching ought to have reminded the Church of its task and its promise for the life and fellowship of men. We have failed to take up the cause of the poor and unprivileged as a Christian cause, in accordance with the message of God's Kingdom."[1]

Although the break between the Church of England and the working class was never so complete as was the case with churches on the European continent, Anglicans also point to real failure here on the part of their church. A group of Anglicans, of whom the present Bishop of Sheffield (Dr. Leslie Hunter) has been the spokesman, have been encouraging the most drastic self-criticism within their own church. In a pamphlet published by the group in 1937 they say of the Anglican Church : " From some points of view, occupied by an increasing number of spectators, it (the church) wears the ungracious character of a vested interest. Many clergy, especially in industrial areas, who are serving Christ and the people in their spiritual care devotedly, feel that they have toiled all the night and caught nothing, because the Church of England as a social and economic organisation frightens the fish away—except the small fry who are not aware of the organisation. The industrial worker may often honour and even revere the priest of his parish, but he turns away from the institution because, rightly or wrongly, he thinks that it belongs to the other camp and that, in spite of what some of its members say, it does in fact support the economic and social *status quo*."[2]

In the United States the situation is quite different. There is no particular social stratum as such from which all the churches are alienated but the divisions within the church do to a considerable extent correspond with social divisions in the nation. The Roman Catholic Church is strong among the industrial workers who come in large part from the later waves of immigration from Catholic countries in Europe. That church has shown both astuteness and ethical insight in identifying itself with the

---

[1]Ecumenical Press Service, September 12, 1947.
[2]*Men, Money and the Ministry*, p. 5.

social aspirations of its own people. The Roman Catholic Archbishop of Boston in an address to the C.I.O. Convention emphasised the Roman Catholic solidarity with labour by saying : " In all the American Hierarchy, resident in the United States, there is not known to me one Bishop, Archbishop or Cardinal whose father or mother was a college graduate. Every one of our Bishops and Archbishops is the son of a working man and a working man's wife." Most of the influential leadership of Protestantism is identified with the comfortable middle classes. The Federal Council of Churches appointed a committee on the state of the church in 1936 which came to the conclusion that " the leaders of the local Protestant churches, particularly those which have largest influence, do not belong to the stratum of the American people whose incomes are below $2,000 a year." The committee added that " they are likely to look with hesitation and fear upon the struggle of the masses for better conditions of life." A scholar who is also an acknowledged leader of one of the major American denominations prepared a memorandum for this chapter in which he summarised the situation within his own Church. His name and the name of his denomination will be omitted because it would be unfair to single out one such denomination and say things about it which also apply to many others. He says that his Church contains members of all classes and that there are more local churches made up of members of the working class than is sometimes supposed. But he makes it clear that the " prevailing and determining element in X church is middle class." He characterises the attitudes characteristic of that class in the following passage :

" To state it otherwise, this element is composed of people whose interests and social ties put them on the side of the main-tenance of the economic and social *status quo*. The majority of the lay people are Republicans, conservative in economic and social thinking, accepting the capitalistic order. It would have to be said that in the present controversy many of them are unsympathetic to organised labour. Thus in part, but only in part, the church is a class church. All this is the involvement of the church in society."

There are other factors that a full discussion of this and other denominations should bring out, such factors as the greater freedom of the clergy as compared with the laity from control by these middle class assumptions and the earnest effort of much of the leadership of the church to counteract prejudice within the membership against organised labour. But this statement gives a fair picture of the actual situation in many of the strongest American denominations. Even where churches are not composed of the more privileged middle-class people their outlook is often much the same, especially in rural America.

Local churches are more completely representative of this social stratification in the United States than denominations. This is natural in view of the fact that each local church usually serves a particular residential area in which one social class predominates because of economic factors that are beyond the control of the church. This involvement of the Church in the stratification of society has at least three results that need to be emphasised. The first and most obvious result is that the Church in its own life denies the fellowship which it professes. Unity in Christ comes too much to resemble social congeniality. A second result is that the Church fails as a solvent for social conflict within the community. How different it might be if it were the normal thing for those on opposite sides of a political or economic conflict to stand together in a common confession of sin before God and in a common commitment to His righteous will. The third result is the extent to which in churches that are made up of different social classes there is a tendency for the Christian religion to come to mean quite different things. The churches of the poor are too likely to emphasise elements of comfort in the Gospel and to turn them into a means of escape from the problems of this world. The churches of the more privileged are too likely to make Christianity a sanction for the *status quo*. Even where the " Social Gospel " has been preached for decades it has not had the effect of disturbing the complacency of the congregations but has instead been little more than a tolerated peculiarity of the minister.

There is no more flagrant illustration of the accommodation of the Church to the social disorder than the racial practices of American churches. It is generally admitted that in the United States the Church is as segregated as any social institution. There is a bad conscience about this in both the North and the South and we may hope for some improvement. But is it not a sign of the very involvement of the Church that this bad conscience about racial segregation becomes most vocal at the time when many thoughtful men outside the Church have become convinced that there is an absolute conflict between racial segregation and the moral pretensions of democracy ? Ninety per cent. of the Negroes who belong to Protestant churches are to be found in purely Negro denominations. Most of the other ten per cent. are to be found in local churches that are limited to their own race. The words of the leaders of the Church about racial justice are now excellent, but the drag of prejudice and social custom (not limited to the majority race) have kept them from being translated into action or even into significant plans for action.

The fact that stands out above all others in this connection is that the practices of the churches both reflect and give religious sanction to a pattern of *involuntary* segregation in the community which is the source of great injustice and which is an institutionalised insult to the minority race. It is for this reason that the Federal Council of Churches in 1946 in one of the most important utterances in its history said : " The Federal Council of the Churches of Christ in America hereby renounces the pattern of segregation in race relations as unnecessary and undesirable and a violation of the Gospel of love and human brotherhood. Having taken this action, the Federal Council requests its constituent communions to do likewise. As proof of their sincerity in this renunciation they will work for a non-segregated church and a non-segregated society." Those words show the Church in the act of confessing its own involvement in the social disorder and they point beyond it.

INVOLVEMENT AS AN ECONOMIC INSTITUTION

A final form of involvement in the social disorder that should be mentioned is the Church's practice as an owning, investing and employing institution. Here problems differ so much from country to country that there is very little that can be said that would have general relevance. In all of the variations the fact seems to be universal that the Church as an institution is not easily distinguished, so far as the moral sensitivity shown in its practices is concerned, from institutions that have less moral pretensions.

A vivid form of involvement of the Church in existing economic institutions is the investment of its funds. It has no principles governing investment except economic advantage and the avoidance of a few types of economic activity that conflict flagrantly with some quite specific teaching of the Church such as, in the case of some denominations, the production of liquor. A critic of an earlier draft of this chapter says : " I cannot see why the Church should be particularly or notably distinguished in its institutional aspects from other institutions which conduct their business honestly." If we maintain that the Church should have a more sensitive and exacting standard in these matters than ordinary commercial enterprises, we must admit that those who have the responsibility of trustees for church property must give full consideration to the security and the economic advantage connected with investments and that they have no moral right as trustees to subordinate such mundane considerations to some theories of their own. One obvious test of policies in this area is whether or not concern for investments in any way influences the mind of the Church in regard to economic questions that come up for decision. It must be admitted that there is less danger of this happening in the case of investments than in the case of pressure from living donors upon whom the Church may depend for its income !

There are great inequalities everywhere in the payment of the ministers of the Church. Often these inequalities have no sense at all because they are due to the accident of endowments. More generally the principle seems to be established that the rich pay higher prices on the market for such valued gifts as eloquence, and the poor take what they can get at a lower figure. There is a great deal of the commercial spirit in the Church. Some churches are attempting to correct the grossest forms of injustice by establishing minimum salaries and to achieve this is a great gain but the discrepancy between the maximum and the minimum causes little worry. The dealing of the Church with its unordained employees has been callous to the point of scandal. In America it has been noted that the policies of church agencies that have occasion to hire labour sometimes disregard the Church's public teaching in regard to the desirability of the organisation of labour.

One common result of involvement in the existing institutions of private property is that the accidental possession of property by particular units of the Church, perhaps an endowed local church or a denominational court or agency, may prevent wise use of the total resources of the Church. Within the same community one church may use its income upon itself to an extent that is far beyond the point of diminishing returns while another, not far away, is unable to secure adequate resources to care for its work with a large but less privileged congregation. Sometimes control of property may act as a barrier to a union between local churches or denominations that would otherwise be possible. Undoubtedly there is value in having many centres of initiative with economic resources within the Church and it would be a mistake to have all Church property controlled by a central authority. But this does not excuse the general disregard of the total needs of the Christian community that is the result of ideas of property that are taken over uncritically by the Church from the secular order.

The Oxford Conference in 1937 made great demands upon the world and the world has consistently fallen short, but it is doubtful if these demands have been less heeded by the world than the standards which were set forth at Oxford for the ordering of the economic life of the Church itself. The following passage from the Oxford report can be read to-day as setting standards that are as remote from application as ever :

" The economic organisation of the Church ought to help and not hinder the comity of Christ which should be the feature of its common life. There should, therefore, be a reasonable uniformity in the payment of those who hold the same spiritual office and they ought to be paid according to the real needs of themselves and their families, and sufficiently to allow them to give themselves, without too great anxiety concerning daily bread, to their spiritual service. It is not tolerable that those who minister to the poor should be poor for that reason alone. It is not right that those who have great responsibilities or greater gifts of utterance than their brethren should for that reason alone have much larger incomes. It does not express Christian solidarity that churches in poor and depressing districts should be handicapped by an inefficient and unlovely plant, which would not be tolerated in the assemblies of the rich. So long as the institution has these defects in its organisation it will corrupt most subtly the vocational sense of its ministry and prejudice its witness in the world. On the other hand, if its members were more continuously critical of its economic structure and were quick to reform the evils in it, such concrete action would release spiritual power."[1]

---

[1] *The Churches Survey their Task.* The Report of the Conference at Oxford, July, 1937, on Church, Community and State, p. 126.

IX

NEW BEGINNINGS
IN THE RELATIONS OF THE CHURCH WITH
SOCIETY

E. C. Urwin

IN this chapter we inquire whether there are any new beginnings, significant of a change of heart or awakening of fresh social responsibility on the part of the Christian Church in recent years. We shall confine ourselves to a few illustrative examples, chosen from a large material.[1] They may be grouped under the following heads :

I. *Penitence*

Are there any signs of corporate penitence on the part of Christian churches for past failures and mistakes in the social field ? Three tokens of it are briefly offered.

The war ended to the reverberation of two atomic bombs dropped without warning on the Japanese cities of Hiroshima and Nagasaki. Christian minds were deeply disturbed by it, not least in the U.S.A. It evoked a poignant acknowledgment of guilt from a Commission appointed by the Federal Council of the Churches of Christ in America in these terms :

" We would begin with an act of contrition. As American Christians, we are deeply penitent for the irresponsible use already made of the atomic bomb. We are agreed that, whatever be one's judgment of the ethics of war in principle, the surprise bombings of Hiroshima and Nagasaki are indefensible. They repeat in a ghastly form the indiscriminate slaughter of non-combatants that has become familiar during the World War II. They were loosed without specific warning, under conditions which virtually assured the death of 100,000 civilians. . . . Both bombings, moreover, must be judged to have been unnecessary for winning the war. Japan's strategic position was

---

[1]Contributions have been received from observers in Europe, the U.S.A. and among the younger churches of Asia, and the resultant picture is based on this material. In particular, acknowledgment should be made of papers by Dr. F. Ernest Johnson, New York, on the American situation, and by Dr. Paul Holt, Copenhagen, on the Continent of Europe.

already hopeless, and it was virtually certain that she had not developed atomic weapons of her own. Even though use of the new weapon may well have shortened the war, the moral cost was too high. As the power that first used the atomic bomb under these circumstances, we have sinned grievously against the laws of God, and against the people of Japan. Without seeking to apportion blame among individuals, we are compelled to judge our chosen course inexcusable."

Few acts of penitence can be more striking than that offered in the name of the Evangelical Church of Germany after the termination of hostilities in 1945. The war had loosed unmentionable cruelties and wrongs on the world, and the fellowship of Christians was severed or strained in consequence. The restoration of fellowship became one of the first tests of the Christian churches. On October 18th-19th, 1945, representatives of the World Council of Churches were present at a meeting of the Council of the Protestant Church at Stuttgart in Germany and were thus greeted by the leaders of that communion :

" We are all the more grateful for this visit as we know ourselves to be with our people in a great company of suffering, but also in a great solidarity of guilt. With great pain do we say : through us has endless suffering been brought to many peoples and countries. What we have often borne witness to before our congregations, that do we now declare in the name of the whole Church. True we have struggled for many years in the name of Jesus Christ against a spirit which has found its terrible expression in the National Socialist régime of violence, but we accuse ourselves for not witnessing more courageously, for not praying more faithfully, for not believing more joyously, and for not loving more ardently.

" Now a new beginning is to be made in our churches. Grounded on the Holy Scriptures, directed with all earnestness on the only Lord of the Church, they now proceed to cleanse themselves from influences alien to the faith and to set themselves in order. Our hope is in the God of grace and mercy, that He will use our churches as His instruments and will give them authority to proclaim His Word and to make His will obeyed among ourselves and among our whole people. That in this new beginning we may be aware of our whole-hearted unity with the other churches of the ecumenical fellowship fills us with deep joy."

In 1940 began in Great Britain the Religion and Life Movement, an outcome of the Oxford Conference in 1937 on Church, Community and State. The Movement, sponsored by the British churches unitedly, was a movement to bring home to the people of Britain their responsibility for the social disorder so manifest in the nation and throughout the world. It began with a call to penitence. The campaign began in the City of Bristol in September, 1940, and spread during the ensuing two years to no less than 150 other centres. The central issue was : Why has life in its varied aspects—domestic, educational, industrial, national and international—become so terrible a scene of confusion and disorder ? The answer given was that it has everywhere slipped away from its bearings in the will of God, and that this calls for repentance.

II. *Concern for Persons*

What have the churches done in the way of restoring personal relationships, and to ensure the right valuation of persons ?

Modern society has seen a breakdown in personal relations, through the disintegration of home life and the atomisation of the individual by mass work and mass leisure, and above all by the grim and bitter dislocations of war. Obviously it was in the latter situation that the opportunity to care for persons provided the clearest call to new beginnings in the restoration of personal relations. Could Christian concern for persons overcome hate and revenge, and provide for the succour of the homeless and dispossessed ?

Take, for example, the problem of the transfer of the Sudeten Germans from Czechoslovakia. From the Christian point of view the real task was to check the spirit of revenge. The omens were not too favourable, the legacy of hatred and wrong was too recent, and the start was bad. After the German atrocities committed particularly during the last days of occupation when women and children were not spared, retaliation was easy and understandable. But this lasted only a few days and then peace and order were once more instituted. This was the time when the Church had a great opportunity to call Christians to perform their duties as citizens in a Christian way. The technical difficulties of transfer were terrible, but with the full knowledge and consent of the government Protestants gave help to Germans in danger.

At the receiving end, the care of displaced persons who came crossing the frontiers in their thousands and tens of thousands, and whose aggregate numbers totalled millions, was a colossal task, testing the resources of government and voluntary services. Across the frontiers the refugees streamed from Poland and Czechoslovakia into Germany. German pastors wore themselves out in refugee service, and church workers from America and Britain, Sweden and Switzerland, reinforced by material aid, came to help. Through the offices of the Ecumenical Refugee Commission and of the Department of Reconstruction and Inter-Church Aid, set up by the Provisional Committee of the World Council of Churches in Geneva, flowed and still flows a steady stream of assistance, which is at once indicative of the unity, faith and fellowship triumphing over the divisions of war, and of practical care for persons.

The Christian Church in China is not a century and a half old, and its membership is but one in 800 of the total population of China. But its record in the field of relief and in the care of persons alone during the prolonged and bitter upheaval of the last ten years is simply superb, whether behind the Japanese lines or in Free China during the war with Japan, or in the continuing civil war and widespread destitution since. In the colossal distress, the Church ministered to those who were suffering or in need, irrespective of colour or faith, wherever it found them. It could not have been easy, for the material means were often lacking, and the Church itself suffered from the general dislocation. Its hospitals might be disbanded and its doctors and nurses placed in concentration camps. Food was in scarce supply, and the need was immense. Yet we read of a Christian at the head of the National Relief Commission, and of Societies for the Relief of the Wounded and their care in transit inspired by Christian solicitude. The words of Dr. W. Y. Chen seem entirely apposite : " In danger and privation, the Church served with the people she served. In the hour of despondency and despair, she brought to the people the good tidings, tidings of faith, hope and love. At the time of victory, she called the whole nation to turn to God, to repent, to humble themselves and to give thanks to Him. Through the storms the Church has led her people and advanced without faltering. She has been tested, and has not been found wanting."

One other particular effort to deal with broken personal

relations may be quoted from Great Britain. The disintegration of home and family life, of which signs are widespread in the modern world, and which war inevitably accentuates, was acutely felt in Britain as elsewhere. The situation compelled the attention of the British Council of Churches. It initiated a series of Home and Family Weeks in many centres of population, where Christian standards of marriage and home life and all that concerns the relations of men and women were upheld. A notable feature was that in many of these weeks there was welcome co-operation with the local authorities for health and education. Again, conspicuously under Christian inspiration and leadership, a Central Marriage Guidance Council was set up in London, and under its initiative similar local councils have been set up in town after town. The work at present is largely remedial, offering skilled advice—legal, medical and psychological—to those whose marriages are threatened with disruption. Marriage Guidance Councillors are generally drawn from the ranks of doctors, clergy and ministers of religion, and trained and voluntary social workers. Already a considerable volume of case work shows appreciable results in restoring personal relations and saving marriages threatened with break-up.

It is interesting also to note the rise in both China and India of a Christian Home Life Movement not dissimilar to the Home and Family Movement in Great Britain. That in China, indeed, ante-dates the British Movement by a decade, for its inception goes back to the Five-Year Movement initiated by the National Christian Council of China in 1930. It has now spread to India and appears to have been widely taken up by all branches of the Christian churches working in India.

III. *Vocation*

Are there any indications that the churches are recognising the role of the laity in their secular vocations as agents of the Christian witness to society?

What is happening in this field belongs undoubtedly to the most striking and promising new beginnings in the leavening work of the Church in society. A forerunner was the Sigtuna Foundation in Sweden, which for a number of years has brought together ministers and people from various groups, like doctors, journalists, representatives of labour and management, for common study of their professional problems in the light of the

Christian Faith. Similar movements have sprung up in several countries during and after the second world war.

Among the most distinctive instances are the "Evangelical Academies" in Germany. They bear testimony to a new and deeper concern on the part of Christian leaders in individual social strata and their demands, and their desire to liberate both theology and the Church from their entanglements with bourgeois society. This has also made possible fruitful contacts with the representatives of the Socialists. The movement, which found its first centre at Bad Boll, has spread among the churches of Western Germany. Its characteristic feature is the holding of periodic conferences and courses of study for a deeper understanding of how Christians shall be able to live out their faith in their vocational life. Both clergy and laity attend these conferences, along with some non-church people. Industrial and professional groups, e.g. doctors, scientists, trade unionists, thus meet. Particular problems are first studied in such expert conferences, and the results are then diffused in larger training courses.

The Christian Frontier Council in Great Britain, formed in 1942, pursues the same aims. It is an association of Christian people in industry and professional life, the purpose of which is thus described :

"No one can doubt the gravity of the present situation in the world, nor the urgent need for action to reverse the present drift of things. To promote such action the Christian Frontier Council was formed in 1942, with the approval of the Church of England, the Church of Scotland and the Free Churches. It reports regularly to the British Council of Churches, but is not part of its organisation and has complete freedom as to the means by which it seeks to attain its ends. *The Christian News-Letter* is published under its auspices.

The Christian Frontier seeks to explore new territory, and new endeavours are never easy to describe in words.

It is based on the threefold belief :

(1) That effective Christian action is urgently necessary in a world threatened with disintegration.

(2) That the real meaning of the principles of Christian action in secular society needs to be re-discovered and reaffirmed.

(3) That action upon these principles, to be effective, must

be expressed, not only in the great and necessary task of proclaiming the Christian view of God and the world, which is the direct and primary responsibility of the Christian churches, but in day-to-day decisions in political, social and industrial life taken by men and women in responsible positions in those spheres.

Centres and groups of a kindred nature are now developing in other countries as well, like Kerk en Wereld in Holland, Associations Professionelles Protestantes in France, and the Centre Protestant d'Etudes in Switzerland.

The new Ecumenical Institute at Bossey outside Geneva, with its conferences of leaders of such lay centres and its periodic courses for teachers, doctors, politicians, etc., has already become an important international rallying point for all these endeavours to mobilise Christian laymen and women and to enable them to face their responsibilities in the world of secular affairs.

Another noteworthy experiment in Great Britain is the institution of " works chaplaincies." With the consent and goodwill of both workers and management in factories and work-shops, Christian ministers have been appointed as voluntary chaplains, able to visit the factories at any time and converse with the workers, to serve them in the case of family trouble and to be at call as occasion demands. While the holding of religious services is not the primary aim of these appointments, the chaplain is there at hand for this purpose when occasion arises, as in the case of great national celebrations.

In the United States of America, also, there are encouraging signs of an awakening of lay responsibility for leadership. The earlier " prophetic " era was characterised by a vigorous minis-terial leadership, and there was a big gap between the social pronouncements so widely promulgated and the actual beliefs and sentiments of the laity. Now there are signs of increasing lay activity in relating the churches to social and economic issues, encouraged by official quarters. A notable illustration was the recent Pittsburgh Conference on " The Church and Economic Life." The members were largely laymen, designated by official church bodies and co-operating agencies.

A significant expression of the growing lay concern was the founding in 1942 of the Laymen's Movement for a Christian World. Its purpose is set out in the member's pledge, " As a Christian layman, I will try to find my part and exert my strength in building Christianity into the everyday life of the world." It has attracted to its membership a considerable number of men of affairs. It publishes a monthly bulletin—*Christian Laymen.* The Movement emphasises prayer, discipline of life and the relevance of Christianity to the common life. A recent conference included in its programme " working groups " dealing with education, housing, labour-management relations, the Church, race relations, international relations, and politics.

Economic conditions are a matter of concern to the younger churches of Asia and Africa, as the reports of the Missionary Conferences of Jerusalem, 1928, and Tambaram, 1938, abundantly demonstrate. A conspicuous example is afforded by action taken by the General Synod of the Methodist Church in India, Burma and Ceylon; 1946. The Synod expressed its deep concern regarding the low economic level of life obtaining particularly in the rural areas, and strongly urged the church to give its immediate attention to the situation. It recommended the appointment of Synod committees in every district to deal with economic and social questions, development of village crafts, the encouragement of producers' and consumers' co-operatives, persuasion of young people to remain in the villages, evoking self-help and the co-operation of the villagers themselves ; and sending promising students for agricultural and technical training. The recommendations also envisage the necessity of reviewing the policy of schools, colleges, evangelistic and other training institutions, so as to consider in what ways their curricula may be adjusted to the training of students in methods of social, agricultural and industrial developments.

IV. *Political Responsibility*

In what new ways have Christian churches faced the challenge of the modern state, and what fresh awareness of political responsibility can be discerned among Christians ?

The most vivid answers have come from those countries where governments forced demands on the Church, the acceptance of which would have compelled betrayal of the faith. This was exemplified in the witness of the Confessing Church in Germany, both prior to and also during the war, and received further illustration from the stand taken in " occupied " countries like Norway, Holland and Greece in resistance to un-Christian pressure from the occupying power.

The moving story is too recent and too well known to require recapitulation here. What does call for emphasis is the realisation that the witness for the faith was itself, in certain circumstances, an act with immediate political consequences. We need only recall the terms of the Norwegian bishops' pastoral letter read at the Easter morning service 1942 :

" We declare that it is our highest duty to God and to man to preach God's word entire and unchanged, for our comfort, for guidance in life, and for our salvation after death, without regard to those to whom it may be displeasing. Here we stand by God's command, servants of the Church, and we therefore cannot without the ruling of the Church receive instructions on how God's word should be preached in any particular circumstances. . . . No earthly power or authority can make conditions contrary to the order of the Church, or to our right to do the work of God, or to serve as preachers of the Gospel. We proclaim the freedom of the word of God and we declare that we are bound by that word."

There is ample evidence, also, of politically significant Church action of another kind in many quarters. That is when churches feel led to make representations or pronouncements on issues which are primarily the responsibility of government, but where Christian principle or Christian opinion is relevant and may even point towards the right action in the situation. One typical instance may suffice.

On October 24th, 1940, six church bodies in the Netherlands united in sending a letter of protest to the Reich Commissioner for occupied Holland, protesting against the regulations according to which officials of Jewish birth and blood had to be dismissed. The letter amply illustrates how the collective Christian judgment may operate in a political issue of this kind :

" We feel impelled to appeal to your Excellency in view of the regulations recently issued in Holland forbidding the nomination or promotion of officials or other persons of Jewish blood. We· hold that the spirit of these regulations is contradictory to Christian mercy. Moreover, these regulations also affect members of the Church itself who have joined within the last few generations and who have been received as equals as is expressly commanded in Holy Scriptures."

We turn now to the situation of bewildering political confusion in which Christians are likely to find themselves as old political landmarks are swept away and new decisions on principle and application are required of them, especially in the face of aggressively secular or totalitarian forces.

Norway, for example, presents us with the attempt to form a specifically Christian party : *Kristeligt Folkesparti* (Christian People's Party). The stand taken by the Norwegian church in resistance to the occupying power quickened the sense of the significance of Christian faith for social and political life. It was hoped to see a Christian renewal within the old political parties but this was not realised, for these parties seemed to revert to their previous materialistic attitude. Hence many Christians felt the need for a more adequate political outlet for their social convictions, and so the *Kristeligt Folkesparti* came into existence. The representatives of the party do not vote according to any party formula, are independent of different theological trends, church organisation or churches. The aim is to work for a realistic and practical policy, independent of current class politics and of different political ideologies.

Holland supplies another variant of Christian political action, based on a strong reaction against the traditional Christian political parties of the country and on the belief that Christians should take their stand along with others in the social and political struggle. After the war a number of prominent church members took action which resulted in the formation of a new Labour Party, to replace the old Social Democratic Party. Christians were included in the leadership of the new party, the previous marxist outlook abandoned, and a positive attitude towards the Church and Christianity taken up.

Likewise in Germany new political alignments are to be noted, both in the emergence of new parties and in a changing attitude of older parties towards Christianity. From the side of the Church, this springs from a new awareness of the social and political significance of the Gospel over and above its meaning for individual redemption. Thus the Christian Democratic Union has brought together Roman Catholics, Protestants, humanist non-Christians and believing Jews. Equally a change has come over the relations between the Social Democratic Party and Christianity. Some significant declarations have been made by responsible party leaders, indicating a movement away from materialism and class warfare, and a new friendliness to the Church and religion. " We bow in respect," says one such declaration, " before all who take Christianity in earnest, and we are determined to allow to the concerns of Christianity the significance which rightly belongs to them."

Or let us take the problem of " isolationism " which has been so politically divisive in the life of the people of the U.S.A. and so crucial for the rest of the world. What ought Christian churches to say on an issue of that kind? Ought a great nation to assert its resolution to live its life alone, even assuming it could, oblivious of responsibility to the rest of the world? One great Christian communion, the Methodist Church of America, largest single Protestant community in the U.S.A., resolved to challenge its own people on that very score, as part of a campaign to bring home the universality of the Gospel and the Christian obligation to take thought for all mankind. Or, in a kindred field of interest, discerning eyes would find in the Charter of the United Nations signed at San Francisco in May, 1945, a feature that strikingly distinguished it from the draft previously drawn up at Dumbarton Oaks, namely, the first article on essential human rights. If enquiry were made as to how it came there, it would be found that at that point the voice of the Christian churches was heard, as it can be heard in the United Nations' Commission on Human Rights.

In the Far East the younger churches of India, China and Indonesia have also been faced with pressing problems of political decision, springing from the rising tide of nationalism and demands for self-government. The challenge of communism is felt in Asia as in Europe, but with a conspicuous difference. In Europe, a system which links the liberation of the common man with atheistic materialism and violent revolution seems hostile to Christian faith and liberty. In Asia, seen over against what is described as Western Imperialism, it supports national aims, and so appears to be a friend to liberty and independence as well as to offer a check to economic exploitation; in this guise it more easily wins the sympathy and support of Christians.

V. *The Church as Prophet of Social Righteousness*

In what ways can we see the Church resuming her proper rôle as prophet of the Word of God to men and nations at this day and hour?

There are abundant evidences that in times of great stress, peril, confusion, or moral declension the voice of the churches is to be heard, upholding faith and proclaiming righteousness.

In Great Britain, on December 21st, 1940, the following letter from the Anglican Archbishops of Canterbury and York, the Moderator of the Free Church Federal Council, and the Roman Catholic Archbishop of Westminster appeared in *The Times* :

Sir,—The present evils in the world are due to the failure of nations and peoples to carry out the laws of God. No permanent peace is possible in Europe unless the principles of the Christian religion are made the foundation of national policy and of all social life. This involves regarding all nations as members of one family under the Fatherhood of God.

We accept the five points of Pope Pius XII as carrying out this principle :

1. The assurance to all nations of their right to life and independence.

2. A mutually agreed organic progressive disarmament, spiritual as well as material, and security for the effective implementing of such an agreement.

3. Some juridical institution which shall guarantee the loyal and faithful fulfilment of conditions agreed upon, and which shall in case of recognised need revise and correct them.

4. The real needs and just demands of nations and populations and racial minorities to be adjusted as occasion may require, even where no strictly legal right can be established, and a foundation of mutual confidence to be thus laid, whereby many incentives to violent action will be removed.

5. The development among peoples and their rulers of that sense of deep and keen responsibility which weighs human statutes according to the sacred and inviolable standards of the laws of God.

With these basic principles for the ordering of international life we would associate five standards by which economic situations and proposals may be tested :

1. Extreme inequality in wealth and possessions should be abolished.

2. Every child, regardless of race or class, should have equal opportunities of education, suitable for the development of his peculiar capacities.

3. The family as a social unit must be safeguarded.

4. The sense of a Divine vocation must be restored to man's daily work.

5. The resources of the earth should be used as God's gifts to the whole human race, and used with due consideration for the needs of the present and future generations.

We are confident that the principles which we have enumerated would be accepted by rulers and statesmen throughout the British Commonwealth of Nations and would be regarded as the true basis on which a lasting peace could be established.

Some definite results followed from that letter. A campaign throughout the whole country, in which the Roman Catholic Sword of the Spirit Movement worked on parallel lines with the Religion and Life Movement of the Anglican and Free Churches, brought the message of the letter home to great numbers of British citizens, Christian and non-Christian, and in some cases led to permanent instruments of Christian co-operation in the social field.

We turn for a second example again to the Reformed Church of the Netherlands. In October, 1941, the Synod protested to the authorities against the renewed legalisation of prostitution. The protest was followed by a public proclamation from the pulpit, in which the Synod expressed to the parishes its great concern about the moral dangers which threatened in ever-increasing measure the older as well as the younger generation. It had learnt with indignation that prostitution had again been legalised. It felt bound to declare that the compassion which is of the nature of the Church rebelled against the wrong that stamps a number of unhappy women as dishonourable and treats them accordingly. It must resist the tendency to minimise the danger of this sin.

We quote finally the pronouncement of the National Christian Council of China, assembled for its biennial meeting in Shanghai from December 3rd-11th, 1946 :

" We are profoundly aware of how earnestly the nation is hoping for reconstruction. In this desire we fully share. Representing a majority of the Protestant churches of China we therefore feel a compelling responsibility to strengthen and gird ourselves the better to perform our part in the spiritual life of the nation upon which all successful political, economic and technical achievement must ultimately depend. To this end, therefore, we are launching a Forward Movement which will be pressed with vigour during the next three years and which will aim at strengthening the inner life of the Church and at making the service of the Church to the nation more far-reaching and significant.

" The Church itself belongs to no party. But as Christians we can neither be blind to the dangers which threaten the foundations of the nation nor refrain from passing moral judgment on social and political evils which are in opposition to what we know to be God's holy will and the moral standards of Jesus Christ. We are united in our opposition to all corruption, to all types of human bondage, inequality, unrighteousness and inhumanity, to all lawlessness and Godlessness.

" The moral life of the nation, largely as a result of the war, is at a low ebb. Standards of moral conduct are lacking. Both individuals and social groups have condoned corruption and lawlessness, and their evil influence predominates almost everywhere. The people suffer, they lie weak and helpless, victims of inhuman cruelties, and know not where to turn for aid. The Church, in the face of such evils, cannot but cry out to the whole nation to repent, and that quickly, so that by a change of heart it may find deliverance and the people be brought forth into safety and peace."

VI. *Creating Fellowship and Building Up Community*

Is there evidence that the churches are contributing to the growth of new community life ?

It is in this field perhaps more than any other that the life of the Church is being continually renewed. By their very nature such new beginnings are local and endlessly varied. Illustration in detail is consequently impossible.

But we may mention one remarkable instance from France— the movement known as the *Cimade*.

The work was initiated at the beginning of the war by the leaders of the French Protestant Youth Council. *Cimade* placed teams in numerous refugee camps, and opened reception centres for liberated prisoners. The work still goes on in a new setting, both among the hundreds of thousands of exiles from Central Europe and Spain, and in bombed regions of France.

Cimade has established barracks in which teams of three or four young people live in conditions like those of the surrounding population, and there a little Christian community is formed. Each post creates its own work programme according to the needs of the locality and the capacities of the team members. Some become young people's clubs, some medical-social centres, others cultural centres. All provide a roof, a table at which one is welcome, a community life inspired by daily worship. *Cimade* now is also engaged in supporting a plan for penal reform, and is sending team members into prisons and camps for " collaborationists."

The teams who undertake this work are both international and ecumenical. They usually consist of young men and women from 20-30 years of age, and include pastors, students of religious education and lay people from various countries. Their underlying conviction is in this faith : " There is a force in the world stronger than the war gods, a completely new beginning, a power which can make a new man of an old one, a liberation for the prisoners, a forgiveness for the guilty, a restoration for the destitute and energy for the defeated . . . and all this lies in Jesus Christ, who creates new men and nations."

Concern for the quality of Christian fellowship and the creation of community is showing itself in another way among the British churches. Here the concern is related to Great Britain's housing problem, not only rebuilding her bombed and battered cities, but dispersing her vast city swarms into new towns and so creating new urban communities. Faced with this question, the British Council of Churches has undertaken a survey of the whole field of the relation of the Christian congregation to the local community where its work must be done and its witness made. One sharp issue has immediately arisen. Must the local congregation itself seek to serve as a community centre, especially for making provision for leisure and other services, or accept the provision made by the local authority, contenting itself with being a centre for worship and religious teaching and fellowship ? There are advocates of both views. Some affirm with conviction that the Church has a community around it. The alternative view sees a new way of Christian service in impregnating with Christian spirit and influence all sides of local community life, as Christian men and women, fortified by the spiritual faith and fellowship of the Church, take up vocational and voluntary service in local government, education, nursing and medical services, care of juvenile delinquents, provision for leisure, and so forth.

SUMMARY

Our survey of Christian new beginnings must end here. Only the briefest critical summary can be attempted, and along three lines :

1. Are they really *new* beginnings ? In one sense, obviously not. The call to repentance is age-long and perpetual in the Christian Church, for the Gospel began with it. Nor is care for persons new, for the value of persons is of the very essence of Christianity. Neither is Christian concern for industry and politics new, nor awareness that the Church has a prophetic function to discharge and a unique fellowship to offer. What is new is a new and challenging situation, and the question is whether the Church is aware of that situation and able and willing to adjust itself to it in a new and realistic way, in the strength of its perennial but ever freshly to be discovered resources in the Gospel.

Put in that way, there is not a little to enhearten us in the preceding review. There are signs of penitence, real and deep, and wide-flung ministries to persons. Neither Churches nor individual Christians placed in situations of great peril and perplexity have shown themselves without courage in facing oppression and tyranny. They have been ready to declare the truth as they saw and felt it to be, and to offer fellowship in new and untried ways.

2. A striking feature of the new Christian outlook here reviewed is the stress laid on the function and witness of the laity in the modern world. A new sense of Christian vocation is breaking through, with the conviction of a God-given function to be discharged in the secular world of affairs. It is felt in the care of persons, not only in the administration of relief to the victims of war, but in a whole range of peace-time callings, as for example, those directed to the care of families. It finds expression in a new sense of responsibility for social life, for industry and for politics and government. The roots of this new sense of lay vocation are in a new awareness of the Gospel and the universality of its claim. The reign of God must penetrate everywhere. In a fresh way, the familiar doctrine of the priesthood of all believers is becoming luminous with meaning.

Not that the awakening is universal throughout the Church. It is most evident in the stirrings of groups of Christians, ready to learn and experiment, and patient in their search for wisdom and understanding of the will of God for them.

3. The greatest hesitancies are in the fields of economics and politics. Christians can feel penitence sharply, uphold their faith with courage in the face of testing, and move quickly to the relief of persons, but in economics and politics judgment is divided. The Church has not made up its mind finally what are the Christian incentives for industry in a world of economic change, nor on the claims of a collective society (distinct from anti-religious systems with which it is too often associated) as over against an individualist society, nor what ought to be the political alignments in which a Christian man will most effectively discharge his social and political responsibility. It is in regard to past failures in that field that the call to repentance is most acute, for everywhere the Churches are suffering from a time lag when their awakening was delayed by too close identification with reigning political power or the interests of a class. Yet in this field the deepest disquiets are felt, and Christian men are obviously searching their hearts and looking for light. While they are everywhere on guard against identifying the Church with any one political system or party, there is clear recognition that the Christian must concern himself with social justice, economic order and political action if Christian values are to prevail.

It is here that the challenge of marxian communism is most acutely felt. In many countries it is in control of power and therefore demands an immediate decision by the Christian as to what he shall think and do. Everywhere it is a pervasive influence, setting before Christian communities and Christian men the dilemma of a system claiming to ensure social justice for all, allied with doctrines of historical materialism and violent revolution that deny both faith and liberty. If anything calls for insight and wisdom it is the solution of that dilemma.

Sharp, however, as that dilemma is, it is not the Church's main problem. That is its own re-birth in Divine power and truth, giving fresh insight into the human situation, and in the daring of its faith in the redemptive purpose of God, leading men out to social adventure and experiment, and bringing the regenerative power of the Gospel to create men and society anew.

X

A RESPONSIBLE SOCIETY

J. H. Oldham

THE subject of the present chapter is the right ordering of human society. The approach to that subject in an earlier chapter from the side of the advances in science and technics makes it clear that the crisis of society is at bottom a crisis of man himself.

A CRISIS OF MAN

We do not mean that every man is affected by the crisis directly in equal degree. We must never generalise about man in general without having in the back of our minds the remark made to a theoriser by a friend immersed in practical affairs : " The difficulty I have, when you start talking about man, is that none of the things you say about him seem to apply to any of the men I actually meet." In affirming that man himself is involved in a crisis, we are speaking of long-term tendencies which affect the lives of individuals and of different communities in varying degrees.

To assert, moreover, that the tendencies dominant in society menace the personal life of man is not to deny that contrary tendencies are also at work. The forces of life everywhere are at war with the forces of death. If it were not so, the battle would already be lost.

These necessary qualifications, however, do not detract from the truth of the statement that what we are facing to-day is a crisis in the life of man. Through the advances of science and technics men have acquired altogether new powers of shaping their environment and of changing themselves. Conscious of their successes in the transformation of nature, they are addressing themselves to the vaster task of transforming society and man in society. In the past men have acknowledged the necessity of submitting to forces they could not control. With the new powers at their command there is opening before their eyes a greater vision. They can picture themselves as taking on their shoulders the responsibility of forging their own destiny. In this outlook capitalism and communism in spite of their differences are at one. It may be said that these are the dreams of the nineteenth rather than of the twentieth century. It is true that belief in the inevitability of progress has been severely shaken, more particularly on the continent of Europe. But it would be a hasty and superficial judgment to regard this as an abandonment of the resolve to exercise conscious control over the process of evolution. In an adventure of such magnitude mistakes and set-backs, even of a grave and disastrous kind, are only to be expected, more particularly in the early stages. It is an unwarranted assumption that men are incapable of learning from their failures and rectifying their errors. The surprising thing is that, in spite of all the disappointments and sufferings that have been experienced, mankind as a whole is proceeding persistently on its course. There could be no stronger evidence of the strength and depth of the impulses by which it is driven forward.

How are we to regard from the Christian standpoint this radical revolution in the life of man in which with consciousness of increasing powers he takes his future into his own hands? There are many Christians who are ready to condemn out of hand the ambition of modern man to transform his environment as a supreme manifestation of human pride—a diabolic revolt of man against his Maker. But there is in many quarters a growing recognition that this is too simple a way of disposing of a real and profound problem. How could man have developed the astonishing powers he has shown himself to possess unless they had been implanted in him by the Creator? There is an old saying that no one contends with God except God Himself, and, if there is a God, the " Promethean powers " which antagonise Him must in some manner be ordained by Him ; they must be understood as His most imposing and awe-inspiring manifestation.[1]

No modern thinker has shown a greater awareness of the reality and depth of this problem than the Russian philosopher, Nicolas Berdyaev, who constantly in his writings recurs to the theme that Christian thought must come to terms, as it has never yet done, with the creative faculties of man. Is man in seeking to transform his environment responding to a demand of God? Michael Foster has recently drawn attention[2] to the crucial issues raised for Christian thought by the fact that by the new powers

[1]Erich Frank, *Philosophical Understanding and Religious Truth*, p. 130. Oxford University Press. 1945.

[2]*The Christian News-Letter*, No. 299, Nov. 26th, 1947. 20 Balcombe Street, London, N.W.1.

which man has acquired he has been emancipated in large degree both from the tutelage of nature and from his dependence on his social environment and cultural tradition. All these have in an unprecedented degree become subject to the control of his will.

In a remarkable article on " The New Man "[1] Père de Lubac, one of the most powerful and influential thinkers in France, asserts that we are witnessing to-day not only extraordinary changes on the surface of the globe, but, at a deeper level, a new type of man coming into being, transforming the more or less accepted idea man has hitherto held of himself, his history and his destiny ; and that Christian thought must reach out to take this tremendous fact into its reckoning. Man, in the Christian view, is not placed in the universe as one thing among other things. He is not, for weal òr woe, installed in a ready-made world ; he co-operates in its genesis. Providence is not fate, but the power that conquers it. " Providentialism, in the sense in which it is too often invoked, is not a Christian truth. It is not encroaching on Providence to work for the improvement of an order of things which has been established mainly through man's own historical activities."

If the Church is to fulfil its mission in a world in which such radical changes are taking place, its own thinking must change. There must be an enlargement of the Christian imagination, which perceives that the range of man's freedom is vaster than we had supposed. The great Christian doctrines of creation, sin and redemption have to be thought out afresh in this far wider context. But while we must strive to achieve this larger vision, we cannot as Christians be blind to the greater perils by which the new possibilities are attended. The discovery of new values may so engross men's interest that they may lose sight almost completely of others that are of equal importance, or are even more fundamental.

Through the forgetfulness of these other, deeper truths, men's efforts to obtain mastery over the world have brought them face to face with problems, the range and gravity of which have hardly yet begun to be generally understood. In the first place, in the process of gaining control over physical nature, men have called into existence a vast network of forces and intricate organisation which they are not able effectively to control. This " second

[1]Published in *Études* for October and November, 1947, and in English translation in the *Dublin Review*, 1948 (First Quarter).

nature " which has come into existence by human decision is in many respects far more alien and unfriendly to man than original nature. Of physical nature it was possible to believe that God created it to serve as a home for man, and that man's task was to co-operate with its processes. Men could believe that the process made sense, if they could discern it. But no such belief is possible about the second nature which has been brought into existence by man. No one could suppose that the evils attendant on the industrial revolution, which were the result of human selfishness, stupidity and shortsightedness, called for any reverence, submission and co-operation from those who were their victims. Because the effects of modern large-scale organisation are the product of human will, and bear the manifest traces of human blindness and injustice, they are apt to provoke resentment, bitterness and conflict.

Secondly, the attempt of man to order the world by his own unaided efforts lays on him a terrifying and well-nigh intolerable responsibility of choice. In all directions the range of man's choice is being indefinitely extended. In an unprecedented and increasing degree he holds in his hands the issues of life and death.

It is no accident that the philosophy of atheistic existentialism should be attracting wide attention to-day. In its more serious forms it is an attempt to face honestly the predicament of modern man. Men are now beginning to discover in their own experience the implications of the assertion that God is dead. They are coming to see what it means to inhabit a universe which cannot be conceived as in any sense the expression of an intelligent Creator's will. The traditional understanding of truth has been shot through with a sense of an order to which our thought must conform. But suppose that there is no sense of speaking of such an order, no sense in speaking of a universe, what, then, is the status of our thinking ?

And what is true of thought is abundantly true also of conduct. Men are only just beginning to see what follows in respect of their judgments of value, if there is no order of values posited and sustained in the universe itself. The old-fashioned hedonist wanted to displace one code of conduct, accepted on the authority of tradition, by another, believed to reflect more adequately the nature of things. To regard pleasure and the absence of pain as the highest good was to make an assertion about what is. But if there is no "nature of things," what then?

If the universe is without intrinsic meaning, the responsibility for man's future must rest wholly on the shoulders of men, since there is nowhere else for it to rest. Without support, without security of any kind and without succour from any source man has to decide at every moment what man is going to be.

This disbelief in any intrinsic meaning in the world makes its appearance at a time when both in thought and practice we have been made aware of the perversions of which human nature is capable. Dostoevsky opened up a new world of understanding in penetrating beneath the surface of civilised life and revealing the secrets of the underground man. Freudian psychology has disclosed the dark depths of the unconscious. The bestialities of concentration camps and other horrors perpetrated in Europe have shown the impulses of cruelty and lust that are latent in human nature. If man decides everything by his own unfettered choice, if we live in a world in which everything is permissible, there can be no guarantee that it will not be the underground man who will in the end decide. It is this incalculable creature man with his explosive liberty who is the centre of the human scene and holds human destiny in his hands.

The concentration of interest in recent centuries on the mastery and acquisition of things has brought about an impoverishment of the human spirit. Man develops as a person through his relations with other persons and in striving towards a Perfection beyond and above himself. The subordination of these expressions of his nature to an excessive pre-occupation with things has led to the progressive decay of *human substance*. In their absorption in the task of exploiting the material resources of the earth through technics, men have lost sight of the ends of living. In the exciting pursuit of knowledge, wealth and power they have ceased to ask what these things are for. They have in consequence lost in a large measure even the capacity to understand the meaning and importance of ends, which arise only in the sphere of personal living, *i.e.*, through living in responsible relations with other men and in loyal response to the claims of God. They have acquired all knowledge, but have not love and, in so far as this is true, they have, as the apostle tells us, become nothing. This loss of his true being is the crisis of man.

In the recently published life of Albert Schweitzer[1] there is a striking passage which describes the trend given to his whole thought and life by a chance remark of one of the guests at a social evening. The remark was, " Why, we are all of us nothing but *epigoni* !" As long ago as the closing years of last century Schweitzer had observed " symptoms of a kind of pernicious anæmia which was sapping the life of western civilisation " and which seemed to him to be " the growth of a peculiar intellectual and spiritual fatigue." It appeared to him that the ethical was in danger of being ousted by the expedient or opportunist, as a norm for personal and political conduct. The *Realpolitik* of German origin was being adopted by other countries. Governments were pursuing, and their people condoning, courses of action that were fundamentally inhumane. Everywhere the sacredness and freedom of human personality were being violated. " My own impression," Schweitzer writes, " was that in our mental and spiritual life we were not only below the level of past generations but were in many respects only living on their achievements, and that not a little of this heritage was beginning to melt away in our hands."

A CRISIS OF CULTURE

The crisis of man is inseparably bound up with a profound and far-reaching crisis of his whole social and cultural life. We are referring here, in the first instance, to western man. But the disintegrating influences of science and technics are invading the ancient civilisations of Asia and the more primitive cultures of Africa and threatening their foundations.

The late Archbishop Temple in an article written shortly before his death asserted that the real crisis of our time is not primarily a moral or political but a cultural crisis. He explained that what he meant is that " man is not a being ruled wholly by his reason and conscious aims. His life is inextricably intertwined with nature and with the natural associations of family and livelihood, tradition and culture. When the connection with these sources from which the individual life derives nourishment and strength is broken, the whole life of society becomes enfeebled. The present plight of our society arises in large part from the breakdown of these natural forms of associations and of a cultural pattern formed to a great extent under Christian

[1] *Albert Schweitzer.* By George Seaver. A. & C. Black. 1947.

influences. New dogmas and assumptions about the nature of reality have taken the place of the old. New rituals of various kinds are giving shape to men's emotional life. The consequence is that while their aims still remain to a large extent Christian, their souls are moulded by alien influences."[1]

Canon V. A. Demant has exerted himself in his writings to impress this truth upon his contemporaries. Thus he says in a broadcast talk : " I want here to interpret the crisis of our time as the breakdown of a civilisation. As a sociologist and a historian of human cultures I am sure, not only that this is the truest interpretation, but in the end the most hopeful one. If we go on thinking and acting as if this civilisation of ours is assured of its survival, or as if its strains could be cured by better political systems or economic methods or even more heroic morals, then— I contend—the breakdown will deepen into complete dissolution. On the other hand, if we frankly recognise that our western civilisation is showing, on the largest scale ever known, all the signs which have marked the disintegration of cultures in the past, we may be able to plant the seeds of a renewal which will not have to wait until after a long period of utter decay. If men feel they are on the right track, even if it is still very unpleasant, they will work for the future. Civilisation dies when men do not anticipate the possibility of its death."[2]

The soil in which the life of the individual is planted has become impoverished and humus has to be put back into it before there can be any fruitful growth.

If the Church is to make an adequate response to the crisis, there are four major tasks to which its attention and energies must be directed.

(1) The Practice of Communal Living

The first indispensable task is to restore substance to the human person through the revitalisation of personal life in the living give-and-take, the mutual obligation and responsibility of a society of persons. If our diagnosis is true, the world cannot be set right from the top but only from the bottom upwards. There is no way of restoring substance and depth to the life of man except by living. Preaching and programmes in themselves effect no change. Ideas and emotions have an effect on

[1] The Christian News-Letter, No. 198. December 29th, 1943.
[2] The Listener. June 26th, 1947.

character only by being translated into action. The nature of man is not something fixed and static, but an energy and activity. Human living is living in relations with other persons and can acquire meaning and depth only in those relations. Since the number of persons with whom an individual can have direct and close relations is limited, the art of social living has to be learned and practised in small groups, of which the family is the chief.

The essential problem of modern society is, as Professor G. D. H. Cole has put it, " to find democratic ways of living for little men in big societies. For men are little, and their capacity cannot transcend their experience. These little groups are the forces out of which the new Europe must be built, if democracy is to be its ruling spirit. They are the nuclei of the new social consciousness on which alone the practical architects of the social order of to-morrow can hope to build a society in which men's higher faculties of love and creative service will have soil to grow."[1]

The Church is concerned with the primary task of re-creating a true social life in two ways. In the first place, its greatest contribution to the renewal of society is through the fulfilment of its primary functions of preaching the Word and through its life as a worshipping community. It is the worship of God that is the source of all genuine renewal. It is only from His fulness that the impoverished human spirit can receive fresh life. It is only in response to the demands of His perfection that it can reach out to new tasks. It is His grace and truth which in the last resort guarantee and sustain the personal and cultural values which are essential to the health of society.

There is nothing greater that the Church can do for society than to be a centre in which small groups of persons are together entering into this experience of renewal and giving each other mutual support in Christian living and action in secular spheres. Such groups will find their vital inspiration in Word and Sacrament and in the fellowship of such gatherings as the parish meeting.

These things are true and fundamental, but to say them in the context of the present chapter is almost dangerous. They may easily suggest to us that all that is needed is for the Church to go on in the teeth of difficulties in the way it is going. There is no real understanding of the human crisis which does not bring

[1] *Christian News-Letter*, No. 90. July 16th, 1941.

with it a realisation of the remoteness of the present life of the Church from the realities of the life of society, and of the magnitude of the effort that is required if that remoteness is to be overcome.

It is only too easy for groups of the kind suggested to become self-centred, with the main emphasis on personal religion, as has been common enough in the past. The demand of to-day is for an effort that is shot through with a deep awareness of the contemporary situation. It must not be a retreat from society but a task undertaken in the conviction that the essential need of society is a new depth of the personal life. Everything hinges on the fulness of meaning that can be put into that conception.

Secondly, the Church has a direct concern also with the wider field of human relations, since it is in *society* that the meaning of personal living has to be re-learned. It is in the secular sphere that the real challenges have to be met, and it is in the meeting and overcoming of these real difficulties that spiritual growth takes place.

It is an essential Christian concern that as wide a sphere as possible must be kept open in which men can have direct and responsible relations with other persons. This sphere is the indispensable training ground for political life. Only those who have been moulded by their experience in these human associations smaller than the State—whether they be voluntary societies for religious, cultural, recreational, philanthropic, civic or economic purposes, or agencies of local government—are capable of exercising the decision and thought that are required by healthy political life. Where the individual is without roots in a vigorous and rich cultural life, and all, or nearly all, his relations are directly with the State, he becomes a mere unit in a sandheap of separate atoms, and the advances of totalitarianism meet with no resistance.

The vital necessity of a rich variety of associations subsidiary to the State is constantly insisted upon in the series of papal encylicals dealing with Christian social doctrine. For example, in *Quadragesimo Anno* it is said : " It is an injustice, a grave evil and a disturbance of right order, for a larger and higher association to arrogate to itself functions which can be performed efficiently by smaller and lower societies. This is a fundamental principle of social philosophy, unshaken and unchangeable . . . . Let those in power, therefore, be convinced that the more faithfully this principle of subsidiary function be followed, and a graded hierarchical order exist between various associations, the greater will be both social authority and social efficiency, and the happier and more prosperous the condition of the commonwealth."

The importance of this doctrine in relation to our present mass society is obvious. Nothing can deliver men from becoming members of a herd and restore to them a genuine personal life except the widest diffusion of responsibility of initiative and of opportunities of co-operation with their fellows.

There is nothing in the results of disinterested scientific research, as Mr. Aldous Huxley points out in his *Science, Liberty and Peace*,[1] " which makes it inevitable that they should be applied for the benefit of centralised finance, industry and government. If inventors and technicians so chose, they could just as well apply the results of pure science for the purpose of increasing the economic self-sufficiency and consequently the political independence of small owners, working either on their own or in co-operative groups, concerned not with mass distribution but with subsistence and the supply of a local market." He maintains that recent economic studies show that mass-producing and mass-distributing methods are technologically justified in perhaps about one-third of the total production of goods. In regard to the remaining two-thirds there are grounds for believing that even from the economic point of view the advantages lie with local production rather than with huge centralised factories. From the point of view of providing opportunities for a humanly satisfying life, a policy of encouraging and fostering smaller groupings has everything in its favour.

A German collaborator in this chapter who has wide experience in these matters writes : " We believe that the breaking up of our mass society into smaller associations of various kinds in which genuinely human relations are possible is the foundation of a healthy political life. We regard this matter as so important, because only on these lines do we see a chance of working against the tendency to transfer decisions from the individual to a hypertrophied bureaucracy and so to reduce progressively the area in which he can exercise responsibility or share in its exercise."

It is in the wide field of rebuilding vital social tissue through

[1]Chatto & Windus. London. 1947.

the experience of communal living that the direct service of the Church to society can best be rendered. Service in this field lies closest to its specific and central concerns. It is also a service which, by reason of its traditional activities and its widespread parochial and congregational organisation, the Church is peculiarly qualified to render. It is one on which opportunities of endless variety lie everywhere ready to hand. Every available energy can at once be thrown fruitfully into the task.

The task of multiplying opportunities of co-operation and of building up small communities with common interests and shared responsibilities may often seem humdrum and commonplace. The scale is so small that it is difficult to see how what is done can have any appreciable effect on the forces which are determining the course of history and the fate of mankind. Its results may often appear to be meagre and disappointing and may be brought to nought by forces beyond our control. The strength to persevere comes from the knowledge that relations with persons are the stuff of life and that through loyalty to personal obligations in a multiplicity of individual instances social tissue is being restored and new vitality is being infused into human society. In these relations with other persons we are living man's true life and the results can be left in the hands of God.

(2) *A Christian Doctrine of Work*

The attempt to lay new social foundations cannot be carried very far without coming up against the question of men's *work*. A man's work fills so large a part of his waking life that unless his Christian faith can impart a meaning to what he does in his working hours it can have little vital significance for him. The restoration of substance and depth to personal living will amount to little unless it finds opportunities of expression in the large slice of the day which for the vast majority of men is devoted to earning a livelihood. The crisis of man, with which this chapter is concerned, will not be surmounted without a Christian doctrine of work. To develop such a theology of work is quite outside the scope of this chapter.[1] We can only emphasise its importance.

Taking as his starting-point and text the doctrine of work

[1] Reference may be made to the relevant chapters in Brunner's *The Divine Imperative* ; R. L. Calhoun, *God and the Common Life* ; an essay on " Man and Work," by T. M. Heron in *Prospect for Christendom* ; and a pamphlet by W. G. Symons on *Work and Vocation* (S.C.M. Press).

implied in the statement *laborare est orare*, Mr. T. M. Heron, who is both an industrialist and a competent theologian, frankly recognises that the assertion is of merely academic interest, unless it can be related to the conditions and problems of to-day. " Can a financier or a machine-tender," he asks, " really pray at his work to-day ? Can he practise the presence of God as he plans his next deal or struggles against the monotony of his nut-tightening ? Can he see in the thing he is making or causing to be made something which is being made for Christ's sake ? Let us admit without reservation that, unless in each case the Christian can answer these questions with a simple affirmative, he must if he is logical give up either his Christianity or his activity in relation to money or the machine. Full acceptance of the doctrine that work is prayer leads in fact to the conclusion that many of our present industrial activities should be classed, as lending money at usury and the gladiator's occupation were once classed, as callings which no Christian can pursue. . . . We have either to translate ' *laborare est orare* ' into modern English and mould our civilisation upon it, or else acknowledge as pretentious survivals every remaining bastion of the Christian culture."

There could hardly be a stronger challenge to Christian thought. Men cannot rest satisfied unless they can find a meaning, or at least some gleam of meaning, in their work. In the judgment of many observers the apparent lack of value in work is the crucial problem of our civilisation.

Meaning is present when a man finds in his work something of the joy of creation, the satisfaction of good craftsmanship. In doing something as well as it can be done a man has the sense of self-fulfilment ; his powers are absorbed in doing what he is meant to do. "As a focus and framework for developing self-hood," Professor Calhoun says, " there is clearly no substitute equivalent to absorbing and cumulatively significant work." The complete, self-forgetting absorption of a man in his task can be at the same time an act of worshipping God. The giving of the self to God in his work of creation may be a form of prayer.

But not all men have the opportunity of being artists or of engaging in creative activities that absorb the whole of their faculties. Monotony, drudgery, plodding and unexciting toil belong to the human lot, and spells of these, in lesser or greater degree, have their place in all work. Where the satisfaction of craftsmanship and creativity is absent from work, or is present only in a minimal degree, meaning must be sought elsewhere.

Part of the task of restoring meaning to work is that men should be convinced that what they are doing, however laborious and exacting, is contributing to the good of the community as a whole. The connection between the work of a man's hands and the necessities and well-being of the community was self-evident in the small societies of earlier times. It is much more difficult to make the connection apparent in the large-scale enterprises of to-day. Yet it is essential that men should feel that they are making a contribution that is really needed for the life and work of the world. So long as they have this sense, even vaguely, and dimly, they can look on their work as an expression of their life and love.

It would be a mistake, however, to assume, as Christians and idealists are apt to do, that the motive of public service can be in itself, except in a small minority, a sufficient incentive to maintain work at the necessary level of efficiency. Men are influenced far less by distant ends than by their immediate experiences. The few persons with whom they are in daily contact are more real to them than the far-off results of their labours. While a sense that work is worth while because it serves in some way the public good is necessary, it is with the more immediate incentives that we must concern ourselves, if a meaning is to be restored to work. We know at present relatively little about the variety of incentives which impel men to work. Telephone engineers, for example, in executing repairs are probably animated much less by a conscious desire to render a public service than by a professional distaste at seeing their machines go wrong. "The day-to-day structure of activity," as Mr. W. G. Symons says, "in a government office or in a factory depends on a whole complex of motives and incentives—emulation, professional pride, craft interest, hope of promotion, the drive of good leadership, interest in the pay-packet and so on. It is the duty of those who have the responsibility for organising work to see that these various incentives operate so as to maintain efficiency." The relevance in this connection of the Hawthorne experiments in the United States referred to in an earlier chapter[1] is obvious.

All solutions of the problem of restoring a meaning to work

[1] p. 40.

are too simple which fail to take full account of the extent to which modern machine production has isolated work from the rest of the context of men's lives. Large scale production is dominated by rational considerations, and the individual person is viewed in his functional relation to the undertaking as a whole. Instead of the machine serving man, man has to serve the requirements of the machine. We are confronted here with a fundamental contradiction between the claims of the human person and the whole structure of modern industry. Nothing will overcome this contradiction but a revolution in men's ideas by which human labour is conceived in terms not primarily of the technical process and the material product, but of human good ; that is to say, of the human relations of those associated in the productive effort and the human purposes which it is designed to serve, the ultimate end and meaning of the whole process being found in the worship of God.

Is there a call to the Church to help in bringing about such a revolution in men's thinking ? It is plain that little or nothing is gained by formulating a few abstract principles of a Christian conception of work. The Christian doctrine of work that is needed is not one that can be elaborated by theologians sitting in their studies. Any doctrine so framed would inevitably be remote from life. The only doctrine that can be expected to have any practical effect is one that grows out of an active wrestling with actual problems of industrial life to-day. It can be formulated only by those who have first-hand experience of these problems, aided in this task by such illumination as theologians and pastors can bring to them. Industry can be redeemed only by those engaged in industry. If the churches are convinced that for the effective Christian service of society to-day a Christian doctrine of work is essential, they must realise that it cannot be provided in any adequate form through present machinery. New means must be devised for encouraging lay men and women in secular callings to wrestle in Christian obedience with the problems which they encounter in their daily work, and new provision must be made for giving them the help they need in addressing themselves to these tasks.

(3) Collective Morality

New complexities arise for Christian action in society from the fact that for the majority of men most of the decisions which they have to make or execute are collective decisions.   It has always been true that most men have had to execute orders given them by their superiors.   The difference to-day is that the growth of organisation has for immense numbers of people greatly restricted the sphere in which they are free to take independent responsible decisions.   The nature of the acts which they daily perform is determined by conditions beyond their control and where, as members of a party, a trade union or an employers' association, they have a partial, or at least nominal, responsibility, the power of an individual to influence the collective decision may often seem negligible.

The significance of this change is as yet very inadequately understood by the Church.   It is not easy to feel " on our pulses " difficulties which lie outside our own experience. Theologians, clergy and professional people are withdrawn from many of the acute pressures of modern society.   " The Clydeside shipbuilding apprentice," writes a minister of the younger generation, " the delicatessen proprietor, the accountant or the New York longshoreman knows in his bones more about the essential moral problems and tensions of contemporary life than the average minister can compass with his imagination." Yet it is just these moral problems and tensions that the Church must understand and take account of in its teaching, if Christianity is to be a faith by which men can live and from which they can receive guidance in the rough and tumble of life.

Much has been written about the decay of Christian belief. Far less attention has been paid to the rejection and distrust of the Christian ethic.   In a sense the second may be regarded as an outcome of the first.   Men's moral uncertainties are, no doubt, a consequence of their loss of belief in all absolutes.   But their moral perplexities arise also from the fact that they can see little or no connection between Christian morality as it is ordinarily presented and the problems with which they have to deal in their daily life.

Mr. Middleton Murry among contemporary thinkers has seen with exceptional penetration what is really happening in modern society.   In his latest book, *The Free Society*,[1] he maintains that a point has been reached in human development when the reality of the individual person no longer resides in himself.

[1]Andrew Dakers. 1948.

It is the socialised man who is the contemporary reality. The individual person of traditional religious and liberal-political thinking has become largely an illusion. Willy-nilly the socialised man, which each one of us in greater or less degree is to-day, does what society as a whole does. He may as an individual *think* what he pleases ; he may *say* at least a good deal of what is contrary to the ideas prevailing in society ; but in the realm of action he is compelled to a large extent to *do* what society as a whole does.

In a society in which decisions in practical affairs have become collective decisions it is within the smaller groupings that the exercise of responsibility must, in the first instance, be asserted. It is in the individual factory, the party, the trade union, the employers' federation, that the battle for freedom of conscience has to be fought and won. Political decision, for example, is generally understood as joining a political party, but it is a disastrous mistake to suppose that a man who becomes a member of a party is thereby relieved of all political responsibility and has simply to do what the party tells him. To remove any area of life basically from the realm of responsible decision is to withdraw it from the rule of God over the world. That does not mean that the decisions of his political party may not in most instances be in accord with the general outlook on political questions which determined his original choice. Nor does it mean that an individual, even when he differs from the party, may not quite properly decide to give greater weight to its collective judgment than to his own. But it does mean that for the man who is resolved to obey God in all his acts, direction cannot be substituted for responsible decision.

Group morality, in which the achievement of justice is the highest norm, must always differ from individual morality in which, in the Christian view, love is the guiding principle. But the problem is intensified by the un-Christian character of our present culture and by the increasing social cohesion.

In a society in which Christians are a minority, we cannot expect that collective decisions will be based directly on Christian assumptions, which most of those who make the decision do not share. It is not by the full light of the Christian faith, but by some " refraction," as M. Jacques Maritain has put it, of that light that in the circumstances of to-day we may hope that the collective decisions of society to-day may be guided.

The insistent task which confronts the Church in modern society is to help to provide ethical guidance for collective decisions and actions. Without such guidance the relations between groups must degenerate into a struggle of naked power. The problem of the morality of states in distinction from that of individuals has for long engaged the attention of Christian as well as of general political thought. It has been widened in scope, brought closer to the ordinary man and made more insistent by the extension of collective action by groups. There is no more urgent need than for the supplementation of an ethic for the individual by a morality of group action. Unless men have such a morality to guide them in their decisions and actions in group life, and unless they are enabled to see a connection between this working morality and Christian faith, Christianity will seem to have little significance for life in this world.

Christians have to carry the dual responsibility of doing their utmost to further in the various areas of social life the growth of a group morality, which as we have seen can never be identical with the Christian ethic, and of maintaining at the same time a critical attitude towards it. The temptation, to which the Church has too often succumbed, of equating the ordinary human virtues of honesty, fair dealing, toleration and general decency with Christianity must be resisted. These virtues are not confined to Christians, and it only creates difficulties to assume that they are. Christians have to exemplify these virtues in their own lives and to do what lies in their power to make collective decisions conform to them, but they cannot rest satisfied with them. They are not bearing their full Christian witness if they are merely keeping in step with what is best in social endeavour. There must always be a certain awkwardness in the relation of the Christian to society. Life for him is not conformity with abstract ideals. It is a daily meeting and confrontation with other persons and with God in Christ. To what new and unexpected actions that confrontation may lead him he cannot foresee. It is by his openness to these encounters, and not by complacent conformity to prevailing custom, that he can introduce a new leaven into society.

What is involved in furthering the growth of a group morality may be made clearer, if we ask how the task may be carried out. If we limit ourselves to the contribution of the Church to the undertaking, a possible way of dealing with the matter would be to establish a number of chairs of Christian ethics in theological colleges, and to instruct the holders of these to devote special attention to questions of group morality. If this were the best means of achieving the object in view, it ought to be given a high priority among the many claims on the resources of the churches. But in actual fact it would be quite ineffective in meeting the real need. There is undoubtedly a contribution to be made by reflective thought. But the practical problems which arise in real life are so endless and varied that general formulations and theoretic discussions afford only a modicum of help. The only hope of dealing with the problem effectively is that it should be approached from the other end. In the crucial question of Christian action in the complexities of modern society the answer can be found only by those who are involved in the activities of society, though theological insight and knowledge can be of great assistance to them in finding it. Few would probably dispute this truth in the abstract, and instances of the right kind of approach are not wanting either in the life of the churches or in the work of some theological seminaries. But a genuine acceptance of what has been said would result in very far-reaching practical changes in the life and methods of the Church.

(4) *The Political Task*

We have considered, first, the task of re-creating the substance of human life through personal living in relation with other persons, a task which lies in the main in the social and cultural sphere ; secondly, the need of restoring meaning to *work* in the economic sphere ; and, thirdly, the need for giving content to a group morality which will guide collective decisions in the economic and political spheres. It remains to consider the *political* crisis in which mankind is to-day involved and the tasks to which it calls.

The crisis is acute and things are moving rapidly. This chapter may be read in an international context widely different from that in which it is written in February, 1948.

Science and technics, as we have seen, have brought about a new form of social existence, which is manifested in the free as well as in the totalitarian societies. What these have in common is almost as significant as the radical difference between them. If the new fact in history is that men to-day, with the new knowledge and skill at their command, are embarking on the adventure of taking conscious control of their destiny, it is to that tremendous fact that the Christian gospel has to be related. If the courage for such an attempt is lacking, the whole of human life will be progressively moulded by anti-Christian forces.

The political scene is so confused, and the difficulties of finding the right course of action so overwhelming, that many Christians are tempted to throw in their hand and look on Christianity as having to do only with personal relations and a private morality. There is a pietistic as well as a liberal *laissez-faire*. However pious the intention, it is a denial of God's reign in the world, of the Lordship of Christ over history.

The political issue which dominates the whole life of mankind to-day is the tension between the western democracies and Soviet Russia and its satellites. The question of the Christian attitude towards this controversy cannot be evaded.

In this political controversy, vital human and Christian interests are involved. But it must be asserted with equal emphasis that the Church cannot identify itself unequivocally with either side in the dispute. It is debarred from doing so both by Christian principle, since no earthly political society can claim to be an embodiment of the Kingdom of God and all alike stand under the judgment of God, and by impartial examination of the facts. The Church, if it is true to itself, has its own criteria of judgment, which differ from those of the world. An independent attitude towards the idolisation either of communism or of democracy will win greater respect than an uncritical endorsement of one or the other. The Christian task is to discern elements of truth and goodness wherever they may be found, and to unmask and denounce unrighteousness in every quarter. The function of the Church in the present political crisis which threatens to overwhelm mankind in disaster is a dual one. It has to bear fearless and uncompromising witness to the truth which it sees, and at the same time to exercise a catholic sympathy and fulfil a ministry of reconciliation.

It is by communism with its totalitarian claims that the issues in the political debate to-day are posed. There is no space to consider here, important as the question is, what relative importance is to be attached to the present ascendancy of a communist ideology in comparison with the deeper and more enduring forces of the character, environment, tradition and historical experience of the Russian people ; nor, in spite of its relevance to present political realities, the question how far the original purpose of marxism to deliver the workers from economic exploitation has been replaced by a rigid system controlled by a relatively small political élite and directed to the expansion of Russian power. What we are concerned with in this chapter is the Christian attitude to the conception of life implied in communism, which is a powerful ferment throughout the world and aims at a complete transformation of human existence.

It is necessary to distinguish between communism as a political and economic system and as a totalitarian control of life. From the former there may be much to be learnt ; with the latter Christians can make no compromise.

The Federal Council of Churches in America in a statement regarding American foreign policy in relation to Russia, published in 1947, assert that the critical and supreme political issue of to-day is *not* " the economic issue of communism versus capitalism or the issue of state socialism versus free enterprise. As to such matters, it is normal that there should be diversity and experimentation in the world." That a body representative of the American churches should commit itself unreservedly to this important distinction is in view of the general state of public opinion in America a noteworthy fact. The same statement goes on to affirm that " the basic international issue is the simple issue of the police state as against the free society." This is, however, too great a simplification. The questions involved are wider than the police state and, while the police state is an intolerable denial of the Christian view of the proper relations of men in society, it may in revolutionary periods claim a relative and temporary justification. If the party in power has reason to believe that its political opponents will, if they succeed in ousting them, send them and their friends to death or a concentration camp, it is natural for them to take all possible precautions to prevent this from happening. An established tradition of toleration is necessary for the working of free institutions.

The forms of society which men create are determined by the responses which they make to the challenges of their environment and of history, and these responses depend in the last resort on their conception of the nature and destiny of man. Between the Christian and the marxist views of man there is an irreconcilable antithesis. It is true that there are many affinities in detail between the two conceptions, so far as the structure, as distinct from the content, of the thought is concerned.[1] There is also, owing to the influence on Marx's thinking of the Judæo-Christian tradition, a considerable measure of common ground over against rival philosophical anthropologies. But underlying these analogies and resemblances there is a fundamental and insurmountable opposition, which makes itself felt in divergences all along the line. In Christianity the central meaning of man's life is found in a transcendent relation to God. In marxism the meaning of his life is found wholly within his earthly history. In the former the dynamic of human existence is grounded in a divine redemption ; in the latter in human actions under the compulsion of the social structure.

This ultimate opposition is, however, for two reasons not decisive in regard to our attitude to communism in the political sphere which we are here considering. In the first place, it might be claimed for communism, whether justly or not, that, while it rejects the doctrine, it performs the works and that, like the son in the parable, while refusing to obey the Father, does actually fulfil His will. Secondly, in the world as it is to-day atheism is not confined to communism. It is inherent, whether professed or not, in the claims of fascism, and it is widely prevalent among the leaders of thought and action in the western democracies. It was liberal thought which undermined belief in supernatural reality and laid the whole burden of the guidance of life on man's shoulders alone. Atheism is a characteristic of the whole climate of the age. None the less the professed and militant atheism of communism is a factor that cannot be disregarded in the present political crisis.

It is the grandeur of marxism and no small part of its strength and at the same time, from the Christian point of view, the root of its deadly error that, at least in its original form, and still in the belief of many of its adherents, it offers men a complete scheme of salvation. The fundamental concern of Marx, as Père Lubac reminds us in the article already referred to, was the spiritual liberation of man. The emphasis which he laid on man's social liberation arose from the fact that it is an indispensable means to the other. He insisted against Feuerbach that the human essence is no abstraction inherent in the individual but the

---

[1] These analogies have been worked out in a remarkable way in an unpublished paper by Professor Paul Tillich.

ensemble of his social relations.[1] The question of men's social relations is of overwhelming importance because they affect and determine the very being of man. This insight of Marx is a perpetual challenge to Christianity.

What is said about the marxist position in the following passage in Père Lubac's article deserves our close attention : " Of the marxists we can say," he writes, " something analogous to what St. Augustine, with his own implied reserves, said of neo-Platonists : in one sense they rightly see the end but they prevent themselves from ever attaining it by mistaking the road. They foresaw a liberated and united humanity, completely possessed of its own essence and reconciled with itself and the universe, living in utter fulfilment to the end of history. Do not our own Scriptures promise us the same ideal . . . the ideal St. Augustine summed up in *unus Christus* and *Christus integer* ? But by believing that, to be attainable, the ideal must be shorn of all transcendence and realised in time, they deny its conditions and render it inconsistent. Moreover, by seeking it in history by incongruous methods, they prevent themselves from even approaching it or laying its foundations."

It is the promise of salvation, even though it be an earthly and material one, that gives to totalitarian societies the attraction which to-day they undoubtedly exert. " The totalitarian State," as Canon Demant has observed, " is engendering a conviction that men may work for the future." The appeal of the totalitarian movements is especially felt by those peoples who have been deprived hitherto, or feel themselves to have been deprived, of an adequate share of material advancement. If men are confronted with a choice between economic security and political freedom, they will unquestionably choose the former.

There is no reason in principle why material advance should not be achieved on a basis of political freedom, which has, in fact, been the foundation of American prosperity. But when the matter is viewed historically, it is apparent that there may be conditions in which only a strong centralised government wielding despotic power can overcome the obstacles to economic advance and provide a framework of security within which other freedoms may later develop. It is at least arguable, for example, that the present régimes in the Balkans, or some of them, are the only governments that in existing circumstances possess the necessary

[1] " Theses on Feuerbach," *Ludwig Feuerbach.* Martin Lawrence.

strength to solve the basic economic problems of the peoples over whom they rule.

There are, as we saw earlier, no Christian grounds for condemning the effort of men to better their earthly lot and to bring to the task the widest exercise of their powers. But the actual results of the endeavour, as they manifest themselves to-day, cannot but raise serious questions. The consequences of an attempt to find the whole meaning of man's life within the temporal are becoming increasingly evident. If man is not made in the image of God, he has to be made in the image of society. He becomes a function of society, the instrument of impersonal ends. In the end he ceases to be man. Life loses its sacredness. Where the interests of the state seem to require it, the individual may be ruthlessly sacrificed. While in important respects they are completely opposed to one another, communism, national-socialism and fascism are alike in making the impersonal might of the collective an end in itself and in sacrificing individuals without mercy to this god.

This is not, of course, the whole truth about existing totalitarian states. No government could survive that failed to satisfy in some measure the aspirations of the majority of its subjects. In every human society men's natural impulses towards community and co-operation seek some expression. It would be quite misleading to leave out of the picture of Russia its achievements in education, the promotion of health and the care of children and in giving to the ordinary man the sense that the country belongs to him and that he shares fully in a common life.

We are speaking here only of the *logic* of totalitarianism, when no higher authority is acknowledged to which the rulers of the state must have regard, and the state becomes a " mortal God." But the actual facts are terrible enough. Even when full allowance has been made for revolutionary fury, the Bolshevist determination to eliminate ruthlessly an entire class is the expression of a complete disregard of the claims of human beings as such. A recent carefully documented account of forced labour in Russia,[1] on which the Soviet economy seems to be irrevocably based, estimates the number of those employed in slave labour in labour camps at fifteen million persons, condemned to a brutish life of unmitigated toil in intolerable

[1] Dallin and Nicolaevsky, *Forced Labour in Russia.* Hollis & Carter. 1948.

conditions. The expulsion of eighteen million people from eastern Europe, depriving them at a stroke of their homes, tearing up the roots of their historical existence, and leaving their lives at the mercy of an unknown fate, is a similar manifestation of callousness to every human right.[1]

The question which concerns us here, however, is not to pass judgment on communism in the light of an ideal standard but to consider it in relation to the practical political alternatives to-day. These may be described, briefly and inadequately, as the liberal, capitalist society of free enterprise, of which the United States is the outstanding example, and the attempt which is being made by the British Government, and by governments or parties in various countries in Europe, to work out a new synthesis of the claims of freedom and equality in the form of a democratic socialism. How are these alternative political systems to be viewed in the light of the fundamental Christian understanding of the meaning of life ?

It cannot be too strongly emphasised or too often recalled that the marxist movement, whatever sinister forms its later developments may have assumed, was in its origins a moral revolt against the injustices of a system in which man was exploited by man. Christians must often be put to shame by the readiness of young communists to sacrifice themselves recklessly for the attainment of what they believe to be a higher justice and fuller humanity. We cannot oppose to the totalitarian systems the conception of a " free society " without a constant realisation of the ambiguity of the term "freedom." It may mean the freedom of the Christian man to obey God and to serve his fellow-men according to his conscience. It may mean, on the other hand, freedom to indulge greed and lust, freedom of the strong to exploit the weak, the freedom of property rather than of men.

The question needs to be asked to what extent " free societies "

[1] Callous indifference to the individual is common to all forms of totalitarianism. National-Socialism, which deified not a chosen class but a superior race, deliberately put to death ten million persons and carried out experiments on the bodies of its victims with every refinement of cruelty. The infection of this inhumanity has penetrated into the western democracies. The facts which have been cited in the text show that slavery, which the nineteenth century did its utmost to eradicate from the world, has been re-introduced on a vast scale into Europe. By the retention of prisoners of war for labour purposes long after the cessation of hostilities Great Britain and France have shown how far they have succumbed to the contagion. It would be difficult also to point to a more signal instance of callousness to human life and suffering than the dropping of the bombs on Hiroshima and Nagasaki.

have actually succeeded in realising freedom. We may take the United States as the outstanding present example of a capitalist economy, though the same things could be said in varying degrees of other capitalist countries before the war.

An exposition of the policies of the National Association of Manufacturers in the United States is given in Robert A. Brady's *Business as a System of Power*,[1] which also includes a long section describing, with full documentation, the economic, social and political policies of the central employers' organisations (*Spitzenverbände*) throughout the world. The facts given in this volume have an important bearing on the question how far capitalist societies can claim to be free societies. In addition to various measures of defence against labour action, there have been developed in recent years extensive programmes for the " re-education " of the labour masses. The aim is, on the one hand, to change the ideological outlook of the ordinary worker and, on the other hand, by a special ideological training and by a carefully worked out system of incentives to attach to the interests of management the more ambitious youth who might otherwise become future leaders of labour. The more fully developed of these programmes of what is sometimes called " welfare capitalism " are all inclusive and attempt " to control both form and content of the *totality* of worker ideas and activities." In many of these welfare and educational programmes there is a considerable blend of idealism, to which Mr. Brady appears to do less than justice, and the benefits in many instances to the workers are undeniable. But it is a question how far such educational and welfare activities, directed from a single autocratic centre, are in accord with the nature of a free society.

What is, perhaps, of more immediate importance for our present purpose, is that these central employers' organisations are directing their attention to means of influencing or controlling political action and are creating for the purpose their own staff of expert advisers, constituting a business " civil service." They are also devoting a considerable part of the large funds at their disposal to the formation of a public opinion favourable to the policies which they wish to have carried out. Mr. Brady is of opinion that " nothing fundamental in history, structure of organisation or social outlook divides clearly the policies of the *Spitzenverbände* within the totalitarian countries

[1]Columbia University Press, New York. 1943.

from those of the liberal-capitalist states." No discussion of the free society is realistic that does not take full account of the growth within the economic system of a vast structure of political influence and power outside the recognised democratic processes. There is nothing which distinguishes the outlook that has been described from the ambition of state planners to shape history by means (in the phrase of Engels) of " a collective will according to an all-embracing plan."

It is not only in the field of government, however, but also in the social and cultural spheres that the influence of the large-scale organisation of the machine age makes itself felt in free as well as in totalitarian societies. " In the U.S.A. no less than in U.S.S.R.," writes Mr. Christopher Dawson,[1] " we are conscious of the victory of the mass over the individual. Moreover, we see in America how material prosperity and technical efficiency produce social conformity, so that without any intervention on the part of the state, men of their own accord tend to think the same, and look the same, and behave in the same way. None of these things is peculiar to the United States. It is only that in America the standard of material prosperity is higher and the counter-balancing forces of authority and tradition are weaker. And consequently the United States has been the pioneer of a popular hedonistic mass civilisation which is the chief alternative to the totalitarian ascetic mass civilisation of communism."

The conflict between the democratic and totalitarian States has its roots in the tearing apart, and the espousal by one side or the other, of two things that belong inseparably together—liberty and equal justice. A philosopher of the younger generation in Great Britain writes : " The conflict between marxism and liberalism is a conflict between the need for economic equality and the need for political equality in the ideal state. Marxism will be the ideology of those who feel the one need acutely, liberalism that of those who feel the other. The economic need is felt first. In plain terms poverty is more unpleasant to the poor than being regimented, at least when the regimentation is held to be in the interest of a higher standard of living and more equitable distribution of wealth. . . . You will never convince the bulk of the population of the importance of liberty (I am speaking from five years' experience as a wage-earner), until you

[1] In an article in *The Month*, January, 1947.

convince them, by espousing their claim for equity, that you are not using ' liberty ' as a catchword for reaction."[1]

There is no reason why the free societies should not offer to men greater social justice than a totalitarian state. There are strong grounds for believing that it is only the free society that can in the long run ensure progressive approximations to social justice. It alone provides the opportunities by which men can discover by common discussion and by experiment what social justice means and thereby progressively achieve it. Unless the free societies can by their accomplishments convince the masses of the truth of this, they must inevitably suffer eclipse.

When we take a world view of the situation, moreover, the defenders of western democracy cannot pay too close heed to the fact, to which Mr. Thomas has called attention in an earlier chapter,[2] of the impression made on Asiatic and African peoples by the racial attitudes and political and economic imperialisms of the western democracies. Many of these peoples feel that their aspirations for independence and freedom meet with greater understanding and sympathy in Russia than in the West. The existence of this feeling, whether justified or not, may be of enormous importance in shaping world history. For the Church it is a matter of supreme concern, since Christians in Asia and Africa are torn between the ties which unite them with the western churches from which they have received their Christianity and the attraction of the greater social and racial equality which appears to be offered them by an atheistic communism.

It might seem appropriate at this point to consider what has been called the third force—the attempt in Great Britain and elsewhere to establish a form of democratic socialism. But an adequate discussion of the movements in Great Britain and other countries to find a middle way between American free enterprise and Russian totalitarianism would require far more space than is available. Moreover, the attempts to strike out a new course are still in their beginnings and the shape they will take is not yet clearly visible. The ideas and convictions which will carry them to success have still to be defined.

It is not for the Church to prescribe to its individual members the political decisions they should make, and it is obvious that in an ecumenical assembly the political decisions that are open

---

[1] Ian Crombie in the *Christian News-Letter*, No. 280, March 5th, 1947.
[2] pp. 71 ff.

to its members and are demanded of them must vary greatly from country to country. All that ecumenical discussion can provide is aid towards an understanding of the general principles by which Christian action must be guided.

In an attempt to define the beliefs and attitudes which ought to govern the judgments and actions of Christians in relation to the political issues we have been considering, we must beware of lapsing into a moral idealism which supposes that the mere enunciation of moral aims can arrest or deflect the strong tides which are shaping our present social existence. The powerful biological, economic and political forces that hold men in their grip can be mastered not by ideals and aspirations but only by a higher and stronger reality.

The social order which Christians in virtue of their faith must seek to realise will include the following elements :

There can be no question, in the first place, that Christians must stand firmly for the freedom of men to obey God and to act in accordance with their conscience. This is the foundation of a responsible society. What is at stake is not merely the rights of the individual, but the moral progress of society as a whole. Only a society which respects the consciences of its members is open to the creative impulses by which it can attain to a fuller moral and spiritual life.

The question of conscience, which is crucial to spiritual growth, presents itself to-day, in a new form, since, as we have seen, humanity has entered on a new kind of existence. If the way in which men live and the things that they do are determined to a large and increasing extent by corporate decisions, the life of the individual, as expressed in his daily actions, can possess a moral quality only if moral purpose permeates the whole life of society and governs its collective decisions. It is only if men are able freely to participate in the making of these decisions that their life as a whole can have a moral character.

Secondly, to obey God men must be free to seek the truth, to speak the truth and to educate one another through a common search for the truth. Only through the freedom of its members to expose error, to criticise existing institutions and to express fresh creative ideas can society advance to fresh levels of life. In order that this may be possible, there must be free access to sources of information, freedom of expression in speech and writing and freedom to criticise authority.

Sir Norman Angell has written an arresting book[1] in which he directs attention to the widespread disregard of, and even contempt for, facts in public controversy, and the alarming extent to which men refuse to allow their actions to be guided by them. " The present generation," he concludes, " is a generation more perilously threatened by the results of unreason than any which has preceded it."

This grave depreciation of truth is by no means confined to communists, but communists have done much to encourage it. Professor Harold Laski is certainly not an unfriendly critic of communism, and yet he writes in a pamphlet,[2] as chairman of the British Labour Party, as follows : " The communist parties outside Russia act without moral scruples, intrigue without any sense of shame, are utterly careless of truth, sacrifice, without any hesitation, the means they use to the ends they serve. . . . The only rule to which the communist gives unswerving loyalty is the rule that a success gained is a method justified. The result is a corruption both of the mind and heart, which is alike contemptuous of reason and careless of truth."

Sir Norman Angell adds two quotations from Lenin. The first is : " We must be ready to employ trickery, deceit, lawbreaking, withholding and concealing truth " ; and the second : " We can and must write . . . in a language which sows among the masses hate, revulsion, scorn and the like towards those of different thought." Mr. Angell adds the quite proper comment that " Lenin's code, as reflected in the words just quoted from him, is the moral code of war ; a code adopted towards the enemy by every one of the combatants in the struggle just ended. The communist believes that he is engaged in the greatest of all struggles and that if he renounced those means of deceit and deception all good soldiers employ, then he would be beaten and the cause of the People would perish." We could not have a more forcible reminder of the way in which war, and the threat of war, threatens to engulf all the values which make man a human being.

Thirdly, the Christian is committed by his faith to respect for man as man. Every other individual is equally with himself the object of God's love. He can never allow the individual

---

[1] *The Steep Places.* Hamish Hamilton. 1947.
[2] *The Secret Battalion : An examination of the Communist Attitude to the Labour Party.* Labour Publications Department, London, 1946.

person to be absorbed in a hated class or disliked race. Every man has the right to an opportunity of expressing his point of view and of having it listened to in affairs that concern him. The principle was given classic expression in a conference between Oliver Cromwell and the officers of his army almost exactly three hundred years ago in the remark of Colonel Rainboro : " I think the poorest he that is in England has a life to live as the richest he."

This religious respect of man for man is the basis of true toleration. Toleration, like all qualities most worth striving after, may easily degenerate into something scarcely deserving of the name. It may mean a supine indifference to intellectual, æsthetic and moral values and a refusal to distinguish between good and bad. True toleration has its ultimate root in the religious belief in man's finitude. Truth is too large and rich to be apprehended in its fulness by any single individual group, school or party. It can be found only by the collaboration of many minds and the clash of opposed opinions. Those who are animated by this conviction will be ready to acknowledge the elements of truth in their opponent's case. They will be prepared to listen to his exposition of it with a view to discovering points which they themselves have missed and to understanding the reasons for what seem to them to be errors. Where no reconciliation between conflicting views can be reached, they will still believe that out of the clash of opinions a larger synthesis will in the end emerge.

This belief in a truth beyond the grasp of any individual or party, in a universal moral law by which all alike are bound, is the indispensable basis of the free society. Those who refuse to acknowledge a spiritual reality of truth and justice to which all owe an obligation can have no valid objection to being totally directed by the state.

What has been called the free society might also (and for some purposes more advantageously because of the ambiguity in the meaning of freedom) be called the non-violent society—that is, a society which has recourse to violence only in the last resort. A fundamental difference between the believers in democracy and communists is that the former believe, as a result of experience, in a way that communists do not, that violence defeats its own object and perverts a good cause. No one who has a sense of realities will deny the necessity of putting restraints on those who seek to overthrow a régime that has the support of the majority of the people. But democrats believe that no un-necessary violence should be employed ; that in broad historical issues what you think you are going to attain is never what you do in fact attain, and that you can be much more sure of the injury to social health from intolerance and ruthless violence than of the consequences that will in the end result from this or that particular action.

Fourthly, the Christian will always attach a greater import-ance to the direct relations between persons than to the collective relationships which threaten to dominate our life. The latter are instrumental to the former and must be judged by the extent to which they foster a genuinely personal life in which true community is achieved. Institutions have an essential place in human life and may become the vehicles of personal living. But this can come about only if there is a revolutionary reversal of values.

We owe a debt to Martin Buber[1] for his persistence in recalling our minds to the immeasurable significance of the living relations between persons, which is the common stuff of every-day existence, and which powerful forces operating in society to-day may filch from us before men are fully awake to the incomparable value of what is in danger of being lost. Neither the individual as such, he insists, nor the aggregate as such, is the fundamental fact of human existence. The fundamental reality is *man with man*. What is peculiarly characteristic of the human world is something that takes place " between " one being and another. The essence of human life is what *happens* between man and man. It is in the communication that man is man. To this profound truth the present age is largely blind.

It is evidence of the prevailing confusion of thought that there can be prolonged discussions on the relation of the indi-vidual to the community without any sign of an awareness that there are not two possibilities to be considered but *three*. The first step, as Buber rightly says, " must be to smash the false alternative with which the thought of our epoch is shot through—that of individualism or collectivism." What we are speaking of here is not to be confused with the " third force " which was referred to earlier. That was a possible alternative to com-munist and capitalist systems in the political field. The third

[1]More particularly in his latest book *Between Man and Man*. Kegan Paul. 1947.

possibility referred to here is a different dimension of life from the political. To recognise this other dimension which is " a primal category of human reality " would make a radical difference to all political thinking and action.

Acknowledgment of this higher dimension is not a way of escape from the realities of man's historical and collective existence. History is always " political " history—the struggle of competing groups to maintain themselves. Christians can refuse to take their part in these struggles only at the price of renouncing all influence on historical life. To occupy themselves only with relations with persons, the very condition for which is dependent on the forces they ignore, would be disloyalty to Christ, who is the Lord of history. The relation between the two worlds of personal relations and of historical reality is one of the most urgent questions which needs to engage Christian thought.[1] What we are urging here is that the extent to which men are inevitably subject to the operation of impersonal forces makes it all the more necessary that these should be balanced by the experience of real community. In a society in which men retain the power to enter into relations with other persons, the working of institutions undergoes a subtle change, because those who work them know something of the true life of the spirit. New possibilities of action present themselves to those who govern. The health of society depends on the permeation of all its activities with the leaven of a rich and full personal life.

Fifthly, belief in the responsibility of men to God and knowledge of human sinfulness will impel Christians to set restraints on irresponsible power and, as has already been urged, to work for the widest distribution of power, responsibility and initiative throughout the whole community.

Sixthly, there are theological grounds for believing that all the varied activities of man, religious, cultural, political and economic, should be given the maximum independence of one another. A tradition in which the independence of each of these is respected is the most powerful of all bulwarks against the all-embracing claims of the omni-competent state.

Seventhly, it must be the aim of a just society, exercising responsibility for all its members, to ensure that the material rewards of the common national enterprise are equitably distributed.

[1] The issue is raised in a challenging form in a pamphlet by Dr. Gerhard Ritter, *Christentum und Selbstbehauptung*. Furche-Verlag, Tübingen, 1946.

This has already been emphasised so strongly that it is unnecessary to say more about it here.

We come finally to the question of political freedom, by which we mean here the freedom of a people to control, criticise and change its government. If that freedom is lost, there is no longer any check to prevent those in power from yielding to the temptation, to which all who bear rule are exposed, to gather more and more power into their hands and to destroy progressively all social, cultural and religious freedoms.

Political freedom is the foundation and guarantee of all other freedoms. It is not the *source* of all freedoms. The ultimate source of all freedoms is Christian freedom rooted in Christian faith. But, so far as freedom in an earthly society is involved, no freedoms are in the long run secure without political freedom.

It may be said that for long periods and over large areas men have had to live without political freedom and that for many peoples to-day it is not a practicable alternative to authoritarian rule. That is certainly true. Men have had in the past, and many have to-day, to be content with such freedom as they can get. But those who appeal to the experience of the past are in danger of leaving out of account the changes brought about by technics. If it is true that the advances in science and technics have effected a radical change in human existence, the consequences must be fully faced.

In earlier societies, when tyranny became excessive, there always remained the possibility of rebellion. The knowledge that, if things were pressed too far, the subjects might rebel had a tempering effect on despotic rule. In the days when weapons were staves and pikes, or even muskets, numbers were a factor to be reckoned with. Modern inventions have placed in the hands of the ruling group not only weapons of mass destruction but means of technical control through the Press, radio and postal system which make successful rebellion virtually impossible.

Of still greater significance is the fact that modern inventions have enabled rulers not merely to control the actions, but to give direction to the minds and to play upon the emotions of their subjects. In former days despots could do what they liked with men's bodies, but men's souls remained free. The new powers in the hands of rulers, the potentialities of which are only beginning to be realised, enable them to invade the citadel of the soul. By education and propaganda through school, Press, radio and cinema they can mould men's thinking in conformity with their own desires. They can deny them access to sources of information which might lead them to form opinions contrary to those which the wielders of power want them to hold. By these means modern dictators can go a long way towards depriving man, not only of the capacity, but even of the desire to resist. Technical advances have weighted the scales so heavily in favour of despotic rule, that it is a question whether political freedom, if it is once lost, can ever be recovered.

No one supposes that political freedom can be immediately achieved throughout the world. It has to contend with widely accepted ideologies which deny its value. In some places conditions are not yet ripe for its exercise. But in the western world there have been developed through the slow growth of the centuries institutions which, with whatever partial denials and shortcomings, are informed by the conception of political liberty. There is also an accumulated experience of the working of free institutions. It is an interest of mankind as a whole that these freedoms which have been won by long and sustained effort should be preserved and extended as an example, and for the benefit of all.

It has been our aim to show that the conflict between liberty and totalitarianism is not identical with the international tension between the western democracies and the communist societies grouped under the leadership of Russia. The forces opposed to one another in the international sphere are not a white against a black but two differing shades of grey. There are elements of freedom within communist societies which, however restricted in scope, contain possibilities of growth. No picture of Russia is complete which does not include the Christian Church with all its unknown potentialities for the future. In the western societies there are those who, both consciously and unconsciously, are the enemies of freedom. The real struggle for liberty cuts across all existing fronts..

But, true and important as this is, it is essential not to fall into the opposite and, as it may prove, more deadly error of supposing that, because we have to do not with a difference between white and black but a difference between two shades of grey, there can be no vital issues involved. The difference between a violent and non-violent society, between tolerance and intolerance, is a matter of life or death for the human spirit. It is a complete abdication of responsibility to suppose that because everything human is relative there are no decisive turning-points in history. Where the highest values are at stake, to refuse to make up one's mind and take a stand, because the issues are confused and there seems to be much to be said on both sides, may be a betrayal of humanity. In spite of the relativities attaching to all political systems and political actions the defence and service of political freedom may assume the form of an imperative religious decision. What is involved may be the whole question of what man is in the sight of God and of what God means him to become.

XI

THE STRATEGY OF THE CHURCH

C. L. Patijn

AFTER this broad analysis of the state of our communal life, forced into unprecedented crises by technical evolution, a chapter on the " Strategy of the Church " with regard to social, economic and political life rouses expectations which cannot easily be fulfilled. One fundamental issue must be made clear at the start. The Church's task *vis-à-vis* the community in its social and political life is an indirect one. The Kingdom it proclaims is not of this world. Its task is to incorporate men in a different realm, to serve a Lord different from any the world knows. Its message is unto Jews a stumbling block and unto Greeks foolishness. Mars, Mammon and Dionysos are living spirits, and will always be more real in the eyes of men—even if their names are no longer known—than the Invisible in His mystery.

It is a mistake to think that the Church as an institution must adapt itself to the ways of society in order to exert its influence. It creates an impression of impotence when preachers speak more about what is in the newspaper than in the Gospels, or appeal to the same interests as those of non-church societies or the entertainment world. Men do not turn to the Church to hear a more or less intelligent discourse on what is happening outside, but to hear its own message. In this three-dimensional, matter-of-fact, materialistic world, the world of the " Euclidian intellect " as Dostoievsky termed it, they want the Church to be a channel for the spiritual forces from God's dimension. The Church lives on the biblical revelation, an absurd mythology in the eyes of the world ; on a never-ceasing stream of prayer, likewise incomprehensible in the eyes of the world ; on the community of the saints, transcending all worldly categories. Only a Church filled from within from these sources can be of any use in our disintegrated society. The primary factor is not its good will, its good theology, its activity, its moral influence, but its prophetic and priestly reality as the Body of Christ.

Before we start to study the specific problems of the present situation, it is therefore necessary to define as sharply as possible the way in which the Church can and must use its influence on practical events in the social field. We need to be clear in the first place what we mean by the word " Church." The Body of Christ has two very different aspects. On the one hand it is an institution, organised for the purposes of preaching, administration of sacraments, worship, teaching and the pastoral ministry. On the other hand it includes millions of men and women who are actively engaged from day to day in the conduct of public administration, industry and the affairs of the public and common life. There is an important practical difference between clergy and laity in dealing with the influence of the Church on society. It is the latter that have to bear the brunt of the difficulties of the relation between God's dimension and our three-dimensional world. Our churches have been so thoroughly clericalised that they have lost sight of the fact that it is far easier for the Christian ministry, standing in its pulpits or acting in its corporate capacity, to declare its views on the social and political order than for the individual laymen to relate Christian worship and teaching with their task in society. They are more deeply involved in the problems of society, especially in its technical aspects, than the clergy. As members of the Body of Christ and as responsible for the affairs of social, economic and political life, they are citizens of two different worlds. Their special problem is " to keep the unity of the Spirit " in their own life. Their task is to bring to bear the influence of the Church on society from within, by their own decisions in the conduct of public and common life. Do they get the kind of help from the institutional Church which they need? The really spiritual encounter between Church and society begins in the hearts and minds of these laymen.

What is the influence of the Church on our communal life? Often the Church is incapable of exercising any beneficent effect, either because it is too unworldly or too conformed to the world.

It often happens that ministers and congregation are so absorbed in the biblical material which is the core of the sermon that contact is lost with real life. The wealth of Christian thought and tradition is so great that current social problems may sometimes not enter into the preacher's range of vision. The biblical words have become dissociated from their concrete meaning, spoken in concrete circumstances, and as dead letters they dominate the life of the Church, without any relation to the actual conditions of its members. On the other hand, the Church has from its earliest days shown an almost startling talent to cover itself with the skin of the social conditions under which it had to live. By the acceptance of natural law, by excessive admiration for Aristotle, by legitimist theories, by theological constructions such as orders of creation and corporative groups, by the too unquestioning acceptance of liberal philosophy, by identifying itself too much with the interests of nations and classes, at different periods it absorbed large portions of the world's life and thought into its own thought and life. It was not for nothing that Paul gave the warning that the Church should not allow itself to be beguiled " after the tradition of men, after the rudiments of the world " (Colossians ii, 8). Not only did all this human wisdom obscure the light of the revealed truth, but also—and this is important in our discussion—society and the state were able to develop practically according to their own laws. As a result, there were often but few signs of the Church affecting the community. Charity was never entirely lost. The poor, the widow and the orphan, so frequently referred to in the Bible, were not forgotten. But there have been many centuries during which there were no signs at all of the Church influencing society, because the world had subjected the Church to its own categories.[1]

It is not a pure coincidence that the other-worldliness of the Church and its worldly-wisdom often occur simultaneously. When liturgy and personal spiritual life are the sole concern of

[1]Note by Professor John Bennett : " This paragraph presupposes a conception of the relation between the Christian revelation and human wisdom that is open to criticism. Dr. Patijn makes much of the importance for the Church of technical knowledge but he fears the development of general principles, theories and philosophies because these come to be the expression of self-sufficient and pretentious human reason. He is right in insisting that in the Christian revelation we have the criterion by which all human wisdom must be tested. But there is more to be said than is suggested in this chapter for a spirit of openness to the wisdom of the world on the part of the Church, even to its theoretical systems. The use of ' natural law ' by the Church may have been mistaken when it allowed too detailed elaboration of classical natural law to become part of its official teaching, but it is not a mistake for the Church to open its mind to the moral wisdom of the classical world so long as this wisdom is kept under the Christian criterion and so long as its transformation by the Spirit of Christ is also emphasised. An illustration of an attitude toward the wisdom of the world that is somewhat different from the one underlying this paragraph is to be found in Dr. Patijn's own treatment of Marx and Engels in this chapter. He says of them : ' It is better to admit that Marx and Engels saw the moral side of this problem (the problem created by the industrial revolution) better than the Christian Church, even though they based their theories on an untenable materialism which will never be acceptable to Christian thought.' "

the Church the world is left to the State and to other powers. Whenever the law (or theology, or confession) which was received with fire and thunder on Mount Sinai is no longer the expression of a living relationship between God and His people but has congealed to a juridically manageable system of principles, the Church ceases to have any real influence on the life of the community.   When belief becomes a matter of routine, ethics become irrelevant.   Every Church, whatever its theology or order, is threatened with the danger of losing contact with reality—either with God or with society.

This danger is greatest in times of great social change.   In these circumstances the Church is no longer able in social matters to live on its traditional spiritual treasures, as is possible in ages of social stability.   That is why the Church's decisions in the social field in times of stress are of such tremendous importance. It is true that the Church is a socially weak phenomenon, that its members are perplexed in a hostile world, but it is also true that they can be a " saving remnant " with a very special function in society, so that the Church's attitude to the problems of society may become of fateful importance for the future of both Church and society.

Although most Christians will agree that the Church ought to influence society, great confusion prevails with regard to theory about the relations between Church and society.   Professor John C. Bennett in a recent publication[1] has given a stimulating survey of the difficulties that confront Christian " strategy " in relating ethics to social policy.   He examines in turn different types of strategy that have been adopted in the past.   He shows the ever-present dangers of a strategy of withdrawal from those activities of public life which create special problems for the Christian conscience.   He rejects the absolute identification of the Christian ethic with particular policies and stresses the necessity of keeping every human programme and every human institution under judgment.   He strongly criticises a double standard for the Church and state, for personal life and public life.   Coming to the positive part of his book, he shows the practical significance of central biblical ideas, such as the commandment of love, Christian humility and self-criticism, for the everyday life of society, and lays great stress on the importance of determining the goals which represent the purpose

[1]*Christian Ethics and Social Policy.*   Scribners, New York.   1946.

of God for our time. As an example of the latter he quotes some of the guiding principles of the report of the Oxford Conference of 1937 with regard to important problems of society and thus brings us to the heart of the question.

Here, however, we are also in the heart of our difficulties. No one will deny the ethical relevance of the spirit in which Christian individuals, standing in responsible positions or dealing with the interests of other people, fulfil their tasks, nor the extreme importance of the problem of restoring personal relations in a depersonalised society. Our deepest perplexity is, however, that the problems of society are for the most part of such a technical character that there is little or no apparent relation between many decisions to be taken and the driving ethical principles of Christian faith.[1] In such cases the best decisions are the technically best decisions. Not the intentions of the driving spirit, but the knowledge and skill of the responsible man are in many cases from an ethical point of view decisive. Again, a great deal of Christian discussion, especially when it emphasises the personal character of human relations, is apt to forget the lesson of the nineteenth century, when Christians limited

[1] Note by Professor John Bennett : " Dr. Patijn does not seem to me in this chapter quite to do justice to the place of the proximate norms that should guide the social strategy of the church or, as they have been called in the literature of the Oxford Conference, ' middle axioms.' Middle axioms are those goals for society which are more specific than universal Christian principles and less specific than concrete institutions or programmes of action. An example of a middle axiom is the conviction that the Church should seek the development of an organised world community that can overcome the anarchy of international life. Another example of a middle axiom is the conviction that the Church should seek to overcome involuntary racial segregation. Both of these are objectives of the churches but neither of them prescribes the institutions or the programmes by which they are to be made possible. Dr. Patijn sees clearly that the statesman must be concerned about the technical means by which such objectives can be realised. He stresses primarily the problem of how we may know what is, from the technical point of view, the best next step. But even if the statesman or the expert knows the answer to that question, whether or not a community—a nation or the world of nations—takes the next step depends upon the convictions of the people who are neither statesmen nor technicians about the objective itself. To use an illustration from the decisions which confront the American people, it is quite as important for the churches in America to see clearly American responsibility to aid in the recovery of the economic health of the European continent as it is for. the experts to decide on the best methods by which that objective can be reached.

" In the last part of this chapter Dr. Patijn presupposes objectives of this kind when he discusses the ' third force.' Commitment to social structures that would make possible order and justice in the economic sphere together with political and spiritual freedom could be analysed into several such objectives which must control the mind and the imagination of Christians, if the more precise proposals of statesmen and experts are to have a chance of success. As the Church comes close to concrete problems in its teaching its main emphasis will have to be on these goals, commitment to which does involve real moral decisions and yet leaves the door open for differences concerning technical and political methods."

themselves to charity to the individual victims of social circumstances, leaving it to the socialists to attack the institutional development of society which was the source of the evil. In our days more than ever we must not cure symptoms but deal with causes— with the institutional problems of society.

It is undoubtedly of the utmost importance to determine " the goals which represent the purpose of God for our time." Here also, however, things are more difficult than most churches so far have realised. The guiding principles of the Oxford Report, for instance, although in themselves without any doubt right and deserving of serious consideration, are not always very helpful for men in responsible positions, as the real problems lie beyond such general statements. The difficulties are not solved as soon as charters for international relations, human rights, trade and industry are established, but begin with their application. The Church in dealing with problems of society must be aware of the real centres of difficulty and of the battlefields where the future of humanity will be decided. The Church must help its members and the world at large by subjecting these social phenomena to God's judgment.

How can the Church—and its laymen in responsible positions—do this ? In the first place, there must be a real knowledge of the problem. Too often representatives of the Church in ethical zeal jump to conclusions while having in view only a small part of the complex reality of a problem. In such cases they bring the weight of biblical indignation to bear on the wrong point and ring the wrong bell. No one in a responsible position can be impressed by irrelevant statements, even when they are completely well meant.

On the other hand, the Church must not be overawed by the argument that it cannot judge the institutional problems of society because of their purely technical character, since in the most important institutional problems of our day ethical issues are interwoven with the technical aspect. Around every great problem of society in our days a fierce political battle is being fought, in which the destiny of millions of human beings is in the balance. It is the duty of the Church and its members to examine the ethical aspects of these problems and to judge them in the light of biblical testimony and of Christian experience. Here the central guiding principles of Professor Bennett come back on the institutional level. The commandment of love involves a sense of responsibility for those on the other side of every social or national or racial barrier, even though their interests conflict with ours. It is useless in such cases to proclaim theories about the true natural order for economic or international life since no one in real difficulty will get help from mere abstractions. To remind a godless society in its burning points of conflict of its responsibilities, will only have effect if the full weight of prophetic judgment is thrown into the balance at the heart of the real difficulties and at the right moment, with the greatest possible knowledge of the facts.

For all this there must be a lively interaction between the institutional Church and its lay members who are responsibly concerned with the affairs of society. The clergy must contribute the light of revelation, the appeal to faith and spiritual courage, the laymen their expertness and open-mindedness to fact. Serious thinking will be necessary about the technical complexity as well as about the ethical and spiritual ambiguity of the great problems of society, before it will be possible to see a clear line of Christian strategy in relation to these problems.

The problem is not a new one. The Church has for a long time been adopting attitudes, deciding and forming new ethics. The important question is whether the Church is pursuing the right path ; in other words, to what extent has it taken a stand on really Christian grounds, with knowledge of the facts, in burning, concrete and living problems ? The question may be examined with reference to a few important problems of our present-day society.

NATIONALISM

Uncritical acceptance of, and even complete submission to, nationalism has been one of the most dangerous temptations of representatives of the Church when the interests of their own nations were at stake. Complete rejection of the national interests of other peoples is another side of the same attitude. In recent decades, however, the tide of Christian feeling with respect to nationalism is turning, and the churches have given proof of greater independence in their judgment. The first signs of this development can be observed in the mission field.

When, in the course of the past hundred years, the stormy encounter of the East and West produced a rising tide of

nationalism in the colonial world, or among peoples threatened
by western imperialism, the missions, themselves representatives
of the western world, were faced with the question of combating
the urge for freedom as inimical to the West, or releasing themselves from the political and cultural background of the West
and greeting the new consciousness joyfully. Fortunately there
were some leaders in missionary work who, many years before
clear decisions were taken in other fields, elected decisively for the
development and self-government of colonial peoples. The
importance of this choice was that this was done not for tactical
reasons, i.e., to remain on good terms with their surroundings,
but because they rightly saw that, just as Paul refused to bind the
non-Jewish world to Judaic law and the guardians of the church
of Jerusalem, but aimed at an independent church government,
the new churches of the East should be allowed to stand on their
own feet. Spiritual growth can only take place in freedom. For
that reason in later years the missions were increasingly sympathetic to national aspirations, since colonial domination was
seen to mean the removal from entire nations of the responsibility
for their own destiny, a responsibility which cannot be withheld
from persons and peoples without spiritual damage. Therefore
this encounter between the freedom movement and the Christian
Church in Asia has for the present come to a favourable decision,
even if in some countries there are still large sections of the
Church which are enmeshed in their own national interests
and theories, and for this reason find it very difficult to follow the
missions on this path. The choice was made late, but not too
late, and may in the future be regarded as an extremely important
and happy decision.

In western countries the Church is on the right road so far
as too close association with the national life of peoples is concerned. In the first world war it was not yet given to most
churches to see beyond the national view. In the belligerent
countries Christian preaching only too often yielded to the
temptation of simply identifying God's purposes with those of the
nation. I- the last world war there was a clear change for the
better. In most churches there was less of a tendency to identify
their own country's cause with God's aims. Generally speaking,
a certain critical distance was maintained. The world-wide
community of Christ's Church was never entirely disrupted
and the Una Sancta proved to be a reality, although still a weak

one. Great admiration is due to the Church in Great Britain, which throughout the war displayed in its radio broadcasts responsibility not only for its own afflicted country but for the spiritual life of others, even the enemy.

THE TOTALITARIAN STATE

One characteristic sign of our communal life being exposed to great spiritual dangers is the historically entirely new phenomenon of the totalitarian state. In the history of the Church it will remain the undying glory of that section of the German Church which constituted itself as the *Bekenntniskirche*, that it immediately countered this danger on biblical grounds with great courage and self-sacrifice. When the totalitarian state in the countries of Europe occupied by Germany opened its terrible onslaught upon the rights and spiritual life of the subjugated peoples, the churches generally offered resistance which was of the greatest significance. The threatened churches did not base themselves on the national reactions of the peoples entrusted to their care, but saw in the totalitarian state a manifestation of anti-Christ, of demoniac nihilism, and so founded their attitude on the Word of God and not on any national aspiration.

The way in which the churches withstood the German attack has been of the greatest importance in this stormy century. In a certain sense, however, the choice was not difficult. National Socialism cut at all the principles of human society so deeply that almost everyone in the western world, whatever his spiritual outlook, had to offer resistance. The Church did not stand alone in its resistance. The political benefits bestowed by the French Revolution were in jeopardy. The allies of the Church included all shades of opinion from conservatives and liberals to socialists and communists. It remains the Church's merit that it recognised the danger more profoundly and formulated it in truer terms than its associates ; but this does not detract from the fact that it had many associates, at least in occupied territory.

This struggle is by no means ended. The coming years will show how deeply the Church has learnt its lesson, when new dangers of a totalitarian nature threaten, perhaps in less extreme forms. In the coming years the Church will again have to find a clear standpoint in the light of Romans xiii. For instance, in the strength of the living experience of the past few years, it will have to realise that a government can claim our obedience as the minister of God, only if, and in as far as, it is bound in its actions by the rule of law.

THE SOCIAL PROBLEM

The nineteenth century confronted our communal life with a social struggle increasing in extent and intensity. This brings us to a more general problem in our cultural crisis, even though this problem is itself a consequence of the disruptive evolution of economic life under the influence of technical advances. Since the industrial revolution in England in the first half of the nineteenth century, the social struggle has been one of the most active symptoms of ill-health in our western civilisation. It is bitter to admit that Marx and Engels saw the moral side of this problem better than the Christian Church, even if they based their theories on an untenable materialism which will never be acceptable to Christian thought. The question at issue here, however, is not a struggle of ideas against ideas. If that were the case, the Christian Church would have had an easy task with the social tensions which have afflicted us in the past few decades. What was at stake was the living needs of great groups of the community which had sunk to such economic dependence, that their existence threatened to lose its human values. There is no doubt that in the social problem the Church generally made the wrong choice. In this its close association with certain social classes has avenged itself, and Professor Bennett has rightly pointed out " that the working people and the democratic forces in Europe came to believe that the Church was against them." Naturally, there were exceptions to this rule, just as there are countries where from the outset considerable Christian influences have been operating in the labour movement. None the less the social struggle throughout the world has tended to estrange large sections of the community from the Church and its message.

If Hitler's whip did any good at all, it was in this field. Without his absurd folly, inimical to every aspect of society, the working classes and other social groups might have lived in different camps for a long time. Now over extensive areas of the world all the participants in the social struggle were thrown together in one heap and subjected to the heavy jackboot of the totalitarian state. It may not be as hopeless as it seemed twenty years ago to find points of contact in Europe between the church communities and the socialist workers' movements. Wherever common enemies have been at work, problems have shifted and human beings begin to show a little more understanding for each other's aims. In the Christian Church too—and this is perhaps the most important point—a readier comprehension has come about of the implications of social justice. It is therefore late, but perhaps not too late, to make an effort to break with the old faulty divisions in the social field.

In this, however, we are in the midst of the most difficult part of our task. The social problem is not capable of solution in abstract terms but is involved in the conditions of living of our present society. By demanding a philosophically defined *justum pretium* or a merely protective and rigid social policy, we run the risk of not protecting the conditions of living for large sections of the population, but in the long run doing just the opposite, injuring them by sinning against economic laws. Nor is the final solution one of improving the relative position of the least favoured sections of society, because, as Professor Ellul rightly remarks, even our best efforts at creating social security tend to " make the individual still more a mere cog in the larger unit and force him to give up more of his personal life." Even our good intentions may become dehumanising forces. Behind the social problems there is the sphinx-like phenomenon of our material civilisation, grown beyond all proportion, which we are endeavouring to measure economically or psychologically, but about which we know only one thing, that we are still completely in its grip.

THE ECONOMIC DISORDER

So far the Church has provided no clear answer to the question how it should behave towards our completely new technical society. Most that has been said about it is just kicking against the pricks. How are we to bring some order in our thinking, to enable the Church to make its choice in this most important question?

Opposition to the materialism which threatens to stifle our spiritual life often assumes the shape of resistance to the forms in which it manifests itself—to blind economic forces, to technique, to the machines, the " robots," to all those enemies of the soul, of honour, of personal relations, of nature itself. But this is still theory. It is not a question of opposing spiritual to material principles. Nor is it primarily a question of putting another type of human relations against the dehumanising forces of our century, although this may be important in concrete, limited circumstances. The call is for decisions in concrete situations. It is not enough to point out and disqualify dehumanising forces. It is a question how far it is possible and necessary to control and repel them.

In our century we have witnessed two formidable attempts to bind the material forces of our communal life and subject them to a controlling principle—communism and national socialism. The fact that they have aroused enthusiasm in so many millions of people is due in no small degree to this attempt to simplify life, to effect cohesion, to bring about integration in a society conformed to one pattern. We have also been witnesses of the terrible consequences. They have themselves deteriorated into new, virulent, dehumanising and mechanical forces, at the expense of righteousness and morality, mercy and love.

The dilemma with which we are confronted in the present phase of our material evolution has been characterised by Dr. Niebuhr in the following words[1] : " The age of ' free enterprise,' when the new vitalities of a technical civilisation were expected to regulate themselves, is over. But the age in which justice is to be achieved and yet freedom maintained by a wise regulation of the complex economic interdependence of modern man is powerless to be born."

One of the features of such an " age between the ages " is that there is great confusion both in theory and practice, and struggles of very different kinds are in progress, while the structural crisis in economic life is in rapid evolution. The Church cannot eliminate this confusion, because it is itself in the midst of it and will find little in its own sources, in the Bible and church history, on which to stand, because our situation is different from any we ever went through before. No one, however, requires an answer from the Church in any field beyond its competence. On the other hand there is a call for spiritual help in matters of life and death. Therefore the Church should not aim in the first instance at a theoretical solution, but rather at a comprehensive pastoral insight into the existential needs of society in all its ramifications.

The economic developments of the twentieth century grant no respite to anyone. Industrialists, labourers, governments

[1]*Discerning the Signs of the Times*, p. 40.

and peoples are fighting for their existence. But the fight is on different fronts and partly internal, because the interests to be guarded are in some cases contradictory. This means that none of the parties is capable of achieving alone a result satisfactory for the whole by logically putting its own views into practice. A world governed solely by " free enterprise " would tend to subordinate everything to blind economic forces. It would produce no solution, because it is precisely through these forces (increase in the fixed cost of the enterprise, growing international competition, the ineffective operation of the price mechanism) that we have become involved in the present economic difficulties. An economy based solely on social security might prove fatal. A compromise achieved by producers and workers in joint consultation likewise offers no hope, because they would shift the burden of price increases on to the consumer. An economic life regulated solely by the state would be untenable, owing to inefficiency and threats to spiritual freedom. An economic effort guided purely by national views offers no other prospect than continued chaos.

The economic disorder of our society is a structural one. By declaring that the deep crisis through which we are passing is a consequence of sin or a loss of belief in eternal life, as the Church has declared time and again in days of crisis and anxiety, we would give no answer to the structural aspect of the situation and thus turn a theological truth partially into a lie. First of all, the Church and its representatives in society must take this aspect of our crisis quite seriously. It is clear that we are involved in a long and painful process of adaptation to a new equilibrium of economic and social forces. In such a period producers, labour, civil servants, groups and nations fight for interests and social values which are in danger of being overrun by events, and they are therefore inclined to forget the partial character of their own interests and views. The Church believes that human society is meant to constitute one body with many members, in which every component part is responsible for the well-being of the whole. But what is the whole? A mediæval dream of an organic society, such as that of the Roman Catholic Church, produces as its only result a certain preference for the corporate ordering of society instead of free enterprise. Of itself, however, it is a construction, a pseudo-solution, a form adaptable to practically every economic or social policy.

Nevertheless, it is certain that the economic disorder must be brought under human control " by a wise regulation of the complex economic interdependence of modern man." Most people agree on the necessity of such a regulation, but violent disagreements begin as soon as practical policy is broached. Therefore it is no use for the Church to recommend a directed economy in an abstract way, for the point at issue is invariably concrete, involving measures which may be technically good or bad. The Church is as a rule incompetent to judge the technical aspect of those measures. There is, however, a spiritual element in human resistance to the necessary transition from the old to the new age. For as Niebuhr states cogently and rightly[1] : " The lower and narrower loyalties which stand against newer and wider loyalties are armed not merely with the force of human inertia, but with the guile of spirit and the stubbornness of all forms of idolatry in human history." Here is the Church's task in the materialistic chaos of our years.

In the political arena to-day, especially on the European continent, the three most important approaches to our problem are those of the " managers," representing the economic power in our society, the communists, and the representatives of the so-called " third force," the coalitions of the centre parties in many countries.[2] With respect to the first group—the Church will have to refute and combat a number of common arguments against directed economy and state intervention, because, as typical expressions of narrower loyalties, they represent obstacles on the road to a just and more integrated society. It is not true that increasing restriction of " free enterprise " is in itself a danger to liberty in our social life. On the contrary, without state intervention to ensure economic stability, to secure standards of individual welfare and to regulate international economic relations, there would have been no hope for the economic liberty of large sections of the community (workers, agriculturists, the middle classes) in many countries of the world. It is equally untrue to pretend that planning for economic order is to be resisted because it entails bureaucracy and unshackles new

[1] Op. cit., p. 43.
[2] The words " third force " (*troisième force*) are borrowed from the situation in France. In most countries a clear distinction between three great political trends cannot be made, as public life is more complicated. Nevertheless the French situation is more or less characteristic of the position into which many countries have been brought by political and social-economic events.

dehumanising forces. The danger of bureaucracy and de-humanising forces is no less present in the big concentrations of economic and material power, which have arisen in our days in trade and industry, without any intervention from the side of the state. Since we are faced with this problem under all circumstances, we can better meet it on the level of the " wider " than the " narrower " loyalties. Nor is it true that the intervention of the state will automatically lead to totalitarian measures. The biblical concept of the state as existing for the sake of law and order does not by any means restrict this to policing (as was thought by the liberalism of the nineteenth century) but aims at that order which will enable the community " to lead a quiet and peaceable life " (1 Timothy ii, 2). There is no doubt that nothing jeopardises a quiet and peaceable life so much as our material chaos.

To sincere defenders of " free enterprise " the Church can point out the absurdity of a philosophy aimed at producing harmony, while it clearly only results in economic instability and dynamic conflicts of power, in which the weaker groups must submit to the interests of the more powerful. Moreover, there are quite a number of business men who see the dark sides of our economic system but who are unable to withdraw from it. Under the pressure of competition and economic necessities they experience the truth of Romans vii, 15 : " For that which I do I allow not ; for what I would that do I not ; but what I hate, that I do "—in this case in consequence not of a " law in their own members," but of the economic laws of society. There is, however, no doubt that many representatives of economic power in society are not willing at all to take the interests of society as a whole into consideration at the cost of part of their own interests. Their wilful harshness, arrogance and lack of social imagination have given the capitalistic system its bad name in the ears of millions of people. The Church must not only appeal to their personal sense of responsibility, but must stress the point that irresponsible power is in any circumstance unacceptable. No society will work without individual initiative and enterprise, but equally no society will work where irresponsible power cannot be called to account and brought under control. This applies not only to capitalist undertakings but also to abuse of power by organised labour.

The communist approach to the social-economic problems of

society is well known. It needs hardly any explanation that, even if it were possible to run a whole economy on the principle of " from each according to his means, to each according to his needs " (the Russians made the experiment and achieved some economic miracles, but have abandoned it), the decisive factor for the Church is the spiritual aspect of communist practice. Not only is the materialist philosophy of marxism unacceptable, but also in everyday life its subordination of the human person and spiritual freedom to the ultimate aims of collectivism, its justification of any and every means and its bad faith. In communism we witness the decadence of an originally sincere social protest. Even more than its materialism its disregard of the most elementary notions of law as a guarantee of personal freedom has caused this decline. The Church must understand the social needs that open the way to communism in many countries. It must never forget that, whatever may be the evils of communism, it is a symptom of the existence of human suffering calling for justice and help.

Most Christians will not be seriously tempted to adhere to extreme capitalism or marxism. Our analysis of the economic disorder of society and of the different approaches to it leads us to the conclusion that the representatives of the churches will as a rule be found on the side of what is called the " third force " or the centre parties, ranging from moderate conservatism to socialism, for only these centre groups are aware of the necessity for both freedom and order in a democratic society. We draw this conclusion, however, very reluctantly, not only because the Church must not identify itself with any political group, but because of the relatively small results these groups so far have obtained in tackling our economic disorder. Freedom and order are still conflicting principles, and synthesis is not yet within our reach ; we see only compromises of limited order and limited freedom. In many countries we can see the danger of a society, in which the state, recognising the necessity of intervention in economic affairs, seeks to control virtually all activities while taking responsible initiative in none.[1]

Several reasons for this weakness of the democratic forces are evident. It is not only economic enterprise that has its " narrow loyalties," but also parties, groups and lower organs of government. It is extremely difficult to-day to bring about a

[1] Cf. *The Economist*, January 10th, 1948.

homogeneous policy in democratic society. This is partly for technical reasons, but spiritual elements are also involved. Professor Niebuhr has pointed out[1] that there is no possibility of bringing social stability and a measure of social justice to an impoverished world so long as the conflict between Christianity and socialism is not resolved. It is distressing to see the component groups of the " third force " in many countries repeating the quarrels of twenty-five years ago. Many representatives of the churches are not at all aware of the necessity of " a wise regulation of the complex economic interdependence of modern man." It was not long ago that in almost every Church the business cycle was passively accepted as a natural visitation by God, and the thought of binding Leviathan was regarded as pure arrogance.

Once a better economic integration of our society has been achieved, the material forces will be just as great a threat to the spirit and soul as now, but in a different way. Then it will be less a question of material existence than of culture, a problem which lies beyond our present discussion, but which pervades everything. At the moment, however, the primary thing is the struggle for economic existence itself, which forces human beings to think more of material things than is good for them.

THE INTERNATIONAL PROBLEM

Another problem of extreme importance, in which the Church's influence has so far been insignificant, is international relations. This does not apply to the approach of some churches within a nation to international relations on the national level. The work of the Commission on a Just and Durable Peace, in which the American churches dealt with international relations, has greatly contributed to the acceptance of international responsibility by American public opinion. On the international level, however, influences of the Church are hardly perceptible. Since this subject is being dealt with in another volume, more need not be said here. But it is clear that international chaos affects our present life at least as much as the economic problem.

. . . .

We have mentioned a number of political and social-economic subjects on which momentous decisions are being taken in our days. Other topics could have been mentioned, such as the racial problem or the extremely important problem of cultural

[1]Op. cit., p. 22.

education. We have argued that in these fields the Church is confronted with decisions. We have tried very briefly to indicate between what possibilities and on what grounds decisions must be reached by the Church. How is the Church to put this into practice?

As we stated at the outset the primary consideration is that the Church's task with respect to communal life is an indirect one. Less than ever may the Church forget its priestly function. In a society sick with materialism, there must be one institution which is different. People become spiritually atrophied in the struggle for existence. What would be the use to them of a Church which, as soon as they enter, continues with them discussions at the point where they left them at their work? The Church must not fight merely for the preservation of spiritual values or take up a defensive position against the wicked world which threatens it on all sides. The human being turns to it as to his mother expecting and hoping for rest, understanding, wisdom, a place to bring his troubles and gain a glimpse of other things than the daily round. The churches must learn to arouse the desire of Psalm xlii, 1 : " As the hart panteth after the water brooks, so panteth my soul after thee, O God." The Church must also take counsel with those who have knowledge of facts. It must not be of this world, but it must know this world through and through. It must be wise, but not surrender uncritically to worldly wisdom.

In its approach to the problems of society it is more necessary than ever that the Church should learn from the prophets of Israel. Their characteristic note was to establish a relation between God and a concrete section of the life of their people. This means that in sermon and pastoral care the Holy Scripture— and not simply a number of isolated Christian thoughts—must be interpreted and applied to real situations, to the political and social-economic conditions in which people live. For this Professor Karl Barth and others have used the words " political preaching." This term has frequently been misunderstood, because it was held that the Church must take no part in politics. But the Church is always taking part in politics, even when it is silent. It must ; for only when it does so are the words applicable to it " Ye are the light of the world." The earth and the world are political terrain.

The Church will need from time to time to make official

pronouncements on concrete problems, as was done by some churches during the German occupation in the last war. Such definitions of attitude, often made under great stress, were milestones on the road to decisions by subjected peoples in their resistance against national socialism. Last year the Federal Council of Churches in the United States in an official pronouncement renounced the pattern of segregation in race relations as a " violation of the Gospel of love and human brotherhood " and requested its constituent communions to work for " a non-segregated Church and a non-segregated society." We can learn from such clear and forthright statements how vital it is for the churches to sound a spiritually responsible note at critical moments.

In many cases, however, it is unnecessary and may be undesirable for the Church to take direct action officially.[1] Archbishop Temple, who was not afraid of expressing his individual views about concrete political measures, was very decisive in his warning against corporate action on controversial public issues by the Church. When difficult technical decisions are involved, the Church as Church must be careful not to commit itself to a particular policy. It is possible to secure collective Christian guidance in other, less authoritative, forms. There are many examples of unofficial action by groups of ecclesiastical leaders and of policies of permanent church agencies, which have exercised a great influence. Especially in issues of a social-economic character the Church should make use of the method of appointing a commission to issue a report for which it alone is responsible. Such groups speak only for themselves, but their word may have a great weight and a beneficial influence in our social perplexities.

Here again we must stress the importance of a lively contact between clergy and laity. Many of our churches are dangerously dependent on their clergymen, while at those points where Christian knowledge must be related to concrete decisions the clergy can often learn from the laymen more than they can teach. The Church should bring together in vocational groups or other associations its members bearing social responsibilities, to help them to come to clear decisions with respect to concrete and burning problems of central social importance. We need not be too much concerned about the authority of such groups

[1] Cf. John C. Bennett, *Christian Ethics and Social Policy*, pp. 108-15.

and organisations. Unofficial guidance of this kind may miss the formal authority of councils and confessions, but when its action or pronouncement represents in specific circumstances the penetration of God's dimension into our three-dimensional world, it will have an intrinsic authority which needs no further legitimation.

There are in several countries Christian political parties with related Christian social organisations. From time to time Christians will make use of such bodies for the realisation of certain aims. Parties and corporations are machinery, formal bodies, which may work with good or evil effect, and in the light of existential needs it may be necessary to work with such apparatus. They are emergency posts, however, which soon show a tendency to maintain themselves for their own sake. In that case they threaten to become Christian protected positions which acquire their own interests and soon find some theory or other, sometimes even a theology, on which they can base their continued existence. Then the danger arises that the Church may become identified with specific worldly interests. In countries where the Christian sections of the population have entrenched themselves in Christian organisations and parties, they have generally remained conservative and less sensitive to the real needs of society than elsewhere. Moreover, the growth of Christian parties outside the Church, splitting the life of a country between Christian and non-Christian groups, has often obstructed for the latter the path to the Church. On this point it will never be possible to draw up general rules. In a free society it must be possible for Christians to unite for definite purposes ; but the Church should keep its distance, and remain critical even of those who call themselves its friends.

Partly for this reason the Church will not be able to do without its own organs for dealing with the problems of society—not in order to go beyond its own proper functions, but that it may fulfil expertly and efficiently its priestly and prophetic task. The Church needs eyes and ears, hands and feet, and not only a mouth. It must be well-informed, must know how to attack a problem properly and must not merely stay in its sanctuary. The best church order does not guarantee, however, that the Church will handle these problems in the right way. Christian life is always moving between two poles. On the one hand there is rigidity, blindness and deafness, which threaten us as human beings in all our work—we who are nothing but " foolish people, and without understanding ; which have eyes and see not ; which have ears and hear not " (Jer. v, 21). And on the other there is the promise : " They that wait upon the Lord shall renew their strength ; they shall mount up with wings as eagles ; they shall run and not be weary ; and they shall walk and not faint " (Isaiah xl, 31). *Veni creator spiritus !*

XII

AND NOW?

Emil Brunner

THE preceding pages have made it plain that the sickness from which contemporary society is suffering is characterised by two outstanding pervasive and closely connected features—the reduction of the human person to a cog in the social machine, and the disintegration of organic community life. The manifold aspects of social pathology are simply variations of this basic theme.

We may recall briefly some of the points to which attention has been drawn :

The depersonalisation of human life and the dissolution of natural communities such as family and neighbourhood, by the impact of modern technics and its production of mass-man ;

the predominance of material, economic factors and the neglect of spiritual realities ;

the destruction of the sense of personal responsibility and of originality of expression as a result of the standardising influence of modern methods of mass-psychology and mass-propaganda ;

the persistence—even the accentuation—of the contrast between degrading poverty and slave-like conditions on the one hand, and the senseless accumulation of wealth and power on the other ;

the destruction of natural community life and the degeneration of personal life among populations threatened by western capitalist imperialism in Asia and Africa.

But it is evident from what has gone before that the problem by which our age is dominated is the emergence of the totalitarian state—the new Leviathan begotten by economic materialism and by the deliberate negation of personal freedom and responsibility.

The danger of totalitarianism would not be so overwhelming, if it were merely a matter of political dictatorship as opposed to democratic forms of government. Totalitarianism is something more pernicious than dictatorship. It is the attempt to direct and mould the entire life of the community and of its individual members in accordance with the dictates of an omnicompetent state machine, using for this purpose all the powerful methods of mass-suggestion and police control provided by modern technics. The disquieting feature of our situation is that totalitarianism—in the sense indicated—is in the ascendant everywhere, even in those countries which are regarded as traditionally democratic.

All these symptoms of social disorder are known to many thoughtful people outside the orbit of the Church. It is our task as Christians to judge them in the light of God's purpose for the good life of man, as revealed in God's Word. This will lead us to see some at least of the deeper causes, and even, in some cases, to reverse the order of cause and effect which appears on the surface. Thus it is certainly necessary to be alive to the perils inherent in the increasing maladjustment between personal living and the stupendous expansion of modern technics. But it is even more necessary—and this may be our specifically Christian contribution—to see that technics is not the *cause* of the real evil, but, at least in part, its *effect*. The technical revolution of the last two hundred years is not the cause but the product of technical man. It is a society which has lost its sense of direction and a proper scale of values and is obsessed by the mania of technical salvation and by a crazy over-valuation of production and material goods, that produces the type of " wild " technical development in which man dominates the forces of nature, but is no longer able to dominate his technics or himself.

But in all these observations of facts and causes we are still on the surface of things if we fail to perceive the deepest cause and its omnipresent effects—the progressive secularisation of life during the last few centuries, beginning in the West and gradually corroding all the religions and civilisations of the globe. While there has never been a genuinely Christian civilisation, the mass-atheism of to-day, the prevalence of agnostic philosophy in higher institutes of learning, the disregard of absolute standards of right and wrong, the complete " this-worldliness " of men's outlook are entirely new phenomena. These things have never existed before, either in antiquity or in the so-called Christian era of the West. The modern world has lost the horizon of transcendence. This is the basic fact of the social disorder. If man does not believe in any superhuman moral authority, if he does not believe in the eternal destiny of man, if the very concept of human dignity has faded away (as it must do when severed from its religious roots), if the idea of responsibility has lost its sacred meaning—how can we expect anything but social chaos or its alternative, tyranny ?

The Christian Church is not entitled, however, to pass judgment on the process of secularisation and de-Christianisation, without confessing at the same time its own large share of responsibility for this development. It is under condemnation for what it has done, and still more for what it has not done ; for what it has been and what it has not been. It is not without good reason that large sections of the labour world have lost confidence in the Church because of her compromise with capitalistic bourgeois society or with predatory imperialism. We Christians have to accept the verdict that during the critical period, when industrialisation began to revolutionise social life within the civilised world, the Church was not awake to what was going on, and therefore was unable to speak the helpful word and lead in the helpful action that was rightly expected from those who proclaimed a Gospel for the poor.

It is fair to say that in recent times there has been an awakening of the Church, and that it has tried to make up for its previous blindness and inactivity. But this process of restitution is only in its beginning, and the guilt of the past is not easily forgotten. Above all, organised Christianity has failed, and still fails, in one essential thing—to show the world by living example what true brotherhood and community are. Both by a false conformity with the powers that be and a false aloofness from the life of ordinary men, the Church failed in its mission to show a wayward society a compelling picture of its true purpose. Among the outstanding leaders of human society in recent generations we find few Churchmen ; other voices have possessed greater power of conviction and other minds more prophetic vision. Moreover, the lives of church people have not convinced others that it makes any significant difference whether one is a Christian or not. The Church has therefore little reason to put the blame on those who found it more inspiring to follow marxism or some other ideology rather than to listen to the Christian message. The present social disorder is thus above all a judgment of God upon the Church.

None the less, the charge is laid upon us to call the world back to the way of God which it has deserted. It would be a false kind of penitence if the Church, because of its guilt, dared not hold up before the world the shining light which has been entrusted to it. That is why we must persist in doing what we have been trying to do in the ecumenical interchange of convictions and insights of which the present volume is the outcome, namely, to discover and to set forth what we Christians believe to be God's will for society. It is not enough to preach and to teach. We must act, and call to action, wherever a way to improvement is open. The Church must once more become what she has been at her best—a pioneer of true community life, and the conscience of the nations.

It would be a fantastic illusion, however, to assume that the Church is capable of curing the desperate sickness of society. The limits of our wisdom and of our power become evident as soon as we seek to come to grips with the complex forces operating in society. We stand on relatively firm ground so far as general principles and criteria are concerned. But when it comes to discriminating between right and wrong in the realm of concrete social and political decisions, dark and light are not easily distinguished. We have to remember how often the " good causes " to which many Christians have given themselves with wholehearted devotion have turned out to be bad ones, or to have had evil effects. How often has the good intention to " hold fast that which is good " led to a conservatism which stood in the way of real progress. How often, on the other hand, has a purposeful will—in itself a necessary pre-requisite in the struggle for social justice—led to a utopianism and radicalism, the result of which has been increased depersonalisation and destructive libertarianism. We dare not be too sure of our social programmes and postulates. Yet it is more Christian to err than to remain inactive in face of flagrant evil.

There is one thing, however, which the Church has to do at all times and in all circumstances, and which can never be wrong, that is, herself to be a real community. We must pray and work that the Church may *become* a real Church. If there were kindled in Christians the fire of love, they would become a leaven in society, inspiring fresh hope, dissipating hatreds, breaking down barriers between men and creating new possibilities of understanding and co-operation. The effects of such a regenerating and healing ministry, in society, if through divine miracle it were to come about, would be incalculable. Without this all proclamations and social activities will be in vain. There has never been, nor will there ever be, a Christian state or a Christian international order, but there ought to exist in every locality a Christian community imbued with the spirit of brotherhood and love. And where it exists, there alone can the world learn what real community is. " See how these Christians love one another "—it was this persuasive, spontaneous example which opened the world of antiquity to the gospel.

The future is completely hidden from us. The Church may suffer persecution and may be relegated to a position of diminishing influence in public life. Or we may be on the threshold of an age in which God may accomplish great things in society through a Church reborn. We must meet the future as it comes. The vital matter is that the Church should make a fresh surrender of itself to the realities in which it believes. We need to allow to be re-born in us a living faith in the God whom Christ revealed—a faith which governs all our actions and which is intense enough to be contagious. We need to believe in the depths of our souls that God is greater than all the aggregations of human power, that the life of the spirit is more real than the technical mastery of things, that love is stronger in the end of the day than force. What matters is not the assertion of this truth in words, but living by that faith in the confidence that God will not disappoint or betray those who trust in Him.

MEMBERS OF ASSEMBLY COMMISSION III ON

" *The Church and the Disorder of Society* "

(The list includes those members of the Commission who were appointed before the end of 1947 and who therefore were able to participate in the preparation of the volume.)

PROFESSOR REINHOLD NIEBUHR, New York, *Chairman.*
DR. J. H. OLDHAM, London, *Vice-Chairman.*
THE REV. NILS EHRENSTROEM, Geneva, *Secretary.*

PROFESSOR W. BANNING, Driebergen.
PROFESSOR JOHN C. BENNETT, New York.
PROFESSOR N. BERDYAEV, Clamart/Seine.
MRS. KATHLEEN BLISS, London.
PROFESSOR EMIL BRUNNER, Zürich.
PROFESSOR JACQUES ELLUL, Bordeaux.
DR. PAUL HOLT, Copenhagen.
DR. F. ERNEST JOHNSON, New York.
THE RT. REV. BISHOP WILLIAM SCARLETT, St. Louis, Missouri.
MR. M. M. THOMAS, Trivandrum.
THE REV. E. C. URWIN, London.
PROFESSOR ERIK WOLF, Freiburg i.Br.

INDEX

(a) Subjects

Afghanistan, 61

Africa, 16, 28, 94, 110, 125, 146, 176 ; South, 75

Agriculture, 62, 73, 110

America, United States of, 17, 22, 36, 44, 54, 57, 65, 70, Ch. VI *passim*, 92, 94, 97, 98, 99, 101, 103f., 106, 109, 113, 132, 139, 143, 144, 145, 159n., 171 ; universities of, 38 ; South, 18

Anglicanism, *see* Church of England

Animism, 68

Artificial insemination, 42

Asia, 16, 28, 44, Ch. IV *passim*, Ch. V *passim*, 94, 103n., 110, 113, 125, 146, 162, 176

Associations Professionelles Protestantes, 109

Atheism, 96, 140

Atomic bomb, 64, 71f., 104f. ; energy, 32

Austria, 19

Bad Boll, 108

Balkans, 141

Beveridge Plan, 59

Bible, The, 71, 157, 166, 172

Biology, 32, 42, 56

Bishops, 94, 96, 98, 111

Bolsheviks, 65, 142

Bossey, Ecumenical Institute at, 109

Bristol, 105

Britain, 17, 22, 34f., 36, 44, 52, 53, 58, 59, 81, 94, 105, 106, 107, 108, 109, 114, 143n., 145, 146, 149, 163

British Council of Churches, 107, 108

Buddhism, 68

Burma, 61, 110

Calvinism, 20

Canada, 61, 80

Capitalism, 31, 38, 51, 60, 66, 96, 120, 139, 143, 170, 178

Caste, 69, 74

Catholicism, Roman, 13, 18, 19, 20, 52, 60, 69, 95, 96, 97f., 112, 114, 115, 167

Centre Protestant d'Etudes, 109

Ceylon, 110

Chaplaincies, industrial, 109

China, 63, 64, 67, 68, 95, 106, 113 ; Christian Church in, 106 ; Christian Home Life Movement in, 107 ; National Christian Council of, 107, 115f.

Christian Ethic, 50f., 134, 137, 158

Christian Frontier Council, 108f.

Christianity, 13, 14, 20, 21, 22f., 26f., 41, 44, 46, 48, 50, 68ff., 94, 95, 96, 112, 113, 140, 141, 171

Church, The Christian, 24, 75, 76, 78, 79, 83, Ch. VIII *passim*, 104, 106, 111, 116, 118, 119, 122, 126, 127, 133, 134, 146, 153, Ch. XI *passim*, 178, 179, 180 ; and politics, 20, 28n., 52, 110ff., 119, 138, 146f., 151, 155ff. ; and society, 24f., 28n., 30, 45ff., 59f., 76, 77, 78, 98, Ch. IX *passim*, 113ff., 127f., 130, 136, 137, 155ff., 179 ; and the crisis of our age, 27f., 127 ; and the State, 60, 77, 94, 110ff., 127 ; and the working-class, 97 ; as an economic institution, 100ff. ; fellowship in, 116ff., 179f. ; national, 93f., 95 ; payment of ministers in, 101, 102 ; racial segregation in, 100 ; social doctrine of, 52, 113ff.

Church of England, The, 93f., 95, 97, 108, 114, 115

Church of Scotland, The, 108

Cimade, 116, 117

Cinema, 59, 67, 153

Civilization, commercial, 16 ; European, 16, 21, 50, 51, 52 ; humanist, 54 ; industrial, 16, 40 ; western, 30

Class warfare, 112

Collectivism, 24, 66, 119, 129, 133ff., 150f., 170

Colossians, Epistle to the, 157

Communication, means of, 43

Communism, 22, 23, 44, 50, 51, 58, 65, 66, 72, 74, 79, 96, 113, 119, 120, 138, 139, 140, 142, 143, 145, 146, 148, 149, 153, 163, 166, 168, 169, 170

Community, 15, 16, 17, 18, 20, 21, 23, 25, 48, 65, 73, 76, 80, 82, 116ff., 126f., 142, 151, 179f. ; centres, 117 ; women in the, 85

Concentration camps, 55, 59, 106, 124, 139

Confucianism, 67, 68

Congress of Industrial Organisations (C.I.O.), 98

Conscience, 147

Co-operative movement, 35, 110

Corinthians, Epistles to the, 92, 93

Czechoslovakia, 105, 106

Democracy, 17, 25, 34, 53, 58, 64, 65, 80, 100, 127, 140, 145, 146, 149, 150, 153, 176, 177

Displaced persons, 105f.

Dominions, British, 17, 65, 115

Dumbarton Oaks, 113

Economics, 54, 100ff., 119, 145, 165ff.

Ecumenical Movement, 28n., 93, 147

Ecumenical Refugee Commission, 106

Education, 85, 86, 107, 114, 118, 153 ; popular, 17, 38, 66f.

Ephesians, Epistle to the, 91

Étatisme, 53

Ethics, 67, 68, 158

Europe, 17, 28, 44, Ch. III *passim*, 61, 62, 64, 70, 71, 72, 78, 80, 81, 82, 89, 96, 97, 103n., 113, 116, 121, 124, 127, 143, 159n., 163, 165, 168

" Evangelical Academies," 108

Evangelical Church in Germany, 97, 104 ; Stuttgart Declaration (1945), 104

Existentialism, 123

Factory legislation, 38

Family life, 56, 67, 87, 107, 115, 125

Far East, 113

Fascism, 19, 21, 50, 66, 140, 142

Federal Council of Churches (U.S.A.), 98, 139, 173 ; Statement on racial segregation (1946), 100 ; Statement on Atomic bombing, 103f.

Feudalism, 67, 72, 80, 96

Formosa, 62n.

France, 57, 58, 109, 116, 143n., 168n.

Free Church Federal Council, 114

Free Churches, 95, 108, 115

Free enterprise, 81, 139, 143, 166, 168

Freedom, 15, 19, 22f., 60, 66, 69, 70, 76, 78, 81, 82, 113, 125, 135, 141, 143, 147, 152, 153, 170

Generations, relations between, 88f.
Geneva, 106, 109
Germany, 57, 58, 59, 61, 65, 66, 104, 106, 108, 110, 112, 163 ; Confessing Church of, 110, 163
Greece, 67, 110, 155

Hawthorne works (of the Western Electric Company), 40, 132
Hinduism, 68
Hiroshima, 71, 103, 143n.
History, 141
Holland, 58, 75, 109, 110, 111, 112, 115
Home, The, 86ff., 107
Home and Family Weeks, 107
Humanism, 75, 112
Hunger, 63, 66, 73

Illiteracy, 66
Imperialism, 17, 28, 38, 72, 73, 74, 75, 77, 79, 95, 113, 162, 178
Incentives, 40, 119
India, 61, 62, 63, 64, 67, 68, 69, 77, 78, 95, 110, 113 ; Christian Home Life Movement in, 107 ; National Congress of, 77
Individual rights and liberties, 17, 113
Individualism, 74, 150
Indo-China, 61
Indonesia, 61, 62, 63, 64, 68, 75, 78, 113
Industrial revolution, 32, 34f., 83, 123, 164
Industrialism, 17, 62, 63f., 84, 119, 131

International Missionary Council, 71
International problems, 171ff.
Invention, 29, 30, 32, 38, 152
Investment, 100f.
Islam, 61, 68
Isolationism, 113
Israel, 24 ; prophets of, 24
Italy, 19

Japan, 61, 62, 63, 64, 65, 66, 68, 72, 103, 104, 106
Java, 62n.
Jerusalem, 162 ; Missionary Conference (1928), 110
Jews, 111, 112, 162
Judaism, 162
Just and Durable Peace, American Churches Commission on, 171
Justice, 14, 15, 16, 17, 19, 21, 22, 25, 26, 49, 51, 60, 79, 151f., 171, 179

Kerk en Wereld (Holland), 109
Kingdom of God, 26, 138
Korea, 61, 64

Labour camps, 142
Labour Party, 112, 148
Laissez faire, 19, 80, 138
Law, 26f.
Laymen's Movement for a Christian World, 109f.
Leisure, 59, 87, 105, 117
Liberalism, 19, 22, 54, 80, 81, 145, 169
Lutheranism, 20, 95

Machine, The, 30ff., 33ff., 37ff., 62, 63, 69, 71ff., 74ff., 84, 133
Manchuria, 64
Manufacturers, National Association of (U.S.A.), 144

Marriage, 86ff., 107 ; Guidance Council, 107
Marxism, 18, 21, 22, 57, 74, 80, 97, 112, 119, 139f., 141, 145, 170, 178
Materialism, 50, 62f., 97, 112, 113, 119, 157n., 164, 165, 170, 172
Mediterranean, 61, 67
Methodist Church, 110, 113
Missionary enterprise, 16, 17, 71f., 75, 76, 77f., 95, 162
Moralism, 75, 147
Morality, 133
Mysticism, 75

Nagasaki, 103, 143n.
National Socialism, 50, 51, 57, 59, 104, 142, 143n., 163, 166
Nationalism, 51, 64f., 66, 69, 72, 73, 74, 75
Natural Law, 19, 74, 157
Negroes, 100
Neighbours, relations between, 89f.
New Testament, 91
Norway, 110, 111, 112

Orthodox Churches, 93, 95
Osaka, 62
Oxford Conference on Church, Community and State (1937), 28n., 74n., 75n., 102, 105, 159, 160

Papal Encyclicals, 128
Patriotism, 51
Peace, 26
Penitence, 103ff., 118, 119
Personal relationships, 105f.
Philippines, 61, 62n., 64, 68, 69
Philosophy, 59, 67
Pittsburgh, 63 ; Conference on " The Church and Economic Life," 109

Planning, 36, 38
Platonism, 141
Poland, 106
Political Parties, Christian, 75, 112, 174
Politics, 56, 57, 58, 60, 79, 137ff., 154, 172
Population, 62f., 73
Poverty, 63, 64, 65, 66, 69, 81
Power, 43, 49, 63
Press, 153
Prisoners of war, 143n.
Production, 53f.
Propaganda, 55, 56, 153, 176
Property, 22, 54, 101f.
Protestantism, 13, 18, 19, 20, 69, 75, 93, 96, 105, 112, 113, 115, 116 ; German, 96, 104
Psychology, 42, 124, 176

Quadragesimo Anno, 128

Racial segregation, 75, 100, 159n., 173
Radio, 153, 163
Rationalism, 77
Reason, 50
Reformed Churches, 95, 115
Relativism, 75
Religion, 67, 68, 69, 112
Religion and Life Movement (Great Britain), 105, 115
Research, 38, 44
Riddell Lectures, 49
Romans, Epistle to the, 163, 169
Rome, 76
Ruhr, 63
Russia, 44, 53, 54, 57, 61, 65f., 78, 138, 139, 142, 145, 146, 148, 153

San Francisco, Charter of United Nations (1945), 113
Scandinavia, 22, 61

Science, 29, 30, 31, 33, 38, 42, 43, 44, 45, 46, 47, 48, 49, 56, 59, 72, 88, 129, 137, 152
Secularism, 14, 20, 24, 68
Sex relationships, 86ff.
Sigtuna Foundation, 107
Slavery, 143n.
Social Democratic Party, 112
"Social Gospel," 99
Social organisation, 14, 15, 120ff., 164f.
Social sciences, 42
Social security, 58, 59
Socialism, 22, 52, 54, 58, 59, 65, 108, 139, 143, 146, 160, 163, 170, 171
Society, agrarian, 18 ; industrial, 17, 18, 19, 20, 23 ; technical, 22, 25, Ch. VII passim
Spain, 18, 19, 58, 116
Spitzenverbände, 144
State, The, 53ff., 58, 77, 142, 158
Sudeten Germans, 105
Sweden, 106, 107
Switzerland, 58, 106, 109
Sword of the Spirit Movement, 115

Tambaram Conference (1938), 110
Technical Society, Ch. VII passim

Technics, 16, 17, 18, 19, 23, Ch. II passim, 54f., 56, 57, 81, 137, 152, 177
" Ten Points " Letter to Times (1940), 114
Thailand, 61, 68
Toleration, 149
Totalitarianism, 22, 23, 25, 58f., 64f., 66, 68, 69, 77, 112, 141, 142, 143n., 145, 146, 153, 163f., 176, 177
Trade Unions, 34, 35, 38, 108, 134, 135
Tribalism, 65, 69

United Nations' Commission on Human Rights, 113
United Nations Organisation, 78, 79
Utopianism, 179

Vocation, 107f., 115, 118

War, 37f., 55f., 148
Women in industry, 84, 85, 86
Work, 40f., 86, 115, 130ff. ; Christian doctrine of, 130ff. ; women and, Ch. VII passim
World Council of Churches, 95, 104 ; Department of Reconstruction and Inter-Church Aid, 106

(b) Names

Angell, Sir Norman, 148
Aristotle, 157
Augustine, St., 141

Barth, Karl, 172
Bates, M. Searle, 61ff.
Bennett, John C., 91ff., 157n., 158, 159n., 160, 164, 173n.
Berdyaev, Nicolas, 121
Bliss, Kathleen, 83ff.

Brady, Robert A., 144
Brunner, Emil, 130n., 176ff.
Buber, Martin, 150
Burnham, James, 57

Calhoun, R. L., 130n., 131
Chen, W. Y., 106
Cole, G. D. H., 127
Constantine, 69
Crombie, Ian, 146

Cromwell, Oliver, 149

Dawson, Christopher, 145
De Lubac, Père, 122, 140, 141
Demant, V. A., 126, 141
Devadutt, V. E., 95
Dostoevsky, 124

Eliot, T. S., 41
Ellul Jacques, 50ff., 165
Engels, Friedrich, 145, 157n., 164

Feuerbach, Ludwig, 140, 141n.
Florovsky, George, 93
Foster, Michael, 121
Frank, Erich, 121
Franks, Sir Oliver, 36f.
Freud, Sigmund, 42

Gandhi, Mahatma, 76, 77
Goldsmith, Oliver, 40

Heron, T. M., 130n., 131
Hitler, Adolf, 164
Holt, Paul, 103n.
Horton, W. M., 75n.
Hunter, Leslie, 97
Huxley, Aldous, 129

Jeremiah, 24, 175
Johnson, F. Ernest, 103n.

Kagawa, Toyohiko, 62
Kraemer, H., 76n.

Langenfass, Friedrich, 96
Laski, Harold, 148
Lawrence, Martin, 141n.
Lenin, 148
Luther, Martin, 75, 96

Mairet, Philip, 33
Mannheim, Karl, 43
Mao Tzetung, 62
Marcel, Gabriel, 47, 48
Maritain, Jacques, 96, 135
Marx, Karl, 74, 140, 141, 157n., 164
Mirams, A. E., 73
Mumford, Lewis, 31, 32, 35
Murry, J. Middleton, 134f.

Nehru, Jawaharlal, 62, 77
Niebuhr, Reinhold, 13ff., 34, 80ff., 166, 168

Oldham, J. H., 29ff., 120ff.

Patijn, C. L., 155ff.
Paul, St., 24, 27, 92, 157, 162
Polanyi, Michael, 49

Rainboro, Colonel, 149
Reckitt, Maurice B., 33n.
Ridenour, Professor, 38
Ritter, Gerhard, 151n.

Schweitzer, Albert, 125
Seaver, George, 125n.
Smuts, Jan, 78
Stalin, 65
Symons, W. G., 34f., 130n., 131

Temple, William, 125, 173
Tennyson, Alfred, Lord, 72
Thomas, M. M., 71ff., 146
Tillich, Paul, 140n.

Urwin, E. C., 103ff.

Voltaire, 74
Vidler, A. R., 93

REPORT OF SECTION III
"THE CHURCH AND THE DISORDER OF SOCIETY"

*Received by the Assembly and commended to the churches for their
serious consideration and appropriate action.*

I. THE DISORDER OF SOCIETY

THE world to-day is experiencing a social crisis of unparalleled
proportions. The deepest root of that disorder is the refusal
of men to see and admit that their responsibility to God stands
over and above their loyalty to any earthly community and their
obedience to any worldly power. Our modern society, in which
religious tradition and family life have been weakened, and which
is for the most part secular in its outlook, underestimates both the
depth of evil in human nature and the full height of freedom and
dignity in the children of God.

The Christian Church approaches the disorder of our society
with faith in the Lordship of Jesus Christ. In Him God has
established His Kingdom and its gates stand open for all who will
enter. Their lives belong to God with a certainty that no disorder
of society can destroy, and on them is laid the duty to seek God's
Kingdom and His righteousness.

In the light of that Kingdom, with its judgment and mercy,
Christians are conscious of the sins which corrupt human communities and institutions in every age, but they are also assured
of the final victory over all sin and death through Christ. It is He
who has bidden us pray that God's Kingdom may come and that
His will may be done on earth as it is in heaven; and our obedience
to that command requires that we seek in every age to overcome
the specific disorders which aggravate the perennial evil in human
society, and that we search out the means of securing their elimination or control.

Men are often disillusioned by finding that changes of particular
systems do not bring unqualified good, but fresh evils. New
temptations to greed and power arise even in systems more just
than those they have .replaced because sin is ever present in the
human heart. Many, therefore, lapse into apathy, irresponsibility
and despair. The Christian faith leaves no room for such despair,
being based on the fact that the Kingdom of God is firmly estab-

lished in Christ and will come by God's act despite all human failure.

Two chief factors contribute to the crisis of our age. One of these is the vast concentrations of power—which are under capitalism mainly economic and under communism both economic and political. In such conditions, social evil is manifest on the largest scale not only in the greed, pride, and cruelty of persons and groups; but also in the momentum or inertia of huge organisations of men, which diminish their ability to act as moral and accountable beings. To find ways of realising personal responsibility for collective action in the large aggregations of power in modern society is a task which has not yet been undertaken seriously.

The second factor is that society, as a whole dominated as it is by technics, is likewise more controlled by a momentum of its own than in previous periods. While it enables men the better to use nature, it has the possibilities of destruction, both through war and through the undermining of the natural foundations of society in family, neighbourhood and craft. It has collected men into great industrial cities and has deprived many societies of those forms of association in which men can grow most fully as persons. It has accentuated the tendency in men to waste God's gift to them in the soil and in other natural resources.

On the other hand, technical developments have relieved men and women of much drudgery and poverty, and are still capable of doing more. There is a limit to what they can do in this direction. Large parts of the world, however, are far from that limit. Justice demands that the inhabitants of Asia and Africa, for instance, should have benefits of more machine production. They may learn to avoid the mechanisation of life and the other dangers of an unbalanced economy which impair the social health of the older industrial peoples. Technical progress also provides channels of communication and interdependence which can be aids to fellowship, though closer contact may also produce friction.

There is no inescapable necessity for society to succumb to undirected developments of technology, and the Christian Church has an urgent responsibility today to help men to achieve fuller personal life within the technical society.

In doing so, the churches should not forget to what extent they themselves have contributed to the very evils which they are tempted to blame wholly on the secularisation of society. While they have raised up many Christians who have taken the lead in movements of reform, and while many of them have come to see in a fresh way the relevance of their faith to the problems of society, and the imperative obligations thus laid upon them, they share responsibility for the contemporary disorder. Our churches have often given religious sanction to the special privileges of dominant classes, races and political groups, and so they have been obstacles to changes necessary in the interests of social justice and political freedom. They have often concentrated on a purely spiritual or other-worldly or individualistic interpretation of their message and their responsibility. They have often failed to understand the forces which have shaped society around them, and so they have been unprepared to deal creatively with new problems as they have arisen in technical civilisation; they have often neglected the effects of industrialisation on agricultural communities.

II. ECONOMIC AND POLITICAL ORGANISATION

In the industrial revolution economic activity was freed from previous social controls and outgrew its modest place in human life. It created the vast network of financial, commercial and industrial relations which we know as the capitalist order. In all parts of the world new controls have in various degrees been put upon the free play of economic forces, but there are economic necessities which no political system can afford to defy. In our days, for instance, the need for stability in the value of money, for creation of capital and for incentives in production, is inescapable and world-wide. Justice, however, demands that economic activities be subordinated to social ends. It is intolerable that vast millions of people be exposed to insecurity, hunger and frustration by periodic inflation or depression.

The Church cannot resolve the debate between those who feel that the primary solution is to socialise the means of production, and those who fear that such a course will merely lead to new and inordinate combinations of political and economic power, culminating finally in an omnicompetent State. In the light of the Christian understanding of man we must, however, say to the advocates of socialisation that the institution of property is not the root of the corruption of human nature. We must equally say to the defenders of existing property relations that ownership is not an unconditional right; it must, therefore, be preserved, curtailed or distributed in accordance with the requirements of justice.

On the one hand, we must vindicate the supremacy of persons over purely technical considerations by subordinating all economic processes and cherished rights to the needs of the community as a whole. On the other hand, we must preserve the possibility of a satisfying life for "little men in big societies." We must prevent abuse of authority and keep open as wide a sphere as possible in which men can have direct and responsible relations with one another as persons.

Coherent and purposeful ordering of society has now become a major necessity. Here governments have responsibilities which they must not shirk. But centres of initiative in economic life must be so encouraged as to avoid placing too great a burden upon centralised judgment and decision. To achieve religious, cultural, economic, social, and other ends it is of vital importance that society should have a rich variety of smaller forms of community, in local government, within industrial organisations, including trade unions, through the development of public corporations and through voluntary associations. By such means it is possible to prevent an undue centralisation of power in modern technically organised communities, and thus escape the perils of tyranny while avoiding the dangers of anarchy.

III. THE RESPONSIBLE SOCIETY

Man is created and called to be a free being, responsible to God and his neighbour. Any tendencies in State and society depriving man of the possibility of acting responsibly are a denial of God's intention for man and His work of salvation. A responsible society is one where freedom is the freedom of men who acknowledge responsibility to justice and public order, and where those who hold political authority or economic power are responsible for its exercise to God and the people whose welfare is affected by it.

Man must never be made a mere means for political or economic ends. Man is not made for the State but the State for man. Man is not made for production, but production for man. For a society to be responsible under modern conditions it is required that the people have freedom to control, to criticise and to change their governments, that power be made responsible by law and tradition, and be distributed as widely as possible through the whole community. It is required that economic justice and provision of equality of opportunity be established for all the members of society.

We therefore condemn:

1. Any attempt to limit the freedom of the Church to witness to its Lord and His design for mankind and any attempt to impair the freedom of men to obey God and to act according to conscience, for those freedoms are implied in man's responsibility before God;

2. Any denial to man of an opportunity to participate in the shaping of society, for this is a duty implied in man's responsibility towards his neighbour;

3. Any attempt to prevent men from learning and spreading the truth.

IV. COMMUNISM AND CAPITALISM

Christians should ask why communism in its modern totalitarian form makes so strong an appeal to great masses of people in many parts of the world. They should recognise the hand of God in the revolt of multitudes against injustice that gives communism much of its strength. They should seek to recapture for the Church the original Christian solidarity with the world's distressed people, not to curb their aspirations towards justice, but, on the contrary, to go beyond them and direct them towards the only road which does not lead to a blank wall, obedience to God's will and His justice. Christians should realise that for many, especially for many young men and women, communism seems to stand for a vision of human equality and universal brotherhood for which they were prepared by Christian influences. Christians who are beneficiaries of capitalism should try to see the world as it appears to many who know themselves excluded from its privileges and who see in communism a means of deliverance from poverty and insecurity. All should understand that the proclamation of racial equality by communists and their support of the cause of colonial peoples makes a strong appeal to the populations of Asia and Africa and to racial minorities elsewhere. It is a great human tragedy that so much that is good in the motives and aspirations of many communists and of those whose sympathies they win has been transformed into a force that engenders new forms of injustice and oppression, and that what is true in communist criticism should be used to give convincing power to untrustworthy propaganda.

Christians should recognise with contrition that many churches are involved in the forms of economic injustice and racial discrimination which have created the conditions favourable to the growth of communism, and that the atheism and the anti-religious teaching of communism are in part a reaction to the chequered record of a professedly Christian society. It is one of the most fateful facts in modern history that often the working classes, including tenant farmers, came to believe that the churches were against them or indifferent to their plight. Christians should realise that the Church has often failed to offer to its youth the appeal that can evoke a disciplined, purposeful and sacrificial response, and that in this respect communism has for many filled a moral and psychological vacuum.

The points of conflict between Christianity and the atheistic Marxian communism of our day are as follows: (1) the communist promise of what amounts to a complete redemption of man in history; (2) the belief that a particular class by virtue of its role as the bearer of a new order is free from the sins and ambiguities that Christians believe to be characteristic of all human existence; (3) the materialistic and deterministic teachings, however they may be qualified, that are incompatible with belief in God and with the Christian view of man as a person, made in God's image and responsible to Him; (4) the ruthless methods of communists in dealing with their opponents; (5) the demand of the party on its members for an exclusive and unqualified loyalty which belongs only to God, and the coercive policies of communist dictatorship in controlling every aspect of life.

The Church should seek to resist the extension of any system, that not only includes oppressive elements but fails to provide any means by which the victims of oppression may criticise or act to correct it. It is a part of the mission of the Church to raise its voice of protest wherever men are the victims of terror, wherever they are denied such fundamental human rights as the right to be secure against arbitrary arrest, and wherever governments use torture and cruel punishments to intimidate consciences of men.

The Church should make clear that there are conflicts between Christianity and capitalism. The developments of capitalism vary from country to country and often the exploitation of the workers that was characteristic of early capitalism has been corrected in considerable measure by the influence of trade unions, social legislation and responsible management. But (1) capitalism tends to subordinate what should be the primary task of any economy —the meeting of human needs—to the economic advantages of those who have most power over its institutions. (2) It tends to produce serious inequalities. (3) It has developed a practical form of materialism in Western nations in spite of their Christian background, for it has placed the greatest emphasis upon success in making money. (4) It has also kept the people of capitalist countries subject to a kind of fate which has taken the form of such social catastrophes as mass unemployment.

The Christian churches should reject the ideologies of both communism and laissez-faire capitalism, and should seek to draw men away from the false assumption that these extremes are the only alternatives. Each has made promises which it could not redeem. Communist ideology puts the emphasis upon economic justice, and promises that freedom will come automatically after the completion of the revolution. Capitalism puts the emphasis upon freedom, and promises that justice will follow as a by-product of free enterprise; that, too, is an ideology which has been proved false. It is the responsibility of Christians to seek new, creative solutions which never allow either justice or freedom to destroy the other.

V. THE SOCIAL FUNCTION OF THE CHURCH

The greatest contribution that the Church can make to the renewal of society is for it to be renewed in its own life in faith and obedience to its Lord. Such inner renewal includes a clearer grasp of the meaning of the Gospel for the whole life of men. This renewal must take place both in the larger units of the Church and in the local congregations. The influence of worshiping congregations upon the problems of society is very great when those congregations include people from many social groups. If the Church can overcome the national and social barriers which now divide it, it can help society to overcome those barriers.

This is especially clear in the case of racial distinction. It is here that the Church has failed most lamentably, where it has reflected and then by its example sanctified the racial prejudice that is rampant in the world. And yet it is here that to-day its guidance concerning what God wills for it is especially clear. It knows that it must call society away from prejudice based upon race or colour and from the practices of discrimination and segregation as denials of justice and human dignity, but it cannot say a convincing word to society unless it takes steps to eliminate these practices from the Christian community because they contradict all that it believes about God's love for all His children.

There are occasions on which the churches, through their

councils or through such persons as they may commission to speak on their behalf, should declare directly what they see to be the will of God for the public decisions of the hour. Such guidance will often take the form of warnings against concrete forms of injustice or oppression or social idolatry. They should also point to the main objectives towards which a particular society should move.

One problem is raised by the existence in several countries of Christian political parties. The Church as such should not be identified with any political party, and it must not act as though it were itself a political party. In general, the formation of such parties is hazardous because they easily confuse Christianty with the inherent compromises of politics. They may cut Christians off from the other parties which need the leaven of Christianity, and they may consolidate all who do not share the political principles of the Christian party not only against that party but against Christianity itself. Nevertheless, it may still be desirable in some situations for Christians to organize themselves into a political party for specific objectives, so long as they do not claim that it is the only possible expression of Christian loyalty in the situation.

But the social influence of the Church must come primarily from its influence upon its members through constant teaching and preaching of Christian truth in ways that illuminate the historical conditions in which men live and the problems which they face. The Church can be most effective in society as it inspires its members to ask in a new way what their Christian responsibility is whenever they vote or discharge the duties of public office, whenever they influence public opinion, whenever they make decisions as employers or as workers or in any other vocation to which they may be called. One of the most creative developments in the contemporary Church is the practice of groups of Christians facing much the same problems in their occupations to pray and to take counsel together in order to find out what they should do as Christians.

In discussing the social function of the Church, Christians should always remember the great variety of situations in which the Church lives. Nations in which professing Christians are in the majority, nations in which the Church represents only a few per cent of the population, nations in which the Church lives under a hostile and oppressive government offer very different problems for the Church. It is one of the contributions of the ecumenical experience of recent years that churches under these contrasting conditions have come not only to appreciate one another's practices, but to learn from one another's failures and achievements and sufferings.

<h2 align="center">VI. CONCLUSION</h2>

There is a great discrepancy between all that has been said here and the possibility of action in many parts of the world. Obedience to God will be possible under all external circumstances, and no one need despair when conditions restrict greatly the area of responsible action. The responsible society of which we have spoken represents, however, the goal for which the churches in all lands must work, to the glory of the one God and Father of all, and looking for the day of God and a new earth, wherein dwelleth righteousness.

MAN'S DISORDER AND GOD'S DESIGN
Volume IV

THE CHURCH
AND THE
INTERNATIONAL
DISORDER

THE
CHURCH AND
THE INTERNATIONAL
DISORDER

AN

ECUMENICAL STUDY

PREPARED UNDER THE AUSPICES OF THE

WORLD COUNCIL OF CHURCHES

VOLUME FOUR

CONTENTS

List of Contributors

I CHAIRMAN'S INTRODUCTION Kenneth G. Grubb   13

II THE CHURCHES' APPROACH TO INTERNATIONAL AFFAIRS Roswell P. Barnes and Kenneth G. Grubb   19

III THE CHURCH AND THE DISORDER OF INTERNATIONAL SOCIETY F. M. Van Asbeck   47

IV CHRISTIAN RESPONSIBILITY IN OUR DIVIDED WORLD
    (a) The Christian Citizen in a Changing World
        John Foster Dulles
    (b) Our Responsibility in the Post-war World
        Joseph L. Hromadka   73

V FREEDOM OF RELIGION AND RELATED HUMAN RIGHTS
   O. Frederick Nolde   143

VI CHRISTIAN RESPONSIBILITY IN A WORLD OF POWER
    (a) Power. Emil Brunner
    (b) The World of Power. Kenneth G. Grubb   190

Membership of the Commission   211

Index   213

Report of Section IV

CONTRIBUTORS

BARNES, Roswell P., Associate General Secretary, Federal Council of Churches, U.S.A. Author of *A Christian Imperative*.

BRUNNER, Emil, D.Theol., Professor of Systematic Theology, Zurich. Author of *The Mediator, Justice and the Social Order*, etc.

DULLES, John Foster, LL.D., Chairman of Committee on Policy, Department of International Justice and Goodwill of American Federal Council of Churches ; Member of United States Delegation to many international conferences, including United Nations Assembly. Author of *War, Peace and Change*.

GRUBB, Kenneth G., C.M.G., Chairman, Commission of the Churches on International Affairs, and of International Department, British Council of Churches ; Secretary General, Hispanic Council.

HROMADKA, Joseph L., D.D., Professor of Systematic Theology, John Hus Faculty, Prague. Author of *The Legacy of Calvin, Doom and Resurrection*, etc.

NOLDE, O. Frederick, D.D., Professor, Lutheran Seminary, Philadelphia, and Director of the Commission of the Churches on International Affairs. Author of *Power for Peace*, etc.

VAN ASBECK, Baron F. M., LL.D., Professor of International Law, Leiden, formerly Government Secretary, Netherlands Indies. Author of *Le Régime des étrangers dans les colonies*, etc.

I

CHAIRMAN'S INTRODUCTION

Kenneth G. Grubb

THE papers in this volume treat some of the problems in the field of international affairs which claim the attention of Christians, and frequently require the adoption of definite attitudes. The Disorder of Man is to most men nowhere more painfully apparent than in international relations ; the Design of God for the nations is difficult to perceive. It is often said that national socialism, communism and democracy are the great designs of the present time to overcome Man's disorder and to evoke order. The differences between these systems or the nations that adopt them account for no small part of international disorder.

It is tacitly assumed that the relations between nations are reasonably satisfactory, if their differences are not expressed with such violence as to threaten harmony and provoke rupture, and perhaps war. The nations, indeed, desire peace, not usually at any price, nor even at the price of national sovereignty, and most nations are willing to adopt an attitude of " live and let live " in regard to their neighbours. It is possible that societies with very diverse outlooks may live side by side for long periods on such terms, but the possibility is less than it has been at any previous stage in history. For, whereas there is a widespread appreciation of tolerance and a desire to secure basic rights and liberties for all men, there is also a more general consciousness of nationality and dignity, a closer contact through modern communications, and an unprecedented recourse to sources of power.

How far, therefore, nations which have built up their domestic policy on contrary principles can live side by side to their mutual peace and profit, it is not unreasonable to question. It is easy to disclaim any desire to export the domestic political product, and this intention is often genuine. But the appetite grows by what it feeds upon : and all aspects of national policy are infected, as they should be, by a nation's fundamental assumptions

about the state and the citizen and the purposes of national
existence.

It is a mistake to suppose, therefore, that conduct in the
kitchen has no bearing on conduct in the park. International
relations will not be harmoniously solved if there is unresolved
disharmony between men as men, and between man and God.
The truth of essential human interdependence has yet to be
learned : attitudes that are wrong at home cannot be right
abroad. If this is so, it must have a bearing on the Christian
approach to international affairs. If the ordinary members
of the Christian churches of the world succumb to the feeling
that they can do nothing to influence the clash of the nations,
then they are right, because they have succumbed. But if
they do not succumb, then they can do something simply by their
attitude. How much they can do varies greatly from country to
country, for in some countries it is difficult for the ordinary
citizen or churchman to defend publicly what he has chosen
privately.

Some will be surprised that little is said in this volume
about the problem of peace, as such. This is due to both a
reaction from the past, and a realism in the present. Much more
is said about human rights and liberties. Christians must
repudiate the search for peace merely as an insurance for selfishness or as scope for overweening ambition. Subordination of
the life of the nations and of individuals to God's will is indispensable to peace. Peace, as a supreme end in itself, has ceased
to be the final objective of men's efforts.

A lot is said in the volume about Great Powers. In most
historical eras there have been great Powers. Their position
is one of more than ordinary responsibility to-day. They have a
preponderant influence at the United Nations ; their military,
naval and air resources are vast, and their differences not easy to
harmonise. The situation for small Powers has deteriorated.
The Second World War showed once more that they have no
security in being small and professing neutrality. Great Powers
can exercise a beneficent influence if they are tolerant and
responsible ; if not, they may be fatally dangerous.

The fear and fact of power overshadows men's minds. But
it remains true that states as well as individuals subsist under
the governance of God. All power, small and great, and all
persons in authority, need to be reminded of this truth, especially

in an age of atomic power. But although men may fear power, they cannot forgo its use and its fascination. Christian men, for their part, stand for the reality of moral power. It is slow in its effects and incapable of determining situations which have got out of hand when passions are enraged, or issues decided without reference to the people. But it counts, as the course of history shows, if there exist those who express it.

Moreover, although there is much human cause for misgivings and apprehension in the world of nations, God still reigns. His intervention in history, centred above all in the Incarnation, is history's most decisive feature and the basis of eventual and Christian hope. He is not deaf to prayer, nor indifferent to pain. The sufferings of the just are still the saving principle in human experience. Evil brings its own retribution, and righteousness its reward, not to-day, nor to-morrow, but equally not in a future so distant as to be irrelevant to life.

National diversity is a creative element in international life, but its beneficent ends have repeatedly been prevented by an excessive nationalism. The ideal of world government is to many a legitimate objective, but practical schemes are in advance of world opinion, and the present development of man's moral capacities. The risk of a centralised tyranny is, in any case, great. The immediate possibility is to work for an international order based on a rule of law, limiting national sovereignties and providing procedures for peaceful changes. This means the development of international law from a contractual law between nations to a law above them.

A step towards this end lies in the more constructive use of the United Nations. So far, the United Nations has not shown any capability of succeeding at one of the important points where the League of Nations failed, namely, the formation of a body of authority, experience and policy which will truly be above the nations. The decisions of the United Nations are the decisions of nations agreeing or differing from one another. The emergence of a truly supra-national body with influence and standpoints of its own, and policies which are not merely the highest degree of possible compromise between the nations, is a matter for the future. If it is unobtainable, it is even more impracticable to think in terms of such a limitation, or even abolition of national sovereignties, as would make world government a possibility. Meanwhile, it is urgently necessary that the rule of law and the recognition of moral responsibility in international relations be extended.

The demand for guarantees of human rights and freedoms has occupied men's minds in many countries. The state assumes the prerogatives of God when it supposes that it is free to grant or to deny fundamental rights and freedoms to men. The authority of the state must support that law which expresses these rights and safeguards such freedoms. Internationally, a constructive step lies in the acceptance of an international covenant of rights with adequate measures to protect it. Since the churches are concerned with ultimate loyalties, the state's recognition of their essential freedom is the crucial test of its own moral responsibility.

The effectiveness of securing human rights, however detailed the measures of enforcement may be, depends largely on good faith. The whole structure of international relations, in so far as it is expressed in agreements, depends on respect for the plighted word. If a world of restraints can be removed by the mere decision to regard none except those of brute force, then trust gives way to suspicion and suspicion to war or anarchy. Up till recently the history of human development was one of gradually increasing respect for justice and honourable dealing. The main problem of statesmanship must be to restore that respect, and at the same time to allow room for adjustment of the reasonable demands that arise from the social vitalities of the peoples.

It is the essence of the dilemma that such respect cannot be restored by statesmanship alone. The sanctity of solemn obligations depends on the recognition of absolute justice. Else, all conceptions of justice are relative both as to their bases and the respect due to them. Justice becomes the will of the state symbolised in its leader or the voice of the people heard in its assemblies. There is no higher corrective to either. The decay of justice has been hastened by oppression exercised in the name of order, especially in war ; its restoration can only be effected by a legal order which expresses rights and freedoms derived from man's ultimate loyalties.

The defeated nations of the Second World War, Germany and Japan, deserve special consideration from this standpoint. In the administration of conquered peoples it is inevitable that the victors should be to some extent judges on their own behalf. No man, or group of men, who live in the fear and obedience of God, can sustain such a responsibility with equanimity. The demands of government and of proper discipline are only respected when justice is not only done, but is seen to be done. If justice cannot in some measure be achieved in the legal order, it is unlikely that it can be secured in the economic order where its demands are difficult both to define and to satisfy.

The modern world is the stage of a new movement of national emergence and popular consciousness. The short period since the war has witnessed the acquisition of autonomous nationhood by some 500,000,000 persons. The nations of the East have suddenly taken an active part in world affairs, and precisely at the time when many in the West are disillusioned about progress, in Africa and the East men are embracing it with new fervour. From now on, the statesmen and people of the newly born nations will be concerned not so much with self-government as with good government. For the one, passion and combative conviction are mainly required ; for the other, righteousness and wisdom.

Finally, the whole international scene is the scene where communism and Christianity meet. They meet not only as rival ideologies or faiths, but as ingredients in the total attitude of peoples to concrete situations. Their confrontation as systems of thought and faith extending dominion over the allegiance of men is not the subject for this volume.

So much has been written on this that it is hard to choose words. The deterioration in relations between the U.S.S.R. and the U.S.A., and to a lesser extent, Great Britain, has been a sad feature of the post-war years. The obstructive use of the veto in the Security Council, the failure of the Foreign Ministers' conferences with consequences for the future of Germany, the apparently uncompromising character of Soviet policy in special incidents, and the tone of Soviet propaganda (sometimes, however, rivalled by irresponsible journals elsewhere) are all well known. Men differ over the interpretation of these things. There seems no real reason to believe that the U.S.S.R. wants war on a global scale ; primarily nations want security. No nation wants war if it can obtain its fruits otherwise. But a limited demand easily becomes unlimited, and passions and anger of expression lead to positions from which shame or pride prevent retreat.

What contribution can the fellowship of churches represented in the World Council of Churches make ? To their regret, the churches of the West know little of the real influence of Christianity in Russia, and have little opportunity for seeking a clearer understanding with Russian Christians. It is easy to advocate an experiment in friendship between the peoples of the U.S.S.R. and the other nations, East and West. It is also easy to affirm that, above all political differences, Christians believe in certain fundamental assertions about the nature of God and His redemptive action in human history. But if there is no form of access and contact, what progress can be made ? It is difficult to answer this. At least, Christians can strive so to form their views and influence those of others as to exercise a moderating influence where matters of fundamental conviction are not involved ; to forgive while conscious of their own need of forgiveness ; and to recognise all that communism has done for peoples for whom Christianity had apparently accomplished little. In the larger view, it may yet prove that the fellowship of Christians may be the most effective starting point for a development of open relations between the U.S.S.R. and other countries.

In the field of international affairs the ecumenical nature of the Church is of particular significance. This is a truth so obvious that it hardly needs repeating. But there is need for a more thorough exposition of the meaning of this luminous idea. At what points does the ecumenical Church effectively touch the world of international relations ? What Biblical truths, common to the faith of all the churches, provide the foundation for a Christian approach ? What is involved in bringing the influence of ecumenical bodies to bear on international ones ? The World Council of Churches has undoubtedly been well advised in including the intractable field of international relations in its official purview, but in so doing it has raised more questions than can readily be answered, and some that cannot be answered in print, and only by a divine miracle in life.

THE CHURCHES' APPROACH TO
INTERNATIONAL AFFAIRS

II

THE CHURCHES' APPROACH TO INTERNATIONAL AFFAIRS

Roswell P. Barnes and Kenneth G. Grubb

THE particular purpose of this section is to enquire how the influence of the churches can best be employed in the field of international affairs. It is widely felt in the churches that some of the most crucial questions that confront the Christian conscience are being posed by the relations between the nations ; and yet spiritual and moral influence seems to be impotent. The renewed possibility of war, a continuing testimony to sin and to inability to define the purpose of the power of the state and to confine it, still gloomily dog men's minds. The discovery of the means of using atomic energy has multiplied a thousand-fold the danger, but has also offered new possibilities for peaceful control of power, which it is a duty of the Churches to use. What Christians can do must be done now and maintained constantly ; for when conflict between nations has once broken out, the opportunity for remedy by Christian action, or the chances of limiting the conflagration, are small.

The relations between nations are therefore of importance to the churches long before they reach the stage of threatened conflict. Wars may be planned, or they may be the almost unavoidable consequence of attitudes which have been nursed and fed until they have grown into uncompromising demands. It is often difficult to foresee what will be the ultimate outcome of economic or political tendencies. They may appear capable of harmonisation with the ambitions of others but, even if the spectator holds that they are, the actors on either side may not believe it. It is similarly difficult to know what will be the ultimate result of any policy. Benevolence of intention provides no assurance of effectiveness. There are many situations in which inaction or a gesture intended as conciliation leads, to all seeming, to greater disaster than the timely, if vigorous, use of power. To the Christian, the difficulty is not to find situations which are interesting because they appear to involve the application of Christian principles, but to refuse to squander energy over the relatively secondary.

THE CHURCHES' APPROACH TO
INTERNATIONAL AFFAIRS

I. TYPES OF PROBLEMS

A. *Aspects of International Relations*

What does the task of exercising influence in international relations mean for the churches? In a narrow sense, international relations are direct relations between states as such, negotiating directly with one another through their governments. A dispute over a frontier, a treaty, the exchange of plenipotentiaries are examples. The interests of the churches may be involved in international exchanges of this type, although it more frequently happens that their concern is not sufficiently evident to justify special action. But it is impossible to say so in advance and constant vigilance is needed. The exchange of a few square kilometres of forest may conceivably affect freedom of education or preaching. A treaty may contain conditions safeguarding the rights of minorities or omitting to do so. Such actions as the removal of large masses of people must, on any count, affect the situation of religion as well as the organisation of human welfare.

In a broader sense, international relations are relations between peoples. Governments generally represent in some measure the will of their people, though this representation may vary from a considerable measure to an almost negligible degree in totalitarian régimes. Even in a " police state " it is likely that the government will seek to influence and control the will of its people so as to induce acceptance, if not support, of the government's policy. Consequently, any contact or communication between people across national frontiers may have some bearing on the relations between their nations. " Since all relations within a State, and all supra-national relations, are ultimately relations between one human being and another, the Christian understanding of man is the starting-point for all questions of international relations."[1]

[1] Max Huber, *The Universal Church and the World of Nations*, p. 99.

Thus it is important, in considering the approach of the churches to international affairs, to keep in mind the distinctions between the narrower and the broader aspects of international affairs : between the state and the nation, the government and the people, the technical and the psychological, the scientific and the moral, the impersonal and the personal. While these distinctions are useful for purposes of analysis, the close relationship between the two sets of factors is also important ; for example, the codification of international law and the development of a common moral atmosphere must go hand in hand ; the negotiation of tariff agreements, a highly technical task, is futile unless the government will ratify and the people will support the resulting measures ; an international convention on human rights would be of little value without the will in the several nations to support it.

A different type of relationship was introduced by the League of Nations, and resumed by the United Nations and its Specialised Agencies, including such bodies as UNESCO, and the International Labour Office. The Charters of such bodies frequently contain principles or provisions which are of special importance to Christians. Article 71 of the Charter of the United Nations is an example. The Constitution of UNESCO, by the very nature of its subject, is in this class, and it deserves careful study. It is a feature of the basic documents that govern the policy of some of these recent bodies that they specifically express a willingness or desire to co-operate with recognised non-governmental international bodies. This, perhaps, is not so significant as the more general considerations of the obligations involved and stated in a Charter. The nations which are members of the United Nations do, in effect and in respect of certain policies, agree to accept certain standards of conduct. Constant exposure to comments, strictures and possibly measures of an international body, and the public opinion which is liable to form, can be very effective, but just in what degree depends ultimately on the respect of members for the authority in question, and on the provision for the use of sanctions, or force, against offenders. The effectiveness of this type of internationalism is precisely one of the great issues at stake to-day. In the past it has been effective in minor but useful decisions, but has broken down in great and crucial ones. It is hoped that the curative and creative work of the United Nations will become proportionately

more important.   At least, it is worth while for the churches to be
so organised as to make their voice heard and views felt in all
such organisations, and this is best done if they make their
own international instrument for the purpose.

There are occasions when an internal situation may arise
within any nation which is repugnant to the Christian conscience
outside national bounds, but which is defended on grounds of the
sanctity of national sovereignty.   There are also general standards
of conscience which do not needlessly interfere with the customary functioning of national governments.   Thus the right of
every man to obey his conscience is to be safeguarded by the
churches.   But special communities or sections of the populace
may be treated wrongly, done out of their reasonable rights, or
even persecuted, and the offences condoned if not defended on
the ground of the inviolability of domestic sovereignty. Justification of these lapses from standards of behaviour expected from
members of the United Nations may be sought on grounds of
public order or the necessity of homogeneous national development.   Remedies may be available but may not be effective.
There is an alleged lack of information, differences about the
facts, and delay in establishing them.   These cases are apt to be
intractable ; in the end the world loses interest and passes on to
the next sensation.

There is also widespread doubt whether the world can go
any further on the lines of separate national sovereignty without
courting disaster ;   but, in practice, nationalism remains a
powerful and almost irreducible force.   It is the responsibility
of the churches to remind governments and peoples that nations
subsist under the governance of God.   Aside from this consideration, the nation tends to regard itself as morally autonomous
and therefore to accept what is, in effect, moral anarchy in the
world community.   The Oxford conference stated : " A true
conception of international order requires a recognition of the
fact that the state, whether it admits it or not, is not autonomous
but is under the ultimate governance of God."

B.   *The Position of the Churches*

In regard to all these different situations the question has not
merely to be asked whether the churches have the right to
recommend certain action, but what is their competence to do
so.   It can be argued that if Christian principles are ignored

in the handling of public affairs, Christians must at all costs at least protest. Protest they may, and in so doing relieve their consciences, but it does not follow that the situation will be relieved. The effectiveness of action depends on its being closely matched to the real demands of the situation which are not always candidly declared, or, indeed, easy to identify. Moreover, to endeavour to correct injustice by the application of absolute justice, is not usually possible, and if not possible, to seek to do so may merely mean the creation of tensions in which further injustices will be committed.

On the other hand, immediate effectiveness is not the only consideration in determining Christian action. It is not necessarily demanded of the Christian that he be successful ; it is demanded of him that he be faithful. The churches must raise their voices even if they do not seem to be heard. The Christian always labours in tension between the seeming irrelevance of the absolute on the one hand and the questionable validity of the immediately practical on the other hand.

It is true that Christianity is concerned with the whole life of man. Nevertheless, a useful practical distinction can perhaps be drawn between those questions on which the churches can claim special competent knowledge and others on which they can advance no such claim seriously. An individual Christian may be a first-rate economist, and as such he may have something of weight to say on the technical aspects of an economic question. It is not for the churches, as churches, to claim competence to make similar pronouncements. But the churches can take a firm stand on their own ground : they can expose the fallacies that underlie some of the aims and many of the methods which the modern manipulations of economic society embrace, in the light of the Christian view of the purposes of man's life. They can also speak out of much experience, and from a broader than national or class perspective, on the nature of those inner forces and compulsions which compel men, in spite of natural misgivings, to be ready to suffer for convictions. Thus they may condition the decisions of the Christian economist. They can add to this a wealth of practical wisdom in the promotion of welfare, literacy and the healing of disease of mind and body, and these are questions which are receiving much attention in the discussions of international bodies.

But it is one thing to admit the competence of the churches

to exercise an influence on certain aspects of international affairs, and another to secure agreement as to the objectives they should seek and the methods they should use. The relations between the nations are fraught with such critical potentialities that it can be argued that every major international issue should engage the close attention of the churches. At the other extreme stand those who contend that it is impractical to hope to influence the general relationships of the nations or the standards of human rights which they will, in practice, observe, and the churches should concentrate on securing those minimal rights and freedoms which are essential to their own existence. Another wide body of Christian opinion finds a middle ground and claims an intimate concern in all international measures and national policies designed to promote the social rights and welfare of men, the stability of family life, the advance of literacy, and the improvement of public health, the maintenance of peace and the access to opportunity. They would not consider that complicated international financial settlements or transport agreements should make detailed claims upon their attention ; but they will recognise a responsibility to create a favourable atmosphere for the negotiations of even such agreements and to comment on broad relevant principles.

The main difference is between those who hold that it is the duty of the churches to influence and form a view upon international relations as such, and those who hold that it is their duty to state and guide the attitude of Christians to them. It is difficult to draw this line with exactitude, and may not be desirable to do so. The advocates of the first of these views are faced with an immense task. The advocates of the second assume that certain political outlooks are unlikely to be changed and that the appetite for power takes little real account of formal and legal obligations. Therefore, they seek to define the attitude of the churches in the face of these conditions, and to identify a few points where Christian action seems unavoidable.

These differences in approach and temper are partly traceable to the theological and historical background of the churches. Examined more factually, they are also due to the different positions occupied by nations in world affairs, and the very different degrees of influence exercised by the Church within the nation. A vigorous church movement, exercising influence in its own nation while that nation commands weight among the world of nations, finds no field of international action alien to it. Great Britain was in this position in the nineteenth century when religion was conventionally popular and the nation energetic and assertive. The United States, for different reasons, occupies a place of great influence in the world to-day and the churches are, in turn, influential in the country. But when a church is very small, or is shrinking rather than growing, or has been the victim of persecution, or is faced with an unsympathetic and restrictive political régime, it tends inevitably to concentrate on the maintenance of its own essential life, and to limit its interest in international affairs to a minimum. It is, therefore, impossible to say that either of the two tendencies in question is right to the exclusion of the other. Which is followed will, in practice, depend on the standing of the churches in a nation, their tradition and their relation to the state. A lively sense of interdependence and mutual obligation between churches all over the world is one way by which to fortify their influence and incidentally to strengthen their own position. But no one who is conscious of the strength and jealousies of national-ism and the conscious repudiation in many quarters of a Christian approach to politics will underrate the difficulties in practice.

Despite these differences, there has been a tendency during recent years to converge upon a common ground where there is a large measure of agreement. This agreement, already hinted at above, is furthered by emphasising the distinction between the more limited and technical aspects of international relations, on the one hand, and the broader moral and psychological aspects on the other hand. It is recognised that the churches seldom have a responsibility to advocate one specific technical measure among several when their respective merits can be judged only on the basis of highly specialised knowledge and information. But behind the technical questions there are usually questions of purpose and motive, upon which, it is generally agreed, the churches must speak. By speaking in this field, decisions are conditioned rather than determined. The distinction between conditioning and determining decisions cannot be clear-cut, but it implies that influence intended to condition decisions is less direct and specific than influence intended to determine decisions. Even in the technical field, the proficiency and effectiveness of the experts and professional diplomats has not been so conspicuous during recent decades as to justify the relegation of all responsibility to them.

The churches possess certain assets and suffer from certain limitations or disadvantages in organising to influence international affairs. Their most obvious and valuable advantage is the widespread distribution of Christians. Thanks largely to the past 150 years of missionary expansion and to the character of emigration to the British Dominions, Christian churches of Protestant, Orthodox or Anglican allegiance are scattered over the world. Much has been said of the significance of this : Archbishop Temple called it this " great new fact " of our time. Potentially it is unquestionably a development of great significance, for it means that between and among the nations there are numbers of persons, themselves citizens of " sovereign states ", who owe obedience to our Lord and Master, and are constantly striving to maintain that obedience amid the cogent and necessary loyalties of national life.

The Christian testimony to the permanence of absolute principles, to the existence of values which have not been, and cannot be, created by the unaided effort of statesmen, philosophers or scientists, is a contribution to an approach to international affairs that is badly needed. Belief about man's place in society and the unconditional obligations which the existence of God and his neighbour lay upon him, is an essential constituent in enduring human relationships. The churches may be divided on many questions of order, theology and tradition, but in those beliefs which are the decisive ones for the establishment of human rights they are very largely at one. It is certainly the case that there have been and will continue to be differences about the precise relationship between church and nation which may best express the truth of such assumptions, but there is a Christian conception of the relation of man to his neighbour, of the reverence due to personality and of the obedience to be held towards reasonably and properly constituted authority and the inviolability of the pledged word, which are not to be found, and may be explicitly repudiated, where the Christian conscience is unheard.

But to leave the matter at that is to overstate the case. The value of this world-wide witness of the Church is seriously reduced by its actual condition. In most nations the churches are small, and it is correspondingly more difficult for them to maintain their own due freedom and rights under circumstances of discrimination, and to influence the international conduct of the nation. The Christians of India, of every ecclesiastical allegiance, are two per cent. of the population ; of China, less than one per cent. In the Near and Middle East the question has to be asked whether the ancient Orthodox and Eastern minorities can prosper. There are, however, hopeful signs in many places that Christian influence is not solely dependent upon numerical strength. While in most countries there are not many citizens who vote for a policy because it appeals to an enlightened Christian conscience, yet it is true that where Christians are few in number they are sometimes prominent in leadership. In a democracy, however, the quality of counsel is commanded by its popularity, and any estimate of the international influence of the churches must be tempered by a sense of these limitations, and of the final aims of human society.

It follows that the concerns of the churches, even if acutely involved in any situation, will be only one of many factors which will weigh in the formulation of official policy. A general negotiation which in its consequences may affect the interest of the churches, may be pursued and completed on grounds only remotely connected with it. It may often be right for the churches to endeavour to secure that due attention should be given to their case, but it cannot be right that they should overstate it, or press it beyond a due point. The consequences of human actions are frequently very different from the intentions of human agents, and a certain prudence must be exercised in pressing for policies whose ultimate repercussions may be unexpected and not generally profitable.

In practice, religious motives are usually found in dilution, not in a pure state. The protection of weak Christian minorities may be assumed by powerful Christian neighbours desiring to advance national influence under the guise of religious zeal. In such cases a genuine Christian approach is rendered nugatory almost from the start. It is partly the sense that these situations involve so many tangles that caused enlightened opinion to advocate a general approach to human rights as the best way to attempt to solve the specific problem of the rights of minorities.

Finally, it must be remembered that the international action of the churches is frequently powerless in the face of the extraordinary resistant amalgam produced by the integration of religion and national life, and constantly hardened by the nationalist appeal to cultural homogeneity. In some countries the attitude of the State to its own political and social problems has been powerfully, if insensibly, affected by the outlook of popular religion, and the attitude of religion similarly influenced by the State. The massive and impressive religious and national cultures of the East are not easily penetrable. In the Christian world the same resistance is found in the hardening of the Roman Catholic centres of influence and power in Latin America against the liberties and rights of other Christians. These tendencies and attitudes of nations may effectively nullify the paper decisions of the most solemn international guarantees.

Moreover, it frequently happens that influence can be exercised only or mainly through ways that are uncongenial to Christians. Christianity makes unconditional claims. The execution of policy in international relations is, as is the case in politics generally, the art of the possible. Only in certain countries can the churches arouse popular interest, and then only over certain questions. Matters of some importance to the Christian conscience may be settled in negotiations between governments and only a few people will be aware, and then too late for action. In the long run, the advocacy of general principles does have its effect, or rather in the past it has had, but in the process many just causes may be lost and apparent injustices done.

The Christian is, therefore, faced with the task of tirelessly pursuing valid objectives by the methods of compromise and adjustment to the possible. In this process the objectives lose their clarity and not infrequently their original value. Ends are inevitably coloured by the kind of means used to achieve them, and it is always questionable how far it is right to lower the level of even proximate aims in order to enjoy a partial success. On the other hand, in such an atmosphere it is frequently possible to combine forces with those who are moving in the same direction, although they start from different assumptions. All who believe generally in the respect due to human personality, although they may not agree with Christians on the ultimate grounds on which that respect must be based, are concerned in the struggle to secure effectively certain human rights. Most minorities appeal to a broad cultural liberalism and some hold to the same principle when they become majorities. The advisability of the churches correlating efforts with those of other faiths or of no fundamental faith in the struggle for standards and conditions rests upon considerations of prudence and convenience rather than of principle or conviction. But even while they accept compromise in a given situation, the churches must remember that it is their responsibility always to maintain a tension between the absolute and the immediately possible.

2. ACTION OF THE CHURCHES

Whereas the political forces of the modern world are to-day so aligned as to offer some new possibilities for Christian action, they also present very serious obstacles. In the nineteenth century the British influence was at its height and was widespread throughout a large part of the world, and this corresponded with a period when nascent nationalisms of the modern regimented type were only beginning to rise to self-consciousness. It was, therefore, possible for Britain to champion humanitarian causes whether on disinterested or self-interested grounds, to intervene actively for the protection of missionaries, and to press for and often obtain substantial concessions to the demand for religious and cultural freedom. Britain was not alone in these aims and such accords as the Berlin Act, establishing minimum standards for the powers in Africa, were the joint result of the efforts of several nations. But Britons played a prominent part, which in the view of some should be assumed by the United States. But to many the idea that any one nation should enjoy excessive power, even if it uses it beneficently, is distasteful, and inevitably savours of an imperialism meaning little more than the domination of one people by another to the latter's advantage, or at the best complacent and unprogressive patronage.

By the end of the War of 1914-1918, the growth of modern nationalistic feeling was in full swing. The break-up of the Turkish Empire marked the end of the old order in the Near and Middle East ; the constitutional struggle was soon to develop intensely in India ; China and Japan were in various stages of national growth, internal coherence or assertiveness. But a totally new factor was introduced by the creation of the League of Nations. This raised the question of the ultimate meaning and possible limitations of national sovereignty, but this proved incapable of solution. After the war of 1939-1945, the same question remained and, in the view of many, is still the most crucial single one in this field. All nations claim the right of national self-government but, through the United Nations, an attempt has been made to secure adhesion to certain standards of conduct, and to provide, in some cases, for measures by which they will be observed. But the difficulty of reconciling national sovereignty with international obligations is still unsolved in practice.

It seems inadvisable that reliance should be placed on the direct intervention of any one nation in order to sustain the principles of Christian action in the affairs of other states. Politically it is impracticable and, religiously, it is a principle of inadequate strength and justice. If, in special cases, pressure is to be brought from outside on any nation to ensure the fulfilment of agreed standards of human rights, it should only be through the process of representation at the United Nations and its specialised agencies, and through other appropriate international institutions. The times are past when any one or more nations can, or should, assume the position of advocates of special privilege or status for Christians or for churches. The fact must be faced that the modern atmosphere of cultural relativism and the sanctity accorded to national autonomy make this difficult. But the dangers of the present international situation must be taken into full account. The Charter of the United Nations is not regarded by most Christians as an ideal international instrument : it represents, as was plainly stated at the time, what was possible under all the circumstances. Moreover, it is as well to remember that a great war necessarily undermines the effective moral assumptions current in international relations. The success of force, however justified, breeds respect for force. The repudiation of accepted codes under the supposed necessity of circumstance, and the pressure to sacrifice standards of moral conduct for the sake of victory, lower the temperature of international sensitivity. The public conscience becomes hardened, and the motive of self-interest, always dominant, becomes overpowering. When even the strong are preoccupied with the problem of survival, the rights and liberties of the weak receive scant respect. While, on the one hand, it should be recognised that in such an atmosphere it is sheer optimism to expect that the representations of churchmen will easily result in positive and favourable action, on the other hand it should be remembered that the calculation of immediate success or failure is not for Christians decisive.

It is pertinent to ask whether the churches are equipped to maintain in this field the activity necessary to make their influence felt. Theoretically, there is no reason why they should not be. The expansion of Christianity, the leadership which the churches possess, and the basic assumptions of the Christian Faith are all assets. The formation of the World Council of Churches has come at a time when not only the internal consciousness of the churches has demanded it, but when also the external situation may only be susceptible to a central and united approach. The younger churches may express their concerns through the International Missionary Council as well as the World Council. Moreover, ever since the Edinburgh Conference of 1910 the churches have been at work improving their own techniques of co-operation across the boundaries of the nations and the divisions imposed by their own traditions. More recently (1946) these two representative bodies have combined to establish a Commission of the Churches on International Affairs.[1]

But certain conditions must be observed if Christian action in international affairs is to be appropriate. It is important to decide whether, in general, the churches should pursue those requisites which belong especially to their own life or should immerse themselves in the struggle to secure the general conditions which they believe to be essential to the well-being of the peoples. Should they concentrate on the fight to obtain effective guarantees, and the effective practice of religious liberties, or should they join with all those who are promoting a general and effective Bill of Human Rights? Should they seek privileges for any religious minority, Christian, Moslem, Jewish or other, or should they advocate the acceptance of a general standard and formulate a broad policy accordingly? It will probably be agreed that they should not be concerned to seek any privileges at all, but such rights as all men should enjoy; but when energies and resources are limited there will be differences of opinion over the priorities. It may be argued that unless the churches protect their own interests, no one else will do so. But the churches do not have interests which they do not earnestly desire to share with all men. In the long run, therefore, they may be well advised to pursue a standard of general human rights to which at least all members of the United Nations will be expected

[1] For a review of its programme and work, see Section 3, p. 37

to conform. But, within such a programme, the rights and liberties of special value to organised religion are committed to their special care.

Agreed provisions could only express the churches' policy in the limited field discussed. If the concern of the churches is with such matters as disarmament, the conditions of dependent peoples, the assumption of a true international culture and a host of other questions, it is clear that agreement could only be reached among the churches on very general statements. This is not to say that the churches cannot take any action, but it is often the case that the most effective action in such negotiations is not inspired by any very clear or detailed understanding of policy. It is impossible to lay down hard-and-fast rules in advance for the elaboration of the best procedure. Every situation requires to be studied on its own merits and with reference to its own importance and the vigour and weight of the forces which seek to control it. All that can be done here is to point to some of the various approaches which may have to be followed.

It is a commonplace that the soundness of a policy depends largely on accurate, continuous and up-to-date intelligence. Large sums are spent by the departments of external affairs of the governments of the world, and millions of cabled words translated into cypher or code in order that the policies of states may be perceived, the state of public opinion foreshadowed and the probable moves in the game correctly estimated. Much of this work of accumulating information and compiling intelligence must be done with great secrecy : no reasonable person would expect it to be a transaction of the market-place. It is not suggested that the churches should imitate such a system. It would be contrary to their habitual outlook and would require expenditure which they ought not to contemplate when the more urgent primary needs of mankind are so largely unsatisfied. Nor would the situations which the churches may be called upon to consider usually be such as to require so elaborate an apparatus.

It is nevertheless true that to determine policy in any situation without good intelligence is to court disaster from the start : it implies what is too often true, that the churches underrate the resources both of governments and of other organisations in the field. The churches are not badly equipped for the development of a centralised system of necessary intelligence. Their own members are scattered throughout the world. In their ranks are found persons of judgment and experience in contact with many aspects of the national life and capable of forming reliable estimates on the trend of official policy and the real outlook of different sections of the people. The churches naturally speak with authority and understanding on the movements of religious thought and the temper of the religious life. But if they are to render good service to internal relations, it is essential that their analysis should not be vitiated by undue optimism or over-simplification.

An international Christian body equipped with a good service of intelligence from informed church sources on matters which by general consent touched immediately the Christian conscience might render useful service. This would be enhanced if such intelligence proved to be a reliable shadow of events actually to come—but prophecy is dangerous because it is usually misleading. Anyhow, a really adequate scheme could hardly be envisaged as it would require a central staff, for the digestion of material, which could not be provided without considerable resources. At present the opposite error is frequently inevitable. Action is frequently suggested at the last moment and backed up by a presentation of the case that may be informative and accurate to men on the spot, but unconvincing to men off it. Time is not allowed for facing coolly the objections that those less interested in the cause of religion may very properly raise, and, in fine, the case proves difficult to sustain.

But information is not enough, either for governments or for churches. Wisdom is as essential as knowledge, and no amount of knowledge evaluated and analysed within a pattern of reference of secular pragmatism can provide sound policy. A Christian understanding of history is fully as important as political science for understanding the behaviour of people. Consequently, the churches should give attention to supplementing the competence of governments rather than to attempting to duplicate it.

But to possess the facts and understand them and leave it at that is inexcusable in a world where anxiety is more common than hope, and war easier to organise than peace. Action can take one or all of six forms—prayer, negotiation, consultation, reconciliation, education and publicity.

A. *Prayer*

It is a duty of Christians to pray for constituted authorities and for international bodies, and if it sometimes seems all that can be done it is never the least important thing to do. The efficacy of prayer should not be questioned, for not only does Biblical history testify to the influence of prayer upon political events, but also the experience of present-day Christians corroborates the faith of prophets, apostles and martyrs who called upon God in prayer. Spiritual forces are liberated by prayer which create peace and destroy evil.

B. *Negotiation*

Action through negotiation can take various forms. An international, non-governmental body, as is the World Council of Churches, can properly negotiate directly with international organisations, the United Nations and its specialised agencies including such bodies as UNESCO, the International Labour Office, the International Refugee Organisation and others. These bodies sometimes have, as in the case of the Economic and Social Council of the United Nations, elaborate provisions for co-operation in certain questions with the non-governmental organisations. In other cases they allow for the appearance of recognised observers at conferences and for consultative committees of a " mixed " type when non-governmental representation may be admitted. It can be determined only by a careful examination in each separate case whether the churches, through the World Council of Churches or any body acting on its behalf, should avail themselves of these opportunities. On the one hand, the expenditure of mind and time may be considerable if policy is to be thoroughly and continuously discussed and the churches' viewpoint effectively pressed. On the other hand, it is useless to complain afterwards that the process of international debate and possible agreement has ignored the legitimate interests of the churches, if use has not been made of the openings afforded for representation.

There are, however, many questions which are not international in the broad sense: they only concern the interests of one or two countries or are matters which are most likely to be settled by negotiation between two or three states or powers, without being raised at the United Nations or its councils and specialised agencies. In such cases, if action is to be taken by the churches at all, it is often better taken by the competent representative national organisation, by national councils of churches, or one influential church. If such matters are raised with the World Council of Churches or any of its agencies, it may or may not be desirable for the World Council or the appropriate committee to express an opinion, but it is usually proper to refer action to the national church bodies concerned. This is not a universal procedure, but unless it were clearly evident that agreed Christian principle had been flagrantly transgressed, it is difficult for a body such as the World Council to press for any particular solution. The same principle usually applies to the not infrequent case of an appeal by a Christian minority against a constitutional injustice. It may be possible for the World Council to have the matter raised at the United Nations, but frequently the only remedy lies in access to the seat of power of the one or two countries concerned.

C. *Consultation*

Consultation with those directly responsible for governmental policy and action is generally more appropriate and effective than formal negotiation. Or it may be a correlative to negotiation. A conference, formal or informal, of a church leader or group of leaders with government officials provides an opportunity to ask questions and offer suggestions and warnings which may correct perspective, deepen insight, or call attention to a neglected interest. It may serve also to inform the churchmen and to increase their understanding of the government.

Consultation may also serve to encourage the responsible government leaders to give due weight to Christian considerations, including the wider interests of humanity. Such leaders are under constant pressure from groups seeking to further their own interests. They are also under pressure to serve the immediate and obvious interests of the state to the neglect of the welfare of other peoples. One of the functions of the Church is to keep the leaders of the state under tension in the face of the demands of the moral law, lest the necessary compromise in political action go farther than is necessary in the direction of mere expediency and so bring disaster. Moreover, public leaders need to be assured that, in their highest purposes, they have the fellowship and support of the Christian forces. A consultative visit may be more helpful than a carefully formulated petition.

D. *Reconciliation*

The churches in their own life, relationships and behaviour can set an example of reconciliation for the world of nations. This example may have a more persuasive influence on international affairs than hortatory resolutions. On at least these three propositions there is widespread agreement : (1) The several churches, in their relationships and in their life as members of a world-wide fellowship, should give a demonstration of the achievement of an orderly and mutually helpful community. The basic problem of world order is that of achieving world community in a moral or spiritual sense. This requires that peoples of different nations, races and cultures should learn to live together as members of a community. If the churches in their fellowship can achieve mutual understanding and community of essential purpose, they can bind the world together and thus build the necessary foundations for political order. (2) The churches in the ecumenical fellowship should achieve common agreement on the basic moral principles of national and international policy inherent in their common faith. Such agreement among the peoples of various nations, races and cultures is the basic need of the world to-day. Moreover, the aggressive promulgation of such principles is generally the most appropriate and most effective way of influencing and guiding political policies. (3) The churches of various communions and in all nations should continue and enlarge their programme of mutual aid, bearing one another's burdens. By extending assistance in relief and reconstruction across national, racial and ecclesiastical boundaries, Christians show the better way, strengthen faith, and further reconciliation.

E. *Education*

Education is another form of action. The churches have a responsibility for educating and influencing public opinion concerning the basic ethical and moral principles which should underlie national policy with regard to international relations. The basic Christian principle that all men are brothers presupposes the need of educating mankind in the recognition of the great human family. The churches should urge upon their members especially the acceptance of the responsibilities of Christain vocation in citizenship which requires (1) that the individual, on the basis of his enlightened Christian judgment, support as a citizen those national policies which most closely approximate to an application of Christian principles and oppose measures that are objectionable ; and (2) that he vote for, and support, public leaders who are committed to such policies. The educational programme may include the publication of analyses of current government policies in the light of Christian principles.

F. *Publicity*

The value of publicity in relation to international questions varies enormously from one country to another. In the United States, for example, it is relatively easy to secure and the American people are influenced by publicity when it is done with skill. The public nature of modern official conferences creates an atmosphere which is favourable to the use of publicity. But it is precisely in countries where publicity might be most helpful that it is impossible to secure. There are usually one or more of four reasons for this. Either the Press and radio are strictly controlled by the authorities and access cannot be had by unofficial bodies ; or the question which may be of great importance to the Christian community has little or no general appeal ; or editors and radio directors wish to avoid controversy ; or the churches, representing only a small minority ; are unable to carry the necessary influence.

3. THE COMMISSION OF THE CHURCHES ON INTERNATIONAL AFFAIRS

Effective Christian action in international affairs calls for an organisation which will give due regard to the responsibilities of churches in different countries and which will at the same time capitalise on the world-wide resources of non-Roman Christianity. A brief description of work now being carried on under international Christian auspices may serve as a basis for fashioning a plan for further procedure.

The Commission of the Churches on International Affairs (C.C.I.A.) has been set up jointly by the World Council of Churches and the International Missionary Council to work on their behalf in the field of international affairs. The Commission was established at a conference at Cambridge, England, in 1946. It consists of twenty-eight members in different countries of the world, many of whom are laymen. While the duties of the Commission member have not been formally

specified, initial experience has suggested the following functions :
(a) to correspond with the officers of the Commission, drawing
their attention to matters which call for study or possible action
and advising them on relevant data ; (b) to co-operate with
recognised church agencies and committees in his own country
in educating public opinion or in making representation to
public authorities on matters in the international sphere that are
of concern to the Christian conscience ; and (c) to participate in
duly convened meetings of the Commission.

The primary responsibility of the Commission is to serve the
churches, councils ; and conferences which are members of the
World Council of Churches and the International Missionary
Council as a source of stimulus and knowledge in their approach
to international problems, as a medium of common counsel and
action, and as their organ in formulating the Christian mind on
world issues, and in bringing that mind effectively to bear upon
such issues. The specific purposes of the Commission are
defined in the statement which was adopted at Cambridge and
subsequently approved by the parent bodies. (See Appendix
A.) In accordance with these provisions, the Commission, which
has offices in London and New York, has begun the work
committed to it.

Contacts with International Authorities

Contact with the United Nations and its organs is maintained
in two ways. The Commission is officially registered with the
United Nations Department of Public Information at its New
York headquarters ; by this provision it regularly receives all
unrestricted documents and is entitled to be represented by an
observer at all open meetings. The documents are catalogued
and filed daily with a view to communicating any items of
importance to appropriate church leaders or agencies. A staff
member of the C.C.I.A. attends most of the United Nations
meetings where matters of concern to the churches are under
discussion. Moreover, the Commission holds consultative status
with the Economic and Social Council (Category B), as provided
under Article 71 of the United Nations Charter and is represented by an officially accredited consultant. This offers a
channel for bringing to the Council and its commissions any
views which the Churches' Commission itself may desire to
submit or which churches request it to transmit.

Contact is further maintained 'with related and specialised agencies. Through arrangements at the London office, the Commission has been represented by an observer at the Paris and Mexico City Conferences of the United Nations Educational, Scientific and Cultural Organisation and has maintained continuing contact with the work of this agency. While such informal, friendly relations have proved helpful, there are strong arguments favouring a more formal relationship in accordance with arrangements which UNESCO has set up. Through unofficial relationships at London and Montreal, the Churches' Commission has also followed the activities of the International Labour Office.

National or Local Commissions

It was recognised at Cambridge that the strength of international Christian action in international affairs would be in proportion to the interest and activity of the churches in their national settings. In accordance with the first aim of its Charter, the Commission has sought to encourage the formation of national commissions through which the conscience of Christians may be stirred and educated as to their responsibilities in the world of nations. The World Council of Churches and the International Missionary Council supplied lists of addresses, including existing ecumenical committees, Christian councils, correspondents, and the like. Circular letters and inquiry forms were sent to these inviting their advice on the best means of establishing contacts within their particular countries.

Nine national commissions concerned with international affairs are now known to be in existence, and one has been authorised but not yet established. In sixteen countries, correspondents have been appointed, either provisionally or by official church bodies, to serve as a point of contact with the international Commission. In a few countries two correspondents have been named to care for the local church and the missionary interests. Where commissions have not yet been set up and correspondents not yet named, church leaders, including members of the C.C.I.A., have been temporarily designated to receive communications and to refer them for study and action to the proper agencies of the churches. While the results thus far achieved by letters are encouraging, there is general agreement on the need to strengthen and extend these contacts through personal visits.

Information to the Churches

Utilising the points of contact thus provided, the officers of the Commission have sought to keep its constituency informed about its activities. They have brought to the attention of the churches certain issues with which Christians were apparently concerned or on which judgment could helpfully be expressed. Memoranda on United Nations activities in the field of human rights and on the general work of UNESCO have been distributed. Information has been sent out covering the decisions of the United Nations General Assembly and of other organs. A few statements by national church commissions have been circulated.

Particular attention has been given to the process of writing an International Bill of Human Rights. Drafts of the first Working Papers for a Declaration and Convention, prepared by a United Nations drafting committee, were widely distributed and critical reactions solicited. Similarly, the draft Declaration and Covenant prepared by the United Nations Commission on Human Rights at Geneva in December, 1947, were forwarded to church leaders in over forty countries with a request for appraisal.

It should be recognised that only a meagre beginning has been made in the effort to keep the churches informed about international developments. While the contacts with the United Nations and related agencies make available relatively full information, the resources of the Commission have been inadequate for necessary analysis and distribution.

Representation to International Authorities

By its Charter, the Commission of the Churches is authorised to represent its constituency before international bodies such as the United Nations and related agencies. The contacts which the Commission maintains with the United Nations, particularly by virtue of its consultative status with the Economic and Social Council, open the way for a ready transmission of Christian views. In a few instances, the officers have presented to the Secretariat of the United Nations statements which were formally adopted by national church bodies or by their officially constituted departments. Since the Commission is known to represent many churches throughout the world, such transmission has been possible on behalf of a single church group without implicating others or the parent bodies.

In only one field—human rights and, more particularly, religious freedom—has there been sufficient evidence of a common mind to enable the Commission to speak directly on behalf of the churches. Here it drew upon statements of the Oxford and Madras Conferences, current actions by officially constituted groups of the World Council and the International Missionary Council, and the replies received from critical study of the draft Declaration and Convention on Human Rights. As a result of this representation, numerous changes were brought about at the next stage of drafting : the United Nations proposals for provisions to safeguard religious freedom and related human rights, as provisionally accepted in the Geneva drafts of the Declaration and Covenant, conform closely to the position taken by representatives of the churches. On behalf of the Commission, the Executive Chairman and the Director addressed a letter to the Secretary-General of the United Nations urging prompt action on a convention to outlaw genocide.

On many other subjects where an expression of Christian opinion could reasonably be expected, the Commission has been unable to take a stand, primarily because (1) the churches have not formulated the general principles to express a Christian mind on these subjects ; and (2) the speed with which action was required could not be matched by the present facilities for communication with churches all over the world. However, by processes of informal consultation and clearly without commitment of the Commission or its constituency, officers of the Commission have conferred with officials of the United Nations and related bodies on numerous matters in which the churches are vitally interested.

Action by Separate Church Groups

As occasion demanded, churches in various countries have taken independent action on problems of international relations or have communicated directly with their own governments. In a number of cases, the Churches' Commission on International Affairs has brought problems with relevant information to the attention of various agencies of the churches of their national councils, and constructive steps have followed. A limited number of issues are here cited to illustrate this type of procedure : (1) revision of original Trusteeship Agreements to include more adequate safeguards for religious liberty and missionary freedom ; (2) provisions for human rights with special reference to religious freedom in treaties with the Axis satellite powers ; (3) consideration of the Palestine problem, to make available important information and to stress especially the historical and contemporary interests of the Christian community ; (4) investigation of the refugee problem with a view to possible representation by the C.C.I.A. when the basic information had been compiled by·the Ecumenical Refugee Commission ; (5) provisions for religious freedom in the Italian constitution and the import of these in face of discriminatory articles in the Lateran Pacts ; (6) the alleged treatment of natives in S.W. Africa ; (7) violations of religious freedom in Spain ; (8) protection of German missionary property and the status of German missionaries ; (9) general problems of the peace settlement with Germany, with special reference to human rights.

International issues will continue to arise in which Christians in one or another country have particular interest or peculiar competence.   Moreover, many problems will appear on which a common world Christian mind is difficult to reach, or to reach rapidly enough.   While international Christian action must be sought wherever imperative and feasible, the procedure through separate church agencies or national churches will obviously play an important part.

Study Programme

The Commission of the Churches on International Affairs has been made responsible for special studies on international issues in preparation for the Amsterdam meeting and, in that connection, has served as Commission IV of the study programme.   This assignment has involved considerable time and effort, as well as correspondence and travel.   Little opportunity has been at hand for additional investigations.   However, the Commission has under consideration various studies, among which those projected in co-operation with the Younger Churches of the Far East hold a prominent place.

This report is in no sense an exhaustive description of the work thus far attempted under the auspices of the Commission of the Churches on International Affairs.   While it recounts in part what has been undertaken, it is intended primarily to illustrate a programme which, with necessary modifications, will permit Christian testimony in current world affairs. The examples cited are largely within the types of action described above as negotiation, consultation and education, but prayer, reconciliation and publicity have played an important part. The churches will have to decide whether the kind of organisation here projected and the kind of work here done represent the manner in which their responsibility can be most adequately met. They will further have to decide whether their activities in the field of international relations shall be carried on at a minimum level, or whether the resources which they make available shall be more nearly in proportion to the gigantic nature of the task.

All private bodies dealing with international affairs are at a disadvantage in matters of technical skill and information compared with official ones. The expansive strength of bureaucracy, the discipline of organised departments of state in the best civil services, and the quality of personnel employed, give governments a long lead. This is increased by lavish expenditure on cables, transport and accommodation. Even so, their achievements leave something to be desired. On the other hand, the churches enjoy the advantages of clearly defined and limited aims, of spiritual cohesion and world-wide extension, and of the service of mind and heart which derives from deeply-felt loyalties. It should not be impossible to devise means to use these assets to the best advantage in a world which sorely needs justice between the nations and mercy between men.

APPENDIX A

CHARTER OF THE COMMISSION OF THE CHURCHES ON INTERNATIONAL AFFAIRS

The primary responsibility of the Commission on International Affairs shall be to serve the Churches, Councils and Conferences which are members of the World Council of Churches and the International Missionary Council, as a source of stimulus and knowledge in their approach to international problems, as a medium of common counsel and action, and as their organ in formulating the Christian mind on world issues and in bringing that mind effectively to bear upon such issues. More particularly, it shall be the aim of the Commission :

1. To encourage the formation, in each country and in each church represented in the parent bodies, of commissions through which the consciences of Christians may be stirred and educated as to their responsibilities in the world of nations.

The influence of Christians upon international problems must be made effective mainly through individual governments and inasmuch as the relation of public opinion to official action varies, the methods of expressing this influence will vary. It must be a major purpose of the Commission to assist churches in the several lands to express their judgments on world issues to their governments.

2. To gather and appraise materials on the relations of the churches to public affairs, including the work of various churches and church councils in these fields and to make the best of this material available to its constituent churches.

Thus the Commission will draw spiritual sustenance from our Christian people. If the Commission is to be an effective body, there must be channels through which the hopes and fears of Christian people can flow into the Commission, and through it to Christians in other lands.

3. To study selected problems of international justice and world order, including economic and social questions, and to make the results of such study widely known among all the churches.

Only a limited number of carefully chosen problems can be given the thorough study required. Such study should utilise the best available thought from any quarter, should seek counsel of informed experts, and should bring to bear on the problems insights derived from Christian faith.

4. To assign specific responsibilities and studies to sub-committees or special groups, and to claim for them the assistance of persons especially expert in the problems under consideration.

Much of the Commission's most important work will have to be done through groups, smaller and more readily accessible than the Commission as a whole. Special effort should be directed to assure that such sub-committees, while necessarily limited in scope of membership, shall be as fully representative as possible.

5. To organise study conferences of leaders of different churches and nations.

Through such conferences, meeting in an atmosphere of Christian fellowship, significant Christian judgment on international issues may be reached, and the work of the churches in the several nations may be guided and advanced.

6. To call the attention of the churches to problems especially claimant upon the Christian conscience at any particular time, and to suggest ways in which Christians may act effectively upon these problems, in their respective countries and internationally.

7. To discover and declare Christian principles with direct relevance to the relations of nations, and to formulate the bearing of these principles upon immediate issues.

In preparing and issuing public declarations, the Commission should build upon the results of earlier work by the parent bodies in this field, such as the Stockholm, Jerusalem, Oxford, and Madras Conferences. In general, the character and scope of such declarations may well follow the general lines thus established. More specifically :

(a) When the World Council of Churches or the International Missionary Council as a whole is meeting, in an Assembly, conference, or committee, the Commission might recommend statements which, if adopted, would have importance as representative of Christian opinion (outside Roman Catholicism) all over the world.

(b) Since the Councils meet infrequently, the Commission on International Affairs would, in the interim, have liberty to speak in its own name, making clear that the Councils had not endorsed the statement.

(c) If occasions arise in which the officers or sub-committees of the Commission feel impelled to speak without waiting for consultation with the Commission as a whole, they should make clear that they are not committing any group other than themselves.

8. To represent the World Council of Churches and the International Missionary Council in relations with international bodies such as the United Nations and related agencies.

The Commission should maintain such contacts with these bodies as will assist in :

(a) the progressive development and codification of international law ;

(b) the encouragement of respect for and observance of human rights and fundamental freedoms ; special attention being given to the problem of religious liberty ;

(c) the international regulation of armaments ;

(d) the furtherance of international economic co-operation ;

(e) the acceptance by all nations of the obligation to promote to the utmost the well-being of dependent peoples, including their advance toward self-government and the development of their free political institutions ;

(f) the promotion of international social, cultural, educational and humanitarian enterprises.

9. To concert from time to time with other organisations holding similar objectives in the advancement of particular ends.

III

THE CHURCH AND THE DISORDER OF INTERNATIONAL SOCIETY

F. M. Van Asbeck

I. THE TASK AND ATTITUDE OF THE CHURCH

WE speak of the task of the Church, of the word of the Church, of its message, its power and weakness, and of its guilt. In the international field especially, where we are concerned with different nations and with the different churches of non-Roman Catholic creed, where we cross frontiers and denominations, the question is forced upon us : What do we mean in using the word " Church ? " In these contexts " The Church " does not mean the sum of all the existing churches, nor the *Una Sancta* itself. In the words " The Church " we express our firm belief in a new reality, which is taking form and substance in the efforts of the different churches to reach, through all divergencies of opinions and attitudes, theological and ethical, a consensus concerning the central and vital problems of the present.

That new reality, the ecumenical fellowship, compels us to reconsider and to re-think international relations, in the midst of which the Divine Message has to be proclaimed and the outlook towards the *Una Sancta* kept open. In all its preaching, in all its admonitions and warnings, the Church has to be conscious of the existence of the *Una Sancta*, transcending all the cleavages and divergencies on earth. But it would be arrogant, godless presumption to equate our ecumenical fellowship with the *Una Sancta*, as though the Kingdom of Divine Love were already present in this world.

New theological reflection leads to new concrete and practical conclusions on the relations between Church and world, and on the witness of the Church. The Church cannot keep silent upon the conclusions arising from its reconsideration of world affairs.

The world wars have shaken the conscience of the churches and roused them to a clearer perception of their task in the international sphere ; of their special responsibility for the founding and the foundations of a world order, in which all the peoples of the earth may " lead a tranquil life " (1 Tim. ii, 2). Till the first world war the Church had almost totally neglected its duty towards the international society ; and even after that pandemonium its response to the burning questions of international order, authority and liberty was at first lamentably weak. This plain default of the Church, however, can be explained, though certainly not justified, by the general conception of international questions as " *arcana imperii*," as the private preserve of the governments of the so-called sovereign states, and in particular of the Great Powers. Ordinary men, so doctrine and practice since the eighteenth century have taught us, have no legal standing in, and no concern with international relations and their law (or lack of law). They were only " objects " of that peculiar branch of law, debarred from a voice in its application, from judgment and criticism. The same passive rôle was assigned to the churches, and they acquiesced—that was their fault. The Church, then, has been unfaithful to its divine vocation of proclaiming the gospel to the powers of the world in their dealings and decisions, of exhorting and warning them. It has failed to subject the international society to the test of the Christian message; it has not risen above national conceptions, national interests, judging them all in the light of God's revelation. In so behaving the Church lost the confidence of many but, worse, it failed to bring its own unique contribution to the founding of peace and justice between the nations.

Since Oxford 1937[1] the Church has been painfully aware of opportunities missed, of tasks neglected, and of its sin against its Lord. And it cannot give more sincere proof of repentance and conversion than by applying itself now to its full task in the international field, that of proclaiming God's Holy Will for or even *against* the world of nations.

In this task the Church has to recognise its limitations : the Church is neither competent nor called to recommend concrete decisions in the international field. Individual Church-members may do so in virtue of their personal knowledge and competence, and it is their high duty to fulfil this task according to their lights. In the present time of searching for new solutions the duty of the Church towards those members is to bring them

[1] It is very important to re-read, in connection with this paper, the relevant part of the report of the Oxford Conference (*The Churches Survey their Task*, pp. 167-187).

together in order to deepen and strengthen their testimony. As a body the Church has another, a higher, a spiritual task; that is, to put relations, situations, facts in the light of the biblical message, to throw new light upon them from that eternal source. This is the inalienable contribution of the " *Oikumene* " towards the re-ordering of this world ; it is at the same time a task of unparalleled difficulty and magnitude : to point out the sole foundation, namely, that God, Creator of heaven and earth, is the Lord of all the nations and their governments—" the earth belongs to the Eternal, all earth holds, the world and its inhabitants " (Ps. xxiv, Moffatt translation). He who has delivered us and who will continually deliver us from all evil, He who has given peace unto us and who requires peace from us in this world, requires fervent and continual prayer for peace and justice. It is the Church's duty to translate the meaning of the words of Micah vi, 8 into various spheres of life, and to proclaim this message on the foundation that its Lord Jesus Christ is the real Lord of the world ; to Him ". . . full authority has been given in heaven and on earth " (Matthew xxviii, 18, Moffatt translation), and His authority calls all worldly authority, all powers, all thrones, all governments to account, and passes judgment on them by the standards of justice and mercy. The Church, itself human and frail, can know in the light of Christ's authority the treasures of obedience and faithfulness. It is its solemn task and responsibility to proclaim Christ's universal authority in the society of nations also and to offer its treasures to it.

In the world of nations the Church has a wider field to till than specific Church—and mission—interests. The establishment of a real international order on the foundation of justice and law must claim a prominent place in its concern, an order for all men, irrespective of origin, race, creed, nationality or class.

Wherever this task of proclamation, of exhortation and warning is neglected, especially in the field of international relations, the highest court of appeal against worldly authority, against might and power of whatever nature and substance, collapses, and all curbs and checks on the use of power disappear. The absence of such appeal, of checks and restraints, means that there and then the way lies open to a totalitarian régime of any type—even a democratic type which may conceal a dictatorship of mighty material or non-material interests. That is why freedom of creed and cult constitutes the very foundation of any legal order, including the international.

Whenever the Church speaks, it must, in order that its word be effective and practical, have a clear vision of the world, in the midst of which it speaks, and to which it addresses its word, and a clear knowledge of facts and currents, fancies and motives, secret or open. The Church must know and take into account, first, the character and the organisation of the world society to-day and the mechanism of its behaviour ; second, the actual, concrete tensions and adjustments, conflicts and co-ordinations such as : problems of transition from war to peace, the spirit and attitude of the Great Powers, the supply of primary necessities, the German problem, the poverty and weakness of Europe, the race problem, the colonial problem, the Jewish problem and Palestine, the confrontation of Christendom and Islam, protection of minorities, and a host of other problems.

2. THE CHARACTER AND ORGANISATION OF WORLD SOCIETY

When speaking of our present-day world affairs, what do we mean by advocating the establishment of an international legal order ? What is the significance and the rôle therein of national sovereignty ? What should be the relation between power and law under such an order ? What of an international authority ? All those questions need reflection and rethinking in the Church, for at every moment, in its action and in its silence, the Church will be confronted with them.

The apostle Paul (1 Cor. xiv, 33, Moffatt) makes a sharp contrast between disorder and harmony, saying that God is a God not of disorder but of harmony. In the international sphere war is in sharp contrast to peace. War means disorder, it is the very negation of a legal order. " Peace " translates in the international sphere Paul's " Harmony " ; it is the worldly aspect of harmony, for the word means the compacting or fitting together of views and interests, attitudes and behaviour into a stable whole. Peace is something very much more profound than non-violence, non-war. Peace in the international world is only present where and when men are earnestly, sincerely striving to attain and to maintain a legal order. We cannot, and we should not, in this earthly dispensation, deny the existence of opposition, of clashes of power ; but over and against them we should affirm, and surely the Church should affirm, the paramount obligation of maintaining and strengthening a legal order above states and nations, under which differences may be solved, clashes prevented, and in which power finds its right place.

Now, an " order " presupposes a permanent relationship and hierarchy, like the " orders " of animals and plants in biology. A legal order means such a relationship and hierarchy in human interests and values, determined as far as possible by an unselfish agency, following a settled method controlled by standards of justice, not by temporary and casual power-relations, in the interests of the deciding person or group. A biological " order " is purely descriptive, a legal order has to fulfil a purpose, has to give a meaning to the life of its participants, which is always and everywhere in the last resort the protection and fostering of human physical and spiritual life, in order that men may develop all the gifts God gave them, for His glory and His Kingdom. The international legal order has to fulfil this purpose in all relations which extend beyond the frontiers of national communities.

To understand the world society of to-day it is indispensable to keep in sight the following main characteristic.[1] In that society various religions, social conceptions, legal orders, ideologies, exist side by side, insulated or interrelated, some of them politically or even fundamentally disunited, connected by no common conviction ; and inseparably bound up with that pluriformity is a difference of economic systems and of standards of living.

For the world of states has not re-integrated itself into a " community " of states or nations since the mediæval " *corpus christianum* " disintegrated. It survived only as a rather loose " society," and the French appellation for the League of Nations, " Société des Nations,"[2] revealed in a striking manner its very nature. When at the end of the middle ages the " *corpus christianum* " of Europe broke up, the existing unity lost its common basis. That process went further and during the nineteenth century the society of states came to be suspended in the air of relative power. Since the nineteenth century we have

---

[1]Cf. the Oxford Report, pp. 171-174.
[2]Concerning the League of Nations, cf. the Oxford Report, p. 175.

been confronted with a new historical situation, viz., the existence side by side of isolated states, between which there is no moral or spiritual bond. Some rudiments of former conceptions survived, but less and less remained of such a common conviction regarding moral values as governs a homogeneous national community— a *pre-legal* " existential " decision (often taken unawares and so to say unconsciously) concerning the purposes of human life in society, a decision which for Christians derives from the Gospel and confronts us with the fundamental relationship between God and man, and between man and man as redeemed by Christ.

Indeed, between the states of the world in general, the essential conditions for a real " community " of nations have never been fulfilled; they lacked always and still lack the distinctive features of a true community : a pre-legal decision on its purpose and basic convictions ; the firm solidarity, transcending national interests, of purposes and attitudes and behaviour ; and, bound up with that solidarity, a binding authority. On the contrary, it has mostly been only the varying need of adjusting their parallel, or diverging, or even opposing national interests, or sometimes an acute common danger, which determined the weak inner cohesion of that society of states—notwithstanding some more or less fruitful endeavours towards a more solid structure, like some of the international administrative unions or the two Hague Courts of Arbitration and of Justice. The hierarchy of values and interests found —and still finds—its definite expression in the power of the single states or of their alliances and other combinations at any moment available, and in their potentiality in case of conflict ; it is not expressed in a principle based on moral and spiritual unity, in which power has found its right subordinate place. A solidarity, and consequently a community, in the true sense of that beautiful term, was and is found only in some of the partial or limited, regional or functional combinations of states, which live or act together on a common ground.

Looking at the world at large, we can only recognise that, since the first world war, conditions making for greater unity have deteriorated. For the superiority of the West, unquestioned up to 1914, exercised a certain levelling influence between the states of the world through the westernised upper classes of the non-European states. During the first war that superiority received a deadly blow ; new peoples came to the fore, dormant civilisations were awakened to a new life. And now after the second war, bringing strengthened nationalisms and new antagonisms in its train, the world stage is prepared for the interplay of four or five civilisations, which have practically no common ground. Within such a civilisation perhaps there will reaffirm itself or there may grow up a community of states, based upon common descent, a common creed, common conceptions, or perhaps upon a common hostility to some other group.

International society thus being still weak, there is no true authority above the states, nor even, save in the International Court of Justice, tentative beginnings of one. Such an authority would comprise—side by side with the existing governmental bodies, which are mostly exclusively composed of official representatives of the state-governments, acting generally, save in a few exceptions, under instructions from and responsible to them—bodies, which, although created by the states in a treaty or otherwise, would be composed of individual members, chosen for their personal competence and integrity, bodies which would function without any further intervention, instruction or approval by governments, as the direct organs *of the international society itself*. (Under the League of Nations, the Permanent Mandates Commission belonged to this category of supra-national organs, though acting only in an advisory capacity.) The present world society, however, shows only a juxtaposition of states and, except in the International Court, most of the international organs are composed of purely official representatives. Where the prominent rôle is played by the national state, and more particularly by the Great Powers which hold the limelight, intercourse between and co-operation of the states is carried on primarily to serve national interests. But we ought gratefully to record the growing discussion of subjects of common international interest. Nothing is gained by disguising patent facts ; even the *United Nations* constitutes only a loose *confederation*—although, especially in the cultural and social domains, a new outlook for integration of world society is opened up—for the United Nations itself does not rest upon a pre-legal decision, a common conviction of all its nations regarding moral values. It rests principally and overwhelmingly on the various, diverging, legal orders of the member-states ; it represents, itself, a political, unstable order, in which considerations of influence and power, only weakly restrained by conceptions of right and justice, define decisions and demarcate responsibilities.

This weakness of our world society manifests itself again in its law.[1] The law of the international society shows clearly the marks of a law lacking supra-national validity. It has retained the character of a private law contract between parties, although already some features of an institutional, a public rule of law are visible in the contractual form. However, institutional as over against contractual law requires the sanction of a firm authority over and above the " state parties." The states thus have the double task of implementing and executing the international rule and, at the same time, of establishing laws and maintaining law and order within their own society. Confronted with the huge problems of the international society, international law in most cases proved weak ; for in these great problems, involving the vital interests of states, governments, falling back on their national conceptions, decided according to their national views, pride, prejudices and convictions.[2]

The binding force, the power to effect order of international law has diminished rapidly since the decline of the so-called natural law of the Middle Ages and Renaissance, *pari passu* with the limitation of its sanctions to mere persuasion and self-help. The classical doctrine of international law went on to deny the binding force of that law, to destroy the subordination of sovereign states to international precepts, or propounded some formalistic theory which tried to combine fire and water, such as the formula of the self-limitation of states, which in fact is no limitation at all. The age of great uncertainty in all matters regarding international law, international authority, international obligation began. Our plight is, that even now, after two wars, we have not yet wholly overcome the fatal suggestions of the classical doctrine of international law, its insincerities, inconsistencies and uncertainties.

In consequence the sun in the solar system of world politics is still always the national state, called an independent and sovereign power and considered equal to its fifty or sixty partners. Here and there, for various political, social, economic, cultural purposes, there exist general unions ānd *ententes*, or regional understandings, various forms of international co-operation in special fields, closely or loosely knit. But even in the most

---

[1] Cf. the Oxford Report, pp. 174-5.
[2] Cf. the Oxford Report, p. 173.

modern mechanism for general co-operation between states, the United Nations, the national so-called sovereign state forms the foundation. It would not be otherwise possible to erect such a superstructure ; nevertheless the great central question for our generation remains this : What kind of relationships between member-states does this general organisation provide ? And can this organisation meet the growing needs of an inter-dependent world ?

The prominent rôle and unique significance of the national state finds a striking expression in the loyalty, that is the obedient subservience generally of man towards his state, his readiness for unlimited sacrifices on behalf of his state. Broadly speaking, loyalty found until the world war its highest expression and farthest extension in relation to a man's own country. His native land meant for him his social and spiritual home, a place of security as well as a source of inspiration. No such loyalty existed towards " humanity," towards his continent, nor even, save in exceptional periods, towards congenial nations. Now, the world war has given rise to a new sense of obligation, an obligation not felt towards one's native land directly, but towards the defence of human dignity. It was shown by the splendid acts of all those self-sacrificing men and women, who voluntarily enlisted against the " hostis generis humani," the foe of all mankind. Ths new, but as yet undeveloped, loyalty may prove an important element in a future, more integrated, world organisation. On the other hand we should not forget conscientious objectors[1] and the problems concerning loyalty, originating from their attitude, the age-long problems of the tension between loyalty towards God and towards Cæsar.

It is this leading rôle of the national state, which in ordinary and in legal speech is indicated by the word " sovereignty." In every community and in every society and in every group of men, there must be, unless it is to crumble to pieces, a central point of authority and power, towards which in time of decision, emergency and danger, people may turn their eyes, for which they will curb their personal wills. In the international sphere this pre-eminent place is still occupied by the national states, each acting by itself or in consultation with others, in ententes, in alliances. It is one of the main functions of the United Nations to provide a room and a table, around which national representa-

[1] Cf. the Oxford Report, pp. 178-183.

tives may promote the interest of all by frankly facing the threats to law and order. One of the chief needs of the world is that this work may be done in a manner and a spirit, adequate to the interests of the world *as a whole* and not only to the particular interests of one state or another or of a certain group. But as long as an effective authority above the states has not been installed, national authority will wish—in this disunited, unintegrated world—to control, as long as possible and to the utmost degree, political influence and power as well as the obedience of its citizens. So long as no international agencies exist, deemed worthy of confidence and invested with effective authority, the normal seat of authority will remain with the national state. Such agencies do not exist at the present moment. Least of all does the Security Council of the United Nations command confidence, nor has it effective authority, being hampered by the discord of those permanent members, from whose unity its practical measures must derive their very birth and efficiency. Sovereignty should mean, then, not unlimited power used and exercised according to the *bon plaisir* of the sovereign states, but, in the absence of effective supra-national authority, employment of state-competence and power, for the benefit of the world society, according to law and justice. Again it clearly appears that our world, as its primary social and political need, demands the gradual development and growing effect of true authorities above the states.

But that original sovereignty of the national state means indeed a temptation, especially, but not only, for the great states, who combine sovereignty with power, and are thereby in a position to use their high competence not for the benefit of the society of states, for the ordering of international life, but for selfish interests to the detriment of others or of the world as a whole. Such power may be exercised and applied by military means (but that looks too brutal nowadays and entails dangerous consequences), or by economic influence and pressure, open or disguised, or by the quite modern means of terrorism and of adroit, venomous propaganda.

The world of states is a hard, impersonal world, composed of impersonal, primarily self-regarding national states, which are entrusted with a splendid, most responsible task, but in its discharge have to be restrained by their subservience to a higher society ; and in the service of higher permanent interests, they must co-operate in a system of law and order. This demands a *legal* organisation which is more than a loose *political* co-operation *ad hoc*. The world has to combine all its efforts towards the founding and strengthening of an *institutional* organisation, based on a *common* principle. We are far away from, and not at all inclined to, the unitary world state, a leviathan which might crush the smaller states, and destroy all that is valuable in the life of all states, great and small.

That does not, however, imply that we have to sit down quietly and be content with the present imperfect organisation of our world, which is so poorly equipped for the handling of common interests. Up till now, generally speaking, the regulation of international interests lies in the hands of the states directly concerned, mostly without the concurrence of disinterested third party judgment ; though the United Nations are in a position to provide help if desirable, if only by means of friendly advice or indirect pressure from other governments. But governments they are, and as such must look first to their own national interests, and take into account possible repercussions of an attitude or a decision on other policies. The world still lacks an agency which will safeguard international interests on their own merits within the whole fabric of international life.

There lies the reason why change in inter-state law presents itself as a distinct and difficult problem. International law in its written form (in treaties and agreements, etc.) is for the most part not the expression by a superior authority of the common conscience of a community, as is national law in homogeneous states, but—especially in treaties of limited participation, and more particularly in so-called " political " treaties—a compromise between group-interests determined by their relative power.[1] Change under such circumstances means a new adjustment, to be negotiated by the parties directly interested, possibly under some pressure. In this respect the world needs a body higher than the single states, by which the fortuitous pressures might be institutionalised and constitutionally directed.

Again, the reference of international disputes to arbitration or judicial decision depends, save under the optional clause of the Statute of the International Court of Justice, upon the voluntary agreement of the parties concerned.

<hr/>

[1] See page 54 above.

Above all, the maintenance of international peace, of the embryonic international legal order, is closely interwoven with the protection of specific interests of individual states, and so depends upon their voluntary consent. No direction and no action come from a central agency of impartial, supra-national standing. So long as no such agency, disposing of effective force to uphold decisions and maintain order, has been created, in the last resort, the Great Powers feel that these tasks are their responsibility. There lies the cause of armaments and the armaments race, the increasing burden of which is shouldered in the belief that national security must be protected by national means. In a non-integrated society of states reduction of armaments seems an almost hopeless task, because, as history teaches us, it opens up at once questions of relative power between the big states. International security calls for international protection by international means, by pooling of defence-systems and defence-instruments, or rather, by the institution of a real international defence-system, aiming at security for the world *as a whole*. The United Nations Charter contains a relatively bold approach to such an international defence-system, but its realisation depends upon a preceding growth of the sense of interdependence rising to a supra-national level. And we have learned to regard an effective method of regulating international interests as a pre-condition of such a defence-system, which implies the discovery of a method for changing the existing law along peaceful paths (to which we invited attention a moment ago), or, in current language, for the settlement of disputes of a non-legal character.

We should not, however, close our eyes to some curious features of the complementary rôle of the Great Powers in the exercise of international authority. They have often furnished some substitute, though a weak one only, for a supra-national authority, in their hegemony in the world of States. More than a century ago that substitute could be discerned in the " Concert of Europe " consisting of the five Great Powers of that time ; to-day we all know the permanent members of the Security Council, whose hegemony, however, is distracted by their discord. Nevertheless, such hegemony, if justly and responsibly and consciously exercised, could develop into a kind of virtual supra-national authority. Hand in hand with it goes pressure, one of the instruments of that very primitive authority. But Great Powers being what they are, always provide a mixture of self-interest and of wider and higher interests, in which the former predominates.

The crux of our present-day world organisation lies in the canalisation of hegemony and pressure into some institution, even in a tentative, provisional form, of a real supra-national authority. Such a reform surpasses our imagination, but, nevertheless, is the major end which we seek to attain in our quest for peace, for an international legal order.

So long as the national state is the only basic sub-structure of the society of states, it seems natural that the agencies of that society should be composed by the governments, and consist of members designated as their representatives. It seems equally necessary, that the society should acquire its own, direct, autonomous organs for the handling of its common interests.

Therefore we come back to the question touched on above : whether in the organisation of world society we ought not to try to pass, with circumspection and discipline, but with courage and imaginativeness, from the present purely *confederate* to what might be called a more *federal* stage, in all those domains where common interests must have precedence over national group interests— even if it were provisionally only between those states whose life and work rest on a common basis of moral and spiritual values. In other words, must the governmental, the " official " principle be always or nearly always followed ? Or can there be found a *useful preparation of real supra-national authority* in connecting that governmental principle with what we might call the " popular " principle of inviting qualified persons to sit on international bodies, perhaps during an initial stage only in an advisory capacity ? This was done in the former Permanent Mandates Commission, and works in connection with the Executive Committee of the Food and Agriculture Organisation, or, in quite another field, the Research Council, auxiliary to the Caribbean Commission. It seems unfortunate that a body such as the Commission on Human Rights of the Economic and Social Council of the United Nations must, because of a general decision taken by that Council in 1946, consist only of governmental representatives, although each government indeed remains free to refrain from giving instructions to its delegate on the Commission.

It has been shown in the preceding argument, how and why the present world organisation is built on group-(state-) co-operation and group-representation. But it is a common lesson of experience in all parts of the world and in all walks of life, that a purely group-organisation always shows a tendency (for example in communal representation in colonial territories) to stiffen relations between men, to obliterate those general interests which transcend the group-interests, to diminish the chance of appeals to a higher justice than that of the groups, and to enhance the power of the mighty, or to produce a series of deadlocks.

The organisation of the United Nations, its possibilities, and also the weakness inherent in its almost purely governmental structure, has already come under review several times, in passing. As the United Nations is the most notable, the highest and most far-reaching attempt of our day in the search for an international order, in our quest for peace—as was the League of Nations in the inter-war period—it deserves our closest, most earnest and objective attention, and the strong support of the Church. It is of primary importance that we should be conscious of its value, and above.all of its limitations, in order neither to be unduly optimistic, nor perforce condemned to suffer a black disillusionment. The Church in particular should avoid ordinary optimism concerning this and other worldly affairs, knowing full well that man is a frail earthly vessel.

It is easy to underrate the value and importance of the United Nations when we look at the practical results it has achieved. Suppose for a moment, however, that the United Nations collapsed, our heavy loss would at once be apparent. It is, of course, too early as yet to draw up an exact balance-sheet of its achievements. Yet it is already certain that its Assembly is the most important gathering in the world for the exchange of thoughts and opinions, for reconciling interests, for the settlement of grievances and for the gradual upbuilding of an international order, precisely because it provides a forum for the nations, a meeting-place where they can learn to know each other better and thereby try to overcome their differences of basis and outlook. The Economic and Social Council, in its more limited membership, in its flexible decentralisation of business, through auxiliary commissions and the various specialised agencies, is capable of making a valuable contribution to the prevention of friction and conflict ; and the same applies to other permanent organs of the United Nations.

The attainment of satisfactory results, however, depends upon the fulfilment of two conditions : first, that governments and nations combine wholeheartedly in the earnest endeavour to make the noble preamble of the Charter a living reality instead of only another document ; and, second, that governments (until now the sole sub-structure of the Organisation) should spare no effort to draw their peoples into this international work.

What, then, are the limitations of the United Nations? They are many. But the principal limitations have their origin in the following causes. Firstly, that governments and peoples, in their practical behaviour, do not as yet seem to be entirely free from antiquated conceptions and obsolete legal theories on sovereignty : the Charter of the United Nations itself cuts through the old concepts and theories in many places, but its deadly weakness lies in the comprehensive veto provisions for the Security Council, securing to the Great Powers individually the unfettered appeal to their own sovereign judgment, maintaining by this privilege the old " halo " of unlimited sovereignty, and thus weakening the political integration of our world.

The second cause of limitation is this : The United Nations has maintained, up till now, an almost exclusively governmental structure in its organs. This structure appears, on the one hand, unavoidable in the present dispensation, because of the power-centres in the world. On the other hand it is a brake on the successful functioning of the United Nations organs, because its purely governmental organisation makes it susceptible to all the political influences which disturb the life of the nations.

Thirdly : the quasi-universality to which the United Nations tends is at once a source of strength and a cause of weakness. The world of nations having become a whole—still incoherent but nevertheless interrelated in several fields of action—the United Nations does indeed need that quasi-universality if practical and useful results are to be attained in those fields. But throwing together, as it does, states of unmistakably different character, it erects at the same time a barrier to strong and united action.

The absence or deficiency of a common " ethos " is indeed the basic cause of the weakness of the United Nations. As the members are so widely different, their differences in first principles, in outlook, in moral and spiritual convictions, are too glaring to be overlooked. Whenever those differences are overshadowed by the practical necessities and needs of the world, taken as a whole—*primum vivere*—the organs of the United Nations, working in their governmental structure, may arrive at voluntary common decisions, taken by governments in juxtaposition, by means of reciprocal consultation, persuasion and exchange of views, but not by a common superior authority.

On the other hand, in all cases where concerted action is dependent upon the existence of common moral and spiritual convictions, i.e., on a common " ethos," the unavoidable necessity appears of confining co-operation to a smaller circle of states and nations, who adhere to the same or to congenial principles of life and work ; a co-operation less universal, but precisely for that reason much more close and intense, which may find its effective expression in the unreserved handing-over to an impartial agency of the settlement of international interests between members of the group.   It will then be possible to try to form within such smaller circles common institutions which would be composed of men of expert knowledge and personal value, working independently of their governments.   Such institutions would lead their own corporate life in virtue of the confidence in the members of the group, but would be independent in their day-to-day activities.   The organisation of such groups of more closely associated peoples for specific purposes would seem to be all-important in the useful development of the United Nations ; and also, wherever possible, the range of such institutions, acting on their own authority and responsibility as organs auxiliary to governmental agencies, should be extended.

The question might now be asked : does all this mean that we have to strive for a " world government " ?   Yes, and no. If the expression " world government " has to be taken in the sense of a unitary government of the whole world on the pattern of national governments, clearly the answer must be " No." It must be emphasised that such a Leviathan would crush us all. But if this means stressing the need for a gradual building-up of a common authority in the appropriate fields of activity, the answer should be " Yes."   But we should avoid too ambitious schemes and high-flown terms such as " world government." We should be content with the unpretentious aim of a common authority to be set up in any and every field where the objectives and the moral structure of the participating states promise valuable practical results.   The United Nations must always be on the watch for opportunities of strengthening a more truly federal co-operation between states in a certain group, by their common subjection to a superior authority. This would help to remove obstacles which arise from the existence of national frontiers—the stereotyped tokens of isolated national spheres.

Such institutionalised co-operation would tend to strengthen security, to prepare the way for an international legal order and unity between nations, and provide an approach towards the unity of the " *Oikumene*."

All the preceding problems and questions are presented to our world with urgent intensity by the new weapons of mass destruction. Their discovery has again brought home to us—and this time in appalling explicitness—that the world in regard to armaments has grown into a whole, into a single scene of deadly peril for us all, that all the nations of the earth are forming now, even against their professed views and dealings, a community. And for what purpose? What community? Not a free, spiritual or social community for the service of peace and welfare, but an inescapable community of danger and fear. All that their growing interdependence has not been able to impress upon them, all that their interrelation of interests in other walks of life has not succeeded in creating, the modern means of mass destruction, of blowing up this earth created by God, are bringing into existence : namely, an unorganised community of eventual death and destruction, which, however, mankind either refuses to recognise or, by reason of its inveterate conceptions and its insuperable suspicions, can only dimly perceive.

Under this modern threat all questions of sovereignty, of autonomous national defence, take the aspect of a caricature, even in the case of the big powers. Now, in 1948, there has sprung into being one supra-national common concern, far elevated above national interests and national *noli me tangere* ; and the first task and prime responsibility of our disfigured, mutilated world, lies in the sincere facing of our exact situation as it is now and the bold endeavour to remould our world institutions so that they may become adequate to our wants. That is to say, that we resolve to build up, stone upon stone but at high speed, real supra-national authorities which can be effective in parrying the imminent danger, and in ensuring co-operation in the field of defence and armaments, and eventually restore security. In this field the world has to pass at one giant stride from the present loose confederation to a closer integration, into a community—

even if it is provisionally of limited interests only—bearing more distinctly federal marks. That implies a withdrawal of national governments in favour of an international authority, representing our world as a whole in its perilous plight. Indeed, the discovery of the means of mass destruction might constitute a blessing in disguise, if it could compel us to a reform which till now has been beyond our vision, but which in these days is imposed upon our faltering wills, if we are to preserve the lives and souls of fellow-creatures, of our brothers of whom each of us in turn is the keeper.

Let us meanwhile not forget the other, the brighter side of this medal : the new discoveries in the field of nuclear energy contain at the same time a promise of new possibilities for our distracted world, possibilities which in their turn can only be put to the service of the peoples of this earth by an agency which is able to protect our common interests, regarded and handled as belonging to the world as a whole.

Now let us look back for a moment at the ground we have tried to cover. The nations are living in an exceedingly pluriform society, strongly interdependent in interests, united *under*, not yet *by* a common menace, yet always still without a common moral and spiritual basis and without adequate institutions. The sense of obligation under a common international law, elevated above the fragmentary treaty-law, remained weak. A national obligation, expressed as loyalty to a man's own state, was recognised. On the other hand, an international obligation, which in its essence is a social obligation towards a community of nations, is mostly still lacking. What is the reason for this lack of a sense of international obligation, and for the consequent weakness of international law ? It is the absence of a supra-national community. Why is it that such a community is still non-existent in the world taken as a whole ? Here we arrive at the limits of rational thinking and intellectual research. Here we are faced by a bare fact : the *concordia* on which the *pax hominum* (Augustine) must be based does not exist.

The founding and maintenance of an international legal order, i.e., of peace as the prerequisite of " harmony," depends upon the fulfilment of a *condition*, and on the other hand makes a stringent *demand* upon us. The condition is this : the existence of a community, living by a common conception of justice and human dignity. The demand : the establishment of a solid organisation, capable of dispensing law and justice according to that common conception, and of maintaining law and order. This demand can only be satisfied when the condition has been fulfilled, according to the measure (geographical and otherwise) of its realisation ; that is to say, so far as a common conviction of law and justice exists among the members of the community. Thus an international legal order will be determined by (1) the degree of integration (oneness) of the world, which is a social and spiritual fact, not dependent for its consummation upon our wills, but indeed on our hopes and prayers ; and (2) the degree of our readiness for new steps and efforts towards new designs of international authority ; these are not facts outside our will, but are directly and essentially dependent upon it. From the extension (geographically and as to specific matters) and the intensity of that integration there will be born a community of *nations*, in which juxtaposition of *states* and co-ordination of sovereignties will no longer alone determine an essentially political structure, but, along with these, also a hierarchy of values and a common subordination of states to an authority above them. A combination of juxtaposition and hierarchy : this is the typical feature of a federal structure.

It should be clear from this argument that a legal order above the states, which is the one and only aim of our quest for peace, is for the time being only gradually and partially attainable, and will assume different aspects in relation to different matters of common concern. We shall not have to fight *against* war and national sovereignty, but to arm ourselves *for* a legal order above the states, for an international law with binding force, for " peace."

In matters which are not deemed of universal concern for the whole world, we shall have to strive for a legal order over those nations only which are already united by a common conviction. The gain, even as an example, might prove to exceed all expectation.

On the other hand, in matters concerning which a common conviction has not yet grown up, the world will have to content itself with the beginnings of a purely confederate form of organisation which prevails to-day, a form which now, as always, can only be workable if the participants act in good faith and mutual respect, faithful to the plighted word, and if they can succeed in freeing themselves from greed for power and profit. This may seem wishful thinking and a platonic incentive to good behaviour. In fact it is the one and only condition for ordered life, national or international.

Slowly and gradually the conviction has gained ground that some fundamental principles of order and conduct exist even for impersonal political institutions such as the states. Among these good faith stands first. But the most important point in this connection is not the recognition of the principle itself, it is the fixing of the means controlling the observance of the principle in the practice of states. The final opinion on the observance of good faith ought not to be left to the exclusive judgment of the interested state or states, but should be referred to impartial, " third party " judgment. In particular, this is true for appeals to the well-known *clausula rebus sic stantibus* (a treaty considered binding only " so long as things stand as they are "), or to the still more indefinite " law of necessity." Such impartial control amounts to creating an effective restraint on the use of power (economic, journalistic or otherwise), and the rendering of power subservient to higher justice. It means at the same time the strengthening of solidarity, i.e., the common responsibility of states and nations for the well-being of the whole world. But to speak of solidarity is to be driven back to the fundamental problem of the moral and spiritual unity of nations, their mutual obedience to a higher order.

3. THE CHALLENGE TO THE CHURCH

The lack of solidarity between the nations of the world to-day is the life and death challenge presented to the Church in the field of international relations. The Church cannot remain unmoved before the spiritual disunity which nowadays looms large on the international horizon and tends to paralyse the world, and, more dangerous still, to foster the forces of war and destruction. In the political arena there may hang an iron curtain, there may be an apparently impassable gulf between groups of nations, but in the spiritual realm this is an unbearable situation. At such a juncture the Church must feel a deep unrest which should make it alert to prayer, thought and action. The burning question of the clash of the diverging pre-legal existential decisions[1] must never be forgotten.

[1] See pages 50-53 above.

The first duty of the Church in this respect is to look the facts squarely in the face ; it must recognise the existence of those facts and their implications, but it cannot leave the matter there. For the Church is an ecumenical fellowship, transcending all human divisions and groupings. The Church recognises only one Christian decision, above all the political or politico-spiritual decisions : that is, the duty of obedience to the Lord of the whole earth. From this starting-point the Church must follow consistently the lines of approach to the existing disunity. First, it must investigate the origins of the divergencies, their historical as well as sociological sources and backgrounds ; and to that end the churches of the world must listen to each other in true fellowship, as servants of one Truth. Secondly : from that true knowledge and Christian understanding the churches should search for points of contact, for lines of communication between the different world conceptions. There is no time to lose, and the work demands a long, strenuous, tough effort. The Church is not a disinterested onlooker : the whole work of the Church in the domain entrusted to it, i.e., the " Oikumene," is dependent for its progress or failure upon the results of this effort.

All this may seem rather facile verbiage in a conference paper, or only a veiled proof of the unavowed but nevertheless all too real embarrassment of the Church. It may be considered unduly and falsely optimistic, or even as " sounding brass " ; but when we look closely at this task of understanding and uniting, we cannot fail to be impressed by its magnitude as well as by our seeming audacity, remembering our human frailty and limitations. It is, however, *the* task *par excellence* in the international world, and if the Church does not undertake it with haste and devotion, we shall be regarded as unprofitable servants.

In undertaking this task, the Church must clear itself from all bias, all uncritical assumptions, all unconscious leanings towards traditional conceptions and superstitions, and all contemptuous self-righteousness ; and this applies to all churches, each in its own field.

The point of contact between the several churches is, now as ever, the consciousness of mutual responsibility. We are all threatened by the danger that Matthew xxv is not a real, a stirring force in our lives. All that happens in the West is part of the life of the East, and vice versa, and all suffering, all privations there are the direct concern of the churches here : where one member of Christ suffers, all the others suffer with him. In the political sphere it may be that when something happens behind an iron curtain there, or a silk curtain here, the rest of the world may become resigned or lose interest, but the Church can never accept an attitude of aloofness.

By seeking to know, to understand, to clarify, to reassemble under common obedience to the higher·commands of Christ, the Church must remain active and alert, must maintain spiritual contacts, foster ecumenical unity, heal wounds and console.   It is clear that the first and essential condition is that all the churches should enjoy liberty for their individual confession or creed, for common understanding, for unhindered intercourse with one another, because they are all enlisted in the *militia Christi*, a unity of mankind beyond politics, breaking through the idolatry of nation, race or class.

In so living and acting, the Church would form a new " front " of spiritual solidarity, in which it would express its consciousness, in the first place, of the value of dignified human existence, and then above all, of a life of *purpose*, destined to fulfil the Lord's commandments.   In practical terms, this means that the Church must take a clear stand for the disinherited, for the weak, the downtrodden, all over the world, i.e., must work for social justice in its different forms, for social security as a pre-requisite to true human life.   As Christians we must give a clear demonstration · of solidarity and justice, both within the Church's walls and outside, in national and international life. The indispensable witness of the Church, by which it will be judged in the eyes of the world, is to defend that solidarity and justice.

4. THE WORD OF THE CHURCH

The disorder of the world, then, seems due to two causes, and therefore we look on it as fate and guilt.   The one cause lies in the profound differences of civilisation, insight, outlook, purpose. This seems to be due to fate ; but looking more deeply into Holy Writ, we begin to perceive in it many sinful aspects of a secularised world.   The other cause of present disorder lies in greed for power and profit, as they manifest themselves in a self-righteous sovereignty or an equally arrogant nationalism, both striving for their own ends regardless of other people's interests and claims, and of higher justice ; or in tendencies towards economic monopoly, anti-social exploitation of the weak, whether weak social groups or of weak peoples. There is no real, enduring cure for this all-pervading disease of group egoism but a return to obedience to God's commandments, and, in the worldly sphere, the building of a just social and economic and political organisation, based on good faith and mutual respect, both within the states and in the international world of states. Christians have, as statesmen or as private individuals, the duty to show to the world the leaven of their faith in their private lives and in their public offices, and in their dealings with other groups and nations, to devote themselves to the cause of " peace " in all its manifold aspects, to convince the world of their sincerity, and to learn from other nations, where these seem to have progressed farther than their own on the path of social justice in the broadest sense of the word.

It is amidst this disorder of world society, due to lack of coherence and egoism, that the Church has to speak its word. Though international in outward appearance, being planted in different national soils and living in different surroundings, the Church is doomed to failure if its life remains confined to its different national embodiments. For in the Church, in contrast to any other agency, is *the* real supra-national community, a community not created by man, but by God's intervention in this worldly dispensation ; having within its purview the " whole earth and all it holds " and charged with the care of man, a creature after God's image. *Oikumene* means something which is radically different from the world of states and of nations, and the *ecumenical* work transcends by the call of the Church's Master all human *international* co-operation.[1] The ecumenical leaven should revolutionise the international world. That means that, as the *Corpus Christi*, the Church has first of all to put its own house in order, so that in its form and appearance it may be obedient to the call of its Master.

In obedience to Him the Church must proclaim that the state is not an end in itself, nor does it establish its own law, but it is God's instrument for the establishment and maintenance of a legal order in this world, a legal order both for *national* life and for *international* life, for there are no watertight compartments. The sole foundation of world society, which has already been

[1] Cf. the Oxford Report, pp. 168-169.

mentioned (viz., that God is the Lord of all nations ; that Jesus Christ has been given full authority in heaven and on earth), leaves no room whatever for self-righteous sovereignty : all authority exists by the grace of God.   The state has to maintain order for the protection of human life and dignity; the Church's duty is to point out to the state, when necessary, this prime responsibility.   And secondly, the Church has to put all existing law, all existing situations, to the test of justice.

Instead of appealing to national sovereignty as binding together the loose rights of any individual state, all states, however divergent in outlook, must arrive at a common recognition of their duties, tasks and responsibilities, for the protection of basic principles of law and justice, of human rights and fundamental liberties.   It is the function of the state to ensure a tolerable realisation of these basic principles in any society, national or international.   They are to maintain the external expression of the belief that man as a human being has a dignity, being delivered by Christ from sin and decay.   The Church must preach the fore-ordained Kingdom of God among men.   It must point out that human rights and other basic principles can never be equated with the reign of Divine love and of man's responsibility before God ;   but it must insist that without those basic principles of public and private behaviour declared and guaranteed, demonic forces are free to obstruct the penetration of God's commandments into human life.   There will never be a Christian state ;   still less, a Christian " United Nations."   But the Church must exhort governments and ordinary men to found a society on justice and law, national as well as international.   The administration of justice in this world calls for independent, conscientious, responsible persons, to whom the task of maintaining justice and order can safely be entrusted.   Justice here on earth takes its deepest meaning from the observance of God's commandments in this shattered world. The Church must continually bear this in mind, as part of its apostolic and missionary task.

From all this it will have become clear that the Church cannot plead for one definite political system, for in every one of them lies the danger of the demonism of power.   The Church must, however, denounce the irreconcilable antagonism between any state, or class, or any other totalitarian system, and justice. The Church must protest with all its might against the destruction of human dignity and freedom and genuine solidarity. Apart from this, it can only show a preference for that system which leaves the way open for man to obey the call of Christ, and which gives the best protection for man to live and act as a responsible person in his family, in his community, above all in his Church. The first and last word of the Church should be responsibility, and it must therefore defend such systems as recognise the real public responsibility of a government. Only under such a system, coupled with an independent judiciary, is the way open to a tolerable protection of fundamental liberties, i.e., those liberties under which the relationship between God and man is not destroyed or restricted.

In the world of states likewise, that system has a claim to the Church's preference which promises the best chances for nations to live and act as responsible communities under a rule of law. It must be emphasised that the over-accentuation of the national sovereignty of the isolated state, such as we witnessed often in the past, and which still occurs in our interrelated world, is fraught with the deadly danger of lawlessness. The history of the last century has abundantly taught us this, especially in a world like that of to-day, in which states and nations have grown so markedly interdependent.

The Church is, therefore, entitled to say, and indeed must stress, that some form of federative co-operation between the states of the world is a demand of the Christian conscience. This co-operation must do justice of that growing interdependence, and is a pre-condition of that international order which is our declared ultimate aim. The Christian conscience demands this above all, for the realisation of the ecumenical fellowship (*cf.* page 47) which is our starting-point and our goal.

If Christ is the " *Kurios*," the Church must urge the establishment of an international legal order. But the Church as a body is neither called on nor entitled to indicate exact legal ways leading towards the end in view, nor to make pronouncements concerning the organisation of such an order and the form of its institutions. The task of the Church is to awaken the consciences of men in and outside its precincts to the urgent necessity of such an order, supported by authority ; to foster the recognition of such an order and authority ; and to see that that great work be undertaken and duly accomplished with all possible energy.

In other fields too the Church has kindred tasks to accomplish.

International disorder originates partly in disorders within national frontiers. In its preaching of love to our neighbour the Church should insist that the community must open to all its members, within the national states as well as in the international sphere, the possibility of work which has a purpose and a meaning, and that the community should provide social security for its members. Again, in those fields the Church must plead for the protection of fundamental rights and freedoms of man as a responsible person. The social and economic anarchy of the world in several respects, a characteristic feature of our world, which is one of the forms of disowning Christ's message, must be overcome. This means that the Church should urge the duty of all who wield economic power to serve the world as a whole and to be accountable for its stewardship. If the Christian principles of justice, service, stewardship and responsibility are earnestly observed, the disintegration of world society might be attacked at its roots.

The highest task of the Church still remains to call man to repentance and conversion, to a sincere denial of hatred and egoism, and to lead in prayer and supplication *ut omnes unum sint* (" that all may be one ").

The Church of Jesus Christ, a community which transcends all differences of nations and states, races and cultures, classes and groups ; the embodiment of a once mercifully given, supra-human reality created not by men, must posit Augustine's maxim : *Pax hominum ordinata concordia* (" Peace among men is the tranquillity of order "). When churches and nations obediently exert all their forces for the attainment of such a concord, then they on their side accomplish all which is within their power, in order that God's mercy may deliver us from all our evils and distresses, and that He may fulfil His design for this world.

IV

CHRISTIAN RESPONSIBILITY IN OUR DIVIDED WORLD

It is necessary in this chapter to set together two distinct viewpoints, for it is only by a careful consideration of all the factors involved that the light of truth may be brought to bear upon the tensions of the present world situation.

(a) THE CHRISTIAN CITIZEN IN A CHANGING WORLD

John Foster Dulles

FOREWORD

THIS paper is written by a layman who has been active in the field of international affairs. It is primarily an action paper, not a theological paper. It accepts, explicitly or implicitly, basic Christian beliefs and suggests how, in the actual situation, they may impose on Christian citizens a duty of practical conduct.

There is no thought that the Church should endorse the conclusions reached or the lines of action suggested. The writer is, indeed, one who believes that the Church ought not to make authoritative pronouncements with respect to detailed action in political, economic or social fields. Practical political action is not often a subject for authoritative moral judgments of universal scope. Those who act in the political field must deal with the possible, not with the ideal; they must try to get the relatively good, the lesser evil; they cannot, without frustration, reject whatever is not wholly good; they cannot be satisfied with proclaimed ends, but must deal with actual means. Those necessities prevail conspicuously in the international field where tradition, national interest and group loyalty have accumulated to an unusual degree. They place limits on what is practically possible; they introduce error into every human judgment; they increase the ever-present risk that men will see as " right " that which is self-serving.

Facts such as those mentioned require that the churches should exercise great caution in dealing with international political matters. They should not seem to put the seal of God's approval upon that which, at best, may be expedient, but which cannot wholly reflect God's will.

It does not, however, follow that Christian faith and Christian political action are unrelated. All citizens have to act in relation to political matters—inaction being only a form of action, a clearing of the way for others who do act. Also, Christian citizens, when they act, will try to be guided by Christian insight and Christian inspiration. Political institutions moulded by those who take a Christian view of the nature of man will be different from those moulded by atheists. What the churches elect to say will have political consequences. What they elect to keep silent about will also have political consequences. So the churches, too, have a relationship to practical politics that is inescapable.

Since that is so, it seems that the churches ought to know what are the problems which Christian citizens face. "Thy word is a lamp unto my feet and a light unto my path." But the churches cannot throw the light of the Word upon the Christians' paths unless they know where those paths lie and what are the obstacles that need to be illumined lest the Christian pilgrim stumble and fall. It is useful, no doubt, for Christian citizens to be inspired by the vision of a distant, heavenly scene. But also it is useful to have light upon the way.

Obviously, Christian citizens throughout the world do not all face identical problems or have identical duties. No single presentation can adequately inform the churches. There are, in the world, many paths for Christians, all leading toward a central point, the doing of God's will on earth. Some paths lead from the East, some from the West; some from the North, some from the South. Each of these paths has obstacles of its own. In turn, these obstacles constantly shift. What is described now may be irrelevant by to-morrow. Despite the fact that the scene is world-wide and shifting, the churches should seek to keep informed. Otherwise, they cannot keep each way illuminated with shafts of the divine light.

This paper seeks to show, in relation to international affairs, what is the political path which some Christians have to tread, what they see as the obstacles ahead, and how they think they can, perhaps, overcome these obstacles and wrest the initiative from forces of evil, ignorance and despair which exist in every land and which seem to be conspiring to overwhelm mankind with awful disaster.

The writer recognises, quite frankly, that the path he describes is a path which leads from the West. He knows full well that that way differs from other ways. These, too, should be known, for the Church concedes no priority or privilege to any nation, race or class.

As the churches come to know better the practical problems which Christian citizens have to face and the lines of action in which they may become engaged, the churches in turn will be better able to minister to the actual needs. They will be better able to show, to each and to all, that Christ is indeed the Way, the Truth and the Life. As Christ is so revealed, He will draw all men unto Him, and that supreme loyalty will provide the unifying force which otherwise men seek in vain.

I. THE INEVITABILITY OF CHANGE

The basic political and social fact that citizens must face up to is the fact of change. Life and change are inseparable. Human beings constantly change. So, too, do human societies. There are always some who unthinkingly wish that they could stop change and freeze a moment into eternity. That cannot be and, indeed, we should not want it to be. If it happened, it would mean an end and the replacement of life with death.

Christians do not regret the inevitability of change. Rather, they see in it a cause for rejoicing. Some religions see man as bound to a wheel which turns and on the turning of which he can exert no influence. As a result of that assumption, it follows, for them that the ideal mental state is one of indifference and renunciation of hopes and efforts which can end only in frustration. The Christian believes that he can do something about change to determine its character and, accordingly, he looks upon the inevitability of change as something that provides opportunity. That opportunity has a dual aspect. Outwardly, there is the opportunity to make the world more nearly one in which God's will is done on earth as it is in heaven. Inwardly, there is the opportunity for personal growth and development which comes out of grappling with situations and trying to mould them.

When there is change, something that *is* disappears and something that *was not* appears. Also, whenever there is change there is a means, a force, that brings change to pass. The Christian seeks the disappearance of that which he deems imperfect. But the disappearance of something imperfect is not, of itself, sufficient to make change good. If that were so, all change, by whatever means, would be good, for everything is to some extent imperfect and there cannot be change without the disappearance of some imperfection. The Christian tries to appraise change not merely in terms of what disappears, but also in terms of what replaces that which disappears. This appraisal involves an appraisal of means as well as ends, for the means by which change is accomplished makes an indelible impression upon the result and becomes, indeed, a part of the result.

For Christians, the great social task is to deal with the forces that make *some* change imperative so that (*a*) these forces will make their principal impact on what can be and will be replaced by something better ; (*b*) the forces for change will leave relatively immune what at the moment cannot be replaced by something better ; and (*c*) the forces for change will not themselves be evil and un-Christian in character.

2. THERE IS NEED THAT CHANGE BE INSTITUTIONALISED

Political leaders who have, or want, power, usually talk much alike as to the social ends they seek. They all propose to increase the sum total of human happiness. The manifestos of communism, nazism and democracy have much in common. Many people pick their leaders simply on the basis of their promises and on the basis of the zeal which they seem to manifest. Sometimes the very violence with which leaders would seek their ends seems a recommendation, as being a proof of zeal.

The Christian citizens will consider not only the social ends which are professed in words, but also those elements which, we have seen, make up the nature of change. They will inquire into whether the changes proposed will replace something imperfect by something better ; will leave immune what cannot be improved and will avoid means which are evil. They have learned that the actual result will probably be determined more by the means than by the professions of long-range ends. Also, they know that a choice of violent means may not indicate honest zeal, but a lust for the increased power which comes to political leaders whenever violent means are sanctioned.

Difference of opinion about means is often the critical difference. Christians prefer means of the kind which, they believe, Christ taught. They are not inclined to look with approval upon means of violence and coercion. They have seen that, over the ages, war, revolution and terrorism have been repeatedly invoked for noble ends. But change brought about in that way is hurried and it usually gets out of control. It crushes blindly what happens to lie in its path. At times it inspires fine and sacrificial qualities, but also it develops in men hatred of fellowman, vengefulness, hypocrisy, cruelty and disregard of truth. History seems to show that when these evil qualities are invoked to produce good ends, in fact they vitiate or postpone the professed ends. Change sought by methods of force, violence and coercion seldom produces lasting, good results. The Oxford Conference of 1937 said :

" Wars, the occasions of war, and all situations which conceal the fact of conflict under the guise of outward peace, are marks of a world to which the church is charged to proclaim the gospel of redemption. War involves compulsory enmity, diabolical outrage against human personality, and a wanton distortion of the truth. War is a particular demonstration of the power of sin in this world and a defiance of the righteousness of God as revealed in Jesus Christ and Him crucified. No justification of war must be allowed to conceal or minimise this fact."

Some Christians believe that the use of violence is of itself so un-Christian that it should never under any circumstances be resorted to. Most Christian citizens, it seems, do not accept that view. The vast majority appear to believe that while they ought not themselves to initiate the use of force as a means, once force is invoked by others to do injustice and to impose conditions violative of the moral law and of the Christian conception of the nature of man, then to use force to prevent those results may be the lesser of two evils. Christians would generally agree that methods of change other than violence are to be preferred because violence, unless it be the dispassionate force of police power under law, almost always generates un-Christian qualities which cancel out, or at least greatly dilute, the value of the changes which violence brings about.

If force is discarded as the accepted means of change, then there have to be established procedures and political organisations for the purpose of making peaceful change. Such procedures have, to a considerable extent, been established within states, but they are lacking in the international field. There, as elsewhere, history teaches the inevitability of change. If one examines an historical atlas and looks at the political arrangement of the world 100 years ago, 200 years ago and so forth, one cannot but be impressed by the magnitude of the changes that have occurred. Most of these changes have been effected by war or the threat of war. Each war brought about the disappearance of something that was imperfect. Often it involved the doing away of power in some men and nations which had become disproportionate to their ability or readiness to use that power for the general welfare. In that sense, the change was good. But, also, the method of violence has done terrible things to the hearts of men. It has not brought individuals to greater love of God and neighbour in accordance with the great Commandments. Indeed, the result has been, on the whole, quite the contrary. The prestige of Christianity in the world has been gravely impaired by the frequency with which the so-called Christian nations have used violence as a method of international change. Furthermore, the hatred, falsification, cruelty and injustice incident to each war has, we can see in retrospect, done much to provoke new war and all the evil that that entails.

3. INSTITUTIONS FOR CHANGE REQUIRE DECIDING WHO CONTROLS

Christian citizens can readily conclude, as a generalisation, that there ought to be political institutions which will enable international change to take place in a peaceful way. But that conclusion is not, of itself, very significant. It cannot have any practical consequence unless also there is another decision, namely, whose judgment will determine the timing and the nature of peaceful change. Change *ought* to be based upon reflection and deliberate choice, not upon accident and force, of course. But *whose* reflection and choice are to be controlling?

That is a hard question. Within nations there is no uniform answer. In the international field few have attempted seriously to answer it and those few are not in agreement. Uncertainty, disagreement and competition about that largely explain why, in the international field, change has so far been left mostly to accident and violence.

It used to be widely held that political decisions should be made by rulers who were not responsible to their people. To-day, it is generally agreed, at least in theory, that it is better that men should be self-governing through some representative process which they control. But that theory is seldom carried out in practice, even within nations. In many countries of the world power is exercised by dictators. Of these, there are many types. Some are men who, loving power, have taken it and make no attempt to rationalise their action. Often, by written con-stitution, their government is a " republic " or " democracy." Some dictators are benevolent, taking power only to tide over a real or imagined crisis. Some exercise dictatorial power in order, professedly, to train the masses and discipline them into a common mould which, it is thought, ought to precede self-govern-ment. Such purposeful dictatorships are often termed " totali-tarian."

There are other countries where the peoples do in fact, through representative processes, exercise a very large measure of influence upon the choices that are made as to change. These societies customarily describe themselves as " free societies." Some call them " responsible societies " or " self-disciplined societies." We use the phrase " free societies " because it has wider popular use, although we recognise, and hereafter emphasise, that there is interdependence between freedom and self-discipline and sense of responsibility. We also recognise that even in the so-called " free societies " there are usually some who are, in fact, excluded from equal opportunity to participate in the deliberative process which determines when and how change shall be effected.

In no country is there a " pure " democracy in the sense that all of the people have equal and direct participation in all of the deliberations which determine change. Also, in no country are dictatorships so absolute that those who possess the governmental power wholly disregard what they sense to be the wishes of the people. Even so, the organisation of the different nations shows that there are great and momentous differences, both in theory and in practice, as to whose choice should determine change. These differences are a great obstacle to institutionalising change at the international level. Therefore, the matter deserves further consideration.

4. FORMS OF GOVERNMENT COMPATIBLE WITH CHRISTIAN IDEALS

Christians tend to favour the free society of self-discipline. That is probably because Christians think of man primarily in terms of the individual and his relations to God and to fellow man. It is only individuals who have souls to be saved and God, it seems, is not concerned with nations, races and classes, *as such*. He is concerned with individual human beings. Christians, who believe that, want a political society which, recognising the value and the sacredness of individual personality, gives the individual the opportunity to develop in accordance with the dictates of his own conscience and reason, and also puts on him a responsibility to exercise freedom with regard for the welfare of fellow men.

Christians believe that for one man to possess arbitrary power over his fellow men is an un-Christian relationship. It usually corrupts him who rules and it tends to debase those who are ruled, if in fact they acquiesce in being ruled.

Furthermore, Christians believe that civil laws, made by men, should, so far as possible, reflect the moral law. We believe that there is implanted in every individual a potential awareness of right and wrong and that under favouring conditions the composite of such individual judgments will reflect the moral law better than the judgments of absolute and self-perpetuating rulers. Also, as a practical matter, unless laws reflect and codify the moral judgments of those subject to them, they are not apt for long to be enforceable.

For such reasons, Christians tend to prefer the free society. But also they recognise that peaceful and selective change is not assured merely by giving people a right of suffrage. The voice of the people is not always the voice of God. It is easy to arouse masses for destruction without regard to the problem of replacement. Mob psychology is seldom conducive to selective change and it does not in fact represent individual reflection and choice.

A free society, if it is to effect peaceful and selective change, must be a society where, in addition to the right to vote, the people possess and use personal freedoms and access to information and the opportunity to exchange and propagate thoughts and beliefs so that there is, on an individual basis, genuine reflection and sober choice of minds and spirits which are both free and developed by use and self-discipline. There is also need of tolerance, particularly in the sense that political power may not be used to promote any particular creed.

The free society may at times of emergency, such as the emergency created by war, grant one man or a few men very extraordinary, even dictatorial, powers. But the people will reserve effectively the opportunity to end these powers when the occasion for them has passed.

Economically, a free society does not have to be a *laissez faire* society. There are some who profess to believe that only a *laissez faire* society adequately encourages individual development. There are, however, few who to-day would put that belief wholly into practice. In all states, even those most dedicated to " free enterprise," there is governmental control of at least some of the tools of production, such as railways and public utilities, which are endowed with a special public interest. In most countries, there are important collective and co-operative enterprises. It would seem that there is no inherent incompatibility between the Christian view of the nature of man and the practice of economic communism or state socialism. Communism, in the sense of " from each according to his abilities, to each according to his needs," was early Christian practice.

In the modern world, particularly where there is industrialisation, there is much interdependence and necessity for co-operation. In part, this necessity can be met by individual knowledge of how, in a complicated society, individual acts affect others. To that knowledge there needs to be added self-control and sense of duty to fellow man, so that individuals will voluntarily refrain from acts which they see have injurious consequences more than offsetting the benefits to self. But even where the people are possessed of much self-control and sense of duty, there may have to be added public controls and centralised direction to promote the equitable distribution of goods in short supply and to insure co-operative and co-ordinated action on a scale adequate to the needs of our complicated economies.

One may have different judgments as to what economic

structure is best adapted to modern conditions and as to the kind of incentive which is required to insure needed productivity. There are times and conditions when the most effective appeal is to self-interest. There are other times and conditions when the greatest appeal may be to men's sacrificial spirit. The Christian Church seeks constantly to make men's motives more lofty, and to invoke concern for others rather than for self. Christians believe that those that are strong ought to bear the infirmities of the weak, and not to please themselves. But there are few who fully heed that injunction. Christian citizens, in seeking to organise society, have to take account of what men *are*, not what the Church thinks they ought to be.

From the Christian viewpoint, the essential is political and economic conditions which will help, and not stifle, growth by the individual in wisdom and stature and in favour with God and man. We want conditions which, in so far as practical, will, in fact, exalt the dignity of man. The essential in this respect is the content, not the form. The conditions which best assure that will doubtless vary from time to time and from place to place.

It is not possible to attach the Christian label to any particular political or economic organisation or system to the exclusion of all others. It is not possible to say that " free enterprise " is Christian and socialism un-Christian—or *vice versa*. It is not possible to say that a popular representative system of government is Christian, or temporary dictatorship inherently un-Christian. It is, however, possible to condemn as un-Christian societies which are organised in disregard of the Christian view of the nature of man. This would include those which are totalitarian in the sense that they recognise the right of some men to seek to bring the thoughts, beliefs and practices of others into conformity with their will, by processes of coercion.

It could be argued that if Christians really believe that the truth is uniquely revealed by God through Jesus Christ, they ought to seek an organisation of the state which would make it possible to use every power, including police power, to compel acceptance of that truth and the liquidation of heretics and non-conformers.

There have been times when that viewpoint prevailed. Christianity, over its two thousand years, has had many experiences and has learned much. It has learned that when Christians use political power, or any coercive or artificial means, to give special advantage to their distinctive sect, the outcome is apt to be an ugly thing. We reject methods which, history seems to teach, pervert Christianity. If we reject totalitarianism for ourselves, we, *a fortiori*, reject it for others. Believing that our own faith cannot remain pure when coupled with methods of intolerance, we also believe that no faith can enter into that partnership without corruption.

5. PEACEFUL CHANGE IS POSSIBLE

Practical experience seems to show that where the people have a considerable degree of self-discipline, where they recognise duty to fellow men and where they have considerable education, then they can operate political processes which make for change which is peaceful and selective. In the western democracies, the political institutions have to a great extent been influenced by Christianity. (By Christianity we do not mean clericalism which may be an impediment to peaceful and selective change.) In these countries, conditions approximating to those of a free society have on the whole existed for 150 years or more. During that period, social and economic change has been so immense that conditions in any one of these countries to-day would completely bewilder those who lived there a hundred or fifty years ago.

The changes have, in the main, been peaceful changes. There has been little coercion, terrorism or civil war. The conspicuous apparent exception is the United States' war of eighty-five years ago, called in the North the " war of the Rebellion," but in the South the " war between the States." It was, in essence, more international than civil war. The basic issue was whether certain sovereign states had, by prior compact of union, given up the right to resume full sovereignty.

The social changes effected by free political processes have in the main tended to increase the opportunity of the individual to develop according to the dictates of his conscience and reason. Slavery has been abolished. There has been a definite trend away from treating labourers as animals or machines are treated. Women have been freed from grave disabilities. Economically, individual initiative, experimental and competitive, has produced great richness. The " industrial revolution," while it has brought evils, has shown men how, with less physical effort, they can produce much more. Infant mortality has been greatly reduced, health generally improved, and the span of life lengthened. Education is general and the development of spiritual life has been kept free of political inhibitions. Graduated income taxes and death duties effect a very considerable distribution of production in accordance with need.

To say these things is not to be self-righteous or complacent. There are many great blots and many deficiencies. One notable blot is the persistence in the United States of a considerable, though diminishing, measure of race discrimination. There persist inequalities of many kinds, economic, social and political. There is no assurance that ways have been found to prevent the cyclical breakdown of production process and the vast misery consequent therein. By no means is God's will done as it is in heaven. To be satisfied would be un-Christian.

But it is not un-Christian to point out that where political institutions show evidence of Christian influence, the result is good fruit. If that were not so, one could doubt that Christianity did in fact reflect God's ultimate revelation to man. Christ said : " By their fruits shall ye know them."

It seems, both on the basis of theoretical reasoning and on the basis of practical experience, that peaceful and selective change can be assured under the conditions of a free society of self-discipline. There is no comparable evidence to show that under a despotic or totalitarian form of society there can be sustained change that is peaceful and selective and which progressively increases the opportunities for individual growth.

6. WORLD SHORTAGE OF FREE SOCIETIES WITH TESTED POLITICAL INSTITUTIONS

There are not in the world many societies which have tested political mechanisms whereby decisions reflect the choice and reflection of the people as a whole. That, in the main, is not because such institutions are not wanted, but because various conditions have militated against their realisation. Many peoples have been long in colonial dependency. Some, like the peoples of India and Pakistan and certain Arab states, are only now moving from dependency to full independence. Some, like the peoples of China and Indonesia, are in chaos and strife. Some, like the Germans, Japanese and Italians, are still under, or just emerging from, the military control of the victors. Some live under constitutions which, in words, vest sovereignty in the people ; but they are, in fact, ruled by a small group which perpetuates itself in power by force, subject to change by periodic revolution. Some live under " dictatorships of the proletariat."

These facts are significant because they affect the practicability of developing internationally processes of change which will be peaceful and selective. It means that there do not exist, on a world-wide scale, tested institutions of political liberty and that there is an absence of the foundation needed for building a world structure which has political power to legislate change. The creation of a World State involves a mechanism of power and the selection of individuals to direct it. If the power is to be sufficient to make possible change which is adequate to replace violent change, there must, somewhere, be large discretionary authority. But it would not be possible to-day to assure that the discretion would come from peoples who were free, and morally and intellectually trained for the use of political freedom.

Theoretically, it is possible to devise a world representative system so " weighted " in favour of the societies of tested freedom that their representatives would have the preponderant voice. The others, who are the majority, would never consent to those few societies being accorded world supremacy. They would, in a sense, be justified. For while the free societies have shown good capacity to govern themselves, they have not shown the same good capacity to govern others, of different races and cultures. It would not advance us to recreate and extend the colonial system under the guise of " world government."

To-day, any world-wide system for institutionalising change would inevitably be despotic. Either it would vest arbitrary power in the persons of a few individual officials, or it would vest great power in the small fraction of the human race who have tested political processes for reflecting the individual choice.

The great majority of the world's population will not, and should not, agree to be ruled by the " free societies." The " free societies " will not, and should not, go back under despotism.

This impasse is a source of great peril. It leaves international change to be effected largely by force and coercion. It does so at a time when the means for corrupting men's souls and destroying their bodies have grown far beyond anything that the world has ever known. Thus, Christian citizens can feel that each, according to his means, has a duty to act to increase the possibility of world political unity and processes for peaceful change. That does not mean that Christian citizens will treat unity as the all-sufficient end, to which they should sacrifice what to them seem justice, righteousness and human dignity. They will seek the conditions for unity with the urgency of those who know that great disaster impends and with the practicability of those who know that such disasters cannot be averted merely by the incantation of fine words.

7. THE DEVELOPMENT OF FREE SOCIETIES

If peaceful change requires deciding whose judgment is to prevail, and if the judgment of a free, disciplined, society is the only reliable and generally acceptable judgment, then the extension of free societies throughout the world is prerequisite to a world-wide institutionalising of change. Many Christian citizens see that as the great long-range political task. Its accomplishment would make it possible to set up and operate in a non-despotic way international mechanisms for peaceful change. That task has two aspects :

(*a*) It is first necessary to preserve and improve free societies where they now exist. Free societies are delicate plants. To grow them is a long, hard task and, once they are grown, they are in constant danger of withering away. The post-war climate has been particularly hard on free societies. The cumulative result of two world wars is grave economic distress coupled with great human weariness and disillusionment. Under these conditions, men have a longing to be taken care of. Also, the economic margin for survival has been reduced to a point where centralised planning has seemed necessary. To men who are preoccupied with the struggle for the basic, material needs of life for their families, bread may be of more compelling and immediate importance than civil rights and freedoms. Such conditions lead to giving great power to a few men.

Delegation of power does not, of itself, necessarily mean an abandonment of freedom. It may be an exercise of freedom to meet an emergency and the people may retain both the legal right and the practical political mechanisms for ending the delegation when the emergency has passed. As we have noted, free societies usually give dictatorial powers in time of great emergency, such as war, and it has been shown that they can withstand temporary dictatorship of this kind. Nevertheless, there is always grave risk in conferring dictatorial power because such power can readily become self-perpetuating.

To preserve the characteristics of a free society within the areas where it now measurably prevails will itself be a difficult task. It will require vigilance and dedication by Christians as citizens. That dedication should not be merely in the interest of *preservation*, but of *improvement*. Only effort motivated by the creative urge can generate the needed energy and enthusiasm. Struggles are seldom won merely by a defensive strategy.

(*b*) New free societies must be developed, and this can be done and should be done rapidly wherever the necessary human foundation exists. Fortunately, much has been done, through varied channels, to create those foundations. The Christian churches have played, in this, a great part. The Christian missionary movement has had a great world-wide influence in developing in men a sense of duty to fellow man. Also, Christian schools and colleges have stimulated education throughout the world. On the moral and educational foundations developed over past generations, much is now being done to erect free political institutions.

Until recently, nearly one-third of the world's population . were the subject peoples of the "free societies." Within the last three years, free institutions have been set up in India, Pakistan, Burma, Ceylon, the Philippine Islands and certain of the Arab states. A large measure of autonomy is envisaged for Indonesia. The total number of peoples thus acquiring political freedom represents about one-quarter of the population of the world and could more than double the total population of the free societies. That is an amazing and encouraging occurrence which should confound the pessimists and inspirit the disillusioned.

Of course, it is not certain that all of these new political entities will, in fact, maintain societies of freedom in the full sense. In part, the present development represents a great experiment. In many of the areas momentous and difficult decisions remain to be made, and there is not yet the kind and degree of individual moral and intellectual development which would easily assure a peaceful outcome. There will be need of sympathetic understanding, material aid, and scientific and technical assistance from the older societies of freedom.

There remain dependent colonial areas which can be developed toward self-government and free institutions. The colonial powers, by the United Nations Charter, have pledged themselves to seek that development; and to aid in attaining the result there has been created the Trusteeship Council.

It should be remembered in this connection that political wisdom generally comes only with practical experience. If people are to be held in guardianship until they have fully developed all the qualities desired, there will be an indefinite prolongation of guardianship. It is better to err on the side of giving freedom prematurely than to withhold it until there is demonstrated proof of ability to use it wisely. To learn by self-experience is apt to involve much suffering. But few learn adequately from the experience of others.

There is in China nearly one-fifth of the human race. Some Chinese leaders have, in recent years, sought to replace despotism with free political institutions. But progress has been slow. The people are materially impoverished and only a few have book-learning. They have had to undergo a war and occupation longer than that of the European continental allies. Individualism, in terms of the family, is perhaps excessive and a sense of community too restricted. But the people still possess richly the qualities which will enable them to make a great addition to foundations of political liberty.

During the last century there developed a sense of fellowship between the Chinese people and the peoples of the West, largely because of the activities of Christian missionaries, educators and doctors. Now, more than ever, such activities need to be continued and, indeed, intensified.

There is a great responsibility toward the vanquished peoples of Germany, Japan and Italy. The victors have made themselves the government of Germany ; they, in fact, direct the government of Japan and will largely influence the post-war development of Italy. The peoples of these countries have education and personal morality in large measure. It ought to be possible for them to develop into free societies. That is a task of great difficulty because of the evil war has bred. But it is a task of unique importance.

A survey of the globe shows that it is possible for upwards of three-quarters of the human race to develop peacefully and quickly—say, within one or two generations—the use of free political institutions. No doubt there would be many inadequacies, as indeed there always are. But it is possible to foresee conditions under which there would be obtainable, from most of the peoples of the earth, judgments which reflect the thinking, on an individual basis, of minds and spirits which are free and developed by political experience and self-discipline. On that foundation it would be possible to establish, internationally, procedures for peaceful change which would not be despotic, but which would reflect that moral sense which, we believe, is potential in every human being.

The programme suggested has a particular appeal to Christians because it is a peaceful programme to which the Christian churches can make a great contribution. There can be parallel effort by the churches and Christian citizens.

The free society cannot be equated with a Christian society and it is possible to have free societies whose institutions are predominantly influenced by non-Christian religions. But the Christian faith especially emphasises those qualities of self-control and love of neighbour which are needed for the good operation of a free society. So, Christian citizens could feel that to extend free societies was a great long-range effort to which they could worthily dedicate themselves and seek to dedicate their nations. Thereby they would be laying the indispensable foundation for world institutions for peaceful and selective change. Those engaged in that effort could feel that they were making the world more nearly one where God's will would be done, and they would be responsive to the appeal of the masses that a way be found to save them and their children from the death, the misery, the starvation of body and soul which recurrent violence now wreaks upon man.

8. CONFLICT OF PROGRAMME WITH SOVIET PROGRAMME[1]

The programme which we suggest is one that, if vigorously espoused, could enlist great support throughout the world. In the countries to which we referred in the preceding section, both

[1] Unless otherwise indicated, quotations are from J. Stalin's *Problems of Leninism*, Moscow, 1940. This volume is currently circulated by official Soviet agencies as an authoritative expression of present-day Soviet doctrine.

the people and their leaders predominantly want peaceful evolution as free societies. There are, of course, everywhere some who put their primary reliance upon means of violence, but in the countries referred to even those do not dare openly to advocate force as an ideal method. In these countries there is freedom for citizens to advocate the use of political processes which are peaceful rather than violent. Our programme would not, however, receive co-operation from the Soviet Communist Party and those in the world who are guided by, or subjected to, its dogma. The reason is not so much difference of opinion between Soviet and non-Soviet leaders as to the final ends to be sought, as difference of opinion as to the means by which those ends can be achieved.

The programme we suggest is one for peaceful evolution toward conditions which will make possible the world-wide institutionalising of change. The emphasis is on *peace*, both as end and means. The Soviet Communist Party does not believe in such peaceful evolution. It believes that only by violence and coercion can it secure its desired ends.

The difference about means creates a great gulf between Soviet practices and the practices of those not dominated by Soviet Communist philosophy. These differences in practice are especially important in the realm of international affairs and they cannot be ignored by those who, as citizens, have to take a stand on the international issues of our time. It makes it necessary to compare theory with theory and practice with practice and not to judge on the basis of comparing the theory of some with the practices of others.

The long-range social ends which Soviet leaders profess to seek are in many respects similar to the ends which Christian citizens seek. As a matter of political organisation, Soviet doctrine does not look upon its " dictatorship of the proletariat " as the final best result. Such dictatorship is to be a preliminary phase which will gradually wither away in favour of a condition where the people are self-governing. Soviet dictatorship is " preparing the ground for the withering away of the State, which is one of the basic elements of the future stateless Communist System " (p. 38).

Economically, Soviet leaders seek " a much higher productivity of labour " (p. 295), " the abolition of exploitation of man by man " (Constitution, Article 4), and ultimately the distribution of the production of labour in accordance with the formula " from each according to his abilities, to each according to his needs " (p. 570).

Socially, Communist doctrine envisages " the equality of the rights of citizens of the U.S.S.R., irrespective of their nationality or race, in all spheres of economic, state, cultural, social and political life " (Constitution, Article 123).

In its foreign policy, the Soviet Union is " the most inter-nationalist of all state organisations " and seeks the amalgama-tion of all " into a single state union " (p. 37). It seeks for colonies the right " to complete secession " and " independent existence as states " (p. 51).

There is nothing in these long-term ends irreconcilable with what Christians seek. Indeed, most of those ends—and more—have been sought by Christians long before there was any Communist Party. Christians seek to develop in individuals such a love of fellow man and such capacity for self-control and self-sacrifice as to reduce to a minimum the need for the State as a dictating authority. As we have noted, the early Christians " had all things common . . . and parted them to all men as every man had need " (Acts ii, 44, 45). Christians have long taught and sought the equal dignity and worth of the human personality without regard to race, nationality, colour, class or sex. They have sought for colonial peoples self-government or independence as rapidly as circumstances might permit. Inter-nationally, they have been the most ardent supporters of plans for world organisation.

There is, we can see, much in common as regards ultimate social ends. But even as to these there is a difference in emphasis between Soviet and Christian thinking. Soviet thinking proceeds from a materialistic premise, whereas Christian thinking proceeds from a spiritual premise. Soviet leaders hold that " the material life of society . . . is . . . primary, and its spiritual life secondary," being merely a " reflection " of material life (p. 601). Christians believe that material and social conditions on earth are primarily important as creating the conditions needed for spiritual development. Christians believe in a moral law which derives from God and which establishes eternal standards of right and wrong. Soviet leaders do not believe in such concepts as " eternal justice " (p. 595).

These differences are important because they lead to the

differences as to means. Where political institutions and practices reflect a materialistic philosophy, they readily subordinate the individual to some group, which may be nation, race or class. The individual who seems to get in the way of the chosen group may be treated ruthlessly and liquidated, or forced to conform, without such treatment involving a violation of any professed belief. It takes a spiritual approach to measure joy in terms of " one sinner that repenteth, more than over ninety and nine just persons, which need no repentance." To those who hold the materialist philosophy of Marx, Engels, Lenin and Stalin it seems permissible to treat the welfare of a particular class as the ultimate end and to use means which will promote that end irrespective of the effect of those means upon the dignity and sacredness of the individual human personality. Many of the long-term social ends professedly sought by Soviet leadership are equally sought by Christian citizens, but the spiritual philosophy of Christianity requires the rejection of means which can logically be accepted by those who have a materialistic philosophy.

Soviet leaders assert that the desired ends cannot be achieved peacefully and should not be sought peacefully. " Force is the midwife of every old society pregnant with a new one " (Karl Marx's *Capital*). " Up to a certain period the development of the productive forces and the changes in the realm of the relations of production proceed spontaneously, independently of the will of men. But that is so only up to a certain moment, until the new and developing productive forces have reached a proper state of maturity. After the new productive forces have matured, the existing relations of production and their upholders—the ruling classes—become that ' insuperable ' obstacle which can only be removed by the conscious action of the new classes, by the forcible acts of these classes, by revolution " (p. 617).

" Can such a radical transformation of the old bourgeois order be achieved without a violent revolution, without the dictatorship of the proletariat ?

" Obviously not. To think that such a revolution can be carried out peacefully, within the framework of bourgeois democracy, which is adapted to the rule of the bourgeoisie, means that one has either gone out of one's mind and lost normal human understanding, or has grossly and openly repudiated the proletarian revolution " (p. 126).

This belief that the desired results are to be sought only by violence, not by peaceful evolution, is not just theory. It reflects itself in the whole structure of Soviet society, and in its policies, domestic and foreign.

Internally, there is the militaristic pattern that is typical of a state of war. Absolute power rests with the heads of the Soviet Communist Party, which functions as a war-time general staff. " The proletariat needs the Party first of all as its General Staff, which it must have for the successful seizure of power " (p. 79). The Soviet proletariat is considered as " the shock brigade of the world proletariat " (p. 538). The Party itself operates under " iron discipline." " The achievement and maintenance of the dictatorship of the proletariat is impossible without a Party which is strong by reason of its solidarity and iron discipline. . . . The parties of the Communist Internationale, which base their activities on the task of achieving and consolidating the dictatorships of the proletariat, cannot afford to be " liberal " or to permit freedom of factions. The Party represents unity of will, which precludes all factionalism and division of authority in the Party " (pp. 81, 82). This internal unity is achieved by periodic purges in the course of which it is necessary " to handle some of these comrades roughly. But that cannot be helped " (p. 542).

The Soviet State is one of the tools of the Party. " The Party exercises the dictatorship of the proletariat. However, it exercises it not directly but with the help of the trade unions, and through the Soviet and their ramifications . . . not a single important political or organisational question is decided by our Soviet and other mass organisations without guiding directions from the Party " (pp. 134,135). The State, in turn, under such guiding direction from the Party, is a militant organisation. " The State is a machine in the hands of the ruling class for suppressing the resistance of its class enemies. . . . The dictatorship of the proletariat is the rule—unrestricted by law and based on force—of the proletariat over the bourgeoisie. . . . The dictatorship of the proletariat cannot be ' complete ' democracy, democracy for all, for the rich as well as for the poor " (pp. 32, 33).

Under this form of organisation, individuality is suppressed. In the field of politics and even of literature and the arts, there is coercion to think and act along uniform Party lines and there is coercion to eliminate any elements that might be discordant.

In its foreign policy, the Soviet Union shows its adherence

to the theory that the ends which it seeks can only be achieved by violent means. As regards the colonial areas, it seeks independence through revolution rather than through peaceful evolution. This is perhaps the fundamental reason why the Soviet Union has so long refused to sit upon the United Nations Trusteeship Council which is charged with promoting the peaceful evolution of dependent peoples toward independence or self-government. It prefers to seek " revolutionary alliance with the liberation movement of the colonies and dependent countries " (p. 52). In non-colonial areas there is penetration, secret and open, designed to bring into key positions those who accept the iron discipline of the Party and, as conditions seem opportune, resort is had to such methods as political strikes, sabotage, terrorism and guerrilla warfare. The Party has well-organised schools to train personnel for such tasks. These tactics have shown themselves in China, Korea, the Baltic States, Greece, Hungary, Bulgaria, Roumania, Poland, Czechoslovakia, Germany, France, Italy and elsewhere. It is not suggested that whenever there is violence in any of these areas the Soviet is wholly responsible for it. In some of the areas internal conditions are of such a nature as themselves to be promotive of unrest. But the Soviet Communist Party openly encourages and seeks to exploit conditions of violence.

The Soviet Union is a member of the United Nations and that membership can be harmonised with the policies of the Soviet Communist Party. The first purpose of the United Nations is " to maintain international peace and security." That is an end to which the Party can subscribe because war is not a preferred method of the Party. The violence and coercion which it invokes are the violence and coercion of internal struggle, the struggle to get the " police power " and then to use it for liquidating the " class enemies." Wherever the processes of the United Nations seem to stand in the way of Soviet efforts to promote such violent effort, the Soviet Union stands aloof. It has boycotted most of the specialised agencies of the United Nations designed to promote peacefully the economic, social and cultural well-being of the members. It has boycotted the Commissions on Greece and Korea which are designed to maintain the integrity of these states as against revolutionary penetration from the Soviet Union or other states dominated by Communist Parties. It refused to sit on the " Little Assembly " as well as on the Trusteeship Council, which is designed to promote peacefully the evolution of colonial peoples to self-government or independence.

The Party doctrines to which we have referred are intensively taught to all Party members and are fanatically accepted. There is ample evidence to show that Soviet policy in fact reflects those doctrines and reflects the view that the changes desired cannot be effected peacefully and that " a ' peaceful ' path of development " is possible only " in the remote future. if the proletariat is victorious in the most important capitalist countries " (p. 35).

We also see that this dependence upon methods of violence brings with it much the same " compulsory enmity, diabolical outrages against the human personality, and a wanton distortion of the truth " which have led Christians to oppose " wars, the occasion of war, and all situations which conceal the fact of conflict under the guise of outward peace " (Oxford Conference, *supra*).

Since the formation of the Soviet Union there has been a constant effort to portray the Union as surrounded by vicious and rapacious enemies. " We must remember that we are surrounded by people, classes and governments who openly express their intense hatred for us. We must remember that we are at all times but a hair's breadth from every manner of invasion " (p. 157, Lenin). There has been constant effort to arouse hatred toward so-called " bourgeois " or " imperialist " peoples, and notably the British and Americans. " Let not our hatred of our foes grow cold " (*Pravda*, January, 1948). Normal social intercourse is looked upon as partaking of treason ; intermarriage is forbidden.

It is taught that the nature of so-called imperialist or bourgeois countries is such that they must attack the Soviet Union and that " the existence of the Soviet Republic side by side with imperialist states for a long time is unthinkable. One or the other must triumph in the end. And before that end supervenes, a series of frightful collisions between the Soviet Republic and the bourgeois states will be inevitable " (p. 156, Lenin).

The militaristic regimentation within the Soviet Union involves many outrages against the human personality. These are reflected by frequent violent purges, by terrorism through secret police and by political concentration camps containing millions of persons.

Soviet propaganda by press and radio makes little effort to base itself on fact. It fabricates freely. Where facts are given, they are usually so given as to create an impression that is far from truth. That, of course, also happens elsewhere, but in a free society there is opportunity to combat falsehood by challenge and contradiction.

Because the Soviet party relies on means of violence, coercion, hatred and falsehood, the good ends it seeks do not, in fact, arrive—as is usual under such circumstances.

At a time when individual political responsibility has been greatly increasing in the world generally, it has contracted within the Soviet zones of influence ; and within the Soviet Union itself the leaders seem to contemplate indefinite postponement of that " withering away," that " atrophy," of dictatorship and that increase of individual self-rule which is one of the proclaimed ends (pp. 656-662).

At a time when economic inequalities have been levelling off in the capitalistic, free enterprise, countries, the Soviet state has found it necessary to reject the idea of " equalisation " and " levelling the requirements and the individual lives of the members of society " (p. 521). Increasing reliance is placed upon the stimulus of individual reward and self-gain (p. 363). Marxism, it is now taught, " is an enemy of equalisation " (p. 521). The workers get " payment for their work in accordance with its quantity and quality " and in accordance with the principle " he who does not work, neither shall he eat " (Constitution, Arts. 118, 12). There is indefinite postponement of the " higher phase " when there will be distribution " to each according to his needs " (pp. 569-570). Money, it is true, is not the primary means to power and special privilege. But other means are widely prevalent.

At a time when earnest and effective efforts are being made to achieve equality without regard to race or class, the Soviet Party intensifies class warfare and its " classless " society is relegated to the indefinite future because, it is said, the struggle of the " new class " against the " bourgeoisie " is not a " fleeting period," but an " entire historical era, replete with civil wars and external conflicts " (pp. 30, 31).

At a time when the Western democracies, notably Great Britain, were peacefully bringing political independence to upwards of 500,000,000 people, Soviet leaders, the great talkers

about the right of peoples to " independent existence as states "
(p. 51), have not themselves produced any freedom for any
people, but the Soviet Union has been annexationist.

At a time when the other Great Powers became increasingly
disposed to increase the authority of the United Nations,
Soviet leaders, while professing to seek a " single state union "
(p. 37) have refused even to discuss moving toward that result
by some diminution of the " veto " power within the Security
Council.

It is not contended that Soviet communism is wholly bad.
We have seen that all change has elements of good because everything that is is imperfect. Certainly, there was so much imperfection under the Czars that any change from that could readily
work some improvement. Also, Soviet leaders do not rely wholly
or continuously on means of violence and there have been some
good, peaceful developments, notably in the field of education.
Also, the very fact that there is a Soviet challenge has had a
stimulating effect upon the Western democracies which, for their
own good, needed the spur of competition.

Unfortunately, however, it seems basic in Soviet doctrine
that there is now no " peaceful path of development." During the
thirty years since the October Revolution, the emphasis, both in
doctrine and in practice, has been on violent and coercive
revolution, with results which confirm what history has so often
taught, that good ends are not readily achieved by means of
violence, terrorism, hatred and falsity such as the Soviet Party
advocates and uses. Those who adopt these methods give an
impression of great zeal and of great concern for their Cause.
What they do attracts great attention just because it is violent,
whereas peaceful change usually attracts little attention. But
close analysis usually shows that when change is sought to be
wrought by violence, the sense of progress, while exhilarating, is
illusory.

So it is that while there is no irreconcilable conflict between
the ultimate social ends which are professedly sought by Soviet
communists and those ends which Christian citizens seek, there
is great difference as to the means which should be used. That
difference derives both from the different philosophical and
moral premises and from conflicting judgments as to the kind
of means that, in fact, can be relied on to produce the desired
ends.

9. PEACEFUL RECONCILIATION OF PROGRAMME WITH
SOVIET PROGRAMME

The Soviet reliance on change by force and violence constitutes a serious obstacle athwart our suggested programme. Soviet influence is considerable and it is now favoured by external conditions.   World War II created a vacuum of power in many areas.   Of the eight so-called " Great Powers," three—Italy, Germany and Japan—have been engulfed by the disaster of defeat.   Three—United Kingdom, France and China—have been enfeebled by the struggle for victory.   Therefore, there is about the Soviet Union a power vacuum into which it has already moved to bring some three hundred million people, representing about fifteen nationalities, under the dominant influence of the dictatorship of the proletariat and its revolutionary theories and practices.

Even more important than this fact of political vacuum is the fact that there has developed in the world much of a moral vacuum.   The so-called western or Christian civilisation has long accepted most of the social ends now professed by the Soviet Communist Party and, indeed, its goals have been even more advanced.   But of recent years, it has seemed to be half-hearted and lacking in fervour or sense of urgency.   The result has been that many people have unthinkingly compared the idealised purposes and theories of the Soviet programme with the worst practices of western nations.   Others, eager for quick results, uncritical of means, have been attracted to the Soviet programme by the very violence of its means, which have seemed a proof of zeal.   The fact that Christian citizens tend to favour non-violent means is taken as proof that they lack zeal.   The consequent degree of following attracted by the Soviet dynamic programme has encouraged Soviet leaders to entertain great expectations of realising their particular " one world."   Their ambitions have mounted so that there is indeed grave danger of that " series of frightful collisions between the Soviet Republic and the bourgeois states " which Lenin and Stalin have forecast as inevitable.

Christians must dedicate themselves to prevent such developments.   There are in the main two ways of doing so.

First, Christians must reject, and see to it that their nations reject, the Soviet thesis of the inevitability of violent conflict and they must not imitate Soviet leadership by placing reliance on violent means.

Secondly, Christians must see to it that their nations demonstrate that peaceful methods can realise the goals which we all espouse.

There is disturbing evidence that the so-called " free societies " are themselves tending to adopt those features of Soviet procedure which Christians particularly condemn. In the United States great emphasis is being placed upon achieving military supremacy and military counsels are more influential than has normally been the case in that republic. Some portions of the American Press are stirring up emotional hatred against the Soviet Union and there is some distortion of truth, principally through the exaggeration of what is true but of minor importance.

It is no doubt desirable that the free societies should be resolute and strong. Also, it is important that the members of free societies should understand the true nature of the Soviet programme so that they do not abet it mistakenly. Also, there is no good in concealing the fact that the Soviet programme is dangerous. Whenever any particular group sets out to dominate the world and to do so by methods of violence, coercion and terrorism, a tense situation is bound to result. No doubt Soviet leaders do not want major war, although we must recall that Lenin has stated, and Stalin has repeated, that " if the ruling class, the proletariat, wants to hold sway, it must prove its capacity to do so by military organisation also " (p. 156, Lenin). But even if, as we believe, Soviet leaders now look upon their methods of internal penetration as more effective than international war, still the situation is risky. It requires a very nice judgment to use force precisely to the degree which will gain the maximum without precipitating actual war. Such an effort also assumes, on the part of others, a degree of self-control which we hope and pray exists, but which is not a certainty. Thus peace is at the risk of incidents or miscalculations. The free societies need to face up to that reality. But also they must strive to exercise iron self-control, being determined not themselves to use force to crush the Soviet experiment. They may not like the Soviet experiment in state socialism and its dynamic world-wide programme, but they must recognise that a free world is a world of difference and that any society has a right to experiment and compete. Marshal Stalin claimed that the results of the Soviet first Five Year Plan proved that " the working-class is as able to build the new as to destroy the old " (p. 439) and that they have confounded the claim of capitalism as the " best of all societies " (p. 440). If, in fact, the Soviet system of state socialism can peacefully confound capitalism, it is entitled to the opportunity to do so. Unhappily, the Soviet does not rely primarily upon such methods of peaceful competition and comparison. But the Soviet methods, while they are in part methods which Christians will generally reject, are so far at least methods short of war and Christian citizens of the free societies must make a supreme effort to do all that lies within their power to keep it so and to see that their nations use peaceful responses which are available and which can preserve and extend the system of free societies.

The most important response to the Soviet challenge will be in effecting peacefully the reforms which Soviet leaders contend can only be effected by violent means. We must by actual demonstration disprove Stalin's dictum that " one must be a revolutionary, not a reformist " (p. 597).

The western democracies won their prestige in the world through their great peaceful accomplishments. The industrial revolution, the concept of " liberty, equality and fraternity " and the experiments in political freedom created world-wide confidence in the dynamic and life-giving quality of their institutions. But for long now, these democracies have faced no serious competition. The quality of their effort has deteriorated and they have, to a considerable extent, been coasting with a momentum that is waning. Many do not like it that a challenge has now arisen. Many would prefer peace which is a condition of tranquillity or stagnation, where all threat and challenge are removed and where men can feel that they can safely relax. Some are inclined to the view that unless we get that kind of peace, we do not have peace at all, and an irresponsible few talk of using force to crush the challenger. That is folly. Those of us who are of the western peoples face the task of mental adjustment to a dynamic peace where there is competition. We need to make it clear to ourselves and we need to make it clear to proponents of other systems that we welcome a world in which there is peaceful competition. Above all, we need to make it clear that we can peacefully, through reform, bring about results which all men want and which they will be apt to seek by the violent methods which the Soviet sponsors unless we can prove that they can be achieved by peaceful means.

Whenever a system is challenged, there is a tendency to rally to support the system " as is." The world becomes divided between those who would maintain the *status quo* and those who would change the *status quo*. As we have seen, those who would sustain the *status quo* inevitably are defeated. And almost inevitably the issue is resolved by violence. The result may not be the particular changes desired by the dynamic powers, but equally, it does not maintain the status which their opponents sought to preserve. So it is that in the face of Soviet challenge we must not rally to the defence of our institutions just as they are, but we must seek even more ardently to make them better than they now are.

In fact, much progress has been made along this line. We have already referred to the action of Great Britain in bringing about five hundred millions of colonial dependent peoples peacefully to self-government. That has been the most effective way to demonstrate that the achievement of self-government by dependent peoples was not dependent upon a Soviet " revolutionary alliance " (p. 52) and that it is possible to achieve by peaceful means results which the Soviet leaders profess to want but which they have said could only be achieved by violent means.

The " free societies " have also made considerable progress in achieving an economy whereby production is on the basis of ability and distribution on the basis of need. The steeply graduated income and estate taxes which now prevail generally in " capitalistic " countries take largely from those who have ability to accumulate and to an increasing extent this is being distributed to those in need, in the form of social security programmes. These countries are in fact much closer to the so-called " higher phase " of communism than is the Soviet Union itself.

Socially, the great blot on the escutcheon of the democracies is the discrimination against coloured persons practised by much of the white population of the United States. Here, however, the problem is recognised and great efforts are being made to deal with it. It is not possible by legislative fiat to eradicate social prejudices, the origins of which go back hundreds of years. There is, however, a vast change which is in peaceful process.

The danger is that those who face the Soviet challenge will feel they must defend themselves on every count. There is some evidence that the Soviet challenge is, to an extent, having that natural result. Christians must stand strong against that, recognising the imperfection of every system and of every nation, not identifying righteousness with anything that is, but constantly striving to prove that the evils that exist can be eradicated by peaceful means.

That demonstration is already gathering momentum, and as that momentum grows, the Soviet menace will become innocuous and Soviet leaders themselves will probably abandon, or at least indefinitely postpone, their efforts to produce change by violent means. Probably they will not do so as a matter of conviction, for the conception of violent change is deeply ingrained. But they can be expected to alter their tactics as soon as there will no longer be available to them in the different countries of the world sufficient support for successful revolutionary measures. Soviet leaders are realists. They do not consider that violence must be continuous or that it should be recklessly undertaken. Their aim is to strike " at the decisive point, at the decisive moment " (p. 63, Lenin). There is not uninterrupted attack and there may at times be strategic retreat. " They have to realise—and the revolutionary class is taught to realise by its own bitter experience—that victory is impossible unless they have learned both how to attack and how to retreat properly " (p. 65, Lenin). " The object of this strategy is to gain time " (p. 65). There must be a " selection of the moment for the decisive blow " (p. 64).

So it is that while Soviet leaders believe in violent means, they do not believe in continuing violence and they do not believe in violence being precipitated until the moment comes when " all the class forces hostile to us have . . . exposed . . . their practical bankruptcy " (p. 64, Lenin).

The years between the Soviet revolution and World War II involved a very large exposure of practical bankruptcy on the part of non-communist nations. During that period the " free societies," at least, were not at their best. Soviet leaders have encountered weaknesses which have afforded them great opportunities and given them great encouragement. Within recent years that situation has begun to change. There have been some great constructive developments. To some of these we have alluded. It is possible to push forward along these lines and it is imperative that this should be done.

It is regrettable that the Soviet Communist Party and those that follow its guiding directions will not co-operate in a world programme to develop peacefully conditions needed for peaceful change. But that non-co-operation need not operate as a veto. If, through fear or morbid fascination, the free societies do nothing, then they do indeed make inevitable those violent revolutionary processes, those frightful collisions, which Soviet leadership would precipitate as its means to its ends.

The Soviet challenge loses its potency once the free societies show a capacity for constructive action. As we have said, the challenge, in its present phase, seems not a militaristic challenge, like that of Hitler, Mussolini and the Japanese war lords. It is a call to revolution. If the non-communist societies, faced by that challenge, stand still and do nothing, for fear of offending Soviet leadership, they are lost. If they quietly move ahead, showing a practical capacity to achieve peacefully the things which Soviet leaders say can come only after an " entire historical era " of violence, then those talkers will quickly be rated as " incorrigible windbags "—to use Stalin's expression (p. 533).

It is important that there be these peaceful developments both domestically and internationally. We have already outlined what might be the grand, over-all, international programme. But such a long-range programme is not enough to meet the present need because it does not contain enough possibility to register quickly decisive results and thus to create general recognition of the capacity of the free societies. Intermediate programmes are needed, where successes can be registered, prestige gained and momentum acquired. We shall go on to consider what might be some of these intermediate programmes.

10. INTERMEDIATE STEPS AT PRESENT PRACTICABLE

It is not necessary to stand still and do nothing internationally until there has been laid the world-wide foundation for a free world society. There is much which can be done, to-day and to-morrow. There are already two great assets with which to work. One is the great and all-pervading force of the moral law. A second is the existence of an organisation—the United Nations—

which brings together in public association most of the nations of the world. On the basis of these two facts, many intermediate successes can be achieved.

Exposure to Moral Judgment

The moral law has universal influence. There are some who deny its existence and who try to educate men to ignore it. It is never immediately and universally effective. But still there is general, world-wide agreement about " right " and " wrong " in their broad outlines. That fact is of immense importance, for it makes it possible to use moral force for peace and justice at a time when there cannot yet be an adequate political mechanism.

Moral power can be a powerful force in the world. That is not a mere pious hope. It is the judgment of every realist throughout history. It was Napoleon who said that " in war, moral considerations make up three-fourths of the game." It was Admiral Mahan who said that physical force was useful only " to give moral ideas time to take root."

Allied leaders during both the First and Second World Wars did much to consolidate and marshal world sentiment to ensure Germany's defeat. They did that through great statements of aims, such as the Fourteen Points and the Atlantic Charter, which appealed to the moral conscience of the world. It is possible also to frame issues and organise moral power in the interest of peace.

The United Nations is a political machine which even now can be used to make moral power work during peace to preserve peace. That is largely due to Christian influence.

Many thought that world organisation should be primarily a military organisation to carry out the will of the Great Powers. That was, indeed, the conception which dominated the representatives of the Soviet Union, Great Britain and the United States when they met at Dumbarton Oaks in the summer of 1944 to make a first draft of the Charter. But our church people did not think much of an organisation which would be primarily military and which would depend chiefly on physical force. So they worked hard to make their point of view prevail. It did largely prevail at the San Francisco Conference of 1945, thanks in great part to the small nations, which did not want to be placed permanently under the military dictatorship of the three big Powers.

So, the San Francisco Conference radically changed the plan of Dumbarton Oaks. It emphasised the United Nations General Assembly as a place where the representatives of all states, big and little, would meet and discuss any problems of international relations, and where even the great nations could be required to subject their conduct to the judgment of world opinion.

The United Nations has now been functioning for over two years. Many are disappointed with the results. They would like the United Nations to be able to dictate and enforce the particular results which they want. As we have seen, the United Nations cannot now be that kind of an organisation. However, it has revealed great possibilities. Of course, it has not settled everything. Indeed, the international situation is gravely troubled. But the United Nations has shown that it need not be a mere spectator. It can do something. It can call every nation's international acts to the bar of public opinion, with confidence that that will have healthy practical consequences.

We have seen how, in time of war, the public verdict of right and wrong exercises a powerful effect. The United Nations has begun to show how, in time of peace, public opinion can exercise a powerful effect. At the San Francisco Conference and at the subsequent Assemblies of the United Nations political leaders from many lands have presented views on many matters. Always the speakers were obviously conscious of the fact that their audience included the representatives of many million people who possessed great power and who were primarily swayed by moral considerations. Every speaker presented his case with regard to what he thought was world opinion and he tried to get its backing. Almost always the different governments presented their positions otherwise than they would have done had they been meeting in secret and not subject to informed world opinion. That is a fact of great moment. It does not make future war impossible. It can make war less likely.

Things equal to the same thing are equal to each other. If world opinion can bring the foreign policies of the different nations toward harmony with the world's moral judgment, then those policies will automatically move toward harmony with each other.

It ought to be normal that major international policies which create fear or resentment anywhere should be subjected to the scrutiny of the Assembly.

The United Nations Charter provides that the Assembly may discuss any situation, regardless of origin, which it deems likely to impair friendly relations among nations. Thus, the Assembly can act as the " town meeting of the world," as was the design. If any nation is afraid to have its international policies discussed, that is good proof that they ought to be discussed. In the Assembly the sponsors of questioned policies would explain them and welcome an expression of the confidence of the Assembly. The verdict would not have any legal consequences. There may not be immediate and clear-cut compliance with it, but an unfavourable judgment would to some degree influence the future of the condemned policy and make more likely its modification or abandonment. No nation, however strong, will lightly defy a verdict which seems to reflect the informed and aroused moral judgment of mankind.

Soviet dictatorship is sensitive to public opinion. It is by no means stupid enough to think that it can prevail merely by force. At home it can, within limits, make public opinion what it will. But only within limits. The Party recognises that it must " properly express what the people are conscious of " and that this is a " necessary condition " (p. 152). Stalin says that the Soviet Union joined the League of Nations in 1934 because it recognised that the possibility of exposure would deter wrongdoers. ". . . despite its weakness the League might nevertheless serve as a place where aggressors can be exposed " (p. 628). The Soviet representatives, more than any others, have used the United Nations as a forum for appealing to public opinion. They recognise that, in the outer world, where police power and control of news are not at their command, Soviet foreign policy cannot prevail unless it can bring people generally to believe in its rightness.

So, while the United Nations cannot to-day be converted into a mechanism directed by a few persons having power to rule the nations, it can be used to subject national acts to the test of moral judgment. Moral power arises from the most humble to reach the most mighty. It works inexorably, even though slowly. It will not suit the impatient. But it can achieve solid results. The important thing is that the United Nations be used for purposes for which it is adapted and not be discredited by attempted use for purposes for which it is ill adapted.

Some relatively minor changes would serve greatly to increase the capacity of the United Nations to serve as a medium for focusing world opinion upon national acts. There should be a permanent organ of the United Nations able, at all times, quickly to bring to light the facts necessary for world opinion to form an intelligent judgment. The Security Council logically should do that. But its freedom to investigate is limited by the Permanent Members' right of veto. If this cannot be changed, then it may be that the General Assembly could undertake this task, perhaps through its " Interim Committee " or " Little Assembly " so as to assure at least what Stalin referred to as " exposure."

Social and Economic Agencies

The United Nations is not designed merely to deal with political problems. It is also designed to promote human welfare. One of the great conceptions embodied in the Charter was that the unity gained in war could be preserved in peace if the war allies went on together to combat the social, economic and physical enemies of mankind. So the Charter branded intolerance, repression, injustice, disease and economic want as the common enemies of the morrow, just as Nazi Germany and Imperialist Japan were the common enemies of the day. It proposed that the united nations stay united to wage war against these evils.

These possibilities of the United Nations have not, as yet, been adequately developed. Commissions and specialised agencies are at work, but they have not yet had time to achieve any dramatic successes and, indeed, their work has largely been lost sight of because political controversy in the Assembly and Security Council has seemed more exciting, more news-worthy and more important. The economic and social tasks of the United Nations should be brought into proper perspective and pushed with effort comparable to that invested in the political phase of United Nations work.

International Bill of Rights

One of the most important of these social tasks of the United Nations is the bringing into force of an agreed international Bill of Rights. The United Nations Charter itself, by its preamble, affirms faith in fundamental human rights and in the dignity and worth of the human person. One of its basic purposes is to achieve international co-operation in promoting and encouraging respect for human rights and for fundamental freedoms for all. Provision is made in the Charter for a commission for the promotion of human rights, which Commission has now been established. It ought to be possible through this Commission to bring about increased acceptance of a Bill of Rights. This, if done, would greatly facilitate the building of the foundation required for transforming the United Nations itself into a more effective political instrumentality. This important subject is being dealt with in another chapter.[1]

Functional Agencies

A further important area of usefulness lies in the development of functional agencies to carry out agreed policies. The United Nations itself, under present conditions, cannot legislate generally. There are, however, some matters as to which a policy could be voluntarily agreed upon between all or most of the member states. Then these agreed policies could be entrusted to some functional agency to carry out. One of the proposals regarding atomic energy illustrates this type of procedure. The fact that that particular proposal has not yet been accepted, does not show that the functional approach is itself unsuitable. The functional approach is the easiest and most painless method of breaking down, or at least breaking through, national boundaries. It does not involve any blanket delegation of power which could be used despotically. It is merely a means of achieving, on an international basis, a concrete result sought by different nations.

In the United States, the State of New York and the State of New Jersey have, through a treaty consented to by the Federal Congress, created the Port of New York Authority, which develops the sea and air facilities of the New York Harbour area. It finances its own projects. It serves an end which is greatly in the interest of the people of both states and it does so by means and methods which are so inconspicuous that few citizens of either state are aware of the fact that they have made a very large surrender of sovereignty to an inter-state body.

[1] See Chapter V. "Freedom of Religion and related Human Rights," by O. Frederick Nolde.

Functional agencies, to advance mutually desired ends, can be set up under the auspices of the United Nations in agreement with the member states or such of them as are concerned. The operations of the agencies within the agreed scope of their authority could be free of any veto power.

It is particularly important that atomic energy should be brought under world rule. There exists a moral basis for such rule because all of the governments have expressed the view that there should be effective means to assure that this new power should be used constructively for man's welfare and not destructively for, perhaps, the extermination of mankind. The United Nations Assembly, as its first important act, voted unanimously to establish a commission to accomplish this result. However, nearly two and a half years have since elapsed and differences as to the means of control have created an impasse. Meanwhile, the knowledge of how to use atomic energy for destruction is doubtless growing and competent persons say that the monopoly of know-how may be broken in the near future. A situation of great gravity would arise if behind the present ideological differences there lay the menace of atomic weapons. It would be particularly grave if these weapons were held by persons who espouse the use of violent means to achieve their ends. Civilisation is drifting dangerously toward the edge of an awful precipice. To save it may require that atomic energy should, on a world-wide basis, be promptly brought under international control.

Regional Agencies

The United Nations Charter provides for regional agencies and agencies for collective self-defence. Through such agencies, international organisation can be developed more rapidly than on a world-wide scale. Inevitably, world-wide development is the slowest ; local development is quicker. Political institutions have developed from cities and principalities to counties and states and finally to great aggregations of states, like the Soviet Union and the United States, bound together by a federal system, and the British Commonwealth, bound together by loose agreement and common loyalties which have become traditional. The Pan-American defence system is a striking illustration of how groups of nations may unite on the basis of common interest and common trust.

Steps toward political, economic and monetary unity are being taken by many nations of Europe. This is a good development. A Europe divided into a score or more of separate unconnected sovereignties can never again be a healthful and peaceful part of the world. To substitute unity and strength for disunity and weakness is precisely the kind of positive action of which the free societies must prove themselves capable.

It is axiomatic that world government is the last step and the most difficult step to take. It is easier to develop political mechanisms on a less than universal basis than on a universal basis. By doing that, men can increase somewhat the possibilities of peaceful and selective change on an international basis. If, for example, ten nations can find a common political mechanism, they should not be prevented from doing so merely because sixty nations cannot do the same thing. It would be as logical to say that the states of the Soviet Union or of the United States should not have come together politically because that unity could not be achieved on a world-wide basis. Regional pacts and arrangements for collective self-defence are expressly authorised by the Charter of the United Nations (Articles 51, 52). They should be encouraged, subject only to the qualification that they should be genuinely based upon legitimate common interests ; should in no sense be a military alliance directed against any other state ; should sincerely seek to maintain and promote universality through the United Nations. To-day there are in the world a series of international groupings. There is the Soviet Union and its several associated states. There is the British Commonwealth. There is the Arab League. There is the Pan-American system. Such groupings can be steps toward the universal world order which is the goal of our long-range programme.

.   .   .   .   .   .

We could go on indefinitely in this vein. We have, however, said enough to indicate that, with a moral law of universal scope and with the United Nations as a place to bring together national acts and world-wide judgments, important intermediate results can be achieved. There is much to be done on a less than universal basis, within the framework of the Charter. Nations and peoples can do much to help each other. Such efforts do not take the place of our long-range programme, because they do not constitute a conscious, planned effort to create, on a world-wide basis, the conditions prerequisite to a general institutionalising of change. But interim measures can gain the time and the prestige needed for successful development of a long-range programme.

What seems urgent—and possible—is to revive in men a sense of moving peacefully toward a state of greater perfection. Many have been beaten and broken in spirit by the violence of the forces that have been loose in the world for now upward of a decade. They temporarily placed hope—perhaps undue hope—in the United Nations. But that hope has largely gone and there is despairing acceptance of the idea that continuing violence is inevitable for an entire historical era.

That is a dangerous mood. It can, perhaps, be broken by acts which, even in a small way, show the possibility of peaceful change. Let us, therefore, not despise what is presently possible, knowing that out of small things can come a rebirth of faith and hope, and that out of faith and hope can come great things, far beyond any that are here portrayed.

CONCLUSION

The Rôle of the Christian Church

Many will feel that the programmes here outlined are quite inadequate ; and those who feel that way may be quite right. Certainly our suggestions seem unimaginative and stodgy in comparison with many programmes, particularly the Soviet programme for achieving its ideal single world state by means of world-wide proletariat revolution. We have tried to write under a self-imposed ordinance, namely, to propose only what we felt might *practically* be achieved by *peaceful* means and without the sacrifice of hard-won human rights. No doubt, even within this limitation, there are better prospects than are here portrayed. But no programme which is both practical and peaceful will seem as exciting and dramatic as a programme which is purely imaginative or violent.

Leaders who invoke violence attract a fanatical following because they seem to know what they want and to be determined to get it. They give an impression of being right just because they seem willing to risk much to achieve their goals. Many seem to feel that " truth " is whatever people are willing to fight and die for, and that unless people advocate killing and dying, they must be doubtful in their own minds. So it is that ways of violence often become exalted and ways of peace are often depreciated.

It would be easy to arouse the so-called " free societies " of the Western " Christian " civilisation to initiate a great crusade, a holy war. Their programme could be expressed in many fine-sounding slogans, such as the " smashing of atheistic despotism " and the " removal of the last remaining obstacle to indispensable world government." Such a programme would evoke great enthusiasm and many fine sacrificial qualities. Many would gladly fight and die for such ends.

We reject any such procedure because of our profound conviction that its violence would end in utter frustration. We consider that such a procedure would be as irreconcilable with Christianity as is the violent procedure which Soviet leaders advocate and that in either case the procedure would produce results quite different from those sought.

We are fully conscious of the fact that peaceful and practical programmes will seem to many to evidence a lack of zeal and to conceal a desire selfishly to preserve the evils of the *status quo*. That appraisal, in our opinion, can be and should be changed. Christians should, we believe, appraise more highly than they seem to do the self-control, the self-discipline and the respect for human dignity required to make change by peaceful means. The Christian churches could, we think, find the way to make peaceful efforts seem more inspirational and be more sacrificial. It is a tragedy that inspiration and sacrifice in large volume seem to be evoked only by ways of violence. If the Christian churches could change that, then, indeed, they would help the Christian citizen along his way.

We have not outlined tasks which could be participated in only by Christians because, we believe, that if Christians advance a political programme which only Christians can support, they logically must contemplate a monopoly of power and privilege on behalf of their particular sect. That, we have made clear, would, in our opinion, vitiate the programme. But the task which we have outlined is a task which should arouse the Christian churches to a sense of special responsibility.

What is the need ? The need is for men and women who

can see what now is and what can be. Christ put particular emphasis on vision and light. He taught men to see truly and to avoid the hatred, hypocrisy and selfishness which blind men or warp their visions. If Christian churches do not produce the needed vision, what can we expect but that mankind will stumble.

The need is for men who have the peacefulness which comes to those who are possessed by the Christian spirit of love ; who have the power which comes to those who pray, repent and are transformed and who have the dedication of those who leave all to follow Him.

The need is for more effective political use of moral power. The moral law, happily, is a universal law. But Christians believe that, through Christ, the moral law has been revealed with unique clarity. The Christian churches ought, therefore, to be especially qualified to help men to form moral judgments which are discerning and to focus them at the time and place where they can be effective.

The need is for full use of the present great possibilities of the United Nations. It was Christians most of all who wanted a world organisation which would depend primarily on moral rather than physical power. They have it. Now it is up to the churches to generate the moral power required to make the organisation work.

The need is to build the foundation for a more adequate world organisation. A world of free societies could be that foundation, and free society depends, in turn, on individuals who exemplify Christian qualities of self-control and of human brotherhood, and who treat freedom, not as licence, but as occasion for voluntary co-operation for the common good. So, again, the Christian churches have the great responsibility.

The need is for effort on a world-wide scale. The Christian Church is a world-wide institution. Consequently, the individual Christian may exert his influence not only as a citizen but also as member of a church which in its corporate life has a contribution to make. The Church demonstrates in its own life the achievement of community out of various races, nationalities and communions. It develops a common ethos. Its missionary movement constantly extends the fellowship of those who share the same loyalties and purposes. Its ecumenical movement deepens and consolidates that fellowship. Its programme of relief and reconstruction restores hope to the despairing and reconciles those who have been enemies. The Commission of the Churches on International Affairs is beginning to give stimulus and leadership to the more direct impact of the churches on the current problems of relations between the nations. Thus the churches themselves in many ways can help build the bases for world order.

So it is that, as we analyse the need, Christian responsibility emerges as an inescapable fact. It is a fact that ought to have practical consequences. The potentialities of Christian influence are great, but the present weight of Christian impact is wholly inadequate. If, in the international field, Christians are to play their clearly indicated part, their churches must have better organisation, more unity of action and put more emphasis on Christianity as a world religion. That, we pray, will come from the Amsterdam Assembly and the final realisation of the World Council of Churches.

(b) OUR RESPONSIBILITY IN THE POST-WAR WORLD

Joseph L. Hromadka

I. THE PERSPECTIVE OF HISTORY

Because of these abnormal times, the Church of Christ has to deal with the basic issues of our present international life both with extreme caution and with courageous clarity. We are living, three years after the end of World War II, on volcanic ground, pregnant with destructive explosions and earthquakes. The old international order is gone. No great issue has been solved, not one area of our earth has achieved stability and security. In the history of the human race it is a unique, unprecedented situation. Never in the past has the *whole* of the world been shaken so profoundly as during the last thirty years. Since the last war the magnitude of the international crisis has manifested itself with such terrific and inescapable pressure that every thoughtful person feels the proximity of an avalanche which at the mere echo of a loud voice may bury what has been left of our civilisation and spiritual heritage. This is why we should approach any big problem of our present international life with extreme caution.

However, for the same reason we urgently need a courageous clarity of mind. Much of our present confusion and perilous tension is due to our lack of understanding of what is actually going on among the peoples and nations of the world. Everywhere we observe frustration and impatience, distrust and fear, and everywhere we sense the danger of an explosion because of an inadequate understanding of the magnitude and dimensions of the international catastrophe. Each one of us knows of instances when human impatience and anger killed a seriously sick man, and when the same impatience and anger had originated and grown because the people around the patient had been unaware of the gravity of his illness. From my own experience I can say that both the most irritated and sanguine critics of the international situation, and of " the other side " in particular, have lacked a clear vision of the nature and the abysmal depth of the contemporaneous crisis. The simple truth is that the rapid changes of history are transcending our normal categories, that, lacking imagination and vision, we are unable to grasp the meaning of the present turmoil and so become either disillusioned and cynical, or angry and hostile towards the nations and the men who seem to thwart our plans so wantonly. Hence it is essential that once again we try to understand courageously and clearly the basic nature and issues of contemporaneous history. Courageously, that is—to go beyond our pleasant and popular clichés, to break through our accepted conventions, and to abandon ideas which are already out of date. We lack courage, but we likewise lack clarity which resists and withstands the intoxicating haze of comfortable simplifications.

How far we are from the days of thirty years ago when the progressive, freedom-loving men were stirred by the great idea of " making the world safe for democracy ! " Ever since those days of " a new spring " many events have taken place which have unveiled the weaknesses and frailties of the modern, free, civilised society ! Then, we earnestly believed that the great ideas of a free, autonomous, self-determining humanity might be adequate to meet the issues of the modern era, not only to destroy the shackles of the feudal, autocratic, monarchical régimes, but also to build up a new Temple of human freedom and justice. We failed to overcome the fatal consequences of World War I and to establish a new, better, durable order on the ruins of the old. The basic issue of our times, both in national and international life, is far more than freedom and democracy. It goes beyond the categories of capitalism and socialism, liberalism and communism, even beyond what we call the alternative of " a free society or a totalitarian system," the alternative of the democratic, free West or the communistic, regulated, controlled East. The whole of the civilised human race is sick, and none is justified to claim a monopoly of means and medicines for the cure of the disintegrated international order. We are living in a crisis that is more than a crisis of democracy and freedom, of liberalism or humanism. What is at stake is much more than modern civilisation and free society. The ultimate principles and axioms of truth, justice, human personality, love, and the organic moral fellowship of men are at stake. Modern man, both in the West and in the East, has lost a real understanding of the supreme authority and the supreme court of appeal to which all men, all nations and races, ought to subordinate themselves in order to understand one another and to discover a common ground on which to start the construction of a new and better order.

2. THE PERSPECTIVE OF THE BIBLICAL MESSAGE

A right historical perspective is needed if we wish to have a right insight into the main issues of our international struggle. This is not enough. As members of the Church of Christ we need a still more adequate vantage point, the perspective of faith. The faith we mean is the certainty of the real presence of the Crucified and Risen Lord in the midst of our present misery and calamity. The place of the Church is beyond all human, political, national and cultural divisions and hostile groupings, beyond all hatreds, fears, suspicions, political devices and platforms of the post-war world. This is by no means to minimise the importance and validity of social, political and international ideals or aspirations. The Church of Christ may be non-political, but she is not indifferent to the problem of bringing order into a chaotic human society. Even he who knows the main *motifs* of the history of our civilisation is not in a position to assess the profound political contributions the Church, as such, has made to the structure of our society. She is not neutral in the struggle between freedom and slavery, justice and lawlessness, order and chaos, civil rights and tyranny. And yet, the Church has a peculiar mission : to go down, to the very abyss, where men as miserable sinners stand before their Lord, and where men commit clumsy blunders and make inescapable personal and political decisions. This is exactly where the prophets and apostles have sent her. The Lord of holiness, justice and mercy has descended from the heaven of heavens into the darkest valley of human corruption and sin, and has broken the bondage of guilt and death exactly where the power of godlessness and destructive evil seemed to triumph invincibly over Christ and His Kingdom. The Church can live only in the presence of her Lord. This means that she has to stand where He stands, and to do what He has done, to identify herself with human helplessness and need.

The present moment of history makes us more responsive to the mystery of the Biblical Testimony, or—at least—it opens our eyes to the fact, so often previously hidden, that the power of sin and confusion, both in the personal and political realm, transcends our capacity to cope with the catastrophic situation. The whole human race has been shaken out of its complacency, and the world's ruins reveal our helplessness. We have been awakened to *what* we are and *where* we are. " They are all gone aside, they are all together become filthy : there is none that doeth good, no, not one " (Psalm xiv, 3 ; Rom. iii, 12). This is not to proclaim a morbid relativism and to deny a real, specific responsibility on the part of individual nations or groups for the catastrophe in which we live ; this is rather to warn us against any effort to identify the Church of Christ with a definite political cause or to use her against any international *bloc*. Here we are : victors and vanquished, " Western " democrats and " Eastern " socialists and communists, citizens of the European-American civilisation as well as heirs of Eastern, Asiatic cultural tradition, different in race and education, but all of us united in common misery and sin, as well as in faith and ultimate loyalty to the Crucified and Risen Lord. Are we ?

Deep as is the difference in the measure of our responsibility for the destruction of the old international peace and order, and for the terrific losses in life and material welfare, we have to look at the contemporaneous international situation from the perspective of our common guilt and suffering on the one hand, and, on the other, of the real presence in our midst of the Crucified.

It is not so easy. Each one of us has been influenced and formed by his particular national heritage and political ideology. Consciously or unconsciously, we justify our political prejudices and concepts on the ground of our own national traditions, being rarely able to draw a clear line between the Biblical message of justice and freedom and the political ideas we share. Furthermore, being under the spell of our national political aspirations, we are historically and psychologically handicapped in our effort to understand other nations and the ways in which they have socially and politically organised the life of society. A Western democrat believes in his brand of democratic methods and processes and is easily impatient or irritated when a nation chooses another way of political action and organisation. There is nothing more important than to be aware of one's own political weakness and shortcomings, and—simultaneously—to look at other nations from the perspective of their historical past and against their social background. Before we engage in controversy and struggle let us understand one another and approach the basic issues in a spirit of self-control and constructive cooperation. If we meet one another as poor sinners equally responsible for the days to come, and if we listen to the word of the Living Lord, present in our midst in His holy compassion and mercy, then we may do something essential for the new order of peace and justice, justice and peace.

3. THE NEW HISTORICAL SITUATION

Let us, again, consider the dimensions of the historical changes and the magnitude of what has to be done. The heavy burden of the restoration of the international order and co-operation has been shifted on to the shoulders of two new Powers which, until 1941, were only in a loose way responsible for the maintenance of world trade and international peace. The American nation and the Soviet people are newcomers, just entering the stage of world architects. Neither of them has undergone an adequate test as to its skill and ability to lead other nations along the lines of peaceful collaboration. This is to a certain extent a fortunate situation. Both the American nation and the Soviet Commonwealth (the Federal Union of Soviet Republics), being comparatively young and new, are unfettered by a petrified political tradition and diplomatic routine, and may approach the big issues of our time with that freshness of mind and courage of imagination which help us to grasp the real, vital needs of the human race and to throw overboard all obsolete inhibitions and outdated, paralysing fears. The peoples of the U.S.A. and the U.S.S.R. have very much in common : they are numerically big, rich in territory and in actual (America) or potential (the Soviet nation) material treasures. Both of them are technically minded, eager to learn, to invent, to organise, and no obstacles will stop them. A European citizen looking at the American West and the Soviet East cannot help being impressed by a touch of titanic dynamism in these two new powerful organisers of the new world. Whereas the old European nations were oppressed by an age-long tradition in politics, social culture and way of life, the two great victors and leading nations of the present era are relatively free and unshackled, and may face the heavy task of the new human order with boldness and a genuine understanding of what the *present* moment demands.

However, the same profound historical change which has pushed the two new Powers into the forefront of international life is causing peculiar anxiety and uneasiness—a mood very different from that after World War I. The present political upheaval itself is a revolution unprecedented in the political history of humanity. The British Empire in the process of liquidation, the breakdown of French power, the dismal fall of Germany, the throes of Indian national independence, the civil war in China, the end of the last feudal tradition in Central Europe and in the Balkans—who can grasp the meaning and the potential consequences of these almost volcanic revolutionary changes ? Let us repeat : We are living in the midst of an international revolution unsurpassed in human history. If we are scared by the very word " revolution," we had better get readjusted to it lest we fail to cope with the abysmal problems pressing us to the wall ! All is fluid, nothing is stable and secure, political life resembles burning lava from a volcano, threatening our dwellings and our treasures. Are the Americans and the Soviet people capable of dealing adequately with the scope and nature of the change, and with what ought to be built on the débris of yesterday ? None of us can possibly make any prediction. There are, naturally, men and women who are terrified by the advance of the Soviet power—unknown, unpredictable, sometimes ruthless and brutal, sometimes irresistible on account of its deep appeal to the mind of common men. There are, however, millions of those who are depressed by the growing military power, economic wealth, and atomic energy in the hands of the American nation, all the more as it is so well protected by two oceans and by very good neighbours. Many of us are inclined to take the present position of the U.S.A. for granted, as a reassuring safeguard and stronghold of what we call Christian civilisation : The United States as the projection of the Western Christian tradition and of humanism with its emphasis upon the dignity of man, the sacredness of conscience, freedom of human personality, civil rights, habeas corpus, tolerance and political self-determination ![1]

And yet, we must not ignore the fact, that the U.S.A. has become the wealthiest nation in the world and that for many millions, not only in the East, it is a symbol of the power of money, and has—rightly or wrongly—ceased to be looked upon as the Promised Land of freedom, progress and happiness. A large section of humanity is afraid of America, of the demonic temptations of money, capital and wealth. This should be considered. What matters in the realm of the international struggle is not only brute, tangible facts, but also moods and sentiments, fears and hopes, prejudices and sympathies.

Here we are, standing at the dividing line of two eras of history, between the Western world, with all its noble tradition, represented by the American people, and on the other hand, the " Eurasiatic " East represented by the Soviet Union, claiming for the first time in history an equal share in the leadership of the world. Now these two giants, instead of co-operating in the construction of a peaceful order, find themselves in a situation of growing mutual distrust and dislike. This is a terrifying situation. The breakdown of the Versailles peace of 1919 was, in a large measure, due to the disunity of the victors. They won the war, signed the peace treaty, and then disbanded without any consistently united effort to organise the peace. We well know that a lack of a reasonable unity among the present victorious Powers might result in a similar international chaos or vacuum, and that one hasty step and panicky action might cause a

---

[1]Nobody who has come in touch with the American people in churches, colleges, universities and many other institutions would be ready to deny that America is in many ways a stronghold of what is dear to any freedom-loving man.

catastrophe of unimaginable dimensions. It is the conviction of the present writer that the situation, though far from being satisfactory and reassuring, is not desperate and that the sinister predictions of an approaching armed conflict of the great victorious Powers only aggravate the main problems of our time, and slow down the process of healing post-war mankind. It is the great mission of Christians in all countries to keep the rival fronts in close touch with each other, and not to allow a petrification of the international *blocs* that would make further discussion and debate impossible. So long as the two " sides " speak to one another, so long as they revile each other, the situation is not beyond repair. Let us talk together ! Do not let us give up ! Do not let us abdicate ! This is not a time for black despair and hopeless resignation ; this is a time of great opportunity. As we walk at the edge of the deep abyss do not let us be paralysed by fear, but let us combat our dizziness in a spirit of faith and hope !

4. THE PROBLEM OF THE WEST

The people of what we call " the Eastern *bloc* " (including Central, South-Eastern and Eastern Europe) have a deep respect for the traditions of life of the European (and American) West. The breakdown of Western civilisation would be a tragedy that would affect all the great values the " Eastern " man loves and adores. The subordination of man to the God-Creator and Saviour, Who is the God of grace and justice and the Lord of history, guiding it to the ultimate victory of truth and merciful justice ; the subordination of human instincts and passions to the clarity of intellect and to the majesty of an awakened conscience ; the norm of justice as superior to power ; love as the transforming force of social life ; the freedom of a responsible personality as against the claims of any human authority to rule the human soul—all these principles have been the underlying *motifs* of Western history, often betrayed and corrupted, and yet invincible and re-emerging as long as there have arisen groups of men and women who believed in them and were ready to work and die for them. The people of the East, whether they tend more to the right or to the left, would shudder, should those great ideas and norms cease to be the leaven of our personal and public life.

There are, however, some warning questions to which a citizen of the West should listen, and take into serious consideration.

1. The prestige of the West, during the years 1919-1940, was greatly shaken and has not recovered. Let us not speak of the Spenglerian prognosis of the " Decline of the West " : It was based on a philosophy of history that proved to be philosophically and politically fallacious and was invalidated by the events of the last ten years. However, the fact that the Western orbit of the world failed to organise and maintain the peace of 1919 cannot be disputed and disposed of lightheartedly. The authority of the Western democratic powers after the Armistice of 1918 was enormous, especially in Central Europe and in the Balkans. A united, socially and politically courageous policy in regard to the post-war world might have been able to cope with the situation. The social and moral aspirations of the masses, aroused by the Russian revolution of 1917, might have been guided into more or less normal channels of human progress if (I apologise for the " if " !) the Western nations had shown a far-sighted understanding of the downtrodden and oppressed peasants and workers of the Central and South-Eastern areas of Europe. The atmosphere of anxiety and fear lest the Soviet revolution should seize the masses of the European nations paralysed the energy of the victors and contributed to their disunity, which eventually resulted in the political decay of Central and Western Europe. The democratic nations were losing their moral prestige, as well as their political influence, until the integrating and creative power of democracy faded away. The fascist and national-socialist movements were indirectly, and in a measure also directly, strengthened by the moral and political vacuum created by the failure of the democratic victors to organise the world.

2. Hence millions of European citizens are doubtful whether the " free democracies " of the West are qualified to meet the needs of the present era, and to organise effectively a new order on the basis of real social justice and equal opportunity. Serious misgivings exist as to the ability of Western democracy to safeguard the progress of a genuine political and national liberty, let alone social security. Is not a material, economic interest on the part of " big " industries and financial concerns looming behind all the high-sounding slogans of " a free democracy," behind all the efforts to protect " individual freedom," " free enterprise " against any control by government, society and state ?

The blind or bankrupt leniency of the liberal democratic governments towards the reactionary régimes which one by one swept away the political life of Europe and after 1920 reinstated the old, seemingly vanquished elements of feudal conservativism in their old positions, has made the common man of Europe rather suspicious of the political tendencies prevailing at present in some leading Western states.

The vigorous and, at times, brutal reactions of the radical movements in Poland, Hungary, Roumania, Bulgaria, Yugoslavia, and also in Italy and France, against the local elements responsible for the pre-war régimes, cannot be interpreted solely as a Soviet machination. They have grown out of indigenous needs and memories. Their dynamism is proportionate to the blunders and failures both of the respective national régimes of the pre-war era and the leading Western democratic powers of Europe. It is essential to keep in mind the historical background of the countries which are undergoing the process of a total social and political transformation. The Soviet Government and the communistic parties may have taken advantage of the failures of the past for their own ends. However, the easy simplification with which many people in the West have been trying to interpret the present events in the Balkans and Central Europe as a sinister Soviet or communistic expansion might fatally blind our eyes and deafen our ears to what is actually going on in those areas. This is not at all to justify or to condone the methods and individual acts of the present rulers in the countries under consideration. This is just to remind ourselves of the failures of the democratic régimes during the Balkan, Austrian, Abyssinian, Spanish and Munich crises in the thirties of our century. Only in this way can we correctly understand the violent resentment on the part of the new politically advancing elements in many European countries against any effort made by " the West " to assist, in the name of formal democracy, the classes and individuals responsible for the previous régimes. There exists a grave danger that the Western democracies are—justly or wrongly—identified with social and political reaction, and that they will lose all political and moral authority. The shadows of Spain and Munich have not disappeared ; on the contrary, they loom as a portentous omen on the horizon.

3. How far are the Western democracies *morally*, intellectually, and spiritually capable and competent to deal with the

basic needs of our era ? This is a question not to be lightly dismissed. The sentiments of anti-Soviet, anti-communistic fear, suspicion and hysteria as they prevail, and seem to be cultivated, behind the official " Western " policy of the present day, seem to reflect an ominous lack of moral and spiritual vigour. What the peoples of Europe, in general, and of Germany, Central and South-Eastern Europe in particular, badly need is a spiritual, intellectual, moral power to cope with their national, political, cultural issues. The " West," as it makes itself known, and the many adherents in European countries of the " Western orientation " are united merely in their negative, hostile attitude to the Soviet Union and communism—and are depressingly weak in their positive, spiritual and intellectual convictions and faith. What is it that the Western man really believes in ? What are his basic convictions ? What is it that he would be willing to live and die for ? The fear and anxiety of a Maginot-line mentality which tries to preserve the old treasures and values instead of creating new ones are not strong enough to meet the challenge of the present day. They reveal a spirit of self-defence. The people who are afraid and uncertain about what they believe or what they ought to establish, are under a constant temptation to yield to a political or social reaction, or to an urge to stop the morally and socially justifiable process of history. They will yield to the peril of being destroyed by the explosive elements accumulated by blindness and weakness, instead of shaping and forming the fluid lava of the present spiritual and social life. From my own experience I know of many instances—even in my own country—where the non-communistic groups have failed, precisely because of their lack of common convictions, and of a united, morally and politically dynamic programme ; whereas the communists know what they want, are well disciplined, and are hard-working people.

Hence, what is urgently needed is an earnest self-examination by the people of the West about their essential heritage and mission. Let me repeat over and over again : all Europeans, Eastern not less than Western, would be terribly impoverished, intellectually, morally and politically, if the " West " should break down under its own weariness, exhaustion and lack of vision. The "East" of Europe, in its present stage of history and way of life, is lacking in many of the great values and achievements of Western civilisation. The destiny and mission of " Mother

Europe " are tied up with the achievements and the heritage of Western Catholicism, the Reformation, the Renaissance, the Enlightenment and Democratic Humanism. If the West should waste its treasures through a lack of faith, through spiritual indifference and self-complacency, an atmosphere of a graveyard would, for a long time, deprive the whole European orbit (the East included) of its inward resilience and creativity. The struggle for human dignity, for the sacredness of human personality and for a responsible freedom, without which our life would become bleak and miserable, would be carried on under very difficult conditions and circumstances.

Everybody who knows through personal contact the real civilisation of Western nations cannot help being impressed by its refinement, decency, tolerance, by its respect for human freedom and individual welfare. However, one cannot be unaware of the growing spiritual weariness, of the hollowness of so many " Western " ideas and institutions. Why is it that it is just those so-called Westerners, in many countries on the border-line between the Western and Eastern orbit of Europe, who indulge in complaining and grumbling without a real understanding of the historical moment, and without a vigorous and constructive plan for the future? The West is losing ground in many European countries not only on account of a tremendous pressure on the part of radical socialism but also because of its own lack of faith and courageous realism. The Western idea of freedom, liberty and democracy is too formal, too unrelated to the basic issues and realities of the present times.

Yes, indeed, the " West " should refrain from blaming one-sidedly the aggressive socialist and communist groups, and examine its own mind, and the reasons why so many Western concepts and institutions have been losing the power to attract the imagination of the masses. A formal democratic process is not an end in itself, hence a formal freedom of thought, expression and speech is not an end in itself. The masses of common men are interested in the goal and the purpose to which human freedom and free institutions ought to be dedicated. The baffling historical changes during the last ten years have shaken the very foundations of the old civilisation and way of life. The destruction of both material and spiritual treasures is such that many nations and countries, primarily in the most devastated areas, are facing the almost insurmountable task of reorganising disintegrated society and of building up more adequate forms of social and economic life. Something new is in the making. Much of the old way of life has got to be given up ; many of our ideas and categories which our fathers took for granted have to be reconsidered, reshaped, re-defined.

Facing the present situation of destruction and devastation (primarily within the area of Soviet influence) many people have come to realise that what really matters is not primarily political freedom, but a well-thought-out, reliable plan of a new society based on social justice, human dignity, enduring peace. · At the danger of repetition let us once more remind ourselves of new or renewed efforts to preserve the *status quo*, the privileges of decaying classes and groups, to stop the progress of history and to destroy what the common people have most longed for. There exists a shrewd, subtle tendency to protect and to preserve the racially, financially and socially privileged groups and parties under the pretext of freedom and formal democracy.

There are peoples whose situation may be compared to a flood inundating and destroying villages and towns, to a fire, sweeping across a city, to a volcanic eruption covering with dust and debris vast areas of a country. Millions of dead are heaped on the ground. How can we under these conditions expect a normally functioning democratic process ? In such a situation, what matters is to help the people, to disarm wrongdoers, to assist, to save, to establish dams, to extinguish fire, to organise reconstruction, not to thrive on individual freedom or on freedom of reporting. In certain circumstances discipline, service, responsibility, self-control, self-dedication are superior to freedom and human rights !

The re-examination of Western ideas against the background of what has been, morally and spiritually as well as politically and socially, the most dynamic *motif* of Western history is needed precisely at the present time. We do not advocate an attitude of compromise and " appeasement " ; we advocate an effort to revitalise what has been the creative genius of French, British and American democracy, and of civilisation. Anyone who is ready to study the legacy of the best architects of Western civilisation will more adequately understand the real process of history within the " Eastern orbit," and avoid a misleading, abstract over-simplification of some of the present policies in the

" East," dictatorship, totalitarianism, Soviet aggression. Such a simplification may partly be justified ; the dangers of dictatorship and totalitarianism are not absent. But it is wrong, and erects a barrier between nations, if it blinds human eyes to the historical urgency of the social and political transformation of the " Eastern " nations, releasing many inward creative forces which for centuries have been kept under the deadening pressure of old institutions and privileges. How difficult it is to ascertain a real fact, the real issue of an event, to understand it rightly, to report it truthfully and to interpret it with a relative correctness ! You may compile a good report of many true facts ; and yet it may be a pitifully false picture if you ignore, miss or misconstrue what is the living kernel of a historical process, and if you push more or less irrelevant details into the foreground.

The living, unfettered Word of God and the fire behind the most creative manifestations of our history may help us to get closer and more understandingly to the heart of things in Central and Eastern Europe, and to realise that a real advance of social and political democracy may proceed through channels and détours which defy our preconceived ideas and institutions, and yet, correspond to the real substance of the present history of those countries more adequately than what used to be the pattern universally accepted by all advanced, civilised nations.

A new, careful study of the basic issues of the Reformation in the light of the Biblical message has helped the Church of Christ (in recent years) to resume her vital mission and to break the shackles of a sterile confessionalism as well as of morbid ecclesiasticism and bourgeois secularism. A new insight into the very foundations of Western civilisation may do the same : it may overcome the weakness of our democratic formalism, which has lost its substance and has become a tool of privileges and vested interests ; it may open our eyes to the aspirations of nations and masses which in a clumsy, awkward, harsh and crude way are trying to arrive at a nobler place under the sun. I see all the potential dangers of the " Eastern " form of social and political progress. But we will not be able to challenge and overcome them unless we see, and sympathetically understand, the longing of the " Eastern " masses for more human dignity, social equality, cultural progress, and for a fair share in the political responsibility for the new world order.

5. THE PROBLEMS OF THE EAST (THE SOVIET ISSUE)

Essential as it is to examine one's own spiritual and political outlook it is not enough. There is another urgent matter we have to face : to know, to understand and to interpret—as adequately as possible—the situation within the " Eastern orbit " of the present world, the orbit which has become one of the two main pillars of any future international order. We must not stop where our statesmen and diplomats have stopped. Even if our political representatives should arrive at the conclusion that further discussions and negotiations are useless, we have to go beyond the political concepts and diplomatic divisions. Here, again, let us keep in mind that the present issues cannot be reduced to an easy, inviting formula. Western man, separated by the barriers of history, geography, and mental processes from the Soviet world, is tempted not only by propaganda but also by the many acts behind the " Iron Curtain," to interpret the ideological and political structure of the Soviet system as another manifestation of modern totalitarianism. For many a Western Christian, the issue of the Soviet Union is— in its essential nature—identical with, or analogous to, the issue of Hitler-Germany. Nazism and Sovietism may, they say, differ on minor points, but are identical in their ideological and practical effort to subordinate man, his dignity, responsible freedom and integrity, to an earthly idol, be it race and blood or social class and state, which has usurped the throne of a divine Absolute and deprives the individual soul of any free, moral, cultural, or spiritual self-determination. Hence, they say, the attitude of " Western man " towards the Soviet orbit cannot be other than that of an uncompromising hostility : The Soviet system based on the philosophy of communism, e.g., dialectical materialism, is the incarnation of an anti-Christian religion. The spirit of communism and its fanatical self-expression reveal the fact that here we have to do not with a merely political platform and system, but with a false, godless religion, with a pseudo-religion, against which we must fight without fear or compromise. This is, broadly speaking, the attitude of a vast multitude of Western men towards the " East."

It is here, however, that I wish to make a distinction of paramount importance. The phenomenon of communism is in its essential structure different from that of nazism. Communism does not adhere to any metaphysic that would elevate an earthly reality (be it the class of the proletariat or the ultimate classless society) to the plane of an Absolute. The philosophy of nazism is based on the concept of the Nordic race and blood as undefiled manifestations of the Absolute spirit of the Universe and as the metaphysically ultimate source of truth, justice and real life. The philosophy of communism (in its Marxian or Leninian and Stalinian version) moves within the plane of history, uninterested in what is beyond history. Its atheism is rather a practical reaction against the forces of the pre-socialistic society than a positive, philosophically essential tenet. In many ways, we may say, the classic theory of communism (as has often been pointed out) is a secularised Christian theology, often furiously anti-Church ; but it insists that communism has done for the poor what the Church should have done, but which she has transformed into a liturgical, mystical, opiate. Communistic atheism is, in a large measure, rather a tool and weapon of an anti-bourgeois or anti-feudal political propaganda than a distinctive faith and metaphysic. It is more agnostic than positively metaphysical. Its dynamism and its religious sentiment are, to be sure, a substitute for religion, but its vigour is due to an engrossing, fascinating idea of a society in which man will be free of all external greed, mammon and material tyranny, and in which a fellowship of real human beings in mutual sympathy, love and goodwill would be established.

We must not forget that what we call communism, which is one of the expressions of an age-long struggle against social exploitation and insecurity, has always had two aspects : one more formal, philosophical, revolting against the official *Weltanschauung* of the feudal and bourgeois society (*e.g.*, dialectical, historical materialism), and the other, more material (in its very essence idealistic), struggling for a social system in which all class differences would fade away, the demonic, tyrannical power of money and private property would be crushed, and all men and women would be united on the same ground of human dignity, freedom and love. The tenet of dictatorship is there, too, and has played a tremendous rôle in the days of revolution and civil war and in the transition era of socialistic reconstruction. It has produced many unnecessary hardships, and has caused much anxiety, hatred and violent hostility. One of the most serious shortcomings of the present communistic leaders in various countries has been the emphasis they have laid upon dictatorship at the expense of the positive idea of a classless, socialistic community. Millions of common men and intellectuals would be awakened to the real issues of our time and other millions would be morally disarmed if the leaders of the new régimes in Europe would point more convincingly to what the end and the goal of the present social struggle actually are.

As we now approach the " problem " of the Soviet Union, let me remind the reader of a distinction to be made between the concepts (categories) of communism, the Soviet régime and the Russian people (including all the other nationalities of the Soviet area). No matter how closely associated they may be they are not identical. The Soviet Revolution of 1917 prevailed under the leadership of the Bolshevik Social Democratic Party, and its Commander-in-Chief, Vladimir Lenin. For many historical reasons, not to be dealt with here, it was they who were able to reorganise the disintegrated and chaotic Russian Empire. The philosophy of dialectical, economic materialism proved to be efficient to concentrate the new ruling class upon the main issue : to transform the feudal, and, as far as it existed, bourgeois society into a socialistic system. However, the philosophy of communism and the Bolshevik (now communistic) Party on the one hand, and the Soviet system, on the other, are not identical terms. If a comparison is in order, the issue with which we have to do is similar to that in France after the Revolution of 1789. The philosophy prevailing in the revolutionary days may have inspired the leaders and the masses to act, to overthrow the " ancien régime," but it was not necessarily and essentially connected with the structure of republican, revolutionary France. The same is true of the Russian situation. Russian political and cultural history since 1917, to be sure, cannot be understood without the impact of the Marxian-Leninian philosophy and without the leadership of the Bolshevik (communistic) Party. Sociologically and politically, the general chaos in the vast area between Poland and the Pacific Ocean was, after the breakdown of the old régime, of such dimension that only a very vigorous, disciplined political group and a distinct philosophy could have gradually checked the anti-revolutionary and other disruptive tendencies, and restored an organic unity out of a totally atomised and disintegrated national life.

The present strict, and, at times, harsh régime under the guidance of the communistic élite, which may, in a way, be compared to a monastic order, can be adequately understood and appraised only against the background of Russian history, the revolutionary era, the civil war of 1918-1922, and the many interventions by foreign Powers. The vast empire, without any genuine democratic tradition, held together by the absolute power of the Tsars and integrated by the politico-religious myth of the emperor wielding the sceptre of a divinely inspired autocracy, fell to pieces and was for a long time threatened by innumerable perils from within and from without. If we objectively, and with fairness, consider the backwardness of the masses, the relatively swift reorganisation of the territory, the defeat of internal and external enemies, and the stupendous transformation of the old social system into a new, socialistic, collectivistic structure of society, we cannot help being impressed by the enormous energy, skill and organiing ingenuity of the ruling party. This is not to be understood as a consent to the very ideas and methods applied by the Revolution ; this is just to emphasise the absurdity of the various ways in which the Soviet situation has been criticised and condemned by applying abstract. political yardsticks or by comparing it with the democratic institutions and processes originated, grown and perfected under an utterly different historical sky. What I have in mind is to interpret the dictatorial régime of the Soviet system as a historical necessity in a country consisting of multiple ethnic, and in part culturally backward elements, and in a nation which for many reasons had not been privileged to enjoy political liberties and popular education.

There is another aspect of the Soviet régime. Communistic philosophers and statesmen stress the temporary, transitory nature of the socialistic, proletarian dictatorship. They reject the nazistic and fascistic idea of a dictator as a permanent embodiment of the divine majesty of the race (nazism) or of state sovereignty (fascism). They entirely reject the idea of a personal dictatorship and maintain the necessity of the collective dictatorship of the proletarian class. It does not exclude—as the Soviet experience bears out—a unique dictatorial prestige and position of a revolutionary leader (Lenin, Stalin) or of a political group (the Politbureau of the Communistic Party in U.S.S.R.). Further, the demonic temptation of power and the lust for power, are a constant danger that the temporary rulers may perpetuate and unduly enlarge their uncontrolled authority. In the Soviet Union, the leader of the state attracts, for historical reasons, a reverence and loyalty which in Western countries is historically impossible and sociologically unnecessary. However, we may say that the very idea of communism in regard to dictatorship differs essentially from that of nazism. The more advanced the socialistic structure the less dictatorial power is needed, until—in a fully developed and safeguarded collectivistic, classless economy—all dictatorship will fade away. The Marxist theory of the state and of a perfect classless society may be false. It certainly is false. But the fact remains that communism, in spite of its idea or practice of dictatorship, is not principally absolutist and totalitarian. It tends—in its philosophy—towards a total liberation of the individual man.

I do not believe (how could I ?) that the communist ideology will, eventually and permanently, be capable of integrating the new, post-revolutionary, society, into a living body of material trust, free responsibility and service, and thus be able to preserve the fruits of the social revolution, unless it appeals to that in man which transcends the material process of history. Even a classless society cannot exist without the testimony of divine judgment, the eternal law of justice and forgiveness. Nevertheless, my point at this juncture is this : communism reflects, in a very secularised form, in spite of its materialism and dictatorship, the Christian longing for the fellowship of full and responsible love.

The Soviet, collectivistic structure of human society can exist without the philosophy of dialectical materialism. As a matter of fact, the vast majority of Soviet citizens, in towns, villages, plants, " kolkhozes," literature and art, are neither party members nor philosophically communist. The Marxian-Leninian ideology has penetrated into all realms of the social and cultural activity. However, after the new social and political order has been thoroughly rooted and entrenched and adequately secured, and after the 180 millions of Soviet citizens have been educated and come of age, the official ideology will undoubtedly undergo—as it actually is undergoing—a process of transformation from within.

6. COMMUNISM AND RUSSIAN HISTORY

That transformation may be expected also for another reason. The Leninian philosophy of dialectical materialism and the Soviet revolution carried out a unique, possibly unprecedented change and break in the history of Russia and of the whole world. Yet both of them had been only to a certain extent an import from the outside Western world. (Socialism and communism were originally Western movements !) Vladimir Lenin was a genuine Russian intellectual, a son of the Russian soil, formed and shaped by the Russian moral, spiritual and intellectual tradition. The history of *Russian* communism as well as Sovietism is scarcely intelligible without the history of the specifically Russian social and literary movements going as far back as. 1825 ; possibly as far as the era of Peter the Great. The deep love for the " insulted and injured," for the miserable peasant (muzhik), for the " scum " of human society, for workers, petty artisans, in a word, for the under-dog of human society, is one of the most creative, impressive and revolutionary tendencies in the life of Russian intelligentsia and in the literary work of all the great Russian writers of the nineteenth century : Byelinski, Gogol, Tolstoy, Goncharov, Dostoyevski, Tchekhov, Gorki. The Soviet Revolution was a culmination of the long preceding struggle. The suffering and the missionary expeditions of thousands and thousands of Russian intellectuals whose social passion, warm love and self-sacrificing sympathy for the exploited is unsurpassed in the history of our civilisation, are products of this Revolution. Just as Karl Marx insisted that the masses of German workers were heirs of the great German philosophers and writers, so the leaders of the Russian revolution insisted on raising the oppressed and despised working classes to a high level of literary education and to a sense of their historical destiny.

If you happen to visit the Soviet Union you may observe a feverish educational process to combat as fast·as possible cultural backwardness and illiteracy. Looking at Russia from outside, you have the impression that Soviet life is reduced to the great social and economic experiment of collectivisation under a strict political and police control. Looking from inside you see another process in full swing : a process of education in schools, theatres, centres of culture, music halls, galleries, exhibitions, museums— a process through which the knowledge of Russian history, of the great classic Russian literature and art are becoming the property and enjoyment of millions. What the non-Russian nationalities and ethnic groups in the Caucasus, Siberia and elsewhere have acquired through the revolutionary transformation of the Russian Empire, only the days to come will reveal in a fully conclusive way. The Revolution had not this end in itself. It was planned and carried out as a violent assault upon the old régime. In a large measure, however, it was a process of liberation, through which the " common man " or " proletarian " could become a citizen, with all rights and honours, and through which all the dormant, fettered moral and cultural forces of the Russian people could be released and developed.

The Russian classics are being read and re-read. Alexander Pushkin, Lev N. Tolstoy, M. Gorki (and many others, Gogol and Dostoyevski included) are obligatory reading in schools and universities.

Soviet literature and art have to consider the rather primitive and naïve taste of the advancing masses, and the writers are over and over again warned by the political leaders not to forget the education and integration of the national life, and not to yield to a refined and decadent " l'art pour l'art." Any cynical or pessimistic interpretation of life and history is frowned upon ; and over-critical literary comments on what is going on in national life are severely criticised, unless they have a constructive attitude to the national process of recovery and rehabilitation.

This is not to be ignored or underestimated. The unique accomplishments of Russian authors both in literary form and spiritual content are a living factor in the life of a growing number of Soviet citizens. To-day, tens of millions of them read them with passion and hunger, whereas thirty years ago only a thin layer of the Russian nation was able to read, enjoy and appreciate the profound wealth of knowledge, wisdom, human understanding accumulated by the long procession of Russian writers who, being almost perfect interpreters of the Russian mind, have become moral and spiritual teachers of all nations. With the elimination of illiteracy country folk and townspeople, intelligentsia and common men read them alike. All the classics severely criticised the sins and evils they had discovered and uncovered in the life of the ruling classes as well as of the so-called lower strata. Some of them confronted what was the best and the worst in the West with what was the best and the worst in the

East and created an atmosphere of human sympathy, understanding and brotherhood which is as yet forming and shaping the soul of nations. Our knowledge of man, of his depth both in corruption and heavenly aspirations, is deeper and broader than it was before the Russian classics were written. A reverence for the sanctity of the human soul was, in them, organically associated with a thorough study of Russian national life, of its blessings and perils, its grandeur and corruption. A tender love of man never ceases to breathe through their writings, even if the author had descended into the deepest depth of human misery and sin or if he had been confronted with the most repulsive aspects of Russian society. There is no sign of cynical disillusionment, pessimism, decadent nihilism or moral abdication in the pages of those writers who once made Russian literature a creative element in world civilisation. Behind all the critical analysis in the Russian classics the reader finds an affirmative, constructive manifestation of human compassion, and a deep longing for truth and the salvation of mankind.

Now, the works of the Russian classical writers are the regular food and nourishment of Soviet students and citizens. Within the framework of the present social and economic experiment a rich stream of moral and spiritual inspiration is flowing into the minds and hearts of the Soviet people. Neither dialectical materialism nor the dictatorship of the proletariat gives an adequate key to open the door of a real understanding of what is going on in the vast spaces of Russia. Nobody can possibly foretell the future of Eastern civilisation. In many ways its process differs from the general trend of Western history. We must not measure it with the criteria derived from the heritage of Western feudalism, the Reformation, the Renaissance and liberalism. The Russian past had its " driving force," its highlights and patterns, its own creative *motifs* and aspirations. All these *motifs* and aspirations are working like leaven behind the revolutionary ideas and methods of Marxian communism in general and of Russian sovietism in particular.

There was a time when the leaders and ideologists of the Soviet revolution tried to interpret the Christian past as a combination of pre-scientific mythology, clerical fraud and gross superstition, or merely as a by-product of the social structure and economic development of Russian society. From the moment, however, that a systematic construction of the new national community started, a new understanding of the Christian Church and her history was initiated. Historical materialism notwithstanding, all the contributions of Christian moral standards, thought, practical life and institutions of the past have been interpreted with a new spirit of appreciation, evaluation and affirmative appraisal.

Nazism was increasingly hostile to the Christian heritage of German history, treated it as a poisonous infection which had penetrated from outside into the healthy body of an originally pure, unpolluted Nordic race. The Nazi ideologists elaborated a thorough philosophy of German history (*völkische Geschichtsphilosophie*) interpreting the German historical process as a continuous struggle between the original genuine German spirit (*Blut, Boden, Ehre, Kraft, Macht*) on the one hand, and the Jewish-Christian· element (and Latin legalism) on the other. All the great figures of German history (Frederick II, Luther, Frederick the Great, Bismarck, Hitler, and many others) were put into the gallery of heroes on account of their vigorous effort to extricate the German soul from the shackles of Jewish-Christian spiritual slavery, and to free it from the poison of Christian faith. The Soviet historians, thinkers, and even the political leaders have adopted an increasingly appreciative attitude to the contribution of Christianity, and point to its " progressive " spirit. The noble Christian doctrine of man, with its emphasis on the family, its deep sympathy for the poor, downtrodden, miserable members of human society, its commandment of love for man, faith and hope with regard to the end and goal of history, its self-denying efforts during the era of foreign domination (" Tartar Yoke ")—all this has been acknowledged as a vital, dynamic and forward-driving factor of social justice, equality and brotherhood.

Family life is cultivated, and the sexual morality of the Soviet young men and young women is, in my judgment, cleaner than in my own country and in many Western democracies. The post-revolutionary moral libertinism affected only a thin stratum of intellectuals and of some " proletarian " snobs who had—in the days of turbulent events and of new, undigested ideas—lost their heads and got confused in their hearts. Since the beginning of the tremendous constructive project of collectivisation and national reorganisation all merely negative, disintegrating ideas (*e.g.*, atheism and anti-religious propaganda) have either been side-tracked or are at least unpopular. Everything that would weaken the working morale or foster sexual anarchy (*e.g.*, the ideals of sexual promiscuity) is vigorously denounced and combated.

I am not competent to deal with the present status of the Church in the Eastern area of Europe. However, some few words on the Church problem must be added. A Western observer is not in a position to judge whether the Eastern Orthodox Church or any other Church in the Soviet Union has enough real spiritual and intellectual vigour to enable it to be a real force in the spiritual regeneration and moral growth of the people. We have no right to question the formal freedom of the Church to perform her purely religious duties, to conduct public worship, to train her clergy, and to educate her children. Furthermore, the churches have undergone a great test and have shown their capacity to assist the people in the days of crisis and destruction, to give comfort and hope in suffering and at the moment of death, and to become a unifying force in the national life. The government and the Communist Party have paid a high tribute to the Church for her great services during the recent war (1941-1945).

However, it is not quite clear to what extent she is free to raise her prophetic voice on great or small issues in public, political, educational and moral life. We are not in a position to assess her active, formative contribution to the inward growth of the moral and spiritual structure of the men and women responsible for the present state of affairs in the Soviet Union. The education of the adepts of the Party (pioneers, komsomols) is based on an entirely non-religious philosophy. The official doctrine is that of Marxian (or Leninist) materialism. The Church seems to stand on the fringe of the national life. And yet, she does stand, praising God and pointing to the glory of the Triune God and to the real presence of the God-Man, Jesus Christ. She is not the only channel of the potential spiritual regeneration of the nation, but she is one element which testifies to the fact that a nation organised on a revolutionary, materialist philosophy cannot permanently live and maintain her human rights and responsible freedom without looking to the Lord of history who speaks the Word of judgment and forgiveness.

One point more should be added. Shortly after the victory of the Revolution, the Church was tragically shaken to her foundations and almost collapsed : partly, because she was so intrinsically associated with the very structure of the pre-revolutionary society, partly, because the atheistic, anti-religious elements of the Communist movement tried to liquidate, in a rather primitive way, all religious activities and institutions. Long before Marxism, Russian atheism had assumed a rather religious fervour. " The protest and revolt against God " was a kind of humanistic evangelism preaching the destruction of the evil cæsaro-papistic system and the establishment of a new, socially free and politically just Russia. The tens of thousands of Christian victims who, during the revolutionary era, suffered persecution or death were only partly " Confessors " (martyrs) ; partly they were just victims of the revolutionary upheaval, confused about the real meaning of the historical events, allied with the " White " (anti-red) counter-revolution, and finally liquidated with the old régime. But the Church survived the collapse of the Tsarist empire. She came to realise that her existence did not depend on the old social system. She survived in her orthodox, historical structure. All the efforts to organise another Church that would adjust her doctrine, liturgy and morals to the new ideology failed almost completely. " The Living Church," a sort of modernistic, theologically humanistic religious body, disappeared, after an initial success and advance, like snow in springtime. It withered away in spite of the backing it had indirectly received from the victorious régime.

This is a great lesson for the present time. Only a Church that understands the meaning of the times, and knows *where* to fight, and *what weapon* to use, is in a position to carry on. Social and political systems may come and go. But the message of the Living God, of the Incarnate Word, the Crucified and Risen Lord, and the Creator Spirit, abides for ever.

7. CONCLUSION

This is the situation within the " Eastern orbit," and in its relation to the West, as it looks to the present writer :

1. The Soviet problem must not be reduced to the issue of dictatorship and totalitarianism, although this forms part of it.

2. The categories of communism, the Soviet system, and Soviet Russia are not identical.

3. The Soviet leaders have long memories and cannot forget

all the efforts (if not the intrigues) which came from the West to thwart the Revolution, to overthrow the Soviet government, to isolate it after it was established, and to give moral support to the anti-Soviet, anti-socialist régimes.

4. The terrific destruction of Soviet territory and the enormous losses in human life (who knows how many millions of the Soviet people perished ?) during the German-Soviet war of 1941-1945 have made the Soviet régime and the Soviet people sensitive to any sign or indication of an anti-Soviet policy of " encirclement " and isolation. What has frequently been interpreted as Soviet expansion, or as a revived Russian nationalistic imperialism may be rather a manifestation of self-protection and self-defence.

5. The strength of the Soviet system is a guarantee against the potential dangers of a new international chaos and anarchy. Who can say what the weakening or the destruction of the present Russian régime would imply ? How dismal the situation of Eastern Europe and Asia, as well as that of Central and Western Europe, would become if the process of reconstruction and con-solidation within the Soviet area were stopped or paralysed ! The Western democracies are neither morally nor politically capable of coping with the crisis that would follow a critical weakening of the Soviet Union.

6. The Soviet system cannot be transplanted into a country of a different historical, moral and cultural tradition. It is rooted, and has organically grown, in the soil tilled and cultivated by the Russian people, the Russian Church, and the Russian intelligentsia.

7. The same system, however, would be gravely affected if the noble tradition of Western civilisation were seriously wounded from outside, or if it withered from within on account of its moral and spiritual decay. The Soviet social and political ideal came into existence under the influence of great Western philosophers, political writers and of the dynamic Western religious history. What would become of the noble Soviet social ideal and goal, if the Western struggle for the dignity of responsible man under the authority of the eternally valid norms of justice, truth, chastity and love ended in despair, cynical pessimism, spiritual indifference and frustration ?

8. It is exactly here that the West should concentrate its

creative ambition. The West will never attract the better elements of the post-war world (in Europe, Asia and elsewhere) by insisting upon the old capitalistic emphasis on " free enterprise," " profit-motives," and " private property," or by talking about comfort or the atomic bomb. It can preserve, revitalise and hand over the great heritage of Western civilisation to non-Western man on one condition : if it adheres to what the creative genius of European and American history has created along the lines of political, intellectual and social progress. Under the present historical conditions of a terrific disorganisation of European society classic capitalism would utterly fail and break down. Freedom and political liberties without social security and without a new, more organic, fellowship of man are, to-day, meaningless. And a real organic fellowship of mutual trust and confidence is fatally weak without a deep faith, warm convictions and an ardent hope. The anti-Soviet and anti-communistic fear in the West is partly due to the fact that the official Western society does not seem to trust the deepest ideas of Western history, or has lost its burning convictions and hopes.

We have dealt with the " Eastern orbit " as positively as possible, since there is little opportunity to look at it from the angle of the Eastern nations or from the perspective of Eastern (European) civilisation. We are, however, not unaware of grave dangers inherent in the ideological, historical and political structure of the system prevailing in the area behind what is called the " Iron Curtain."

First, the very fact of the tremendous power in the hands of the present rulers within that area arouses serious misgivings and well-grounded apprehensions. It is the first time in history that the people of the present Soviet territory have proved so strong and have crushed their enemy so completely. Unlike the period after the first victorious Patriotic War (1812-1815), the present Russia is able to appeal to the radical, progressive, revolutionary elements in the whole world, and thus greatly to strengthen her position. It is the combination of her military victories, the enormous integration of her political organisation and her revolutionary dynamism that makes her present advance so formidable and, in a way, even awe-inspiring. Moreover, the other nations are not without a suspicion that behind the Soviet social revolutionary aspiration looms a revived nationalistic expansion of the old Russian Empire. No matter which of the two historical patterns, revolutionary socialism or Russian nationalism, is stronger and more aggressive, the combination of both may prove to be a terrific temptation to try to dominate the world, and precipitate a fresh historical catastrophe.

Second, the philosophy of historical materialism which denies all the norms, criteria and standards beyond the process of history, reducing man to a mere by-product of his social and economic environment, may—if unresisted and unchallenged—break down moral inhibitions and self-control, and let loose the purely animal passions of envy, hatred, greed and self-assertion. The Church of Christ will have to dig her trenches and establish her walls of testimony at the farthest outskirts of human life in order to shape and form an unshakable framework of moral norms, judicial laws, social standards, without which a new barbarism would sweep across the world ; all the more since the Western spiritual weariness and the fruits of liberalistic indifference have brought about a grave peril of moral decay and cultural disintegration in the realm of the whole civilised community.

Third, it is doubtful whether the revolutionary tradition and Marxian materialism are capable of protecting the sacredness of human personality and freedom. Likewise many honest men are sometimes disturbed at the way in which the representatives of the Eastern régimes deal with political minorities and adversaries, both at home and at international conferences. Instead of carrying conviction they engage too much in propaganda and assault. They may be, here and there, right. The other groups have often done almost nothing to understand Eastern problems and have attempted, in a subtle way, to deprive the Soviet people of the fruits of victory. The Western man is, consciously or unconsciously, self-righteous, and takes his own privileged place in the world for granted ; any advance on the part of the European Easterner arouses in him fear and righteous indignation. And yet, the Eastern people would win much support from the best truly liberal and Christian groups in the West, if they used less noisy propaganda and spoke with a genuine accent of truth, sincerity and honesty.

9. Let us once more appeal to the leaders of the Soviet community and of the communistic parties to rely less on the violent methods of agitation, threat, deportation, trials and police control, and to arouse in man his noblest sentiments of sympathy for the poor, the weak, the helpless and the miserable,

to awaken him to what is after all the core of socialistic humanism.

10. The problem of Germany cannot possibly be solved without a genuine co-operation of the West and the East, a co-operation on the basis of what is best in both of them. If the German people try—shrewdly, cunningly or stupidly—to play one power against the other and to ally themselves with the seemingly stronger side, they will bring final destruction upon themselves as well as upon the whole of Europe. This is not a time for intrigue or malicious revenge, it is a time for earnest responsibility and for a realistic, sober, wise, sincere desire for co-operation.

This is a time for hope and for new beginnings. Nothing is lost, and much can be gained and achieved, if all faithful members of the Church rally in the spirit of unqualified loyalty where the Crucified and Risen Lord is waiting, and if they, in humility and penitence, try to break through the present divisions of the world and speak to one another with undiminished boldness and truth. We cannot make any predictions, but our courage and hope may pave a new highway for reconciliation and peace.

V

FREEDOM OF RELIGION AND RELATED HUMAN RIGHTS

O. Frederick Nolde

Source material for this chapter has been contributed by :—F. Bednar, W. Y. Chen, George D. Kelsey, S. A. Morrison, B. L. Rallia Ram, Alberto Rembao, Emory Ross. The author has himself represented the Churches, through the Commission of the Churches on International Affairs, at meetings of the Commission on Human Rights of the Economic and Social Council of the United Nations. A synopsis of contents is provided to facilitate reference.

SYNOPSIS

INTRODUCTION—Renewed Emphasis on Human Rights (p. 144); Christian Activity (p. 145); The Basis for Christian Activity (p. 146); A Juridical Approach (p. 148).

I. RELIGIOUS LIBERTY ON THE CURRENT SCENE—1. Human Rights and the United Nations (p. 150); The Charter of the United Nations (p. 151); Commission on Human Rights (p. 152); Actions of the General Assembly (p. 154); Analysis of Developments through the United Nations (p. 155). 2. Religious Liberty in Typical Situations (p. 159). 3. Summary of Current Situation (p. 164).

II. THE POSITION OF THE CHURCHES—1. Statements by Ecumenical Conferences (p. 165); Requirements of Religious Liberty (p. 165); International and National Aspects of Religious Liberty (p. 167); Analysis of Ecumenical Statements (p. 168). 2. Developments Following the Ecumenical Conferences (p. 170); Human Rights and the World Organisation (p. 170); Statements on Religious Liberty (p. 171). 3. Recapitulation of the Development in the Christian Position (p. 173).

III. REQUIREMENTS OF RELIGIOUS LIBERTY (p. 173). 1. Man as an Individual (p. 176). 2. The Religious Group (p. 180). 3. Responsibility of Government (p. 182).

CONCLUSION: PROCEDURES FOR ECUMENICAL ACTION (p. 185).

I. A Declaration on Religious Liberty (p. 186).
II. Life and Work of the Churches (p. 188).

INTRODUCTION

THE tensions which agitate present-day society, both domestic and international, threaten the exercise of human rights and freedoms. Under the necessities of war, people in every free community yielded to their governments individual rights which in times of peace they were disposed to guard with jealous care. Efforts to recapture the enjoyment of personal freedoms encounter varying obstacles. Where disrupted economies have followed the devastation of war, the preservation of life has made unavoidable the continuation and, at times, the strengthening of government controls. The inability of the major victorious powers to adjust their differences has cast a shadow over every land. Without measurable assurance of a peaceful world, the traditionally free countries are reluctant to return to their accustomed ways of freedom. Totalitarian governments do little to liberalise their domestic practice and, in fact, seek to extend their view of society to foreign lands.

RENEWED EMPHASIS ON HUMAN RIGHTS

The forces which threaten human liberty have not passed unheeded. Nor has the recognition of them stopped with an awakened desire to reclaim what has been lost. It has stimulated the resolve to interpret man's rights more inclusively and to seek their realisation more universally. With mounting insistence, social and economic rights are being added to classical freedoms such as speech, religion and association. The ultimate goal of observance embraces all men everywhere, without distinction of race, sex, language, or religion.

The renewed and expanded effort in behalf of human rights is not equally vigorous at all points. This is readily understandable. In many instances, an inevitable fatigue has dulled the edge of man's inclination to struggle. Where people suffer from economic insufficiency, they are prone to devote their energies to prior needs. Where their actions are circumscribed by political controls, they submit to a situation which is for the moment unavoidable. Notwithstanding the vast numbers whose struggle has been limited by inclination or circumstance, a sufficient voice has been raised to justify the contention that man's effort to promote respect for human rights stands as an encouraging symbol in our chaotic world.

CHRISTIAN ACTIVITY

Christians, as individuals and through the churches, have played an important part in shaping the current emphasis upon the rights of man. In some instances, their activity has been stimulated by immediate exposure to actual or threatened denial of freedom. Under conditions where it was possible to continue their exercise of human rights, they were prompted to action by the adversities encountered in other lands and by the prospect that their own liberties might thereby be endangered.

It should be recognised that those Christians who suffered curtailment of spiritual freedom at the hands of their own government were placed in a particularly difficult situation. Under national socialism in Germany, issues were not always clarified. Disturbing contradictions appeared in the effort to reconcile opposition to government with loyalty to land and people. Protests raised under such circumstances merit the appreciation of defenders of liberty everywhere. That appreciation must stand even though the voices raised were limited in number and the response to them ineffectual. " They helped to cross Hitler's purpose at a very decisive point by making it possible for free Protestant Christianity, despite all the cunning assaults against it, to survive in Germany and retain all its power of germination. . . . In this one field the National Socialist system met a force which it was able to suppress but not to break."[1]

The struggle of the churches in the occupied countries gave spiritual depth to a resistance that often moved at political and social levels. Aims were variously defined. Procedures were fashioned as the need dictated. In summarising their purpose, a group of prominent churchmen in Norway stated : " We fight this battle so that we may work free and unrestrained. Unrestrained outwardly by the State's illegal encroachment, and free inwardly with a clear conscience before the Church's Master and His Sacred Word."[2] In the Netherlands, the churches resisted especially the effort of the occupying powers to confine religion to a purely spiritual realm. By every means in their power they expressed opposition to " the way in which the three main foundations of our people which are rooted in the Christian

---

[1] Karl Barth, " The Protestant Churches in Europe," *Foreign Affairs*, XXI (1943), 267.

[2] Bjarne Hoye and Trygve M. Ager, *The Fight of the Norwegian Church Against Nazism*, p. 134. (Manifesto of July, 1942).

Faith are being attacked, namely justice, charity, and freedom of conscience and conviction."[1]

In virtually every part of the world, Christians have become alert and active in their defence of the freedom which finds its only sure foundation in spiritual liberty. In lands where new constitutions were in process of drafting, as in India and Italy, the benefit of Christian insights was made available. Where internal difficulties followed the chaos of war, as in China and Korea, movements toward stability have been accompanied by the insistent demand for the recognition of human rights. In Latin America and in Africa, issues of long standing have taken on a new meaning and have been met with an increasingly vigorous attack by Christians. Illustrations are inadequate to convey a true picture of the noble struggle for freedom which has been waged in many lands in face of opposition and persecution.

It is safe to say that Christians in countries which remained relatively free were greatly stimulated by the struggle in lands where freedom was denied. Animated by the sufferings of their fellow Christians and by the desire to safeguard their own liberties, they addressed themselves primarily to long-range plans whereby international action could become effective in the future protection of human rights and freedoms.

THE BASIS FOR CHRISTIAN ACTIVITY

Christians have a valid concern that all human rights—civil, social and economic—should be respected everywhere. As the world comes to be more closely knit together, their sympathy is extended to people in any land where the denial of freedom brings suffering or distress. Christians believe that respect for human rights is essential to world order. When human rights are denied, man's conscience cannot operate adequately in criticism or commendation of national and international policies. The Christian recognises the commission to preach the Gospel of Jesus Christ to the uttermost parts of the world. This commission can, and, if there is no other way, must be obeyed in face of opposition and persecution. Nevertheless, when conditions favourable to the exercise of human rights exist, men are in a

---

[1] W. A. Visser 't Hooft, *The Struggle of the Dutch Church*, p. 46. (Declaration Against the Attempt to Enforce a Philosophy of Life, April, 1942.)

better position to hear the Gospel and freely to decide what their response shall be.

Underlying the motives which prompt Christian action to promote the observance of human rights is the Christian conception of man in relation to his fellow men and to God. This conception is rooted in Christian faith and represents the justification for Christian effort to secure man's freedom in society. It is to be clearly distinguished from the form which the churches use as they seek to bring governments, both national and international, to an assumption of legitimate responsibility in safeguarding human rights. There are three presuppositions which, from the Christian point of view, substantiate the claim that man has the right to freedom, particularly to freedom of religion.

First, *the Christian conception of man's freedom is derived from the faith that man is made in the image of God.* This contention embraces the view of natural law but goes beyond it. Man is a rational being and is entitled to everything that is essential to the reasonable development of his personality. There is a moral law which must be observed as man seeks his own development and which requires full consideration of the equal rights of others. When viewed solely from the standpoint of natural law, the moral law is perceived by intuition and experience. While this mode of perception is not disavowed, the Christian also reckons with the fact of revelation, and therefore finds in the historical reality of Jesus Christ a distinctive basis for man's freedom.

Second, *the dignity which is claimed for man is attested by the demonstration of God's love for him in Jesus Christ.* The conception of man's worth and potentiality reaches its highest point in the understanding of God's redemptive act in history. More than empirical or intuitive grounds are here provided for the contention that man has fundamental rights. God's estimate of man's value in his sight undergirds the contention. A divine appraisal therefore substantiates and magnifies what is claimed for man on the basis of natural law.

Third, *the right of every man to freedom is imperative in order that he may be in a position to respond to the calling wherewith God has called him.* The Christian sees in the life, death and resurrection of Jesus Christ more than a demonstration of God's estimate of man. A purpose is clearly to be fulfilled thereby. In order that man may be in a position to respond to God's call, that is, to seek his fullest growth in the light of the Gospel, he must be free to hear that truth proclaimed and, to the degree of his acceptance of it, give full expression in all contacts of life.

A JURIDICAL APPROACH

Many Christian scholars have developed theological presuppositions for man's rights and freedoms. Unquestionably, further study is needed in order that the Christian position may be clearly and convincingly advanced. Analyses of this kind will more appropriately find place in other volumes of this study series. At the present time, there is immediate and urgent need for the development of the Christian view on human rights in terms which will apply to all men and which can be used in representations to national and international political authorities. The study here projected has this need particularly in view.[1] It places the problem of Christian responsibility for the recognition of human rights in the framework of international affairs. It proceeds on the assumption that agreements thus far reached by Christians are sufficient to permit the churches now to take a united stand before the nations and peoples of the world. The churches can make their contribution to the promotion of respect for human rights only if they draw from distinctively Christian presuppositions the principles which will be universally applicable

---

[1] *Comment*. Reactions which were offered in the process of critical reading revealed two points of view with respect to the manner in which the issues of human rights should be approached by the churches at the present time. One view recognised that Christians must make their position clear to the world, but claimed that there was a prior need to study further the distinctively Christian conception of man and society. This position was advanced in only a small percentage of the responses. The other view accepted the value of further study but, at the same time, saw the immediate demand upon Christians to set forth their conception of human rights in terms which would apply to all men and which could be used in representations to political authorities.

The prescribed limits of the present study made it impossible to develop both approaches. Fully recognising the need for continuing theological study, the author reached his decision to devote this paper to a " juridical " consideration of human rights, particularly of religious liberty, on grounds of immediate world needs. The nations are in process of drafting an International Bill of Human Rights. Peace treaties, as well as bilateral and multilateral treaties of various kinds, are being written. Procedures must be fashioned to cope with violations of human rights. Education for freedom and responsibility is urgently required. If the churches have anything to offer for the solution of these current issues, they must speak now and what they say must be relevant to the immediate situation. The adequacy of the functional analysis—as projected in Part III of this Study and more concisely set forth in the first part of the Conclusion—must be tested by the question : Does the Christian view of man and society, to the extent that it has been defined, permit the claim that the rights and freedoms therein declared represent a goal which should be sought for all men everywhere in their exercise of religious liberty ?

and which can be reasonably expected to find endorsement by men of goodwill everywhere.

While the churches have a concern for all human rights, they hold a special interest and may claim a special competence in regard to those rights which will enable man's conscience to operate effectively in personal and social experience. Concentration upon a peculiar interest and competence of the churches does not limit Christian activity to the promotion of a narrowly conceived religious freedom. On the one hand, man is free to live by conscience only when certain related rights and freedoms are respected. On the other hand, freedom of conscience in society is imperative in order that man may pursue his effort to secure further freedom for himself and for all men.

The concentration thus suggested provides a legitimate focus for Christian action in promoting the observance of all human rights. It does not exclude other concerns. In emphasising the fundamental importance of conscience, its enlightenment and its expression, the churches will be in a position to adjust their efforts with fidelity to an evangelical conception of life.

The interpretation here given of the special interest and competence of the churches establishes the general limits under which the following analyses are projected. Religious liberty will be viewed in the context of all human rights. Upon each succeeding generation rests a continuing, two-fold responsibility : (1) to clarify the meaning of religious freedom ; and (2) to seek conditions of human relationship which will be favourable to the exercise of religious freedom.

The observance of religious liberty must be sought in the stream of life. Any contribution which is to be made through Christian instrumentality must therefore reckon with conditions which mark the current world scene. Part I will describe the present status in man's effort to make religious freedom a reality. Since detailed description will be impossible, attention will be centred upon (1) the nature and extent of the responsibility which the United Nations is assuming in promoting respect for human rights ; and (2) the form in which problems of human rights persist in national settings.

As the churches seek to fashion their most effective contribution, they should take full advantage of earlier studies and conclusions. Part II will assemble and analyse (1) the positions taken in ecumenical conferences, particularly Oxford and

Madras, and (2) actions under the auspices of national church groups during and immediately following the war.

On the dual background of prevailing world conditions and a fruitful Christian inheritance, the churches must determine the requirements which should be met in order that religious freedom may be realised in the society of our generation. Section III will view these requirements in terms of (1) man as an individual ; (2) the religious group ; and (3) the responsibility of government.

There is urgent need for the churches to fashion a procedure for ecumenical action in promoting the observance of religious freedom. The Conclusion will present in condensed form, as a basis for study and discussion (1) A Declaration on Religious Liberty ; and (2) Responsibility of the Churches in their Life and Work.

I. RELIGIOUS LIBERTY AND THE CURRENT SCENE

Clear understanding of the forces and conditions in contemporaneous society which may promote or curtail the exercise of religious liberty is a prerequisite to intelligent and effective action by the churches. Distinctive marks of the prevailing trend in international and in national approaches to the rights of man must be clearly identified. Complete analysis is here impossible. Emphasis will be laid on the manifest tendency to regard the protection of human rights as an international responsibility and on the persistence of varying problems in typical national settings.

I. HUMAN RIGHTS AND THE UNITED NATIONS

The authority to recognise or deny man's rights and freedoms has traditionally been vested in national states. When human rights were violated in any country, a foreign government felt justified in intervening mainly to protect its nationals. In scattered instances, friendly representations have been made to protest against extreme violations on grounds of common humanity.

On the background of traditional concept and practice, the advance toward an unprecedented recognition of international responsibility for the wellbeing of man may be ranked with the most significant achievements in to-day's history. Provisions to safeguard human rights through the United Nations have been developed during the formative period of its existence. These hold the possibility of revolutionising the method whereby man's rights may be secured to him within his own society. An understanding of these provisions is highly important. If the application of them should cease for a time and their effectiveness become temporarily lost, the record of what man sought thereby to achieve ought to be preserved as a stimulus to succeeding generations. If more extensive opportunities for international co-operation appear, a knowledge of the early developments will make for more adequate support by the churches. At all events, any effort of Christian people to promote the enjoyment of religious liberty must reckon with the purposes and projected activities of the United Nations.

The Charter of the United Nations

The Dumbarton Oaks Proposals for the Charter of a world organisation contained only one brief and subordinate reference to human rights and fundamental freedoms. In the period between October, 1944, when the Proposals were made public, and April, 1945, when the Conference on World Organisation was convened at San Francisco, strong popular sentiment was aroused to remedy this defect. Christians in a number of countries were active in their effort to secure in the final draft of the Charter more adequate provisions to safeguard human rights. Church leaders in at least four countries which were to be represented at San Francisco petitioned their national delegations to support the establishment of a Commission on Human Rights. Consultants to the United States delegation were sent by the Federal Council of the Churches of Christ in America and by the Foreign Missions Conference of North America. These consultants had effective opportunity, in formal conferences and in personal contacts, to reaffirm the convictions which Christians had expressed. An international Christian influence played a determining part in achieving the more extensive provisions for human rights and fundamental freedoms which ultimately found their way into the Charter.

The Preamble of the Charter, written in the name of the peoples of the United Nations, expresses determination to " reaffirm faith in fundamental human rights, in the dignity and worth of the human person, in the equal rights of men and women, and of nations large and small." One of the major purposes of the organisation shall be " to achieve international co-operation . . . in promoting and encouraging respect for human rights and fundamental freedoms for all without distinction as to race, sex, language, or religion " (Art. 1, Sec. 3). The Charter relates this purpose to the functions and powers of the General Assembly (Art. 13, Sec. 1, B), of the Economic and Social Council (Art. 62, Sec. 2), and lists it among the basic objectives of the International Trusteeship System (Art. 76, Sec. c). The Economic and Social Council is required " to set up commissions in economic and social fields and *for the promotion of human rights* " (Art. 68).

Commission on Human Rights

The fact that the establishment of a Commission on Human Rights is mandatory evidently centres in it a primary responsibility for " promoting and encouraging respect for human rights and fundamental freedoms." Accordingly, Christian leaders in a number of countries encouraged the prompt establishment of this Commission and sought to point out important responsibilities which the Commission could rightfully assume. Their efforts were attended by considerable success.

The Commission on Human Rights is composed of one representative from each of eighteen members of the United Nations to be selected by the Council. Representation shall be by nations, but each nation may determine whether or not its representatives shall be instructed. The Commission is authorised to call in *ad hoc* working groups of non-governmental experts in specialised fields or individual experts. Members of the United Nations are invited to establish information groups or local human rights committees within their respective countries to collaborate with them in the field of human rights. By subsequent action, two sub-commissions have been authorised, one on Freedom of Information and the Press, the other on Prevention of Discrimination and Protection of Minorities. A Commission on the Status of Women has been established.

The work of the Human Rights Commission shall be directed toward submitting proposals, recommendations and reports to the Council regarding : (a) an international bill of rights ; (b) international declarations or conventions on civil liberties, freedom of information and similar matters ; (c) the protection of minorities ; (*d*) the prevention of discrimination on grounds of race, sex, language, or religion ; (*e*) any other matter concerning human rights. Closely related to this work are arrangements for documentation, including a year book on law and usage concerned with human rights, the human rights activities of other United Nations organs, the bearing of war trial decisions on human rights, and the related activities by specialised agencies and non-governmental organisations. The Commission is further authorised to submit suggestions regarding ways and means for promoting human rights and fundamental freedoms with a view to securing the co-operation of other appropriate organs. It was agreed to accept as a general principle that international treaties involving basic human rights, including to the fullest extent treaties of peace, shall conform to the fundamental standards relative to such rights set forth in the Charter.

The Commission held its first session in 1947 and, among the various assignments accepted in its terms of reference, gave prominent place to the preparation of an International Bill of Human Rights. In June, a drafting Committee prepared working papers on a Declaration and a Convention. The Second Session of the Commission, convened at Geneva in December, agreed that the International Bill should contain two parts. The Declaration is to be a statement of principles or goals the enforcement of which must depend primarily upon the moral obligation accepted by the member states. The Covenant is intended to be a more precise document in the form of a treaty and enforcement measures will apply only to the countries which ratify the Covenant by their constitutional processes.

The texts of the Declaration and Convention as approved by the Commission, together with suggestions for implementation or enforcement, have been sent to the Member States for their reactions, and to the Economic and Social Council. Following consideration by the Commission at its third session in May, 1948, they will go—if acceptable at that time—to the Economic and Social Council, and, if approved by the Council, will be recommended to the General Assembly. According to present indications, the Declaration can be finally adopted by a two-thirds vote. The Covenant, after approval by the General Assembly, must be submitted to the Member States and will become effective only after a sufficient number of them have ratified it. The completion of this process, with respect to the

Declaration and the Covenant, may require a longer time than anticipated. Many conflicting points of view must still be reconciled and acceptable machinery for effective action devised. In a preliminary discussion on the rights and freedoms to be included in an International Bill, the Russian delegate objected to the following either because they were not necessary, were too broad, required further definition, or conflicted with national laws : right to life and personal liberty, right to petition the United Nations, non-retro-activity of penal laws, right of asylum, right of property and prohibition of unlawful expropriation, freedom of movement (migration), and freedom to resist oppression. At the Geneva Session of the Commission, provisional agreement was reached on some points and, where differences appeared, they were debated in good spirit. However, many of the differences which have come to light remain unresolved, and it is to be expected that more will emerge.

The importance of this development from the standpoint of the churches, in their own life and in their effort to promote world order, is clear. The Commission of the Churches on International Affairs, which holds consultative status with the Economic and Social Council, has set forth the views of its constituency through memoranda, informal conferences with many delegates, and formal representation to the Commission on Human Rights. Similarly, Christian leaders and committees in different countries have been instrumental in influencing the positions advanced by their governments. The texts of articles on religious freedom now contained in the draft Declaration and Covenant, as well as in provisions in related articles, strongly reflect the recommendations submitted on behalf of the churches.

Actions of the General Assembly

While the Commission on Human Rights has the initial task of study and recommendation, other organs as appropriate will apparently assume responsibility actually to promote respect for and observance of human rights.

The General Assembly has recognised the need for a further definition of the rights and freedoms which are referred to but not enumerated in the Charter. In its condemnation of genocide, the Assembly related the conception of individual rights to those of racial, biological and cultural groups and authorised the preparation of a Convention. It approved an international conference on freedom of information. It further referred the Panamanian Declaration on the Rights of Man to the Commission on Human Rights and to the member states for study and recommendation. In calling upon the Union of South Africa to treat the Indian minority within its territory in accordance with treaty obligations and with the relevant provisions of the Charter, the General Assembly took unprecedented action. Herein it revealed an intention to lift the violation of human rights from the area of domestic jurisdiction and to regard it as a matter of international concern.

The approval of eight Trusteeship Agreements marks an important step in the definition of the concept of rights and freedoms contained in the Charter. The provisions bear directly upon religious liberty and missionary freedom. The articles on human rights in the Trusteeship Agreement with Togoland under British administration will serve to illustrate these provisions:

Article 13 : The Administering Authority shall ensure in the Territory complete freedom of conscience and, so far as is consistent with the requirements of public order and morality, freedom of religious teaching and the free exercise of all forms of worship. Subject to the provisions of Article 8 (holding or transfer of lands and natural resources) of this Agreement and the local law, missionaries who are nationals of Members of the United Nations shall be free to enter the Territory and to travel and reside therein, to acquire and possess property, to erect religious buildings and to open schools and hospitals in the Territory. The provisions of this Article shall not, however, affect the rights and duty of the Administering Authority to exercise such control as he may consider necessary for the maintenance of peace, order and good government and for the educational advancement of the inhabitants of the Territory, and to take all measures required for such control.

Article 14 : Subject only to the requirements of public order, the Administering Authority shall guarantee to the inhabitants of the Territory freedom of speech, of the Press, of assembly, and of petition.

Analysis of Developments through the United Nations

The United Nations is still in its infancy. Many changes may naturally be expected as it develops to the full strength permitted under its Charter and perhaps beyond that, through processes of amendment, to a form of world government. However, certain lines are rather clearly marked out in the Charter and substantiated by the manner in which the various organs in their early sessions proceeded to put the provisions of the Charter into effect. These provisions and trends should be carefully studied in order to understand what competence the United Nations has to promote the observance of human rights.

The new factor which has been introduced into man's age-old struggle for freedom in society is the recognition of an international responsibility. This is vastly different from the diplomatic protection of citizens abroad or intervention in the name of humanity. It goes beyond previous international action in special fields such as slavery. It is potentially more inclusive than the Versailles provisions to protect minorities and the objectives sought by the Mandates Commission of the League of Nations or by the International Labour Organisation. The Charter provisions seem to indicate that a check of some kind is intended upon the constitutional and legal provisions as well as the practices of separate states. At the same time, it should be noted that the United Nations Charter contains a general article designed to protect the prerogatives of its individual member states (Article 2, section 7) :

"Nothing contained in the present Charter shall authorise the United Nations to intervene in matters which are essentially within the domestic jurisdiction of any state or shall require the Members to submit such matters to settlement under the present Charter ; but this principle shall not prejudice the application of enforcement measures under Chapter VII." (Chapter VII sets forth action which the Security Council may take with respect to threats to the peace, breaches of the peace, and acts of aggression.)

In face of the restriction here imposed, to what extent can international responsibility to promote the observance of human rights be effective ? This crucial question has not yet been definitely answered. At the present stage, one can only point out what seems to be possible under the terms of the Charter as those terms are being interpreted and applied in the early transactions of the United Nations.

The Charter recognises that there are human rights and fundamental freedoms, but does not specify them. Two features of its provisions are important. First of all, the Charter makes only broad reference to rights and freedoms and thus it does not identify any single right such as religious liberty. This general approach resulted from the reluctance of the San Francisco Conference to become embroiled in a specification of particular rights. At the same time, it opened the way to a conception of necessary interrelationships among separate rights and to the possibility of their effective interplay in experience.

In the second place, the Charter stresses observance " without distinction as to race, sex, language, or religion." While non-discrimination is commendable, provision for it without an adequate enumeration of human rights is dangerous. This can readily be seen in the case of religious liberty. A government hostile to religion of any kind could, without discrimination, curtail or deny the right of religious liberty to all its citizens and still comply with the requirements of the Charter. It could say in substance that religious liberty is not a human right, or that the limited construction which it is disposed to place on religious liberty represents the extent to which the right exists. A similar situation could develop with respect to the various social, civil and economic rights. The provisions of the Charter will become full of meaning at this point only when rights and freedoms have been clearly and adequately defined. Encouragement may be found in the apparent intention of the United Nations to proceed with this task of definition and in the modest progress which has already been made.

The Charter states that the United Nations shall seek to achieve international co-operation in promoting and encouraging respect for human rights and fundamental freedoms, but does not specify the methods whereby this shall be done. The task of achieving international co-operation is assigned generally to the entire organisation, and more specifically to the General Assembly, the Economic and Social Council and the Trusteeship System. So far as the Economic and Social Council is concerned, it is required to set up a Commission on Human Rights. Nowhere in the Charter, however, is direct reference made to the manner in which the United Nations or any organ is authorised to proceed in order that human rights may actually be exercised. In all probability, affirmative steps can be taken to encourage member states to move toward the accomplishment of this purpose. The presence of human rights clauses in the Trusteeship Agreements and the current effort to draft an International Bill of Rights reveal ways in which such encouragement can be provided. The atmosphere which is thus created can itself offer an incentive to action by member states.

More baffling than the method of *encouragement* is the method of *action* which the United Nations can undertake. The Commission on Human Rights as presently constituted has no power to act. One indication of this appears in the somewhat evasive method now used in handling those communications which deal with reported violations.

The Charter empowers the United Nations—in most instances, the Security Council—to take action in six types of situations which are understood to fall not within domestic but within international jurisdiction. These are (1) an act of *aggression* ; (2) a *breach* of the peace ; (3) a *threat* to the peace ; (4) a *dispute*, the continuance of which is likely to endanger the maintenance of international peace and security ; (5) a *situation* which might lead to international friction or give rise to a dispute ; (6) a *question* relating to the maintenance of peace and security, to armaments or disarmament, or to general principles of co-operation. Action by the United Nations under these circumstances was clearly designed in the interest of international peace and security. It may therefore be assumed that action on violations of human rights will be possible under the Charter in the first instance when international issues are involved.

Further exploration of methods of enforcement, particularly as related to domestic situations, has been authorised and begun. Preliminary discussions have referred to petition, inquiry, judicial decision, recommendation for action, observation of results, and, if recommendations are not followed, public censure, and perhaps remedial action. The fact that the Covenant on Human Rights is now being viewed as a treaty will permit the use of methods generally followed in bringing compliance with treaty provisions.

In seeking ways to promote universal observance of human rights, education must be given a place of first importance. Whatever specific legal means for enforcement may finally be devised, the weapons of publicity and public censure must be reckoned among the most effective. The nature of the world organisation as now constituted makes reliance upon such means imperative.

2. RELIGIOUS LIBERTY IN TYPICAL SITUATIONS

The emergence of an international responsibility for the protection of human rights is a distinctive and encouraging mark of political developments following the Second World War. It remains a fact, however, that human rights are normally observed or violated in more restricted political and cultural areas. Fair appraisal of religious liberty on the current scene must accordingly take into account problems which appear in national or local settings. The solution of these will first of all command the attention of the people immediately involved. As an international approach is strengthened, its impact may become progressively effective.

The world scene, in so far as it involves conditions affecting the exercise of religious freedom, is extremely complex and varied. By way of illustration, a few typical situations are here briefly described.[1]

Where national independence or autonomy emerges

For the first time in a long history, INDIA is going to have a written constitution for her government. The process of writing it has brought to the fore the question of the fundamental rights of man : Are there any rights which inhere in each and every person apart from affiliation of caste, creed, organisation or race ? While initial developments in answering this question have been encouraging, the division into two dominions carries the dangerous possibility of granting the Hindu a position of advantage in India and of establishing Pakistan along the lines of the traditional Islamic states. Whatever conflicts arise will surely centre in the problem of religious liberty. The limitations of " law, order and morality," particularly as related to conversion, are very wide and therefore open to abuse. Also, closely related social laws, as in the case of marriage and property, can serve to curtail the free expression of religious belief. The

---

[1] For the information on which these descriptions are based, the author is indebted to a group of contributors. The statements as originally submitted have been considerably abbreviated and are now intended primarily to set forth certain types of problems which must be faced. The reader must recognise that political conditions in a country may be radically changed at any time—as, for example, in Czechoslovakia. The extent to which such changes affect the observance of human rights may not be immediately discernible. The types of problems must still be taken into account even though their manifestations in national settings may vary.

solution of these issues at the domestic level can be considerably aided by an international agreement on the rights of man and on the limitations to which these rights may validly be subjected.

Where a stable government is sought following internal dissension

The people of CHINA, whether communists or nationalists, want peace, unity and democracy. However, behind the political conflict, there is the struggle for power, indeed for absolute power. When a country is torn by internal strife, the free exercise of human rights is endangered. Where communists rule, there is a tendency toward a hard and fast regimentation of community life. While the National Government is seeking a democratic pattern, it must contend not only with internal weaknesses, but also with the inertia of immense population and territory, time-honoured customs, widespread illiteracy, and the appalling destruction of the Second World War. In this situation it is of greatest importance that restrictions be kept at a minimum, and that the stage be set for the full recognition and observance of human rights when internal peace has been achieved.

Where a colonial status is apparently continuing

Varying types and degrees of encroachment on human rights, including certain aspects of religious liberty, can be seen in colonial AFRICA. In some portions of French Africa, there is a tendency to impose national points of view, and to favour religious and other bodies from outside which support this position. Where German missionaries have been at work, as in Tanganyika, the effort to identify those who supported the Nazi ideology has carried the danger of impairing religious freedom, even though the Government is committed to an objective study of each individual case. In the Belgian Congo, the manner in which Government subsidies for education have been distributed has resulted in sharp inequalities and in discriminatory practices. While the terms of the Concordata and missionary agreement between the Holy See and the Portuguese Government have not been literally applied, nevertheless the practical identification of church and state results in a curtailment of the religious rights of people in Portuguese territory overseas. Each of these problems demands separate attention. However, the solution of them all can be aided by international action to promote respect for human rights.

Where a long-standing racial minority suffers discrimination

There is no restriction by law on religious freedom in the UNITED STATES. None of the laws in those states where some form of discrimination is made legal bears directly on religion. Yet there is a curtailment of religious liberty, varying in different parts of the country and in local situations, which stems directly from racial attitudes and practices. The system of "racial caste" generally imposes the segregated church upon American Christianity and at times limits inter-church fellowship where racial lines must be crossed. In some parts of the country, there is an apparent correlation between sociological reaction and theological dogmatism. At times, there is manifest a tendency to seek implications of Christian ethics which will not undermine prevailing racial views and practices. Many Christian people are disturbed by the racial situation in the United States and are seeking to come to grips with it. Their efforts may be stimulated by the prospect of a growing international concern and the possibility of a wider international responsibility for the observance of human rights everywhere.

Where strengthened constitutional provisions are desired

Religious freedom and the rights of the churches in CZECHO-SLOVAKIA are legally recognised by two kinds of provisions, namely, the general principles of religious liberty in the constitution and the laws regarding the rights of individual church bodies or groups. A *qualified* majority of the General Assembly is required to change the constitution, while all other laws may be changed by a *formal* majority, that is, fifty-one per cent. of the Assembly. With all eventualities in mind, there would be great advantage if some of the rights now merely set forth by law and therefore subject to change by a formal majority, were made specific in the constitution of the Republic. The solution of this problem calls for united action by all bodies which are represented in the Council of Churches in Czechoslovakia.

Where Christian activity touches the Muslim community

The growing tendency to identify nationalism with Islam in the independent Muslim countries of the NEAR EAST intensifies the critical attitude of governments towards foreign missions, the Christian minority, and the convert from Islam. The first two are charged with introducing an alien element within the cultural unity of Islam, which is now regarded as the foundation of national greatness. The convert to Christianity is in popular eyes a traitor to the Muslim community. Islamic nationalism threatens to oust the democratic principles of equal treatment for all, irrespective of their religious affiliation, which underlies the Constitutions of these countries. This situation bears adversely upon the activities of the churches in worship and evangelism and works hardship upon Christians by restricting their social and economic opportunities. Religious liberty in the Near East is not likely to come through treaties with foreign powers. In all probability, desired improvements can be better encouraged by provisions to safeguard the rights of minorities in an International Bill of Human Rights.

Where Protestant missions involve tension with a Roman Catholic situation

In LATIN AMERICAN countries, religious liberty is theoretically guaranteed in every constitution. The problems which are there encountered arise not so much from relations between the state and the individual as from relations between the minority and the presumed majority churches. Representatives of the Roman Church, operating directly or through such states as are subservient to it, have in numerous instances brought about a denial or curtailment of freedom. The persecution of minorities is often stimulated by the contention that the essence of Latin American culture is identical with the old religion and that any new religion will necessarily destroy cultural and national values. Difficulties occasioned by this contention appear in countries where legislation favours the Roman Catholic Church, but in varying degrees are also encountered in lands where similar freedoms are to be enjoyed by all religions or where certain restrictions are uniformly imposed.

Where a Protestant minority seeks adequate safeguards of freedom

Apparent contradictions in the new constitution of ITALY give rise to some concern about the manner in which its provisions will actually be applied in the case of minority religious groups. The constitution provides that no distinction shall be made among citizens in the enjoyment of their guaranteed rights, and all religious confessions shall be equal before the law. At the same time, relations between the state and the Roman Catholic Church are to be regulated by the Lateran Pacts of 1929. Fidelity to the detailed terms of the Lateran Pacts would make impossible the full application of the general constitutional safeguards of religious freedom. Government authorities have given assurance that the general constitutional provisions will be made to prevail in practice. However, the fact that contradictions continue to stand in the fundamental law makes the basis for religious freedom measurably insecure. The danger of adverse administrative decisions at local levels adds to the concern of the Protestant minority. The position of Italy, by virtue of its commitment to terms in the peace treaty and its prospective relation to the United Nations, opens the way for a beneficial effect of any development to promote the observance of human rights through international action.

Where Christianity encounters political controls

Political conditions in the U.S.S.R., and the distinctive character of the Russian Church in its history and present life, make it virtually impossible to state the problem of religious liberty in a manner acceptable to all parties. Those who view the situation from without welcome the apparent improvement with respect to opportunities for worship and education and the apparent change in public attitude toward religion and its manifestations. At the same time, they are disturbed by what appears to be a relatively complete control over people by a totalitarian government. The failure to provide adequate legal safeguards for religious freedom and the tendency to effect changes by bureaucratic rather than popular decision serve to place more liberal current practice on an insecure foundation. The inability of people to take positions which are critical of governmental policy and their inability corporately to enter into fraternal relations with churches of other lands represent curtailments in domestic practice. Where Soviet influence becomes controlling in other countries, similar restrictions are in varying degree attempted. The disturbance of observers is accentuated by the manner in which U.S.S.R. representatives in international deliberations interpret religious freedom and related human rights, and the part which the state should play in the recognition of them. An appraisal of religious freedom in Russia, acceptable to Christians within and outside, must await the time when the situation can be discussed in unimpaired consultations. Such consultations are earnestly sought by those who are bent upon the promotion of world order, with peace and justice.

3. SUMMARY OF CURRENT SITUATION

The nations have declared their intention to achieve international co-operation in promoting respect for and observance of human rights. Effort is under way to define the rights of man and to devise means whereby the recognition of these rights may become universal. Under present world conditions, it is to be anticipated that the attainment of desired results will require a considerable period of time.

Meanwhile, problems arising from threatened or actual denial of human rights appear in many national and local situations. New constitutions and legal forms are being written which will tend to govern future practice. In many instances, the need for action, both remedial and preventive, is imperative.

Christian effort to promote the observance of human rights must reckon both with the international and national aspects of the current world scene. In normal circumstances, action in national and local situations will have to be taken by the Christians immediately involved. However, the resources of world Christianity must be available when assistance is sought. Moreover, as these co-ordinated resources move to influence the direction of international action, an atmosphere can be created which will have its beneficial effect upon local issues.

To carry on this work with prospect of greatest effectiveness, there is needed a precise statement of what Christians throughout the world believe is involved in the exercise of religious freedom. Such a statement must flow from a distinctively Christian point of view, but must be couched in terms which can win general acceptance. An instrument would thereby be provided both for appraising national problems with a view to remedial measures and for indicating requirements to be met in documents intended to safeguard human rights in the future. As background for a statement of this kind, the position of the churches as set forth in ecumenical conferences and in national church groups must be carefully analysed.

II. THE POSITION OF THE CHURCHES

With a diligence increasing in recent years, the churches have addressed themselves to the task of building a society where the exercise of religious freedom is possible. In ecumenical conferences and in national church groups, they have announced their views on the meaning of religious freedom and on procedures whereby the exercise of religious freedom may be realised. These developments ought to be brought together in brief compass. They ought also to be scrutinised.in the light of recent political procedures and current need. This is necessary in order that the churches may determine what changes are called for to permit their most effective, continuing contribution.

I. STATEMENTS BY ECUMENICAL CONFERENCES

Representatives of the non-Roman churches have set forth the requirements of religious freedom, drawn particularly from the standpoint of the work which the churches seek to do. Further, they have expressed their conviction about the international significance of religious liberty and the responsibilities upon states to create conditions favourable to its exercise. These findings are here reproduced and then briefly analysed to ascertain the extent to which they are pertinent to the current international trend and to the manifestation of problems in national situations.

Requirements of Religious Liberty

Detailed statements enumerating the rights and freedoms which are necessary for the fulfilment of the churches' mission have been offered by the Oxford and Madras Conferences. The first of these is contained in the Report of the Section on Church and State at Oxford, 1937:

" We recognise as essential conditions necessary to the church's fulfilment of its primary duty that it should enjoy : (*a*) freedom to determine its faith and creed ; (*b*) freedom of public and private worship, preaching and teaching ; (*c*) freedom from any imposition by the state of religious ceremonies and forms of worship ; (*d*) freedom to determine the nature of its government and the qualifications of its ministers and members and, conversely, the freedom of the individual to join the church to which he feels called ; (*e*) freedom to control the education of its ministers, to give religious instruction to its youth and to provide for adequate development of their religious life ; (*f*) freedom of Christian service and missionary activity, both home and foreign ; (*g*) freedom to co-operate with other churches ; (*h*) freedom to use such facilities, open to all citizens or associations, as will make possible the accomplishment of these ends ; the ownership of property and the collection of funds."

The second appears in the findings of the Conference on the World Mission of the Church, convened by the International Missionary Council in Madras, 1938.

" There are minimum rights of religious freedom upon which the Church should insist, else it will be unfaithful to its calling, and its own power and effectiveness crippled. Without endeavouring to make a final or exhaustive statement on the content of these rights, we hold that they should comprise at least the right :

(*a*) to assemble for unhindered public worship
(*b*) to formulate its own creed
(*c*) to have an adequate ministry
(*d*) to determine its conditions of membership
(*e*) to give religious instruction to its youth
(*f*) to preach the Gospel publicly
(*g*) to receive into its membership those who desire to join it.

There are other elements of religious freedom closely connected with these, the recognition of which the Church should also claim, such as the right :

(*a*) to carry on Christian service and missionary activity both at home and abroad
(*b*) to organise local churches

(c) to publish and circulate Christian literature

(d) to hold property and to secure support for its work at home and abroad

(e) to co-operate and to unite with other churches at home and abroad

(f) to use the language of the people in worship and in religious instruction

(g) to have equality of treatment in countries pre-dominantly Roman Catholic, similar to that accorded by Protestant governments

(h) to have legal recognition for Christian marriages between nationals."

International and National Aspects of Religious Liberty

The Report of the Section on the Universal Church and the World of Nations at Oxford in 1937 clearly recognised the significance of religious liberty for world order and viewed it as an international problem:

"An essential element in a better international order is freedom of religion. This is an implication of the faith of the church. Moreover, the ecumenical character of the church compels it to view the question of religious freedom as an international problem : all parts of the church are concerned that religious freedom be everywhere secured. We are, therefore, deeply concerned with the limitations that are increasingly being imposed in the modern world. We affirm the primary right to religious worship and the converse right to refuse compliance with any form of worship unacceptable on grounds of conscience. We affirm the right to public witness of religion and the right to religious teaching especially in the nurture of the young. In pleading for such rights we do not ask for any privilege to be granted to Christians that is denied to others. While the liberty with which Christ has set us free can neither be given nor destroyed by any Government, Christians, because of that inner freedom, are both jealous for its outward expression and solicitous that all men should have freedom in religious life. The rights which Christian disciple-ship demands are such as are good for all men, and no nation has ever suffered by reason of granting such liberties."

In an Additional Report of the Section on Church and

State, Oxford cited the general responsibility which rests on the state in relation to religious liberty:

" On the other hand, the church knows that man has been created in the image of God and has therefore an indestructible value, which the state must not impair but rather safeguard. The destiny of man and the different social activities in their proper functioning—such as marriage, the family, the nation and culture—constitute an irremovable limit of the state which it cannot with impunity transgress. A state which destroys human personality or human associations, or subordinates them to its own ends, is therefore incompatible with the Christian understanding of life. The state ought, on the contrary, to employ its resources to ensure that human freedom should find growing expression in the service of the neighbour and should not be used according to the prompting of natural inclination for self-assertion and irresponsible behaviour. In this task it cannot dispense with the co-operation of the church. It is therefore in no sense an attempt to meddle with what does not belong to it, but a simple act of obedience to God who is righteous and loving when the church, so far as circumstances allow it, becomes the champion of true human freedom in co-operation with the state and when necessary in criticism of its measures."

Analysis of Ecumenical Statements

Appraisal of these statements in the light of subsequent international developments reveals that a substantial beginning has been made. It also brings to light the need for further study by the churches in order that their position may be effectively integrated with present-day world movements to protect human rights.

The statements define the *requirements* of religious liberty largely in terms of the claims made by the churches. This is entirely legitimate. The churches must first see what is involved in religious liberty in the light of a Christian conception of man and in the light of the Church's divinely appointed task. An important first step has here been taken. With full recognition of the contribution in this first step, a further development of the Christian position now seems needed. The rights which Christians claim for man in society should be defined in terms of the rights of all men without discrimination on grounds of race, sex, language, or religion. From the rights of man will be derived the rights of the religious group.[1] Moreover, in setting forth the requirements of religious liberty, a clearer recognition of the interrelationship between religious freedom and other human rights is required. Christians may properly contend that religious freedom is primary. At the same time, they know its exercise depends upon the recognition of related rights. This harmonises with the broader approach through the United Nations. It also fits more naturally the needs of man in society where many human rights are complexly interwoven. A formulation which proceeds from the rights of man and which indicates the necessary interplay of various rights will enable the churches to communicate their claims more objectively and more effectively to governmental authorities, both international and national.

Further, the statements call attention to the *responsibility of governments* for the protection of religious freedom. The ecumenical conferences recognised the significance of religious liberty for world order. A foundation of lasting importance was here laid. From this base, national church groups moved to secure acceptance of international responsibility in safeguarding human rights through the United Nations. From this base, the churches throughout the world must now provide moral guidance as to the manner in which international responsibility can be met within the framework of the United Nations. The ecumenical conferences also clarified the responsibility of national states in relation to the work of the churches. The general principles they advanced need to be made more specific in terms of method, and correlation must be attempted between national and international responsibility. In doing this the churches will in no sense be repudiating a previous stand. By moving in the ecumenical tradition they will press for a more effective current application of Christian principles.

The position taken by the Conference on " The Churches and the International Crisis," convened by the Provisional Committee of the World Council of Churches at Geneva in 1939, stands as a connecting link—both in time and in concept—between the

[1] The broad term *religious group* is used here and in subsequent references rather than the specific term *church*. This is necessary because religious freedom must apply similarly to all religious associations. In a world society the churches can claim no rights which are not equally recognised for other religious groups.

major ecumenical conferences and the work of national church groups during the war.

" *All human beings are of equal worth in the eyes of God* and *should be so treated in the political sphere.* It follows that the ruling power should not deny essential rights to human beings on the ground of their race or class or religion or culture or any such distinguishing characteristic."

2. DEVELOPMENTS FOLLOWING THE ECUMENICAL CONFERENCES

During the war and in the period thereafter, activity of the churches in the field of religious liberty was carried on most intensively in separate countries. Effort was made to keep the churches of other lands informed about studies and action undertaken locally. A modest degree of international Christian co-operation was thus attained. In the main, the approaches taken emphasised an international responsibility and recognition of the interplay of religious freedom and related human rights. The correspondence of this approach with the procedures advocated by other than church agencies was in no small measure the result of an influence exercised by Christian action. A brief review of happenings since the Geneva Conference of 1939 reveals the manner in which the lines originally established in ecumenical thinking have been followed in the effort to come to grips with problems of religious liberty in an interrelated world.

Human Rights and the World Organisation

As the Second World War progressed to its conclusion, the nations united against the Axis powers became increasingly committed to the establishment of a world security organisation. From the outset, commissions of the churches emphasised the inadequacy of any world agency which was concerned merely with security and ignored the economic, cultural and humanitarian forces in international society. They sought more comprehensive provisions whereby the peoples of the world might live together constructively and creatively. In this effort, they gave substantial place to the demand for international co-operation to promote respect for human rights. Concurring action was taken by the Federal Council of the Churches of Christ in America and the Foreign Missions Conference of North America in the form of the following resolution :

" That the Department of State of the United States and the

Department of External Affairs of Canada be urged to seek the establishment of an agency on ' Human Rights and Fundamental Freedoms ' along with the Social and Economic Council set forth in the Dumbarton Oaks Proposals."

This action was transmitted to the foreign offices of the United States and Canadian Governments. It was brought to the attention of delegates to the United Nations Conference on International Organisation at San Francisco. Similarly, the British Council of Churches and church leaders in Australia brought to the attention of their national delegations to San Francisco the need to strengthen provisions for safeguarding human rights in the Charter of the proposed world organisation. In behalf of the churches which had given expression to their views, representation was made by the consultants to the United States Delegation at San Francisco. It may be accurately stated that the findings of the ecumenical conferences, when expanded and made more explicit in the thinking of national church groups, became an instrumental factor in achieving the provisions for human rights in the United Nations Charter.

Statements on Religious Liberty

Concentrated study and action on issues of religious liberty, more broadly on all human rights, were pursued in the United States and in Great Britain, under the auspices of Joint Committees on Religious Liberty. The activities of these committees were comprehensive and far-reaching. Reference is here made only to two documents which indicated the further development of concepts which find their roots in the ecumenical conferences. Attention has previously been called to the stand for freedom by Christian people under totalitarian governments and in occupied countries, and to the significance of their contribution in advancing the cause of human rights. It is now necessary to consider activities which quite directly affect the process of drafting international agreements in the establishment and work of the United Nations.

The Statement on Religious Liberty, prepared by the United States Joint Committee on Religious Liberty, was formally adopted by the Federal Council of Churches and the Foreign Missions Conference of North America respectively in March, 1944, and April, 1944. It was used by the Committee as a basis for its various negotiations with the United States Government and was widely distributed throughout the world.

The Statement proceeds from the broad assumption that there are rights which derive from the dignity of the human person as the image of God. It claims that these rights must be set forth in agreements into which the nations may enter and must be vindicated in treaty arrangements, and in the functions and responsibilities assigned to international organisations. It specifies related freedoms which must be recognised in order that religious liberty may be inclusively observed. The Statement concludes with a brief assignment of responsibility both to the state and to the people.

In the American Statement an international approach to the protection of human rights is advocated and at the same time the obligations of individual states are recognised. The point of departure is taken in the broader concept of human rights. However, the manner in which the requirements of religious liberty are advanced does not explicitly reveal the interrelationship of religious freedom and the other rights essential thereto.

A Statement on Human Rights and Religious Freedom, prepared by the British Joint Committee on Religious Liberty, was adopted by the British Council of Churches, April 22, 1947. It was formally submitted to the United Nations Commission on Human Rights.

The Statement begins with a Christian affirmation on the meaning of human freedom and the responsibility of the state for the protection of its citizens. In the form of a Charter, religious freedom is more closely analysed in terms of its requirements and is specifically related to the civil rights which are essential to its expression. The points of the Charter are further broken down to indicate provisions which are needed to make them materially effective. The Statement concludes with a consideration of the problem of religious minorities and proposes the method of making a just treatment for religious minorities incumbent on all states alike, without any special or possibly invidious reference to individual states.

In calling attention to international responsibility and to obligations upon separate states, the British Statement sustains the idea which is rooted in ecumenical decision. With greater clarity than appears in any other statement formally adopted by the churches, nationally or internationally, it relates the exercise of religious liberty to the various civil rights which are essential thereto. Without specific definition, it allows for enforcement through internationally imposed sanctions and through the power of world public opinion.

3. RECAPITULATION OF THE DEVELOPMENT IN THE CHRISTIAN POSITION

The position of the churches with respect to religious freedom in our day has thus been explained and made more explicit. The Oxford Conference recognised the significance of religious liberty for world order and viewed it as an international problem. Oxford and Madras enumerated the requirements of religious freedom from the standpoint of the life and work of the churches. Geneva added the broader setting of all human rights.

Through the action of national church groups, the conception of international responsibility was attached to an emerging world organisation of the United Nations. The relationship between religious freedom and other human rights was pointed out with increasing definiteness. World-wide Christian conviction must now make its impact on the process whereby the United Nations seeks (1) to define, through an International Bill of Rights, the human rights and fundamental freedoms which the Charter refers to but does not enumerate ; and (2) to devise the ways by which the rights and freedoms, when they are defined, may actually be observed in a world society. A more effective Christian impact may result when the findings of ecumenical conferences and of national church groups are brought together. As a step toward this synthesis, an analysis of the requirements of religious liberty is now proposed.

III. REQUIREMENTS OF RELIGIOUS LIBERTY

The requirements of religious liberty in our day may be projected on a two-fold background. On the one hand, there is a Christian approach to the issues of religious freedom which finds its roots in the ecumenical movement and its development in the studies and actions of national church groups. This phase of the background provides in the main the *substance* or *content* which must find place in the requirements of religious liberty to-day. Accordingly, the analysis here following has drawn upon statements in ecumenical conferences, and upon the positions which became clarified under varied experiences of Christians in many countries since the outbreak of the Second World War. On the other hand, there is an emerging international political responsibility which is at least in part a response to Christian insights. This second aspect of the background gives clue to the *form* in which the requirements of religious liberty must be stated. While form is important in the analysis of requirements, it will be even more significant in fashioning an instrument which may be used for Christian representation to political authorities.

The point of view with which the churches should determine the requirements of religious liberty may be characterised by three considerations.

1. *Religious liberty must be sought for man as an individual person moving in the relationships of society.* The point of departure ought to be in the rights and freedoms of man as an individual, and in the responsibilities he must assume as a member of society. This is clearly distinguished from the starting point in the church or religious group. The claims of the religious group upon society are derived from the rights of man and should be considered only after the rights of man as an individual have been established. Whether rights and freedoms are viewed basically from the standpoint of the individual or in derived fashion from the standpoint of the religious group, they must be understood to apply to all men, no matter what their religious faith may be.

Attention is therefore centred upon *individual man in society.* In looking at him, the Christian sees what the biologist, the sociologist and the psychologist see. But he finds something more than human science alone can discern. To the Christian, every man on the contemporary scene is the concern of an eternal God. Beset by the demands of living in a complex world, man may yield to confusion or lower self-interest ; or, utilising most effectively the resources which God has placed at man's disposal, he may become "a living sacrifice, holy and acceptable to God." Whether viewed from the standpoint of science, or of an eternal dispensation, to every man is given an appointed potentiality. The realisation of his potentiality rests with man and with society. Every man ought to have the chance to become what God intended him to be. Upon society rests the responsibility to give every man that chance.

In realising the opportunity which is due to him, man cannot ignore the obligation which he owes to society. He must bring into proper balance the different and somewhat antithetical factors which operate in his growth. These factors find parallels in the paradoxes of life. The individual must be in a position to act freely, but he must also act responsibly. He must use his own resources, but he must combine them with the spiritual inheritance of the human race. He must seek his highest personal development, but he must also seek to contribute most richly to the wellbeing of his fellow men. These factors, which on the surface appear to be contradictory, must become complementary. This is man's responsibility. He will have opportunity to meet it only if he is in a position to experience religious liberty.

2. *Religious liberty which is sought for man in society is subject to biological, environmental and ethical limitations.* In some respects man can never be free. He is born into this world with the limitations of biological inheritance. Not only in physical structure, but also in mental and emotional competence, his boundaries are fixed. To say that all men should be free does not imply that all men are equal. Freedom is forced to operate within the limits of each person's biological inheritance. Man is also born into this world with the limitations of environmental inheritance—religious, cultural, political, economic, social. While these are not perforce permanently binding, they cannot be ignored. Man may rise above the environment of his birth and childhood. Nevertheless, the obvious reality of environment— as a minimum influential and as a maximum determining—makes it impossible to hold all-inclusive claims for religious liberty. Another limitation—to be sure, of a far different kind—needs to be added to those imposed by heredity and environment. It grows out of the point of view with which the Christian insists that religious liberty shall be sought for all men. Freedom is not intended to open an inviting door to the lowest levels of conviction and action. Rather, it is intended to encourage an achievement of the highest that is possible for each individual and for the world society of which he is a member. Religious liberty is properly exercised only when faith and love combine to make a free man his brother's servant. This limitation, while not inherent in the nature of man and of society, flows imperatively from the Christian presuppositions about man in his relation to his fellow men and to God.

3. *Religious liberty must be sought with full recognition of the interdependence of all rights and freedoms.* " Religious liberty is not an isolated reality. It exists or is denied in the midst of a complex of institutions, attitudes and practices. These are inseparable from measures of liberty in general and from certain specific liberties such as those of free expression and free association. Religious liberty is supported by related liberty ; the effort to secure religious liberty is, both in history and in contemporary society, a force working largely toward the associated liberties." [1]

With these considerations in mind, the requirements of religious liberty will be viewed in terms of (1) man as an individual in society ; (2) the religious group ; and (3) the responsibility of government. While separated for the purposes of analysis, the requirements as they affect man, the group, and government are interrelated in actual experiences.

I. MAN AS AN INDIVIDUAL

The achievement of religious liberty in society will require that every man, by freely but responsibly combining his own resources with the spiritual inheritance of the human race, may seek his highest personal development and, at the same time, contribute most richly to the wellbeing of his fellow men. What does man need in order that he may be in a position to exercise the religious freedom which is his right ? To answer this question, the particular functions which man must be free to perform are sketched. A brief discussion of each function is intended to bring to light the completing factors which are necessary to make the freedom personally possible and the limiting factors which are necessary to make the freedom socially beneficial.

(1) *Man in his innermost, personal life should be free to determine his own beliefs.* Here is involved that aspect of conscience which touches the individual alone—the operation of conscience as it was previously formed and the shaping of conscience in the contacts of life. Belief grows out of voluntary acceptance and therefore cannot be the result of compulsion or force. It is frequently claimed that freedom of conscience, in so far as it concerns only individual beliefs and not social actions, cannot be denied. This is untrue. For, while a person is free to believe as he sees fit within the scope of the information at his disposal,

---

[1] M. Searle Bates, *Religious Liberty : an Inquiry,* pp. 343, 344.

the kind and the amount of information open to him decidedly limit the decisions to which he commits himself.

A first requirement for freedom of belief, therefore, is the right of access to information. To say that a person may believe as he desires, and at the same time to prevent him from coming into contact with ideas to which he may react, is an empty gesture. Freedom of access to information should be sought for all men with a clear understanding of its reasonable limitations. Within the limits prescribed for all religious freedom, parents have the right to determine the kind of religious influence to which their children shall be exposed during childhood. A religious group has the right to determine the kind of beliefs and action it seeks to cultivate, subject to a recognition of the rights of other religious groups and to the claims of the larger community to which it belongs. A nation, with representative government, may determine its policies and practices in the light of the religious outlook which at any time is predominant in its constituency, provided its government permits criticism from its own constituency and from peoples of other countries. Neither the religious organisation nor the state has an obligation to *provide* information beyond that which it has customarily made available, except when a consistently open-minded study of " foreign " points of view reveals a worth previously unavailable to its constituency. Both have a responsibility to *permit* the mature individual to relate himself to sources of information in such a way as to allow personal decision and belief.

If the right of access to information as a first requirement for freedom of belief is to be personally and socially beneficial, the individual person, in exercising his rights, must meet related requirements. His mind must be open to entertain new points of view, or when dissatisfied with beliefs he holds, he must actually seek additional information. In the process, he must be held free to change his beliefs. He must use judgment in appraising the information to which he has access or he must rely upon the judgment of others in whom he has confidence. In reaching decisions, he must consciously take into account his higher self-interests and the implications of his beliefs for the wellbeing of his fellow men.

(2) *Man in his innermost, personal life should be free to enjoy the fruits of his belief.* Here is an area where every person can enjoy his freedom to the utmost. A Christian description of the

experience may be given in the words of Galatians v, 22, 23 : " . . . The fruit of the Spirit is love, joy, peace, long-suffering, gentleness, goodness, faith, meekness, temperance ; against such there is no law." The only serious obstacle which arises to interfere with this enjoyment is the impossibility of access to information which a person considers necessary to the refinement, strengthening, or modification of his belief. While freedom to enjoy the inner fruits of faith can neither be granted nor denied by human authority, it must be mentioned as an important aspect of individual religious liberty.

(3) *Man should be free to join with those who hold similar beliefs with a view to carrying on such activities as do not involve direct participation by others who believe differently.* Freedom to organise with people on the basis of common beliefs should carry with it freedom to worship according to conscience, freedom to preach, freedom to educate members of the group and their children, freedom of fellowship and service. The rights of the individual must then be transferred to the group. Pursuit of the group's activities will require that it be granted, through its members, freedom of speech and of Press ; freedom of organisation and of public meeting ; and freedom to acquire and hold such property as may be necessary to corporate life.

In exercising his freedom to join with others who hold similar beliefs and in becoming party to their activities, each person must be alert to implications for himself, for his children, and for the broader society in which the group moves. On grounds of personal belief or on grounds of community good, he should always have the right of withdrawal from a religious group without suffering loss of any privileges beyond those which rightfully attached to his previous membership.

(4) *Man should have freedom to express his belief in a social and political community where differing religious convictions are held.* Many communities are not characterised by cultural or religious homogeneity. The more the nations and peoples of the world become closely inter-knit, the more diverse will the outlook and practices in communities tend to become. Freedom of conscience in its wide sense demands that man as an individual—whether he stands alone or as a member of a religious group—has the opportunity to express his beliefs in all social and political relationships. Objectively conceived, this gives the proponent of one religious view no position of advantage over the proponent

of another religious view. The strength of any religious conviction must ultimately be found in the truth upon which it rests. A social or political community may thwart the effective application of a truth. When the ideal of religious liberty is spun out in society, that risk must be run. Notwithstanding, the individual must be free to express his belief. This freedom is his right. It is also an imperative for social growth. Progress is made not so much by adjusting the conduct of an individual to the accustomed standard of the community, but by adjusting the conduct of the community to a standard higher than that which it had previously accepted.

In order that this freedom may be real, man needs freedom of speech as involved in the spoken word and in publication. Free speech, by way of criticism or commendation, is essential in order that man may make his contribution in shaping the conduct of the community. It is also essential to enable him to propagate his own beliefs ; or, looking at propagation from the side of the recipient, freedom of speech is necessary in order that others than the speaker may have access to the information and beliefs which he holds. The community in which this freedom to propagate beliefs is to operate must not be narrowly conceived in terms of municipality or nation ; it must move from the smallest social unit ultimately to include the world community of nations. In addition to freedom of speech, the individual should have the right to govern his conduct in the political and social group by conscience. The opportunity to act in accordance with belief is indispensable to full freedom.

Individual freedom of speech and action in a society of differing religious convictions becomes possible only when social and political institutions play their part. The right of man to determine what he says and what he does by conscience must first of all be a recognised premise for interrelationships in the community. Responsible people in social and political institutions must be disposed, as a matter of principle, to heed the stand which the individual has taken and to appraise fairly the conviction on which the stand is based. They must grant immunity from discrimination and from legal disability on grounds of a person's convictions, at least to the point where recognised community interests are adversely affected. Their judgment of what actually constitutes community interests may be warped and progress may be accordingly retarded ; but their judgment, in so far as it reflects the will of the people whom they represent, is the only criterion by which they can shape policy and practice.

To this situation, man must bring a measure of competence to justify his freedom. Obviously, he must recognise that other people who hold different beliefs have the same right of expression which he claims for himself. He needs the courage of his convictions. He must have respect for authority, even when his conscience forces him to take issue with the positions advocated by authority. The representation of his beliefs should be accompanied by an open-mindedness which will make him seek to appreciate other views and by a willingness to modify his position when justified. With full recognition of the complementary rights of the individual and of society, he must be ready, if need be, to suffer persecution and deprivation, in order to be true to his conscience.

The effort to place in proper functional relationship the various factors which may foster individual religious liberty in a complex society has forced an anticipation of factors which fall appropriately in the functional consideration of religious groups, and social and political institutions. This need in no sense be disturbing. In fact, it is unavoidable when religious liberty is viewed in the stream of living.

2. THE RELIGIOUS GROUP

The achievement of religious liberty in society will require that any religious group, fully recognising the rights of other religious groups and the demands of social wellbeing in a community, may freely but responsibly pursue its chosen activities among its own members and, at the same time, proclaim its way of life to others for their acceptance or rejection.

In the make-up of current society, whether viewed on a world scale or in the narrower compasses of national states, appears a multitude of different religious groups. Honesty compels us to recognise that each group either believes that it alone is right or that it is more right than any other group. Each group therefore seeks to pursue a programme of life that will not only affect its own constituency, but will also win new adherents to its faith. The intensity of the effort at self-propagation and growth varies considerably. Nevertheless, it must be assumed as valid that when a group holds convictions strongly enough, the desire to have others hold similar beliefs is inevitable. To preserve religious liberty for the individual person, the claims of competing or co-operating religious groups must be adjusted.

As far as the individual is concerned, Protestant Christianity finds a starting point in the recognition of man's right of access to information. In obeying the commission to preach the Gospel to all men everywhere, a commission which roots in the experience of the earliest Christian community, the churches place at man's disposal the information they possess. The evangelical conception of the message thus proclaimed prohibits compulsion or the use of force. Man is free to accept or to reject. Individual freedom of religion is not impaired.

In determining relations among religious groups, imperfection in man and in society must be taken into account. In the provisional dispensation which imperfection establishes, many different religious points of view will inevitably be held and proclaimed. When Protestant Christianity claims freedom for itself, it must also grant freedom to others. While it credits other religious groups with equal sincerity, it will jealously guard its heritage and seek continuously to refine that heritage with the help of God. It will use all its resources to place what it cherishes at the disposal of all men. At the same time, it must grant equal right and freedom to other religious groups. To the extent that its conduct exemplifies this point of view, it can reasonably expect that other religious groups will proceed with similar animation.

The freedoms claimed for religious groups are rooted in the freedoms claimed for the individual. Every person should have the right to organise with others. As he affiliates himself with those who have similar convictions, his individual rights become corporate rights. Freedom for the religious group should be interpreted to include freedom to worship according to conscience and to bring up children in the faith of their parents ; freedom for the individual member to change his religion and his group affiliation ; freedom to preach, educate, publish, and carry on missionary activities ; and freedom to maintain and to develop an organisation, and to acquire and hold property, for these purposes.

Each of these freedoms in varying degree impinges upon, or presupposes the recognition of certain civil and social rights. Governments and social institutions, in so far as lies within the province of each, have an obligation to see that these rights are observed. Freedom to worship, interpreted to include public worship, is dependent upon the right of public meeting and, to a certain extent, of organisation. It may involve freedom of speech and freedom of Press. Freedom to bring up children in the faith of their parents, if it is to include education beyond that which the home provides, is dependent upon freedom of speech, of the Press, of organisation and public meeting. Freedom for the individual to change his religion will call into play most of the civil and social rights as soon as he practises the religion which he has come to profess. Freedom to preach and to educate demand freedom of speech, of Press, of organisation and public meeting. Freedom to publish corresponds with freedom of the Press. Freedom to organise with others and freedom to acquire and hold property are in themselves civil and social rights. Freedom to carry on missionary activities basically bespeaks the right to testify to one's conviction in any part of the world. It may involve all or many of the other freedoms. By its very nature, however, it carries implications which the other freedoms may not contain. These implications grow out of the historical fact that missionary activity more frequently and specially involves the nationals of foreign states, their ingress, egress, and activities as aliens. It is justified in the first instance on the right of individuals everywhere to access to information. It therefore requires that social and political institutions permit freedom of access and exposure to the cultures, ideas and beliefs of other peoples and freedom of cultural exchange.

As religious groups are granted the freedoms here indicated, they will recurringly be brought into close relationship with each other and therefore will encounter the dangers of competition and friction. An ethical code would tend to minimise or remove tensions and religious organisations would contribute materially to the practice of religious freedom by developing and accepting such a code of " professional ethics."[1]

3. RESPONSIBILITY OF GOVERNMENT

The achievement of religious liberty in society will require that governments, both national and international, assure to all citizens, in their individual and group relations, freedom from direct or indirect

[1] Principles for a voluntary code to guide behaviour of religious bodies are suggested in M. Searle Bates, *Religious Liberty : an Inquiry*, pp. 562, 563.

compulsion in matters of religion, and guard them against discrimination and legal disabilities on account of religion.

The purposes and prerogatives of government may be defined in many different ways. When viewed in the light of religious liberty as a·fundamental human freedom, governments bear a clear responsibility to individual man as a member of society. Negatively, it is not within their province to prohibit or to curtail the exercise of religious liberty by their citizens or to impose religious practices upon them. Positively, they have an obligation to create conditions which are favourable to the freest development and expression of conscience consistent with the best interests of the entire community under their jurisdiction. Historically, governments have in varying degree failed to meet this responsibility under two broad conditions : (1) when governments as a matter of consistent policy claimed that the people existed for the state, not the state for the people ; and (2) when governments, under adverse pressure from other states, found it necessary to protect the interests of their people and in the process of aggressive or defensive action, limited or prohibited the exercise of normally recognised rights.

In face of the present situation, the exercise of religious liberty as a human right must in the first instance be made possible through the action of separate national states. The decisions of the United Nations can be an instrumental factor in influencing member states to respect and observe human rights for all persons within their jurisdiction. It is important, therefore, to mark out the requirements which should be met by all forms of governments, international as well as national and local. Many of the requirements upon government have already been indicated in relation to the exercise of religious liberty by the individual and by the religious group. They are here brought together to reveal the part which governments should play.

1. *Governments should assure to all people within their jurisdiction— as individuals and in corporate relations as members of a religious body— freedom of religious belief and action subject only to such limitations as are prescribed by law and are necessary to protect public order and welfare, and the rights and freedoms of others.* This will require the right of access to information, freedom to worship according to conscience, freedom to bring up children in the faith of their parents ; freedom for the individual to change his religion ; freedom to preach, educate, publish ; freedom to carry on missionary

activities ; and freedom to organise with others, and to acquire and hold property for these purposes. These rights and freedoms should be equally assured to majority and minority groups. The group which claims the freedoms when it is a minority in a country has a reciprocal obligation to recognise equal freedom for all when it is a majority in another country. Where such rights and freedoms are observed without distinction, people will be free from external compulsion in matters of religion.

When political authorities reach the conclusion that the exercise of freedoms violates laws designed to protect community wellbeing, they have the right to interfere. However, such interference should not be with the purpose merely of granting one religious group a more favoured position than another· body. It must be on the basis of community wellbeing. It must be with a consideration of man's place in the human family and not his place in relation to the majority religious body. As has been previously pointed out, the judgment of political authorities or the laws by which they judge an action to be harmful may be wrong. This risk cannot be avoided. It will be minimised when, through closer relations among the peoples of the world, a higher " world morality " is achieved.

2. *Governments should create conditions favourable to the exercise of the freedom in religious belief and action which is the recognised right of the individual and of the religious group.* A first contribution of government will be to safeguard its citizens against discrimination and legal disability on account of religion. This responsibility stands even though minorities and individuals, to the extent that they differ from the majority in conviction and practice, normally suffer certain disadvantages. In assuring their people freedom of religious belief and action and in creating conditions in society which are favourable thereto, national governments should seek as a minimum to comply with the highest standards in a world society. To the degree that they exceed such standards, they will be contributing to the progressive elevation of a " world morality." As the prerogatives of national sovereignty yield to the demands of world order and security through international collaboration, national states and the world organisation must co-operate to secure to every man the enjoyment of human rights and fundamental freedoms.

CONCLUSION:

PROCEDURES FOR ECUMENICAL ACTION

A survey of the present status in man's effort to make religious freedom a reality has revealed an emerging international responsibility and, at the same time, the continuation of disturbing problems in national settings. An investigation of the positions advanced by the churches indicates that the ecumenical conferences made substantial progress in their study of religious liberty and that, subsequently, national church groups have further developed these findings in relation to changing needs and practices. An analysis of the requirements of religious liberty in our time has identified the needs of the individual and of the religious group in society, and has set forth the basic responsibilities to be met by government.

There is urgent need for the churches to fashion a procedure for ecumenical action whereby the observance of all human rights and particularly of religious liberty may be promoted. Of primary importance in this procedure is the wide acceptance of a statement or declaration wherein the Christian view of religious liberty is set forth in a form which is designed to guide remedial and preventive action by the churches. Such a declaration will be helpful in appraising situations where violations are reported to have occurred and in revealing what changes in legal provision or practice are needed. It will provide direction for those who are seeking safeguards for religious liberty in national constitutions and laws, and in international treaties, declarations, or conventions ; it will be usable as an instrument to determine the adequacy of proposed or enacted juridical forms. In addition to a statement on religious liberty, the procedure should indicate the distinctive responsibilities to be assumed by the churches. The conclusions here set forth are presented as a basis for the study and discussion from which a needed plan of action may be formed :

    I. A Declaration on Religious Liberty.

    II. Responsibilities in the Life and Work of the Churches in Demonstrating Religious Liberty.

I. A DECLARATION ON RELIGIOUS LIBERTY

An essential element in a good international order is freedom of religion. This is an implication of the Christian faith and of the world-wide nature of Christianity. Christians therefore view the question of religious freedom as an international problem. They are concerned that religious freedom be everywhere secured. In pleading for this freedom they do not ask for any privilege to be granted to Christians that is denied to others. While the liberty with which Christ has set men free can neither be given nor destroyed by any Government, Christians, because of that inner freedom, are both jealous for its outward expression and solicitous that all men should have freedom in religious life. The nature and destiny of man by virtue of his creation, redemption and calling, and man's activities in family, state and culture establish limits beyond which the government cannot with impunity go. The rights which Christian discipleship demands are such as are good for all men, and no nation has ever suffered by reason of granting such liberties. Accordingly :

The rights of religious freedom herein declared shall be recognised and observed for all persons without distinction as to race, sex, language, or religion, and without imposition of disabilities by virtue of legal provisions or administrative acts.

1. *Every person has the right to determine his own faith and creed.*

The right to determine faith and creed involves both the process whereby a person adheres to a belief and the process whereby he changes his belief. It includes the right to receive instruction and education.

This right becomes meaningful when man has the opportunity of access to information. Religious, social and political institutions have the obligation to permit the mature individual to relate himself to sources of information in such a way as to allow personal religious decision and belief.

The right to determine one's belief is limited by the right of parents to decide sources of information to which their children shall have access. In the process of reaching decisions, everyone ought to take into account his higher self-interests and the implications of his beliefs for the wellbeing of his fellow men.

2. *Every person has the right to express his religious beliefs in worship, teaching and practice, and to proclaim the implications of his beliefs for relationships in a social or political community.*

The right of religious expression includes freedom of worship, both public and private ; freedom to place information at the disposal of others by processes of teaching, preaching and persuasion ; and freedom to pursue such activities as are dictated by conscience. It also includes freedom to express implications of belief for society and its government.

This right requires freedom from arbitrary limitation of religious expression in all means of communication, including speech, Press, radio, motion pictures and art. Social and political institutions should grant immunity from discrimination and from legal disability on grounds of expressed religious conviction, at least to the point where recognised community interests are adversely affected.

Freedom of religious expression is limited by the rights of parents to determine the religious point of view to which their children shall be exposed. It is further subject to such limitations, prescribed by law, as are necessary to protect order and welfare, morals and the rights and freedoms of others. Each person must recognise the right of others to express their beliefs and must have respect for authority at all times, even when conscience forces him to take issue with the people who are in authority or with the position they advocate.

3. *Every person has the right to associate with others and to organise with them for religious purposes.*

This right includes freedom to form religious organisations, to seek membership in religious organisations, and to sever relationship with religious organisations.

It requires that the rights of association and organisation guaranteed by a community to its members include the right of forming associations for religious purposes.

It is subject to the same limits imposed on all associations by non-discriminatory laws.

4. *Every religious organisation, formed or maintained by action in accordance with the rights of individual persons, has the right to determine its policies and practices for the accomplishment of its chosen purposes.*

The rights which are claimed for the individual in his exercise of religious liberty become the rights of the religious organisation, including the right to determine its faith and creed ; to engage in religious worship, both public and private ; to teach, educate, preach and persuade ; to express implications of belief for society and government. To these will be added certain corporate rights which derive from the rights of individual persons, such as the right : to determine the form of organisation, its government and conditions of membership ; to select and train its own officers, leaders and workers ; to publish and circulate religious literature ; to carry on service and missionary activities at home and abroad ; to hold property and to collect funds ; to co-operate and to unite with other religious bodies at home and in other lands ; to use such facilities, open to all citizens or associations, as will make possible the accomplishment of religious ends.

In order that these rights may be realised in social experience, the state must grant to religious organisations and their members the same rights which it grants to other organisations, including the right of self-government, of public meeting, of speech, of Press and publication, of holding property, of collecting funds, of travel, of ingress and egress, and generally of administering their own affairs.

The community has the right to require obedience to non-discriminatory laws passed in the interest of public order and well-being. In the exercise of its rights, a religious organisation must respect the rights of other religious organisations and must safeguard the corporate and individual rights of the entire community.

II. LIFE AND WORK OF THE CHURCHES

The ideal of ecumenicity demands that the churches in their various branches set an example to the world of toleration for all, and specifically for members of minority Christian communions. The occasion to further the cause of international understanding lies immediately to hand and is within the power of the churches to use forthwith, namely, " to do good to all men and especially toward them that are of the household of the faith."

1. *Christians should seek to promote respect for and observance of human rights by processes of education and friendly adjustment.*

Upon the agencies of government, both international and national, rests the obligation to create in society conditions which are favourable to the observance of human rights. Even more important is the duty of individuals and groups. The enjoyment of freedom will become a reality only when the people learn to exercise their rights with a sense of responsibility and with charitable consideration for the rights of others.

Whenever violations of human rights occur in relationships among religious bodies, their adjustment should first be sought without appeal to agencies of government. In the event that every conscientious effort meets with failure, petition to national authority or to the United Nations may be considered as a final recourse.

2. *Christians must demonstrate their conception of religious freedom in the life and work of the Christian community, both at home and throughout the world.*

Tensions frequently arise as religious bodies exercise their right to teach, preach and persuade. This situation will be eased by the adoption of a voluntary code to guide all behaviour and action which have bearing upon relationships among religious groups in the community, including such requirements as (a) an emphasis upon positive witness to the truth rather than controversy and conflict in religious enterprise ; (b) respect for the conscience, the sense of moral values, the cultural and religious traditions of those who do not share the same religious allegiance ; (c) full recognition for others of the liberty and regard desired for self ; (d) respect for the right of parents in determining the religious instruction of their children ; (e) frankness and honesty in making known the purposes of religious activities ; (f) regard for spiritual liberty which will keep the appeal of religious truth free from the appeal of social or material benefit ; (g) respect for law and custom in the community, or, if informed conscience requires violation of them, acceptance in good spirit of corresponding penalties ; (h) co-operation with other religious bodies in tasks of community welfare where there are commonly accepted goals and commonly acceptable procedures.

VI

CHRISTIAN RESPONSIBILITY IN A WORLD OF POWER

The work of Study Commission IV was undertaken at a later date than that of the other Commissions. It was therefore impossible to secure truly ecumenical comments upon the two sections in the final chapter. Both writers regard their contributions as extracts and notes rather than as final pronouncements.

(a) POWER[1]

Emil Brunner

AS the word " power " has many meanings, we want to make plain from the start that, by power, we here understand the capacity of man to determine the life, *i.e.*, the doing and not-doing of others by compulsion. In a very strict sense, compulsion is impossible ; even the mightiest and most cruel tyrant can compel no one to do his will if the other one does not want to obey, but rather suffers the consequences of disobedience. In our time, however, scientific cruelty has brought us near the point where even this last resort of human freedom is eliminated. But in this case, man as a human being is eliminated and turned into an automaton.

Apart from these two extremes, compulsion can be exerted by many means, and the sum of these available means we call power. A father can compel his children because they are dependent upon him or because he is physically stronger or because his parental authority is granted by law and the state. A teacher has power over his pupil, the boss has power over the employees, an officer over the soldiers, a judge over the culprit. In a well ordered state, the judge can be sure that the state will use all its means of compulsion in order to guarantee the carrying out of the sentence of the judge. The state has power over every single citizen and over every group of citizens. It can compel

[1]This contribution, which is part of the Gifford Lectures for 1948, published under the title of *Christianity and Civilisation* by Messrs. Nisbet, is included here with their permission and that of Messrs. Chas. Scribner's Sons for the U.S.A.

them to do what they do not like doing. The great powers amongst the nations are those who can, if they wish to, subjugate the small ones to their will, either directly or indirectly. To have power does not necessarily mean to use it, although its mere existence has an effect similar to actual use, wherever it is not certain how this power will be used.

Power over others is desired by most men for two reasons : First, power over another man is as it were reduplication of one's own existence. Instead of one, I have two human organisms at my disposal. I can make the other work and live for me without worrying about his life beyond his utility for me. The second reason is of a more inward nature. Power means also enhancement of value, prestige, whether in my own estimate or in that of others. We therefore understand that men desire power and that few who have it, abstain from using it, whether in the first more objective or in the second more subjective sense.

Power is the more desirable as the goods of this world are already portioned out, because by power this distribution can be changed in favour of the one who has power. That is why a large part of human life is a struggle for power or the use of power in the struggle for goods. This power and its use can take varied shapes. Everything by which the capacity to compel others is increased, can become a means of power : bodily strength and ability ; shrewdness in using one's own superiority in the right place ; possession of things that others must have or desire to have ; these things may be of the most different kind—economic goods or the keys to Heaven—or of the doors to the high places in society or state. It is impossible to separate physical power from spiritual, even with regard to compulsion. The power of the state, for instance, by which it can compel the citizens, is not merely, nor even predominantly, its police and military force which stands behind its commandments, but it is composed of innumerable factors, the sum of which may be called the spiritual authority of the state.

Because power means the ability to compel, it stands at first in opposition to freedom. The power of the one over the other is the dependence of the second upon the first. Power and freedom are related like the convex to the concave. The surplus of freedom of the one, which is power, is the deficit of freedom of the other. Power creates dependence. But not all dependence is created by power, because there is also a dependence due to free will. Furthermore, a dependence created by power may become spontaneous. The good citizen of a good state wants the state to be powerful. He accepts its compulsive power with his free will. The freely chosen leader of a group has power which the group accepts, and is not therefore felt as compulsion. This freely willed power must not be confused with a merely psychic dependence or bondage which is a strange mixture of acceptance and refusal of the power of another.

Because power taken in itself is opposed to freedom, there is a tendency in every society to order and to canalise power in order to limit its danger for the less powerful. The most important means to order power is law, which in itself is nothing but ordered power or order of power. It is a necessity of civilised life that the ultimate use of power, power over the lives of others, should be centralised. This centralisation of ultimate power is the state, or an institution like the state. It originates from the tendency to localise ultimate power in a few hands and to canalise it by certain rules. What we call the state is the centralised monopoly of the exercise of ultimate power. Power, not merely social organisation, is the characteristic essence of the state. The social organisation of society is in itself something quite harmless. The state begins at the moment when this " harmlessness " disappears, *i.e.*, where the state stands behind this social organisation, with its ultimate power, its power over men's lives. This instrument, the state, is necessary as a safeguard of peace, because it is only by this monopolisation of ultimate power that the tendency of men is checked to use their powers to the utmost limit, for their own benefit, to the point of killing. The will-to-power and recklessness in using it is so strong in man that again and again he will not refrain from actual killing. Until this possibility is taken away by monopolisation of this ultimate power by the state, peaceful civilised life cannot develop. In this sense the state is the presupposition of cultural life.

This centralisation of ultimate power in the state, however, is only one step in taming the dangerous power-element. The second step is the ordering of centralised power by law. Ultimate power and the power of the state in general should be exercised only within definite limits, for definite purposes, and in a definite manner. The power of the state should only be used in the service of the life of the people and in defence of their rights. The state must be the guarantee of peace, order and justice. It is clear that the state is not the source of law, but rather its guarantor. The state is the servant of men and not their master. Its *raison d'être* is to protect the lives and the rights of men. That is why the monopoly of ultimate power is given to it. State law is primarily law for the state and not law of the state. State law is limitation and canalisation of the power of the state. We call it public law, in distinction from private law which the power of the state has to protect. It is by public law that society orders and disciplines the dangerous although necessary power of the state, which is monopolised ultimate power.

Private law, however, *i.e.*, law ordering the spheres of individual power, does not originate necessarily or primarily from the state. It precedes the state, but it needs the state for its protection. The rights of individuals and their lawful relation are not created by the state, but they are publicly acknowledged and protected by the coercive power of the state.

A third step, however, is necessary in order to guarantee this purpose of the state. This third step is the plurality of the bearers of power in the state ; what we call the division of power. This explains the creation of Parliament, and this also was the meaning of a much older institution : courts independent of government. The absolute king united all state functions in his person. He was ruler, law-giver and judge. The principle of " division of power " is much older than Montesquieu, but Montesquieu was the first to have clearly recognised its importance. In the people of Israel there already existed a certain division of power: the law was not given by the King, but by God, through prophets and priests, and the King had to obey and to protect this law. The Roman Republic represents a well thought out division of power, which was the result of age-long struggles. Montesquieu's principle *le pouvoir arrête le pouvoir* is the most essential element of a constitutional state as distinguished from absolutism and tyranny.

It would be unfair to claim that this conception of power is exclusively Christian, but it is deeply rooted in Christian faith. The sovereignty of God forbids any human power being made absolute. It excludes both the absolute sovereignty of the state and the absolute sovereignty of the people. All human sovereignty is limited by divine sovereignty and by divine law. Furthermore, the Christian conception of sin reveals the dangers inherent in power. The Christian knows better than anyone else the temptation to the abuse of power. Power is misused whenever it is used against the law of God, and contrary to its God-given purpose.

When St. Paul deduces the power of the state from the divine order and commands Christians to obey it, he is not thinking of the absolute sovereignty of the state or monarch. The divine origin of power is at the same time a divine limitation. According to St. Paul, this limitation is given with the purpose of the state, which is peace and justice. In stressing the power of the sword, as a means of divine revenge, St. Paul gives that interpretation of the state as monopolised ultimate power, which we have just outlined. By this reference to the power of the sword, the state is not reduced to a police function, as has often been said. This reference to the sword is merely an expression of biblical realism. It shows that the monopoly of ultimate power is the very essence of the state, as the basis of peaceful civilised life. This conception of the state and of power is the correlate of the biblical conception of sin. Wherever the power of sin and the temptation to sin belonging to power is seen, it becomes impossible to understand the state as merely social organisation, as is the case on the basis of an optimistic understanding of man as good.

The concentration and canalisation of power in the state is more important the greater are the conglomerations of power within society. Society does not consist of individuals merely, but of groups, some of which wield tremendous power. In our capitalist age there are concentrations of financial and industrial power, compared with which the individual is powerless. The credit system combined with industrialisation has produced an accumulation of economic power unknown in previous times : it is that which is called "big business," mammoth corporations controlling hundreds of thousands of men and enormous capital, capable of limiting the freedom of all these hundreds of thousands, of controlling the economic life and welfare of whole nations and influencing the state machinery to a dangerously high degree. By their more or less monopolistic character, they exert coercive power almost like that of the state. But this is only one side of the picture. On the other side, we see accumulations of power created by organisation of those who individually are powerless, i.e., the tremendous power of Trade Unions, which in some countries are at least equal in power to their capitalist counterparts. Experience has proved that large numbers of men combined by organisation are equal in power to large numbers of dollars, and, in the long run, even superior. The development of these two concentrations of power breeds a new danger. These colossæ, both business corporations and Trade Unions, have become, so to speak, " states " within the state, being capable of challenging the authority of the state and thereby endangering the primary purpose of the state. The purpose of the state is to serve the interests of all. Those economic mammoth organisations, however, are so powerful that they are able to force the state to do their will. This situation explains in part why so many people want to strengthen the economic power of the state, and are calling for a general state-control and even nationalisation of economy.

The last decades, however, have confronted us with a phenomenon more dangerous than any other, for freedom and general welfare—the totalitarian state. The stronger the state, the more dangerous its power. The ·whole constitutional, democratic and liberal movement had sprung from the desire to combat the danger lying in state absolutism. At that time, state absolutism was represented by the absolute monarch. Parliament and constitutional government were an effective attempt to bridle it. Monarchy has either disappeared or been eliminated as the bearer of power. The democratic principle of the sovereignty of the people has conquered the western world.

It is, however, only now that we are beginning to see that this sovereignty of the people, manifesting itself in the election of government by the people, is not in itself a safe guarantee against a new kind of state absolutism. It is possible to conceive a totalitarian state on a democratic basis. To think of democracy and totalitarianism as opposites is just as wrong as to identify totalitarianism with dictatorship. Totalitarianism of the state is not a form of government. The form of a state decides how and by whom political power is to be wielded. Totalitarianism, however, means the extension of political power to life as a whole. The nationalisation of economy is the decisive step towards this totality of political control over life as a whole. If neither individuals nor groups have independent economic means they have no real political freedom. If everyone is a functionary of the state, and if nobody can make his living independent of the state machinery, if the Press, the cinema, the wireless, are state controlled, if there are no other schools but state schools, the free society is lost, opposition and the public expression of independent opinion become impossible. Every deviation from the programme of the state becomes rebellion and sabotage. Even if this state has the democratic form, *i.e.*, government elected by the majority vote of the people, it amounts to a complete suppression of liberty ; it will not be long, before even the so-called " free election " becomes illusory, because the state machinery controls all the means of propaganda.

Compared with this modern totalitarian state, the absolute monarchy of old times looks harmless. Private property of individuals and groups and the absence of state-controlled education and public opinion left a considerable area open for free disposition. In the totalitarian state, however, this space for free decision hardly exists and therefore a free development of cultural life is almost totally excluded, for cultural self-expression is dependent on material means. But all these material means are in the hands of the state. To take one example : if the state decides who is to get the paper available for printing, would you believe that an opposition Press could exist ? The state even controls the time of every individual citizen. No one could say : I prefer to earn less in order to have time for this or that cultural, moral or religious activity. State economy can exist only if it has complete control of the working time of everybody. It dictates almost entirely on what things money may or may not be spent. It not only controls schools and universities, but also the schools and exhibitions of art, it controls the theatre, all the actors being state employees. In theory it is not forbidden to do whatever you like outside of the state ; so long as it does not cost anything and needs no material controlled by the state. All this means that totalitarianism, even at its best, is the grave of freedom.

Furthermore, even a democratic totalitarian state must necessarily degenerate, because state power is unlimited. It produces an all-powerful bureaucracy of functionaries and a semi-militaristic hierarchy. This hierarchy necessarily leads to a supreme Ruler. The principle of the division of powers becomes an illusion. Its place is taken by the rivalry of the different sections of the state machinery, but all of them are hanging from one and the same pinnacle of the bureaucratic hierarchy. The democratic fiction will still be preserved whilst actually there is a tyrannical dictatorship. In all this we are not describing merely one of the totalitarian systems of the present time ; all these are the necessary inevitable results of complete nationalisation of economy. We have seen during war-time how—whether we like it or not—war-time economy produces almost all of these worst features of totalitarianism, secret police, administrative jurisdiction, control of public opinion, etc., and that, even within states of solid democratic tradition and of intact democratic institutions, complete nationalisation of economy is militarisation of the state.

For all these reasons the totalitarian state, being the absolute maximum of accumulated power, is the worst and most dangerous social evil which we can conceive. It is the very devil of our time. Whatever analogies totalitarianism may have had in previous centuries, real totalitarianism became possible only in our age, where the techniques of production and transport, the aeroplane, the wireless and the machine-gun made state power omnipresent, all powerful and all pervasive.

Now we have to turn to a last no less gloomy aspect of the power problem, the power relation between the states. Mankind has somehow succeeded in eliminating the most destructive effects of power within a given territory by concentrating ultimate power in the state. It has succeeded, furthermore, in bridling the power of the state itself by law and the constitutional division of power. But now the formation of the powerful states has created a new problem : the struggle for power between the states, endangering the life and freedom of humanity. Thus far, all attempts to bring the power relations of the states under the control of justice and humanitarian interests have been almost without effect.

It may be said that at a time when the divine law and the moral order exerted considerable influence over the nations and their rulers, this purely spiritual limitation of power exerted a certain smoothing and muffling influence. The states, however ruthless in their international behaviour, did not quite do everything lying within their power. By treaties, they created a certain kind of international law which proved effective to a certain extent, although its effects were limited because the treaties could not be enforced. They created institutions of international justice and peace like the Permanent Court of International Justice at The Hague, and the League of Nations which to a certain extent eliminated the use of power by law.

But these institutions proved incapable of solving the most important and dangerous conflicts arising from the dynamic character of history because they were limited by the principle of the sovereignty of the individual states. The League of Nations certainly was an attempt to limit individual state sovereignty by a supra-national federal structure. This attempt, however, proved futile, because the great powers did not really intend to abandon their sovereignty to the will of the federation, and because some of the most powerful states were not members of the League. Horrified by the disastrous results of the second world war, the nations made a second attempt in the same direction in forming the United Nations. Although a few years only have elapsed since its formation, it must be admitted that this second attempt has also failed, so far as the present is concerned. The condition of international anarchy, therefore, still prevails, which leaves the feeble nation at the mercy of the powerful and which threatens humanity with a new conflagration that, should it become a reality, would most probably mean the end of human civilisation.

There remains the question of a world state. Why should it not be possible to overcome international anarchy in the way in which it has been overcome within a given territory by the little Swiss or by the big American federation, which combine regional autonomy with the overarching supremacy of the federation? Apart from the fact that at present such a proposal is purely academic, the question remains whether such a universal world state having the monopoly of ultimate power would not be the greatest danger for freedom and higher culture. Only a federal structure combined with a strict division of powers would prevent it from degenerating into tyranny. A centralised non-federative world state, or, if I may use the phrase, a monolithic world state, would necessarily become a power monster of totalitarian character, whilst a federative structure always includes a certain risk for the peace of the world.

A truly Christian solution of the power problem from the economic, political or international point of view, does not seem to be a realistic prospect. The ideal of a reign of peace and justice in which the lust for power would not only be tamed, but overcome from within, is not possible in a world of sinful men. Either we believe that within this temporal world sin, lust for power, can be overcome, or we do not see that real peace is irreconcilable with sin. Both these views contradict the Christian conception of man and history. Because as Christians we see the close connection between power and sin, we accept St. Paul's idea, that only by monopolised ultimate power, *i.e.*, by the state, can sinful anarchy be overcome. Whether it will be possible some time to overcome the anarchy between the powerful states themselves by subordinating them to a super-power without endangering justice and freedom, we cannot know, although we may hope for it.

In spite of all this, we cannot follow Jakob Burckhardt in his *Weltgeschichtliche Betrachtungen*, who opposes power to culture and makes culture, so to speak, the innocent martyr of power. How often did it happen that the most generous patrons of science and arts have been also most ruthless in their power politics, misusing their power ! It is not culture, it is only respect for justice, love and reverence for the divine law, which are capable of overcoming the lust for, and the misuse of power. It is only that mind which rather would suffer injustice than do it which is willing to " overcome evil with good " which is capable of resisting the temptation even of very great power. The greater the power, the greater the temptation of being godlike. Against this temptation no education or culture can prevail. The "demonism" of power is overcome by Jesus Christ alone. Therefore the most important thing that can be done at any time against the evil effects of the power motive, is the spreading and deepening of true Christian discipleship. The most dreadful thing, however, is the will to power in a Christian camouflage of which occidental history is full. If anywhere, it is here that we can see the cunning of the devilish power taking the shape of an angel of light, and in so doing, hiding the one who alone is capable of driving out the spirit of power.

(b) THE WORLD OF POWER
Kenneth G. Grubb

I

It is a cause of general apprehension that the world is the scene of the existence and possession of excessive power, and men's minds are dominated by the fear of it. There are many forms of power, and the word itself is used in many different senses.

It is not necessary here to attempt a definition, or to analyse these meanings. Most men, when the word is used in an apprehensive sense, have in mind that sort of power which contains the danger of war. It is with this meaning mainly, but not exclusively, in view, that we have to glance at some of the problems raised by power for the Christian and for all men.

Mainly, but not exclusively. For power in many of its different meanings is a necessary element in human affairs. It is the means of executing authority, and the source of technical progress. In the form of influence, the power of one mind over another, it has moved men to noble action and enduring example. Light on spiritual power, as Christians understand it, the power of the Holy Spirit and the power of God over the ultimate destinies of men, is thrown by the theology of Christianity and by the Bible. But when men speak of power in the political world, and in particular in international relations, they do not have in mind this kind of power. They think of the concentrations of power which will enable small groups of men to coerce the wills and limit the freedom of their fellows. They think also of those manipulations of economic power which deprive men of effective decision about their own lives. They think, also, of the discrepancy between the nations in resources of power, which often dictates their conduct. And, most pervasively of all, they think of all those forms of power which, whatever be their constructive possibilities, clearly imply a readiness, a willingness, or an intention, either to vindicate or to pursue a cause by force. To most men, the final, the supreme act of power, which confers on it its sinister semblance, is the readiness to use force, and to justify power by the success of force. To Christians, the supreme act of power is, in the central Christian paradox, in the weakness of the Cross, the power of God unto salvation.

If the difference between the Christian and the general conception of power is so great, is it possible to define the Christian attitude to power in any terms other than the most hostile? The Church, however, is, in common experience, involved at many points with the world. Christians cannot refuse to come to some terms with the actual existence of power for several necessary reasons. Many of the nations and civilisations that are the large-scale employers of organised power, in the modern sense, are the children of a Christian tradition. The uses of power are not necessarily malevolent, but are very often beneficial. Power is an indispensable concomitant of life : without power love cannot act. The churches are concerned in those aspects of power which construct the social and political order, the power necessary to maintain order and execute the behests of duly constituted authority. The churches have also to consider the relation of power to justice and the acute problems posed by wars which increasingly involve a visitation of destruction for all men, just or unjust.

Political Power

The power of authority, that is of governments, has extended enormously in recent decades. The liberal conception of the function of government as that of keeping order and holding the ring for progressive development and productive inter-play of social and economic forces, has proved inadequate. Accordingly, governments have set themselves the task of social leadership and education. Many of the problems thus raised seem best soluble by some measure of centralisation and uniformity. Inasmuch as authority anyhow tends to favour administrative centralisation for the maintenance of its own prestige, the stage is set for a vast increase of its influence. Behind this development has stood wholly laudable motives of social progress. As that progress has grown, men's conscience and sense of freedom are quickened, and authority has to contain, and benefit from criticism, and at the same time to govern wisely and well. Not always has it been possible to solve this question by a reasonable harmony between order and criticism, and governments have instead increased their own authority, until states which yesterday merely maintained police have to-day become police states. The pace of progress is partly responsible for this, for a due balance between order and freedom requires maturity, and maturity is the fruit of time. Time is of the essence of a rightly ripening and ordered progress, but it is not always available.

The expanding power of political authority has also found expression in empire. Of the modern empires, the British is the most conspicuous example. Yet the conception of imperial power has in general ceased to be attractive to the British mind ; indeed, as a formula, it has never in this century had the attraction of imperial influence. Precisely because the idea of centralisation was absent from its dominant scheme, the idea of power seemed an inappropriate description of its driving motive.

Economic Power

Economic power takes on complex forms : it has had attention in other papers of the World Assembly series[1] and need not receive more than a reminder here. The power of vast corporations is great ; their usual instrument for securing political decisions is not force but influence. Even that influence need not be overtly exercised ; it is usually most penetrative when least felt. The existence of a sufficient aggregation of economic power is sufficient by itself to compel crucial political decisions. This is often wholly right, for man does not live by politics and culture alone, but it may also be undesirable. The feeling that it is undesirable is one of the reasons why economic power is transferred to the state, in the belief that it will be manipulated for the benefit of all. This hope is widely held to be in process of realisation : what is still obscure is not what is gained but what is lost in the process. The state becomes the trading agent of the nation, either as the active promoter and conductor of its business, or as the regulator and guide of its citizens' activities.

Scientific Power

Technical and scientific power has reached enormous development, and volumes have been written on the power of man over nature. Constantly we are told that man's mental stature has outgrown his spiritual : no one seems happy about it, but no one is certain of the next step. It is not only a question of man's control over nature ; but that nature itself is transformed by man, and the transformation, in turn, takes on new forms. Power over nature has found new and unprecedented development through the uses of atomic energy. Power over man himself has been advanced through the control of behaviour by physical and chemical means. It is possible that we are here only on the threshold of developments whose ultimate significance it is impossible not to view with the misgivings derived from initial experience. Yet such is the fascination of power that men will possess it before they can see its uses or envisage any system for its control.

Power in Propaganda

Another use of power is found in the technique of propaganda and the censorship. By the former the mind is fed and by the

[1] See Dr. J. H. Oldham—" Technics and Civilisation," Vol. III, p. 29.

latter the eyes are closed. Those who profess their immunity from propaganda often succumb easily to it, while the suspicion of the existence of propaganda is, among others, an effective inducement to total cynicism. The power of propaganda should be taken seriously by the churches, for the Gospel itself is propagated by preaching, writing and other means. Modern propaganda may finish by defeating its own possibility of success, but not because it has left men capable of a discrimination which goes behind the advertisement, but because it has shouted them into deafness. Meanwhile, it is a powerful instrument in the hands of those who use it ruthlessly and with psychological insight.

The Use and Misuse of Power

Centralised authority, economic organisation, scientific control of nature, and the regulation of public opinion, can be used for peace. But when they are developed together, they form a powerful preparation for war. The classic forms of might, armies, navies and air forces, can also be used for peaceful purposes such as organised relief work, but their primary purpose is war.

National self-consciousness developing into overweening national ambition, sometimes supported by a crusade to impose political forms and doctrines, is an important cause of war. The deep-seated demands and foundations of nationalism cannot be ignored because of the hope of an internationalism which, in the politically effective sense, is still a dream of the future. Nationalistic aspirations may be tribal or economic or imperial or allegedly ideological ; they do not necessarily either grow or decline in proportion to the degree of popular advancement or education. The urge to nationalism in the creation of new "sovereign states" has apparently not yet reached its term. There has been much enthusiasm recently for such development, but every new nationalist state adds to the potential conflicts of national power. Where sources or means of considerable power are controlled by the state, the national cause is easily given an overwhelmingly emotional appeal of honour, and the situation becomes sinister. False, but none the less menacing, concepts of blood and destiny, or the fanaticism of intolerant political convictions, quickly resort to violence and torture for the maintenance of an authority which may be indistinguishable from tyranny, and for the suppression of freedom, criticism and the ability of the people to change the government. At this stage, the problem of power has become acute for the Christian conscience, and only those who have had to experience its effects can properly speak of it.

II

Internationally, it is customary to use such phrases as the " Great Powers," the " Middle Power," " the Balance of Power," " power politics." The idea of power, and the existence of " powers " are inseparable.

The Great Powers are presumably the U.S.A. and the U.S.S.R., and to a lesser degree, in varying gradations, Britain, France and China. Great Powers are such because of their economic resources, fighting strength, possessions, political organisation and certain other considerations. It is not necessary, therefore, that Great Powers should combine and manipulate all the menacing aspects of power described above. Britain has been great through political background and free tradition, imperial expansion and naval strength ; France, for broadly similar reasons but with the emphasis in different places ; the U.S.A. is a Great Power through her extension, economic wealth and political institutions ; the U.S.S.R. through her centralised authority, spectacular administrative and social achievements, and the success of her armies. And so on. These concepts may be remote from the Christian conception of greatness—if there is such which is applicable to the world of nations, but they are the dominant ones in the assumptions of the peoples.

If the desires and policies, legitimate or excessive, of a nation are challenged by others, a settlement may conceivably be reached through arbitration, or through the good offices of the United Nations, but if one of the parties can see their way to superior power, or the issue is hotly contested, war is possible. War is a use of power as a supreme arbitrator among the nations. It is an arbitrator not by the standards of justice, but by its own standards, which is the will and ability of the stronger. Visitors may endeavour to use their conquests justly, but what they win is the right to impose their will. There are some who hold the causes of war to be mainly economic. Others have fought violently against imperial power. Others have taken arms for freedom. The authority and ambition of a few men controlling the instruments of force may commit a nation to war in the name of national honour, to positions from which it has no escape, and the really dangerous wars are those between nations. If the different forms of power are together developed by the state and its policy is challenged, the outcome is likely to be war. But all the instruments of power can be used for good causes or bad and that is true of war. Equally power cannot of itself cause moral advance ; war, even in a good cause, usually hinders it.

In the relations of Great Powers to each other and to lesser powers, arguments of justice may have a place, or ever-dominant national self-interest may be temporarily met by a concession which satisfies honour without yielding substance, but the ultimate sanction is the possession of superior power and the readiness to use it in war. But it is an ultimate, rather than an immediate sanction, for the risks of war are many and its rewards often slight. Power is, therefore, as useful to sustain a bluff as a battle. If a Great Power is great enough, it need not necessarily be bellicose ; if its whip is long, the dogs will not bark. But since power is only decisive when it directs superior force, if one nation is powerful, another will seek to be more so.

Accordingly, it has been argued that the best solution of the problem of power, internationally, is for the world to have a master. That may be so, but it is not practicable to-day. The worst misfortune is for it to have two or three powerful masters, for when they fight the lesser nations will be crushed between them. The best chance of such nations is that one be much better armed than the others, preferably that one whose general outlook agrees with their own fundamental political and moral assumptions, and whose policy most suits their own self-interest. Here again, there is little that is Christian about a world of this kind.

The situation is bad because the Great Powers have become relatively greater ; and the small ones relatively smaller. The massive organisation and supplies needed for modern war can only be compassed by nations of prodigious resources. In such a world, so time-honoured a policy as that of the balance of power, becomes impossible. The enormous technological and scientific equipment required for modern war needs vast wealth and man-power. This is true of the development of atomic energy, and may also be true of other unknown and even more powerful weapons, said to be in preparation. Although scientists have themselves raised their protest, it is unlikely that men will cease from these discoveries, or that they can be limited to peaceful uses. As the world is to-day, the status of a Great Power requires the sanction of superior war potential for the final arbitrament. It is quite obvious that there is no reason to assume that by the use of this sanction anything other than power, for example, justice, is vindicated or advanced. Indeed, power, used as force, is most likely to breed a greater concentration of power.

The discovery of nuclear energy has deepened the problem. At present it seems that only Great Powers, or powers possessed of considerable economic and technical resources, will be able to develop atomic energy on any scale in the near future, especially for the purpose of war. The distance between Great Powers and others is, therefore, increased. That the United Nations should have come into existence at the time when the first atomic bombs were dropped ought to have been regarded as a last chance offered to mankind. In fact, no progress has been made towards effective control. Whatever be the responsibility for the dropping of the bombs, it may be questioned whether a government could, under the circumstances, be expected to go any further than the United States has at the United Nations. The Federal Council of Churches in the U.S.A. stated, some two years ago, that " our nation, having first used the atomic bomb, has a primary duty to reverse the trend which it began." But at present it seems likely that a discovery which ought to enrich the nations will be so handled as to reduce the peoples to poverty and fear.

The Christian attitude to war has not been rendered any easier by recent developments of destructiveness, and Christians are still divided about the issues. There are those who would agree with Machiavelli that " that war is just which is necessary ; and those arms are merciful when no hope exists save in them." Many will feel that an even more earnest concentration by Christians on the causes of war and their removal is possible and urgent. " War consisteth not in battle only, or the act of fighting ; but in a tract of time, wherein the will to contend by battle is sufficiently known. . . . So the nature of war consisteth not in actual fighting ; but in the known disposition thereto, during all the time there is no assurance to the contrary. All other time is Peace " (Hobbes). If the defence of justice is justification for war, it is not a crucial point whether the war be between states, or civil war. There are many who hold that revolution for the overthrow of tyranny is justifiable to the Christian conscience. Those who attach a universal significance to the methods of non-violence practised by Gandhi would say that it is not. But it is also legitimate to doubt whether modern tyrannies of power can be overthrown by such means.

It is instructive to note what the Oxford Conference has said on this matter : " The necessity for the use of force, however difficult and morally questionable it may be, must be admitted in principle, since without it the State would not be able to maintain the system of law and order which it protects. But there is much well-grounded difference of opinion on the question whether certain kinds of force are, under all circumstances, forbidden to the Christian, and at what point, in concrete instances, the line should be drawn ; these differences come out particularly clearly in the attitude to war. But, in spite of these differences, there is a settled Christian conviction that the use of force, however unavoidable it may be for the fulfilment of the distinctive tasks of the State, is in itself absolutely opposed to the commandment of love. It can only be used as the lesser of two evils in reliance on divine forgiveness. It is, therefore, part of the political responsibility of the community to watch the ends for which the State uses its power, and also to see that the use of force is reduced to a minimum. Further, it should be insisted that the exercise of force, apart from exceptional instances of extreme emergency, should take place within the framework of generally accepted law, and should remain the exclusive monopoly of the organs of the State, in order that it should not become the instrument either of caprice or of the private and collective lust of power." [1]

So long as the fear of overwhelming reprisal is the best deterrent to war, there is a strong argument for restricting the use of the atomic bomb to those who now have it. But there is no good reason to suppose that such restriction will remain possible. The majority of Christians will perhaps recognise the legitimacy even of atomic war for a just cause, but the assumption that civilisation can be thus defended must be abandoned. It will be destroyed. Nevertheless, those who believe in the

[1] *The Churches Survey Their Task:* The Report of the Conference at Oxford, July 1937, on Church, Community and State, pp. 262, 263.

defence of justice at all costs will be slow to weaken the hands of governments by non-participation in war. Others will take the opposite view. " We do not believe," stated the Commission of the British Council of Churches on the Era of Atomic Power, " that the Church is able with its present insight to pronounce between the two alternatives. It must throw the shield of its protection and sympathy over those who make either choice. Each is the expression of loyalty to one side of Christian obligation. The one is a response to the claims of what presents itself as a moral absolute, and to an instinctive conviction that the future of the Church as the Body of Christ cannot be staked in a conflict in which there is no place left for mercy and the individual person counts for nothing at all. For those who make this choice the end of citizenship has come, since society has taken a course in which no Christian meaning can be found. The other decision is an attempt to discharge in the most desperate of situations the obligation which by God's appointment men owe to temporal order ; for those who make it the greatness of the crisis is a crowning reason why citizenship should be affirmed."

The competence of the United Nations in the control of atomic energy has yet to be tested. Even if agreement were reached on one Atomic Development Authority, there remain formidable obstacles. The Authority would only be effective if national sovereignty were surrendered to an extent which no nation has hitherto accepted, and surrendered to an international authority in the effectiveness of which no nation can at this stage be confident. Ideally, the stage is set for action. The United Nations is a more fully representative international body than any that has previously existed. It has been created precisely at the time when the uses and dangers of atomic energy have made a vivid impression on the conscience of mankind. It is right, therefore, that Christian influence should be directed to the support of its authority and prestige. In the long run, it should be possible to build up a moral influence through the United Nations which will be expressed in official decisions and pronouncements, but will depend for its effectiveness on the general attitude of the majority of its members.

Throughout history there have been attempts at peaceful international co-operation. The League of Nations was the best organised, most far-reaching, least successful and least durable. Its efforts were supplemented by a host of international instruments, regional arrangements and treaties. Most were mainly ineffective. It is certainly arguable, on this record, that one of the failures has not been the concoction of pacts but the readiness to enter into them too lightly. It is also true that certain uses of power in war, such as gas, have not been revived, and that the horror of an instrument of mass massacre may cause a universal revulsion from it. The relative relationships of the powers of attack and defence must, however, be weighed before gathering any comfort from this argument, and as a long struggle deepens, men will embrace what they profess to abhor.

If the failures of the past be taken with the misgivings of the present, it seems to be the wrong moment for elaborate schemes of international control of atomic power. Such schemes involve sacrifices by the nations of precedent and constitutional authority that they are not prepared to face. They ask for a confidence in the control itself that they are unwilling to give. They demand an understanding and trust in one another that only folly can suppose to exist. For the present, even if it is a situation which is bound to break down, it is better and safer that the matter should be left in the hands of the United States.

It remains to ask whether the relations between the powers, great or small, can be conceived in terms more satisfactory than those of " power politics." This depends on whether the nations can be persuaded that they have common interests and obligations which are essential to their survival. If they have common interests which they believe to be not incompatible with their self-interest, the chances of a conflict of force are greatly reduced. But it is not possible to hold and realise such common interests without some acceptance of common obligations.

The tradition of Natural Law at one time supplied first a common interest in Europe, and subsequently a source for the conception of international law. It failed to maintain its hold when the idea of progress took vigorous possession of men's minds and has never been effectively restored. Perhaps the most pervasive common interest to-day is in the desire for security. It is a most important interest to meet, because until nations enjoy security they rarely indulge in morality. In national life, morality results from having margins to spare. It is a luxury which is not afforded by nations which are struggling for exist-ence, and which imagine themselves to be thwarted and baffled in what they hold to be their legitimate ambitions. Nations which are strong and prosperous have frequently some morality to spare. But if a desire for security is a common interest, it may not of itself be of decisive importance. It does not follow that if a nation were truly and finally assured of security it would be content with its present position and influence.

To some, war seems the worst of all evils. To others, violence in a just cause is better than a state of deception and perfidy, torture and persecution. But modern war itself by its scale and the methods it employs, by its own destructiveness and deception, does not necessarily cure these evils—or rather it may cure a disease to create an epidemic. Nevertheless, the view of fighting which tends to regard it as a supreme wickedness is strange to many Christian minds, and to the history of the Church. It is bad, but there are worse evils. What seems certain is that it cannot be isolated from other evils and eradicated alone. The object of peace is not to make a world safe for covetousness, coercion or unrestricted indulgence. They err who hope to equate the evasion of war with the attainment of pleasure.

Meanwhile, the Churches would be well advised to consider their own strategy and relationship in regard to the situations likely to be created by war. These things should, as far as possible, be planned in advance. This is not a counsel of despair, but one aspect of a reasonable common sense. At the same time, it is not right to forget that power is also being used to-day for beneficent ends ; that, although frustration dulls the edge of high endeavour, yet purpose, pursued by right means for right ends, in and through the strength of God, does not always fail of fulfilment. The ministries of love, even in the presence of war, are not done in vain. Self-deception must be avoided, but despair has no final justification for the Church. Above all, men have yet to learn to tread the hard path of humiliation and confession of need for forgiveness and to throw themselves on the mercy of God.

MEMBERSHIP OF ASSEMBLY COMMISSION IV ON "THE CHURCH AND THE INTERNATIONAL DISORDER"

(The Commission consists in part of members of the permanent Commission of the Churches on International Affairs. The list includes only those members of Assembly Commission IV who were appointed before the volume went to press.)

MR. KENNETH G. GRUBB, London (*Executive Chairman*)
PROFESSOR O. FREDERICK NOLDE, New York (*Director*)
PROFESSOR H. S. ALIVISATOS, Athens
PROFESSOR BARON F. M. VAN ASBECK, Leyden
THE REV. C. BAETA, Gold Coast
SR. A. BAROCIO, Mexico City
PROFESSOR F. BEDNAR, Prague
PROFESSOR N. BERDYAEV, Paris (Deceased)
THE RT. REV. EIVIND BERGGRAV, Norway
PROFESSOR G. W. BROWN, Toronto
THE RT. REV. THE LORD BISHOP OF CHICHESTER, England
THE RT. REV. JOHN CULLBERG, Wästerås, Sweden
MR. JOHN FOSTER DULLES, New York
PROFESSOR J. L. HROMADKA, Prague
DR. C. L. HSIA, China
PROFESSOR WERNER KAEGI, Zürich
MR. JOHANNES LEIMENA, Java
DR. RAJAH B. MANIKAM, Nagpur
REV. W. MENN, Frankfurt
S. A. MORRISON, Esq., Cairo
THE RT. REV. G. A. OLDHAM, Albany, N.Y.
DR. G. PAIK, Korea
MRS. A. A. PEREZ, Philippines
MR. W. F. RENNIE, New York
PROFESSOR R. SMEND, Göttingen
THE RT. REV. J. SZERUDA, Warsaw
MRS. L. E. SWAIN, Craigwill-on-Cape Cod, Mass.

INDEX

(a) Subjects

AFRICA,
  religious freedom in, 160
Arab League, 110
Atlantic Charter, 104
Atomic power, 15, 19, 109, 120,
  206, 207 ff.

BRITAIN, 17, 25, 29, 96, 98, 101,
  104, 171, 204
British Council of Churches, 172
  Joint Committee on Religious
  Liberty, 172
Bulgaria, 94, 123
Burma, 87

CEYLON, 87
Change, 80
  and control, 78 ff.
  inevitability of, 75 f.
  institutionalising of, 76 ff., 85
  peaceful, 83 f., 86, 103
China, 29, 84, 88, 94, 98, 119, 204
Church, The,
  and consultation, 35
  and the Disorder of Society,
    Ch. III passim
  and Education, 36, 87
  and Human Rights, 145 ff.
  and negotiation, 34
  and Politics, 70 f., Ch. IV
    passim, 112, 116
  and Prayer, 34
  and publicity, 37
  and reconciliation, 36
  and religious freedom, 165 ff.,
    188 f.
  and Soviet Russia, 112, 137 f.,
    139, 141, 163
  and the Una Sancta, 47
  and the United Nations, 60, 113
  Approach to International
    Affairs, Ch. II passim, 111 ff.,
    114 ff.

Church, The—continued
  Biblical message and, 127
  challenge to the, 66 ff., 127 f.
  in China, 27
  in India, 27
  Orthodox, 26, 27, 137
  Roman Catholic, 28, 162 f.
  The Word of the, 68 ff.
Civilisation,
  relation of East and West
    European, 121 ff.
  " Western," 125 f., 139 f.
Commission of the Churches on
  International Affairs, 31,
  37 ff., 114
  Charter of, 43 ff.
  relations with U.N.O., 38 f., 40,
    154
Communism, 17, 76, 81, 89 ff.,
  116, 123, 128 ff.
  and Christianity, 91 f., 97, 98 ff.
  and the Free Society, 89 ff., 101
  as a religion, 128 f.
  philosophy of, 90 ff.
Conscientious objectors, 55
Czechoslovakia, 94, 159 n.
  religious freedom in, 161

DEMOCRACY, 76, 79, 93, 100, 115 f.,
  118, 122, 123 f., 125
Dialectical materialism, 128 f.
Dictatorship, 79, 82, 127, 129
  of the proletariat, 85, 92, 93, 98,
    131
Dumbarton Oaks Conference
  (1944), 104 f., 151, 171

EDINBURGH CONFERENCE (1910),
  31

FEDERAL COUNCIL OF THE
  CHURCHES OF CHRIST
  (U.S.A.), 151, 170 f., 206

Foreign Missions Conference of
    North America, 151, 170 f.
Fourteen Points (President Wilson's), 104
France, 94, 98, 119, 123, 204
    Revolution of, 1789, 130
Free Society, The, 79, 80 f., 84 ff.,
    99, 100, 101, 102, 112, 113
    and Russia, 89 ff.
    development of, 86 ff.
Freedom,
    Christian conception of, 147
    of the Press, 182
    of speech, 179, 182
    religious, 41, 149, 150 ff., 157,
        159, 165 ff., 173 ff., 176 ff.,
        180 ff., 185 ff.
    right of every man to, 147 f.

GERMANY, 16, 42, 84, 88, 94, 98,
    107, 119, 124, 142, 145
Great Powers, 14, 48, 53, 58, 97
    98, 104, 204, 205, 206
Greece, 94

HAGUE COURTS, THE, 52, 53, 197
Human Rights, Ch. V passim
    C.C.I.A. and, 40 ff.
    Covenant of, 40, 153, 154, 158
    Declaration and Convention on,
        40, 41, 153, 154
    International Bill of, 31, 40,
        107 f., 148 n., 153, 154, 158,
        173
    Juridical approach to, 148 ff.
    United Nations Commission on,
        see " United Nations "
Hungary, 94, 123

INDIA, 29, 84, 87, 119, 159
Indonesia, 84, 87
    religious freedom in, 159 f.
International Labour Office, 21,
    34, 39, 156
International Missionary Council,
    31, 37, 38, 41, 43, 45, 46

Islam,
    religious freedom in, 162
Italy, 84, 88, 94, 98, 123
    religious freedom in, 163

JAPAN, 16, 29, 84, 88, 98, 107
Jerusalem Conference (1928), 45

KOREA, 94

LATERAN PACTS, 163
Latin America,
    religious freedom in, 162
Law,
    international, 57, 64 f., 70, 71
    moral, 104 ff., 113
    Natural, 147, 209
League of Nations, 15, 21, 29, 51,
    60, 106, 197, 198
    Permanent Mandates Commission, 53, 59, 156
Liberty, see " Freedom " and
    " Human Rights "

MARXISM, 96, 138
Minorities,
    persecution of, 162
    protection of, 31, 152, 155, 156,
        163
Missions, 166
    Protestant, and the Roman
        Catholic Church, 162, 166 f.
Munich Crisis (1938), 123

NAZISM,
    compared with Communism,
        128, 132, 136
Netherlands, The, 145
Norway, 145

OXFORD CONFERENCE on
    " Church, Community and
    State " (1937), 22, 41, 45, 48,
    77, 95, 150, 165 ff., 173, 207

PAKISTAN, 87, 159

Palestine,
  Jewish problem and, 50

Philippine Islands, 87

Poland, 94, 123

Power, 80, Ch. VI *passim*
  Christian conception of, 193 f.,
    200
  delegation of, 86
  economic, 202
  in propaganda, 202 f.
  political, 201
  scientific, 202
  use and misuse of, 203
  The World of, 199 ff.

RELIGION, FREEDOM OF, Ch. V
    passim

Roumania, 94

Russia, 89 ff., 98 ff., 104, 118 ff.,
    124, 128 ff., 139, 204
  and the Free Society, 89 ff.
  and the United Nations, 94
  Christianity in, 18, 141, 163 f.
  foreign policy of, 94, 141
  great writers of, 133 ff.
  relations with U.S.A., 17, 110,
    118 f., 120
  religious freedom in, 163 f.
  Soviet Revolution of 1917, 122,
    130, 131, 138

SAN FRANCISCO CONFERENCE on
    World Organisation (1945),
    104 f., 151, 157, 171

Socialism, 81, 82, 116, 125, 133

Soviet Union, *see* " Russia "

Spain, 42, 123

State,
  national, 55 ff., 70, 71
  Soviet, 93
  world, 85, 111

Stockholm Conference (1925),
    45

TAMBARAM (Madras) Conference
    on the World Mission of the
    Church (1938), 41, 45, 150,
    165 ff., 173

Totalitarianism, 82 f., 195 ff.

Turkish Empire, 29

UNITED NATIONS, 14, 15, 22, 29,
    34, 35, 40, 53, 60, 61, 97, 103,
    104, 105, 106 f., 108, 109,
    110 f., 149, 155 ff., 183, 204,
    206, 208
  Charter of, 21, 30, 38, 58, 61, 88,
    104, 106, 107, 109, 110, 151 f.,
    155 ff., 171
  Commission on Human Rights,
    40, 59, 107 f., 150 ff., 172
  Department of Public Informa-
    tion, 38
  Economic and Social Council,
    34, 38, 59, 60, 107, 152, 153,
    154, 157, 171
  Educational, Scientific and Cul-
    tural Organisation
    (U.N.E.S.C.O.), 21, 34, 39,
    40
  Functional agencies of, 108 f.
  General Assembly, 105, 106,
    107, 109, 153, 154 f.
  International Refugee Organisa-
    tion, 34
  Regional agencies of, 109 f.
  Russia's attitude towards, 94
  Security Council, 17, 56, 58, 97,
    107, 158
  Trusteeship Council, 88, 94, 95,
    155, 157

United States of America, 17, 25,
    104, 108, 118 f., 120, 171, 204,
    206
  Civil War, 83
  race discrimination in, 84, 101,
    161
  religious freedom in, 161

U.S.S.R., *see* " Russia "

VERSAILLES TREATY (1919), 120, 156

WAR, 77 f., 95
First World, 29, 52 f., 104, 119
Second World, 14, 16, 29, 53, 98, 104, 114, 159, 160, 170, 174

World Council of Churches, 17 f., 31, 34, 35, 37, 38, 39, 41, 43, 45, 46
Conference on " The Churches and the International Crisis " (1939), 169, 170

YUGOSLAVIA, 123

(b) Names

AGER, Trygve M., 145
Augustine, St., 64, 72

BARNES, Roswell P., 19
Barth, Karl, 145
Bates, M. Searle, 176, 182 n.
Bednar, F., 143
Bismarck, 138
Brunner, Emil, 190
Burckhardt, Jakob, 199
Byelinski, 133

CHEN, W. Y., 143

DOSTOYEVSKI, 133, 134
Dulles, John Foster, 73

ENGELS, Friedrich, 92

FREDERICK the Great, 136
Frederick II, 136

GANDHI, 207
Gogol, 133, 134
Goncharov, 133
Gorki, M., 133, 134
Grubb, K. G., 13, 19, 199

HITLER, 103, 128, 138, 145
Hobbes, 206
Hoye, Bjarne, 145
Hromadka, J. L., 114
Huber, Max, 20

KELSEY, G. D., 143

LENIN, 92, 95, 98, 99, 102, 130, 131, 133
Luther, 138

MACHIAVELLI, 206
Mahan, Admiral, 104
Marx, Karl, 92, 133
Montesquieu, 193
Morrison, S. A., 143
Mussolini, 103

NAPOLEON, 104
Nolde, O. F., 108 n., 143

OLDHAM, J. H., 202 n.

PAUL, ST., 50, 194
Peter the Great, 133
Pushkin, Alexander, 134

RAM, B. L. Rallia, 143
Rembao, Alberto, 143
Ross, Emory, 143

STALIN, 89 n., 92, 98, 99 f., 103, 131

TCHEKHOV, 133
Temple, William, 26
Tolstoy, L. N., 133, 134

VAN ASBECK, F. M., 47
Visser 't Hooft, W. A., 146

REPORT OF SECTION IV
THE CHURCH AND THE INTERNATIONAL DISORDER

*Received by the Assembly and commended to the churches for their
serious consideration and appropriate action.*

THE World Council of Churches is met in its first Assembly at
a time of critical international strain. The hopes of the recent
war years and the apparent dawn of peace have been dashed. No
adequate system for effecting peaceful change has been established,
despite the earnest desire of millions. In numerous countries,
human rights are being trampled under foot and liberty denied by
political or economic systems. Exhaustion and disillusionment have
combined with spiritual apathy to produce a moral vacuum which
will be filled, either by Christian faith or by despair or even hatred.
Men are asking in fear and dismay what the future holds.

The churches bear witness to all mankind that the world is in
God's hands. His purpose may be thwarted and delayed, but it
cannot be finally frustrated. This is the meaning of history which
forbids despair or surrender to the fascinating belief in power as a
solvent of human trouble.

War, being a consequence of the disregard of God, is not
inevitable if man will turn to Him in repentance and obey His
law. There is, then, no irresistible tide that is carrying man to
destruction. Nothing is impossible with God.

While we know that wars sometimes arise from immediate
causes which Christians seem unable to influence, we need not
work blindly or alone. We are laborers together with God, Who in
Christ has given us the way of overcoming demonic forces in
history. Through the churches, working together under His power,
a fellowship is being developed which rises above those barriers of
race, colour, class and nation that now set men against each other
in conflict.

Every person has a place in the Divine purpose. Created by
God in His image, the object of His redeeming love in Christ, he
must be free to respond to God's calling. God is not indifferent to
misery or deaf to human prayer and aspiration. By accepting His
Gospel, men will find forgiveness for all their sins and receive
power to transform their relations with their fellow men.

Herein lies our hope and the ground of all our striving. It is required of us that we be faithful and obedient. The event is with God. Thus every man may serve the cause of peace, confident that—no matter what happens—he is neither lost nor futile, for the Lord God Omnipotent reigneth.

In this confidence we are one in proclaiming to all mankind:
I. *War is contrary to the will of God.*

War as a method of settling disputes is incompatible with the teaching and example of our Lord Jesus Christ. The part which war plays in our present international life is a sin against God and a degradation of man. We recognise that the problem of war raises especially acute issues for Christians today. Warfare has greatly changed. War is now total and every man and woman is called for mobilisation in war service. Moreover, the immense use of air forces and the discovery of atomic and other new weapons render widespread and indiscriminate destruction inherent in the whole conduct of modern war in a sense never experienced in past conflicts. In these circumstances the tradition of a just war, requiring a just cause and the use of just means, is now challenged. Law may require the sanction of force, but when war breaks out, force is used on a scale which tends to destroy the basis on which law exists.

Therefore the inescapable question arises—Can war now be an act of Justice? We cannot answer this question unanimously, but three broad positions are maintained:

(1) There are those who hold that, even though entering a war may be a Christian's duty in particular circumstances, modern warfare, with its mass destruction, can never be an act of justice.

(2) In the absence of impartial supranational institutions, there are those who hold that military action is the ultimate sanction of the rule of law, and that citizens must be distinctly taught that it is their duty to defend the law by force if necessary.

(3) Others, again, refuse military service of all kinds, convinced that an absolute witness against war and for peace is for them the will of God and they desire that the Church should speak to the same effect.

We must frankly acknowledge our deep sense of perplexity in face of these conflicting opinions, and urge upon all Christians the duty of wrestling continuously with the difficulties they raise and a praying humbly for God's guidance. We believe that there is a special call to theologians to consider the theological problems involved. In the meantime, the churches must continue to hold within their full fellowship all who sincerely profess such viewpoints as those set out above and are prepared to submit themselves to the will of God in the light of such guidance as may be vouchsafed to them.

On certain points of principle all are agreed. In the absence of any impartial agency for upholding justice, nations have gone to war in the belief that they were doing so. We hold that in international as in national life justice must be upheld. Nations must suppress their desire to save "face." This derives from pride, as unworthy as it is dangerous. The churches, for their part, have the duty of declaring those moral principles which obedience to God requires in war as in peace. They must not allow their spiritual and moral resources to be used by the state in war or in peace as a means of propagating an ideology or supporting a cause in which they cannot wholeheartedly concur. They must teach the duty of love and prayer for the enemy in time of war and of reconciliation between victor and vanquished after the war.

The churches must also attack the causes of war by promoting peaceful change and the pursuit of justice. They must stand for the maintenance of good faith and the honouring of the pledged word; resist the pretensions of imperialist power; promote the multilateral reduction of armaments; and combat indifference and despair in the face of the futility of war; they must point Christians to that spiritual resistance which grows from settled convictions widely held, themselves a powerful deterrent to war. A moral vacuum inevitably invites an aggressor.

We call upon the governments of those countries which were victors in the second world war to hasten the making of just peace treaties with defeated nations, allowing them to rebuild their political and economic systems for peaceable purposes; promptly to return prisoners of war to their homes; and to bring purges and trials for war crimes to a rapid end.

II. *Peace requires an attack on the causes of conflict between the powers.*

The greatest threat to peace today comes from the division of the world into mutually suspicious and antagonistic blocs. This threat is all the greater because national tensions are confused by the clash of economic and political systems. Christianity cannot be equated with any of these. There are elements in all systems which we must condemn when they contravene the First Commandment, infringe basic human rights, and contain a potential threat to peace. We denounce all forms of tyranny, economic, political or religious, which deny liberty to men. We utterly oppose totalitarianism, whenever found, in which a state arrogates to itself the right of determining men's thoughts and actions instead of recognising the right of each individual to do God's will according to his conscience. In the same way we oppose any church which seeks to use the power of the state to enforce religious conformity. We resist all endeavours to spread a system of thought or of economics by unscrupulous intolerance, suppression or persecution.

Similarly, we oppose aggressive imperialism—political, economic or cultural—whereby a nation seeks to use other nations or peoples for its own ends. We therefore protest against the exploitation of non-self-governing peoples for selfish purposes; the retarding of their progress towards self-government; and discrimination or segregation on the ground of race or colour.

A positive attempt must be made to ensure that competing economic systems such as communism, socialism or free enterprise may co-exist without leading to war. No nation has the moral right to determine its own economic policy without consideration for the economic needs of other nations and without recourse to international consultation. The churches have a responsibility to educate men to rise above the limitations of their national outlook and to view economic and political differences in the light of the Christian objective of ensuring to every man freedom from all economic or political bondage. Such systems exist to serve men, not men to serve them.

Christians must examine critically all actions of governments which increase tension or arouse misunderstanding, even unintentionally. Above all, they should withstand everything in the press, radio or school which inflames hatred or hostility between nations.

III. *The nations of the world must acknowledge the rule of law.*

Our Lord Jesus Christ taught that God, the Father of all, is Sovereign. We affirm, therefore, that no state may claim absolute sovereignty, or make laws without regard to the commandments of God and the welfare of mankind. It must accept its responsibility under the governance of God, and its subordination to law, within the society of nations.

As within the nations, so in their relations with one another, the authority of law must be recognized and established. International law clearly requires international institutions for its effectiveness. These institutions, if they are to command respect and obedience of nations, must come to grips with international problems on their own merits and not primarily in the light of national interests.

Such institutions are urgently needed today. History never stands still. New forces constantly emerge. Sporadic conflicts East and West, the attainment of independence by large masses of people, the apparent decline of European predominance, the clash of competing systems in Asia, all point to the inevitability of change. The United Nations was designed to assist in the settlement of difficulties and to promote friendly relations among the nations. Its purposes in these respects deserve the support of Christians. But unless the nations surrender a greater measure of national sovereignty in the interest of the common good, they will be tempted to have recourse to war in order to enforce their claims.

The churches have an important part in laying that common foundation of moral conviction without which any system of law will break down. While pressing for more comprehensive and authoritative world organisation, they should at present support immediate practical steps for fostering mutual understanding and goodwill among the nations, for promoting respect for international law and the establishment of the international institutions which are now possible. They should also support every effort to deal on a universal basis with the many specific questions of international concern which face mankind today, such as the use of atomic power, the multilateral reduction of armaments, and the provision of health services and food for all men. They should endeavour to secure that the United Nations be further developed to serve such purposes. They should insist that the domestic laws of each country conform to the principles of progressive international law, and they gratefully recognise that recent demands to formulate principles of human rights reflect a new sense of international responsibility for the rights and freedoms of all men.

IV. *The observance of Human Rights and Fundamental Freedoms should be encouraged by domestic and international action.*

The Church has always demanded freedom to obey God rather than men. We affirm that all men are equal in the sight of God and that the rights of men derive directly from their status as the children of God. It is presumptuous for the state to assume that it can grant or deny fundamental rights. It is for the state to embody these rights in its own legal system and to ensure their observance in practice. We believe however, that there are no rights without duties. Man's freedom has its counterpart in man's responsibility, and each person has a responsibility towards his fellows in community.

We are profoundly concerned by evidence from many parts of the world of flagrant violations of human rights. Both individuals and groups are subjected to persecution and discrimination on grounds of race, colour, religion, culture or political conviction. Against such actions, whether of governments, officials, or the general public, the churches must take a firm and vigorous stand, through local action, in co-operation with churches in other lands, and through international institutions of legal order. They must work for an ever wider and deeper understanding of what are the essential human rights if men are to be free to do the will of God.

At the present time, churches should support every endeavour to secure within an international bill of rights adequate safeguards for freedom of religion and conscience, including rights of all men to hold and change their faith, to express it in worship and practice, to teach and persuade others, and to decide on the religious education of their children. They should press for freedom of speech and expression, of association and assembly, the rights of the family, of freedom from arbitrary arrest, as well as all those other rights which the true freedom of men requires. In the domestic and in the international sphere, they should support a fuller realisation of human freedom through social legislation. They should protest against the expulsion of minorities. With all the resources at their disposal they should oppose enforced segregation on grounds of race or colour, working for the progressive recognition and application of this principle in every country. Above all it is essential that the churches observe these fundamental rights in their own membership and life, thus giving to others an example of what freedom means in practice.

V. *The churches and all Christian people have obligations in the face of international disorder.*

The churches are guilty both of indifference and of failure. While they desire more open honesty and less self-righteousness among governments and all concerned with international relations, they cannot cast a first stone or excuse themselves for complacency.

Therefore, it is the duty of the Christian to pray for all men, especially for those in authority; to combat both hatred, and resignation in regard to war; to support negotiation rather than primary reliance upon arms as an instrument of policy; and to sustain such national policies as in his judgment best reflect Christian principles. He should respond to the demand of the Christian vocation upon his life as a citizen, make sacrifices for the hungry and homeless, and, above all, win men for Christ, and thus enlarge the bounds of the supranational fellowship.

Within this fellowship, each church must eliminate discrimination among its members on unworthy grounds. It must educate them to view international policies in the light of their faith. Its witness to the moral law must be a warning to the state against unnecessary concession to expediency, and it must support leaders and those in authority in their endeavor to build the sure foundations of just world order.

The establishment of the World Council of Churches can be made of great moment for the life of the nations. It is a living expression of this fellowship, transcending race and nation, class and culture, knit together in faith, service and understanding. Its aim will be to hasten international reconciliation through its own members and through the co-operation of all Christian churches and of all men of goodwill. It will strive to see international differences in the light of God's design, remembering that normally there are Christians on both sides of every frontier. It should not weary in the effort to state the Christian understanding of the will of God and to promote its application to national and international policy.

For these purposes special agencies are needed. To this end the World Council of Churches and the International Missionary Council have formed the Commission of the Churches on International Affairs. The Assembly commends it to the interest and prayers of all Christian people.

Great are the tasks and fateful the responsibilities laid on Christians to-day. In our own strength we can do nothing; but our hope is in Christ and in the coming of His Kingdom. With Him is the victory and in Him we trust. We pray that we may be strengthened by the power of His might and used by Him for accomplishing His design among the nations. For He is the Prince of Peace and the Risen and Living Head of the Church.

RESOLUTION

WHEREAS the uprooted peoples of Europe and Asia are far more numerous than at the close of the war, and whereas this problem constitutes a challenge to the Christian conscience

IT IS RESOLVED:

I. That the World Council of Churches give high priority to work for the material and spiritual welfare of refugees; and appeal to its member churches in countries capable of receiving any settlers, both to influence public opinion towards a liberal immigration policy and to welcome and care for those who arrive in their countries.

This priority in work for the material and spiritual welfare of refugees includes not only those within the care of the International Refugee Organisation and refugees of German ethnic origin, but all refugees and expellees of whatever nationality.

Especial attention should be given to the needs of children, particularly in countries where children have been severed from family care.

II. That the International Refugee Organisation, in pursuance of its task of re-settling refugees, be requested to continue to urge governments which recruit able-bodied persons from among these displaced persons, to receive and settle their dependent relatives also, and thus respect the unity and integrity of family life.

III. That the Council authorise the World Council of Churches' Refugee Commission to take such steps as may be appropriate to bring persons of German ethnic origin within the protection of the United Nations International Refugee Organisation. Further, the Assembly directs the Ecumenical Refugee Commission to work for inclusion of all refugees and expellees within the mandate of the International Refugee Organisation.

IV. That the World Council of Churches, having already requested its member churches to support the efforts of the United Nations' Secretariat on behalf of Arab and other refugees from the conflict areas of Palestine, appeal to the Jewish authorities throughout the world to co-operate in this work of relief, and to facilitate the return of the refugees to their homes at as early a date as practicable.

V. WHEREAS the World Council of Churches notes with satisfaction that the United Nations has accepted as one of its major purposes the promotion of respect for and observance of human rights and fundamental freedoms for all without distinction as to race, sex, language or religion,

AND WHEREAS the Assembly, conscious of the magnitude and complexity of the task of placing the protection of human rights under the aegis of an international authority, regards a Declaration of Human Rights, which is neither binding nor enforceable, although valuable as setting a common standard of achievement for all peoples and all nations, as in itself inadequate
BE IT RESOLVED

That the Assembly calls upon its constituent members to press for the adoption of an International Bill of Human Rights making provision for the recognition, and national and international enforcement of all the essential freedoms of man, whether personal, political or social.

That the Assembly call upon its constituent members to support the adoption of other conventions on human rights, such as those on Genocide and Freedom of Information and the Press, as a step toward the promotion of respect for and observance of human rights and fundamental freedoms throughout the world.

VI. WHEREAS the Churches are seeking to promote the observance of religious liberty throughout the world
BE IT RESOLVED

That the World Council of Churches adopt the following *Declaration on Religious Liberty* and urge the application of its provisions through domestic and international action.

A DECLARATION ON RELIGIOUS LIBERTY

An essential element in a good international order is freedom of religion. This is an implication of the Christian faith and of the world-wide nature of Christianity. Christians, therefore, view the question of religious freedom as an international problem. They are concerned that religious freedom be everywhere secured. In pleading for this freedom, they do not ask for any privilege to be granted to Christians that is denied to others. While the liberty with which Christ has set men free can neither be given nor destroyed by any government, Christians, because of that inner freedom, are both jealous for its outward expression and solicitous that all men should have freedom in religious life. The nature and destiny of man by virtue of his creation, redemption and calling, and man's activities in family, state and culture establish limits beyond which the government cannot with impunity go. The rights which Christian discipleship demands are such as are good for all men, and no nation has ever suffered by reason of granting such liberties. Accordingly:

The rights of religious freedom herein declared shall be recognised and observed for all persons without distinction as to race, colour, sex, language or religion, and without imposition of disabilities by virtue of legal provisions or administrative acts.

I. *Every person has the right to determine his own faith and creed.*

The right to determine faith and creed involves both the process whereby a person adheres to a belief and the process whereby he changes his belief. It includes the right to receive instruction and education.

This right becomes meaningful when man has the opportunity of access to information. Religious, social and political institutions have the obligation to permit the mature individual to relate himself to sources of information in such a way as to allow personal religious decision and belief.

The right to determine one's belief is limited by the right of parents to decide sources of information to which their children shall have access. In the process of reaching decisions, everyone ought to take into account his higher self-interests and the implications of his beliefs for the well-being of his fellow men.

II. *Every person has the right to express his religious beliefs in worship, teaching and practice, and to proclaim the implications of his beliefs for relationships in a social or political community.*

The right of religious expression includes freedom of worship both public and private; freedom to place information at the disposal of others by processes of teaching, preaching and persuasion; and freedom to pursue such activities as are dictated by conscience. It also includes freedom to express implications of belief for society and its government.

This right requires freedom from arbitrary limitation of religious expression in all means of communication, including speech, press, radio, motion pictures and art. Social and political institutions should grant immunity from discrimination and from legal disability on grounds of expressed religious conviction, at least to the point where recognised community interests are adversely affected.

Freedom of religious expression is limited by the rights of parents to determine the religious point of view to which their children shall be exposed. It is further subject to such limitations, prescribed by law, as are necessary to protect order and welfare, morals and the rights and freedom of others. Each person must recognise the right of others to express their beliefs and must have respect for authority at all times, even when conscience forces him to take issue with the people who are in authority or with the position they advocate.

III. *Every person has the right to associate with others and to organise with them for religious purposes.*

This right includes freedom to form religious organisations, to seek membership in religious organisations, and to sever relationship with religious organisations.

It requires that the rights of association and organisation guaranteed by a community to its members include the right of forming associations for religious purposes.

It is subject to the same limits imposed on all associations by non-discriminatory laws.

IV. *Every religious organisation, formed or maintained by action in accordance with the rights of individual persons, has the right to determine its policies and practices for the accomplishment of its chosen purposes.*

The rights which are claimed for the individual in his exercise of religious liberty become the rights of the religious organisation, including the right to determine its faith and creed; to engage in religious worship, both public and private; to teach, educate, preach and persuade; to express implications of belief for society and government. To these will be added certain corporate rights which derive from the rights of individual persons, such as the right: to determine the form of organisation, its government and conditions of membership; to select and train its own officers, leaders and workers; to publish and circulate religious literature; to carry on service and missionary activities at home and abroad; to hold property and to collect funds; to co-operate and to unite with other religious bodies at home and in other lands, including freedom to invite or to send personnel beyond national frontiers and to give or to receive financial assistance; to use such facilities, open to all citizens or associations, as will make possible the accomplishment of religious ends.

In order that these rights may be realised in social experience, the state must grant to religious organisations and their members the same rights which it grants to other organisations, including the right of self-government, of public meeting, of speech, of press and publication, of holding property, of collecting funds, of travel, of ingress and egress, and generally of administering their own affairs.

The community has the right to require obedience to non-discriminatory laws passed in the interest of public order and well-being. In the exercise of its rights, a religious organisation must respect the rights of other religious organisations and must safe-guard the corporate and individual rights of the entire community.

FIRST ASSEMBLY
OF THE WORLD COUNCIL OF CHURCHES

MESSAGE

FIRST ASSEMBLY
OF THE WORLD COUNCIL OF CHURCHES

MESSAGE

THE World Council of Churches, meeting at Amsterdam, sends this message of greeting to all who are in Christ, and to all who are willing to hear.

We bless God our Father, and our Lord Jesus Christ Who gathers together in one the children of God that are scattered abroad. He has brought us here together at Amsterdam. We are one in acknowledging Him as our God and Saviour. We are divided from one another not only in matters of faith, order and tradition, but also by pride of nation, class and race. But Christ has made us His own, and He is not divided. In seeking Him we find one another. Here at Amsterdam we have committed ourselves afresh to Him, and have covenanted with one another in constituting this World Council of Churches. We intend to stay together. We call upon Christian congregations everywhere to endorse and fulfill this covenant in their relations one with another. In thankfulness to God we commit the future to Him.

When we look to Christ, we see the world as it is—His world, to which He came and for which He died. It is filled both with great hopes and also with disillusionment and despair. Some nations are rejoicing in new freedom and power, some are bitter because freedom is denied them, some are paralysed by division, and everywhere there is an undertone of fear. There are millions who are hungry, millions who have no home, no country and no hope. Over all mankind hangs the peril of total war. We have to accept God's judgment upon us for our share in the world's guilt. Often we have tried to serve God and mammon, put other loyalties before loyalty to Christ, confused the Gospel with our own economic or national or racial interests, and feared war more than we have hated it. As we have talked with one another here, we have begun to understand how our separation has prevented us from receiving correction from one another in Christ. And because we lacked this correction, the world has often heard from us not the Word of God but the words of men.

But there is a word of God for our world. It is that the world is in the hands of the living God, Whose will for it is wholly good; that in Christ Jesus, His incarnate Word, Who lived and died and rose from the dead, God has broken the power of evil once for all, and opened for everyone the gate into freedom and joy in the Holy Spirit; that the final judgment on all human history and on every human deed is the judgment of the merciful Christ; and that the end of history will be the triumph of His Kingdom, where alone we shall understand how much God has loved the world. This is God's unchanging word to the world. Millions of our fellow men have never heard it. As we are met here from many lands, we pray God to stir up His whole Church to make this Gospel known to the whole world, and to call on all men to believe in Christ, to live in His love and to hope for His coming.

Our coming together to form a World Council will be vain unless Christians and Christian congregations everywhere commit themselves to the Lord of the Church in a new effort to seek together, where they live, to be His witnesses and servants among their neighbours. We have to remind ourselves and all men that God has put down the mighty from their seats and exalted the humble and meek. We have to learn afresh together to speak boldly in Christ's name both to those in power and to the people, to oppose terror, cruelty and race discrimination, to stand by the outcast, the prisoner and the refugee. We have to make of the Church in every place a voice for those who have no voice, and a home where every man will be at home. We have to learn afresh together what is the duty of the Christian man or woman in industry, in agriculture, in politics, in the professions and in the home. We have to ask God to teach us together to say No and to say Yes in truth. No to all that flouts the love of Christ, to every system, every programme and every person that treats any man as though he were an irresponsible thing or a means of profit, to the defenders of injustice in the name of order, to those who sow the seeds of war or urge war as inevitable; Yes, to all that conforms to the love of Christ, to all who seek for justice, to the peacemakers, to all who hope, fight and suffer for the cause of man, to all who—even without knowing it—look for new heavens and a new earth wherein dwelleth righteousness.

It is not in man's power to banish sin and death from the

earth, to create the unity of the Holy Catholic Church, to conquer the hosts of Satan. But it is within the power of God. He has given us at Easter the certainty that His purpose will be accomplished. But, by our acts of obedience and faith, we can on earth set up signs which point to the coming victory. Till the day of that victory our lives are hid with Christ in God, and no earthly disillusion or distress or power of hell can separate us from Him. As those who wait in confidence and joy for their deliverance, let us give ourselves to those tasks which lie to our hands, and so set up signs that men may see.

Now unto Him that is able to do exceeding abundantly above all that we ask or think, according to the power that worketh in us, unto Him be glory in the Church by Christ Jesus, throughout all ages, world without end.